Books by Herbert B. Ehrmann

THE CRIMINAL COURTS OF CLEVELAND

THE UNTRIED CASE

THE CASE THAT WILL NOT DIE

THE CASE THAT WILL NOT DIE

THE CASE THAT WILL NOT DIE

Commonwealth vs. Sacco and Vanzetti

by HERBERT B. EHRMANN

With maps and illustrations

LITTLE, BROWN AND COMPANY   BOSTON · TORONTO

Published simultaneously in Canada
by Little, Brown & Company (Canada) Limited

PRINTED IN THE UNITED STATES OF AMERICA

Dedicated to
Those Gallant Women Who Faithfully
Tended the Flickering Flame
of New England Idealism from
1920 to 1927

Especially to
Alice Stone Blackwell
Katherine Codman
Zara Dupont
Elizabeth Glendower Evans
Alice Hamilton
Jessica Henderson
Catharine Huntington
Cerise Carmen Jack
Virginia Macmechan
Lois B. Rantoul
Margaret H. Shurtleff
Gertrude Winslow

INTRODUCTION

Since August 23, 1927, when Sacco and Vanzetti were executed on conviction for murder, millions of people have been killed on government orders for no offense whatever, and throughout the world multitudes have been slaughtered without trial in the violence of revolution and counter-revolution. In our own country, men and women have been denied fair trials because of the color of their skins. In other instances, numerous cases have come to light in which convictions were obtained through the use of forced confessions and other questionable police and prosecution tactics. Nevertheless, despite this mountainous record of man's inhumanity to man, the Sacco-Vanzetti case continues to hold a unique place in the annals of injustice. What, then, is there in the case against these obscure Italian anarchists and its fatal culmination that should so occupy the attention of writers of all kinds, including jurists, poets, dramatists and novelists, and engage so much research by students, historians and sociologists?

One answer, I believe, lies to some extent in a feeling that the case was a crucial test of our loyalties to the avowed principles of Anglo-American justice. Those in authority were well alerted to the growing conviction among responsible men and women that the case was a departure from the fair procedures required in a criminal prosecution. This fact and the protest were both ignored. Among those who closed ranks against all criticism were seasoned lawyers, university graduates, trial and review judges, college presidents, and a governor who had previously served as a Congressman. It is possible to explain their actions by examining separately the personality and possible motives of each participant. This, however, hardly explains the behavior of the group as a whole. Indeed, so solid was this array of power that one can almost sympathize with the theory of their defenders — that the alleged gross unfairness in the proceedings was simply Communist propaganda (which certainly exploited the case to the fullest).

One explanation for the continuing attention to the Sacco-Vanzetti case in the midst of far vaster cruelties, therefore, lies in the feeling, perhaps subconscious, that it signaled a weakness within our social order far more dangerous than frontal assaults upon it. Our civilization can protect itself against open attacks on its principles by those who deny them, but cannot long withstand desertion by those who affirm them. That such alleged desertion should appear in Massachusetts in 1927 jolted severely much of the Western world. Massachusetts had acquired a reputation as a leader in the fight for freedom and for human dignity. The Sacco-Vanzetti case came as a shocking premonitory warning that similar weakness might appear anywhere at any time. It is therefore understandable that when Nicola Sacco and Bartolomeo Vanzetti were electrocuted on August 23, 1927, a tremor of seismic proportions rolled around the world.

Perhaps there is another reason why the Sacco-Vanzetti case will not die. There is an epic quality to the story. In retrospect the defendants appear to be extraordinary men pitted against a solid phalanx of officialdom. At every turn of the case which might have saved the lives of the accused, fate intervened to thwart the chance. In this contest, the case seems to lose its essential character as a criminal trial. A brooding sense of inevitability seems to permeate the long narrative. And if a chorus were needed to complete the epic analogy, it may be found in the insistent voices of anti-Red hysteria which were then resounding throughout the land.

The execution of Sacco and Vanzetti must have had a traumatic effect upon me, more severe than I realized at the time. I now recall that for years following their deaths I felt reluctant to talk about the case with anyone who had not shared my experience. I could not bring myself to write about any phase of it beyond doing a few character sketches of persons mentioned prominently in connection with the case.

My unwillingness to reopen memories of the proceedings was not due entirely to their fatal culmination. It is probably a shock to any lawyer for the defense to live through the moment when his clients, whom he knew and liked, are deliberately and carefully put to death. This would especially be true if defense counsel were convinced that the defendants were executed for something which they did not do. Yet, some miscarriages of justice are inevitable. In such instances, lawyers for the defense need not necessarily experience the bitter aftermath if they feel that the State has earnestly sought the truth. In the Sacco-Vanzetti case, however, William G. Thompson (my senior counsel) and I knew that the authorities had intentionally refused to consider anything that might indicate that the accused were not guilty, and had even blocked efforts to establish their innocence. We did not have the solace of believing that their deaths were unfortunate accidents, inevitable in the administration of justice. For this reason every renewed memory of the case for several years remained, for me, something painful, to be avoided if possible.

In 1932, however, my friend Norman Hapgood, a noted journalist and former minister to Denmark, prevailed upon me to write about a single phase of the case, namely, our search for evidence against the Morelli gang of Providence. This evidence pointed to these professionals as the real criminals who murdered and robbed in South Braintree on April 15, 1920. The story is told in my book *The Untried Case*, first published in 1933 by Vanguard Press and reissued in 1960. Thereafter, a busy law practice, plus considerable participation in public and communal affairs, foreclosed the time which I needed to write anything further about the case.

Meanwhile a number of books on the subject appeared, some of which I believe fall far short of presenting an accurate picture of what happened in the Sacco-Vanzetti proceedings. Therefore, when I retired from active practice in 1965, I decided to write a plenary story of the case. I am the last surviving lawyer on either side who was involved as counsel for a substantial period of time, although there are still living several lawyers who strove valiantly to obtain judicial relief during the last few weeks of the case. It would therefore seem to be something of an obligation for me to tell the story as I saw it, before it is wholly relegated to writers who had no contact with the proceedings or the personalities involved in them. Moreover, since I have been a trial lawyer, with a long experience in Massachusetts practice, I am perhaps in that respect in a little better position than most writers to interpret for the reader the events which transpired before, during and after the trials.

In planning this book, I became aware of two serious obstacles which needed to be overcome in order to present the facts in a convincing narrative. The first was implicit in the record itself. From the arrest of Sacco and Vanzetti on May 5, 1920, to their electrocution on August 23, 1927, not one person in authority voiced an opinion that the accused were victims of injustice or expressed a doubt about their guilt. Protests against the proceedings, which grew to world-wide proportions, received no sanction from any source responsible for passing judgment on any phase of them. This chain of official silence, whether due to substantive or to technical reasons, would necessarily create a powerful presumption among readers unfamiliar with the history of the case that the accused men were guilty or fairly tried.

The second obstacle to a credible presentation of the story came into view as my research uncovered what actually happened in the Sacco-Vanzetti case. I found that the facts that lay behind the trial testimony were often quite different at critical points from the recitals in the courtroom and the contentions of the prosecution. Some of this discrepancy had become known to Mr. Thompson and me in our capacity as counsel for the defendants, but not its full extent or significance. These became apparent only on close examination and coordination of disparate parts of the record and other relevant material. What this study revealed struck me at first as beyond belief. As a member of the Massachusetts bar, proud of its traditions, I fought against drawing the inescapable conclusions. Since it had this effect upon me, I knew that a mere restatement would most likely be regarded with skepticism by disinterested readers. Opinions and paraphrases of the evidence, especially as coming from one who had been of counsel for the executed defendants, would be subject to discount as partisan exaggerations.

In order to overcome both of these understandable obstacles to the acceptance of a truthful account, I decided to tell the critical parts of my story largely through the actual words of the many actors in the judicial tragedy. For this reason, the book contains a rather large portion of the original records and other documents, together with an unusual number of footnotes. From this material, the reader will be able to gauge the truthfulness of what might otherwise seem to be an incredible story.

In another respect, the telling of my story follows a rather exceptional course. The usual method of relating the history of a trial would be to start at the beginning, and follow through to the conclusion. However, in the Sacco-Vanzetti case, this would not present an understandable account. The different aspects of this puzzling case are related to one another in a most significant fashion but not necessarily in sequence.

A truly chronological account would involve many breaks in the narrative and turns in many diverse directions. This disjointed narrative would tend to obscure the relentless trend of the entire proceedings.

In the hope of aiding the reader to focus attention on the consistent movement of the Sacco-Vanzetti case to its fatal culmination, I have tried to treat separately the various aspects of the case and then to integrate them into an understandable pattern. This has required the use of some basic material more than once, but such occasional repetition is intentional for the purpose of clarifying and synchronizing the case as a whole.

It is possible, however, that the original record and documentary evidence may prove to be so convincing to some readers, both as to the innocence of the defendants and of their unfair treatment, that they will ask themselves whether there must not be "another side" to the story. This also is understandable — but regrettably without foundation. There may be gaps and mistaken emphases in my story despite my efforts to present an accurate account of everything essential to an understanding of the case. I may fail to point out all of the derelictions of defense counsel. Such lapses, however, if there are any, would not constitute "another side."

Sacco and Vanzetti were entitled to be tried on evidence honestly presented. If this did not occur, the failure cannot be cured. For instance, if the prosecution secured a conviction by utilizing contrived testimony and dubious exhibits, what "other side" can erase the unfairness of the proceedings or supply the missing integrity of evidence on which the verdict should have rested? Unless this is understood, the unbalanced impact of this book may create an impression in some readers that it is a "brief." In a certain aspect it *is* a brief, but not in the sense that its contents have been selected and shaped to produce a desired effect. Nor is it a brief on behalf of clients now in their graves for over forty years. My only client today is historical truth and this I have attempted to serve as faithfully as possible for one who is convinced of the innocence of Sacco and Vanzetti.

In closing this personal word, I acknowledge with thanks the encouragement and help I received from many persons, including Professor W. Barton Leach of the Harvard Law School; Shelley Braverman, authority on firearms; the Honorable Michael A. Musmanno, justice of the Supreme Court of Pennsylvania; Osmond K. Fraenkel, Esq., author of the most complete and accurate summary of the evidence at the Dedham trial of Sacco and Vanzetti; Clement A. Norton, lawyer and journalist; and my wife, Sara R. Ehrmann.

CHRONOLOGY *

1919

November 22	Theft of Buick car in Needham.
*December 5	Morellis indicted for freight car robberies.
December 22	Theft of number plates used at Bridgewater.
December 24	Attempted holdup in Bridgewater.

1920

January	Theft of number plates used at South Braintree.
*March 5	New indictment of Morellis for freight car robberies.
*April —	"Mike" Morelli seen with Buick in New Bedford.
*April 15	"Mike" Morelli's Buick seen for last time in New Bedford.
April 15	Murders at South Braintree.
April 17	Inquest at Quincy with regard to these murders.
April 17	Discovery of Buick car in Manley woods.
April 20	Interview of Boda by police.
*April 24	Incident at Fiore's restaurant, New Bedford.
April 25	Vanzetti's trip to New York.
April 29	Vanzetti's return to Plymouth.
*May 1	Madeiros's first arrest in New Bedford.
May 2	Meeting in Boston of Sacco, Vanzetti and others.
May 3	Death in New York of Salsedo.

* Reprinted from Osmond K. Fraenkel's *The Sacco-Vanzetti Case* by the courtesy of Osmond K. Fraenkel. Entries preceded by an asterisk are additions made by Herbert B. Ehrmann.

May 5   Visit of Sacco, Vanzetti, Boda and Orciani to Johnson house, followed by arrest of Sacco and Vanzetti.

May 6   Arrest of Orciani.

May 6   Interview of Sacco and Vanzetti by District Attorney Katzmann.

*May 11 to May 25   Trial at Providence of Morelli gang on federal indictments.

May 18   Preliminary hearing against Vanzetti in relation to the Bridgewater case.

*May 25   Madeiros's second arrest in New Bedford.

May 26   Preliminary hearing at Brockton against Sacco.

*June 3   Sentence of members of Morelli gang to U.S. penitentiary.

June 11   Indictment of Vanzetti for Bridgewater holdup.

*June 14   Madeiros sentenced to five months in house of correction.

June 22 to July 1   Trial at Plymouth of Vanzetti for Bridgewater holdup.

August 16   Sentence of Vanzetti for Bridgewater holdup.

September 11   Indictment of Sacco and Vanzetti for South Braintree murders.

1921

*January   Madeiros goes south with approximately $2800.

*February 10   Mancini murders Alterio on Mulberry Street, New York.

May 31 to July 14   Trial of Sacco and Vanzetti at Dedham.

November 5   Motion for new trial as against the weight of evidence argued before Judge Thayer.

November 8   First supplementary motion filed (Ripley).

*December 21   Sentence of Mancini on plea of guilty in New York.

December 24   Motion for new trial as against the weight of evidence denied.

1922

May 4   Second supplementary motion filed (Gould and Pelser).

July 22   Third supplementary motion filed (Goodridge).

September 11   Fourth supplementary motion filed (Andrews).

1923

April 30   Fifth supplementary motion filed (Hamilton).

October 1   Supplement to first motion filed (Daly).

October 1 to 3   ⎧All five supplementary motions argued before Judge

November 1, 2, 8   ⎨Thayer.

November 5   ⎩Proctor motion filed.

1924

October 1   Decisions by Judge Thayer denying all motions.

*November 1   Madeiros kills cashier at Wrentham bank.

*November 17   Madeiros arrested in Providence.

1925

*May 11   First trial of Madeiros at Dedham.

*November 16   First written confession by Madeiros.

November 18   Madeiros's statement received by Sacco in Dedham prison.

1926

January 11 to 13   Argument of appeal of Sacco and Vanzetti from conviction and from denial of first, second and fifth supplementary motions.

March 31   Conviction of Madeiros reversed by Supreme Judicial Court.

May 12   Conviction of Sacco and Vanzetti affirmed by Supreme Judicial Court.

May 15 to May 20   Second trial of Madeiros.

*May 22   Investigation of Madeiros story begun by Mr. Thompson and Mr. Ehrmann.

May 26   Motion based on Madeiros's statement filed.

September 13 to 17   Madeiros's motion argued before Judge Thayer.

October 23   Decision by Judge Thayer denying motion.

1927

January 27 and 28   Appeal from denial of Madeiros's motion argued before Supreme Judicial Court.

April 5   Denial of motion affirmed.

April 9   Sentence imposed by Judge Thayer on Sacco and Vanzetti.

May 3	Petition for clemency addressed to Governor Fuller.
June 1	Advisory Committee appointed by Governor Fuller.
July 11 to 21	Hearings held before Advisory Committee.
August 3	Decision by Governor Fuller denying clemency.
August 6	Motion filed for revocation of sentence.
August 6	Petition filed for writ of error.
August 8	Motion denied by Judge Thayer.
August 8	Petition denied by Judge Sanderson.
August 10	Petition for writ of habeas corpus denied by Justice Holmes of the United States Supreme Court, and by Judge Anderson of the United States District Court.
August 16	Exceptions to denial of motion and petition argued in Supreme Judicial Court.
August 19	Exceptions overruled by Supreme Judicial Court.
August 20	Petition for writ of habeas corpus denied by Judge Morton of the United States Circuit Court of Appeals.
August 20	Petition for stay and extension of time in which to apply to the United States Supreme Court for writ of certiorari denied by Justice Holmes of the United States Supreme Court.
August 22	Similar petition denied by Justice Stone of the United States Supreme Court.
August 23	Sacco and Vanzetti and Madeiros executed.
October 3	Petition for writ of certiorari dismissed by consent in the Supreme Court of the United States.

CONTENTS

4

Arrest Without Evidence *47*

5

The Search for Evidence *58*

6

Evolution of Identification *66*

7

Fringe Evidence at the Plymouth Trial *85*

8

The Plymouth Shell Mystery *99*

9

A Day of Remembrance *115*

————

PART II

**August 16, 1920, to August 23, 1927
From the Sentencing of Vanzetti for the Attempted
Holdup at Bridgewater to the Execution of Sacco
and Vanzetti for the South Braintree Murders**

————

10

Fateful Changes Presage the Dedham Trial *145*

11

Ominous Interlude *161*

Contents

Contents

ILLUSTRATIONS

MAPS

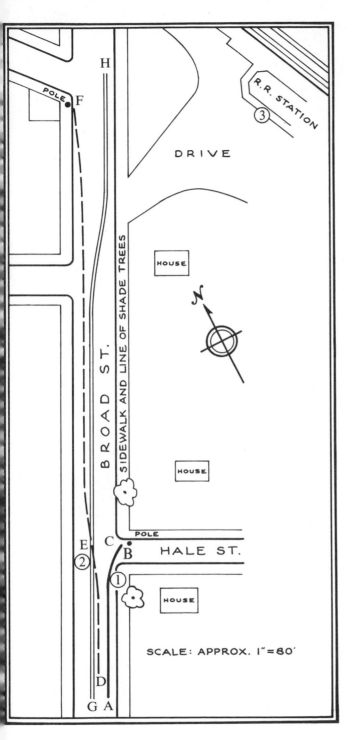

Broad Street, Bridgewater

The scene of the attempted holdup on December 24, 1919. (From sketch plan prepared on November 2, 1920, which is now in the possession of the Harvard Law Library.)

A–B   Course of bandit auto before holdup.

B   Position of bandit auto at time of holdup.

C   Location of holdup.

D–E–F Course of L.Q. White truck.

E   Truck crosses behind streetcar.

F   Truck smashes into pole.

G–H   Course of streetcar.

1   Witness Harding claims he stood here.

2   Witness Brooks claims she crossed Broad Street about here, passing bandit car.

3   Witness Brooks claims to have stood here and seen flashes of firing at C.

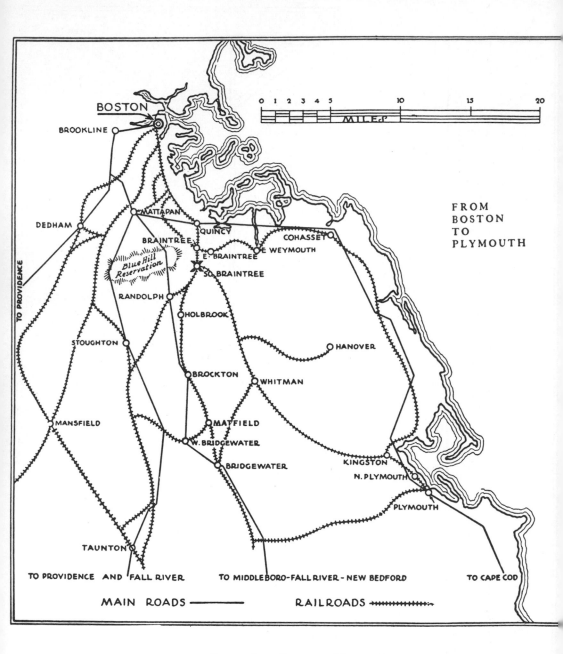

Routes from Boston to Plymouth

(From *The Sacco-Vanzetti Case* by Osmond K. Fraenkel. Courtesy of Osmond K. Fraenkel.)

Pearl Street and Vicinity, South Braintree

(From *The Sacco-Vanzetti Case* by Osmond K. Fraenkel. Courtesy of Osmond K. Fraenkel.)

Before the shooting:

1. Neai
2. Andrews
   Campbell
3. Tracy
4. Heron
5. Foley
6. Frantello
7. Novelli
8. Behrsin

During the shooting:

9. Bostock
10. Wade
11. Nichols
12. McGlone
13. Langlois
14. Carter
15. Pelser
16. Laborers at excavation
17. Liscomb

After the shooting:

18. Splaine
    Devlin
19. Carrigan
20. Levangie
21. DeBeradinis
22. Goodridge
23. Burke
24. Pierce
    Ferguson
25. Cellucci
26. O'Neil
27. Workers on railroad
28. Damato
29. Olsen
30. Gould

xxvii

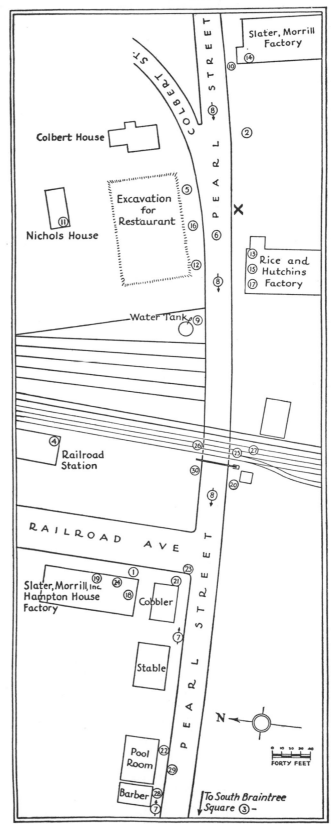

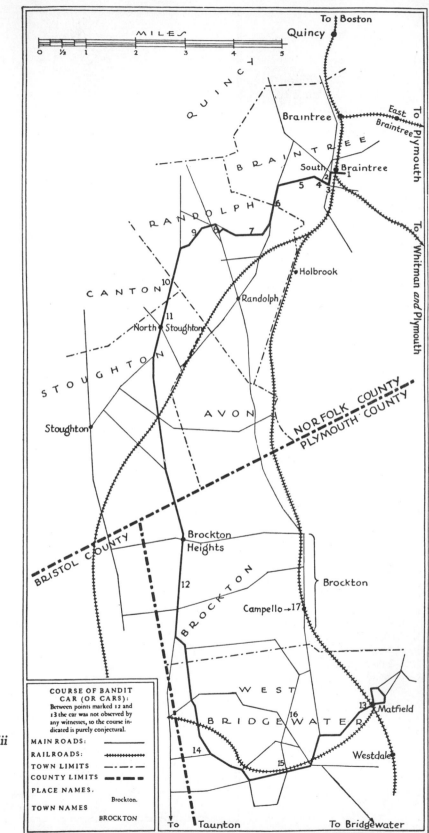

MILES
0 ½ 1 2 3 4 5

To Boston
Quincy

Braintree

East Braintree
To Plymouth

South Braintree

To Whitman and Plymouth

Holbrook

Randolph

North Stoughton

Stoughton

AVON

NORFOLK COUNTY
PLYMOUTH COUNTY

BRISTOL COUNTY

Brockton Heights

Brockton

Campello →17

BROCKTON

WEST BRIDGEWATER

Matfield

Westdale

To Taunton

To Bridgewater

COURSE OF BANDIT
CAR (OR CARS):
Between points marked 12 and
13 the car was not observed by
any witnesses, so the course indicated is purely conjectural.

MAIN ROADS:
RAILROADS:
TOWN LIMITS
COUNTY LIMITS
PLACE NAMES.   Brockton.
TOWN NAMES   BROCKTON

xxviii

Probable Escape Route from South Braintree

(From *The Sacco-Vanzetti Case* by Osmond K. Fraenkel. Courtesy of Osmond K. Fraenkel.)

APPROXIMATE TIME TABLE

South Braintree:

1. Pearl Street—place of crime, 3:05.
2. Hancock Street—Chase—about 3.
3. Plain Street crossing—Buckley, 3:10.
4. Washington Street.
5. Pond Street—Baker—about 3.

Randolph:

6. North Street—Desmond, 3:12; Chisholm, 3:30.
7. Oak Street—Farmer, 3:25.
8. Orchard Street—Hewins.
9. Chestnut Street, Tower Hill.

Canton:

10. Turnpike—Dorr, 3:30; Lloyd, 3:30.

Stoughton:

11. Turnpike—Clark, 3:45.

Brockton:

12. Pearl Street—Kelliher, 3:50.
17. Campello—place of arrest.

West Bridgewater:

14. Manley Woods—where Buick car was found.
15. Johnson house, North Elm Street.
16. North Elm Street trolley.

Matfield:

13. Crossing—Reed, 4:15.

PART I

December 24, 1919, to August 16, 1920

From the Attempted Holdup at Bridgewater
to the Sentencing of Vanzetti

Holdup Attempt at Bridgewater

The Cropped Moustache and the Crystal Ball

On December 24, 1919, the Pinkerton detective agency made an entry in its Boston Journal. It was the initial report in the agency's investigation of an attempt to hold up a payroll truck in the streets of Bridgewater, Massachusetts. In retrospect we now know that this attempt was the genesis of the Sacco-Vanzetti case. However, the Pinkerton reports on the Bridgewater affair remained unknown to counsel for Sacco and Vanzetti until June 1927, little more than two months before the men were executed.

The initial report of the Pinkerton agency follows:

JOURNAL

Executive   N.Y.   Bos.
Boston Journal # 8063   G.D.B. G.E.L.

Account of   L. Q. White Shoe Co.

Operation   Attempted holdup robbery.

Reports to   Mr. Loring Q. White.

Address   L. Q. White Shoe Co., Bridgewater, Mass.

Remarks   Bills to L. Q. White Shoe Co. Bills and reports to Mr. Loring Q. White. Mr. White understands the rate on this matter to be $10.00 per day plus incidental expenses.

Boston, Mass., *December 24, 1919*

Today at 12:15 P.M., Mr. Stone, Vice-President of the Commonwealth Trust Co., telephoned Asst. Supt. H. J. Murray and advised him that an attempt had been just made to hold up the L. Q. White Shoe Co. payroll at Bridgewater,

Mass. Mr. Loring Q. White had telephoned him requesting him to get in touch with the best detective service possible and have them immediately start an investigation at Bridgewater with a view to apprehending the four men implicated in the attempted holdup.

Asst. Supt. H. J. Murray got in touch with Mr. L. Q. White who stated that about 7:30 this morning, three of his men went to the Bridgewater Trust Co. for the payroll which amounted to about $30,000.; that the money for the payroll was placed in a strong box which is bolted to a Ford truck; that while en route from the Bank to the factory, four men drove up in a touring car, three of whom got out and began firing on the men who were guarding the money. One of the men on the truck, — Constable Benj. F. Boles, fired two shots at the men which frightened them and they immediately shot into the car and started off.

The holdup men are described as being either Polish or Russian.

Mr. White stated that he had through the newspapers, offered a reward of $1000. for the capture of the men in question and wished the Agency to make every effort to locate these men.

PLAN: — Opt. J. J. Hayes was immediately detailed to proceed to Bridgewater, Mass. to take up the investigation with a view to apprehending the four men in question; to secure full descriptions and particulars from the employees on the White truck or any other persons in the vicinity who observed the men in question.

Assigned to
Asst. Supt. H. J. Murray

H. J. Murray	*Asst. Supt.*
D. T. Green	*Superintendent*

Operative J. J. Hayes began his investigation immediately. What he found on the first day is best told in his own report for December 24, 1919:

L. Q. White Company
J.J.H. Reports: *Wednesday, December 24, 1919.*

Arrived at Bridgewater on 1:08 P.M. train from Boston today and at once went into conference with Mr. Ralph White at the office of the L. Q. White Shoe Company. From them I learned that at 7:30 A.M. today on Broad Street near Hale Street, Bridgewater, four foreigners attempted to hold up and rob an auto truck containing three of their men who had a box containing $31,000 in the truck. Several shots he said were fired and the attempt to rob was unsuccessful. His men he stated were on their way to the factory from the Bridgewater Trust Co. The money was to be used for paying off the help. The payday is on Thursday but payment was made today because of the fact that tomorrow is Christmas. The men on the White truck which is a Ford were: —

John E. Graves, chauffeur, aged 24 years, residing at 99 No. Main St., Brockton.

Benj. F. Bowles, police officer, aged 47 years, residing at 14 Broad St., Bridgewater.

Alfred E. Cox Jr., paymaster, aged 32 years, residing at 192 Summer St., Bridgewater.

Mr. Graves said, "I have been employed here five weeks. I am married and recently came out of the Army. Before going into the Service, I was also employed by the White Company. Today at 7:30 A.M. I was driving my employer's Ford truck from the Bank to the factory with the money to pay off the help. Ben Bowles, the police officer, sat on the seat to my right. Al Cox, the paymaster, sat on top of the money box which was locked to the floor of the car. There is a top on the Ford truck but the sides and back on it were open. As we came down Broad Street I had the truck on the right side of the street and was following a street car bound for the depot. As the car reached Hale Street it seemed to stop and I saw a dark auto like a Hudson pull in front of it into Hale Street and stop at the corner of Hale and Broad Streets. I was then close to the rear of the car. I saw three men pile out of this Hudson car and walk toward us. One man had a shot gun and the other two had revolvers. I could see we were going to be held up and I pulled my truck across the track and shot by the electric car on the left of it. The man with the shot gun fired four times at us. I did not notice what the men with the revolvers did. It was cloudy this morning and the streets were wet and slippery. When I got past the electric car, I shot ahead as fast as I could and when we got near Perkins Ave., Ben Bowles got excited and caught hold of the wheel and we ran into a telegraph pole. We were not hurt and our car was only slightly damaged. The bandits were about 30 feet away when they fired. The man with the shot gun was 5' 6" tall, 145 lbs., age 35 years, dark complexion and black mustache and looked like a Greek. He wore no hat and had a white shirt on and no collar. He wore a dark suit and no overcoat. I cannot describe the men who had revolvers. I did not get the number of their auto. I noticed the curtains were all drawn on it. The box we had with the money in it is of metal 2 feet long, 14 inches wide and 8 inches deep. I don't know how much was in it. I did not look back after I got by the electric car. Ben Bowles fired two shots at the bandits about the time they fired on us. I think the electric car was moving as we passed it. I did not recognize any of the bandits as persons I had ever seen before."

Mr. Cox said, "I am married and have been a paymaster for the White Company about 10 years. I was on the Ford Truck this morning at 7:30 o'clock when the hold up occured and sat on the money box with my back to the driver Graves and the officer Bowles. The box is of galvanized iron and was locked to the floor of the truck. The box also had a Yale lock on it. As we came along Broad Street near Hale Street I heard a rifle shot. I turned around just as our auto was pulling to the left of a street car and saw a man with a shot gun ten or fifteen feet ahead of us and aiming at us and also a man near him with a revolver in his hand. I saw only two men and noticed a big dark auto standing on Hale Street at the corner of Broad Street. After we got by the electric car the bandits fired after us. Ben Bowles fired two shots at them before we went around the car. The man with the shot gun was a Russian, Pole or Austrian, 5' 8", 150 lbs., dark complexion, 40 years of age, was without a hat and wore a long dark overcoat with the collar up. He had a closely cropped mustache which might have been slightly gray."

Mr. Bowles said, "I am married and am a town constable here and have been in the employ of the White Company 8 years. This morning I sat on the right side of Graves the driver of the Ford truck on our return to the factory from the Bank with the pay money about 7:30 A.M. As we came down Broad Street we were following an electric car bound for the Depot. On nearing Hale Street, I saw a black touring car in Hale Street at the corner of Broad Street and saw three men pile out of it and come toward us. One man remained in the car. He was the driver. We were about 20 yards away when the bandits approached towards us. One of the men had a shot gun another had an automatic gun and I did not see what the third man had. The man with the shot gun opened fire on us at once and when he did I pulled out my revolver and fired twice at him. The fellow with the automatic also fired and as he did Graves pulled our truck to the left of the street car and this blocked the bandits and saved us. We then shot ahead of the electric car and when we got past it the bandits fired on us again. We kept going and near Perkins Ave., Graves lost control of the truck and I caught the wheel of the truck, and the truck ran into a telegraph pole. The street was very wet and there was a slight fog. I can positively identify two of the bandits. The man with the shotgun was 5' 7", 35 or 36 years, 150 lbs., had a black closely cropped mustache, red cheeks, slim face, black hair and was an Italian or a Portuguese. He had no hat on and had a black overcoat on with collar up. His gun was a single barrel affair. The man with the automatic gun was short and thick set, 5' 2–3", 190 lbs., light complexioned, clean shaven, was pock marked and broad shouldered. I think he was a Russian Pole. He wore a gray cap like a police winter cap and a long brown ulster. I had never seen these men before. The third man in the street I cannot describe. The man in the auto who did not get out was light complexioned, wore a black cap, and dark coat with the collar up. The touring car had the side curtains all drawn on it. I did not notice what the bandits did after we got out of their reach. This auto when I saw it was headed down Hale Street toward Plymouth."

After his interviews with the three prime witnesses, Mr. Hayes continued his search for evidence. Edward C. Danforth, a boy fifteen years old, had witnessed the shooting, but was not close enough to be able to describe the men, except to say, "One of them had a rifle [shotgun?] and wore a long black overcoat." Miss Helen Perkins did not see the shooting, but was able to add a few details. She said:

At 7:10 A.M. today I was walking to work and I saw a dark touring car with the curtains all drawn turn into Main Street from Oak Street here and stop. I think it was black in color. It had a dealer's number on it with a zero as the first number. I saw one man get out of the auto. He said 'thank you' to the others in it in broken English. I think he was an Italian. He was of medium height, dark and well dressed. I saw him button the curtains drawn on the side of [the] auto. A few minutes later this man passed me going toward the center of the town along Main Street and he had another neatly dressed foreigner with him about the same size and appearance. This auto also passed and went along Main Street toward the center. I thought it funny the men should leave a car going in the same direction of themselves. The car was a good looking one and I noticed it particularly as a Mr. Flynn here has one like it and I thought at first it was his car and that I might obtain a ride to work in the car. I never saw these men before. I heard none of their talk as they passed.

One of these additional witnesses found by Mr. Hayes turned out to be more informative. He later became a key witness. Frank W. Harding, a salesman for the W. H. Bassett Company, in the garage and automobile supply business, did not see the beginning of the encounter between the robbers and the pay truck crew, but he arrived at the scene in time to see the action. This is what he told Mr. Hayes:

I am 39 years old and live at 171 Walnut St. Bridgewater. This morning at 7:30 A.M. I was walking along Broad Street from Hale Street on my way to work. At Hale Street near Broad Street I saw a black Hudson #6 auto standing with the front wheels on Hale Street and the rear wheels on Broad Street. The car was headed down Hale Street and the curtains were all drawn. It was a 7 passenger affair and bore the Mass. number 01173 C. An electric car was coming along Broad Street toward the depot. I then saw a man step out onto Broad Street from Hale Street as if to take the car. The electric car seemed to stop at Hale Street and I then observed the man drop down on one knee on Broad Street near Hale Street. He had a shot gun in his hands and he fired twice at the White Co. Ford truck as it came along in the rear of the electric car. The truck was then on the left of the car track. I then saw the man who stepped out as if to take the car with a blue Colt-revolver in his hand and he fired at the White truck several times. I also saw a third man in the street but saw no gun with him. He later got into the auto with the bandits after the shooting. Ben Bowles a police officer who was on the Ford truck with the paymaster fired twice at the bandits who also fired at the truck after it passed the electric car. The bandits then slowly got into their Hudson car and sped down Hale Street toward Plymouth Street. The man with the shot gun was slim, 5' 10", wore a long black overcoat and black derby hat. I did not get much of a look at his face but think he was a Pole. The shot gun was one of these pump guns. He dropped on his knee near a large elm tree at the corner of the two streets. The man with the .38 calibre Colt revolver looked like an Italian. He was 5' 5½", 150 lbs., dark complexion, clean shaven, and wore a dark cap. The third man who did not seem to do any shooting wore a black soft hat, brown overcoat of rough cloth, was 5' 8", 160 lbs., stocky build, clean shaven black hair and eyes, hair nicely cut and wore a khaki shirt, soft turndown collar, and dark bow tie. I have seen him hanging around the streets here for four or five days and noticed him as a stranger. I think he is an Italian. Yesterday I saw him around here with the man with the Colt revolver in the holdup. I saw only three men get into this Hudson car. I did not notice anyone in the car. The electric car really saved the men on the White Co. truck and frustrated the plans of the bandits.

Mr. Harding's story was told to the operative on the day of the attempted robbery. Later, on January 3, 1920, he confirmed his statement that he did not get much of a look at the shotgun bandit. When asked whether two suspects he viewed on that date were the two gunmen he saw, he stated to operative A.B.M. that as he did not see the men's faces "on the day of the holdup, he was unable to say whether they were the gunmen or not." (Five months later he positively identified a defendant charged with being the shotgun bandit, describing the accused in detail as he gazed at him from the witness stand.) The foregoing constitute all of the eyewitnesses interviewed by operative Hayes on December 24, 1919.

Mr. Hayes must have reviewed this part of his investigation with considerable satisfaction. Before the day of the crime had elapsed he had established a number of basic facts. No suggestion or pressure had been brought to bear on his witnesses. Their memories were not affected by the passage of time. There was then no suspect around whom their recitals might have tended to converge. Their stories were prime evidence. In an ordinary case, the testimony of these witnesses in harmony with what they told Mr. Hayes only a few hours after the attempted robbery would have served the authorities as a test of the reliability of witnesses. However, no ordinary case was beginning to shape up. Months later, the testimony of these same witnesses (except Graves, who had died) bore little resemblance to the stories told to Mr. Hayes, especially in reference to the shotgun bandit. Instead their recitals at the trial were tailored to convict the prisoner in the dock, an itinerant fish peddler from Plymouth, Massachusetts.

On Christmas Eve 1919, however, one can picture Mr. Hayes taking out his pencil and jotting down the salient facts that he had learned. His notes could have read as follows:

"1. The holdup car was a Hudson 6. It has been so identified by the only two witnesses known to be familiar with the makes of automobiles, namely, Graves the chauffeur and Harding the garage employee. No other witness stated the make of the car. Otherwise, the car was described as a big, black or dark touring car, with the curtains drawn. The registration number was 01173 C.

"2. There were at least four holdup men involved: the chauffeur who remained in the car, the bandit with the shotgun, the man with the automatic pistol or revolver and a fourth who did no shooting.

"3. The only description of the chauffeur came from Mr. Bowles, who said he was light-complexioned, and wore a black cap and a dark coat with the collar up. He probably was clean-shaven, since Mr. Bowles mentioned no moustache.

"4. The descriptions of the shotgun bandit [with which we will subsequently be much concerned] almost reach a consensus. He was between thirty-five and forty years of age, between 5' 6" and 5' 10" in height and weighed about 150 pounds. He probably wore a long dark overcoat (Cox, Bowles, Harding), although Graves thought he wore a dark suit but no overcoat. *He was without a hat* (Graves, Cox, Bowles), although Harding at the time stated *he wore a black derby hat.* Graves and Cox said he was dark-complexioned, Bowles described 'red cheeks,' *Harding did not get much of a look at his face.* His most distinguishing feature was *a moustache described* as *black* by *Graves and Bowles,* and possibly *slightly gray* by Cox and by *both Cox and Bowles as closely cropped.* He was apparently a 'foreigner,' although what nationality is uncertain, since he was variously described as a Greek, a Russian, a Pole, an Austrian, an Italian or a Portuguese. [Emphasis has been added to indicate items which should have been decisive at a later date.]

"5. The man with the automatic or revolver was shorter than the shotgun bandit, stockier, medium- or light-complexioned, clean-shaven, pockmarked (Cox, Bowles), although Harding said he was dark-complexioned. His nationality seems uncertain but was variously guessed as Russian Pole or Italian.

"6. Harding (who apparently got no good look at the shotgun bandit) described in detail the man who did no shooting, stating that he wore a black soft hat, brown overcoat, khaki shirt, soft turndown collar and dark bow tie, and was clean-shaven with black hair and eyes, and hair nicely cut. He had seen this same man hanging around the streets for four or five days and yesterday (December 23) he saw him 'around' with the man who had the 'revolver' in the holdup."

If Mr. Hayes were an experienced police detective he would also have come to certain conclusions about the holdup gang. It is well known in criminal circles that different techniques are characteristic of the work of particular "mobs." In some prisons the incarcerated professionals even play the game of "who done it," betting one another on the identity of the gang that has just pulled off a big-time robbery or attempt.

The Bridgewater attempt was marked by poor planning and execution.

Except for the fact that the criminals had in some way learned that the payroll would be delivered on Wednesday instead of Thursday (which was Christmas) and knew something about the route of the payroll truck from bank to factory, the job had been inadequately scouted.

The payroll was in a two-foot iron box, locked to the floor of the truck and fastened shut with a Yale lock. The bandits would have been unable to make off with the payroll even if its guards had been killed by gunfire or had abandoned the truck.

Instead of staging the attempt on the payroll as the box was being moved from bank to truck or from truck to factory, the gang made a frontal attack on the armed vehicle at a prominent street intersection where traffic was most likely to interrupt the operation. This is exactly what happened. A streetcar arrived during the fusillade, driving between the bandits and the truck, enabling the latter to speed away and forcing the robbers to terminate the robbery attempt and to concentrate on their own getaway.

The bandits did not employ the tactic of surprise but warned of the attack in advance by "piling out" of their car in full view and by ineffectual gunfire. Apparently also, their positions on the street made it improbable that they would hit their targets — if they had any.

There was apparently little evidence of teamwork or assignment of functions among the robbers.

The registration numbers on the stolen plates were clearly displayed instead of being splattered with mud. Whether the bandits had a second or third car nearby for a switch to facilitate their escape was not known to Mr. Hayes. (Since the fleeing car was later traced as far as Randolph, there probably was no other automobile.)

The curtains on the car were properly "drawn," but were buttoned down instead of being left loose at the bottom for easy ingress and egress.

A trained detective, familiar with the ways of criminal gangs, might well have concluded that the Bridgewater attempt was made by individual criminals gathered together, *ad hoc* as it were, for the single purpose of knocking off a payroll which one of their number had heard was a "cinch." [1] This hypothesis would have been strengthened by the apparent lack of national or racial homogeneity in the group. Such a crime is perhaps harder to

---

[1] That the Bridgewater attempt was the work of such an improvised collection of criminals was subsequently related in a number of articles published in *Outlook and Independent,* October 31 and November 7, 1928.

"crack" at the start than when the methods of a well-known gang are evident, unless one of the criminals can be caught and made to talk. For this purpose, Mr. Hayes had turned up some good leads.

Before Mr. Hayes finished his day-long investigation, he interviewed Chief of Police Michael E. Stewart at the Bridgewater Town Hall. From him he learned that the number plates on the bandits' car had been stolen from George Hassam's garage in Needham, Massachusetts, one week earlier. (Actually it was a day or two before the attempted robbery.) Stewart had no clue as to who the bandits were. Nevertheless, the chief had his ideas and expressed them in words that presaged the Sacco-Vanzetti case. Based on no evidence of any kind, he stated that "he believed *that the holdup was the work of an out-of-town band of Russians* with a possible confederate in the White Shoe shops" and *"that there are a lot of Reds and Bolshevists about town"* who *"drift in from Connecticut and elsewhere in Massachusetts."* (Emphasis added.)

Chief Stewart was deeply interested in "Reds" because he had been engaged in rounding up radicals for deportation. This was the notorious period of the Mitchell Palmer Red-hunts. The climax came when, on the evening of January 2, 1920, the Department of Justice under Attorney General Palmer, with five hundred men at his command, operating from Boston and assisted by policemen of the various cities and towns, made a series of raids in Massachusetts cities, towns and villages, including Brockton, Bridgewater and Norwood, and arrested from eight to twelve hundred supposed radicals. (The facts are fully set out in *Colyer v. Skeffington*, D. Mass. 265 F. 17 [1920].) Those seized were later discharged by federal judge George Anderson on the ground that every principle of justice and fair dealing had been violated, in both the preparation and service of warrants, in the detention of the arrested persons and in the "hearings" granted them. In preparation for this drive, the local police had been filled with suspicion that all foreigners of the humbler classes living in their vicinity were anarchists or other types of radicals and dangerous persons.

Chief Stewart was one of these participating in this excitement. It was therefore no wonder that his suspicions were immediately directed against Reds and foreigners, rather than criminals. So far as we know, Stewart had had very little experience with real criminals. Ordinarily there was not much serious crime in Massachusetts towns. In 1919 and 1920, however, there was a decided rise in the number of crimes of violence. This was probably the usual aftermath of a wartime era and partly due to the advent of prohibition, which made bootlegging and hijacking highly profitable. The title "Chief" for local small-town policemen was a somewhat misleading appellation. For instance, "Chief" Stewart had no police force and only one part-time assistant. He knew next to nothing of accepted police procedures. Yet this untrained and inexperienced officer, for whom holdup men were synonymous with radicals, was destined to become the author of the Sacco-Vanzetti case.

After despatching operative Hayes to Bridgewater, assistant superintendent H. J. Murray of the Pinkerton office took another step. The main reliance of a good detective agency in tracking criminals is the down-to-earth business of developing contacts with the underworld. Mr. Murray tells us in his own words what he did.

L. Q. White
Asst. Supt. H.J.M. Reports: *Boston, Wednesday, December 24, 1919.*

Today on receipt of information regarding attempted holdup at Bridgewater, with the information to the effect the same was believed to be committed by foreigners, possibly Italians, I immediately got in touch with two Italian informants who are frequenters of the different resorts, crap games etc. about town, and advised them of the reward of $1000. offered by the L. Q. White Company. Also enlisted their assistance for any information that might be of interest on this matter. I also interviewed a number of local Police Inspectors, furnishing them with descriptions of the men implicated in the holdup.

During the evening, I visited a number of the resorts in company with informant but did not secure any information of value.

I advised each of the parties interviewed that there was an opportunity of claiming the reward offered if they could give the Agency any information leading to the arrest and conviction of these men.

I discontinued at 11 P.M.

Reported
12–26–19–M
Boston

As seen later, this step had most significant and somewhat bizarre consequences.

While Mr. Murray was working through informants, his operatives in the field continued to gather additional important information. On December 26, operative H.H. reported that the number plates seen on the bandits' car had been stolen a day or two before the holdup from Hassam's garage in Needham. The plates had been loaned by Hassam to a man named Miele on December 17 for temporary use on an old Hupp Runabout in driving it a short distance to the garage for repairs. He said he had just bought the car without plates. The Hupp was stored in the rear of the garage with the plates still attached. On Monday, December 22, a stranger approached Mr. Hassam at the garage with a request to borrow number plates, giving almost the same reason as Miele: "He had bought an old car in Wellesley that had no number plates on it so he wanted to borrow number plates in order to drive it home." Hassam refused. On Wednesday evening, December 24, the local police interviewed Mr. Hassam concerning the number plates seen on the holdup car. Then, for the first time, Hassam discovered that the plates were gone. Mr. Hassam gave the Pinkerton operative a description of the stranger which later became significant. He also told the police that whoever removed the plates must have been familiar with the garage as the Hupp was in the rear end surrounded by other cars.

The Pinkerton operatives made a substantial effort to connect Mr. Miele with the stolen plates, or with the stranger who sought to borrow them, including the evidence that he had visited the garage on Monday and Tuesday. Miele denied that he had been to the garage on Tuesday or that he knew anything about the theft. In the end nothing came of the investigation.

On the same day, December 26, operative J.J.H. learned from Chief McKenzie of the Newton police that on November 22 (erroneously printed as *December* 22), 1919, a seven-passenger Buick 192 Model (last digit omitted) had been stolen on the street in Needham. The car was black with a blue stripe around it and an oval glass window in the rear. It was owned by David H. Murphy, a shoe man who resided in Natick, Massachusetts.

Despite the positive and undisputed evidence from qualified witnesses that the bandit car in Bridgewater was a Hudson, the report now contains the notation, "This Buick may have been the car the bandits had." So great was the suggestive force of the discovery that a Buick had been stolen a month before in Needham that from that moment on the bandit car began to be converted into a Buick. Chief Stewart, with Officer Albert Brouillard of the State Police, then discovered two witnesses in Bridgewater who purported to identify the car as a Buick. On December 27, 1919, the report indicates that John D. King identified the car from his window as a Buick as it "tore down Grove St. after the hold up." Richard D. Casey saw some car, before the holdup, stop in front of the rear door of his house. He said it was a Buick. (Mr. Harding, the garage employee, later changed his identification of the car from a Hudson, made on the day of the holdup, to a Buick. Mr. Graves, the chauffeur, who also said it was a Hudson, died before any trial proceedings.)

At the time this shift in the make of the car seemed to have no significance, except, perhaps, to indicate how the police, convinced of a fact, can sway witnesses' testimony to conform to their belief. Months later, however, the (by then) uncontradicted testimony that the holdup car was a Buick became an important link in the prosecution's case.

Another incident that later became of prime importance was the finding of an exploded paper shotgun shell near the site of the attempted holdup. The Pinkerton Bridgewater report of this discovery seems to be missing, but there are later references to it in the Pinkerton reports of operative H.H. (Henry Hellyer) on the double murder and robbery in South Braintree.

The (South Braintree) report for April 19, 1920, states that Police Chief Jeremiah Gallivan of Braintree showed H.H. a shell for a Winchester shotgun, "the same as the one found on the scene of the Bridgewater attempted holdup last December."

In a report dated May 7, H.H. stated that he had "turned the envelope containing shot over to [Norfolk County] Asst. Dist. Atty. Kane." The "shot" is apparently the shot mentioned in the report dated May 10, 1920, which reads in part as follows:

Proceeded to Bridgewater, Dr. J. M. Murphy, who found clue to the bandits in Bridgewater last December, I learned had moved to 80½ Maple Street, Florence, Mass. Telephoning to Dr. Murphy, I got proper account of the circumstances under which he found the shell, which operative J.J.H. described, but not fully. The shell was found by Dr. Murphy near the scene of the attempted holdup along with the wad and a number of shot, and laid in the road after being ejected from the gun only a short time before Dr. Murphy found it. As he now recalls it, same was a # 12 gauge Winchester Repeater shell, and the shot apparently was # 10.

Dr. Murphy was a hunting man and competent to estimate the size of the shot. Number 10 is very small shot, being less than half the diameter of the BB and little more than one-fifth the diameter of "00 Buck." [2] These are facts to be remembered, since Dr. Murphy's find later became a

[2] Shelley Braverman letter to HBE, July 9, 1965.

portent of disaster for Vanzetti and the genesis of an inexplicable ballistic mystery.

The operative's report for May 11, 1920, reads as follows:

Before going to South Braintree, I went to the State Police Dept. and gave Capt. Proctor the # 12 gauge Winchester Repeater cartridge found by Dr. Murphy in Bridgewater on the day of the attempted robbery of the L. Q. White payroll there. I also gave him J.J.H.'s report on the finding of the same.

We do not know whether J.J.H. obtained the shot and shell directly from Dr. Murphy or why they remained in the possession of the Pinkerton detectives from December 1919 to May 1920. Possibly the report given to Captain Proctor was the missing report. However, the State Police have reported to me that they cannot find the report of J.J.H. allegedly given to Captain Proctor.

Operative H.H.'s report for January 6, 1920, states that Chief Stewart had received a letter from the chief of police of Nashua, New Hampshire, telling of information he had received about Greeks coming from Ohio for the purpose of holding up and robbing paymasters. Chief Stewart knew of a Greek named Nicholas Agatkides who had worked in the White shoe factory "last winter." Stewart's characterization of the man is a flash revelation of his own thinking. Agatkides had *"investigated [instigated?] and led a strike that occurred among the help, besides which he was a draft dodger and all-around anarchist and agitator."* The man had left Bridgewater a year before, but was seen in the town a day or so prior to the holdup. Inquiries among the Greeks in Bridgewater brought out the fact that Agatkides bore a bad reputation and was "classed as a bum and a crook," information which Stewart had omitted to impart, possibly because of his obsession with radicals. Agatkides had taken employment in a Greek restaurant in Brockton. He visited his friends in Bridgewater a day or so before Christmas and promised to return on Christmas day "with a lot of booze." However, he never showed up and disappeared from the restaurant about January 4. This is the last entry concerning Agatkides.

Meanwhile Assistant Superintendent Murray was making progress through his underworld contacts. On December 29, he reported that one of his informants "stated that there was an Italian at a certain place on Summer Street [Boston] who had said that he either drove the car used in the attempted holdup at Bridgewater, or that he knew the men implicated in the holdup in question." He also got a description of the suspect. Murray immediately detailed operatives M.J. and E.E.C. to arrange to have the informant designate this man and to place him under surveillance.

On December 29, 1919, operative E.E.C. reported that the suspect was designated to him and that he (with operative M.J.) put the man under surveillance. In this and subsequent reports he was referred to as "the subject." Between noon and 5 p.m. on December 29, the subject visited so many places in Boston, East Boston and Brighton — nine — making so many changes of conveyances that one must admire the shadowing skill of the two operatives. One also wonders whether the suspect was seeking to cover up his tracks. At 5 p.m. the subject entered 31 Waverly Street, Brighton, by the rear door. The shadowers watched the house until 8 p.m. and did not see the subject leave.

On December 30, E.E.C. watched the house from 7:30 a.m. until 9 p.m. but did not see subject enter or leave.

On the same day, Murray had supper with his informant, who stated that he "had learned that the Italian mentioned yesterday had said that the men who were implicated in the Bridgewater holdup had occupied temporarily a shack in close proximity to Bridgewater and that the car that had been used was left there along with some overalls or disguise of a similar nature, used by one of the men implicated in the hold-up; that these men were Italians, had deserted the car, returned to Quincy by trolley; that they are believed to be residing in vicinity of Fore River Shipyard and are known to be anarchists."

Mr. Murray repeated to operative H.H. the story which his informant had learned. On December 31, H.H. relayed the information to Chief Goodhue of the Quincy police and to Officer Frank LeBaron in Bridgewater, assistant to Chief Stewart, who was away. H.H. then interviewed witnesses Cox and Bowles, who told him that they had no recollection that any of the holdup party wore overalls or clothes that were bulky in appearance as if one suit had been drawn over another. He also interviewed Mr. Harding, who could not recollect seeing any overalls or bulky-looking clothes, although one of the men wore a long black coat.

Chief Stewart and Officer Brouillard reported that they had traced the escaping car as far as Randolph but there lost the trail. (Randolph is northwest of Bridgewater.)

On January 1, H.H. reported that he and Officer LeBaron searched among the Bridgewaters for the supposed shack where the car had been stored. There were numerous shacks but only one answered the informant's description "in every respect." This was a place owned by an Italian named Emile Lombardi. Nothing came of this discovery, however.

Chief Sharples of East Bridgewater guided them around all likely places, but they found no trace of the missing car or anyone who had seen a "big Buick" in the vicinity.

By this time Mr. Murray must have become somewhat skeptical of the "subject's" story about the bandits. On January 2, through operative G.E.C. (E.E.C.?), he ascertained that the occupant of 31 Waverly Street was an Italian named C. A. Barr. (He was also known as Barasso.) He then suggested to H.H. that the man be seen and questioned "as to what he really knew of the affair."

On January 3, 1919, Chief Stewart, Officer Brouillard and operative H.H. interviewed Mr. Barr at his residence. The episode is so extraordinary and meaningful that the operative's report of the interview should be quoted verbatim:

L. Q. White
H.H. Reports: *Saturday, January 3, 1919.*

Today I resumed on the above mentioned operation by awaiting Chief Stewart and State Officer Brouillard who had promised to be in Boston at 9 A.M.

At 1:30 P.M. they arrived. We proceeded to 31 Waverly Street, Brighton, to see one C. A. Barr who had made statements in regard to the attempted holdup. On arrival at 31 Waverly Street we found that C. A. Barr had gone to Allston earlier in the day and it was not known when he would return. We waited in the neighborhood until C. A. Barr returned at 7:30 P.M. Then we entered 31 Waverly Street and talked with C. A. Barr who is a man 45 years, 5' 8", 150 lbs., black hair, dark complexion, close clipped black mustache, streaked with gray, black eyes, sharp features. Dressed in brown suit and heavy working shoes. Barr related a rambling statement about a machine that he had invented with which he could detect who had committed a crime no matter where it was committed. He stated that one Mrs. Vetilia of 2 Lexington Street, E. Boston had looked into the machine and saw the holdup happening and saw the men plainly but did not know who they were. He further stated that the men had changed their clothes before attempting the holdup and after the holdup again changed their clothes and left Bridgewater on the train.

Reported
1–5–20–M
Boston

Pinkerton reports do not indicate that Mr. Barr or his story about led anarchist bandits and the car left in the shack received any further attention at the time. Perhaps his fantastic tale of the crime-detecting machine discouraged further investigation. If so, that may have been precisely the purpose of Mr. Barr in telling such a cock-and-bull story. Let us consider the following:

1. Mr. Barr was fingered as a suspect by the underworld connections. The informant said that the subject had implicated himself in talking to associates but the informant may have had additional cogent reasons for his tip which were too hazardous to disclose. The reports indicate that the informant suggested enough to Mr. Murray to make his own investigation, but not enough to involve himself as a stool pigeon.

2. If Mr. Barr feared further police investigation, one way to end it was to create the impression that he was irresponsible. Certainly, the police should not have expected the suspect to invite trouble for himself by telling the truth at his first interview with the Bridgewater police chief, a State Police officer and a private detective.

3. It is astounding that the three professional investigators should apparently have missed the most significant and obvious clue which confronted them on their visit to Mr. Barr, namely, Mr. Barr himself.

Operative H.H. described the suspect he saw at 31 Waverly Street as "*a man 45 years, 5' 8", 150 lbs., black hair, dark complexion, close clipped black mustache, streaked with gray, black eyes, sharp features.*"

On December 24, 1919, the witness Cox had described the shotgun bandit to operative Hayes as a man "*5' 8", 150 lbs., dark complexion, 40 years of age. . . . He had a closely cropped mustache which might have been slightly gray.*"

On December 26, 1919, Mr. Hassam had described to operative H.H. the stranger who tried to borrow the number plates as a man "*40 years, 5' 8", 165 lbs., stocky build, black hair, dark sallow complexion, black eyes, black mustache, clipped close.*"

How was it possible for these investigators to have missed the amazing similarity of these three descriptions? Had the informant delivered into their hands the very criminal for whom they had been looking? We will never know. For Mr. Barr's story received no further attention — at least from the Pinkerton detectives and Officer Brouillard. As for Chief Stewart, he filed it away in his memory, to be brought again into his consciousness by a payroll robbery and brutal double murder four months later.

2.

Murder and Robbery at South Braintree

The Inquest and the Pinkerton Reports

The event which invoked in Chief Stewart's mind the vision seen by Mrs. Vetilia in Mr. Barr's marvelous invention took place on Pearl Street, in South Braintree, at about 3 P.M. on April 15, 1920. At that time and place, there occurred the double murder and payroll robbery for which Nicola Sacco and Bartolomeo Vanzetti were executed just after midnight on August 23, 1927.

As in the case of the Bridgewater affair, there is in existence a mass of data concerning this crime gathered by the police and others prior to the arrest of any suspects. This evidence, obtained when memories were fresh and prior to the arrest of Sacco and Vanzetti, is far more trustworthy than that presented at the trial. It was not selected and shaped with the object of securing a conviction or an acquittal of the accused. Taken together, especially with other evidence which became available after the trial, it makes quite a different picture of the crime than that developed on the witness stand. This material includes the minutes of the inquest (before Judge Albert Avery) into the deaths of Frederick A. Parmenter, paymaster of the Slater and Morrill Shoe Company, and Alexander (Alessandro) Berardelli, his guard, held in the District Court at Quincy on April 17, 1920, and reports of the Pinkerton detectives investigating the crime. The minutes of the inquest were not part of the record of the trial of Sacco and Vanzetti, which was in the Superior Court at Dedham, but were held in the files of the district attorney of Norfolk County, who regarded the proceedings in Quincy as "a private inquest held by the Commonwealth." [1]

[1] Holt Record, Vol. I, 1064. (These six volumes form the chief source for study of the Sacco-Vanzetti case. Hereafter, references to a volume and page number will refer to

Frederick G. Katzmann, the district attorney, had the inquest minutes at the Dedham trial and used them to cross-examine defense witnesses. Under Massachusetts law, he had the right to hold the minutes in secrecy.[2] Defense counsel knew he had them, but never obtained or saw a copy so far as the record discloses. This was the cause of their failure to point out important discrepancies between the inquest testimony and the trial evidence. When Mr. Thompson and I learned about the inquest minutes in July 1927, we persuaded Dudley P. Ranney, then assistant district attorney, to present them from his files to the Governor's Advisory Committee, which he did on July 21.[3] We had copies made for our own use.

The reports of the Pinkerton investigation of the South Braintree crime for the Travelers Insurance Company were unknown to counsel for the defendants until May 1926. At that time Mr. Thompson was alerted to their existence by the late Tom O'Connor, formerly a reporter of the State House News Service, and a copy was made available to us.

If we now turn to the minutes of the inquest of April 17, 1920, we get a description of the crime free from the possible taint of forcing the evidence to convict or acquit any known suspects.

Let us see what happened through the eyes of Mrs. Annie F. Nichols as she sat at the kitchen window of her home on the north side of Pearl Street. Her house faced two shoe factories on the south side of Pearl Street — the Rice and Hutchins factory almost opposite and the Slater and Morrill "lower" factory downhill and somewhat further east. Between her house and Pearl Street some Italian laborers were making an excavation. Her window looked directly at a spot between the two factories, about forty feet east of Rice and Hutchins and about one hundred fifty feet west of Slater and Morrill. This is the spot that was shortly to become the scene of robbery and murder.

At about three o'clock she saw two men leaning against the fence of Rice and Hutchins when Parmenter and Berardelli (called "the detective" by

---

the Holt Record. *The Sacco-Vanzetti Case: Transcript of the Record of the Trial of Nicola Sacco and Bartolomeo Vanzetti in the Courts of Massachusetts and Subsequent Proceedings, 1920–1927. 5 vols. With a Supplemental Volume on the Bridgewater Case.* [New York: Henry Holt, 1928–1929.]) By his use of the word "private," Mr. Katzmann must have meant that the inquest judge had excluded all persons not required by law to attend. G.L. Mass., Ch. 38, sec. 8.

[2] *Commonwealth v. Ryan*, 134 Mass. 223.   [3] Vol. V, 5251.

Mrs. Nichols) came along. Berardelli was in front and Parmenter following. Each carried a black bag, as he always did.

As Berardelli approached, the stranger nearest to him stepped right up to him and fired. *"I think this man that shot the detective spoke to him but I don't know what he said."* Then the man who shot Berardelli chased Parmenter across the street and put two shots into him. Somewhere in his flight Parmenter dropped his bag. The other stranger, who had been leaning against the fence, also fired at the detective. "They both seemed to want to get him."

Then she saw one of the two bandits fire a shot in the air to signal their auto, and the car came up the hill from in front of Slater and Morrill. Each of the robbers picked up a bag and threw it in the car. They then got in the automobile, together with a third bandit who came out from behind a pile of bricks on her side of Pearl Street, and "were gone." She can't describe this third man but the other two were short and stout and wore dark suits and caps. She didn't see their faces. There were five in the automobile, including the chauffeur. It all happened in "two seconds."

The car that came up the hill on signal was a large black touring car ("it may have been a new car or newly painted"). The curtains were drawn on her side.

Such was the scene as Mrs. Nichols saw it.

Mrs. Nichols's next-door neighbor, Maurice Colbert, a railroad man, did not see the actual shooting, but on returning home from work he saw two men against the fence. He paid no attention to them. He had just got into his house when the shooting commenced. He heard five, six or seven shots. The time must have been about 3:06 P.M., because he fixed the time of leaving work at 3:03 P.M. by looking at his watch, and it took him two or three minutes to walk home. He looked out in time to see two men grab the money boxes, run for the auto and jump in. The car had run about fifteen feet past the men. The men were medium-sized. He could not tell what they looked like, it was all done so quickly. Parmenter, before he died, said one was a short thickset man, the other short and slim. The car was a seven-passenger touring car, black or dark, with fairly good paint. The back curtains were drawn on his side and flapping. He did not see the number plates.

James E. McGlone, a teamster, was taking stone out of a cellar just across from the Rice and Hutchins shoe factory. When he heard the first shot he looked across the street and saw two young fellows running with the payroll bags (or boxes) toward Slater and Morrill's. When the machine came up they ran toward it, and jumped into the auto with the boxes. He saw no revolvers in the hands of these two robbers, but a third bandit had hold of Berardelli's shoulder with his left hand, a pistol in his right. He saw this man put two shots into the guard. There may have been two or three other shots, a couple before he saw the shots at Berardelli. He did not see the shooting of Parmenter. As the car moved over the railroad crossing, one shot was fired at Berardelli from the running board by a bandit facing Slater and Morrill's. The guard was then lying on the sidewalk. At the same time he saw a fellow stick a rifle through the window in the back of the car where the isinglass had been removed.

The three bandits were short men, about the same size, but two were not so heavy as the one who shot Berardelli. This man looked like an Italian but he did not get a good look at the others. He did not notice the number plates.

Lewis L. Wade, a shoemaker for Slater and Morrill, came out of the factory at about three minutes past three to operate a gasoline pump for Mr. Slater's chauffeur. He saw a car on the street and a fellow fixing it or pretending to fix it. He heard a shot and saw Parmenter and Berardelli. After the first shot Berardelli sank to the ground. Parmenter tried to run across the road with the boxes. Two men ran after him, leaving "this Italian alone with Berardelli," who shot Berardelli twice. He thought he could identify this man but he did not want to convict an innocent man. This bandit was bareheaded, slightly bald "over the eyes," hair a bit curly, between nineteen and twenty-two, weighing 125 to 130 pounds at most and dark-complected. He noticed the chauffeur particularly, light, fair-haired, a *pale sickly-looking* man, *as if he had consumption*. He described but could not identify the other two bandits. They also carried weapons.

The car was an open one with the top up and curtains down, some flapping. It looked dusty and dirty. He did not take the number plates, although he could have stepped out and touched the car when it went by.

Mr. Wade then offered the following significant comments:

Q. Did anyone try to intercept them? A. Only the gate man tried to put the gates down but they pointed a gun at him and he went into his shanty. I think the reason Berardelli was killed, I think he knew him.

Q. What leads you to that belief? A. I think so and will always think so. It looks as though this fellow wanted him out of the way.

Q. They followed Parmenter and did their best to get him out of the way. A. He held onto his bag. Berardelli didn't hold onto his box. Parmenter held onto his box and they fired at him back to. Berardelli was on the ground and why should this fellow want to turn around and want to kill him when the money box was on the ground? I think they knew each other.

(Forty years later Wade's surmise was confirmed as a fact in the memoirs of Joseph Morelli, who wrote that he had planned the South Braintree crime in every detail. In 1920 Morelli was the senior member of a group of professional criminals with headquarters in Providence.)

Edgar C. Langlois, foreman for Rice and Hutchins, heard shots, looked out of the window and saw two men, just below him, pumping bullets into Berardelli, one in front and one in back. They were short, dark-skinned, with curly or wavy hair. Both had automatic revolvers. He saw their faces but did not think he could identify them. Mr. Langlois then expressed the untrustworthiness of that kind of identification. "Two minutes after I was talking with another fellow out there now that was in the window and he says one thing and I another. . . . I don't think anyone could identify them, it was all so quick." He telephoned the police and when he returned he saw these two and a third man standing near the car. The car was dark green and the *paint* in good condition. The top was up and it was open at the sides. After the men got in, they stood on the running board, holding on with the right hand and firing at the body of Berardelli on the ground. The back window was pulled out and a man projected a rifle through it.

Saul M. Akeke, shoe worker at Rice and Hutchins, looking out of the window, saw two fellows shooting. When the man dropped, another came from behind the auto and picked up the money. The two who were firing looked alike, medium complexions, wore no hats or caps. They were built about the same. The third man wore a hat and overcoat. They put the two boxes in the auto, jumped in and got away. He was twenty or thirty feet from the scene but could not identify the men. It all happened in three or four seconds.

There were three other witnesses near the scene of the actual shooting. Angelo Susi, working on the cellar opposite Rice and Hutchins, added no useful information. Edward Carter, shoemaker at Slater and Morrill, had little to add except that he thought the murder car was a green Buick. He saw no number plates. John Mannix, slugger at Slater and Morrill, contributed little helpful information except that he heard that the "big car" had been nearly in front of the ladies' dressing room window of Slater and Morrill from quarter past two until the time of the shooting. This later led to the discovery of two excellent witnesses. Both Carter and Mannix saw a second smaller car, apparently Mr. Slater's automobile, which left the location a little ahead of the murder car.

The foregoing constitutes a summary of all of the inquest testimony by witnesses in close proximity to the actual holdup and murders. As would be expected from different witnesses, excited and with little time for observation, it was not entirely consistent. However, there is enough agreement to support several conclusions, especially when integrated with other inquest testimony.

There were other witnesses who testified to what they saw on Pearl Street as the murder car left the scene of the crime. Others saw suspicious-looking strangers in the town prior to the holdup. Before considering this testimony, however, it would be helpful to watch the movement of the payroll from the time it arrived in South Braintree by train until Parmenter and Berardelli kept their rendezvous with death in front of the two shoe factories.

Pearl Street runs east from South Braintree Square toward the two factories where the crime occurred. Just before it reaches the New Haven Railroad tracks, a short distance from the square, it passes a large wooden structure known as Hampton House on the north side of the street. The South Braintree railroad station stood nearby slightly further to the north. Hampton House held the office of the American Express Company on the first floor. Slater and Morrill occupied the second, third and fourth floors, and maintained its executive offices on the second floor, just over the American Express Company. The factory in Hampton House was known as number one, or the "upper" factory. The "lower" factory, down Pearl Street, where the murders occurred, was number two.

Thomas F. Fraher, superintendent of the Slater and Morrill factory, explained the routine of handling the payroll money. "This money comes in by American Express [on the train] in the morning and is carried to Miss Mahoney, the girl that puts up the money. She put it up as usual and had it all ready to go down about 3 o'clock."

The money arrived early in the morning, probably at half past nine. The whole payroll was probably over eighteen thousand dollars, but some of the help were paid in Hampton House. "The rest of the money, $15,773.59 was taken by Frederick A. Parmenter and Alexander Berardelli. It is put into wooden cases divided into sections. These are put in two steel boxes with Yale locks to lock them up." The boxes had handles, weighed six or seven pounds apiece and were colored either black or dark brown. "These two men are supposed to have guns in their pockets and they take these boxes, one in each hand and walk down the street," going from number one factory to number two.

Parmenter had been employed by the company eighteen or twenty years, Berardelli about a year. Berardelli was a special officer of the town of Braintree. Payday was Thursday. Until a week before the robbery, another employee, Harold Lewis, had always accompanied the men, but on this day there were just the two. Sometimes they went down by auto, sometimes on foot. It was common knowledge in the community that the boxes contained money going down for the purpose of paying off the help.

This was about the sum of Mr. Fraher's testimony except for a remark at the end which, if known to counsel for Sacco and Vanzetti, might have thrown doubt on some testimony at the trial given by Fred L. Loring, an employee of Slater and Morrill. When asked whether there was anything else he could give the court that would help in the detection of the robbers, Mr. Fraher stated that he had had a talk that very morning (April 17) with Mr. Loring. It was about some remarks by a group of cabdrivers who "answered descriptions" which Loring overheard in a Boston restaurant, but apparently nothing else worth noting by Mr. Fraher. (At the trial in 1921, Loring testified that just after the shooting he picked up a cap lying "eighteen inches" from Berardelli's body. The prosecution then claimed that this cap belonged to Sacco. Loring's failure to mention his "find" to Mr. Fraher on April 17 tends to confirm a fact that did not come to light until 1927, namely, that he did not find the cap on April 15, just after the shooting, but picked it up on the second day following the crime.)

The testimony of Shelley Neal, the American Express agent, constituted an important contribution to the story of the crime. In great detail Mr. Neal told how the bandits checked the arrival of the payroll on the morning of the fifteenth of April, and he gave a rather vivid account of two cars cooperating with one another and three men watching the movement of the money from the railroad station to Hampton House and from the express office on the first floor to the Slater and Morrill office on the second.

(On the witness stand at the trial of Sacco and Vanzetti, however, Mr. Neal told of only one car and only two men, the driver and the man in the doorway.)[4] In order that the reader may later compare Neal's testimony about thirty-six hours after the crime with his amputated version offered to the jury at the trial, his complete inquest testimony follows:

MR. ADAMS. What is your occupation? A. American Express Agent, So. Braintree.

Q. You had some money come out Thursday morning, April 15th for Slater and Morrell? [sic] A. Yes.

Q. Tell us how that money came to you, how you got it, what if any persons were around when you took it from the train and how you took it over to your office and how you delivered it to Slater & Morrell? A. The train arrives at So. Braintree at 9:18. It is always my custom and has been for 12 years for myself and two men to meet this train. I go armed with a revolver and the men who go with me are armed. We go by express wagon. We receive the money from the messenger on the train in an iron safe, or iron box as is used by all express companies. I took that and put it in the wagon and the driver with me. He rides on the seat and I generally either sit on the safe in the wagon or on the tail board. The other man stood up and we started over to deliver it.

Q. Your office is on the first floor of the Hampton House? A. Yes.

Q. Slater & Morrell's office is right over you? A. Right up stairs. In going across this morning, just as I put the money in the team I made the remark to the driver "It seems to me there are a great many autos in front of the building this morning," as we receive notice continually from the head officials of the company to be ever on the alert for anything that might happen. When we arrived in front of the building I had to cross diagonally in front of two autos to get up to our express door. When I arrived at the door I took the safe off and took it in my office. It makes it necessary to take it in there because there is another pay roll in there for Walker & Kneeland, another factory. I opened the safe with a key that comes to me sealed in a package. I opened the safe and took out the Slater & Morrell pay roll and then relocked the safe with the other pay roll in there, leaving that in the office. I next opened the door, the driver follows right behind me, and took the pay roll under my arm. It comes in a bag. I always carry a revolver in my coat pocket with my hand on the trigger. On opening the door it is always my custom to look the ground over and see what obstructions are there. This morning when I opened the door that one car was standing there with a man in the car and the engine running. The car was black, either newly varnished or a new car, but shiny black.

Q. What make? A. I didn't notice the make or the number plate, but I remember very distinctly the looks of the car. The car had the two back curtains partly up, not all up as you would for a rainy day but to conceal anybody in the back seat from me. That car was headed north. Across from him, about 20 feet from him was another car headed south with one man sitting in that car. These

4 Vol. I, 137, 147.

two men, as I opened the door, I heard one man say "All right" and I knew there was conversation between them. As I went through the door a stranger was standing in Slater & Morrell's entry, before you go up stairs to the factory. This man was standing there with both hands in his pocket, and the minute I got to him I looked right at him and he returned the look right at me. It occurred to me immediately that if he was there for any purpose that he no doubt had confederates inside the door with him, and in place of my going close to him on the corner I took the outside of the curb. Before I went up stairs I took care their entry way was clear. I thought everything was all right and went ahead. When I went up stairs there were several men standing on the top of the stairway but I found them to be salesmen who could be accounted for in the factory. I went through the office and put the pay roll in their safe. It is heavy for a lady who handles the pay roll. Just as I got down stairs, almost to the bottom, this man standing there stepped off one step across the sidewalk and stepped into the rear seat of the black car.

Q. Describe that man. A. I should say he was about 5–8, weighed 150 lbs. either a Swede or a Finn. He was of that complexion, with very light hair. Possibly he had not been shaved for two days. I looked square into his face and he looked as though under a great strain, his eyes were sunk and wrinkled.

Q. Could you remember him? A. I could very readily pick him out. He had on a light hat, of light mixture. His coat was dark, not black but something dark, but beyond that his clothing I did not look at as closely as I did himself. He struck me as a man who had either been through some severe sickness or under a great strain. His face was almost colorless, white. He stepped into the car and in that car the engine was running. They started right off north. The other car which I could not describe I think was either dirty color or had not been washed. That started south. Both started very nearly the same time in opposite directions. From that time I did not have any occasion to see them again.

Q. The first car had the curtains in the back down. Do you remember what the back of the car itself looked like? A. I can't describe the back of the car.

Q. Whether the window was broken or the izing glass there? A. I can't describe that part.

Q. Describe the back of the other car? A. I just remember of seeing the car there but didn't notice.

Q. Can you tell whether the window was broken out or not? A. I do remember on this car the curtains were partly up so it would conceal any person sitting in the back seat. I was trying to find out whether this man had any connection with this car or not.

Q. He got into the shiny car? A. He got into the shiny car. After things happened I remembered this man making the remark to this other car. The other two men evidently had conversation between them.

Q. How many men were in the dark car, the first one? A. One man the driver.

Q. How many in the dirty colored car? A. One man, the driver.

Q. You don't remember the makes of the cars? A. No.

Q. You didn't take the numbers on either of them? A. No.

Q. From that time on you attended to the express business? A. I went right along with the express business.

Q. Now on the afternoon of the shots, tell us what you know with reference to that. A. I was sitting at my desk which is the front of the building. There is a glass window overlooking the cars. The clerk was in the next office with me at the time. The first thing I heard was what occurred to me a motor cycle back firing. That was the first thing in my mind. I made no remark to her or she to me although she looked up and stopped writing. Only about a minute elapsed until another or two followed quickly and I jumped off the chair and said "Somebody is shot." I looked out of the window and saw the crossing tender running into the shanty and saw this black shiny car pass up the street. I immediately grabbed my revolver, I am a special officer, pinned the badge on my coat and ran out of the door. By the time I got out of the door the car was too far up the street and I knew there was no use trying to chase it.

Q. With reference to that car. Did it look anything like the car you saw in the morning? A. Exactly the same car I saw in the morning on side view. The moment I saw it I knew it was this shiny black car with the curtains in the same position, drawn enough so you couldn't see the men in the back seat.

Q. Did you notice the back end of this car as it went up the street? A. I did not from where I was standing.

Q. Did you go out onto Pearl Street? A. Yes.

Q. Did you see the car then go up toward So. Braintree square? A. Yes.

Q. Did you notice the back end? A. No.

Q. Did you get the number plate? A. No.

Q. You can't tell the make of it? A. No.

Q. Or who was in it? A. No.

Q. Tell how fast it was going? A. Not very fast.

Q. Could you hear how it sounded, was the engine running all right? A. I can't say that I could, there was so much noise and confusion at that time. There were several hollering. I knew I could not do anything by following it.

Q. Did you fire at the car? A. I did not.

Q. Did you see any other car there ahead or in back of that? A. That was the only car I saw.

Q. Or that you could see until you got to So. Braintree square? A. I saw it first from my window and by the time I got on the street I could not see it until it got to the corner and then it was pretty well up to the Main Street.

Q. Are you prepared to say it was the same car you saw in the morning? A. I could not as I didn't take the number plate and did not see the back of the car to state positively that it was the same car. I feel satisfied that the shiny black, whether new varnish or a new car, what so closely resembled that car in the morning was the curtains being drawn so you could not see the men in front. It was the same in the afternoon as in the morning you could not see anybody there.

Q. In the morning did the engine sound as though it was running all right? A. Yes, just running idly.

Q. How many shots did you hear altogether? A. As they came in such quick succession I thought it was a motor cycle back firing.

Q. How many shots did you hear? A. I heard two that I absolutely know were shots. They were on the crossing.

Q. How many more did you hear? A. I should say 6 or 7.

Q. Right together? A. Right together.

Q. What interval of time? A. At least a minute or mote [*semble,* more] between.

Q. How many? A. Two I distinctly remember.

Q. These two sounded nearer to you than the first group? A. Yes.

Q. They fired as the auto came up the street? A. As they were very near my office when they last fired.

Q. Do you know who they were firing at? A. No.

Q. Did you see anything of a rifle? A. I did not.

Q. Any rifle pointed out from the back of that car? A. I did not.

Q. No more shots as they went toward the Main street? A. I did not hear any.

Q. Anything further you can give as to a clue to these robbers? A. I think I have told all. I feel the only party I could positively identify was this one man. I felt he was watching me or that money.

Q. And the occupants of the two cars were in communication with each other? [A.] This man, after he left the step and got in to his car, they drove off in the opposite direction.

Q. One toward the railroad track and one toward Pearl Street? A. One north and one south.

THE COURT. Which car was the shiny black one? A. The shiny car went north going toward So. Braintree square. I don't know whether he turned up Holbrook Avenue and came up to the Square or French Avenue.

Q. What time did you take the Kneeland pay roll down? A. Right after. I came down and we put the safe on the wagon and we started up there and during the trip down there I did not meet anybody on the road either way. We are always cautioned to try to note anything when we are delivering pay rolls that looks suspicious.

Q. You didn't say anything to Slater & Morrill about your suspicions at that time? A. No.

Q. That was all your own idea? A. Yes.

Q. It was not anything to cause you to comment? A. No, I did not know whether the man stopping there was waiting for someone to come and when they didn't he started to go.

Q. This is as it has occurred to you since? A. Yes.

Q. You could identify that man again? A. Yes.

Q. You think you could identify the car? A. I would not say as to the car. My mind at that time was on whether there was a man sitting on the back seat of the car.

MR. ADAMS. No one was in the back seat? A. No.

Q. Just the driver of each car and this other man out of the car? A. Yes. After I got far enough along I looked back and saw the back seat empty.

Q. Did the man have a smooth face? A. Standing in the doorway, yes. Very pale and looked like a man you sometime see that is a cigarette fiend, yellow.

Q. He got into the shiny car? A. He got into the back seat of the shiny car.

Q. Were the curtains down on both seats or only one seat? A. The left side of the car nearest me. I cannot say about the right side that was from me. On the left side the curtain on the back was down. If that curtain had been up and the other down I could have looked and seen anybody there.

(Trial counsel for the defendants apparently accepted Mr. Neal's trial testimony that only one car was involved. They had never seen the inquest minutes. In 1926, however, Celestino F. Madeiros, self-confessed participant in the crime, deposed that two cars were used in the crime, and that the robbers with the loot had switched from the Buick to a waiting Hudson in the Oak Street woods, two miles from South Braintree. After we obtained the minutes of the inquest, in July 1927, we learned for the first time that Shelley Neal's trial testimony had been cut to fit the one-car theory and that Madeiros had revealed the omitted truth in this respect — six years after the murders. The use of two or more cars to throw pursuers off the trail is a telltale tactic of professional robberies.)

Thomas F. Treacy, a coal team driver, corroborated Mr. Neal with respect to the two cars in the morning in front of the station. He saw one of these two cars about three o'clock in the afternoon in front of the Slater and Morrill factory, and also saw the very light man with a screwdriver before the car, very light hair, very thin; he "thought he was a Swede." He saw another car getting gasoline at the Slater and Morrill plant (apparently Mr. Slater's car). It was not one of the cars he saw in the morning. Toward the end of his testimony there seemed to be some confusion which might have been due to his misunderstanding the questions or, as the court hinted, to his apparently having been drinking.

Patrick J. Walsh, foreman at Rice and Hutchins, was apparently the only witness who saw the occupants of the car before the three bandits on the street leaped into it. He was on the third floor of the first factory, his view partly obstructed, and did not see the shooting because the murders occurred in front of the second factory. He heard shots, looked out of the window and saw an auto coming up. It was a dirty-looking car, like a Buick. There was only one man on the front seat, driving the car, and another man standing up over the back seat with a regular revolver in his hand. The driver was of a stocky build, with a full face and a lighter complexion than the other. The man with the gun was "awful dark" with thin features. He saw no rifle or number plate. He thought he had seen the same car going by the shop "about a month before with four or five in it, a 'hard looking crowd' who looked like foreigners."

Michael Levangie was the crossing tender mentioned by Shelley Neal in his statement that, on hearing the shots, he "looked out of the window and saw the crossing tender running into the shanty and saw this black shiny car pass up the street." Levangie was cleaning the window of his shanty when he heard shots. He heard shooting but didn't know who was shot or what. The auto came over his crossing at about 3:20 P.M. It was a dark automobile, dirty with mud. He started to lower the gates because he heard the bell of a freight coming, but some man on the rear seat pointed a revolver at him and he left the gates and went into his shanty and stayed there. The only man he saw was the driver, on the left, on his side. He had a dark complexion, dark brown moustache,[5] soft hat and brown coat. He did not get the number of the auto; he looked only at the driver and the pistol. The car was going about ten or twelve miles an hour. He could tell the driver if he saw him again.

Ralph L. DeForest, a shoemaker, heard shots when he was going down Pearl Street, and when he got within twenty feet of the crossing (on the side opposite to Levangie) a Buick car, 1916 model, came up and there was firing on both sides. It was a dirty dull green in color and the back window was out. The engine was running in second speed, missing fire. He had seen the same car at about twenty past two o'clock, near the depot headed toward the shop (Slater and Morrill). The driver was tinkering with the engine, he was light-skinned, had light hair, a smooth face, pale cheeks, either from severe illness or fright, and looked like a dope fiend. He wore an army coat. There were two other men hanging around the depot, both dark-complexioned, with pepper and salt suits. One had a dark coat that did not match. One was about 5' 10", the other about two and a half inches shorter. DeForest went into the depot and when he came out they were gone. That was why he thought these were the men who did the shooting. He thought he could identify the men again.

Carl J. Knipps, shipper for Slater and Morrill, was sitting in the window at the Hampton House factory. He heard the shooting and ran out toward the lower factory. As he got to the crossing, a big dark touring car was coming toward him and he saw a gun pointing at him. At least one shot was fired at him. He was on the depot side of Pearl Street. The car seemed to be working on three cylinders, skipping. On the back seat a man looked as if he were standing up. There seemed to be five in the car. He could not

---

[5] This mention of the moustache in the transcript is inexplicable. The very next day, Pinkerton operative H.H. reported that Levangie had described the driver as clean-shaven. On April 21, Captain Proctor broadcasted a description of the bandits as smooth-shaven. (*Boston Herald*, April 22, 1920.) This was four days after the inquest. This subject will be discussed later.

describe any one of them. He was excited and got out of the way. The car had a number plate in front, none in the back. The back curtains were down.

Merle L. Averill, a salesman, was at DeBeradinis's cobbler shop, on the north side of Pearl, just at the corner of the crossing. He heard shots and ran to the doorway just as a big black machine he thought was a Buick went by. There seemed to be something the matter with the car; it was grinding unnaturally. It looked as if it had had ordinary use. The curtains were up on the right side of the front seat; they were closed in back. He could not see who was on the back seat. The man on his side, next to the driver, was smooth-faced, bareheaded, his face terribly white, extremely pallid. He leaned over the side of the car, pointed a revolver at his group and clicked it, but he had used the last shot at the crossing.

Louis DeBeradinis, the cobbler, gave about the same account as Averill. The man who shot had long hair "to his nose" and his face was awfully white. If he saw him, he "probably" could tell him.

Lawrence D. Ferguson, shoe cutter, from a Hampton House window saw the car pass up Pearl Street, the man on the front seat firing a black automatic out of the car. He looked like an Italian with a growth of beard, pretty stocky. He was only about thirty feet away and got a good look at this man, but was pretty sure he could not recognize him again.

Mark Edward Carrigan, shoe cutter, saw the car go by from his Hampton House window. He saw the man with the revolver, on the front seat with the chauffeur, holding out the gun. He was short and stout, weighing 150 pounds, "dark foreign element, 25 to 28 years old."

Winfred H. Pierce, shoe cutter, saw the car from a Hampton House window, saw the car go "racing" up Pearl Street. The curtains were down and flapping from the front seat to the back. There were two men on the front seat; the man who did the firing was on the right-hand side. He got a good look at his face, but all he noticed was that he was a dark man. He didn't think he would be able to tell the men he saw.

Olaf Olsen, shoemaker, was on the left side of Pearl Street going down when the car came across the railroad track. They were going fast, pointed a revolver at him, but did not shoot. The fellow driving was dark, the fellow with the gun had a cap pulled down too far. He could see four men in the car, a couple in the back seat. The car was going too fast for him to get the license plate number. If he had a good look, he might be able to identify the dark one — they were going so fast. He saw the car go up to South Braintree Square and turn left "on two wheels" toward Holbrook.

Donald Wight, bank teller in the Braintree National Bank, about two miles away, saw two suspicious-looking strangers in his bank who cashed a ten dollar check. It was about quarter past two. One in a dark suit and hat seemed Italian, the other Irish. He saw no automobile. The one who looked Irish had light hair, a complexion colored like fingers stained with cigarettes, wore what looked like a service coat and spoke "straight American." The Italian had a very dark beard, was five feet ten inches in height and smooth-shaven. When the men in the bank heard of the robbery, they immediately thought there was some connection.

John C. Hubbard, an expressman, gave some interesting testimony about a car with three men in it. The motor was skipping. He did not see the number plate. He first saw the car at 2:30 in front of his Holbrook home on the Holbrook–South Braintree line. It came from the direction of South Braintree, turned around and parked. There were two windows in the back and the glass was out of one of them. He couldn't say whether it was a four-door or two-door car. The driver may have been American or Swedish. A man beside him got out to tinker with the carburetor and this man had a black moustache. The man in the back seat was very tall; the driver was light-skinned. The car went off toward South Braintree. He mentioned a bit of hearsay that later proved to be a fact. He had heard that rubber-headed tacks had been found in South Braintree. He saw the car again coming back at about 4:20 P.M. The motor was not then skipping. The reason he thought it was the same car was because the curtains were down at the back seat and there were three men in it. (If the men he saw were involved in the South Braintree crime and were the same on both occasions, Mr. Hubbard's testimony suggests that there might have been a switch of cars. The car which was parked in front of his house and headed toward South Braintree at 2:30 had *two* back windows, whereas the murder car had only *one* oval window. The car which passed his house at 4:20 might have been the murder car but could not have been the escape car, which by that time had passed beyond Matfield over ten miles away on a route which did not include Holbrook.)

The medical testimony at the inquest was brief. It was expanded greatly at the trial over a year later.

Dr. John C. Frazer, medical examiner for 4th Norfolk, attended the autopsy on the body of Berardelli conducted by Dr. George Burgess Magrath, medical examiner for Suffolk County. There were four wounds and four bullets extracted. The tracks of three bullets were horizontal, but the fourth was lengthwise in the body and ended up against the hip bone, "Evidently he [Berardelli] was lying down at the time." They were all of .32 caliber, steel-jacketed, indicating that an automatic pistol was used.

Dr. Frederick E. Jones, medical examiner for 3rd Norfolk, was present at the autopsies performed on Berardelli and on Parmenter. There were two wounds on Parmenter and two bullets were extracted. There were four wounds on Berardelli and four bullets were extracted. He deduced from the wounds and the bullets that all six were fired by the same type of pistol. In describing the track of the bullets in Berardelli, he gave the same testimony as Dr. Frazer: three were horizontal and the fourth must have been fired as Berardelli lay prone upon the ground. This last bullet ended up against the ilium bone of the pelvis and was slightly flattened as it came to rest. He mentioned the contents of the clothing of both men, which they searched, but found no firearms.

The foregoing constitutes substantially all of the inquest testimony. According to Mr. Fraher, all who had seen the robbery and shooting had been summoned to the hearing.

The Pinkerton reports began on April 17, the day of the inquest. The operative (H.H.) apparently worked fairly closely with Captain Proctor and some of his State Police. The daily reports add little to the description of the crime itself. The statements of some witnesses, however, are important, especially in the light of later developments. One of these was Mrs. Jenny Novelli, a nurse, who told the operative that on April 15, she was walking down Pearl Street at about 2:55 P.M. and saw a dark green touring car proceeding slowly along Pearl Street with two men in it. It stopped directly below the Slater and Morrill factory. She thought one of the men was a friend of hers, a Mr. Mooney, but on second look saw he was not. She was positive she could identify the man sitting on the right side of the driver. Her description was as follows: "27 years, 5' 8", medium build, light brown hair, fair complexion and smooth shaven and wore a cap."

(Nurse Novelli later became a defense witness at the trial. Her description of this bandit varied somewhat from that recorded by H.H., and the Pinkerton operative was called to the stand to impeach her testimony. H.H. then purported to repeat what Mrs. Novelli had told him on April 17,

1920. The statement — except for age and height of the bandit — that he attributed to her bore little resemblance to the foregoing description contained in his report, but came closer to describing Sacco.)

On April 18, Levangie is reported as describing the driver as "smooth shaven," although the day before at the inquest, the transcript indicates that he had said the man had a moustache.

On April 19, Chief Gallivan of the Braintree police showed H.H. fragments of bottle, the cap, shell for Winchester shotgun, and one of the rubber-headed tacks thrown out by occupants of the bandit car. The cap was an old, dark-color, heavy winter cap about 6⅞ size. It became a most controversial item at the trial. The shell was "the same as the one found on the scene of the Bridgewater attempted holdup last December." [6] The tack was a steel tack, "about ¾″ long, with a rubber head so shaped that the sharp point of tack will stand up straight no matter how thrown."

The operative then interviewed Mary E. Splaine, who told him a long story covering eighteen years, filled with gossip and scandal about conditions inside the Slater and Morrill office and suspicion of various employees being connected with the crime. (Later, on May 11, after the arrest of Sacco and Vanzetti, Mr. Fraher told H.H. that no serious attention should be paid to Miss Splaine's stories, "because she is one of the most irresponsible persons he ever came in contact with.") In the course of her recital, Miss Splaine said that immediately after the shooting she saw from an office window "a large green automobile come up the street at a good speed." She saw a man leaning over the driver's seat from the rear, firing a revolver.

She described the man as follows from the momentary glimpse she got of him: "round, rather full, pale face, black hair, cut pompadour style, powerful shoulders, and wearing gray clothes, no hat. Greenlaw and Knipps [fellow employees] ran out to get the number, but were greeted with a bullet. Knipps retreated, but Greenlaw stayed a moment and says the car carried no registration plate in the rear."

The report continued: "This was the first time Miss Splaine ever saw two men take the payroll and one of the few times those taking it walked. The usual procedure is to take the payroll down in an automobile and Messrs. Fraher, Knight, Lewis, Parmenter and Berardelli acted as guards. . . .

[6] The *Boston Herald* for April 19, 1920, states that Chief Gallivan found an empty rifle shell in the brush near the abandoned car.

Berardelli the guard had not been on the job a great while and was disliked by the office help who felt he was not trustworthy."

On April 20, 1920, H.H. showed a picture of Anthony Palmisano ("Tony the Wop") to Miss Splaine, among others. She "instantly declared that it was a photo of the man she saw standing in the car with a revolver in his hand and wore light gray clothes."

(Miss Splaine, at the trial in 1921, became the "star" identifying witness, positively identifying Sacco as the man she saw.)

Albert Frantello, an employee at the Slater and Morrill factory, took a good look at one of the men on the street just before the murders. He was: "Italian, 20 to 22 years, 5' 2", slim build, black hair, dark complexion, rough unshaven face, dressed in a dark suit, light grey sweater and dark cap, no overcoat." Frantello believed that the photo of "Tony the Wop" was a picture of the man he saw.

Miss Malcolm, of the dressing room of Slater and Morrill, saw the shooting from a distance, too far away for her to distinguish features. She saw one man stand over Berardelli after he had fallen and fire several shots into Berardelli's body, while the second pursued Parmenter across the street and fired on him after he was down.

H.H. then interviewed Miss Louise Hayes and Miss Minnie Kennedy, who had by far the best opportunity to observe the chauffeur of the murder car. They watched him out of the dressing room window:

"For twenty minutes the chauffeur was no more than six feet away from these two girls so they had an excellent opportunity to notice him which they did because he was good looking and well dressed. He stood alongside the hood of the car, lifted the hood, looked in on the engine and walked around the car so they had an opportunity to note his height and build, so described him as follows: 'No more than 20 years, 5' 6–7", very slim build, blond hair, very fair complexion, smooth shaven and regular features.'

"From his appearance, both girls thought he might be in *bad health*." (Emphasis added.) Dressed in a well-cut dark blue form-fitting suit, stiff collar, four-in-hand tie, dark brown soft hat and dark brown shoes, "they thought he was a pretty classy fellow and therefore paid a good deal of attention." H.H. arranged with Mr. Fraher for them to come to Boston to look through the galleries.

On April 21, the two girls looked over photos at the Pinkerton Boston agency and picked out a couple who looked like the man they saw.

They next proceeded with the operative to the State Detective Department and were questioned by District Attorney Katzmann, Captain Proctor and State Police officers Sherlock, Brouillard, Murphy, Wells and Scott. District Attorney Katzmann thoroughly questioned both girls and spoke of reopening the inquest in order to have their testimony included, but finally said that if they each wrote a report on what they saw and gave a description of the chauffeur, it would suffice. The description given by the girls to H.H. was confirmed except that the driver was not a blond, but nearly so.

On April 22, the adjuster for the company insuring the payroll checked with Mr. Slater the statement by Miss Splaine that it was customary to have two guards accompany the paymaster and to use an automobile. When the policy was placed, the insurance agent had been assured by Mr. Slater, Mr. Greenlaw and Mr. Parmenter that this was the regular thing. Mr. Slater told the adjuster who called him that this was the exception, not the rule. The adjuster, however, was inclined to believe otherwise and felt that Mr. Slater did not pay much attention to the details.

On April 22, the operative showed a number of photos to witnesses in South Braintree. Wade, Frantello, Hans Behrsin (Mr. Slater's chauffeur, who saw two men sitting on the fence) and Miss Splaine separately picked out a picture of Anthony Palmisano as a likeness of one of the men they saw.

On April 22, H.H. interviewed James F. Bostock, proprietor of a machine shop in Brockton. On April 15, he was in South Braintree with a crew of men doing work for Slater and Morrill. He left for lunch at about 12:45 P.M. and returned about 1:30 or 1:45. When he left and when he returned he saw two men loitering on Pearl Street near the Rice and Hutchins factory. As he returned he also noticed a large blue-black car parked right under the dressing room windows. He left Slater and Morrill at 3:05 P.M. to catch the 3:15 train for Boston. As he passed up Pearl Street he saw the same two men loitering in front of Rice and Hutchins and a few yards after passing them, he met Parmenter and Berardelli carrying the payroll. A moment after he exchanged greetings with Parmenter he heard shots. Turning around, he saw Berardelli crouched on the ground; one of the men he had seen was standing within three feet of Berardelli shooting into his body. The other man was shooting at Parmenter, and after Parmenter had dropped the box, the bandit fired twice more into his back. The auto he had seen parked under the dressing room window drove up to where the money boxes lay and stopped. The chauffeur got out of the car and picked up one of the boxes. Then one of the two men who had done the shooting picked up the other box and they got into the car followed by the second and smaller man. There were only three men implicated in the affair. As the car proceeded up Pearl Street, one man stood up in the car with a revolver which he discharged one or more times.

The man who shot Parmenter was: "Italian, 20 years, 5′ 3″, 130 lbs., medium build, black hair, dark complexion, smooth shaven, dressed in medium gray suit and cap."

The man he saw shoot Berardelli was: "Italian, 22 years, 5′ 6″, 140–145 lbs., medium build, dark hair and complexion, smooth shaven, dressed in dark suit and cap."

The driver of the car was: "19–20 years, 5′ 6–7″, 130 lbs., slim build, light hair and complexion, smooth shaven, dressed in dark blue suit and cap."

On looking at the operative's photos, Bostock selected the picture of Anthony Palmisano as an excellent likeness of the man who shot Parmenter and later stood up in the automobile as it was driven up Pearl Street. He thought a picture of one Joseph Sando resembled the man who shot Berardelli, and the photos of Willoughby C. Gray and Robert A. Matthews, the driver of the car. These last were the same photos selected by Misses Hayes and Kennedy.

On April 23, at the office of the Massachusetts District Police, the witnesses again selected Palmisano's picture. Captain Proctor then arranged for two of his men to go to Buffalo to investigate Palmisano.

On April 25, H.H. showed his photos to Mrs. Nichols, Mr. Knipps and Mrs. Novelli, but none of them selected a picture.

On April 26, operative H.H. learned from Captain Proctor that Anthony Palmisano was saved by the criminal's finest alibi — he had been in jail in Buffalo since January.

Shelley Neal and Louis DeBeradinis selected the picture of Willoughby C. Gray as the photo resembling one of the men they saw.

The reports continued through April 29, without adding any important information. They were not resumed until May 6, 1920.

Meanwhile, on April 17, a couple of hunters found an abandoned Buick in the Manley woods near Cochesett in the Bridgewaters. It was a 1920 seven-passenger Buick touring car, dark blue with black fenders and a black top, and, according to H.H.'s report of April 19, apparently in fine condition, the only visible damage being a bullet hole in the right side rear door. This bullet hole is something of a puzzle, since it was not perceived at the time and place the car was discovered, although the car was then and there thoroughly inspected by the hunters and the police. The back window was found lying in the rear. Several witnesses identified the Buick as the murder car seen in South Braintree. It was identified as David Murphy's automobile stolen in Needham on November 22, 1919.

3.

Chief Stewart Remembers

The Anarchist Hypothesis Ends the State Police Investigation

It was now fairly easy to make a tentative reconstruction of the crime in South Braintree. Allowing for errors in observation by witnesses, inevitable in a sudden and brief exposure to a scene of robbery and murder, but giving weight to consensus and to witnesses who seemed reliable and had the best opportunity to note what happened, their reconstruction might have been as follows:

1. There were two cars involved, the shiny Buick and an old dark dirty car.

2. The three men at Hampton House in the morning were obviously checking to make sure that the payroll arrived. The two cars then separated and went off in opposite directions.

3. The car seen on Pearl Street was the shiny Buick.

4. The older dark dirty car must have been fairly near. This second car was in South Braintree either to assist in the fray, if resistance had developed, or to supply promptly a car into which the bandits could switch passengers and loot to deceive pursuers. Where it was at the time of the robbery would have to await further investigation. However, its occupants (or occupant) were apparently around South Braintree Square just prior to the

action on Pearl Street. This might explain why the descriptions of several suspicious-looking characters differed materially from those given by eye-witnesses to the crime itself.

5. Shortly before the shooting, the Buick took up a prearranged position in front of the dressing room window of Slater and Morrill, facing up Pearl Street. The chauffeur fiddled around the car with a screwdriver probably as an excuse for remaining parked, although there may have been motor trouble, since the engine was noted to be missing at the start of the getaway a few moments later.

6. Two bandits took up prearranged positions leaning against the fence of Rice and Hutchins at a spot which the paymaster and guard had to pass on their way to Slater and Morrill a short distance down the hill. As Berardelli came up carrying his money box, the first man stepped out and there seems to have been something said. Shots attracted the attention of witnesses who saw this bandit put two bullets into Berardelli who was felled instantly. He might have shot Berardelli one or more times before the witnesses looked on the scene. The testimony is conflicting as to whether the second bandit also shot Berardelli. Later it was found that there were four bullets in Berardelli's body. The witnesses agree that the robbers seemed determined to kill the guard. The man who shot Berardelli then chased Parmenter across the street and shot him twice. In his flight, Parmenter dropped his money bag.

7. The bandit who did all or most of the shooting then deliberately fired a shot into the air. This was thought to be a signal to the driver of the Buick to come up. It might also have been a signal to the second car if it was waiting nearby, to inform its driver that the robbery was accomplished and that it should speed to the prearranged rendezvous.

8. A third bandit then emerged from behind a pile of bricks on the other side of Pearl Street opposite to the place where the other two had waited.

9. The Buick moved up to a point just beyond the murder scene and slowed almost to a stop. As it did this, the bandit from behind the brick pile and the second bandit from the fence each seized a money bag, threw them into the back of the Buick and all three got into the car. The car then began to pull away, and some bandit, either from the running board or from within the car, fired a final shot at Berardelli's prostrate body.

10. As the Buick moved up Pearl Street a man in the back of the car thrust through the rear curtain, from which the window had been removed,

the barrel of a weapon referred to by witnesses as a rifle. This must have been for the purpose of stopping their pursuers. It was not fired (there were no pursuers), but there was pistol-shooting at people on both sides of the street.

11. Rubber-headed tacks were strewn in the street by the occupants and fell point up, to puncture tires.

12. A striking fact was that not one of the many witnesses at the inquest, or interviewed by the Pinkerton operatives, got the registration number of the car.[1] This apparently was because there was no number plate in the rear, and the plate in front had been mud- and dust-splattered. This condition might also explain why a few of the witnesses described this bright new automobile as dirty.

13. The car gathered speed after the boarding party, so much so that as it made a left turn at South Braintree Square toward Holbrook, it spun almost on "two wheels."

14. By May 5, the police must also have learned that the car never reached Holbrook, but made a hairpin turn in about a mile and sped boldly back into South Braintree, where it turned west on Pond Street leading toward Randolph. This ruse effectively threw off pursuing cars, which continued into Holbrook.

15. The State Police would also have suspected that the bandits might have obtained helpful information from someone who knew the inside working of Slater and Morrill's payroll situation. It was even possible that there was some cooperation. Certainly it was an unusual coincidence that the robbery occurred when the paymaster and his guard carried the payroll on foot, with no third man to cover them, and at a time when neither man apparently carried a pistol or revolver. Employees of the factory threw suspicion on a number of the office help, including Berardelli, whose death, however, would have blocked any interrogation. They would probably have concluded from the obvious determination of the bandits to make sure of Berardelli's death and from other evidence that the guard knew the killers and recognized them.

It is not known how much of the foregoing reconstruction was made by Captain Proctor and his state detectives. However, they were men familiar with the ways of criminals and there can be little doubt that they would

---

[1] Contemporary newspaper accounts, however, reported that the police obtained a registration plate number from some source.

have seen the South Braintree affair as the work of a most skillful band of professionals, remarkable for its thorough scouting, planning, assignment of functions, timing and careful attention to details. It is easy to see why Captain Proctor believed that it was a professional job, as did men in the Department of Justice.

The State Police also had made a good start toward ultimate identification of guilty suspects. According to contemporary articles in the *Brockton Times*, they had obtained very good photographs of fingerprints on the abandoned Buick. These had not yet been matched with those of suspects but they held out the hope that eventually their owners would be traced.

The murder team on Pearl Street could be generally described, although except for the chauffeur, the identification of individuals by eyewitnesses seemed doubtful. Kennedy and Hayes, who had by far the best opportunity to observe the driver, gave a detailed description of his features, appearance, weight and clothes. Bostock, who was nearest to him, gave the same description, even to the dark blue suit. Other witnesses tended to confirm their description of a thin, pale, blondish young man who appeared as if he had not been well or was addicted to drugs. The only exception was Levangie, who was recorded as saying at the inquest that he saw a moustache on the driver as he stopped lowering the gates in the face of a gun nozzle and fled to his shanty. As a matter of fact, no other witness saw a moustache on any of the five bandits. The only witness who apparently got a glimpse of the man in the shadow of the tonneau, available to push the weapon through the rear opening (Walsh), described him as "awful dark" with thin features. The three bandits on Pearl Street seemed to be Italians, were medium or short in height, and wore dark clothes and caps. Despite some differences in estimated height and weight (the executioner was the stoutest), they appeared to be the same general type of men. Which bandit or bandits put bullets into the two victims would have to await further evidence, including possibly ballistic examination.

Having in mind the practical impossibility of identifying strangers in a split second during great excitement, the State Police must have regarded this testimony as rather untrustworthy. Especially would this be true of the descriptions by eyewitnesses who got only a fleeting glimpse of the occupants of the murder car as it escaped up Pearl Street firing a fusillade of shots at both sides of the street. Many witnesses expressed doubt that they could ever identify the men they saw. Nevertheless, the police followed

acceptable detection routine in having the witnesses exami'
photos in the State House and Metropolitan District Comm
galleries of criminals. Most of them selected a picture of Anthony
sano as the man who shot Berardelli. Despite the fact that these witnesses
were free of the powerful suggestion that operates when there are actual
suspects, they had picked out the picture of a man who had been in jail at
the time. The difficulty of correct instant observation was again illustrated
in the descriptions of the murder car. It was a new car, with paint in good
condition, yet several of the witnesses described it as dark green. Actually it
was dark blue, with black fenders and top. The only witnesses who said it
was dark blue were Hayes, Kennedy and Bostock. Other evidence, better
than instant observation, was needed for reliable identification.

 Unknown to the State Police (and to the district attorney's office), there
was actually in existence a powerful clue to guide them in their investigation. If their work had not been interrupted by Chief Stewart's pursuit of
anarchist suspects, they would almost certainly have come upon it and perhaps spared Massachusetts a Sacco-Vanzetti case. As in other instances already described, knowledge of this evidence did not reach counsel for the
defendants until the attitude of the authorities had become so rigidly set
against Sacco and Vanzetti that they refused even to investigate anything
that might have led them to change it.

The clue lay at hand in the headquarters of the New Bedford police. One
evening shortly before April 15, 1920, Inspector Ellsworth C. Jacobs saw a
local unsavory character named Michael Morelli driving what looked like a
new Buick touring car. He was with two other men. Inspector Jacobs knew
Mike and suspected that he had stolen the car or was up to some mischief.
(Mike Morelli was also known to the Bureau of Identification of the Boston police, where he was listed as a car thief.) Jacobs noted the number
plate and then made an entry in his notebook to record his suspicions:
"R.I. 154 E. Buick touring car, Mike Morelli."

Mike was a brother of the notorious Morellis of Providence, Rhode Island, three of whom were then facing trial in the Federal Court for robbing
freight cars of shoes and textiles in connection with a widespread operation
in stolen merchandise.

When they received the news of the South Braintree murders and payroll robbery, Jacobs and his associate Inspector Ralph Pieraccini suspected
the Morelli gang, especially because of Mike and the new Buick. A few days

later, on April 15, between five and five thirty, Inspector Jacobs caught the rear end of the same car as it passed him going by the post office. He then made a second entry in his notebook: "154 E. April 15."

Jacobs never saw the Buick again after April 15. However, on the afternoon of April 24, he found a big black dull-looking touring car, a "Cole 8," standing at the curb in front of Joe Fiore's restaurant at the corner of Kempton and Purchase streets. The car bore the same number as the Buick he had seen Mike Morelli driving. He then made another entry in his notebook: "April 24, 1920, 154 E. Black Cole 8, Touring."

The whole thing looked "fishy" to Inspector Jacobs. Although he was unarmed and off-duty, he went into the restaurant to inquire. There he saw four men who looked like Italians, one of whom he knew to be Frank Morelli of Providence, a frequent visitor in New Bedford. The men at the table were extremely nervous and acted apprehensive when they saw Jacobs. One of the men was short and heavyset, with a wide square face and high cheekbones, was smooth-shaven and had dark brown hair. He was about thirty-five to forty years of age, five feet six or seven inches in height, weighed about 170 pounds and had a face that Jacobs would always remember. As the inspector approached, this man made a movement with his hand toward his pocket and Jacobs thought he was going to draw a gun. The unarmed police officer was badly scared but tried not to show it. Fortunately, Frank Morelli spoke up and relieved the situation somewhat.

"What's the matter, Jake," he said quickly. "What do you want with me? Why are you picking on me all the time?"

"Look here, Frank," Jacobs said, "there's a Cole car downstairs with a number plate that I've seen on a Buick that Mike's been driving. How did that happen?"

At that the tension eased somewhat.

"Oh," said Frank, "that's a dealer's plate. You see, I'm in the automobile business and we just transfer plates from one car to another."

At the time Jacobs had no way of contradicting Frank, but the incident at Fiore's restaurant greatly deepened the suspicions of the New Bedford police that the Morellis were connected with the South Braintree crime. Shortly thereafter, on May 5, Sacco and Vanzetti were arrested and the New Bedford police, having in the meantime secured no further evidence, dropped the matter. The preliminary sample gathered by the alert New Bedford inspector would have led the State Police to a rich mother lode of evidence against the Morellis. Yet the New Bedford story never reached Captain Proctor to spur the search for evidence then being conducted by him and his detectives. By May 5, Chief Stewart's hypothesis, and Chief Stewart as well, took over an entirely different line of investigation and the Morelli gang remained unsuspected until 1926.[2]

In a substantial sense, Stewart's hypothesis predated the South Braintree crime by some two years. Thus, in 1918, Stewart had arrested one Ferruccio Coacci as an anarchist for deportation by the Immigration Department office. Coacci gave bond for his appearance. On April 15, 1920, the day of the South Braintree crime, Coacci's bond expired, but he failed to present himself. The service notified his bondsman. Coacci was then living in West Bridgewater on the corner of Lincoln and South Elm streets, with another anarchist known as "Mike" Boda. The Coacci property included a shed, and in the shed was stored Boda's automobile, an old broken-down Overland. Here was the perfect fulfillment of the Vetilia vision — anarchists who kept a car in a shed near Bridgewater. Stewart's memory was stirred by Coacci's failure to appear on April 15, the expiration date of his bond, the very day of the murders. The coincidence of dates would seem to be meaningless, since the next day Coacci was located at his home. With the expiration of his bond, he had reached the end of the line and was willing to give himself up for deportation. For Stewart, however, the episode held a sinister significance. The story was told by Tom O'Connor in the *Vanderbilt Law Review*.[3] Mr. O'Connor had made an exhaustive investigation of the origin of the Sacco-Vanzetti case. The following is his account of the moment of revelation:

The crucial incident in the development of Chief Stewart's theory came on the night of April 16, when Immigration Inspector Root of Boston came down to Bridgewater to look up Coacci. Chief Stewart directed Officer LeBarron to help Root locate Coacci. As it turned out, according to Chief Stewart's version of the incident, although Inspector Root was loath to take Coacci away that night, Coacci, whose simple luggage was packed, "insisted" on going with the Immigration inspector. According to Chief Stewart, the Sacco-Vanzetti case was "born" that night. As he sat there musing in his little office, something happened. "I've got it," he said; "Coacci!" In one blinding flash Chief Stewart "solved" both the Bridgewater holdup and the South Braintree robbery and murders. On a visit to Chief Stewart at his home in Scituate on May 29, 1927,

[2] The New Bedford episode as evidence that Madeiros told the truth will be subsequently considered in a chapter dealing with evidence against the Morellis.
[3] Vol. 14 (1961), 993.

the writer obtained confirmation of what he had uncovered concerning the origin of the case. In the course of Chief Stewart's recital, he recalled that when he joined the group of police officers and others who viewed the supposed bandit car, a Buick, found in the Manley Woods, West Bridgewater, on April 17, two days after the South Braintree holdup, he had declared to the gathering: *"The men who did this job knew no God."* [Emphasis added.]

In Stewart's investigation which followed, he learned that the Overland car, on April 19, had been towed to the garage of Simon Johnson at Elm Square, West Bridgewater, another suspicious circumstance. He learned further that Boda, another anarchist, had been living with Coacci. He then "made preparations to apprehend Boda and whoever should appear with him to pick up the car when repaired." He asked the Johnsons to notify the Brockton police when they called for the Overland.

On the night of May 5, 1920, at about 9 P.M., four men called for the Overland. Two came in a motorcycle and sidecar, the other two on foot. They were told that the car could not be removed since it had no 1920 registration plate. Mrs. Johnson went to a neighbor's house to telephone the police. Mr. Johnson had gone to bed but dressed and had some talk with the men. The men spoke briefly to one another in a foreign language. Boda started the motorcycle and left with one of the men. The others departed on foot and caught an interurban streetcar at Sunset Avenue, for Brockton.

At about ten minutes after ten that night, on Main Street in Brockton, Officer Michael J. Connolly of the local police boarded the streetcar and arrested two men. He had taken into custody the two pedestrians who had called at the Johnson garage. Neither of the arrested men was suspected or wanted by the police. Neither had a police record. One of them was Nicola Sacco, edge trimmer and night watchman at the 3–K shoe factory in Stoughton, where he lived with his wife and family. The other was Bartolomeo Vanzetti, fish peddler and radical orator in Italian from the town of Plymouth. Except for the fact that they were in the group that called for the old Overland at the Johnson garage, they would not have been accused of any connection with either Bridgewater or South Braintree.

The other two men, who left by motorcycle and sidecar, were Boda and his friend Ricardo Orciani, both anarchists. Chief Stewart was now convinced that he had found his band of anarchist robbers.

4.

Arrest Without Evidence

*The Trap for Anarchists Catches a Shoemaker
and a Fish Peddler*

While Chief Stewart was setting his trap to catch anarchists who kept an automobile in a shack near Bridgewater, a fateful series of events was drawing Sacco and Vanzetti into the net.

In mid-May 1919, one Luigi Galleani had been taken to the East Boston Immigration Station for deportation. Galleani was the editor of an inflammatory paper, *Cronaca Sovversiva*, and a leading anarchist. Sacco and Vanzetti were among the followers of Galleani. After Galleani's deportation, the bombings increased. On June 2, 1919, an explosion occurred at the home of Attorney General Palmer. This bomb apparently exploded prematurely and blew its carrier to bits. Scattered over the scene, however, were printed flyers entitled *Plain Words* exhorting the "proletariat" to violence and signed "The Anarchist Fighters."

The trail of the paper flyers led agents of the Department of Justice to Canzani's printing shop in Brooklyn, New York. Canzani did general printing, including anarchist literature. In February 1920, FBI agents picked up Roberto Elia, a printer at the shop, and Andrea Salsedo, a typesetter. These men were later taken to the headquarters of the Department, a building at 21 Park Row, New York, for interrogation.

The continuous detention of Elia and Salsedo, never explained satisfactorily, alarmed their fellow anarchists. Some of them in Massachusetts had been collecting money for the defense of the men, and sending it to New York. On Sunday afternoon, April 25, a small meeting was held in East Boston to consider what more should be done. Sacco, Vanzetti and Orciani attended the conference. Aldino Felicani,[1] a Boston anarchist, was also there. It was decided to send Vanzetti to New York to find out what was

[1] Felicani was to organize the Sacco-Vanzetti Defense Committee and to become its treasurer. He later acquired and operated the Excelsior Press. He was respected and loved by all who knew him. He died in 1967.

happening to Salsedo and Elia. Vanzetti took the train that same evening for New York, where he received disturbing news from Luigi Quintiliano, secretary of the Italian Workers' Defense Committee.[2] This New York committee had apparently lost confidence in its lawyer, Marciso Donato, and on April 20, 1920, had retained Walter Nelles, Esq., as counsel. Nelles predicted a step-up in antiradical activities by the Department of Justice and advised Quintiliano concerning the disposition of the literature which the New York group had been distributing. Vanzetti spent two days with Quintiliano, who passed on to him the warning advice of Walter Nelles.[3] However, nothing was learned concerning the fate of Elia and Salsedo.

On Sunday, May 2, 1920, Vanzetti reported to the group in East Boston. Sacco and Orciani were again present, as was Felicani. Vanzetti told of Nelles's warning to dispose of the anarchist propaganda material which had been distributed. Most of their talk was about how to get rid of this material. Orciani, who had recently seen Boda, reported that the latter still owned a car which might be used to collect the literature. Sacco suggested that he and Vanzetti and Orciani should meet with Boda sometime early in the week. Vanzetti reminded everyone that there would be a meeting in Brockton on May 9 to raise money for Salsedo and Elia.

On the morning of May 3, the body of Salsedo, crushed to a pulp, was found on the pavement of Park Row, fourteen stories below the window of the room in which he had been held. The news of Salsedo's tragic end added the dread of physical injury to the fear of deportation. The proposed disposition of incriminating literature acquired a new urgency. On May 5, Sacco, Vanzetti, Orciani and Boda had supper at Sacco's home in Stoughton and arranged to meet later that same evening at the Johnson garage in West Bridgewater to take out Boda's Overland, which had been left for repairs. Boda and Orciani arrived in a motorcycle and sidecar. Sacco and Vanzetti, coming from Stoughton, had to travel on two different streetcar lines. En route to West Bridgewater, Vanzetti drafted a notice for the Brockton meeting on May 9. The notice, as translated in the trial record, read as follows:

Fellow Workers, you have fought all the wars. You have worked for all the capitalists.[4] You have wandered over all the countries. Have you harvested the

[2] Vol. II, 1710.   [3] Vol. II, 1710, 1982, 2048.
[4] By agreement of the interpreter, it is noted that the word *padrone* is subject to the interpretation of "owners" and "employers" as well as "capitalists."

fruits of your labors, the price of your victories? Does the past comfort you? Does the present smile on you? Does the future promise you anything? Have you found a piece of land where you can live like a human being? On these questions, on this argument, and on this theme, the struggle for existence, Bartolomeo Vanzetti will speak. Hour —— day —— hall —— Admission free. Freedom of discussion to all. Take the ladies with you.[5]

For Sacco and Vanzetti, the call at the Johnson house was the start of seven years' imprisonment ending in the electric chair. It is therefore a point in the Sacco-Vanzetti story worthy of a pause for reflection. They were about to be held and accused of murder and robbery. Quite apart from the character of the men, their previous life and the bitterly contested evidence offered against them later in court, the very sequence of events which brought them to the Elm Square garage would ordinarily have eliminated them as suspects. Experienced police detectives had only to ask themselves a few questions. Would robbers in possession of two or more automobiles and a variety of number plates seek to take out and use a broken-down old Overland which did not even have a 1920 registration? Would such men ride around in interurban streetcars? Would highwaymen in possession of nearly sixteen thousand dollars, recently stolen, have any interest in the picayune process of collecting coins in dribs and drabs? Would they risk displaying themselves to make appeals at public meetings to obtain the kind of small change customarily produced?

We do not know whether the State Police asked themselves some such questions, but it would seem inevitable that they did. In all likelihood the obvious answers, coupled with what was learned later, were a factor in convincing Captain Proctor that the wrong men had been arrested. Not so Chief Stewart. Convinced that he had caught the murderers, he was not concerned with probabilities or even facts. In his mind, the episode at the Johnson garage had little or nothing to do with disposing of anarchist propaganda. Since the callers at Elm Square were criminals, they must have wanted the ancient Overland for use in another robbery.[6]

Usually when police make an arrest for a serious crime, they know of some evidence, whether tenable or not, tending to implicate the suspects. This was not the case in the arrest of Sacco and Vanzetti. When apprehended, there was no evidence against them. They were men unknown to

---

[5] Vol. II, 2120.
[6] Michael A. Musmanno, memorandum of visit with Stewart, September 15, 1962.

the police. Even in the thorough and carefully tabulated files on anarchists kept by the Department of Justice, the names of Sacco and Vanzetti appeared only as subscribers to Galleani's publication *Cronaca Souversiva*.[7] However, they were in the company of men who filled Mrs. Vetilia's prescription for the bandits: (1) Italians, (2) anarchists, (3) who kept a car, (4) in a shack, (5) near Bridgewater. It was Mrs. Vetilia's vision, not evidence, that when viewed in the context of Stewart's dealings with anarchists seems to have occasioned their arrest. This was sufficient to convince him that he had now solved both the Bridgewater and the South Braintree crimes. In Stewart's mind, Sacco and Vanzetti were already convicted by reason of their chance arrest. The word went out immediately that the guilty criminals had been caught.

On May 6, 1920, the morning after the arrest, H. J. Murray, assistant superintendent of the Pinkerton detective agency, reported that he had received information "to the effect that the Brockton police had under arrest two Italians, one Nick Sacco of So. Stoughton, and Bert Vanzetti of Plymouth, *who were implicated in the Slater and Morrell [sic] holdup*." (Emphasis added.)

Stewart's theory was promptly adopted by the Norfolk district attorney's office. It blocked all further search for professional criminals by the State Police. Evidence indicating that Sacco and Vanzetti were not the South Braintree bandits was thereafter ignored. Clues pointing to others as the guilty parties were dropped or discredited without investigation.

Since the Stewart theory was that both the Bridgewater and South Braintree crimes were committed by the same suspected anarchists, the district attorney's action not only stopped the State Police in their rolling investigation of the Slater and Morrill robbery, but also headed off any further hunt for the Bridgewater bandits. Actually there was evidence in existence indicating that this attempted stickup was the work of several Boston yeggs and jailbirds rather hastily assembled to raid the L. Q. White pay truck in Bridgewater. The alleged participants appeared to be "loners" who did not comprise a preexisting gang or mob.

It will be recalled that the lack of planning and clumsy execution of this attempt stamped it as a reckless affair by criminals who lacked the techniques and teamwork needed for a successful holdup. The possible evidence which might have been secured was published in *Outlook and Inde-*

7 *Boston Traveler*, August 22, 1927.

pendent, October 31, 1928. Although there is no place in this book for any exhaustive examination of this material, some indication of its nature may be in order. In the *Outlook* articles the participants were named by one of their own number, Frank Silva, alias Paul Martini. In addition to Silva, the alleged bandits were Joseph San Marco (alias Joe Knapp), "Guinea" Oates and "Doggy" Bruno. The L. Q. White Shoe Company was originally "cased" for a payroll robbery in 1917 under the direction of "Big Chief" Mede, who had a cigar store on Hanover Street, Boston, a favorite hangout for local crooks. However, Mede rendered himself unavailable by incurring a prison sentence and the project got no further at the time. After the war, however, in 1919, Silva and San Marco revived the idea of knocking off the L. Q. White payroll and they proceeded to tackle the job without the leadership of Mede. They enlisted the aid of Oates and Bruno, who were recommended to them as trustworthy and qualified confederates. Bruno was named by Silva as the "shot-gun bandit." His photograph in *Outlook* seems to answer the description by witnesses given to Pinkerton operative H.H. shortly after the Bridgewater attempt, at least to the extent that it pictures a man with dark complexion, hair and eyes, and a closely cropped moustache.

Some of the facts related by Silva had already come to the attention of Fred H. Moore when he became counsel for Sacco and Vanzetti. Mr. Moore sought to confirm them by visiting Silva at the federal penitentiary in Atlanta but the result was inconclusive. In 1927, however, Mede finally agreed to tell his story. Largely through the continued efforts of Mr. Thompson, who believed that Mede told the truth, Governor Alvan T. Fuller had an interview with Mede on July 12, 1927. After Mede told his story, the governor called in a captain of the State Police attached to his office. This was precisely what Mede feared would happen and he refused to talk with the police alone. (He had reasons cogent to himself for not doing so.) This was the end of the matter, until *Outlook* broke the entire story more than a year after the executions of Sacco and Vanzetti.

The authority of the *Outlook* account is weakened by the fact that money was paid for some of the disclosures. Nevertheless, there is so much "spot" confirmation of it from various sources that despite errors in details, it is difficult not to believe that it told the essential truth. Unfortunately, however, the Silva version lacks the solid basis for positive documentation which is present in the testimony and other relevant material in the Sacco-

Vanzetti proceedings. For this reason, the task of confirming the *Outlook* articles was always a formidable one and today, with the passage of time, it has become practically impossible.

The available data, however, is interesting enough. In addition to the *Outlook* issues for October 31 and November 7, 1928, the reader will find a summary in Osmond K. Fraenkel's book, *The Sacco-Vanzetti Case*,[8] and more extensive discussions in Francis Russell's work, *Tragedy in Dedham*.[9]

In 1926, a hitherto unnoticed incident growing out of Mr. Moore's investigation of the Silva story acquired an unsuspected significance in connection with another crime investigation — our own hunt for the South Braintree killers. This will be related in a later chapter dealing with Madeiros and the Morelli gang.

The adoption of the Stewart theory had another result fated to lead the defendants to the chair. From then on, objective search for the criminals gave way to the quest for evidence to convict men already presumed guilty. Local and State Police officers were enlisted to assist the district attorney's office in finding evidence. As a natural consequence, some of them came to believe in the theory they were called upon to prove. Even the Pinkerton detective agency dropped its previous impartial pursuit of evidence. For instance, operative H.H., in his report for May 13, 1920, the last of the series, relates his interview (through an interpreter) with one Langlei, an Italian laborer, who was working near the scene of the murders. On showing Langlei photos of Sacco, Vanzetti and Orciani, the witness stated that the men he saw did not look like the pictures, although he hesitated at Vanzetti's photo. At the end of his report, H.H. adds: "he ought to be interviewed by someone who can talk and understand Italian, *as, at present he, if located by the attorneys for the defence of Sacco and Vanzetti, would go on the stand and say they were not the men who did the shooting.*" (Emphasis added.) Langlei was never called as a witness. H.H., however, later testified for the prosecution against a defense witness without revealing the existence of the daily reports to his supervisor.

Because of the official theory that both the Bridgewater and South Braintree crimes were committed by the same gang, the ensuing investigation was aimed at obtaining any evidence against Sacco and Vanzetti whether pertaining to either or both affairs. It is therefore impracticable to split the

[8] New York: Knopf, 1931, 199–201.
[9] New York: McGraw-Hill, 1962, 271–278 and 318–325.

story of the district attorney's search for a case into two separate investigations. In some instances the same items were used to prove guilt in both cases.

Before following the efforts of the authorities to find incriminating evidence, two features of the case should be noted which greatly encouraged the prosecution.

When arrested, both Sacco and Vanzetti were armed. Sacco carried a .32 caliber Colt automatic pistol containing a full clip and in his pocket a number of loose extra cartridges. Vanzetti had with him a Harrington and Richardson revolver, .38 caliber, fully loaded, but no extra cartridges. He also had in his pocket three or four unexploded shotgun shells adapted for firing in a 12-gauge shotgun. None of the automatic bullets or shotgun shells was marked by the police for identification later in court. Nor was any description noted of these items by manufacture, type or caliber which might later have served as some evidence of authenticity, nor was any record made of the number of cartridges taken from the men. Therefore, there was never any assurance that those later offered in evidence were more or less than the number taken from the defendants, or that the critical ones were authentic. The possible consequences of these omissions will be discussed later.

But for the fact that Sacco and Vanzetti were armed, it may well be that the Stewart theory would not have prevailed over the belief of the State Police that the criminals were professionals. Sacco and Vanzetti had gone for a few months to Mexico to avoid service in the First World War, claiming to be pacifists. However, the possession of weapons seemed to belie them. In a real sense, then, there was an inconsistency between their claim of pacifism and their being armed. Sacco and Vanzetti, like most self-labeled pacifists, were opposed to violence except on behalf of causes in which they believed. But the carrying of weapons did more than negate pacifism. To the native Yankees of Norfolk County it suggested something sinister and thereby conferred an initial qualification on Sacco and Vanzetti for the role of robbers and murderers. Nor did later explanations by them and other witnesses erase this impression.

Nevertheless, the carrying of weapons by Italians in southeastern Massachusetts was not unusual. Thomas McAnarney, associate justice of the Quincy District Court, in his testimony before the Governor's Advisory Committee, stated: "It is that we are more or less accustomed to seeing

Italians armed here in this City of Quincy." [10] Judge McAnarney was co-counsel for Vanzetti, but Frederick G. Katzmann, the district attorney of Norfolk County, who prosecuted the men, also testified in his answer to my questioning that "it has been my experience that Italians carry some sort of weapon." [11]

The carrying of weapons among the Italians of Norfolk County was therefore not in itself evidence of an unlawful purpose. Like the common practice of pistol-toting in my own native state of Kentucky when I was a boy, it was a cultural pattern without significance. (In those days the South was popularly designated as lying below the "Smith and Wesson Line.") Nevertheless, although known to Judge McAnarney and Katzmann because of their official contacts with Italians, the habit of carrying weapons was not a matter of general knowledge. The weapons seemed to confirm to the public the assumption that Stewart had trapped a couple of highwaymen.

On receiving the news that two of the men who called for the Overland had been arrested, Stewart immediately rushed to the Brockton police station to examine his catch. There his belief in their guilt was strengthened by the fact that they gave false answers to some of his questions. (The prisoners were not under oath and they were not obliged to answer at all.) These lies were used later as important prosecution evidence in the attempt to prove that Sacco and Vanzetti were conscious of being guilty of murder and robbery. At the trial in Dedham, the defendants testified that they thought they were arrested as radicals and lied to protect themselves and their friends. The following questions and answers on the very night of their arrest may bear on the reasonableness of their fears:

Sacco was asked and answered as follows:

Q. Are you a citizen? A. No.
Q. Do you belong to any clubs or societies?
(Excluded)
Q. Are you a Communist? A. No.
Q. Anarchist? A. No.
Q. Do you believe in this government of ours? A. Yes. Some things I like different.

Vanzetti was asked similar questions:

[10] Vol. V, 5063.
[11] Vol. V, 5042. See also John W. McAnarney, Vol. 4997. Aldino Felicani told me that he, too, carried a revolver.

Q. Are you an American citizen?
(Not pressed)
Q. Do you belong to any clubs?
(Excluded)
Q. Are you an Anarchist? A. Well, I don't know what you call him. I am a little different.
Q. Do you like this government? A. Well, I like things a little different.
Q. Do you believe in changing the government by force, if necessary? A. No.
Q. Do you subscribe for literature of the Anarchistic party? A. Sometimes I read them.
Q. How do you get them, through the mail? A. A man gave one to me in Boston.
Q. Who was the man? A. I don't know him.
Q. Did he know you? A. I don't think so.
Q. Why do you think he gave you a paper? A. Well, he was an Italian man and maybe he know I am.[12]

Both men misrepresented the purpose of their visit to West Bridgewater that night, claiming that they intended to visit a friend. They said they had seen no motorcycle. They denied knowing Boda or Coacci. Vanzetti also denied knowing a man named by Stewart as "Ericol Parochi." [13]

Neither man was told he was held on suspicion of murder and robbery, nor did Stewart even mention these crimes.

On the next day, May 6, 1920, District Attorney Katzmann examined Sacco and Vanzetti. This in itself was an indication that his purpose was to get statements about the murders and robbery, since he would not have bothered to intervene in deportation proceedings. *Nevertheless, he did not tell them that they were being held on suspicion of the South Braintree crime.* Both Sacco and Vanzetti testified later that they were ignorant of the charge of murder and robbery. In the midst of a long examination, however, Katzmann did ask some questions concerning their whereabouts on the "Thursday before Patriots Day" (April 19, 1920), and whether they knew about Berardelli's murder. Since Katzmann believed the men guilty, he apparently thought that the men should have inferred the charge from these questions. Had they been guilty, they might have made the connection, but, if innocent and convinced that they had been arrested as radicals, they would hardly have guessed that they were held for murder and robbery. In either case, it was the district attorney's duty to tell them plainly the reason for their arrest.

[12] Vol. III, 3387–3389.   [13] Vol. I, 842, 850.

No transcript of Katzmann's interview with the men was ever put into evidence. For this reason, we have no record of what actually happened. At the Dedham trial, Katzmann based some of his cross-examination of the men on alleged questions and answers in the Brockton police station on May 6, 1920. From these we learn that Sacco and Vanzetti admittedly gave false or evasive answers to some of the questions. At the Dedham trial, they stated that they did not remember a number of the questions which Katzmann alleged he asked and Vanzetti denied having given some of the answers.[14] Mr. Katzmann presumably had the complete transcript in his possession and could have proved who was right. However, he put into the record only two short excerpts.[15] The first contained Vanzetti's answer that he did not know where he was the "Thursday before Patriots Day." The second contained Sacco's confused statements as to the date in April when he lost a whole day at the factory to see about his passports. The excerpt quoted Sacco further as saying that he had read about the South Braintree affair the next day with friends at the shop and that he thought he had worked on the previous day.

Under certain circumstances, falsehoods told by the accused to the police can be evidence of "consciousness of guilt." However, the import of this kind of evidence needs careful evaluation. Among other reasons, the lies may have been told to protect family or friends, or to conceal facts which might disgrace or ruin the suspect, or to prevent discovery of minor offenses; or the failure to tell the truth may not be due to any reason at all.

It is common experience that people in the humbler strata of society fear to answer questions by the police until they know what they are all about. Often the answers furnish a bit of humor. When Marshall John J. Richards and I were seeking out members of the Morelli mob in Providence, Richards stopped to ask a grocery store proprietor for the address of Joe Imondi, one of the milder members of the gang. He came out laughing. "He never heard of Joe Imondi," Richards reported. When I asked what was funny, Richards replied, "The man is his uncle!"

A similar incident, but with nearly fatal implications, occurred in the

14 Vol. II, 1779–1783, 1799–1800.
15 Vol. II, 2117–2118. Mr. Katzmann's questioning of the two suspects will be more fully discussed in the chapters dealing with his later cross-examination of them at the Dedham trial.

rather celebrated Beret-Molway case. Eight witnesses to robbery a[...] der in a Lynn theater had picked out the photographs of Louis Be[...] Clement Molway, two taxicab drivers, as the bandits who had stood against the wall of the theater lobby. The police questioned Beret [...] room. When asked where Molway was, Beret denied knowing him. During the interrogation, Molway walked into the room. He was Beret's room-mate! Coupled with the positive identification testimony, Beret's lie might have cinched the conviction which the foreman of the jury later said was assured. Fortunately, while the trial was in progress, the arrest of the Millen brothers and Abraham Faber for another robbery saved the taxicab drivers from the chair. It was found that the bullets and shells fired by the arrested men matched those found in the Lynn theater and that all had been fired from the Millen-Faber weapons.

Sacco and Vanzetti, however, had very good reasons for not telling the whole truth during their interrogation at the Brockton police station. They were indeed conscious of guilt — the guilt of being hunted and hated radicals and draft dodgers subject, as they thought, to arrest and punishment. Except for the fixed belief that they were the bandits at Bridgewater and South Braintree, the sufficiency of their later explanation for their lies could hardly have been challenged. Their evasion of the draft was a fact, their affiliation with anarchists was a fact, their agitation against the existing order was a fact, the Mitchell-Palmer raids were a fact, the arrests of fellow anarchists and their deportation were facts, the long detention of Elia and Salsedo was a fact, the warning by Attorney Nelles was a fact, the crushed body of Salsedo fourteen stories below the room where he was confined was a fact. There was therefore no need to speculate concerning the reality of their fears. So far as they knew, true answers, even to seemingly harmless questions, might have led to serious trouble for themselves or their friends.

On the other hand, the theory that Sacco and Vanzetti lied and were armed because they were conscious of having committed robbery and murder was (and remained) pure speculation. There was then no factual basis for this assumption. Nevertheless, it acted as a curious, circular proof of guilt. Since Sacco and Vanzetti were already seen as the criminals, their suspicious actions at the time of the arrest convinced Stewart and Katzmann that they were on the right track. The Norfolk authorities then undertook to find evidence sufficient to indict and convict the suspects whom they already knew were guilty. When this was accomplished, the "consciousness of guilt" theory (with later embellishments) became a most effective weapon in the hands of the prosecution. It dominated the cross-examination of the defendants at the Dedham trial. Judge Thayer in his charge devoted more time to "consciousness of guilt" than to all the other claims of the prosecution put together.[16] He later declared that the verdict rested on this type of proof.[17]

Such developments, however, still remained in the unforeseeable future. The district attorney's office was then facing the formidable task of producing a first degree murder case against two unknowns, arrested, as it were, by accident.

5.

The Search for Evidence

One has to remember that when one's interest is keenly excited evidence gathers from all sides around the magnetic point, and that one must mistrust the suggested conclusion.

MR. JUSTICE OLIVER WENDELL HOLMES, JR.

Sacco and Vanzetti could not be indicted for murder and robbery, much less convicted, simply because they were armed and lied at the time of their arrest. In order for "consciousness of guilt" to become evidence against them, there had to be specific proof to which it could adhere. It was therefore necessary to find such proof. In the quest for a case on which to hold the arrested men, the authorities, and many prospective witnesses as well, were profoundly influenced by the conviction that the arrested men were the bandits and the murderers — the magnetic point described by Mr. Justic Holmes.

An example of the repellent power of the magnetic point is the fate of the fingerprints taken from the murder car. Fingerprints are regarded as the most reliable method of identification, since no two prints from different persons are exactly the same. As competent detectives, the State Police promptly took fingerprints from the suspected men and had them com-

[16] Vol. II, 2256.　　[17] Vol. IV, 3514.

pared with the prints on the murder car. Afterwards there was a conference between high State Police officers and the district attorney in the latter's office. Following the conference, there were no further releases about fingerprints. We may reasonably conclude that the prints did not match. If they were in the car, the fingerprints of the prisoners should have been among those previously photographed by the police, especially since the chauffeur was initially identified as Vanzetti, while the man claimed to be Sacco was described in detail as pressing his left hand on the back of the front seat. According to the journalist Fred J. Cook, it was the result of the fingerprint comparisons, made under direction of the State Police, that convinced Captain Proctor that the wrong men had been arrested.[1] He probably had other compelling reasons, but the fingerprints must have been an important factor in his mind, especially when added to the other reasons for doubt which an experienced policeman would have felt. However, since the evidence did not support the State's assumption of guilt, it was apparently repelled by the magnetic point and was never mentioned or ever revealed in the trials that followed. To the prosecution, Sacco and Vanzetti were guilty — period.

Similar oblivion, if not suppression, was accorded the outcome of the Commonwealth's efforts to trace the payroll money to the little group of suspected anarchists. As in most robberies, the possession of the stolen money would have been regarded as almost irrefutable proof of guilt.

To Chief Stewart, obsessed with the coincidence of Coacci's surrender for deportation on April 16, 1920, it seemed logical that the reason for Coacci's willingness to leave was his intention to escape from the country with the loot. Accordingly Stewart caused Coacci's trunk to be intercepted and searched. None of the stolen money was found.

This initial failure to confirm Stewart's theory did not end the prosecution's efforts to connect the stolen money with Sacco and Vanzetti. The idea that the men robbed for personal gain (which was Stewart's first assumption) was apparently not entirely plausible. Sacco was a skilled edge trimmer earning good pay. He had over fifteen hundred dollars in savings accumulated bit by bit from his weekly wages.[2] He had no need to steal.

---

[1] Fred J. Cook, "The Missing Fingerprints," *Nation*, December 22, 1962, 442.
[2] It was this facet of Sacco's character, interestingly enough, which convinced Justice Brandeis of his innocence, according to Felix Frankfurter. People who save methodically, according to Brandeis, are not the kind of people who steal or rob. (Not a hard and fast rule, however.)

Vanzetti's whole life had demonstrated his indifference to money or material possessions. Neither had altered his manner of living after supposedly obtaining nearly sixteen thousand dollars. Therefore, if the arrested men had not robbed and killed for their own benefit, they must have done so for the "cause." This apparently became the prosecution's private explanation for their failure to find any evidence that Sacco or Vanzetti or their associates had any of the stolen money. However, this theory also was soon proved to be without foundation — a fact which remained hidden from the defense and the public for seven years.

Even without investigation, the hypothesis that the anarchist "cause" had received nearly sixteen thousand dollars from the robbers should have seemed at the outset to be quite inconsistent with the actions of Sacco, Vanzetti and Orciani after the robbery. Having just obtained such a large sum, it was hardly credible that they would have pressed their efforts to collect small contributions from other radicals. Having other cars at their disposal, and with plenty of money in their pockets, they would have had no need of seeking to borrow a broken-down car. Such inconsistencies, however, were not necessarily conclusive proof that the prosecution's theory was wrong. District Attorney Katzmann requested the Department of Justice to investigate and report on whether the anarchists had received any large sum of money following the holdup and murders in South Braintree. If the Department found that a large sum of money had been received, the hypothesis of anarchist participation, despite inconsistencies, would be greatly strengthened; if the investigation showed that no such money had come into the possession of the anarchists, this finding, when integrated into all the other known improbabilities, would ordinarily have caused the Commonwealth to review its hypothesis and probably to discard it altogether. At no point, however, did the Sacco-Vanzetti case follow the usual course.

By enlisting the services of the Department of Justice, the district attorney called upon the agency best qualified to ascertain the facts. The need to protect the nation against violence and sabotage had already caused the Department to follow closely, from the inside, the activities of anarchists and other radicals. The ranks of these agitators were thoroughly infiltrated with undercover men of the Department.

FBI agents even infiltrated the Sacco-Vanzetti Defense Committee. According to Lawrence Letherman,[3] formerly the local agent of the Department in Boston in charge of the Bureau of Investigation, a number of his undercover men had been assigned to watch the activities of the Sacco-Vanzetti Defense Committee: "One or two of them obtained employment by the Committee in some capacity or other. I think one of them was a collector." Fred J. Weyand,[4] special agent for the Department in Boston, deposed positively that undercover men had been assigned to win the confidence of the Sacco-Vanzetti Defense Committee and that one of them had become a "collector." (Weyand was special agent during the entire administration of Mitchell Palmer, participating in the arrests and deportations of radicals and in the wholesale raids of January, 1920.)

The Department undertook the investigation requested by Mr. Katzmann. Knowledge of this fact also was not revealed to trial counsel. In 1926, Mr. Thompson, then senior defense counsel, learned that there had been some kind of cooperation between the district attorney and the Department. As counsel, he repeatedly demanded that the Department of Justice open its files for inspection. Despite Mr. Thompson's persistent efforts, reinforced by the pleas of some sympathetic citizens, the Department refused to open its files to counsel. District Attorney Ranney justified the failure to disclose such evidence on the ground that it was a government secret.[5]

Finally, on August 22, 1927, the Department gave what purported to be a summary of its records to W. G. Gavin, Washington correspondent for the *Boston Traveler*. Some of the things reported had already been related by former agents of the Department. In the midst of the story, however, there was a new revelation — the first mention anywhere of the request by the Norfolk district attorney for an investigation of anarchist funds and the Department's report. It read as follows:

The local prosecuting authorities asked the Boston office of the Department of Justice if radicals in New York had come into any large sum of money subsequent to the hold-up and murder of Paymaster Parmenter. The Boston office, as a matter of routine, sent an inquiry to the New York office and was informed that the radicals there had not come into any large sums. . . . That is the gist of what these much discussed records show. *Summed up it shows but one thing, that the Department of Justice did investigate to see if the New York anarchists had received any large amount of money after the South Braintree hold-up and murders and found that they had not. This bit of investigation was favorable to Sacco and Vanzetti rather than harmful.* [Emphasis added.]

[3] Vol. V, 4506.   [4] Vol. V, 4500.   [5] Vol. V, 4385.

Indeed the report *was* favorable to Sacco and Vanzetti — or would have been had the defense known of the investigation and its outcome. The *Boston Traveler* reached the news counters at about 3 P.M. Shortly after midnight, nine hours later, Sacco and Vanzetti were dead.

It may not be entirely fair to place the onus on the Department of Justice for withholding this important information. In making the investigation, they were acting for the district attorney of Norfolk County, pursuant to his theory that the robbery was for the anarchist "cause." They advised Mr. Katzmann of the result. This information, "favorable" to Sacco and Vanzetti, was Katzmann's to divulge or conceal. As with the fingerprint evidence, he chose to let it remain in oblivion where it could have no effect on his course of action. The report of the Department of Justice failed again to divert Mr. Katzmann from his determination to convict the defendants. For him, it meant simply that other evidence must be found.

One type of proof was not available to the prosecutor. In the usual arrest for murder, at that time, the police in the first instant would have sought to secure a confession. This once routine step to obtain a most important type of evidence was not explored by the authorities. Perhaps Mr. Katzmann felt that it was futile to ask plain, direct questions. Whatever the reason, the Sacco-Vanzetti prosecutions proceeded without any evidence in the nature of a confession.

Unknown to the defendants and their counsel, however, Mr. Katzmann took surreptitious steps to secure admissions of guilt. His first move was to contact one Feri Felix Weiss, a "private eye" who had been until 1919 a special agent of the Department of Justice in charge of investigating "anarchists and similar criminals whose aim was the overthrow of the government of the United States." When asked what he thought of Sacco as a participant in the South Braintree holdup, Weiss explained to Katzmann that "anarchists do not commit crimes for money, but for a principle and that banditry was not in their code." (This may explain why Katzmann shortly thereafter turned from asking the help of a private detective to requesting the services of the Department of Justice.)

Weiss further stated that Katzmann suggested to him that he write to one of Weiss's undercover informants, named John Ruzzamenti, to ascertain whether that individual was "willing to go to jail and share the cell with Sacco to find out what Sacco had to tell about his connection with the

Braintree affair." [6] As a result, Ruzzamenti conferred with Weiss in Boston on December 28 and 29, 1920, and with Katzmann on December 30. Ruzzamenti swore that Katzmann said in part to him substantially the following:

that he, the said Katzmann was right hard up against it; that he, the said Katzmann, had no evidence as against the said Nicola Sacco or as against the said Bartholmeo Vanzetti, that they, the said Sacco and said Vanzetti had not talked and would not talk; . . . and that it was necessary that he secure other and additional testimony to that which he already had. Whereupon, with this preliminary explanation, the said Katzmann made the following proposition, to wit:

That Rosina Sacco or Rose Sacco, the wife of Nicola Sacco, resided in the town of Stoughton, Commonwealth of Massachusetts and there had a small home and had an extra and unused room in said house by reason of the arrest and incarceration of her husband, and he, the said Katzmann, then proposed to the affiant that he, the affiant, should undertake to secure employment in the said town of Stoughton or some place adjacent thereto and should as an Italian and a member of the same race as the said Rosina or Rose Sacco, secure a room in her home, and that for and by reason of the fact that the said Rosina or Rose Sacco was undergoing great physical, mental and spiritual suffering by reason of the incarceration of her husband, it should be easy for the affiant to establish friendly relations with her, and said relations once established, it would then be easy for the affiant to secure confidential communications from her as to any criminal activities of her husband, the said Nicola Sacco. That the affiant agreed to undertake this plan.[7]

Mr. Katzmann filed an affidavit admitting that he had an interview with Weiss, but charged Weiss with making the suggestion to place a spy in the Dedham jail. He said he told Mr. Weiss that he "was not inclined to follow his suggestion." He admitted that he had an interview with "the man to whom Weiss had either written or wired," but stated that he had never authorized his employment. Katzmann further stated that the interview was short and that he refused to reimburse his visitor for his expenses. He denied that he discussed any plan with the man and especially denied "that any suggestion whatever was made about his going to Stoughton, or to the Sacco residence there or that any mention was made of any such plan between himself and myself." [8]

Whatever the truth in the Weiss statement and the Ruzzamenti affidavit, Katzmann, later operating through the Department of Justice, did have

[6] Vol. V, 4570.   [7] Vol. V, 4493.   [8] Vol. V, 4611–4612.

a spy named Antony Carbone placed in the cell next to Sacco's. This was not mentioned in the Katzmann affidavit, but first came to light in the affidavits of Letherman and Weyand.[9] (Weyand also stated that Ruzzamenti had told him in January 1921 about the Weiss-Katzmann arrangement for him to board in the house of Mrs. Sacco and obtain her confidence and thus obtain information, but that the arrangement had never been carried out.)

Following the disclosures by Weiss, Ruzzamenti, Letherman and Weyand, the district attorney, in 1926, stipulated with Mr. Thompson and myself:

that one Carbone, alias Carlone, was under an arrangement between the Boston agents of the Federal Department of Justice and the District Attorney of Norfolk County, placed in a cell in the Dedham jail next the cell of Sacco for the purpose of obtaining information from Sacco concerning the South Braintree crime of April 15, 1920, and other information for the benefit of the Federal Government, but that he obtained none.[10]

In its release to a reporter of the *Boston Traveler* on August 22, 1927, the Department finally admitted that it had sent its agent, Carbone, to Boston to occupy a cell next to Sacco as a matter of "routine" in the hope that he might get information about the Wall Street bombing, but failed to state, as did the stipulation with the district attorney, that it was a joint arrangement to secure evidence for the prosecution in the criminal case. The *Traveler* story also stated, "It is said" that Mr. Thompson (then no longer counsel) refused an invitation to inspect the Department's files when he happened to be in Washington, and, "It is stated" that the reason was that Thompson knew that the files contained nothing and that this would be a sad blow at the Sacco-Vanzetti defense propaganda. However, the spokesman knew little of Thompson's character. Thompson would have nothing to do with propaganda in connection with the case. If anything, he was overscrupulous in not using publicity even when it might have helped a great deal with public opinion.

Here again the district attorney's attempts to get evidence that Sacco and Vanzetti were the South Braintree criminals came to a dead end. And here again Sacco and Vanzetti had to be guilty, regardless. In this connection it is interesting to note that both Letherman and Weyand held the opinion

[9] Vol. V, 4500.   [10] Vol. V, 4369.

of Sacco and Vanzetti expressed to Mr. Katzmann by Weiss, the former special agent of the Department.

In Mr. Letherman's affidavit, he said:

It was also the general opinion of such of the agents in Boston as had any actual knowledge of the Sacco-Vanzetti case, that Sacco and Vanzetti, although anarchists and agitators, were not highway robbers, and had nothing to do with the South Braintree crime. My opinion, and the opinion of most of the older men in the Government service, has always been that the South Braintree crime was the work of professionals.[11]

And Mr. Weyand's affidavit, after referring to Sacco and Vanzetti as anarchists, continued as follows:

But I am also thoroughly convinced, and always have been, and I believe that it is and always has been the opinion of such Boston Agents of the Department of Justice as had any knowledge of the subject, that these men had nothing whatever to do with the South Braintree murders, and that their conviction was the result of co-operation between the Boston agents of the Department of Justice and the District Attorney. It was the general opinion of the Boston agents of the Department of Justice having knowledge of the affair that the South Braintree crime was committed by a gang of professional highwaymen.[12]

Because of the close and confidential relationship between the Boston office of the Department and the district attorney's office, it may be safely presumed that Mr. Katzmann was advised of the opinion of those experienced detectives.

Two other sources for obtaining incriminating evidence against the prisoners still remained. Efforts to secure eyewitness identification began immediately on the arrest and continued to the time of the trials. The nature of these attempts and the results will be considered in later chapters. The other source consisted of physical articles such as the bandits' cars, the exploded shotgun shell found in Bridgewater, the cap picked up in South Braintree, the weapons taken from the men, the extra pistol cartridges in Sacco's pocket, the unused shotgun shells taken from Vanzetti, ejected pistol shells found at the murder locus, the bullets extracted from the bodies of the slain men. Such items are known in the law as "real" evidence. Before they could be used to incriminate Sacco or Vanzetti, however, they had to be connected with the men by oral testimony. The manner in which this

[11] Vol. V, 4506.   [12] Vol. V, 4505.

connection was sought to be made came out at the trials and was largely a surprise to defendants' counsel. Since we have very little pre-trial information as to what was done by the prosecution to prepare their case with respect to the use of this real evidence as exhibits at the trials, we must rely mainly on the trial records themselves. These records show enough deviation from accepted ethical standards to have stirred up storms of criticism by many writers. However, the subject has received only spot attention. No examination in depth of the prosecution's use of physical exhibits has yet been made. This will be done in later chapters dealing with the trials for the Bridgewater attempt and the South Braintree robbery and murders.

6.

Evolution of Identification

> HAMLET: Do you see yonder cloud, that's almost
> in the shape of a camel?
> POLONIUS: By the mass, and 'tis like a camel indeed.
> HAMLET: Methinks, it is like a weasel.
> POLONIUS: It is backed like a weasel.
> HAMLET: Or, like a whale?
> POLONIUS: Very like a whale.
>
> HAMLET, *Act III, scene ii*

In seeing whatever shapes Hamlet pointed out to him, Polonius was exhibiting a very common human weakness. All of us, like Polonius, are prone to yield to the power of suggestion. That power permeates much of our lives. Its influence is recognized in various branches of medicine, in the teaching profession, in psychology and in criminology. It is the basis of the magician's art of creating illusions. It is the secret of what we call brainwashing. The law recognizes the effects of pre-trial publicity on the minds of potential jurors. Its role in shaping trial testimony, however, has seldom been fully explored. A witness will occasionally give positive but false testimony on the stand believing that he is telling the truth. Ordinarily we do not know what suggestive forces had worked on the mind of such witnesses.

In the Sacco-Vanzetti case, however, we are in an exceptional position to observe the effects of suggestion because of our unusual knowledge of what preceded the trial testimony. For instance, two especially qualified witnesses on the day of the Bridgewater crime had stated unequivocally that the bandit car was a Hudson. They were Graves, the chauffeur of the pay truck, and Harding, in the automobile business. At that time no one said the car was a Buick. However, after it was learned that a Buick had been stolen in Needham, several weeks previously, it was immediately assumed that the stolen car was the bandits' automobile. Chief Stewart then located witnesses who apparently assumed that they had seen a Buick in Bridgewater. Even Harding, who saw a Hudson during the attempted robbery on December 24, 1919, testified from the witness stand in June 1920 that he had seen a Buick. He was not cross-examined concerning this memory shift since trial counsel for the defendant did not know of the Pinkerton reports made almost contemporaneously with the crime./

In no area of trial practice are witnesses so prone to error as in the matter of eyewitness identification. Here suggestion operates at its maximum strength. A suggestible witness soon believes that the suspect in custody is the man he saw and the belief rapidly grows into conviction.'

The administration of justice is replete with such cases. Reference has already been made in Chapter 4 to one of the little-known instances which occurred in Massachusetts in 1934. There had been a series of robberies in different places, including a Lynn motion picture theater where an employee was fatally shot. Eight witnesses either saw the crime at close range or the escaping bandits. Several, held prisoners in the lobby, watched the robbers at work for about ten minutes. Later they selected photographs of two Boston taxicab drivers, Beret and Molway, as the robbers they saw. The men were arrested, positively identified and indicted. While their trial was on, a group of criminals consisting of the Millen brothers, the wife of one of them, and Abraham Faber was arrested for another crime, committed in Worcester. It was then found that the bullets and shells left on the scene matched those found in Lynn, and that all of them had been fired by the Millen-Faber weapons. Beret and Molway were cleared; the Millen brothers and Faber were tried, convicted and executed.

The witnesses who mistakenly identified Beret and Molway had an excellent opportunity to observe the criminals at close range. What reliance then can be placed on identification testimony where the witnesses, as in the Sacco-Vanzetti case, had little or no opportunity to see the features of the men they identify? Difficulties in identifying individuals were further intensified by reason of the fact that the suspects belonged to an ethnic group unfamiliar to the observers. Such witnesses might be able to describe the general appearance of the criminals they saw, but reliable identification was impossible. Lack of opportunity to observe, however, was not the only flaw in the trustworthiness of the identifications. The manner in which the identifications were made would have rendered them worthless in any event.

No precautions whatever were taken to guard against mistaken identification. On the contrary, every means was employed, out of ignorance or by design, to assure a maximum of suggestibility. There was no lineup. Witnesses were taken to the jail or police station to view Sacco and Vanzetti alone, as if they were animals in a zoo. The prisoners were occasionally made to imitate the movements of the bandits, pull down caps and point as if they held pistols.[1] If witnesses were still uncertain, they were asked to take additional views until their original flash images of the actual criminals tended to become overlaid with the recollection of the prisoners they saw.

As if to make the zoo analogy even more apt, Orciani was driven over the countryside in an automobile to be inspected by a large number of potential witnesses. These exhibitions of the prisoners must have convinced the viewers that the police had arrested the right men. This alone would have been a powerful inducement to make an identification.

After the arrest of Sacco and Vanzetti, the role of the Pinkerton detective agency became a minor one. A large part of the reports from then on is based on hearsay. The display of photographs became a senseless procedure, since the witnesses had already viewed the prisoners. However, some of the reports are instructive, especially as indicating the thinking in the office of the district attorney. Assistant Superintendent Murray attended Katzmann's examination of Vanzetti on May 6, 1920, and he reports that it produced no incriminating evidence. He adds, "A number of witnesses brought in during the day failed to identify either Vanzetti or Sacco positively as two of the men implicated in the Slater and Morrell [sic] holdup and murder at Braintree." He reports that Levangie (whom he calls Angelo) said he believed Vanzetti was the driver of the car, although Vanzetti "stoutly denied having any knowledge of automobiles or being able to drive

[1] Vol. I, 248, 252, 404–6, 473, 509, 606–616; Vol. II, 1861; Vol. III, 2780, 2802; Pinkerton South Braintree reports, May 7, 1920.

them." He then states that the men "tomorrow will be stood up for identification by witnesses, not only from South Braintree, but also from Bridgewater." Chief Stewart's hypothesis is now in operation as Mr. Murray reports that Orciani and Boda (whom he calls Orciano and Bono) have been located at Hyde Park and will be turned over to the Brockton police for examination and possible identification.

On May 7, 1920, operative H.H. showed his "photos to Miss Mary Splaine, Miss Hayes, Miss Kennedy, Messrs. Wade, Frantello, DeForest and several others known to have seen the bandits. All of the foregoing had been to Brockton to see the suspects." The inclusion of Hayes and Kennedy in the visitation to Brockton is important, since these ladies were the only eyewitnesses who had both a close-range and a sustained opportunity to study the driver of the car, described by them as a thin, blond young man. Of the group, three stated that "Sacco looked like the man they saw," but only Wade is mentioned as making an identification of Sacco's picture. Over a year later, Miss Splaine's "looked like the man" was to grow into a positive identification. The report then adds that Levangie, the crossing tender, *who also had been to Brockton, identified Vanzetti* as the driver of the car. H.H. then adds, "Levangie's identification is doubtful as those who saw the chauffeur prior to the holdup and murders say that Vanzetti was not the man driving the car." H.H. then speculates that Vanzetti probably "occupied the front seat along with the chauffeur." This must have been a reflection of the thinking in the district attorney's office, since, over a year later, Assistant District Attorney Harold P. Williams, in opening the Dedham trial, described the chauffeur as blond and emaciated, and then claimed that Vanzetti was sitting beside him on the front seat.

On the same day, May 7, 1920, H.H. "proceeded to Bridgewater and showed the photos to Messrs. Cox, Bowles and Harding. *These people had been to Brockton and seen Vanzetti and Sacco.*" (Emphasis added.) Harding said that "as soon as he saw Vanzetti in the Police Station, he immediately recognized him as the man he saw at the Bridgewater attempted holdup." On December 4, 1919, the day of the attempt, he had said that he did not get much of a look at his face, but thought he was a Pole. On January 3, 1920, on looking over a couple of suspects, he stated that as he had not seen the men's faces on the day of the holdup, he was unable to say whether they were the men or not. Cox and Bowles stated that Vanzetti bore a "strong resemblance" to one of the men in the holdup party, although on the day of the attempt they (and Graves, the chauffeur, who had died) had described quite a different-looking individual. Given a little time, Cox and Bowles would see much more than a "strong resemblance" in Vanzetti's features. We shall shortly examine the full effect of their inspection of the prisoners at the police station.

On May 8, 1920, H.H. interviewed Mrs. Novelli and reported that she looked at the photos of Vanzetti, Sacco and Orciani. She thought Sacco's photo greatly resembled the man she saw in the bandits' car, but she could not be positive.

H.H. then recounted several clues that led to dead ends. He also investigated the neighborhood of the Boda-Coacci home. At this time, the persons interviewed were aware of the arrest of Sacco, Vanzetti and Orciani and that the police held a Buick, suspected as the murder car.

Paul McDonald, who used to deliver milk to the house, did not recognize any of the operative's photos. *He had never seen a Buick car.*

Mrs. Smith, who lived on South Elm Street, saw Coacci frequently. She saw parties there on Sunday nights "with a big car." She picked the photo of Orciani as the man she saw frequently going in the direction of the Coacci home.

Mr. Kirzian, who lived across the street from Coacci, heard a motorcycle there during the night and also *knew that Coacci had an Overland.*

Mrs. Encker, who lived on South Elm Street, said, however, that Coacci had a large Buick car. She picked photos of Sacco and Vanzetti as two men she saw in the house on the Sunday before the Braintree murders when she made a first (and last) call on Mrs. Coacci.

The last Pinkerton South Braintree report covers May 12, 1920. It reports that on that day Sacco was arraigned in the Quincy court for the South Braintree murders, and Vanzetti for attempted murder and robbery at Bridgewater in December. It states further that "Ricardo Orciani was released, lacking identification."

This last notation indicates that H.H. was no longer in the confidence of the district attorney. The real reason for Orciani's release was that he had an unshakable alibi. His claim to have been at his place of employment, a Norwood foundry, on both December 24, 1919, and April 15, 1920, was backed by time clock records.[2] Actually, the traveling exhibition of Orciani

2 Vol. V, 5039; Russell, *Tragedy in Dedham*, 94.

around the countryside had produced — or induced — several identifications.[3]

According to Stewart's theory, the band of anarchist-robbers consisted of five—Sacco, Vanzetti, Orciani, Boda and Coacci. The case against Orciani now had to be dropped. That left Coacci and Boda as the hypothetical associates of Sacco and Vanzetti. Coacci had been deported. His trunk had been intercepted and searched, his room in West Bridgewater had been frisked, some of his property stored in the garage of a friend in Hyde Park had been examined.[4] Nothing had been found to connect him with either Bridgewater or South Braintree. Nor does it appear that there was any other evidence against Coacci on which a case could be built. Boda was just a little over five feet tall, weighing about 120 pounds. No witness of either crime had described such a small man as one of the bandits. Although, later at the trials, Mr. Katzmann indulged in a lot of damaging loose talk and insinuations about Boda, he himself eliminated Boda completely as a participant when I questioned him before the Governor's Advisory Committee in 1927. He then stated that he thought Boda could give him information about the car and other matters, that he had heard that before or after the Bridgewater affair that Boda in the preceding winter had been seen by someone driving "this car," but that the "witness did not bear out what we had understood by hearsay was the information in his or her possession." [5]

So far as the South Braintree crime was concerned, there was also the admission of Assistant District Attorney Williams that Coacci, Orciani and Boda could not be placed in South Braintree on April 15, 1920.[6] That left only Sacco and Vanzetti.

There was some identification evidence of a sort that Sacco was a South Braintree bandit. This enabled the district attorney to hold him for that crime, although for his own reasons, he did not seek an indictment of Sacco until September 11, 1920. Unlike Orciani, Sacco had no workshop alibi for April 15, 1920. Sacco claimed to have been in Boston on that day to arrange for a passport for his planned trip to Italy with his family. However, this alibi had to be proved and Sacco therefore remained as a member of Chief Stewart's now truncated murder party.

---

[3] O'Connor, *Vanderbilt Law Review*, Vol. 14 (1961), 995; Michael A. Musmanno, *After Twelve Years* (New York: Knopf, 1939); Russell, *Tragedy in Dedham*, 69–70.
[4] Russell, *Tragedy in Dedham*, 97.
[5] Vol. V, 5083; Supp. Vol., 350–351. For further samples of Mr. Katzmann's "loose talk," see Supp. Vol., 161, 214–215.   [6] Vol. I, 726.

Except for Levangie's obviously mistaken identification of Vanzetti as the chauffeur, there was nothing to connect him with the South Braintree affair. Vanzetti was therefore not held at this time for the South Braintree affair and not indicted for it until months later. District Attorney Katzmann in 1927 gave the following explanation of his failure to seek an indictment of Vanzetti despite Levangie's positive identification on May 6, 1920: "Apparently there was not then enough information in the hands of the prosecuting officers, or the investigating officers, to bring a charge of murder against Mr. Vanzetti." [7] "And it was not until later investigation which produced identifying witnesses that evidence commenced to accumulate against Vanzetti." [8]

Mr. Thompson then asked Katzmann a question, the answer to which implied a more sinister reason for not proceeding against Vanzetti for the South Braintree murders at that time:

Q. (By Thompson) That evidence did not accumulate in sufficient amount until after you had tried Vanzetti for robbery [the Bridgewater attempt] and had convicted him, is that true? A. That would be so.

How "true" Mr. Katzmann's explanation was may be judged by the fact that on May 18, 1920, the assistant district attorney of Norfolk County assured Judge Herbert C. Thorndike in the Quincy District Court: "We have witnesses that positively identify him [Vanzetti] in connection with the South Braintree affair." [9]

Sacco and Vanzetti were both indicted for the South Braintree murders on September 11, 1920. By then the prosecution had "accumulated" evidence against Vanzetti far more powerful than any questionable identification. He had publicly placed on Vanzetti's brow the mark of a convict. He had also branded Sacco as the friend and companion of robbers. Whether Katzmann's decision to try the payroll attempt case before the murder case (an unusual procedure) was a tactic or not, he had utterly destroyed the presumptions of innocence to which the two men, with crime-free records, would otherwise have enjoyed. It was an absurd fiction to suppose that the Dedham jurors did not know about Vanzetti's conviction merely because the rules of evidence were supposed to keep it out of the trial. Those men read the local and Boston papers, lived in the area, and for over a year had been breathing an atmosphere permeated with widely circulated suspicions

[7] Vol. V, 5079.   [8] Vol. V, 5078.   [9] Supp. Vol., 35.

and gossip. Stewart's hypothesis that the Bridgewater and South Braintree crimes were committed by the same gang was well known. He had finally produced powerful, if inaudible, proof of it. From then on, an otherwise implausible case seemed quite logical and probable.

Of the anarchists suspected by Stewart of committing the Bridgewater attempt, Vanzetti was now left alone to face the Commonwealth. Coacci had been deported without a trace of participation. Orciani had a copper-riveted shop alibi. No witness had described a little-over-five-feet-tall, one-hundred-and-twenty-pound bandit like Boda, and we have Katzmann's 1927 exculpation of him to complete his elimination. Either because there was no satisfactory identification of Sacco, or because investigation had shown that he was working on December 24, 1919, or for both reasons, Sacco was left out of the Bridgewater prosecution. In 1927, Mr. Katzmann testified: ". . . there was not any time that Mr. Sacco was involved in the Bridgewater offence." [10]

The prosecution, however, was not discouraged by the evaporation of the Stewart hypothesis. Vanzetti remained. There was Harding, who had made a positive identification. There were Cox and Bowles, who saw a resemblance. Perhaps, upon another look, or on reflection or after discussion, their memory picture might develop into an image of Vanzetti.

Preliminary hearings were held before Judge Thorndike on May 18, 1920, "on complaint of Michael E. Stewart for assault to rob."

The Commonwealth was represented by Frederick G. Katzmann, district attorney, and William F. Kane, assistant district attorney. Vanzetti's original counsel was William J. Callahan, Esq., a young lawyer from Brockton. However, late at night on May 12, 1920, the date when Vanzetti was charged with attempted murder and robbery at Bridgewater and held without bail, Vanzetti was visited in jail by a delegation. The party included several of his Plymouth friends, now badly frightened, one Doviglio Govoni, a Plymouth "fixer," and John P. Vahey, Esq., well known in Plymouth as a lawyer of experience in criminal cases. They persuaded Vanzetti that he needed Mr. Vahey for his lawyer. He was a brother of a prominent Boston attorney, James Vahey, also known to the Italians as a "big" lawyer — even bigger than John. Besides, Mr. Vahey was a special justice of the District Court at Plymouth. Mr. Vahey associated himself with a young lawyer, James M. Graham, who had been retained by Sacco's Boston

[10] Vol. V, 5078.

friends. Vahey was the active trial counsel at the preliminary hearing and at the Plymouth trial later, assisted by Mr. Graham. On the same night, in jail, Vanzetti signed a prepared paper retaining Mr. Vahey and discharging Mr. Callahan.

At the preliminary hearing the principal witnesses were Cox, Bowles and Harding. During the testimony, Vanzetti was in the courtroom "behind the rail" where the witnesses could view him.

The first witness, Alfred E. Cox, the paymaster, said that the shotgun bandit wore a long dark overcoat with the collar up and was bareheaded. This is what he originally told the Pinkerton operative on December 24, 1919. He now added that the robber's dark felt hat had fallen off and lay on the ground before him. He described the man's moustache as short and croppy, well trimmed, not varying substantially from his earlier description of it, but leaving out that it might have been slightly gray. However, as Mr. Cox gazed at the prisoner, he now added some of Vanzetti's features. The shotgun bandit he had seen had "high cheek bones, hair that stood up" and a complexion that was "medium" (originally described as "dark"). Asked whether he could identify any of the bandits, Mr. Cox answered, "I can identify the man with the shot-gun." Asked, "Where is he now?" the witness answered significantly, *"The man might look different today."* (Emphasis added.) Obviously, Mr. Cox, looking at Vanzetti's long bushy moustache, was troubled by the fact that it could not possibly be described as short or croppy. Since Cox did not know that Vanzetti's moustache had always been the same, he might have been thinking that perhaps it had grown since December 24. "I think it is this man behind the rail, the man with the moustache" (Vanzetti) and "I think he looks enough like the man to be the man." [11] Mr. Cox had conscientious scruples, however, and despite the suggestive influences around him, stated: "I think there is a doubt." [12] He ended his answers in the cross-examination on the same note by admitting that he was not sure enough to swear positively that Vanzetti was the man with the shotgun. [13] In a few weeks, however, the power of suggestion overcame his conscientiousness.

Benjamin F. Bowles, the police officer on the pay truck, followed Cox. He described the shotgun bandit as dark-complected with red cheeks, bareheaded, wearing a long black coat. He still described the man as "having a short, croppy moustache." [14] Like Cox, he added several of Vanzetti's fea-

[11] Supp. Vol., 10.   [12] Supp. Vol., 9.   [13] Supp. Vol., 15.   [14] Supp. Vol., 17.

tures: "Prominent cheek bones, high, a stary look to his eyes, a glary look. Hair not very long, he did not have a hat on, hair just stuck up a little on top." He identified the man with the shotgun as "the man with the black moustache in the dock there" (meaning Vanzetti). He was sure of it.

Since Vanzetti had a medium-brown moustache, the assistant district attorney asked him, "Is that what you call a dark moustache?" Bowles answered, "Yes, I call it a dark moustache." We shall later see how the moustache grew more like Vanzetti's when he testified at the trial a month later. Bowles was cross-examined on the assumption that when he first saw Vanzetti he was not "sure" that he was the man. (The Pinkerton operative's report for May 7, 1920, confirms this.) He did not deny this implication, but said he "was pretty positive, yes." He admitted that he had had conversation with Chief Stewart. The power of suggestion was getting a firmer grip on the testimony and would tighten it further.

Frank W. Harding, garage employee, followed Bowles.

Just after the attempt on December 24, 1919, Harding had stated to the Pinkerton operative that he did not get much of a look at the shotgun bandit. On January 3, 1920, after viewing two suspects, he was unable to say whether they were the gunmen or not, as he did not see the men's faces on the day of the holdup. Four months later, at the Brockton police station, he instantly recognized Vanzetti as the shotgun robber. Then, at the preliminary hearing before Judge Thorndike on May 18, 1920, he described the man, whose face he did not see, as follows: "He was a man of medium height, dark complected, a long black overcoat and no hat. Hair cut close in back. Moustache, dark."

Q. Large or small? A. Call it medium. It seemed to be croppy. Not little and small, but one trimmed up.
Q. Did you notice anything else about his features? A. High cheek bones.
Q. About his complexion? A. Swarthy, dark complected.
Q. Was he pale or rosy? A. His cheeks were red.[15]

Harding then identified Vanzetti as the bandit he saw on December 24. *"There is no question in my mind."* [16] (Emphasis added.)

The only other witness at the preliminary hearing was Mrs. Georgina Frances Brooks, who, *before* anything happened, claimed to have seen four men sitting in an automobile parked on Broad Street in Bridgewater, not

[15] Supp. Vol., 23.   [16] Supp. Vol., 26.

far from the scene of the attempted holdup. She was going to the railroad station. She was in the station for about five minutes when she heard two shots.[17] She then looked out and saw fire coming out of some weapon. Mrs. Brooks, who had previously been to the Brockton police station to look at Vanzetti, identified him from the witness stand as the man she saw sitting behind the wheel in Bridgewater on December 24.[18] There was no doubt in her mind. He was the only one of the four occupants she noticed. The man at the wheel had a soft hat on and a dark coat. He had a moustache "like this man's moustache" (indicating Vanzetti), but she did not notice his hair or his eyes.

Aside from the inherent unlikelihood of Mrs. Brooks's being able to identify any occupant of the car five months later, her story did not integrate into the testimony of other witnesses. The Vanzetti identified by the others was not the driver but the bandit on the street firing the shotgun.[19] All of the others claimed they saw a bandit with a closely cropped moustache, not a long bushy affair such as Vanzetti's, which she pointed out in the courtroom. She heard only two shots while in the station, but on looking out saw fire coming from some weapon — apparently an instance of sound traveling faster than light. Later investigation — not in the record — indicated that Mrs. Brooks could not have seen the shooting from the window of the railroad station because two buildings would have directly obstructed her line of vision. Also off the record is the virtual certainty that Vanzetti knew nothing of motorcars and was unable to drive. At the trial later, Mrs. Brooks showed even more imagination. She proved to be only one of such persons whose imaginations helped to send Sacco and Vanzetti to their doom.

Defense counsel cross-examined the witnesses ably, but offered no evidence, a not unusual practice at preliminary hearings. Judge Thorndike then announced that he would hold Vanzetti for the Grand Jury. Defendant's counsel asked that Vanzetti be freed on bail, since it was essential that he be at liberty in order to properly prepare his case. He stated, "All his friends in my town [Plymouth] who have known him all his life are prepared and are willing to offer their property at his service until he is to be tried. The whole Italian settlement down there are prepared and are willing to put their property for his appearance . . ."

17 Supp. Vol., 31, 117.   18 Supp. Vol., 31.
19 The driver remained in the car, Supp. Vol., 365. See opening, Supp. Vol., 82.

It was at this point that Assistant District Attorney Kane told the judge that *"we have witnesses that positively identify him in connection with the South Braintree affair,"* a claim that was later contradicted by Mr. Katzmann in 1927. Vanzetti was not admitted to bail and remained in jail.

On June 11, 1920, two indictments were found against Vanzetti for assault with intent to rob and for assault with intent to murder. The trial began on June 22, 1920, before Judge Webster Thayer and a jury.

In the trial that followed, the main reliance of the prosecution was on eyewitness identification to prove that Vanzetti was the shotgun bandit. On this issue the chief witnesses were the three men interviewed by Pinkerton operative J.J.H. on December 24, 1919 — Bowles, the police officer; Cox, the paymaster; and Harding, the sidewalk observer. (Meanwhile, Graves, the chauffeur of the pay truck, had died.) It was largely the testimony of these witnesses that convicted Vanzetti.

In order to complete our evaluation of eyewitness identification, it might be helpful to get ahead of our story a bit and see how these three witnesess changed their earlier descriptions so as to identify Vanzetti "beyond a reasonable doubt." Vanzetti's counsel, Mr. Vahey, cross-examined these witnesses skillfully and would have done so even more effectively had the Pinkerton reports been revealed to him. However, testimony shaken by cross-examination still compels a jury to decide whether the witness is telling a straight story. If Bowles, Cox and Harding had told the jury what they told the Pinkerton operative on the day of the attempted payroll robbery, the jury would not have had to guess where the truth lay. Vanzetti would surely have been acquitted.

Bowles was the first witness. The shotgun bandit he remembered no longer had the *"black closely cropped mustache"* such as he saw on December 24, 1919. Looking at Vanzetti, he now remembered that it was *"very dark, trimmed on the ends. Bushy."* [20] Cross-examined as to his testimony at the preliminary hearing on May 18, 1920, he said, "I believe I made the remark cropped. *It was not cropped.* I mean trimmed on the side . . ." [21] He admitted that there was a difference between a "cropped" moustache and a "trimmed" one, saying, "Yes, but at the time *I did not stop to think. I meant trimmed instead of cropped.*"

On direct examination, Bowles said, *"I am positive"* that the man in the dock is the man he saw with the shotgun. Cross-examined as to his less

[20] Supp. Vol., 49.　　[21] Supp. Vol., 65.

certain identification at the Brockton police station, he replied, "I was always pretty sure he was the man." [22]

After some fencing, he finally admitted that he had talked with Chief Stewart "about once every week or two." [23] We do not know what caused Mr. Bowles to "stop to think that he meant trimmed instead of cropped" when he described the gunman's moustache on May 18, 1920, and — unknown to Mr. Vahey — shortly after the attempted holdup on December 24, 1919. Possibly Stewart convinced him of his mistake — at least his reluctance to admit talking with Stewart suggests it.

Mr. Cox then took the stand to identify Vanzetti. Like Bowles, he now omitted the description of the bandit's moustache as "closely cropped" (December 24, 1919) or "short, croppy" (May 18, 1920). He now described it as a "short, well trimmed moustache. That is, not what you would term an awful small moustache, but short." [24] His identification was not as positive as Bowles's. When asked whether he had seen the shotgun bandit "since that day" he answered, "I feel that I have . . . the man in the dock here." [25] On cross-examination he did not at first remember saying "I think there is a doubt," but recalled it when his memory was refreshed by the record.[26] He then repeated his doubt by saying, "I can't say that I am positive that he is the same man." [27]

Cross-examined as to his earlier different description of the bandit's moustache on May 18, he reluctantly admitted, "I might have used the word 'croppy.' I have left that word out because *I don't know that I know just what a croppy moustache is.*" Asked whether he had been "aided in that at all by anything you heard," he replied, "*Only in arguments between someone and myself as to just what a croppy moustache was and I decided I did not know what it was and that I would leave it out.*" [28]

Who argued with Mr. Bowles and convinced him that he did not know what he meant at the preliminary hearing on May 18, 1920, and (again unknown to Mr. Vahey) in his interview with the Pinkerton operative on December 24, 1919?

Frank W. Harding was next. He was the sidewalk witness interviewed by the Pinkerton operative on December 24, 1919. On that date he was a salesman for the W. H. Bassett Company,[29] but by the time of the preliminary hearing and of the trial of Vanzetti he had become an employee of

[22] Supp. Vol., 50.   [23] Supp. Vol., 52.   [24] Supp. Vol., 75.   [25] Supp. Vol., 77.
[26] Supp. Vol., 78.   [27] Supp. Vol., 88.   [28] Supp. Vol., 81.   [29] Supp. Vol., 96.

the L. Q. White Company,[30] whose payroll was on the truck attacked by the bandits. (Bowles and Cox were also employees there.)

It will be recalled that on the day of the attempt, Mr. Harding told the Pinkerton operative, among other things, that: (1) the bandits' car was a Hudson; (2) he thought the shotgun bandit was a Pole; (3) this bandit wore a black derby hat; (4) he did not get a good look at his face. On January 3, 1920, he viewed two suspects and reported that: (5) he was "able to get a good look at these men's faces but as he did not see them on the day of the holdup, he was unable to say whether they were the gunmen or not."

On the witness stand at the trial, Mr. Harding described the bandit car as a "seven passenger Buick." [31] This was what he had called it at the preliminary hearing, but now he went further and identified the car as one he had seen at the courthouse the day before the trial began. Since this car was the murder car used in the South Braintree crime, on April 15, this identification firmed up the basis for Chief Stewart's theory that the two crimes were connected by the same Buick. *Mr. Vahey did not know that Harding, on December 24, 1919, had identified the bandit car as a Hudson.*

Mr. Harding identified the man with the shotgun as "the man in the dock." [32]

To anyone interested in the evolution of identification testimony, Mr. Harding's description of the shotgun bandit from the witness stand on June 22, 1920, is a fascinating study in the tailoring of such evidence to fit the accused. Looking at Vanzetti in the dock, he now described the face he had not seen as follows:

. . . no hat, high forehead, hair was short, dark complected man, I should say, high cheekbones, rather hard, broad face, and the head, perhaps, more of a round head bullet-shaped, I should call it. . . . A heavy dark moustache. As I recollect, it was a moustache that had been trimmed, the ends had been cut off, anyway. It was not what you would call a flowing moustache . . . a dark complected man, or swarthy complexion, . . . his face was red . . . the upper part at the cheekbones . . .[33]

From the above it will be noted that the shotgun bandit as now remembered by Mr. Harding had removed his black derby hat and was now bareheaded, and the man who looked like a Pole on December 24 had now acquired a swarthy complexion, and the face he had not seen on the day of

[30] Supp. Vol., 23.　　[31] Supp. Vol., 93.　　[32] Supp. Vol., 94.　　[33] Supp. Vol., 90–91.

the attempted holdup he now remembered in great detail to match Vanzetti's features as he saw them at the trial. He recognized him at first sight through a crack in the door.[34]

There was even some subtailoring. At the preliminary hearing, Harding, like Cox and Bowles, had described the moustache as "croppy," and, like the others, he now omitted the expression. At the trial, it became a "dark, heavy moustache." Cross-examined by Mr. Vahey, he denied that he had used the word "croppy" at the preliminary hearing, but on being pressed with the record, finally admitted that he had "a recollection of making some such answer as that." [35] He did not "intentionally" keep away from the word "croppy." [36]

Mr. Harding had been sent for by Chief Stewart to look at suspects Sacco and Vanzetti, arrested the night before, in the Brockton police station.

If we analyze the foregoing testimony of the three star identifying witnesses, it is not difficult to divine what may have caused the change in their testimony. All three of them, at the preliminary hearing on May 18, had described the shotgun bandit's moustache as "short, croppy" or "croppy." Two of them who described it on the day of the shooting (unknown to defendants' counsel) had used the phrase "closely cropped." *All three, in their testimony at the trial, left out the description "cropped" or "croppy."* On cross-examination, all three fought against admitting that they had previously used these graphic descriptive words. All three gave lame excuses to explain why they had changed their testimony from what they said at the preliminary hearing, including talking it over with others and thinking it over. All three now relied on the words "trimmed" or "well trimmed" to avoid using the word "cropped." The expression "trimmed" had been added by two of them on May 18, along with the words "cropped" or "croppy." However, neither Bowles nor Cox on the very day they saw the shotgun bandit had mentioned the word "trimmed." (Harding had not then described the bandit's face at all, claiming that he did not get a good look at it.)

This wheeling in unison by the three witnesses means only one thing to a trial lawyer accustomed to being suspicious of changes in testimony. On May 18, the prosecution had simply relied on the witnesses to identify Vanzetti, paying little attention to the most outstanding feature of his face, namely, his long, flowing moustache. Sure that the right man had been

[34] Supp. Vol., 95.   [35] Supp. Vol., 104.   [36] Supp. Vol., 101.

arrested, Stewart and the district attorney must have felt confident that Vanzetti had permitted his short croppy moustache to grow in length after December 24. As Mr. Cox had stated at the Quincy hearing, looking at Vanzetti's moustache, "the man might look different today."

It was inevitable, however, that between the preliminary hearing at Quincy on May 18 and the beginning of the trial in Plymouth on June 22, those preparing the prosecution's case would learn that *Vanzetti had always had a long, flowing moustache*. They then knew that the jury would not accept an identification of Vanzetti as having a closely cropped or croppy moustache. However, this did not convince the prosecution that there was a mistake in the identification. For them, Vanzetti was still the shotgun bandit. In order not to let him escape, therefore, changes now had to be made in the testimony to be offered at the trial. It must have been agreed that Cox, Bowles and Harding drop their description of the shotgun bandit's moustache as "short, croppy." A possible escape from the expression was already at hand in the introduction of the further description "trimmed" at the May 18 hearing. (Defense counsel did not know that neither Cox nor Bowles, on the day they saw the shotgun bandit, had said the bandit had a "trimmed" moustache.) If the witnesses so testified, Mr. Katzmann could contend that Vanzetti had "trimmed" his moustache to alter his usual appearance for holdup purposes. It must have been under this prearrangement that these most important prosecution witnesses changed their previous testimony in a practically uniform manner.

Why were Cox, Bowles and Harding, apparently honorable men, willing to go along with this plan? Regardless of their sincere convictions, they knew that they were consciously changing their testimony. Chief Stewart's conviction that he had arrested the guilty parties and his method of securing identifications through the dangerously suggestive, but discredited and primitive, process of bringing witnesses to view the suspects alone while in custody at the police station or the police court must have been persuasive factors in obtaining the changes in testimony. There are also the further facts that all three were then employees of the L. Q. White Company and that Stewart himself was paid by the company. This is not to suggest that the witnesses were influenced by officials of the shoe company. However, convinced that Vanzetti was the shotgun bandit, they may have been swayed by a mistaken sense of loyalty to their employer, to make sure that the robber did not escape conviction.

The plan deserved to fail. Not only did Mr. Vahey's cross-examination of these witnesses make their explanation for changing testimony sound positively silly, but Vahey's partner, Mr. Graham, established beyond question, by a host of reliable witnesses, that Vanzetti had always had a long flowing moustache, never "cropped." Their testimony also made it incredible that Vanzetti had temporarily "trimmed" the flow of his long moustache in order to stand unrecognized for a day in the Bridgewater streets firing a shotgun. Let us look ahead a bit at some of the witnesses put on the stand by Mr. Graham at the trial.

John Gault had been a police officer in Plymouth for five years. He testified he had known Vanzetti for four years, and prior to his arrest had seen him three or four times a week. During that time he had seen no difference in his moustache from its appearance in the courtroom.[37] His beat was the Italian section of Plymouth. Asked on cross-examination whether Vanzetti's moustache might have been trimmed on the twenty-fourth day of December, he responded, "I don't know that I saw him on the 24th of December or that week. I don't remember."

Joseph W. Schilling had been a police officer in the town of Plymouth for ten years. He knew Vanzetti since the previous fall, saw him two or three times a week, might have been four. He testified that he never remembered Vanzetti's moustache being any different from what it was in the courtroom. Asked on cross-examination whether it was always the same, he said, "It always looked the same to me." He could not tell "the jury that it was always the same." [38]

Andrew Christophori (occasionally spelled Cristofori), who was in the shoe and express business, had lived in Plymouth for about twenty-two years. He had known Vanzetti for about five years, lived opposite to him when Vanzetti boarded in Suasso's Lane. He saw him many times going down or up the street. Vanzetti's moustache was always the same "as it is now." He had never seen him "with a moustache that was trimmed off." [39]

On cross-examination he was asked about moustaches of various other people, including that of a Mr. Douglas whom the witness knew by sight, but saw at intervals of months. Mr. Christophori stated that Mr. Douglas had had a "light, small moustache" when he saw him about a month previously. Mr. Douglas testified in rebuttal that he had no moustache. Mr. Katzmann made quite a little drama out of Mr. Douglas's clean-shaven

[37] Supp. Vol., 327.   [38] Supp. Vol., 328.   [39] Supp. Vol., 321.

appearance. Whether or not this was a trick, as later claimed by Christophori[40] (and by Vanzetti), the episode should have had no bearing on Mr. Christophori's ability to describe the facial appearance of an old friend and neighbor whom he had seen frequently for years. Mr. Christophori stuck to his testimony. He said that he had never seen Vanzetti "go about at times with the ends cut," but that he could not say whether his moustache had been in that condition on December 24.[41]

John Vernazano, a barber, sixteen years at the same address, had shaved Vanzetti or cut his hair for five or six years. Vernazano could not speak English. He had never seen Vanzetti's moustache "trimmed," had never cut the ends of his moustache and had never seen it "any different from what it is today." He did, however, state that sometimes he cut off "two or three hairs" on "the top of his lip." This statement was sufficient for Mr. Katzmann to make the Italian barber, who knew no English, appear as a liar to the jury. He accomplished this by ridicule after inquiring into the possibility that Vanzetti might have kept his own moustache. Mr. Katzmann went on:

Q. How long were these hairs cut off, these two or three or four? A. No, I only know they were hairs that reached the mouth therefore I cut them.
Q. When you cut three, were there two on the right of the centre or only one? A. Just the one that reached the mouth.
Q. But taking the exact mathematical center of the mouth, when there were three hairs, were two on the right of his mouth or how was that? A. He had them right here. (Indicating the center)
Q. Three in the center? A. I can't remember.
Q. Were three of them over here? (Pointing to the right) A. I don't know.
Q. How long did you say those hairs were? Show us the length of those hairs, the three hairs?
(The witness draws with a pencil on a piece of paper representation of the hairs and shows it to Counsel.)
Q. Is that the first hair? Give the second hair.
(The witness makes another drawing of the hair.)
Q. And then the third?
(The witness draws the line of a hair and shows it to Counsel.)
MR. KATZMANN. That is all.[42]

No doubt it amused the jury to watch Mr. Katzmann bait the Italian barber. For us, however, it has a significance transcending entertainment. It furnishes an insight into Mr. Katzmann's low regard for Italians who came

[40] Vol. V, 5107.   [41] Supp. Vol., 326.   [42] Supp. Vol., 315–316.

forward as defense witnesses. This will become more apparent in a later chapter. Some of Mr. Katzmann's contemptuous attitude must have been imparted to the jury. Otherwise it would be difficult to explain how they happened to ignore the testimony of all of Vanzetti's Italian neighbors who testified that his moustache had been the same around Christmas 1919 as it appeared in the courtroom in June 1920 and that it had not been "trimmed up." These included (in addition to his old friend Christophori and the barber Vernazano) the following: Vanzetti's landlady, Mary Fortini; Vincenzo Brini, a friend for seven years, who had worked in the Plymouth Cordage Company for sixteen years; Beltrando Brini, thirteen-year-old son of Vincenzo, born in Plymouth, who had known Vanzetti for six or seven years; Enrico Bastoni, the neighborhood baker, who had known him for six or seven years; Adelaide Bonjionanni, housewife, whose husband had worked in the Plymouth Cordage Company for fourteen years; Margaret Fiochi, housewife, whose husband had worked for the railroad for twenty to twenty-two years; Rose Forni, worker in the Puritan Mills for fifteen years, who knew Vanzetti well; and Alfonsini Brini, housewife and worker in the Puritan Mills, wife of Vincenzo, in whose home Vanzetti had boarded for four years. It would add little to our story to repeat their evidence as to Vanzetti's moustache, since, in legal language, it would be "merely cumulative." Mr. Katzmann did not expend much effort in cross-examining these Italian witnesses on their moustache testimony. In any event it would be incidental to their story as to Vanzetti's alibi, which was Mr. Katzmann's main target in his cross-examinations. This will be dealt with in a later chapter.

The principal task of the prosecution at the Plymouth trial was to get the jury to accept the identifications by Messrs. Cox, Bowles and Harding. As we now know, their eyewitness identifications were virtually worthless. Why did the jury believe their testimony? If we understand this, we will be better able to explain the entire course of the Sacco-Vanzetti proceedings. This much we can say — the jury did not have all the facts concerning these identifications. Like defendant's counsel, they knew nothing of what the three principal witnesses had said on the day of the attempted robbery. There had been some cross-examination as to what they had said at the preliminary hearing on May 18. However, contradictions with previous statements elicited in cross-examination are no substitute for direct, truthful testimony. Cross-examination still leaves to the jury the burden of evaluating the apparent contradictions. Had Cox, Bowles and Harding told the jury at Plymouth the same stories of what they saw at the attempted holdup which they gave hours after it occurred, Vanzetti would surely have been acquitted.

And yet even so, doubt crept into the mind of at least one juror. On February 4, 1966, the *Boston Herald* printed the following letter from Arthur S. Nickerson:

To the Editor of *The Herald*:
I read the recent article about Mr. Donnell's conviction. It reminds me of about 40 years ago, when I sat as a juror in the Vanzetti case. (He was up for robbery at that time: the murder case was later.) During that trial I sat for days watching him, and all during that time I thought that he was a man who worked in the rope walk of the Plymouth Cordage Co. I did not know his name, but had occasion to see him quite often with his big, flowing moustache. What was my surprise, on returning to work after the trial, to find him still working there.
If a person could be so mistaken as to identity as I was, who could I believe? From that day onward I have never believed a person's ability to identify another (unless it was unimportant).

ARTHUR S. NICKERSON

What, one wonders, would Mr. Nickerson and his fellow jurymen have said if they had known the full truth?

7.

Fringe Evidence at the Plymouth Trial

. . . corroborative detail intended to give verisimilitude to a bald and
unconvincing narrative.
THE MIKADO, *Act III*

The trial of Vanzetti at Plymouth resulted in his conviction for assault with intent to rob and assault with intent to murder. The conviction was primarily the result of testimony by eyewitnesses who identified him as the shotgun bandit at the holdup attempt. There was, however, other evidence used to convict Vanzetti. This consisted of a number of physical items known in the law as "real" evidence. Although probably not as decisive as the identification testimony, the nature of this real evidence at Plymouth tends to deepen suspicion as to the methods of the prosecution. The process of molding oral identification testimony by suggestion and pressure is better known and not so unusual. Trial lawyers are prepared to suspect it. They do not, however, ordinarily anticipate that physical exhibits, introduced by the prosecution, may be lacking in integrity.

In the Sacco-Vanzetti cases, defense trial counsel apparently accepted the exhibits as they were presented, without much suspicion, nor were they alerted to the omission of important evidence which might have affected the use of such items in the courtroom. Especially was the defense handicapped by reason of the fact that counsel who represented Vanzetti at the Plymouth trial were replaced by new counsel at the subsequent Dedham trial. The same counsel at the later trial might have noticed that the use of the physical evidence at the Dedham trial was related to the handling of this type of evidence at the Plymouth proceedings. A review of the use of the physical evidence at both trials suggests what is sometimes called the "same signature" or "same handwriting," meaning a common authorship. It may go even further. A comparison of the methods employed in producing and handling such evidence (as well as eyewitness identification) creates an uneasy feeling that perhaps the Plymouth trial became a crude rehearsal for the more finished performance which was to come later in the Dedham courthouse.

Before considering the use of the real evidence at Plymouth, however, we should complete our analysis of the eyewitness identifications. The testimony of Bowles, Cox and Harding, on which the indictment of Vanzetti rested, became also the prosecution's main reliance at the trial itself. Their trial testimony has already been examined in the previous chapter.

The other identifying witness at Plymouth who had testified at the preliminary hearing in Brockton was Mrs. Georgina Brooks. She positively identified Vanzetti again as the man sitting behind the wheel of the car on Broad Street. She saw four men in the car, but she could not describe the other men,[1] except that the man beside the driver wore a soft hat. [2] She was looking at the driver "through the windshield."

She now added a touch not infrequent with imaginative witnesses: "He was sitting at the wheel watching me." He looked at her "very severe." [3]

[1] Supp. Vol., 121.   [2] Supp. Vol., 165.   [3] Supp. Vol. 116.

"He turned and watched me cross over [Broad Street] and as I walked down he watched me." [4]

Mrs. Brooks apparently gave as good as she received. As she went down Broad Street she continued to watch him in return. She kept looking back all the way until she got to the station. (Mr. Vahey estimated the distance as four-tenths of a mile, and there were trees in between.) [5]

She first saw the driver again after December 24 at the Brockton police station, perhaps the last day of April. He was brought in for her to look at in the room where the captain was. There were three other men, but she does not know whether they came in at the same time. Although it had been five months since she had engaged in her looking contest with the bandit chauffeur, she immediately recognized the man who had been behind the wheel — he "was the man in the dock over there." [6]

Probably the jury placed little credence in the story of Mrs. Georgina Brooks.

The next identifying witness was Maynard Freeman Shaw, a fourteen-year-old boy who was delivering newspapers. He witnessed the holdup scene at an angle, about 150 feet away. He saw three bandits, but couldn't "describe anybody except the man with the shotgun." [7] Asked to describe the man with the gun he replied: "No hat on and I was just getting a fleeting glance at his face, but the way he ran I could tell he was a foreigner.[8] I could tell by the way he ran."

Like the other witnesses, he said the gun bandit wore a large dark overcoat, and had a well-kept dark moustache, but he "did not stop to study the moustache." The man's face had "a foreign look in it, sort of sallow." [9]

Maynard next saw the man with the moustache "when I was in the Brockton Police court [May 15, 1920]. I was brought in by Mr. Stewart." He went in twice to look at the defendant. He had a talk with Mr. Stewart in the corridor. Mr. Stewart accompanied him in the courtroom.[10] The defendant in the dock is the man he "saw on the morning of December 24, with a gun in his hand in Bridgewater." [11] Although he was at the Brockton court, he was not called to testify at the preliminary hearing.

It was Maynard whose interrupted testimony tended to confirm the statements to the Pinkerton operative by chauffeur Graves and automobile

[4] Supp. Vol., 119.   [5] Supp. Vol., 120–122.   [6] Supp. Vol., 117.
[7] Supp. Vol., 134.   [8] Supp. Vol., 128.   [9] Supp. Vol., 129.   [10] Supp. Vol., 136.
[11] Supp. Vol., 132.

supply salesman Harding that the bandit car was a Hudson. Note the following:

Q. Do you know what type of car it was? A. It was a late model; I know what type it is *now*, but at *that time I thought it was a* —
Q. You say you know *now* what the make of it is? A. Yes.
Q. What is the make? A. Buick.
Q. (By the Court) Did you know what type of car it was *at the time you saw it?* A. No sir, *not exactly*.
Q. (By Mr. Kane) Do you understand the question? It is not *did* you know, but do you *now know?*
[Here the court interrupted with a statement about the possible source of Maynard's knowledge. The statement began with:
"THE COURT. Of course he should get his information from what *he saw then*."]
Q. Can you describe the car further, the car you saw that morning? A. Well, I thought — well that —
THE COURT. Do you have any judgment as to that car what make of car it *was?* . . .
THE WITNESS. I did not take particular notice of the car.
Q. What? A. I did not take any particular notice of the car.
[This last answer apparently emboldened Mr. Kane to ask the question he should have asked in the first place.]
Q. (By Mr. Kane) Did *you* form any judgment at all that morning as to what type or make of car it was? A. Yes.
Q. What type or make of car was it? A. *Hudson* or Buick. [Emphasis added.] [12]

Quite obviously young Shaw had been worked upon to remember that he had seen a Buick. The suggestion was not wholly successful, since, in 1919, many boys of Maynard's age prided themselves on knowing the many different makes of automobiles then in existence. Despite leading questions as to the type of car *now*, Maynard could not quite bring himself to admit (to himself or to Mr. Kane) that he was mistaken as to the make of car he saw on December 24, 1920. Apparently he had seen a *Hudson*, regardless of the Buick *now* shown him as the Bridgewater bandits' car. Since Mr. Vahey did not know of the Pinkerton report of the December 24, 1919, interviews, he did not, unfortunately, sense the significance of the Shaw-Kane dialogue about the make of the car.

Unknown to the defense, there was at hand the means for Mr. Vahey to wrench Bridgewater apart from South Braintree and thereby break the backbone of the Stewart theory.

[12] Supp. Vol., 126–127.

However, the defense had no such vital information and the jury had no course other than to conclude from the testimony that the Buick automobile in the custody of the police was the one seen at Bridgewater. They must have been confirmed in this conclusion, as were many of the witnesses, by the powerful suggestion implicit in their own inspection of the Buick itself. It was the first physical exhibit offered at the trial. This was the car found on April 17, two days after the South Braintree murders, in the Manley woods (sometimes called the Cochesett woods). The finding of this car was mentioned by Pinkerton operative H.H. in his report for April 18, 1920. In his report for April 19, he noted that the State Police had taken the car away from the Brockton police garage. The *Brockton Times* for April 20 also reported that the car had been taken to Boston by the state officers after photos of fingerprints had been made.[13] Operative H.H. reported that the car was in fine condition with one exception — a bullet hole that went through the right side of the rear door. The testimony concerning the condition of the abandoned car when found, however, would seem to indicate that there was *no such bullet hole in the door when it was first seen on April 17,* and that the hole was shot through the door after the car left the Manley woods. This bullet hole played no part in convicting Sacco and Vanzetti, other than to help place the Buick at South Braintree, where the bandits had done considerable shooting as the car sped up Pearl Street. Nevertheless, it has a deeper significance for us. It suggests that the police in Brockton (or other policemen) *may have been ready to tamper with important exhibits in order to make sure that evidence in their possession would be accepted as proof of their contentions.*

Now let us see when and where the bullet hole in the door made its appearance. In order to do this, we must jump ahead in our story to the testimony given in Dedham at the trial for the South Braintree murders.

The Buick was discovered by two hunters on horseback from Brockton, Charles L. Fuller and Max E. Wind. They entered the woods on a bridle-path leading from Manley Street. Mr. Fuller testified first. He said there was no window in the back of the car and the glass lay on the floor. It carried no license plates. There was no tire in the rear. It had the appearance of having been out overnight, judging from its dampness. There seemed to be tire tracks of another car smaller than the Buick. Mr. Fuller reported the find to the police in Brockton.

[13] *Nation,* December 22, 1962, 450.

The assistant district attorney who examined Mr. Fuller asked many questions about the car, *but did not inquire as to the bullet hole* — a remarkable omission. This was opened up by Jeremiah McAnarney, counsel for Sacco and Vanzetti at the Dedham trial. In answer to several questions, Mr. Fuller replied that he had examined the car and that if there was a bullet hole through the door he would have seen it.[14]

His hunting companion, Mr. Wind, took the stand next. He told approximately the same story as Mr. Fuller. *He too was asked no questions about a bullet hole.* Again, Mr. McAnarney opened up the subject.

Q. You looked the whole thing over pretty carefully, didn't you? A. Yes.
Q. When you left there, you were pretty clear in your mind that you saw no bullet hole in that car? A. I haven't seen any.
Q. And so far as you would say, there was no bullet hole there? A. I did not see any.[15]

After the police arrived they natur?"y questioned the hunters and examined the car.

Q. During the discussion and examination of this automobile by you [Mr. Wind], Mr. Fuller, the police officials or any inspector that may have arrived there, if they did, there was *no mention made whatever of any hole in the side of that automobile, was there?* A. No. [Emphasis added.] [16]

Brockton police officer William S. Hill and city marshal Daniel M. Ryan were the officers who responded to the telephone call. Their arrival was awaited by Mr. Fuller, Mr. Wind and a Mr. Hastings, another horseback hunter who had joined the party. Officer Hill testified that he examined the car carefully, in the presence of the hunters, described the condition of the car and its contents, including the glass window on the floor, the felt strip and tacks that had held it in place, a tank half full of gas, sixty-two cents under the back edge of the front seat and an overcoat. Then followed this:

Q. Did you find anything else about the car? A. No, sir, — yes, I found down there in the garage I found a bullet hole in the right rear door.[17]

Mr. McAnarney's cross-examination concluded:

Q. During the ten or fifteen or more minutes that you four gentlemen spent in looking that car over, none of you had seen that bullet hole? A. No.[18]

[14] Vol. I, 626.   [15] Vol. I, 634.   [16] Vol. I, 634.   [17] Vol. I, 636   [18] Vol. I, 651.

A bullet hole through the door of an automobile suspected as a murder car would have been the most dramatic detail spotted on any inspection. And yet the two hunters who found the Buick never saw it, the two police officers never noticed it on their examination of the car in the woods and did not mention it in their discussion with those present. The assistant district attorney never asked any witness a question about it until defense counsel brought it up, and the Brockton police officer, after giving a detailed description of what he found, threw in this *evidence of a shooting as an afterthought!* Could any lawyer or judge, trained to evaluate evidence, reach any conclusion other than that the bullet hole had been created after the car left the Manley woods? Since this occurred some eighteen days before Sacco and Vanzetti were caught in Chief Stewart's trap, the police were not then under pressure to justify their actions against any particular persons. Yet even without such compulsion, there does exist a suspicion that this most important piece of evidence may have been doctored. And if so, what confidence can we place in the integrity of questionable physical proofs introduced later at crucial stages of the Sacco-Vanzetti case when they were under maximum pressure to produce evidence to justify prosecution of the accused?

The Plymouth trial began with a view of the supposed locus of Mrs. Vetilia's vision in the crime-detecting machine — a shed near Bridgewater in which the criminal radicals kept their motorcar. The jurors were taken to the Coacci-Boda house and shed on an inspection tour. We do not know what bearing the view had on proving that Vanzetti was the shotgun bandit, but it certainly created a background of suspicion.

Unfortunately we do not have a complete transcript of the proceedings at the Plymouth trial. What we have is an incomplete record which we found in 1927 among the papers left by Fred H. Moore, counsel for Sacco and Vanzetti at the Dedham trial. Certain important parts of the record were missing. Mr. Moore must have obtained his copy of the minutes from one or more court stenographers after he came into the South Braintree case in the fall of 1920, several months after the close of the Bridgewater case. In opening the later trial at Dedham, however, the assistant district attorney told the jury (who, like the Plymouth jury, also viewed the premises) what he thought was significant about the shed:

After the South Braintree shooting, police officers visited the Coacci house and shed and they there discovered the remains of curtains which had been nailed over the four windows of the shed in which you went yesterday, and witnesses will tell you that that shed had been curtained. That is, the windows curtained for some time, a rough shed, with a rough floor and a rough interior, but for some reason curtained by curtains nailed over the windows, and they found inside evidence of the dirt floor — there wasn't all that wood in the floor at that time — of the dirt floor having recently been raked over, and later two officers found traces of a hole having been dug in the dirt floor and having recently been filled up, and they found marks of a car, not going straight into the door, but going in to the left, following the angle of that cut across the beam in front, which I particularly call your attention to yesterday.[19]

The foregoing part of the opening was intended to suggest mysterious goings on at the Boda-Coacci shed, including the burying of money boxes and the hiding of a Buick car in the same shack with Boda's Overland. It also is proof of the thoroughness of the prosecution.

Actually, the shed was an old cow stable with an entrance in one corner, measuring overall thirty-one by sixteen feet, but with a usable width of fourteen and a half feet because of heavy twelve- by twelve-inch wooden sills. The sill at the door had been cut down six inches, apparently to permit the use of the opening for entrance and exit by an automobile.[20] A pencil and a piece of paper would quickly indicate the difficulty of moving a seven-passenger car into the shed with Boda's Overland, turning it lengthwise and hiding it from public view.

Now let us look at the testimony of Samuel Johnson before the Governor's Advisory Committee in July 1927. Mr. Johnson was a brother of Simon Johnson and a partner with him in the Elm Square garage to which Boda's Overland had been towed for repairs. He was also an assistant postman on the rural free delivery route. He knew Boda very well, giving him an occasional lift in his car. The following questions and answers have a bearing on the innuendos about the Coacci shed:

Q. Did you have occasion to pass a house where Coacci was living at that time, frequently? A. I used to pass it two or three times a day.

Q. Do you recall an Overland car that was later towed to your brother's garage for repairs? A. I seen it setting there in the garage.

Q. Did you see it being operated at all during the winter of 1920? A. No, sir.

[19] Vol. I, 74. See Vol. I, 708.
[20] Edward Holton James, "The Story of Mario Buda," February 14–16, 1928. Mimeographed report of interview. Sacco-Vanzetti Collection, Harvard Law Library, Cambridge, Mass. (In the record the name is Boda.)

Q. Was the door of the garage open occasionally so that you could see? A. Once in a while, yes, sir.

Q. Do you recall whether there was any glass in the window of the garage? A. No, I don't know of any; *I think there was a bag or something tacked up* to keep the storm out.

Q. That is, there was no glass there, but there was a bag tacked up to keep the storm away? A. Yes, sir.

Q. *Did you ever see a Buick car in that garage?* A. No. [Emphasis added.] [21]

Mr. Johnson also stated that the Overland must have been all of six years old, since it was a right-hand drive. (Boda later stated it had to be cranked by hand.)

Later, in 1928, Boda told Edward Holton James (in Lipari, Italy, in the province of Messina) that he might have hung some bags over the windows to keep the cold out. He further stated that he "leveled the floor inside" and that "there were some big stones inside. I dig them out of the ground and make everything level." [22]

So much for the reality behind the suspicions sown by the prosecution. Nor could the prosecution produce any admissible evidence to back them up in its insinuations. There was no evidence that the Coacci shed was used for any purposes connected with the Bridgewater attempt or that it ever housed a Buick car. In the Dedham trial, Judge Thayer observed to the jury that he recalled no connection of Coacci with the South Braintree affair. [23] And finally, at the very end of the Dedham trial, just before the jury retired, the Boda-Coacci shed (and Mrs. Vetilia's divination) received its legal coup de grace in the following stipulation announced by Jeremiah McAnarney: "Mr. Foreman and gentlemen of the Jury: It is agreed that all evidence obtained by the jury on the view at the Coacci barn or shed be entirely disregarded." [24]

Except to suggest evil doings, it may be doubted that the Plymouth jury's view of the Coacci shed had much influence on their verdict. For one thing, the Bridgewater crime involved no stolen payrolls or money boxes which could be buried behind curtained windows. Moreover, the trial at Plymouth in 1920, shortly after the arrest, was conducted in a very different atmosphere from the later trial at Dedham. The radicalism of Vanzetti did

[21] Vol. IV, 5160.   [22] James, "The Story of Mario Buda," 7.   [23] Vol. IV, 4319–4330.
[24] Vol. II, 2265; see Vol. IV, 4320; *Commonwealth v. Sacco*, 255 Mass. 420. Vol. III, 3432.

not enter the Plymouth trial. There was little publicity to stir up community excitement. To the jury the case must have appeared to be simply a trial for an attempted robbery without overtones of conspiratorial activities. Nevertheless, the view which opened the Plymouth trial may be seen as another step in the prosecutor's case which was repeated with more elaboration at the later trial for the South Braintree killings.

The effect of a similar view on the Dedham jury in 1921, on the other hand, must have been considerable. At the time the atmosphere was permeated with wild rumors, suspicions, fears and regional hysteria. By that time it was well known that the defendants were anarchists and it was believed that the bombings reported in the press were the work of anarchists. The brief admonition to the jury after weeks of trial to ignore their view of the Coacci shed could hardly have removed from their minds what the assistant district attorney pointed out to them at the scene, by the repetition of it in his opening statement, the testimony of witnesses who described its condition during the trial, and the photographs of the Coacci house, barn and shed introduced as exhibits. Literally, the barn door was closed much too late. The Dedham jury may not have based their verdict principally on what they saw in the shed, but it generated an atmosphere which prepared them to accept the prosecution's theory of the crime together with the other questionable evidence offered to support it.

We now come to a cap, suddenly produced as evidence in the Plymouth trial. It presaged the use of another cap to connect Sacco at the Dedham trial.

It will be remembered that the witnesses who identified Vanzetti described him as bareheaded, or with his soft felt hat lying on the ground before him, or (Mrs. Brooks) wearing it in the automobile. The only exception was Mr. Harding, who described him to the Pinkerton operative on December 24, 1919, as wearing a black derby hat, but at Plymouth synchronized his testimony with the others by remembering him as bareheaded. *No one had described the shotgun bandit as wearing a cap.*

On May 11, 1920, Chief Stewart went to Vanzetti's room in Plymouth, without a warrant, and searched it.[25] In doing this he "was acting for myself, working independently." [26] On his theory that Vanzetti was the shotgun bandit, he must have hoped to find a shotgun, or the long overcoat or felt hat described by witnesses. *He found none of these things.* This did not

25 Supp. Vol., 169.   26 Supp. Vol., 168.

discourage him, however. He brought away a coat, a sweater and a cap,[27] but did not produce the coat and sweater in court until Mr. Vahey requested him to do so.[28] Apparently these articles did not answer the descriptions by any witness. However, there was Vanzetti's cap. He found a new witness to identify it.

Richard Grant Casey, a college student, stated he saw an auto, at about 7:20 A.M. (just before the holdup), come down Pearl Street in Bridgewater and stop in front of the rear door of his house. The assistant district attorney showed Mr. Casey the cap he had taken from Vanzetti's room.

Q. I will ask you to look at this cap (showing cap), did you ever see that before? A. Yes.
Q. Where? A. In Chief Stuart's [Stewart's] office.
Q. Is that the one you are now referring to as having seen about a week ago? A. Yes.
Q. Where did you see the cap before? A. As I said, it *appeared to be on this man in the machine on the right of the driver*. [Emphasis added.] [29]

Previously he had stated that there were six other caps in Chief Stewart's office, where the chief asked him to "pick out a cap which resembled the one that I saw." He admitted he had some talk with Chief Stewart.

Mr. Casey gave a description of the driver, but said he noticed nothing about the cap wearer except his clothes and the cap. He never saw his face. The driver was a shorter man with a short moustache wearing a dark velour hat. He had not seen the man in the driver's seat before or since.

At the preliminary hearing on May 18, 1920, Mr. Cox had stated about the shotgun bandit's hat:

A. . . . His hat was on the ground as though he had lost it off.
Q. You saw the hat on the ground? A. This is the impression that comes to me, his hat just fell off.
Q. Describe the hat. A. A dark hat.
Q. Whether a stiff or soft hat. A. A *dark felt hat. It was not a cap.* [Emphasis added.] [30]

At the trial, Mr. Cox *omitted* this testimony. Why did he do this? Was it due to "arguments between someone and myself," as was his omission of his earlier description of the bandit's moustache as "croppy"? [31] Whatever

---

[27] Supp. Vol., 167.   [28] Supp. Vol., 211.   [29] Supp. Vol., 107.   [30] Supp. Vol., 7.
[31] Supp. Vol., 81.

the reason, the omission cleared the way for the appearance of Vanzetti's cap on the head of a robber sitting in the seat taken by the shotgun bandit.[32]

When we later examine the Dedham trial for the South Braintree murders, we shall meet the other cap episode used even more unfairly, but with far greater effect, against the defendant Sacco.

Mr. Casey was also one of the witnesses who called the bandit car a Buick — describing it rather accurately as to color, curtains and rear window. However, after a conference at the bench at the close of his testimony, he admitted that he had looked at the Buick then in the custody of the police, on the day before he testified.

Although Mr. Casey could not describe the man on the front seat whose cap he said resembled Vanzetti's, his description of the driver, sitting next to him, was the basis of a great deal of loose talk by Mr. Katzmann. The meager description, he contended, identified Boda as the chauffeur of the holdup car. Casey had described the driver as "having a kind of soft hat and a short moustache, rather swarthy complexion, looking like an Italian, and having a prominent nose." (Mr. Katzmann had previously put on Georgina Brooks to identify Vanzetti "positively" as the chauffeur. Mrs. Brooks also saw a soft hat on the driver, but unlike Mr. Casey, she saw that he had a moustache such as Vanzetti wore in the courtroom, viz., long and flowing.)

The government was then permitted by Judge Thayer to introduce the testimony of Napoleon J. Ensher to connect Boda, and thus Vanzetti as a friend of Boda, with the Bridgewater crime. Ensher testified in the Bridgewater case at Plymouth at the end of June 1920. He said he saw Boda "two or three times last winter" (the winter of 1919–1920), and "once in an automobile sometime this spring in the morning — it was a Buick — going past our house in the direction of the village." Asked to fix the time, he said it was "about seven or eight weeks ago . . . when the roads were muddy." He said it was "a large dark Buick." [33]

In order to connect this testimony with the Bridgewater crime, Mr. Katzmann called Stewart to testify that on the night of his arrest Vanzetti denied that he knew Boda; then got Stewart to describe Boda in a manner tending to fit the loose description given by the witness Casey of the man who drove the Bridgewater car; and then referred to the testimony of Mr. and Mrs. Johnson that Sacco and Vanzetti were with Boda on the night of

[32] Supp. Vol., 42.   [33] Supp. Vol. 143.

May 5 when Boda came to the Johnsons to get his Overland car. No explanation was given by either Stewart or Brouillard why, after conferring with Boda on April 20, they did not arrest him and why he was not indicted; or, if secretly indicted, why no effort was ever made to find him or get him back from Italy, if he had gone there.

When pressed by Judge Thayer with the question whether Boda "also had a Buick car," Mr. Katzmann gave the following remarkable answer: "Yes, some seven or eight weeks ago, not *the* Buick car, but a Buick car answering this type." [34] (Emphasis added.)

This admission seems to deprive Ensher's testimony that he saw Boda with a Buick car of any relevancy if it was not claimed to be the Buick car used at the Bridgewater crime. Nevertheless, the testimony was permitted to remain in the case. The effect of it, in spite of Mr. Katzmann's disclaimer, was to arouse the suspicion that Boda had been concerned in the stealing of Mr. Murphy's Buick car, and to implicate Boda in the Bridgewater crime, and to show that Vanzetti had denied acquaintance with Boda because he (Vanzetti) was conscious of guilt of the Bridgewater crime (and not because he did not wish to get Boda into trouble as a radical).

Here we have a strange extension of the "guilt by association" proof made so familiar to us during the McCarthy era. Boda had not been shown to be guilty in the Bridgewater attempt. The argument of guilt by association with the guilty, never valid proof, had now degenerated further into a contention that Vanzetti was guilty because he associated with a party who was merely the object of suspicion by the district attorney.

When a similar attempt was made later at the Dedham trial to connect Boda with the Buick car and with the South Braintree crime, it utterly broke down. The Dedham episode reflects light on the effort to tie Boda into the Bridgewater affair. Ensher was again called to furnish the connecting link. When asked whether he knew Boda, Ensher said that he had seen him "once or twice." Then followed:

Q. Do you know whether or not Boda had an automobile while he was there [West Bridgewater]? A. Yes sir.
(Objections)
Q. What kind of a machine was it? A. *He told me an Overland.*
Q. Not what he told you, but what you know of your own knowledge and from observation. A. *I haven't seen it.*

[34] Supp. Vol., 160.

Q. Did you ever see it?

THE COURT. You are called upon, Mr. Witness, to testify, not as to what anybody has told you, but what you know of your own knowledge and from your own observation.

THE WITNESS. Now what is your question? I beg your pardon.

Q. Have you ever seen that machine? A. Yes.

Q. How many times? [Emphasis added.] [35]

Mr. Ensher had begun quite inauspiciously for the prosecution's purposes, but we will never know how he would have changed his testimony (if at all) to conform to what he had said at the Plymouth trial. At this point, the jury was excused for the court to hear argument from Assistant District Attorney Williams as to the competence of the Ensher testimony. At the end of a lengthy argument for its admission, Judge Thayer excluded it with the comment: "But he [Boda] is not connected in any way with the murder. Anybody else driving a Buick car, if it was a 7-passenger car, would stand in almost the same relationship." [36]

Six years later, Mr. Katzmann, despite his contentions at different times that Boda was a participant in the holdup and murder parties, testified before the Governor's Advisory Committee, in answering my questions as to what witness had described a man that looked anything like Boda, "a small man, a slight man (a little over five feet, 120 pounds), with a moustache":

. . . I have not said so, that I knew he was in the car at the time of the murder, and I have not said so at all. The information we had was that he had been seen driving *the* car after this theft in Needham, and before or after the Bridgewater affair, but in any event before the South Braintree affair, in the preceding winter. He was a man that could give us valuable information about the car and about many other matters. [Emphasis added.] [37]

After all of the prosecution's talk in both the Plymouth and Dedham trials, the tenuous Boda-Buick link was excluded by the court in Dedham and reduced by Mr. Katzmann from a claim of participation in the crimes to the status of possible "valuable information."

During the Plymouth trial, the prosecution had withheld offering evidence to the effect that Vanzetti, when arrested, had in his pocket a loaded revolver. Judge Thayer had reserved his ruling on the competence of this testimony. At the close of the Plymouth trial, Judge Thayer ruled that the

[35] Vol. I, 725–728.   [36] Ibid.   [37] Vol. V, 5083.

evidence should be admitted and so informed the jury. It was no doubt unintentional but rather unfortunate for Vanzetti that the last words heard by the jury before the closing arguments began were those of Mr. Katzmann stating that the arresting officer, if called, would testify that the defendant "when arrested in the electric car in the Campello section of Brockton on his person was found a loaded revolver of .38 caliber, 5 chamber." [38]

The final pieces of "real" evidence used against Vanzetti at the Plymouth trial were the exploded Winchester shotgun shell found by Dr. Murphy after the Bridgewater attempt and shotgun shells purporting to be the cartridges removed from Vanzetti's pocket on the night of his arrest. The use of this evidence is filled with so many inexplicable puzzles, unanswered questions and foreshadows of the later Dedham trial for murder that it merits a separate chapter.

8.

The Plymouth Shell Mystery

Of all the perplexing things that occurred during the Sacco-Vanzetti proceedings, one of the most confusing is the mystery of five shotgun shells introduced as exhibits in the Plymouth trial. Four were loaded cartridges, alleged to have been the ones taken from Vanzetti on his arrest, but they were never identified as such or even properly marked as exhibits when admitted in evidence. The fifth, duly identified, was an exploded shell found by Dr. John A. Murphy on the street in Bridgewater.

Pinkerton operative H.H. told about the finding of the Murphy shell in his report for May 10, 1920:

The shell was found by Dr. Murphy near the scene of the attempted holdup along with the wad and a number of shot, and laid in the road after being ejected from the gun only a short time before Dr. Murphy found it. As he now recalls it, same was a # 12 gauge Winchester repeater shell and the shot apparently was #10.

[38] Supp. Vol., 332.

In his report for May 7, 1920, H.H. reported that he turned over to Assistant District Attorney Kane the envelope containing the shot and in his report for May 11, that he gave "the # 12 gauge Winchester Repeater" shell to Captain Proctor, head of the State Police. Proctor produced the exploded shell at the trial. The shot was not produced and was never mentioned, nor was the wad.[1]

It meant very little to say that the shell was "# 12 gauge." This referred to the caliber of the whole shell, not its contents. The size of the shot within the shell, however, would have been quite significant. For one thing, it had an important bearing on whether the shotgun bandit fired with intent to murder. If the shot was quite small, the jury could find a lack of such intent; if the shot was large (such as buckshot) the intent to kill could be easily inferred. Dr. Murphy, a hunting man, guessed the shot to be # 10, very small pellets indeed. This was only an estimate, but it indicated that the shot appeared to be quite small. At the trial, Dr. Murphy stated that he did not know what size the shot was, but agreed with defense counsel Vahey that "such a shell was used in hunting small birds." [2] No hunting man would use buckshot for such a purpose.

For another thing, the caliber of the shot within the shell would have tended to answer the question as to whether the exploded shell was one of a lot similar to the shells taken from Vanzetti's pocket. The mere fact that

[1] The following may be helpful to a reader who is unfamiliar with shotguns and their ammunition:

a. The "gauge" of a shotgun designates the bore of the gun barrel as well as the size of the shells which it is adapted to fire.

b. A "cartridge" is a loaded shell, usually two and one-half or more inches long. The word "shell" is used variously to designate a cartridge or an empty shell. It is made of paper and metal — the base is metal and usually shows the name of the manufacturer.

c. The word "shot" designates the pellets contained within the shell.

d. The term "wads" or "wadding" refers to paper or fiber discs inside the cartridge as well as crimped over the shot to hold the pellets tightly in place within the shell.

e. The size of the shot refers to the diameter of the pellets. "Buckshot" is either .32″ in diameter (0), or .33″ (00); this size is used for deer hunting and guard duty. "Air rifle shot" is .175″, marked "B," or .18″, marked "BB." "No. 4" is .13″ in diameter. These smaller sizes are recommended for hunting geese and turkey. They are dangerous up to 250 to 300 yards; usual range is 25 to 40 yards; "reliably fatal" range would be from zero to 25 yards (approximately). While this is technically true, the small pellets lack "stopping power." For larger animals (deer and human), buckshot is used; buckshot is currently advertised for riot-duty police. "No. 10" shot, referred to in this chapter, is .07″ in diameter — a very small caliber.

f. In factory-made shells of this type, the size of the shot within was visibly stamped on the top disc, either by symbol or word, or both.

[2] Supp. Vol., 142.

one of the shells taken from Vanzetti was a 12-gauge Winchester repeater and the exploded shell was also a 12-gauge Winchester repeater (two very common-type cartridges) would not in itself suggest that the shells came from the same lot unless it could be shown that the caliber of the shot within was also identified. If, on the other hand, the two shells contained entirely different-sized shot, it would appear obvious that there was no relationship between them. The prosecution, however, throughout the trial kept away from any questions concerning the size of the shot inside the shells. This puzzled the jury and led them, in the secrecy of their jury room, to open two of the shells alleged to have been in Vanzetti's pocket. This was a flagrant violation of the defendant's rights. If we consider the objective of the prosecution in using the shotgun shell evidence, we can perhaps better understand why the subject of the shell contents was so thoroughly avoided during the trial.

In his opening of the Plymouth trial to the jury, Assistant District Attorney Kane outlined his purpose as follows:

MR. KANE. He [Dr. Murphy] went out on the road afterwards [just after the shooting], this witness we shall produce, and picked up a shell, a shot gun shell, within five or six feet of the curbing and that was a Winchester 12 gauge shotgun shell. . . . When this defendant at the bar was arrested they found on his person four shells, three of them of the Peters type of shot gun shell, and one of them a No. 12 Winchester shell. In addition to that, we shall produce evidence from the State Officer that when this car was found in the woods off Manley Street, he found a shell near it on the ground and that it was a No. 12 Winchester shell. . . . Gentlemen, I am corrected by the District Attorney who says that the shell that was found on the ground in the woods in the morning was a Peters shell and not a Winchester and that the defendant had three Peters shells on his person when arrested and one Winchester.[3]

This opening of the assistant district attorney indicates an intention to use the shotgun shells for two different purposes, as follows:

The *Winchester* cartridge alleged to have been carried by Vanzetti would connect Vanzetti with the Bridgewater attempt, because an exploded Winchester shell was found on the scene;

The *Peters* shell alleged to have been found in the woods off Manley Street would connect Vanzetti with the abandoned Buick, because there were Peters cartridges in his pocket when he was arrested. (The Buick was claimed to be the car used by the Bridgewater bandits.)

[3] Supp. Vol., 42–43.

Probably Mr. Katzmann thought that the mere finding of the Peters shell in the woods was too remote a connection with the abandoned Buick. The evidence showed that the Manley woods was a hunting area and it was known that No. 12 gauge was the most popular shotgun. No doubt there were numerous 12-gauge shotgun shells on the ground in these woods. At any rate, during the trial, in arguing for the admission of the shotgun evidence, Mr. Katzmann strengthened the relevance of the shell found, as alleged by Mr. Kane, to have been on the ground by making the following different claim to the court:

MR. KATZMANN. . . . we have shown by direct eye witness that the defendant was firing a shot-gun and immediately after the shell was found, or two months [minutes] after and that it was a Winchester. We have shown that the car the witnesses saw at the Brockton Police Station was the same type of car which was used in the Bridgewater affair and *in that car was found another shell of the Peters type which Officer Connelly found among the four* . . . [Emphasis added.] [4]

Confusion now begins to accumulate. At first Mr. Kane said a *Winchester* shell was found, but Mr. Katzmann interrupted his opening to tell him it was a *Peters* shell. Mr. Kane said it was lying *"on the ground,"* but Mr. Katzmann, arguing for the admission of the shotgun shell evidence, told the court it was found *"in that car."*

The confusion becomes even more confounded. At no time during the trial was any *shotgun shell offered in evidence as having been picked up on the ground or in the car. Nor was there any testimony about the finding of such a shell.* Daniel M. Ryan, city marshal of Brockton (not a State Police officer), was called to tell of seeing the car in the Manley Street woods, but did not mention a shotgun shell. We already know that Marshal Ryan was the companion of Brockton police officer Hill when these two responded to the telephone call from the hunters who had found the Buick. We also know that Officer Hill later reported in detail at the Dedham trial on his search of the contents of the car but said nothing about finding a shotgun shell.[5]

[4] Supp. Vol., 146.
[5] Pinkerton operative H.H., in his report for April 19, 1920, stated that Chief Gallivan of South Braintree showed him a "shell for a Winchester shotgun . . . Same as the one found on the scene of the Bridgewater attempted holdup last December." No details were given. The shell was never heard of again.

Why was no shell produced as having been found in the Manley woods? Where was the promised State Police witness? We do not know. However, we do know that when Captain Proctor, head of the State Police, testified later at Plymouth as an expert, his testimony was noteworthy for the absence of anything really relevant. It was after the Plymouth trial that Captain Proctor was formally removed by Mr. Katzmann from further direction of the investigation, and Bridgewater Chief Stewart thereupon received the official appointment from Mr. Katzmann.

Let us now turn our attention to the shotgun cartridges taken from Vanzetti's pocket in the Brockton police station at the time of his arrest. At the Plymouth trial, four unidentified shotgun cartridges were produced by the prosecution as shells carried by Vanzetti. Since Vanzetti did not testify at Plymouth, we must find the defendant's explanation of the shells in his pocket from the later testimony at the trial for the South Braintree murders.

At Dedham, Vanzetti stated that he was at the Sacco home on May 5, 1920, where they had supper before meeting with Boda and Orciani at the Johnson garage. Mrs. Sacco was cleaning up things in preparation for a trip of the Sacco family to Italy. Vanzetti testified that he found *three* shotgun shells on a shelf and asked her if he could take them to give to friends who hunted in the winter, that she assented and he took the shells.[6] In cross-examination, Mr. Katzmann pounded Vanzetti to admit that there had been *four* shells instead of *three*. Vanzetti stated that he believed he took three shells, but finally said: "I don't remember exactly. I don't want to insist at all about it."

Nicola Sacco testified that Vanzetti saw the shells on a shelf in the Sacco home where Mrs. Sacco had put them in her cleaning-out operation; that Vanzetti took them, saying: "I will bring them to Plymouth to a friend of mine so I could make fifty cents for the benefit of the prisoner and other things." Sacco testified further that a friend and his wife had visited them in 1919 or 1918 and had brought a gun and a box of shells. He continued: ". . . we went in the woods that day, me, him and his wife, playing and shooting in the wood, — mostly destroyed moths, but there were left in the box about three. So the three were always in the house." [7]

Rose Sacco, Nicola's wife, explained how she found the shells while cleaning up the closet and put them on a shelf where Vanzetti saw them

[6] Vol. II, 1715.   [7] Vol. II, 1863.

and picked them up, saying, "I am going to take these, if you don't need them, and give them to a friend of mine, and he will probably give me fifty cents for propaganda." [8]

Jeremiah McAnarney, who put Mrs. Sacco on the stand, had not been at the Plymouth trial and apparently did not realize the significance (as Katzmann and possibly Vanzetti did) in Katzmann's insistent cross-examination about the number of shotgun shells. He opened the subject with Mrs. Sacco by saying, "I call your attention to three or four shells . . ."

From the foregoing we cannot be certain whether there were three or four cartridges. If Sacco told the truth when he said that the cartridges were the remnant of a box of shells, one would have expected that they would be of the same make (in this case, of Peters manufacture), whatever the number. However, as we shall see, the fourth cartridge produced at Plymouth was of *Winchester* make, *the same manufacture as the exploded shell found by Dr. Murphy, thereby tending to link Vanzetti to the Bridgewater attempt* which had occurred more than four months before the cartridges were found in his pocket.

It could be a coincidence that the alleged connection with the Bridgewater attempt should come through a fourth cartridge, whereas Sacco and Vanzetti remembered only three on the Sacco shelf, and that this fourth cartridge was of a different make from the other three but of the same manufacture (Winchester) as the exploded shell found by Dr. Murphy. However, as we shall see, Vanzetti's possession of a single Winchester cartridge to match the make of one found at the scene was one of a series of such "one-in-four" coincidences which helped to convict the defendants. Others will be considered later. For the present, however, we can go no further than to wonder whether the fourth cartridge of Winchester manufacture was actually one carried by Vanzetti on the night of his arrest. It was never identified as such.

When the arresting officer, Michael J. Connolly, took the stand at Plymouth, the jury was excused and Mr. Katzmann stated he expected to show by his testimony that when Connolly searched Vanzetti he found three Peters shells and one 12-gauge Winchester, "the same size and type that Dr. Murphy picked up." Mr. Katzmann then argued for the introduction of the shells. A part of his speech has already been quoted.

[8] Vol. II, 2057–2058.

Mr. Vahey battled against the admission of these shells. In his argument he said: "It seems to me so absolutely remote and incompetent to say a man on the 5th of May, twenty weeks afterward happened to have a couple of shells in his pocket was the man who had the shot-gun."

Judge Thayer ruled that Vahey's argument went to the weight of the evidence, not to its competence. Then followed:

MR. VAHEY. It seems to me it would be doing this defendant a gross injustice.

THE COURT. I will protect his rights to the limit. There will be no gross injustice done.

To this Mr. Vahey replied: "I am simply arguing as to my point of view. I have never said at any place or time that the defendant's rights were not protected in your Honor's hands." [9] He then renewed his argument that the admission of the shells would be doing the defendant a gross injustice.

The court concluded: "I will admit the testimony and save your rights, Mr. Vahey."

At this point the jury was sent for and returned to the court, and the examination of Officer Connolly continued:

Q. When you arrested this defendant on the night of May 5, did you search him? A. I did.

Q. Did you find some shells? A. I did.

Q. How many? A. Four.

Q. I will ask you to look at those shells (showing) and see whether or not these are the shells. A. *They look like the same ones.*

MR. KANE. I offer these in evidence. [Referring to the shells the officer produced.]

MR. VAHEY. *Not on that identification I suppose, — that they look like the same ones.* [Emphasis added.][10]

Nevertheless, the shells were admitted after the court was told that those taken by the officer had been handed over to his captain at the desk, and that they were all No. 12 gauge.

The shells should never have been admitted. The failure to prove that they were actually the ones taken from Vanzetti was not cured by the statement that some shells were given to Officer Connolly's captain or that they were 12-gauge. Proper identification was still lacking. No identification marks had been placed on the individual shells, nor was there any memorandum showing the receipt of the cartridges, their number, make or condi-

[9] Supp. Vol., 148.   [10] Supp. Vol., 149.

tion. Even Officer Connolly, who took the cartridges from Vanzetti, obviously avoided identifying those produced in court as the same ones.

As the shells were left with the stenographer, presumably to be held with other exhibits, Mr. Vahey noted that there were three Peters and one Winchester. No further notation appears on the record.[11] Here there occurred another irregularity. It does not appear that each shell was marked as an exhibit for identification during the trial. The failure to mark the shells separately as exhibits made for further confusion. Not only do we not know whether all of the shells admitted in evidence as exhibits came from Vanzetti's pocket, we now have no means of being sure that the four loaded cartridges actually introduced in evidence will be the same shells that later went into the jury room. This further lack of authentication makes it difficult to trace the strange events that ensued.

Confusion and mystery were further created by the ballistic testimony of Captain William H. Proctor, head of the Massachusetts State Police. He was the only ballistic expert to testify at Plymouth. To identify the Winchester cartridge allegedly taken from Vanzetti as a shell similar to the shell picked up by Dr. Murphy, there should have been some testimony concerning the similarity of the shot caliber. Also, having in mind the important bearing of the size of the shot, one would have expected Captain Proctor to discuss the caliber of the pellets or balls. This he did not do. Possibly the stenographer at the Plymouth trial (who had some reporting difficulties) did not get all of his testimony. A statement by at least one of the jurymen, after the trial, suggests that parts of his testimony may not have been fully taken down. But this only deepens the mystery.

The transcript of Proctor's testimony, with cross-examination, covers only three and one-half pages. Over a page is used up in giving Proctor's experience with firearms, beginning with a shotgun at the age of twelve. For years he loaded his own metal shells, then paper shells, but afterwards he bought them already loaded.[12]

He looked at the four cartridges and the one exploded shell. Three dark-colored cartridges he identified as Peters manufacture adapted for a 12-gauge shotgun. He then looked at the fourth loaded shell and the empty shell, stating that they were both Winchester shotgun shells, 12-gauge, bearing the name "Repeater." He then stated that Winchester made an-

[11] Supp. Vol., 149.   [12] Supp. Vol., 208–209.

other shell named "Leader" that had more brass and a longer base. In substance, this constituted his entire testimony on direct examination.

Factory-made shotgun shells bear a symbol on the wadding, such as "B," "BB," "# 4," "0," "00," etc., to indicate the size of the shot within. *No question was asked of Captain Proctor by the assistant district attorney concerning marks on the wadding of the shells.* Just as Proctor read off the names "Peters" and "Winchester" and the word "Repeater" on the shells, he could have read the caliber of the shot on the wadding. All he had to do was to turn the cartridge over and look at the wad. *This he was not asked to do.* There was some reference to the shells being "12-gauge," but this meant nothing so far as the caliber of shot was concerned.

On cross-examination, Mr. Vahey brought out the fact that any kind of 12-gauge shell could be used in any kind of 12-gauge shotgun. The following questions and answers are the only ones in the transcript of Proctor's testimony, even implied, touching on the important issue of the shot caliber:

Q. Is the 12 gauge ordinary hunting gun used more than any other gun? A. Yes.

Q. *In hunting birds and that sort of thing?* [Emphasis added.] A. Yes.[13]

If at this point Captain Proctor had been holding in his hand a shell marked "buckshot" would he not have replied, "Not with this caliber shot!" or something like that? The answer, however, seemed to satisfy Mr. Vahey, since the two men were discussing shells, not the gun. That was the end of Captain Proctor's testimony.

Why did the assistant district attorney avoid asking Proctor about the caliber of the shot? Was it because the prosecution faced a dilemma? Assistant District Attorney Kane had received from the Pinkerton detective some of the shot that lay with the shell found by Dr. Murphy. The doctor had also indicated that the shell could be used for shooting small birds. If so, Mr. Kane knew the approximate size of the shot that had been in the exploded shell. If he had asked Captain Proctor the caliber of the shot within the loaded Winchester shell, claimed by the prosecution to be identical with the exploded shell found by Dr. Murphy, the answer might have been damaging. If, for instance, Captain Proctor had replied that the cali-

[13] Supp. Vol., 211.

ber was quite small, there might be a verdict of not guilty on the indictment for assault with intent to murder; if, however, Captain Proctor had answered that the caliber was buck, or otherwise of large size, the Winchester shell alleged to come from Vanzetti would fail to match the exploded shell found in Bridgewater which would impair, if not destroy, the evidential value of the Murphy shell. Was the dilemma solved, as a similar dilemma was later solved in the Dedham trial, by avoiding a direct question which might have brought out Captain Proctor's real opinion? The talk about both shells being "12-gauge" enabled Captain Proctor to keep away from the real issue. His honest opinion, however, may have leaked out tangentially when he agreed with Vahey that a 12-gauge gun is used for "hunting birds and that sort of thing." This was encouraging, but it was not followed up by the defendant's counsel, and possibly favorable evidence died on the vine as it did later at the Dedham trial.

Just what were the shells concerning which Captain Proctor was testifying? In the light of what came later, the mystery will grow even more insoluble.

The Plymouth jury retired at 10:50 A.M. to their room. Nearly five hours later, they returned to the courtroom for additional instructions. They wished to know whether they could return a verdict of assault with a dangerous weapon in the indictment for assault with intent to murder. To this, Judge Thayer answered yes. In further explanation, the court discussed the matter of intent to murder, including the following: "A deadly weapon is one likely to produce death or grievous bodily harm. That means something if you find that a gun was an instrument that was liable to cause death or grievous bodily injury."

The jury then retired, but returned in about half an hour with a verdict of guilty of assault with intent to murder as well as assault with intent to rob. Unknown at the time to the court, the jury had been conducting its own examination of the shotgun shells. The charge for assault with intent to rob had been settled, and the jury had been discussing at length the indictment for assault with intent to murder. Some jurymen suggested opening the cartridges to inspect the caliber of the shot within, and this was then done in the secrecy of the jury room without the knowledge or presence of defendant's counsel.

Judge Thayer and District Attorney Katzmann learned of this gross violation of the defendant's rights on the day after the close of the Plymouth trial,[14] but did nothing about it at the time. A juryman later quoted Mr. Katzmann as saying that "he did not want it known." [15]

Nearly five months later, after Mr. Moore had replaced Mr. Vahey as counsel, the matter of the secret opening of the shells was investigated by the defense. In November and December of 1920, William J. Callahan, Esq., associate counsel for the defense, with Mr. Moore, interviewed all of the Plymouth jurors. Some of the statements were in affidavit and question and answer form. Coming five months after the verdict, it is understandable that some of the statements might not agree on all of the details concerning what happened at the trial or in the jury room. All agreed, however, that: (1) one or two cartridges were opened in the jury room; (2) they were found to contain buckshot; (3) The size of the balls in the opened shells settled all doubt as to the defendant's intent to murder.

The primary object of Mr. Callahan's quizzing of the jurors was to show that the surreptitious tampering with the shells affected the jury's verdict. At the time, the number and kind of shells that went into the jury room was of secondary interest. For this reason, no certain conclusions on these points can be drawn from the questions and answers. Had the exhibits been separately identified as those introduced in evidence, there would be no problem. However, the exhibits were not so marked. The foreman, Henry S. Burgess, who opened the shell or shells, went no further than to "suppose" they were the same shells about which Captain Proctor testified.[16] Ordinarily the court reporter, to whom the exhibits were given, would have marked them for identification. However, Alfred M. Shaw, Jr., a juryman who, with Mr. Burgess, seemed to be quite knowledgeable about shotgun cartridges, stated that he did not see *any* identifying marks on the shells made by the court reporter. Except for a presumption of regularity, the question is therefore wide open as to what actually went out with the jury into their room. Mr. Vahey had stated for the record, as the loaded shells supposedly taken from Vanzetti were handed to the reporter, "Three Peters and one Winchester." Previously the exploded Winchester shell found by Dr. Murphy and properly identified by him had gone into evidence.[17] Therefore the jury should have received four loaded shells (three Peters and one Winchester) and one empty Winchester. However, nearly all of

[14] Statement of juryman Poole, 85–86; statement of juryman Sullivan, 95.
[15] Affidavit of juryman Frawley, 30; Poole, 79.
[16] Affidavit of juryman Burgess, 4.
[17] Supp. Vol., 141.

the jurors who remembered stated that there were *three* loaded shells and one exploded shell. Mr. Callahan assumed throughout his questioning that there were only three loaded shells.

One of the best, and also one of the most puzzling, accounts was given by the foreman, Mr. Burgess, who opened the shells himself. He apparently knew the most about shotgun shells, and instructed the jury on their power and carrying limits. At first Mr. Burgess thought that the testimony was that "four or five" shells were taken from Vanzetti, but later he thought that he might have remembered two exploded shells, leaving only three loaded shells (as stated by the other jurors).[18] He stated that he saw Captain Proctor, while he was testifying, reading from both ends of the shell, the cap end and the wad.[19]

Then followed this surprising question and answer:

Q. It is now your present recollection that he did say there was bird shot, # 4 and B. shot? A. Best recollection # 4 shot in one shell and as he took up another one "B." That is the one I opened.

The very brief transcript of Proctor's testimony does not contain this reading from the wadding. Some jurors did not recall that Captain Proctor testified as to the caliber of the shot, but juryman Poole stated that "three men in the jury said that the balls that were taken from the shell were of a different kind of a ball from what Proctor said." [20]

Later Mr. Burgess recalled that he opened two shells. It "seemed" to him that both were Winchester repeater. Before opening them he read on the wad side B or two B, but did not remember if this was on the wads of both shells.[21] There were nine bullets in one shell and eleven in the other. The bullets were buckshot. Yet neither B nor two B designates buckshot, but pellets only a quarter as large.

Not all the jurors recalled that Mr. Burgess had opened *two* shells. There should have been only one loaded Winchester among the exhibits. If he opened two and there were only three loaded shells, only one should have remained. The count of the loaded shells (if they were of the same make) became even more confused when two loaded Peters shells were introduced later at the Dedham trial.

A juryman whose knowledge of shot and shotguns seemed to be on a par with that of the foreman was Alfred M. Shaw, Jr. He, too, thought there

[18] Burgess, 2.   [19] Burgess, 3.   [20] Poole, 91.   [21] Burgess, 7.

were only three unexploded shells.[22] He stated that Burgess opened one shell only.[23] (This was also stated by juryman Andrew J. O'Connor.)[24] When asked if there was any printing on the wads of the three unexploded shells, he replied, "It seems there was an '0.'" Juryman Wilbur seemed to remember that one shell that was opened was marked "0" on the wad and another was marked "00." [25] To anyone who knew shotgun shells, both symbols would have indicated buckshot. If the wads (on any of them) were actually so marked, and these were the shells handled by Captain Proctor, it becomes even more inexplicable that neither Assistant District Attorney Kane, nor District Attorney Katzmann, nor Captain Proctor, nor Mr. Vahey made any observation about so patent a fact at the trial.

A possible explanation of the confusion in regard to the contents of the opened shells is that they may have been previously filled by hand. One would ordinarily be reluctant to consider such a solution, yet there seems to be little reason to have the usual confidence in any of the exhibits.[26] There is some evidence, not very convincing, that the shells had been filled or refilled by hand.

The two most knowledgeable jurymen, Burgess and Shaw, stated that they did not think the shells had been previously opened.[27] Juryman Litchfield, however, thought that the shells had been opened previously because of the easy manner in which they opened — a new shell would have been harder to open.[28] Juryman O'Connor saw nothing to indicate a previous opening, but the shells could have been reloaded. He observed that the wadding in the shells was down from one-half to three-quarters of an inch, a rather unusual condition for factory-made shells.[29] This has a significance in another respect which will be mentioned later.

The mystery of the shotgun shells grows deeper when we consider two shotgun cartridges produced by the prosecution at the Dedham trial. They were alleged to be two of the four shells used as exhibits in the Plymouth

[22] Statement of juryman Shaw, 44.
[23] Statement of juryman Shaw, 49.
[24] Statement of juryman O'Connor, 65.
[25] Statement of juryman Wilbur, 58.
[26] The same lack of confidence was expressed by Major Calvin Goddard, who made ballistic tests for the district attorney's office in June 1927. *Harvard Law Review*, Vol. 79, No. 3 (January 1966), 578.
[27] Burgess, 7; Shaw, 48.
[28] Statement of juryman Litchfield, 42–43.
[29] O'Connor, 67–69.

trial to convict Vanzetti of the Bridgewater attempt. The basis for their admission as evidence against Sacco and Vanzetti for the South Braintree murders was the following:

As at the Plymouth trial, Officer Connolly testified that he had found four shotgun shells in Vanzetti's right-hand pocket, 12-gauge, three Peters and one Winchester.[30] He did not, however, identify the two shells offered as having been ones taken from Vanzetti, nor did anyone else.

Witnesses of the South Braintree affair reported that they had seen a rifle protruding through the opening in the rear curtain of the fleeing Buick.[31] (We shall later learn what it really was and who held it.)

Defense counsel objected to the admission of the shells, claiming that there was no evidence of a shotgun seen at the crime. At first Judge Thayer excluded the shells. However, the prosecution called attention to the testimony of the witness Hans Behrsin, who had stated: "As that [the escaping car] passed me by there was some one in the back there beckoning with a gun or shot-gun, whatever it was, through the back light where you got the celluloid glass, whatever it is. That was broken out." [32]

There was no testimony, however, that anyone fired a shotgun at South Braintree, or that any shot was found at the scene or that anyone really saw a shotgun.

On the reference to Behrsin's vague testimony, the two shotgun shells were admitted in evidence against Vanzetti, and became Exhibit 37. In this way, the same shells were used as evidence that Vanzetti was implicated in the Bridgewater attempt on December 24, 1919, and in the South Braintree crime on April 15, 1920.

At the close of the prosecution's case at Dedham, the following stipulation was entered:

It is agreed on behalf of the defendants Vanzetti and Sacco that of the four shot-gun shells found on the defendant Vanzetti at the time of his arrest, two have not been introduced in evidence because they are not in the same condition as when found on him, and this through no fault of either the Government or the defendants, and that the two shot-gun shells that are hereby admitted are subject . . .[33]

In June 1927, I examined these two shells. They were in perfect condition, as if they had come from the factory. Unlike the wads in the Plym-

[30] Vol. I, p. 756.
[31] McGlone, Supp. Vol., 422; Langlois, Supp. Vol., 446; Vol. I, 269, 280, 285.
[32] Vol. I, p. 328.   [33] Vol. I, 939.

outh shells described by juryman O'Connor, these were close under the crimping. On each wad there was plainly stamped the legend "00 Buck." Had these shells been in Captain Proctor's hands at Plymouth, neither he, nor the assistant district attorney, nor Mr. Vahey could have overlooked the clear indication that they contained buckshot, so identified not only by symbol but also by word, and if they had been in the jury room, no jurors would have been in such doubt that they would have wanted to see them opened.

The stipulation would seem to indicate that the Plymouth jury foreman, Burgess, was correct in his first memory that four loaded shells came into the jury room and that he had opened two of them. No testimony was given as to the size of the shot count in the two shells.

Mr. Katzmann, in his summation to the jury at Dedham, however, utilized his knowledge of the secret opening of the shells at Plymouth to designate the contents of the missing shells excluded by the stipulation, and possibly his reading on the wads of the two shells introduced in evidence. He argued as follows:

. . . they had or Vanzetti had four shells — no weapon in which to fire them at the moment that we found, but you will remember, gentlemen, that sticking out the back of the bandit's car on April 15th was either a rifle or a shot-gun, and in Vanzetti's pocket were four 12-gauge shells loaded with buck shot that they were going out to shoot little birds with, with some friend that had visited them at some time before.[34]

This statement not only violated the stipulation, but was inaccurate to say the least. The talk about shooting "little birds" did not come from Sacco or Vanzetti,[35] but from the dialogue at the Plymouth trial between Vahey and Dr. Murphy, and between Vahey and Captain Proctor. Mr. Katzmann's remark about shooting "little birds" with buckshot was seized upon years later by Judge Thayer, who blew it up into a statement remarkable for its multiple inexactitudes. He then assigned his own statement as a reason for exercising his discretion to deny motions for a new trial in the Dedham case. In his decision on the last motion, before the sentencing, he wrote:

At the trial two shot-gun cartridges were in evidence that were found in the possession of one of the defendants; and this same defendant testified he under-

34 Vol. II, 2204.   35 Vol. II, 1894.

stood they were to be used for small birds; and yet, when these cartridges were opened at some time during the trial it was found that they contained buckshot.[36]

Vanzetti gave no testimony whatever as to what the shells were to be used for and said nothing about "small birds." The shells were not opened during the trial at Dedham; they were opened at Plymouth, but surreptitiously and not as part of that trial either. The two opened shells were excluded as evidence by a stipulation and Judge Thayer had no right to treat them as evidence.

Judge Thayer's misstatement had repercussions. In 1927, Dean John Wigmore, in his attack on Professor Felix Frankfurter for writing his famous article "The Case of Sacco and Vanzetti," cited Judge Thayer's false statement as fact and then pointed to Frankfurter's omission of this nonexistent testimony as proof of Frankfurter's untrustworthiness.

But let us return to the Plymouth case and complete the saga of the shotgun shells. When Judge Thayer, on the day after trial, learned of the surreptitious opening of the shotgun shells in the jury room, he knew that Vanzetti's rights to be tried on evidence in open court had been violated. Some judges would have ordered a mistrial or a new trial on their own initiative. So far as we know, neither Mr. Vahey nor Mr. Graham knew at the time of the violation of their client's rights. Certainly the court file contains nothing to indicate any move by them to set aside the verdict for this reason, nor any other paper indicating any knowledge by defendant's counsel. Without making any note for the record of what happened in the jury room, Judge Thayer postponed sentencing Vanzetti until the next sitting of the court. Then, on August 16, 1920, more than six weeks after the verdict, he disposed of the troublesome issue in his own unique way.

First, he "filed" without penalty the indictments for assault with intent to murder on which Vanzetti had been found guilty. By doing this, he could forestall any move for a new trial based on the wrongfully obtained "buckshot" evidence by finding that Vanzetti was not injured thereby since he was not sentenced on the verdict for assault with intent to murder.

Second, the court sentenced Vanzetti from twelve to fifteen years on the verdict for assault with intent to rob. (The maximum penalty for assault with a dangerous weapon with intent to rob and assault with intent to murder was the same in 1920 — not more than twenty years).[37] Ordinarily a

36 Vol. V, 4737; see also Vol. IV, 3517.   37 G.L. Mass. (1921), Ch. 265, sec. 18.

much less severe sentence would have been imposed where there were no aggravating circumstances. Here nothing was stolen, no one was injured, and Vanzetti had no criminal record whatsoever. The stiff sentence would seem to indicate that the buckshot discovery influenced Judge Thayer's judgment even though technically he did not sentence Vanzetti for the assault with intent to murder. As we have seen, he even kept it in mind for years, citing it as a reason for denying a motion for new trial in the South Braintree case.

The effect of Judge Thayer's actions on August 16, 1920, was to cut the ground from under any moves by the defense based on the jury's wrongful act, and still give due weight to the buckshot evidence by imposing a heavy sentence on Vanzetti.

Eventually it made very little difference to Vanzetti what prison sentence was meted out to him in the Plymouth proceedings. In fact, as a convict serving a sentence, his lot was easier than that of Sacco who, as a prisoner awaiting trial, had fewer privileges. The verdict on either indictment made the subsequent verdict of guilty in the South Braintree trial almost a certainty.

9.

A Day of Remembrance

For the little Italian settlement in Plymouth, the day before Christmas was always a very particular fast day. It was not only a day on which good Catholics ate no meat, but had the extraordinary distinction of being the one day in the year which Italian Catholics observed by eating eels at the evening meal. This had become a traditional folk custom, such as turkey for Thanksgiving, or matzos for the Passover. (The eating of matzos, however, is commanded in the Bible. Exodus 36:18.) It was a very important fast day. As some of the defendant's witnesses expressed it at the Plymouth trial, it was "a day of remembrance."

December 24, 1919, was destined to become a very special day to remember. At that time, Bartolomeo Vanzetti, an obscure Italian immigrant, had been living and working in Plymouth for about seven years. Once he had been employed by the Plymouth Cordage Company and had taken an active part in a strike at that plant. Later he left the company to become a construction worker because he preferred outdoor labor.[1]

In the spring of 1919, Vanzetti interrupted his work as a construction laborer and turned to selling fish. At about the same time, he took out a license to dig clams, which he did when he had no job or no fish to sell.

He peddled fish for a few weeks and then returned to construction work. After the summer, he resumed his occupation as a fish peddler.[2] It therefore fell to him to supply his Italian neighbors with eels for the day before Christmas 1919. Vanzetti ordered a barrel of eels from a fish dealer in Boston.

On Sunday, December 21, before he received the eels, Vanzetti called on many prospective customers. Among those from whom he took orders for eels were Rosa Balboni, Adelaide Bonjionanni, Margaret Fiochi, Emma Bonjionanni and John DiCarlo. On the following Monday and Tuesday he took further orders. His price was the same to all — forty cents a pound. On Monday or Tuesday a wagon driven by a large elderly expressman brought the barrel of eels to the address of Frank and Mary Fortini, where Vanzetti boarded. Vanzetti was not at home to pay for the shipment and the barrel was carted away. The expressman returned on Tuesday, December 23, just as Vanzetti arrived. The delivery was made and Vanzetti paid for it.[3]

Vanzetti cleaned the fish that evening and made up various lots of eels for his customers according to the weights they had ordered. December 24 therefore became the only time when Vanzetti could deliver the orders in time for salting the eels and cooking them for the evening meal. The calendar itself confirms the testimony of the many witnesses to Vanzetti's delivery of eels on the morning and afternoon of December 24, 1919.

On December 24 at about 7:30 A.M. in the town of Bridgewater, nearly twenty miles away, there occurred the attempted holdup of the L. Q. White pay truck. The bandit who stood out in the street firing a shotgun was described the same day as having a dark or black closely cropped moustache. No one could then have foreseen that the same witnesses, five months later, would point to Vanzetti as this robber and change their pre-

[1] Vol. II, 1694.   [2] Vol. II, 1696.   [3] Supp. Vol., 245.

vious descriptions of the bandit's moustache from "short, croppy" to "trimmed." Nor would it have seemed possible to destroy what appeared to be an unassailable alibi for Vanzetti, that at the time of the holdup attempt he was delivering eels in Plymouth. The day before Christmas was perhaps the one day of the year when Vanzetti could absolutely count on reliable witnesses to his presence in Plymouth. It was the unique day of eels and it was Vanzetti's business to deliver these fish to his customers in time for them to prepare the evening meal. This combination made it exceptionally easy for his customers to recall seeing Vanzetti in Plymouth on December 24, 1919. It was "a day of remembrance."

Vanzetti's counsel at Plymouth have been criticized for lack of thoroughness. This may have been the fact in certain aspects of the defense, but was certainly not true of the alibi mounted by James Graham, Mr. Vahey's junior counsel. The evidence he produced on this aspect of the case was massive, coordinated and seemingly unanswerable. Defense counsel's justifiable reliance on this evidence may explain why some other aspects of the case received less preparation. This was a mistake. The defense underestimated Mr. Katzmann's skill in exploiting the inexperience of the jurymen with memory testimony and their unconscious tendency to believe that Italians, even of unimpeachable repute, would conspire to shield criminals from the law if they were also Italians.

Trial lawyers know that witnesses who testify to happenings on a particular day have prepared themselves to connect the date with other events which help them to fix the time. It means little that they cannot remember offhand events on other dates as to which they have given no prior thought. They may have lied about their recollection of events on a particular day, but their failure to recollect happenings on other dates suddenly sprung upon them does not prove it. Yet this was one of Mr. Katzmann's favorite methods of discrediting a witness who would not admit error. The Plymouth jurymen apparently were not alerted to this cross-examining tactic.

Also, some of the witnesses who knew Vanzetti well may have seemed a bit overeager to tell the jury that he was delivering eels at the time when the prosecution claimed that he was trying to hold up a payroll truck. Mr. Katzmann made this appear as proof that the Italian alibi witnesses were bursting to tell a false, prepared story. It should have been obvious, however, that if they knew Vanzetti was innocent, they would have been even more anxious to clear him by telling the truth. But it was not obvious to the jury. Mr. Katzmann was able to make the anxiety of the Italian witnesses look like a cover-up for lying.

The action of prejudice on the minds of jurors is little understood. Yet, as we follow Vanzetti's movements on the evening of December 23 and the morning of December 24, and listen to his witnesses, we have only to ask ourselves whether a jury would have found that sixteen native Americans of good repute, long resident in the community, had committed wholesale perjury to protect a local highwayman. And we might also ask ourselves whether Mr. Katzmann, if he had been cross-examining native Yankees, would have displayed the same amused contempt for their honesty and indulged in the same insulting innuendos as he did toward the humble Italians of the town of Plymouth.

Although Mr. Katzmann's style of cross-examination confused some of the Italian witnesses, it failed to shake their testimony. They maintained the truth of their stories despite the difficulty of grasping the meaning of questions in an alien tongue requiring answers with precise shades of meaning when translated. Mr. Katzmann was able to bring out the fact that some of the witnesses were friends of Vanzetti and had discussed their testimony before testifying. This was to be expected. It would have been most unnatural if some of these people had not checked and rechecked their recollection in order to present their stories as convincingly as possible. This, however, was not proof in itself that they were lying. Defense counsel, on redirect examination, might have put more questions to some of these witnesses to enable the jury better to devaluate the effect of much of Mr. Katzmann's cross-examination. Possibly Mr. Graham, accustomed to more sophisticated Boston juries, believed that the men from the Plymouth County countryside could discount this sort of an attack on the witnesses without further questioning by him. If so, this proved to be a mistake.

As his first witness, Mr. Graham wisely chose Mary Fortini, Vanzetti's landlady since October. Prior to boarding at the Fortinis', Vanzetti had lived for several years in the home of his very good friends the Vincenzo Brinis. (The correct spelling is "Brini" but the transcript spelled it "Breni.") Mary Fortini's testimony was fairly inclusive of Vanzetti's movements on and around the day before Christmas. Other witnesses filled in the gaps in her story. As we follow the accounts by the witnesses, we get not only a close view of Vanzetti, but also glimpses of life in the Italian community of Plymouth in 1919.

The Fortinis' home was at 35 Cherry Street, in the heart of the Italian community. They had lived at the same address for twenty-two years. Frank Fortini worked at the Plymouth Cordage Company. Mrs. Fortini said she spoke no English, and it was apparent that occasionally she failed at first to grasp questions translated into Italian, but she finally got their meaning.

It was Mrs. Fortini who told of the old man with the express wagon bringing the barrel of eels to her house and going away because Vanzetti was not there and she had no money. "Either December 22 or the 23rd, I do not remember exactly . . . After one Monday [Monday was December 22], Vanzetti and the express came back." [4] The barrel was left in Mrs. Fortini's kitchen.[5]

Mrs. Fortini stated that Vanzetti came home for supper about six o'clock on December 23, went out again at about half past six and came back about eight. (Mrs. Brini and her son Beltrando later stated that he had been in their home during the interim to request Beltrando's help for the next morning.) He then went into her kitchen to prepare the fish for the next day and remained there until twelve o'clock.[6]

The next morning, December 24, a neighbor, one Balboni (Carlo Balboni), came to her back door at about quarter past six to pick up his order for eels. (Balboni later stated that he stopped on his way home from the night shift at the Plymouth Cordage Company.) Vanzetti was in bed. Mrs. Fortini called to Vanzetti to come down to give Balboni the fish. He came down in three or four minutes dressed in a blue jumper, overalls and a sweater, stockings but no shoes. He got the fish ready for Balboni, who took them away in a basket he had brought with him.[7]

Mrs. Fortini then warmed up milk for Vanzetti, which was all he had for breakfast. After drinking the milk, Vanzetti put on his shoes and went out, but returned before eight o'clock.[8] He had some talk with her about a horse. (Enrico Bastoni, the baker, later stated that Vanzetti had been to his shop "for a horse" at about five or ten minutes of eight.[9]) Vanzetti had only a wheelbarrow and a "small little push-cart" for delivering his fish. After eight o'clock Vanzetti went out again with the boy Beltrando Brini. Mrs. Fortini saw him later that morning "coming in and getting the fish in my yard." [10] At noon he came to eat lunch, remained about half an hour and went out again with the fish. He returned between five and half past

---

[4] Supp. Vol., 245–246.   [5] Supp. Vol., 227.   [6] Supp. Vol., 226.
[7] Supp. Vol., 225.   [8] Supp. Vol., 226.   [9] Supp. Vol., 251.   [10] Supp. Vol., 227.

five, and had a Christmas Eve supper consisting of "spaghetti and ancho-vies, eels and we had some Italian dish, chestnut." [11] He went out after supper at about eight or half past eight. She did not know when he re-turned. (The Brinis later testified that he was at their home.)

Mr. Katzmann began his cross-examination on the subject of Vanzetti's arrest. Except as she was told, or had it read to her, Mrs. Fortini would not have known that it occurred in Brockton, on May 5, 1920. The opening questions and answers indicated that her memory was quite accurate as to days of the week, but nonexistent as to dates and the following is a fair sample of Mr. Katzmann's method of seeking to discredit Mrs. Fortini and other Italian witnesses.

Q. On the day before Christmas what were you doing at half past seven in the morning? A. I don't know.

Q. What time did Vanzetti get up on the day after Christmas? A. I don't remember.

Q. What time did Vanzetti get up the first day of this year? A. I don't know.

Q. What time did Vanzetti get up on Washington's birthday of this year? A. No, I don't know.

Q. What time did he get up East [Easter] Sunday morning this year? A. I don't know.

Q. What time did he go to bed the Saturday night before Easter morning of this year? A. I don't know, no sir.

Q. You have not talked it over with anybody, have you? A. Yes sir, I have talked outside.

Q. With whom did you talk? A. I spoke with the ladies and people outside.

Q. When? A. When we got the news that Vanzetti was arrested.

Q. Up to the time that you got the news that Vanzetti was arrested you have never thought what time he got up the day before Christmas, had you? A. No sir, I never stopped to think.[12]

Mr. Katzmann then examined Mrs. Fortini about what she told police officers when they interviewed her after Vanzetti's arrest. The talk was in English. She told them that Vanzetti was at her house the day before Christmas, but they did not ask her how she remembered it.

Mr. Katzmann went on:

Q. Did you tell the police officers anything about the Breni boy or what time he got up, or about cleaning fish?

THE COURT. You had better separate those questions.

[11] Supp. Vol., 231.   [12] Supp. Vol., 229.

Q. Did you tell the police officers anything about the Breni boy? A. No.
Q. Did you tell the officers anything about Balboni? A. No.
Q. Did you tell the officers anything about your horse? A. No.
Q. Did you tell them anything about his first using a wheelbarrow and then coming back for the other cart. Yes or no? A. I don't know if I told them that or not. I don't talk English.[13]

On redirect she said that she did not tell them more because she needed an interpreter. Then Mr. Graham brought out the following:

Q. Did they ask you anything about Breni? A. No.
Q. Or ask you about Balboni? A. No.
Q. Did they ask you anything about a horse? A. No.
Q. Did any of them say anything to you about getting into trouble? A. Yes sir.
Q. What did he say? A. When they left to go away they told me that I was going to be into trouble because they told me that I was not telling the truth.[14]

Mr. Katzmann then got the court's permission to examine Mrs. Fortini in English. He then resorted to ridicule to discredit her testimony.

Q. Do you know what language I talk? Do you know my language? A. No.
Q. What is a horse — do you know? A. I don't understand nothing.
Q. Do you know what a horse is? A. No sir.
Q. Do you know what a Breni is? A. No sir.
Q. Do you know what a Balboni is? That is something you hang out on the line washday isn't it? A. Me don't understand you. You come in my country and you don't understand nothing, and me just the same. . . .[15]

The next witness was Carlo Balboni, who lived on South Cherry Street. He had been in this country thirteen years and had been a foreman at the Plymouth Cordage Company for ten years. He met Vanzetti two days before Christmas passing the Fortini house on Cherry Street on his way to work and asked him to save two pounds of eels for him. He picked up his order at the Fortini house December 24 on his way home from his night shift at the Cordage Company. He told of Mrs. Fortini calling to Vanzetti, who came down and made up two pounds of eels for him to take home.

On cross-examination, Balboni said he had told "an Italian fellow, the shoemaker," of buying eels from Vanzetti the day before Christmas. This was after Vanzetti's arrest, but Balboni was uncertain about the dates. Then followed:

[13] Supp. Vol., 233.   [14] Supp. Vol., 235.   [15] Supp. Vol., 235.

Q. How long before that was it that Vanzetti was arrested? A. I don't know.
Q. Give us your best memory? A. Well, if I don't remember, how can I?
Q. You think a little about it and then tell these Gentlemen. A. I don't know, I am sure.
Q. Was it about ten days? A. I ain't sure.
Q. Was it not about the 23rd of April you heard of his being arrested? A. I don't know.
Q. You saw it in the paper or heard of his being arrested, did you not? A. In the paper I did not see it because I don't read.
Q. Before you talked with the shoemaker you knew he had been arrested, didn't you? A. Yes.
Q. How long before you talked with the shoemaker did somebody tell you that he was arrested? A. I don't remember.
Q. You don't remember that? A. No.
Q. But you remember where you were at six fifteen in the morning on the day before Christmas? A. Yes, I remember that.
Q. Who else did you meet on the day before Christmas on the way home? Did you talk with anybody? A. No.
Q. Whom did you meet the day before Christmas as you were going to your home? A. I don't know.
Q. Do you know Easter? A. Yes sir.
Q. Whom did you meet going to work the day before Easter? A. I don't know.
Q. What did you have to eat on Easter? A. I don't know.
Q. What did you have to eat the day before Easter? A. I don't know; my wife gets it.
Q. You knew what you were eating? A. I don't remember now. I don't remember what I eat yesterday some time.
Q. How is it you can remember about the day before Christmas but can't remember what I just asked you about? A. I don't know.[16]

The last question above (and similar cross-examination of subsequent witnesses) seems strange coming from Mr. Katzmann, who *knew that the Italians ate eels on the day before Christmas*. After badgering many Italian witnesses about their claim of the unique observance of the day by eating eels, he finally admitted his own knowledge of this custom. This came almost at the end of the defendant's case when Mr. Graham started to question the last Italian witness. The following exchange occurred:

Q. (By Mr. Graham) Do you know the custom of the Italians with reference to arranging about the day before Christmas? A. Yes I do.
Q. What is it?
MR. KATZMANN. I am prepared to admit that. The Commonwealth does not contend about the custom and use of eels.[17]

[16] Supp. Vol., 239.   [17] Supp. Vol., 321.

The foregoing admission should be kept in mind in considering whether the Italian witnesses told the truth in tying their recollection of Vanzetti's presence in Plymouth on December 24 to their purchase of eels from him on that day.

Before following Vanzetti through the Italian quarter with Beltrando to deliver eels to his customers on December 24, let us first see what he did on the evening of December 23 when he left the Fortini house at about half past six.

Alfonsini Brini, wife of Vincenzo Brini and mother of Beltrando, stated that Vanzetti came to her home that night and talked to Beltrando about helping him to sell fish the next day.[18] While Vanzetti was there, "two Americans" brought in half of a pig and put it in her cellar and then came upstairs. They left before Vanzetti, who stayed until about eight o'clock. (She worked daytimes for the Puritan Mills and was home in the evenings, but her husband worked the night shift at the Cordage Company.) Vanzetti brought with him the eels which she had ordered. She remembered that this was about seven o'clock, "because that was the time the other two men delivered the pig at my house." [19] She salted the eels that night. Mr. Katzmann apparently thought that this was a falsehood and cross-examined Mrs. Brini as follows:

Q. What time? A. After seven o'clock.
Q. Morning or evening? A. In the night.
Q. How much after seven? A. I don't know, maybe just before or a little after.
Q. Well, it was not as late as eight o'clock? A. No, seven or after seven. I don't know I remember just because that was the time the other two men delivered the pig at my house.
Q. Did you salt them? A. Yes.
Q. When did you eat them — what time? A. Christmas Eve.
Q. That is about twenty-four hours late, is it not? A. Why, before we eat them about half past five.
Q. Do you do your own cooking in the house for your family? A. Yes. I prepare the food the night before and start to cook it and then my husband finish them in the morning.
Q. I did not ask that. I was asking if you do the cooking in your home or do some of it? A. Yes.
Q. You said yes, — why do you want to say any more. The Jury know it. You said yes and then started as usual.
THE COURT. Perhaps it would be better to put it in another form.

[18] Supp. Vol., 305.   [19] Supp. Vol., 207.

Q. You do some of the cooking for your house, don't you? A. Yes.

Q. You have been doing it for a number of years? A. Yes.

Q. And you have cooked eels a great many times since you have been married? A. Yes, many times.[20]

Beltrando Brini's testimony concerning his helping Vanzetti on December 24 will be considered shortly. Here we may note his graphic account of the pig incident on direct examination as follows:

Q. Do you remember the 23rd of December? A. Yes.

Q. How do you remember that? A. I remember it that Mr. Vanzetti on the 23rd, that night came and asked me if I —

Q. Not that. He came to your house, did he? A. Yes.

Q. Did he talk with you? A. Yes.

Q. Now what was the talk about? A. About helping him.

Q. Helping him where? A. The next day, the 24th.

Q. Is there anything else that happened that night at your house that helped you to remember that night? A. Yes.

Q. What else was there? A. A pig.

Q. Tell us what about the pig that helps you to remember. A. Well two men came there and brought half a pig to the house.

Q. What did they do with half a pig? A. They brought it down the cellar.

Q. Was Vanzetti there when the pig was brought into the house? A. Yes sir.

Q. Do you know who brought the pig to the house? A. I know it was two men but I don't know their names.

Q. Do you know what time they brought the pig to the house? A. I could not tell exactly, but about half past seven.

Q. How do you fix it, the time that they brought it there? A. Because at that time Mr. Vanzetti was in there too.

Q. Any other way? A. We just finished supper when Mr. Vanzetti came there.

Q. Were you all through supper? A. Yes.

Q. Was the table all cleared off? A. Yes, all cleared off.

Q. How do you know that? A. Because I helped myself to clear off everything.

Q. Were the men that brought the pig there — was there anything happened that enables you to remember that the table was cleared? A. After they brought the pig down stairs they came up and drank, one did and one didn't.

Q. Where did they have a drink? A. They drank in the kitchen.

Q. At the table? A. Yes at the table.

Q. Do you know how long Mr. Vanzetti stayed there at your house that night? A. Not exactly.

Q. How long? A. About half an hour or more.

Q. Do you know about what time he left? A. Somewhere around in the vicinity of half past seven.[21]

[20] Supp. Vol., 312.　　[21] Supp. Vol., 258.

Under cross-examination, Beltrando was asked what day of the week was December 22. He replied, "Tuesday — no, Monday," then when asked whether he was sure, went back to Tuesday. Actually, the twenty-second was Monday, which Beltrando soon recognized. Pouncing fiercely on this error, Mr. Katzmann tried to get Beltrando to admit that the pig was delivered on Monday, December 22, and that his entire account of events was one day off. Beltrando stuck to his story, explaining that his mistake about the day of the week was due to his thinking that the twenty-fourth, when he helped Vanzetti, was a Thursday, whereas Thursday was Christmas, the twenty-fifth.[22]

Beltrando and Alfonsini's statements that the half-pig was delivered to their home on the night of December 23 were corroborated by Vincenzo Brini, who said it was delivered on December 23 after he had left his home at 5:30 P.M. to work on the night shift at the Cordage Company[23] and partly by Rose Forni, who lived upstairs in the Brini house.[24]

Matthew Sassi, through whom Vincenzo had ordered the half-pig, told about his buying five quarters of a pig from Ed Manter (who had two pigs) for himself and Brini. He said that Manter slaughtered it on the twenty-third, that his three quarters were left in his cellar by "Jack Kinsley and another man" at about 5:15 P.M. and that he instructed them to take the other two quarters to the Brini house. Again, Mr. Katzmann sought to get an admission that the pig was delivered on December 22, not December 23, but he failed to shake Sassi's story.[25]

He next tried to prove a close friendship between Vanzetti and the witness, but got no further than to show occasional socializing at the Brinis' when Vanzetti was visiting them. Mr. Katzmann then threw out these innuendos to the jury:

Q. Do you belong to any organization that Vanzetti belongs to? A. No, I don't know anything about him.
MR. GRAHAM. I object. He is assuming that Vanzetti belongs to an organization.
Q. Do you know anything of his political beliefs? A. No sir.
Q. Have you ever heard him make any speeches to fellow workers at the Cordage? A. No.[26]

At the end of the defendant's case, Mr. Graham put the following stipulation into the record:

[22] Supp. Vol., 269.   [23] Supp. Vol., 248–250.   [24] Supp. Vol., 293.
[25] Supp. Vol., 296–297.   [26] Vol., 298–299.

In the absence of the Jury Mr. Graham addressed the Court as follows: — I understand that the District Attorney agrees that if Mr. Edward Manter, who is not here, were here he would testify that the day before Christmas, he killed two pigs and one quarter of one pig went to Mr. Sassi who testified yesterday and he kept the other quarter himself and Mr. Kingsley was the man who took them on his team and that Mr. Kingsley would testify that he brought part of the pig because it was that pig, one quarter to Mr. Sassi's room in the Breni house before Christmas, — the date we cannot fix.[27]

The foregoing demonstrates the sloppy result of trying to save the time of witnesses by orally stating what counsel understands they would say if called. Such statements, like all hearsay, are apt to contain errors which cannot be corrected in the absence of the witnesses. On its face the stipulation quoted, although generally corroborating the witnesses, states the number of pig quarters erroneously, describes Mr. Sassi's home as a room in the Brini house — he lived quite a distance away on Obery Street — and says that he slaughtered the two pigs "the day before Christmas" — instead of two days before — which would bring the delivery to the Brinis' to Christmas Eve, a most unlikely time.

The pig episode on the night of December 23 had been mentioned by Beltrando only as an unusual incident in the life of the Brini household which helped him to place the time when Vanzetti had come to request his help the next morning. Mr. Katzmann made a big issue of it by charging Beltrando with telling a contrived lie. Unless four other people also perjured themselves, the evidence that Beltrando told the truth was overwhelming. No evidence whatever supported Mr. Katzmann's charge that the pig was delivered on Monday, December 22. His rough assault on the boy's honesty should have backfired — but it did not.

We are now ready to follow the movements of Vanzetti after he drank his warmed milk and pulled on his shoes on the morning of December 24. Mrs. Fortini had said that he then went out but returned before eight o'clock.

Enrico Bastoni was a baker with a shop on Cherry Street about three doors from the Fortini house. He had lived in Plymouth for eight years and had known Vanzetti for six or seven years. Vanzetti came to his place at five or ten minutes of eight to borrow his horse, but Bastoni had use for his horse that day to make his own deliveries. He knew it was the day before Christmas because "that comes but once a year and that is the day we

27 Vol., 329.

celebrate good." He also spoke to Vanzetti with reference to eels. He knew this was just before eight o'clock because the eight o'clock whistle at the Cordage Company blew a few minutes later.[28]

Rosa Balboni, wife of Joseph Balboni, a driver at the Cordage Company (not the witness Carlo Balboni), corroborated Bastoni. She testified through an interpreter that she saw Vanzetti at about five minutes past seven in the morning on the street near Bastoni's bakeshop as she was delivering bread to the baker. She thought he had a basket and a wheelbarrow. He was delivering fish to a woman. He went into the bakeshop. She was expecting eels from him herself. (They were delivered later in the day.) She knew it was December 24 because the day before Christmas "was a day of remembrance." She also remembered it because it was the day her husband took her little girl to the hospital in Boston.[29]

The woman to whom he was delivering fish must have been Mrs. Therese Malaquisi, of 48 Cherry Street, near the bakeshop and the Fortini home at number 35. She was a widow and had lived on Cherry Street for twenty-four years. She said that Vanzetti delivered her a pound and a half of eels just after seven o'clock on the morning of December 24. The seven o'clock Cordage whistle had just blown. She remembered the day because she got the eels on the day before Christmas.

John DiCarlo had been a shoemaker in Plymouth for about seven years and had known Vanzetti during that time. He spoke no English. He opened his store at seven o'clock and started cleaning up at about a quarter past seven. While he was cleaning up, Vanzetti delivered his package of eels done up in a newspaper. He recalled it was the day before Christmas that he got the eels.[30]

In cross-examination Mr. Katzmann recurred to his innuendos:

Q. Have you ever heard Vanzetti make any speech? (Objected to; allowed) A. No.

Q. Are you sure of that Mr. DiCarlo? A. Yes. . . .

Q. Do you belong to any organization he belongs to? A. No. . . .

Q. Have you not discussed governmental theories over there between you? A. No.

Q. Have you discussed the question of the poor man and the rich man between you? A. No sir.

Q. Do you mean that answer, Mr. Witness? A. Yes.

---

[28] Supp. Vol., 250–253.   [29] Supp. Vol., 256.   [30] Supp. Vol., 240.

Q. You want to leave it with this jury that you are not an intimate friend of Vanzetti? A. Yes, sir.[31]

There had been no testimony that Vanzetti had done the things on which Mr. Katzmann had based his questions. Such evidence would have been inadmissible. However, Mr. Katzmann knew that Vanzetti was an anarchist (that was the reason he had been arrested in the first place). His questions were obviously designed to get Vanzetti's views across to the jury anyway.

The boy, Beltrando Brini, thirteen years old, stated that he met Vanzetti about 7:30 on the morning of December 24, near Maxwell's Drug Store just beyond Suasso's Lane, where he lived. Di Carlo's shoe store was nearby. He saw a lady between the shoe store and the drugstore (Mrs. Malagusi?).[32] He talked with Vanzetti and then talked with his father near the end of Suasso's Lane. His father sent him into the house to get his rubbers. (Beltrando's father, Vincenzo, confirmed Beltrando's statement that he had talked with the boy about getting something for his feet.) [33] He had to hunt for his rubbers and finally found them "under the cellar steps." He put on the rubbers and went to Vanzetti's boardinghouse at 35 Cherry Street, getting there around eight o'clock. "Because at half past seven, around there, I walked down the street and maybe a half an hour or less I hunted for my rubbers . . . and because the Plymouth Cordage whistle blew and I had not eaten my breakfast." Vanzetti was preparing his fish in the wheelbarrow, "wrapping it in some newspaper and under the string was a white paper on which was written the name whose fish it was and the price and how much it cost," and how much to collect.[34] He talked with Vanzetti about the horse mentioned the previous evening and then Vanzetti sent him to deliver fish. He stayed with Vanzetti, delivering fish with him, until sometime between one and two o'clock.

Their deliveries took them throughout the Italian section — Cherry Street, South Cherry, Cherry Place, Cherry Court, Standish Avenue, Court Street and Suasso's Lane. Beltrando did not know the names of all the customers, but remembered two because they did not have change.

When he delivered the eels to Mrs. Adelaide Bonjionanni, of South Cherry Street, "she gave me a two dollar bill for the fish which cost a

[31] Supp. Vol., 243–244.   [32] Supp. Vol., 259–260.   [33] Supp. Vol., 248.
[34] Supp. Vol., 260.

dollar twenty, and because I did not have the right amount of change she came down and paid it to Mr. Vanzetti."

Q. Where was Vanzetti when she paid him? A. At the steps.
Q. When you came and delivered the fish what was Vanzetti doing? A. He was also delivering fish.[35]

Later Mrs. Bonjionanni told of the incident mentioned by Beltrando as seen through the eyes of a busy Italian housewife. She wanted her eels delivered on December 23 so that she could salt them a day before cooking. She liked them better that way.[36] However, they were not delivered on the twenty-third and she was therefore watching for the delivery on the twenty-fourth, the day when they were supposed to be eaten. That is how she remembered that they were delivered on the twenty-fourth. The eels were brought to her house by the little Brini boy "between nine and ten o'clock, I am not decided." [37] She bought three pounds at forty cents a pound, but the boy did not have the change for a two dollar bill. Therefore she went down with the Brini boy to get change from Vanzetti, who was then in her yard.

Mrs. Bonjionanni's fixing of the late delivery of the eels on December 24 was aided by a vivid recollection that its arrival had caused her to suspend momentarily her watching the pot of polenta on her stove. Mr. Katzmann, however, bypassed entirely the eel-polenta association. His cross-examination was based on the assumption that there was no reason for her to remember cooking polenta on any particular day. He concluded his questioning of this Italian housewife in the following manner:

Q. What were you doing between nine and ten on the 24th day of last January? A. I was making polenda [sic].
Q. What were you doing between nine and ten on the 24th day of last February? A. I don't know.
Q. What were you doing the 24th of last March between nine and ten o'clock? A. I don't know.
Q. What were you doing on the 24th day of April last between nine and ten o'clock in the morning? A. I was washing.
Q. What day of the week was it the 24th day of last April? A. I don't know.
Q. You say you were washing? A. I don't say that for sure.
Q. What were you doing on the 24th day of last month between nine and ten o'clock in the morning of May? A. I don't know.

[35] Supp. Vol., 261.   [36] Supp. Vol., 286.   [37] Supp. Vol., 284.

Q. What were you doing on the 24th of this month between nine and ten o'clock in the morning? A. I can't tell.

Q. Did you salt the eels? A. Yes.

Q. What day did you eat them? A. The 24th, in the evening.

Q. Gave them a half a day of salting, wasn't it? A. Yes.

Q. Were you putting polenda on the stove on the 23rd day of February? A. Yes sir.

Q. What day was the 23rd of February when you were boiling polenda? A. Monday.

Q. Were you boiling polenda on the 17th day of March? A. I don't remember.

Q. You mean to say you don't know what day the 17th of March came on? A. I don't know.

Q. Was that a fast day? A. I don't know.[38]

Beltrando also recalled another customer to whom he could not give change. He gave a number of details of the delivery in four short answers.

Q. Do you remember up there [Suasso's Lane] of any time that you could not make change for anybody? A. Yes.

Q. At whose house was that? A. At Mrs. Christophori's house.

Q. What did you do? How did you get the change? A. I went back to Mr. Vanzetti. He was giving some fish to some other lady and he gave me change.

Q. And you took it up to Mrs. Christophori's? A. Not to Mrs. Christophori, but to Esther here. [Esther was in the courtroom.]

Q. Do you remember that you came out by the front door and got the change? A. Yes.[39]

Esther Esteno Christophori told of the same incident. Esther, not quite eighteen years old, was born in Plymouth and had lived there all of her life. She was in the third year of high school. Her account, rich in details, follows:

Q. Do you recall the day before Christmas, last year? A. What, 1919?

Q. Yes. A. Yes.

Q. Perhaps you will tell the Court and Jury how you recall that day? A. Well, I recall that day, the 24th of December 1919, as a day in which all the good Catholics, and that is all of us, think they can only eat fish and nothing but fish and nothing that comes from any meat or from animals can be eaten and I remember that night, the 24th I went to confession to get myself ready for Holy Communion on Christmas.

Q. Are there any special dishes of special preparation that Italians make for that day? A. They don't have any special dishes but they have fish for dinner, they eat eels and at night they have spaghetti and have it with tuna fish, a little bit of fish with chestnuts or any nuts.

[38] Supp. Vol., 287.   [39] Supp. Vol., 262.

Q. Is spaghetti made that day made differently from other days? A. Yes, spaghetti with tuna fish and eels and on other days they have it with meat.

Q. On that day did you see the little Breni boy? A. Yes, I saw him in the morning when he brought the fish.

Q. Where did you see him? A. I was cleaning the other room, the front room and dining room and I went to the kitchen to get the furniture polish and the little boy brought the fish into the kitchen to my mother.

Q. What was it? A. It was two pounds of eels.

Q. Do you recall anything in connection with that? A. He brought the eels in the house a little bit past eleven o'clock and my mother was supposed to cook them for dinner.

Q. Did he leave the house? A. Yes, my mother gave him a dollar bill.

Q. Did he come back again? A. Yes, he came back again right there.

Q. What did he do when he came back? A. I went into the front room and he knocked at the front door and gave me twenty cents change.

Q. Did you see where he went to? A. No, I did not see where he went to because I was in the kitchen and I saw when he came back where he came from.

Q. Where did he come from? A. He was returning from the street or rather he was running through the street up and down Suasso's Lane from Court Street.[40]

Mr. Katzmann sought to impeach Miss Christophori's testimony by asking her whether there was any relationship between getting furniture polish, a knock on the door or receiving communion and the day before Christmas. Miss Christophori readily admitted in each instance that there was none. However, she stated that she had a clear recollection of the day before Christmas. She denied that it was unusual to get eels on the day they were to be cooked. Asked whether she was an "expert on eels," she said, "No, — because I don't care for them very much." Mr. Katzmann then inadvertently brought from her a unique reason why she should have remembered Beltrando's delivery of the eels to her home before Christmas 1919.

Q. Is that the only occasion you can recall that he brought fish to your home? A. *That is the only time that I saw him.*[Emphasis added.][41]

Beltrando stated that he saw Vanzetti again on Christmas Eve. Here we get more details and a different glimpse of Vanzetti:

Q. Did you see Vanzetti again that day, the 24th? A. Yes.

Q. Where did you see him? A. At home.

[40] Supp. Vol., 301–302.   [41] Supp. Vol., 304.

Q. When, what time, at whose home? A. My home.
Q. At what time did you see him? A. About half past seven or eight.
Q. In the evening? A. Yes.
Q. Was there anybody there? A. Sure.
Q. Who was there? A. My mother and my sisters.
Q. How long did Vanzetti stay there that night? A. Quite late.
Q. Did you do anything that night before you went to bed? A. Yes sir.
Q. What did you do? A. I practised on my violin.
Q. Anything else? A. Talked with my sister and played.
Q. Did you get any presents the next morning? A. Yes sir.
Q. Well now does that recall whether you got anything before you went to bed that night or not? A. What do you mean?
Q. Where did you get presents? A. In my stocking.
Q. Now did you do anything before you went to bed Christmas Evening? A. Yes.
Q. What did you do? A. Fiddled.
Q. Anything else?
MR. KATZMANN. I admit that he hung up his stocking.
Q. Did you hang up your stocking? A. Yes, sure.
Q. What did you find in your stocking next morning? A. I found some peanuts, some nuts and I found a pocket book, I found two half dollars and a two dollar bill, I found some candy and I found a necktie and maybe some other things, but I forget.
Q. Did you see Vanzetti Christmas Day? A. Yes.
Q. When did you see him Christmas Day? A. At noon.
Q. Where? A. In my house.
Q. What was he doing there? A. Sitting on a chair.
Q. Was it before dinner or after? A. While we were waiting after we almost finished the dinner.
Q. Did you have any talk with Vanzetti? A. Yes.
Q. Now what did you talk about, — not what you said? A. Talked about the presents.
Q. Any particular one? A. Any particular present?
Q. Any particular present? A. Yes.
Q. What particular present? A. About the two half dollars.[42]

Rose Forni, who had a room in the Brini house, stated that she saw Vanzetti on Christmas Eve "putting some money in the stockings for the children." [43] Beltrando's mother, Alfonsini, told of seeing Vanzetti putting two half dollars in each of the children's stockings.[44]

Mr. Katzmann's cross-examination of Beltrando covers about thirteen printed pages of the record. Almost the entire examination was directed to showing that Beltrando was telling a story which he had told a number of times to his parents and others. This the boy freely acknowledged. To the

[42] Supp. Vol., 262–263.   [43] Supp. Vol., 293.   [44] Supp. Vol., 307.

jury, perhaps, this was proof that the boy was lying, despite his obvious earnestness and the corroboration by other witnesses. Beltrando's testimony indicated his desire to give an exact account, leaving out nothing he thought was important. For instance, his mother stated to Mr. Katzmann: "He kept on saying to me many times because the first time he could not tell me the whole story, he did not remember the whole story, and as the days went along something came to his mind and he told me about what he remembered about that particular day." [45]

Actually the only point which Mr. Katzmann made against Beltrando's account was the boy's error in stating that December 22 was Tuesday. This Beltrando had promptly corrected. The momentary error in counting back from the wrong day weighed heavily on Beltrando's mind. This came out as Mr. Katzmann cross-examined Alfonsini about her conversation with Beltrando on the night after he had testified. She said: "Of course I don't understand English very well, but he told me that they [Mr. Katzmann] were asking about the date of the Monday or Tuesday in December and he says, 'They won't listen to me because it wasn't true that he did this.' That is all." [46]

Mr. Katzmann cross-examined Alfonsini as to Beltrando's friendship with Vanzetti:

Q. (By Mr. Katzmann) How many years did Mr. Vanzetti live in your home? A. I was forty years old. — I understood you to say "How old are you?"
Q. No, I said how many years did Vanzetti live at your house? A. Four years.
Q. Your family like Vanzetti very much? A. Yes.
Q. They are good friends? He was a very good friend with all the family? A. Yes.
Q. He was very fond of your little boy that testified yesterday, was he not? A. Yes, he liked my boy just the same as the rest of my children.
Q. The boy was very fond of him and is today, is he not? A. I never noticed the difference. [47]

Seven years later, in the summer of 1927, shortly before Vanzetti was electrocuted, a greatly agitated young man came to my office. I had never seen him before. He was Beltrando Brini. The imminence of Vanzetti's death had thrown him into a state of near panic. He wanted to see Governor Fuller instantly to tell him that Vanzetti could not have been in Bridgewater on the morning of December 24, 1919, because at that time

[45] Supp. Vol., 310.   [46] Supp. Vol., 340.   [47] Supp. Vol., 307.

Vanzetti was with him delivering eels in Plymouth. Beltrando had seen the governor early in his investigation but the boy felt that he had been given too little time to fully disclose his story. The governor invited him to return. At that time, Governor Fuller was conducting his own interviews with witnesses from which Mr. Thompson and I were excluded despite our protests. We knew that the governor believed Vanzetti's guilt or innocence of the Bridgewater affair was a touchstone for testing the entire Sacco-Vanzetti proceedings. I took Beltrando immediately to the governor's office. There we saw the first secretary, known by the adopted name of Herman MacDonald. I asked for an appointment for Beltrando to talk with the governor. Mr. MacDonald insisted that this was impossible, because the governor was overwhelmed at the time. He flatly refused to ask him for an appointment, but volunteered to listen to Beltrando's story and tell it all to the governor at the first opportunity. Since we were getting nowhere with Beltrando's request to see the governor personally, the only alternative was for Beltrando to take the slim chance that perhaps something of his story would actually reach the governor through Mr. MacDonald. I had little faith that it would. Mr. Thompson and I had had some experience with the futility of trying to get anything to the governor through Mr. MacDonald. It distressed me to listen to this brokenhearted young man pour out his story to Mr. MacDonald, who watched him impassively with the unsympathetic eyes of a dead mackerel. Of course, nothing came of it.

So far as I am concerned, I do not need the testimony of Vanzetti's other friends and acquaintances in his hometown to know that he was in Plymouth on the morning of December 24, 1919. Beltrando's passionate presentation is enough for me.

In order for the reader to weigh the extent to which unconscious prejudice against foreigners affected the jury at Plymouth, it would be helpful to consider the list of witnesses to Vanzetti's alibi. Old residents of Plymouth already mentioned are Mary Fortini, Carlo Balboni, John DiCarlo, Vincenzo Brini, Enrico Bastoni, Rosa Balboni, Beltrando Brini, Therese Malaquisi, Adelaide Bonjionanni, Esther Esteno Christophori and Alfonsini Brini. Others who testified that they had received eels from Vanzetti on December 24 were the following:

Mrs. Margaret Fiochi, of 1 South Cherry Street, wife of Rismo Fiochi, who worked for the railroad at the Plymouth depot. She said she and her husband had lived in Plymouth twenty or twenty-two years. Vanzetti delivered one pound of eels in her kitchen between nine and ten o'clock on December 24. Like Mrs. Bonjionanni she had asked that her eels be delivered on December 23, but Vanzetti was a day late in making delivery. She remembered the date they came because the day before Christmas was "one of the most impressive days we have." Mr. Katzmann revealed his opinion of the honesty of Italians by directly charging perjury and subordination of perjury. He asked her to tell him what kind of a moustache the court stenographer had "without looking at him." Apparently she glanced at the stenographer and said:

A. Yes, I can tell you now.
Q. And that is the way you tell us about the eels — because you talked with somebody before you took the stand, is it not? *Some of those Italians up there told you what to say?* A. No, sir. [Emphasis added.] [48]

Mrs. Fiochi added a family touch when asked about buying only one pound of eels for eight in the family: "The husband and I like it, but the children don't."

Mrs. Emma Borsari had lived with her husband at 6 South Cherry Street for eleven years. Her husband had worked for Walter Brown in the Cordage business for twenty-one years. Vanzetti delivered two pounds of eels to her at about half past ten or at forty-five minutes past on December 24. She fixed the hour because she had to have enough time to prepare half of the eels for dinner (the midday meal) and the rest for "the other meal." [49] She remembered that it was December 24 "because of that day, it is the fast day for us."

Vincent Louis Longhi, of 42 Cherry Street, was born in Plymouth. He was twenty-five years of age. He was a weaver in the Puritan Mills, where he had worked continually for nine years except in 1917, 1918 and part of 1919, when he was in the army. He had never spoken to Vanzetti, although he had met him on the street a few times when he came to town. He remembered seeing Vanzetti in his home on December 24 about five minutes past seven in the morning. He placed the time because "I go to work at twenty minutes to [past] seven in the morning and I generally leave the house at five or six minutes past seven on the car that goes by at ten minutes past seven. . . . I was just putting on my coat. He was in the cooking room, a little kitchen in the house where we do all the cooking. . . . Yes,

[48] Supp. Vol., 219.   [49] Supp. Vol., 295.

my mother was there at the time. . . . She is sick at present." [50] They had eels for supper at half past five.

In cross-examination, he said that he had not thought about the matter until "this morning down to the mill" (presumably because his mother was ill and he was substituting as a witness for her). He knew when he saw Vanzetti because "he came in that morning and brought the eels and that night we had them and it was the 24th of December when we had supper, the spaghetti and the eels." [51]

> A. That is the only time we eat them [eels] with spaghetti.
> Q. With spaghetti? A. Yes sir, we eat them with spaghetti.
> Q. Is that how you remember? A. We don't care for fish.
> Q. Is that the only day in the year that you eat eels? A. That we do.[52]

Mr. Katzmann was getting nowhere with this line of cross-examination. He then shifted to his favorite last-ditch tactic of firing a battery of some fifteen or twenty questions about unchecked and meaningless dates.

Since all of Vanzetti's alibi witnesses were from the Italian community, the Plymouth trial furnishes an excellent casebook for a study in prejudice. These men and women were stable, longtime residents of the town. The prosecution was apparently unable to find a single blemish on their reputation as law-abiding people. Many of them had lived in the same homes and held the same jobs for years. They were a very industrious folk. Some of the housewives worked in the local factories besides maintaining the family home. Their number included a thirteen-year-old boy and a seventeen-year-old high school girl. Their testimony remained unshaken except for those who believed Mr. Katzmann's unsupported insinuations and assertions. Nevertheless, the jury believed that Vanzetti was in Bridgewater, engaged in crime, at the time when these witnesses stated under oath that he was in Plymouth delivering the eels which they had ordered. Evidently they, the jurymen, must have believed these reputable men and women had conspired to commit perjury with "some of the Italians up there" because Vanzetti was an Italian.

The bias of the Plymouth jurors was spotlighted by their acceptance, apparently without question, of the identification of Vanzetti by the "star" witnesses, Cox, Bowles and Harding, three Yankees like themselves. The jury believed these witnesses despite the fact that under cross-examination

[50] Supp. Vol., 316–317.   [51] Supp. Vol., 319.   [52] Supp. Vol., 320.

they first denied or "forgot" and then reluctantly admitted that they had changed their description of the shotgun bandit from that previously given by them under oath. Unlike the Italian alibi witnesses, whose testimony remained essentially unshaken throughout derisive cross-examinations and obvious language difficulties, these three native Americans impeached themselves by claiming that they did not know what they had meant by their own earlier language — after thinking it over and arguing with some persons "up there," to borrow a phrase from Mr. Katzmann.

In analyzing the causes of the Sacco-Vanzetti tragedy, we should not overlook the part played by this unconscious prejudice. Of course the Plymouth jurymen believed that they were fair. It would be unjust to blame them for yielding to an influence of which they were not aware. On the other hand, we would throw away one of the important lessons of the case if we did not recognize the effect of unperceived prejudice. It is a problem in human relations which intrudes itself into the administration of justice. Mere resolves to treat all alike, regardless of race or religion, do not solve it. To administer justice equally to members of all groups, "in" or "out," we need to be alerted to the subconscious forces which direct our minds. Until we set up standards for judging members of different groups on their own merits as we judge those of our own kind, we always face the danger of trial by prejudice such as nullified Vanzetti's alibi in the courthouse of Plymouth in June 1920.

As we ponder the reasons why the Plymouth jury did not believe the powerful alibi presented by Vanzetti's witnesses, we inevitably come to an imponderable factor. The alibi lacked its principal witness — Vanzetti. Under the law, he could not be compelled to testify. If he chose to remain silent, the jury was supposed not to consider it evidence of guilt. Judge Thayer so instructed the jury at Plymouth. There might be compelling reasons, other than guilt of the crime charged, why an accused might not want to expose himself or endanger others to the risks of his cross-examination. Vanzetti had such reasons. Nevertheless, without an adequate explanation, the human mind cannot rid itself of conviction that an innocent defendant would insist on clearing himself of the charges against him.

There was no explanation available to the Plymouth jury as to why Vanzetti did not testify in his own defense except the natural assumption that he was guilty. Except for Mr. Katzmann's insinuations, implicit in his questions to a couple of the alibi witnesses, Vanzetti's radical views and affiliations did not enter the Plymouth trial. Prior to the trial, the jurors had probably never heard of Vanzetti. Only one of the jurymen, Arthur S. Nickerson, resided in Plymouth. As we have seen, Nickerson knew so little about Vanzetti that he thought he was another man whom he had observed at the Plymouth Cordage Company. Therefore, although the atmosphere of the period was surcharged with fear and hatred of radicals and resentment against those who had evaded the draft in the war just finished, it would not have occurred to the Plymouth jury to connect Vanzetti's silence with these manifestations of public emotion.

The dilemma confronting Mr. Vahey defied any safe solution. The decision whether to take the stand had to be (and was) Vanzetti's. Yet Vanzetti, a foreigner, ignorant of American judicial processes, had no basis for judgment other than the presentation of the alternatives by Mr. Vahey, his counsel, the "big" lawyer retained by his friends.

Although Vanzetti, in his pamphlet *Background of the Plymouth Trial*,[53] blames his decision on Vahey's insistence that he stay off the stand, any experienced trial lawyer might readily believe that Mr. Vahey revealed his own positive preference that Vanzetti should abstain from testifying, but still not agree that Vahey was clearly wrong. In reviewing the case with Vanzetti, Mr. Vahey would have been right to emphasize the wreck he had made of the prosecution's eyewitness identification and the strong alibi evidence which had come through the trial practically unscathed. Buttressing the government's weak case, there was only the rather irrelevant testimony of the call at the Johnson garage, the negative evidence that Vanzetti was armed and had lied when arrested, and the unpermissible presumption of guilt due to Vanzetti's silence. On the other hand, once Vanzetti took the stand, a Pandora's box of new troubles would be opened. He could not possibly explain the alleged "consciousness of guilt" evidence without going into his activities as an agitator and anarchist, or without involving Sacco and other associates. Nor would it have done him much good if he had been able to accomplish such a miracle of evasion.

Under the law of Massachusetts as it then stood, there would have been nothing to restrain Mr. Katzmann's cross-examination into every facet of Vanzetti's life, except the "discretion" of the court.[54] And in the Plymouth trial, the exercise of Judge Thayer's "discretion" had already admitted prac-

---

[53] Boston: Sacco-Vanzetti Defense Committee, 1927.
[54] *Commonwealth v. Sacco*, 255, Mass. 439; Holt Vol. IV, 4339.

tically every bit of dubious evidence, however damaging to Vanzetti. With Vanzetti on the stand, Mr. Katzmann could have stirred up, without limit, the hostile emotions of the jury. He did this later at the Dedham trial. This is what makes so unrealistic and unfair the claim that the defendants, at Dedham, "introduced the issue of radicalism." There was no escape from it once the defendants had taken the stand. A kind of hypocrisy is implicit in the charge that the defendants were responsible for "introducing radicalism" into the trial, considering that they were originally caught in a net intended to trap anarchists and that Chief Stewart's entire questioning on the night of the arrest was directed to this subject, not to the crimes of murder or robbery.

Mr. Vahey must have been especially fearful of Vanzetti as a witness. Trial lawyers are most jittery about their witnesses who like to talk too much — and talking was Vanzetti's forte. In criticizing Vahey in his pamphlet on the Plymouth trial, Vanzetti naively relates the following as an example of his lawyer's bad advice:

He asked me how I would explain from the stand the meaning of Socialism, or Communism, or Bolshevism, if I was requested by the District Attorney to do so. At such a query, I would begin an explanation on those subjects and Mr. Vahey would cut it off at its very beginning.
"Hush, if you tell such things to the ignorant, conservative jurors, they will send you to State Prison right away." [55]

No doubt Vanzetti, like most devotees of a cause, felt confident that he could explain these philosophies satisfactorily. For Mr. Vahey, however, the prospect of Vanzetti lecturing the Yankee jurymen on the nature of several forms of social revolutions must have struck terror into his lawyer's heart.

Vanzetti's failure to take the stand at Plymouth had effects far beyond that trial. Governor Fuller regarded it as highly significant. He had early concluded that if Vanzetti was guilty of attempted robbery at Bridgewater, it was quite believable that he and his companion, Sacco, participated in the South Braintree murders. And as I will discuss later, he referred to it repeatedly in 1927 during interviews with numerous persons when he was considering the petition which we had filed on behalf of the condemned men. Our explanation of Vanzetti's dilemma had no effect upon him.

There has been considerable debate in the years since the trials concerning the placing of "blame" for Vanzetti's failure to testify. Those who be-

[55] Vanzetti, *Background of the Plymouth Trial*, 34.

lieve that Sacco and Vanzetti were guilty emphasize the fact that he made the decision himself. Those who maintain that the men were innocent claim that Vanzetti wanted to testify, but Mr. Vahey prevented it. The argument seems to be without an issue. Both statements would seem to be correct. The choice had to be Vanzetti's. On the other hand, his decision had to be made on the basis of his counsel's presentation. There is no "blame" to be allocated. Still, the Plymouth jury knew nothing about the conflicting considerations which finally led to Vanzetti's silence. For them, it must have pointed to guilt. From the vantage point of our knowledge of the facts today, any such inference would be without foundation in reality.

There is, however, at least the possibility that if Vanzetti had testified at Plymouth, Mr. Katzmann's predictable evocation of prejudice in his cross-examination might not have prevailed over Vanzetti's already powerful alibi now backed by his own testimony. The fact that Sacco and Vanzetti were later pilloried on the stand at Dedham does not necessarily prove that Mr. Katzmann would have had the same success at Plymouth. For one thing, the juries were different. The men at Plymouth obviously reflected on the conflicting evidence and took quite a few hours to come to a verdict. Even their surreptitious opening of the shotgun shells indicated that they wanted to be sure of the facts. In Dedham, however, after five weeks of testimony and other evidence which even today presents puzzling problems to eminent jurists, the jury was ready to vote the defendants guilty of murder (carrying a mandatory death penalty) on the first poll.

For another thing, Mr. Burgess, jury foreman at Plymouth, was a man with no apparent prejudice against the defendant, while the record indicates that Walter H. Ripley, foreman at Dedham, was accused of having expressed very strong feelings against Italians long before the Sacco-Vanzetti case.[56] Later, when he was called for jury service at the Dedham trial, he had a conversation with an old friend of twenty-eight years, one William H. Daly, a Quincy contractor. Mr. Daly swore that he said to Ripley that he did not believe those "Guineas were guilty," and that Ripley replied, "Damn them, they ought to hang them anyway!"[57] Judge Thayer gave no reason for disbelieving this sworn statement except to assert baldly that Daly "must have misunderstood him or that his recollection is at fault."

There was still another important difference. At Plymouth, Vanzetti still had his unsullied reputation as a law-abiding resident. There would

[56] Vol. V, 5253.   [57] Vol. IV, 3579; Vol. V, 5378.

have been no predisposition to doubt his word. The jury might have believed his story, especially as Vanzetti's personality was expressive of a native honesty. As a witness at Dedham, however, he was known throughout the area as a convicted robber,[58] and Mr. Katzmann's innuendos reminded the jury of the previous trial.

There was a vast difference between the quiet, relaxed air at Plymouth and the mood of excitement and fear which dominated the later murder trial. Four times a day for thirty-seven days Sacco and Vanzetti were manacled and marched through the streets of Dedham, flanked by guards in civilian clothes and surrounded front and rear by uniformed police officers. Five nearby towns lent part of their police force to help protect Dedham from the "desperate radicals" who, it was feared, might attempt a street delivery. Seven hundred prospective jurors witnessed these processions through Dedham before a jury was impaneled. At the courthouse itself, the sense of fear was intensified. Prospective jurors were first met by guards who also stopped and searched all visitors. There were guards at the entrance, at the foot of the stairs, at the head of the stairs, in the courtroom and parading in the corridors.[59]

Unlike Vanzetti at Plymouth, Sacco and Vanzetti at Dedham were certain to appear to the jurors as dangerous men whose alibis and explanations were not to be taken seriously.

Apparently the strength of Vanzetti's alibi, even without his testimony, tipped the scales in favor of his not taking the stand. This was indicated by a statement attributed to him in 1955 by Mr. James Graham, associate defense counsel with Mr. Vahey. He quoted Vanzetti as concluding the discussion about taking the stand by saying, in substance, "I don't think I can improve upon the alibi which has been established." The decision might have been otherwise if his alibi had been weak. Therefore, it may be that among the many tragic ironies of the Sacco-Vanzetti case we should include the seemingly irrefutable testimony of Vanzetti's friends and neighbors as a possible contributing cause of his conviction.

In concluding this chapter, it is somewhat of a pleasant relief to record that Vanzetti's chief alibi witness has had a good and satisfactory life. "The little Brini boy" who delivered eels with Vanzetti on December 24, 1919, is

[58] This fact was even announced in the press at the start of the Dedham trial. *Boston Evening Globe*, May 31, 1921; *Boston Globe*, June 1, 1921.
[59] Vol. V, 4995, testimony of John W. McAnarney, Esq.

now principal of the Willard (elementary) School in Quincy. He was also conductor of the Brockton Symphony Orchestra for ten years, but had to give this position up because of the load of administrative duties on him when he became a school principal. Recently I had lunch with Beltrando. He talked a great deal about Vanzetti. During the four years when he boarded at the Brini home, Vanzetti and the little boy had become close companions. On long walks in the woods together, Vanzetti would point out the different trees, shrubbery, flowers and animal tracks. He helped Beltrando with his schoolwork, and instilled in him a love of reading and a curiosity to learn many things. It was Vanzetti who stirred in him the then novel ambition to go to college. Often when Beltrando "fiddled," Vanzetti would sit, listen and criticize. Once Vanzetti pointed out that two notes were flat in a piece which he was playing. He urged Beltrando to train himself to become an orchestra conductor. Mr. Katzmann's charge that Beltrando was friendly with Vanzetti was a gross understatement — the boy loved him.

Beltrando made some interesting observations about the Italian residents in Plymouth in 1920. Although most of them knew Vanzetti, few of them shared his unpopular radical views. They knew also that Vanzetti had been a leader in the strike against the Plymouth Cordage Company where many of them, or members of their families, were employed. They feared reprisals if they testified against the prosecution. (There were no such reprisals in Plymouth. However, in South Braintree, at least four employees of Slater and Morrill and Rice and Hutchins were discharged, apparently because their testimony at Dedham failed to please the district attorney.) Beltrando thought that the Italian witnesses who came forward showed great moral courage in testifying to the truth at the risk of endangering their livelihood.

We discussed the events of December 24, 1919. In a double sense it was "a day of remembrance" for Beltrando, as it was for his mother, Alfonsini (who is still living at present writing), and for the Italian settlement in Plymouth, and for all interested in the administration of justice.

PART II

August 16, 1920, to August 23, 1927

From the Sentencing of Vanzetti for the Attempted
Holdup at Bridgewater to the Execution of Sacco
and Vanzetti for the South Braintree Murders

10.

Fateful Changes Presage the Dedham Trial

On July 1, 1920, the jury at Plymouth brought in their verdict of guilty against Vanzetti for assault with intent to rob and assault with intent to murder. The way was now cleared for Mr. Katzmann to proceed against Sacco and Vanzetti for the South Braintree murders. On September 11, 1920, both Sacco and Vanzetti were indicted by the Grand Jury for these crimes, the earliest possible date following the sentencing of Vanzetti. Sacco had been held for the Grand Jury on May 26, 1920. Vanzetti had not been held for the murders, but only for the Bridgewater attempt. On July 14, 1927, seven years later, Mr. Katzmann claimed that he did not have enough evidence to indict Vanzetti for the South Braintree crime at the time of the Plymouth trial.[1] However, now that Vanzetti was a branded highwayman, he moved fast and procured indictments against both men. Later, motions to obtain separate trials for Sacco and Vanzetti were denied by Judge Webster Thayer.

Two days after the Bridgewater conviction, William H. Proctor, captain of the Department of Public Safety in charge of the State Police, was formally removed by District Attorney Katzmann from further direction of the investigation into the South Braintree murders. Too little attention has been paid to this most extraordinary action by Mr. Katzmann. Major crime occurring outside of the cities fell normally into the province of the State Police to investigate. Just as trying Vanzetti for the highway robbery attempt before prosecuting him for murder was a departure from the usual procedure, so the removal of Captain Proctor was also an unusual step away from the accepted procedure in murder cases.

Proctor had been an officer in the Department for twenty-three years and captain for sixteen years.[2] His official experience with serious crime had

[1] Vol. V, 5078.   [2] Vol. I, 884.

been extensive, including participation as an expert witness in over one hundred capital cases.[3] Following the South Braintree killings, he had directed the State forces in an all-out effort to track down the murderers. From his office in the State House, he commanded all of the crime-detecting resources of the Commonwealth, including rogues' galleries, records and descriptions of known criminals, fingerprint-photographing facilities and data, skilled technicians, modern apparatus and equipment, and a staff of officers whose training requirements were at least considerably higher than those of the municipal police, and far above the standards, or lack of standards, for rural policemen in the small towns, euphemistically entitled "chiefs." Although not a Scotland Yard, the Department of Public Safety contained the elite police force in the Commonwealth. Captain Proctor had a personal qualification himself which went beyond the advantage of office. His experience of sixteen years as police captain and his many prior years of service, during which his abilities had earned him promotion to head of the State Police, could not have failed to develop a judgment of crime and criminals entitled to the greatest respect.

Why then was Captain Proctor removed from further direction and investigation of the murders in South Braintree? There is no express explanation in the record to justify this action by the district attorney. The facts, however, suggest a most compelling reason. *Captain Proctor believed that Sacco and Vanzetti were innocent*. This apparently made him an unsatisfactory person to prepare the prosecution's case for trial.

We have already considered his puzzling and innocuous testimony at the Plymouth trial about the shotgun shells allegedly taken from Vanzetti's pocket. Later we shall examine his misleading testimony at the Dedham trial, prearranged with the district attorney to keep from the jury Captain Proctor's real opinion, namely, that he had found no evidence that bullet No. III, which killed Berardelli, was fired through Sacco's pistol.

However, Captain Proctor's belief in the innocence of the defendants was probably not solely the result of his ballistic opinion. After he had testified at the Dedham trial, he was overheard in the corridors by Judge Thomas F. McAnarney, of defense counsel, to say, "These are not the right men. Oh, no, you haven't got the right men."[4]

Over two years later, on August 7, 1923, he said in the presence of Elias Field, Esq., a distinguished Boston lawyer, in discussing the Sacco-Vanzetti

[3] Vol. I, 886.   [4] Vol. V, 5055.

case, "I have been too long in the game, and I'm getting to be too old to want to see a couple of fellows go to the chair for something I don't think they did." [5]

In 1927, Mr. Thompson asked Mr. Katzmann, before the Governor's Advisory Committee, whether Captain Proctor had ever before the trial given him the idea that he did not think Sacco and Vanzetti were guilty.

Q. (By Mr. Thompson) Will you give me your answer on that on your honor? A. My answer is that *I have no recollection* of him saying that.
Q. You will not go so far as to positively deny that he said that? A. *No. I cannot do that.* [Emphasis added.] [6]

Trial lawyers would have no difficulty in interpreting Mr. Katzmann's inability to deny that Captain Proctor had advised him that he did not think the men were guilty. At the time, the district attorney was preparing an important murder case for trial with the head of the State Police, the officer who had directed the government's investigation from the beginning. Surely, if the head of the State Police had advised him that in his opinion the men were innocent, Mr. Katzmann would have recalled it, and if he had not, Mr. Katzmann could and would have denied it.

Mr. Katzmann's motive in removing Captain Proctor would also seem to be revealed in the fact that he transferred further preparation of the case to Chief Stewart, the rural policeman, who had little known experience with serious crime. Unlike Captain Proctor, Chief Stewart believed, almost fanatically, that Sacco and Vanzetti were guilty. Stewart, not Proctor, had contrived their arrest, on his personal theory but without evidence. It is obvious, therefore, that in discharging Captain Proctor and placing control of the gathering of evidence in Chief Stewart's hands, Mr. Katzmann was not seeking more skillful assistance, but rather an aide who would willingly, if not enthusiastically, go along with his own ideas of how to construct the case for the prosecution. And so the preparation of the prosecution's evidence passed from the control of a competent professional into the hands of a credulous amateur, who had a sort of proprietary interest in securing a conviction. Although the head of the State Police was now excluded from the investigation, Mr. Katzmann secured the appointment of State Police officer Brouillard to assist the Bridgewater chief. Placing the production of evidence in the control of Stewart may account for much of the crude

[5] Vol. V, 4975.   [6] Vol. V, 5084.

disregard of the usual safeguards against error which vitiated so much of the prosecution's case.

Some writers about the case make the simple assumption that Captain Proctor's belief in the innocence of the defendants was based on his own expert opinion as to the ballistic evidence. On the other hand, Fred J. Cook, as noted earlier, suggests that Captain Proctor was influenced by his comparison of the fingerprints which he had lifted from the murder car with those which he took later from Sacco and Vanzetti.[7] No doubt these things entered into his conclusion. However, he probably did not need them to reach a preliminary opinion that the wrong men were being prosecuted. Since he had directed the investigation himself, he knew all the details of the South Braintree crime, as well as the statements of all witnesses. This special knowledge must have enabled him to compose a picture of the robber-murderers consonant with the ways of criminals. In his mind, this picture did not include a group of anarchists inexperienced in crime. Just as an able physician with a long and varied experience in diagnosis can often make a good guess as to what disease is afflicting the patient even before making tests, so a much-practiced and skillful detective can frequently form a preliminary opinion as to the type or types of criminals involved in a certain crime. To Captain Proctor and the men in the Boston office of the Department of Justice, South Braintree beckoned to the criminal underworld.

Contrary to the earlier opinion of Captain Proctor held by Mr. Thompson and myself — that he was a sort of supporting villain in the Sacco-Vanzetti tragedy — more intimate knowledge of the record has now convinced me that he was in fact a hero in the technical dramatic sense. It is apparent from his testimony and later statements that there was a conflict in his soul between his conscience as a human being and his official duty to support the case of the Commonwealth. In his earlier years, as he later suggested, he had perhaps not been as scrupulous about aiding the prosecution, regardless of his own views. In the Sacco-Vanzetti proceedings he apparently tried to serve both masters with a compromise. His brief testimony as a witness at Plymouth in the Bridgewater case avoided the real issue, namely, whether in his opinion the exploded shell found in the Bridgewater street matched the loaded shells allegedly taken from Vanzetti. As we shall see, his testimony at Dedham in the South Braintree trial employed a for-

[7] Cook, "The Missing Fingerprints," 442.

mula agreed upon with the district attorney and his assistant which, though it satisfied his conscience, nevertheless conveyed to the judge and jury an impression that he believed that the fatal bullet had passed through Sacco's pistol, whereas his real opinion was exactly the opposite.

In both cases, defense counsel was apparently afraid to probe further into Captain Proctor's opinion. They naturally assumed that the head of the State Police was on the side of the Commonwealth and that cross-examination would boomerang. His reputation was most impressive and widely known. Even his physical appearance was such as to overawe counsel and jury. As Judge Thomas F. McAnarney put it: "There he was, a great big powerful man with that gun and pistol before him." [8]

By the summer of 1923, however, Captain Proctor had begun to talk about his role in the prosecution. He resented his removal as chief investigator and no longer spoke to Mr. Katzmann. There was also the matter of a small bill which Mr. Katzmann refused to approve.[9] At any rate, Captain Proctor's removal apparently relieved him in his own mind of further obligation to repress his true opinion. On October 20, 1923, he signed an affidavit for the defense revealing that his ambiguous answer about bullet No. III was prearranged with the prosecution.[10] This allegation was not substantially denied in the government's counteraffidavits. (The affidavits themselves will be set out in a later chapter.) Had Mr. Thompson then suspected that Captain Proctor had a positive opinion that bullet No. III had not been fired in Sacco's pistol, the affidavit would have been even more of a shocker to world opinion. Inevitably Captain Proctor's complete story of what went on in the preparation of the case, his inner conflict and the pressure applied to him by the district attorney's office, would eventually have come to the knowledge of defendants' counsel except for another stroke of the bad luck that hounded Sacco and Vanzetti from the moment of their arrest: Captain Proctor died suddenly on March 8, 1924. The death certificate gives the cause of death as chronic nephritis.

Captain Proctor's direction of the investigation of the South Braintree crime ended officially with the transfer of authority to Michael E. Stewart. Actually, however, the investigation by his office and his own views had already been brushed aside in favor of Stewart's independent parallel investigation.[11] It was Stewart who took the identifying witnesses to view Sacco and Vanzetti at the police station, in jail and in court, sometimes repeat-

[8] Vol. V, 5189.   [9] Vol. V, 5085.   [10] Vol. IV, 3641.   [11] Supp. Vol., 168–169.

edly. It was Stewart who apparently discussed with these witnesses their proposed testimony until finally they became positive in their identification and changed their stories from those previously given. It was Stewart who obtained witnesses to identify the bandits' car as a Buick. It was Stewart who made an unauthorized search of Vanzetti's room and helped himself to articles which he hoped witnesses could identify. The Plymouth trial was permeated with suspicion voiced by Katzmann, but originating with Stewart, concerning the purpose of the call for Boda's Overland at the Johnson garage on the night of May 5, 1920, and the reason for Vanzetti's falsehoods when quizzed by Stewart about his radical connections, and about Vanzetti's probable guilt because of his association with Boda (who had never been shown to be guilty of anything).

To repeat, then, there were no apparent conflicts in Chief Stewart's mind. In his first interview with Pinkerton operative H.H. on the night of December 24, 1919, the day of the Bridgewater attempt, he stated that he believed "the holdup was the work of an out-of-town band of Russians" and that "there are a lot of Reds and Bolshevists about town." (It does not appear that Stewart then knew of any difference between Communists and anarchists). We have seen that when Stewart first saw the Buick abandoned in the Manley woods two days after the South Braintree murders, he exclaimed to the assembled group: "The men who did this job knew no God." [12] That is to say, they were "atheistic Communists." When suspicion was thrown on the Greek named Nicholas Agatkides in connection with the Bridgewater attempt, operative H.H., in his report for January 6, 1920, reported that the man bore a bad reputation among the resident Greeks, "being classed as a bum and a crook." Chief Stewart, however, reported that Agatkides "led a strike . . . besides which he was a draft dodger and all-around anarchist and agitator." So obsessed was Chief Stewart with his own identification of radicals with criminals that when he questioned Sacco and Vanzetti at the police station on the night of their arrest, his examination was almost entirely concerned with their associations and activities as anarchists. Not one of his questions dealt with their supposed participation in the Bridgewater or South Braintree crimes — the only reason for arresting them in the first place.

[12] O'Connor, *Vanderbilt Law Review*, Vol. 14 (1961), 993. Reportedly Stewart cited as proof that the bandits were not professional criminals the fact that they killed their victims. There may be many reasons why professionals will kill, such as to wipe out witnesses who know them, to get possession of the money or to prevent armed resistance.

From interviews by various people with him, Stewart seems to have been rather proud of having personally discovered the "real murderers" and brought them to justice. As late as 1962, he told Michael A. Musmanno, justice of the Supreme Court of Pennsylvania, that when Sacco, Vanzetti, Boda and Orciani called at the Johnson garage on May 5, 1920, to get Boda's Overland car, they wanted the vehicle for the purpose of committing another payroll robbery the next day. He seemed not at all disturbed at the thought that robbers who had recently obtained nearly sixteen thousand dollars and who had several automobiles and number plates at their disposal would want to use in another robbery a broken-down Overland, so old it still had a right-hand drive and was lacking a self-starter, and which did not even have a 1920 number plate. In this and other respects, his credulity seems unlimited. Nevertheless, he was an interesting, and obviously a persuasive, personality, possibly because of the strength of his convictions. In the Sacco-Vanzetti gallery of portraits, the pictures of Captain Proctor and Chief Stewart should be hung side by side. They would make a fascinating contrast in types — the trained and sophisticated police officer, torn between duty and truth, and the single-minded, rather naively ignorant policeman from Bridgewater who ousted the head of the State Police and took his place as the directing genius of the Sacco-Vanzetti investigation.

An even more fateful change in personnel was about to occur, this time in the defense.

The indictments of Sacco and Vanzetti on September 11 had produced a near panic among the members of the Sacco-Vanzetti Defense Committee, which had been organized in 1920 following the arrest of Sacco and Vanzetti. Despite the overwhelming evidence of Vanzetti's innocence and his representation by the "big lawyer" of Plymouth, their friend had been convicted of the highway robbery attempt. Vanzetti had lost confidence in Mr. Vahey. As he brooded over the case, he came to suspect that his lawyer had double-crossed him and had aided Katzmann in securing his conviction.[13] (When Mr. Vahey later entered into a law partnership with Katzmann, Vanzetti's suspicion became absolute.) However, there never was much of a chance that the two men would get along together. They belonged to different worlds. Vanzetti, the intellectual, the avid reader of

[13] Vanzetti, *Background of the Plymouth Trial.*

philosophy, the foreign-born rebel against the American way of life, was quite beyond the sympathy or appreciation of his lawyer. Likewise, Mr. Vahey was a frustrating puzzle to Vanzetti. As an idealistic man on trial for a most serious crime, Vanzetti could not understand the type of lawyer personified by Vahey, to whom Vanzetti's defense seemed just another criminal case. Perhaps Mr. Vahey, and Mr. Graham as well, believed that Vanzetti was guilty, like most criminal defendants. A contemporary wise-crack illustrated the cynical attitude of many toward both the lawyers and their clients: when Mr. Vahey sent Mr. Graham to consult with Sacco about their strategy in defending Vanzetti, it was said that the purpose of the visit was to find out from Sacco where the payroll stolen at South Braintree was hidden so that the two lawyers could divide it up between them. Vanzetti was quite able to appreciate Mr. Vahey's brilliant cross-examination of the prosecution's identification witnesses, but he was appalled at what he claimed was Mr. Vahey's failure to make a thorough investigation, including a search for witnesses at the scene of the crime, and his disregard of helpful leads and suggestions.

Accordingly, on the indictment of the two men for murder, the Sacco-Vanzetti Defense Committee decided to get new counsel. Since the criminal lawyer, obtained through local recommendation in Plymouth, had lost their confidence, they now went to the other extreme and turned to anarchists in New York for advice. Aldino Felicani, treasurer of the Committee, requested the advice of Carlo Tresca, a leading anarchist and publisher of *Il Martello*, a radical weekly newspaper. Tresca did not know Sacco or Vanzetti, but undertook the mission. His wife was Elizabeth Gurley Flynn, a flaming agitator, active in the far left labor organization International Workers of the World, known as I.W.W. She recommended Fred H. Moore, Esq., who had acted as lawyer for the I.W.W. and was generally active in radical circles.

Moore came directly to Boston and presented himself to Felicani to become counsel for Sacco and Vanzetti. He agreed to serve for a salary of one hundred and fifty dollars per week and expenses. These terms seemed reasonable to the Committee and Moore was engaged. However, Mr. Felicani soon lost control of Mr. Moore's expenditures, which ran into hundreds of thousands of dollars. According to Felicani, Moore was personally honest but his concept of preparing the defense involved employing numerous friends as aides and investigators and scouring the country for clues and suspects. Most of the funds which he expended came from small contributions from the financially humble, raised in mass meetings and through propaganda. Much of the money seems to have been wasted.

The selection of Mr. Moore as trial counsel caused irreparable damage to the cause of the defense. His reputation as a lawyer among radicals had started from a somewhat mistaken premise. It was believed that he had been an important factor in securing the acquittal on an accessory to murder charge involving Arturo Giovannitti, the radical poet, and Joseph Ettor of the I.W.W. executive board. The two men had come to Massachusetts in January 1912 to aid over twenty thousand operatives in the Lawrence Mills in their historic strike against incredibly low wages and bad conditions of work. During a charge by police and militia against a picket line, a girl worker, Annie Lapizza, was shot dead by some unknown person. Ettor and Giovannitti were charged with being accessories to her murder.

Counsel for the defendants at the ensuing trial in the Superior Court for Essex County were James Sisk, Esq., a conservative Essex County lawyer, and George Roewer, Esq., of Boston. Sisk was subsequently appointed a Superior Court judge and Roewer, also a seasoned lawyer, became counsel for most of the important labor unions in Massachusetts. Fred Moore, then a young lawyer from California, joined the team. It was in this connection that Miss Flynn and Tresca came to know Moore. The trial resulted in an acquittal. George Roewer later told me that Moore's chief contribution was to act as a "leg lawyer," running errands for the Massachusetts counsel and rounding up witnesses for them. He had no responsibility and did not originate any part of the defense. In some way, however, Mr. Moore acquired the credit for the victory among radicals. After the trial, he returned to the West, where he apparently exploited the Ettor-Giovannitti triumph, became counsel for a number of left-wing organizations and gallantly defended accused underdogs in a number of cases, with considerable success.

Mr. Moore entered his appearance for Sacco and Vanzetti on November 18, 1920. On the same date, William J. Callahan, the young Brockton lawyer who had originally represented Vanzetti in the Bridgewater case, filed his appearance as co-counsel.

From almost every point of view, Mr. Moore was the worst possible choice to act as chief counsel to defend Sacco and Vanzetti. To begin with, he was from out of the state and jurors in rural areas tend to resent preference given to outside lawyers over their own bar. Moreover, Mr.

Moore was singularly inept at accommodating himself to local conditions and procedures. His radicalism soon became known and his influence as a lawyer was weakened by the public tendency to identify trial counsel's beliefs with those of their clients. In this case they had reason, if not justification, to do so. Anarchy was anathema to the local population and to Judge Thayer. As if to advertise his outlandish views and personality, Mr. Moore wore his hair long, and dressed and conducted himself in ways which offended the native customs. The headquarters which he established in Boston became a gathering place for assorted offbeat people, many of whom had no reason to be there except a vague desire to prevent injustice or to express their sympathy with a radical cause. The relationship between the sexes was reported to be unorthodox, including Mr. Moore's own conduct. How much of this gossip became general knowledge is not known. It is probable that Mr. Moore's prestige as chief defense counsel suffered far more from his public manners than from his private morals.

As the time for trial drew near, Mr. Moore finally took the sensible, but overdue, step of retaining as associate counsel competent conservative Norfolk County lawyers. On the advice of Judge Sisk, who had been senior counsel at the Ettor-Giovannitti trial, he selected the three McAnarney brothers of Quincy. They entered their appearance on May 31, 1921, the day the trial began at Dedham. They had not had time to prepare the defense and Mr. Moore remained the one lawyer with knowledge of defendants' case. His continuation as counsel was by then a necessity.

The most distinguished lawyer of the McAnarney trio was John W. McAnarney, Esq. He was unable to take part in the trial, but his two brothers relied heavily upon his judgment and advice. Thomas F. McAnarney, Esq., was an associate justice of the Quincy District Court. He sat throughout the trial with his brother, Jeremiah J. McAnarney, Esq., who tried the case as co-counsel with Mr. Moore. The McAnarneys could have been of inestimable help to Mr. Moore had he only been willing to follow their lead or even to be guided by their advice.

At this point it might be helpful to anticipate a bit and give a firsthand account of how the McAnarneys came into the case and the difficulties they encountered with Mr. Moore. Here is the story as told by John W. McAnarney to the Governor's Advisory Committee on July 12, 1927.

Q. (By Mr. Thompson) You have long been a member of the Bar? A. Since 1888.

Q. President of the County Norfolk Bar Association? A. I have been; not now.

Q. What other offices have you held? A. I have held thirteen years City Solicitor of Quincy, on the Judiciary Committee —

(By President Lowell) I don't think we need that.

Q. Will you be kind enough to state what your connection with this Sacco-Vanzetti case was and you might incidentally state what my connection was to be? A. My first connection or either of my brothers T. F. or J. J. was when Mr. Moore came to our office and stated that he had been recommended by one of the judges of the Superior Court to see if he could get the McAnarney brothers to take the defense of these two men. I heard the story and told him on account of the pressure of my other work I personally could not take the case, but, if he was willing, my brother J. J. McAnarney who was one of the trial lawyers of Norfolk County, he would undoubtedly take on the case, if I would recommend him to do so and that T. F. who was associated with me, I told Mr. Moore that I had no doubt that T. F. would help out and advise on any questions that would come up and he would be at liberty to call on me, but I wanted in the first place, because of the nature of the crime, I wanted to find out something about these men myself as to their innocence or guilt. That led to my going to Dedham, me and my brothers. I had a session of a whole afternoon with Sacco and his wife; I think at that time Vanzetti was serving his fifteen years at Charlestown. It was later I had my interview with him. I have closely examined Sacco and put him through every test I could think of. I took Moore out and walked the back streets of Dedham with Moore for an hour; first let me say I suppose I am frank as a lawyer; I suppose I am not going in too far as to statements —

(By Mr. Thompson) I will waive any privilege whatever there may be between attorney and client.

(By Mr. McAnarney) I took Moore out and talked with him over an hour. I wanted to find out if he was holding back anything from me that would have any bearing on the innocence or guilt of these men. As a result of my conference with Sacco and Moore, I came to the conclusion that Mr. Sacco was innocent of that crime. I told my brothers they could go and secure his acquittal as far as they could with a free conscience. I live in Quincy and the offense took place in South Braintree. It was a horrible crime and I did not want to have anything to do with it and have my office concerned in keeping them from getting their right punishment but, if they were not the right fellows, I wanted them acquitted.

Q. Do you know how it happened that Moore got into this case? Who hired Moore? A. I understand he was employed by an I.W.W. committee, a committee of radicals that were active in the West. I understand Moore had to do with defending capital cases in the West, then he was employed by this committee of radicals and that led to his coming on here to take charge of this trial.

Q. He was never chosen by either Sacco or his wife? A. On that I have to refer you to an interview when you were present when Mrs. Sacco stated that in substance. When the case started, I think it was the first, the night of the first day after the preliminaries or possibly the second night, my brothers called on me and they were very much purturbed and excited —.

Q. That is for the jury? A. Yes, when the preliminaries were going through. They came to me and stated a serious situation had developed. It was very obvious an antagonism existed between Mr. Moore and the presiding justice and they were fearful, if Moore continued in charge of the case, it would be impossible for them to render a good account of themselves or protect the rights of the defendants.

Q. On the record it appears that your brothers were counsel for Vanzetti and Moore for Sacco. A. That was only what you might call a trial maneuver. It gave each lawyer the right to argue before the jury and right to cross-examine. Right down below the surface they were acting not only as counsel for Vanzetti but they were doing what they could for both.

Q. (By Judge Grant) At a certain stage of the trial you took the laboring oar? A. At no time was the laboring oar taken out of Mr. Moore's hands. That was the unfortunate part of it. It was obvious there would be a miscarriage of justice and they begged I should go out and take charge of it. I told them about what I knew and I told them I would, if necessary, but I wanted Mr. Thompson, William G. Thompson, whom they knew, I should want him to come out with me. That led me to call Mr. Thompson. I got him out of bed I understand. I pleaded with him for a long time to come out on the case and I told him in substance in my opinion it meant the lives of these two men and the best opinion I could form at the moment they were innocent, and my brothers felt that there would be a miscarriage of justice and it was important for him to take hold of it. Mr. Thompson yielded and we met at the courthouse. We first saw Mr. Moore and we labored for a long time in one of the anterooms to get him to withdraw from the case. He positively refused to do so. Then occurred the interview I referred to that Mrs. Sacco said she had not engaged him. I was given to understand by my brothers that Judge Thayer had under advisement whether he would permit Moore to continue, not being a member of the Massachusetts bar. We advised Mr. Moore of that and he said, if Judge Thayer refused to let him continue, Mr. Thompson and I could take charge of the case. That was the arrangement we arrived at in the anteroom and went into the court room.

(By Mr. Thompson) I told these gentlemen that I sat with you three hours and a half and I heard Moore examining witnesses and it was probably the jurors being examined. A. The morning I was with you it was prospective jurors who were being examined.

(By Mr. Thompson) Somebody was being examined and Thayer would look at Moore and state "Objections overruled," and I told you, "Your goose is cooked." [14]

Unfortunately, Judge Thayer permitted Mr. Moore to continue as counsel in active charge of the case. Mr. Thompson later told me that Mrs. Sacco wept bitterly when he told her that she had no alternative except to proceed with Mr. Moore as trial lawyer for her husband.

[14] Vol. V, 4992.

Judge Thomas F. McAnarney, before the Governor's Advisory Committee, spoke of Mr. Moore as follows on July 11, 1927:

Q. (By Mr. Thompson) Well, now Judge you really wanted me to come in and take Moore's place? A. I wanted either you or my brother, J. W., to supercede Mr. Moore. I felt it was impossible to get a fair, impartial hearing with Mr. Moore being in acting charge of these cases.

Q. (By Judge Grant) Impossible, why? Why did you think it would be impossible to get a fair and impartial hearing? A. Because everytime I wanted a man on the jury whom I felt to be honest, he would make an exception to it, I say this without questioning Mr. Moore's integrity or honesty. He did what he thought was best. Whenever he would address the court it was quite similar to waving a red flag in the face of a wolf. He had other distinctly positive characterizations. Judge Thayer on one side, Attorney Moore on the other, and with all due respect to Judge Thayer, and the same with Mr. Moore, I felt we couldn't make satisfactory progress, and I felt that I should eliminate Mr. Moore if I possibly could. A. (By Judge McAnarney) Then we began the preliminary matters — now I am speaking entirely from recollection as I haven't seen a bit of the testimony for years. We then began to take up certain motions, certain things, certain motions, in regard to the jurors. I think there was a demurrer of Mr. Moore's and some other thing and at that time I noticed the pronounced difficulty of Judge Thayer and Mr. Moore, getting along together. We staggered through that day somehow and I made up my mind —

Q. (By President Lowell) Was that the first day of the evidence? A. No.

Q. (By Judge Grant) Empanelling the jury? A. It took over a week to empanel the jury. This was the first day. I think that time that I finally decided we certainly couldn't get along and make progress with Mr. Moore in active charge. I tried to enlist the aid of my brother, J. W., but he had some important matters on hand and I then tried to enlist the services of Mr. Thompson with us, he came up.

(By Mr. Thompson) I came the day you started to introduce evidence. By Mr. Moore and Mr. Williams also. A. Perhaps you came while the jury was being empanelled.

Q. Well, I saw enough to see that Judge Thayer was down on you. A. Yes. In any event, they had paid my brother a small sum of money, a small matter of $1500 or $2000, whatever it was and we agreed then to try to get Mr. Moore to quit and I offered to write a check and turn over whatever money to Mr. Thompson and we would go on with the case, having got into it, without any compensation at all if we could get Mr. Moore to retire. Well, Mr. Moore wouldn't retire.[15]

Judge McAnarney also told how he was frustrated in the selection of a good jury by Mr. Moore's prejudice against "capitalists."

Q. (By Mr. Thompson) Then this jury was satisfactory to you? A. Oh, no.

Q. Just explain why not. A. Well, there again I ran up against friend Moore.

15 Vol. V, 5044.

For instance, somebody would be called as a prospective juror. I have in mind a man named Biddle, a clean-cut, capable man. He works in a brokerage house in Boston.

(By Mr. Ranney) Page & Company. A. (By Judge McAnarney) His name was called. I remembered that I had met him way back twenty years before or thereabouts, fifteen or eighteen years before, and I knew he was a clean cut young fellow. I wanted him to serve on the jury. Mr. Moore said "No." He didn't want anyone in a banking house, brokerage house or any house of that kind on the jury. The same thing came up —

Q. (By Judge Grant) He didn't want any bankers or brokers? A. He was called and examined and he was challenged; going by the attorneys he reached out and shook hands and Katzmann said, "Well, well, you have lost a friend, brother McAnarney." I said "I haven't lost a friend. I have lost a good man. A good, square deal." The same thing occurred again. A man who worked in the organization of the New England Trust Co. was called, I knew him for a great many years, but I didn't know him personally, but I knew he was a clean-cut capable fellow. There was no reason why he shouldn't be on the jury. There again I said "Leave that man alone. He's a good fellow." But Mr. Moore was in charge. I was not.

Q. (By President Lowell) Moore was in active charge? A. Mr. Moore was in charge and he didn't want anybody who worked in a bank.[16]

Judge McAnarney then went on to describe Mr. Moore's impact on the judge and his behavior in and outside of the courtroom.

Q. (By Mr. Thompson) In your judgment, as a lawyer for these men, as a judge yourself, a lawyer of thirty years experience, do you think Judge Thayer conducted that trial fairly or not? A. I think Judge Thayer was — that he couldn't conduct a trial fairly with Attorney Moore on the other side. I have the highest respect for his character or ability, but this man Moore got under his skin as I said before to such an extent and so irritated him, so that people around could see his re-action on the jury, and so for that reason I would say that.

Q. You mean unfairly conducted?

Q. (By President Lowell) Did the judge treat you fair? A. Yes, that was one of the things that made it embarrassing. He would say to Moore, "Why don't you do the same as Mr. McAnarney does?" and Moore was chief counsel.

Q. Well, didn't he slip out of the case after it was over? I supposed Moore had taken a back seat. A. We got out as fast as we could.

Q. (By Judge Grant) Was he rather a disagreeable person? A. I will tell you now. At the trial, the jury there, there would be friend Moore offering his best interests at the trial, on hand with his coat and vest off and his shoes off.

Q. (By Mr. Thompson) What, his shoes? A. In front of the courthouse, Moore, and I would say to Moore, "For God's sake, keep that coat on in the courtroom, can't you?" [17]

[16] Ibid.   [17] Ibid.

It is regrettable that the decisions of judge and jury may depend on whether they are attracted or repelled by trial counsel. Such, however, is the reality of trial practice. Mr. Moore managed to affront the very persons who held the fate of his clients in their hands.

A grave disqualification of Mr. Moore as defense counsel for Sacco and Vanzetti lay in his hostility to the existing social order. We have already seen how this induced him to exclude good jurymen. It went deeper, however. To him the case was a symbol of the capitalistic society's oppression of the workingman. No doubt this concept was in accord with his clients' views, but it was harmful to their defense. Mr. Moore proceeded to blow the case up into worldwide prominence among left wing groups. For this purpose, he won the support of Communists, labor unions and radicals everywhere. In this process, the lawyer's objective of securing justice in the courtroom became somewhat dimmed by the glare of outside agitation and mass meetings. Mr. Moore's efforts succeeded all too well. The swelling denunciations of the purposes of the prosecution produced the inevitable reaction. However much the outcry might have been justified, especially in that era of almost hysterical pursuit of radicals, its effect was to rally what is known today as the Establishment to the defense of the Massachusetts administration of justice. During my own connection with the case in later years, I heard men, including lawyers, echo the alleged words of Mr. Ripley on his way to become foreman of the jury at Dedham: "Damn them, they ought to hang them anyway." Sacco and Vanzetti might have been convicted even if the attacks on the Massachusetts courts had not been made, but in view of what later became known of the tactics employed by the prosecution, the defense efforts to obtain a new trial or commutation would have been more apt to succeed. The various opinions denying relief suggest a discernible desire to justify the actions of the authorities however wrong their conduct seemed to be. In the next chapter we shall see how Mr. Moore's judgment assured the hostility of practically all persons connected with the administration of criminal justice in the Commonwealth.

The judge assigned to preside over the coming trial at Dedham was again Judge Webster Thayer. Reportedly he requested Chief Justice John Aiken to assign him to this post. Among all the Superior Court judges in the Commonwealth, many of whom were as conscientious and fair as the lot of humanity would permit, he was the one most likely to determine upon securing a conviction. Even before the Plymouth trial, according to an article in the *Boston Herald* on April 24, 1920, he had denounced a jury for acquitting one Sergie Zagroff, tried on an indictment for violating the Criminal Anarchy Statute. The evidence had shown merely that the defendant had expressed his beliefs, but had committed no unlawful acts.[18] Later, we shall consider undisputed evidence of his hatred of Sacco and Vanzetti and their beliefs, and of his sense of having a mission to save the Commonwealth from the Reds. Specifically, moreover, the fact that he had acted as judge at the Plymouth trial of Vanzetti should have disqualified him from serving as judge at the Dedham trial. This is how Judge McAnarney expressed it before the Governor's Advisory Committee:

Q. (By Judge Grant) At what stage of the trial do you think he came to that conclusion [that Sacco and Vanzetti were guilty]? A. We were not far advanced in the trial, and I think he came to that conclusion.

Q. (By Mr. Thompson) Why do you say that? A. From the mere fact that he sat on Vanzetti's trial in a holdup case and had sentenced him to fifteen or twenty, or twelve to fifteen years, something like that, and that the same man coming before him charged with a somewhat similar crime, I couldn't help but feel we were up against a stone wall, any more than we could see the decision, but we had that feeling; we got that impression.[19]

The situation was even more dangerous than Judge McAnarney suspected. For instance, he did not know that at the Plymouth trial Judge Thayer had been subjected to a barrage of loose talk by Mr. Katzmann about evidence which the prosecution never produced and to arguments and bench conferences filled with suspicions, not only about the defendant, but also about Boda, Sacco and others. Judge Thayer's mind was also filled with off-the-record facts, such as the surreptitious opening of the shotgun shells by the Plymouth jury and the discovery that they contained buckshot — knowledge which manifestly influenced his judgment throughout the later proceedings.

Judge Thayer's conduct of the trial has been termed fair by his later apologists. And obviously he was a good enough lawyer to make it possible for the Supreme Judicial Court to sustain his rulings of law on appeal. We shall see, however, how fair he was in other respects, such as in his discretionary (and unreviewable) rulings and other matters. Arthur D. Hill, Esq.,

---

18 Fraenkel, *The Sacco-Vanzetti Case*, 535.   19 Vol. V, 5062.

leader of the Boston bar, who came into the case to help in the last desperate days, summed up the trial in one of his characteristic epigrams: "Sacco and Vanzetti received as fair a trial as was possible — consistent with a determination to convict them."

Mr. Katzmann, who performed so astutely, and perhaps not too scrupulously, at Plymouth, remained to prosecute the defendants at the Dedham trial. The next chapter may suggest a motive which turned him into an even more implacable prosecutor. His fairness, not very much in evidence at the Plymouth trial, sank below the horizon at Dedham.

Mr. Katzmann substituted Harold P. Williams, Esq., also on his staff, for William F. Kane, Esq., the assistant district attorney, who aided him at Plymouth. I do not know why this change was made. The Plymouth trial had been based on Chief Stewart's unofficial investigation and Mr. Katzmann's strategy. The reader may judge whether the replacement of Mr. Kane by Mr. Williams made any change in the pattern established there.

It would seem as if no further bad luck could befall Sacco and Vanzetti as they neared the battle for their lives in the Dedham court. Nevertheless, with the oft-quoted inevitability of the *Phaedo,* there occurred another strange episode to put the seal of death upon them.

11.

Ominous Interlude

In January 1921 there occurred one of those irrelevant episodes which so frequently affect the course of human events. With the help of Mr. Moore's bad judgment, the DeFalco affair, as it came to be known, almost guaranteed the hostility of Massachusetts authorities toward the cause of Sacco and Vanzetti.

It may be recalled that Mr. Vahey replaced Mr. Callahan as counsel for Vanzetti in the Bridgewater case on the solicitation of Doviglio Govoni, a Plymouth court interpreter regarded and used as a "fixer" by the local Italian community. A similar effort was now made in the South Braintree case by another fixer and by a Dedham interpreter. The object was to induce the Defense Committee to get rid of Mr. Moore and to retain as counsel influential Norfolk County lawyers. This sort of thing was not unusual at the time. Frequently, court hangers-on would, on their own initiative, seek to obtain criminal cases for local lawyers whom they knew in the hope that, if successful, they would be rewarded in some way. (Mr. Govoni was retained by Mr. Vahey as his "agent.") It would have been clearly unethical for a member of the bar to authorize such solicitation, but generally the lawyer himself would keep entirely out of the matter until the accused, or his friends, personally requested him to act as defense counsel.

The DeFalco episode began when Benjamin Cicchetti, a fixer for the Italians in Providence, contacted Aldino Felicani, treasurer of the Sacco-Vanzetti Defense Committee. Cicchetti was a brother-in-law of a brother of a Mrs. Angelina DeFalco, a Norfolk County court interpreter who had occasionally acted as such for Francis J. Squires, Esq., an experienced trial lawyer, then clerk of the District Court at Dedham, and for Percy Katzmann, brother of District Attorney Katzmann. Reportedly, she told Felicani and others on the Committee that the defense lawyers Vahey, Graham and Callahan were "cattle," that the Committee could get the defendants acquitted if they would retain Mr. Squires and Mr. Percy Katzmann, that Moore could "stay in" provided he "stayed out" of the proceedings, and that Mr. Fred Katzmann would retire as prosecutor at the trial and would turn the case over to one of his assistants. In her zeal to sell the idea to the Committee, she made statements about her influential connections with what she called the Norfolk County Ring which were probably exaggerated "selling talk."

Mr. Felicani, on July 8, 1954, dictated a tape-recorded interview of what happened for Dean Albertson of Columbia University. The following is part of Mr. Felicani's story:

"On Sunday afternoon, January 2, 1921, I was working in *La Notizia*. A certain Mrs. Angelina DeFalco, accompanied by a Beniamino Cicchetti of Providence, called on me at the place. Cicchetti introduced Mrs. DeFalco to me as a court interpreter at Dedham. He stated that she was a very close friend of District Attorney Fred Katzmann — therefore, in a position to help in the case. With the natural suspicion that anyone would have in a case of that kind, I was curious to know what Mrs. DeFalco had to offer.

"Mrs. DeFalco stated then that Sacco could get off in the trial that was about to come if we were interested to secure his freedom by paying a sum of money. After listening for some time, I decided not to talk with her alone. So I decided to inform Guadagni [another member of the Committee]. Made an appointment with Mrs. DeFalco for the next day so we can talk this matter over. From the very beginning we asked — 'How about Vanzetti?'

"She said, 'Vanzetti is a tough case. He has been sentenced. It's pretty hard. But you can get Vanzetti out too provided you are in a position to pay.'

"To cut a long story short, she said, 'It will cost a great deal of money. The district attorney, and his assistants, and the foreman of the jury, will all have to be fixed. There will be a mock trial and the men will be acquitted.'

"On January 5, Mrs. DeFalco talked to me on the telephone, I presume from Katzmann's office, and said that everything was okay. The evening of the seventh of January she invited me to go to her home at a kind of a banquet [*banquetta*, a meal] to deal with Fred Katzmann, Percy Katzmann, Francis J. Squires and all the others connected with the district attorney's office.

"In spite of the fact that Guadagni promised me not to say anything to Moore, Moore got wind of this affair. Of course, he jumped on me immediately and said, 'I won't permit you to go to this banquet.' The situation was embarrassing. I had already committed myself. I was prepared. Moore said, 'I won't let you go alone. I'll let you go if you let me send Mr. Reid with you.' Mr. Reid was a detective working for Moore.

"I said, 'How can I explain the presence of a detective to those people? That's ridiculous. I can't do that.'

"He took me down as far as Commonwealth Avenue. I was determined to go. They wouldn't let me alone. This was about five-thirty. I had planned to be there in Dedham about six, in time for dinner. I had to telephone Mrs. DeFalco and tell her I couldn't come. We had to find an excuse. I said this to Mrs. DeFalco, 'I am expecting somebody from New York [and mentioned Giovannitti] who promised definitely a large amount of money to help. He hasn't arrived and I'm not in a position therefore to come down there and talk terms.' That was the excuse. She was very much disappointed. She almost cried because I was upsetting the whole business.

"I said, 'Why don't you come down to the office of the Committee tomorrow morning at eight o'clock? We'll discuss terms then.' She promised to come.

"I don't know why Guadagni and Moore prevented me from going to the banquet. I think they feared a trap in two ways. They said so. Katzmann may have accused us of trying to corrupt the prosecution, or there might have been a trap to compromise the whole business. I realized that perhaps the best thing to do was not to go, and I didn't go. They didn't physically prevent me, of course. They just argued me out of it.

"So, when I asked Mrs. DeFalco to come down to the Committee office at 32 Battery Street, she promised to come. We had the idea that without any permission from the people at *La Notizia* — because it was their building after all — we would install a stenographic listening device in the basement of the building. [The "idea" was Mr. Moore's.] We bought the device and I still have it. This was one of the early devices and we placed it in such a way that the stenographer, Gwendolyn Beamish, who handled it, had to go down to the coal bin and take the dictation there. This was done during the night.

"Later that evening I wanted to see who was really at the DeFalco home. So I persuaded Orciani [then acting as chauffeur for Mr. Moore] to take me out there. We went there about nine-thirty or ten o'clock. Mr. Reid, the detective, was with us. Sure enough, there were a line of cars in front of the house and we took down the license numbers. In the morning Mr. Reed checked. There was Katzmann's car, Katzmann's brother's car, Squires's car.

"The next morning Mrs. DeFalco showed up. We had there Marion Sproule. She was the first person in charge, with Daniel Cosgrove, of the Workers' Defense Conference with headquarters on Washington Street, Boston. Mrs. Sproule was contacted by somebody — not by me — and she accepted to come. There we were. I was there. Mrs. Sproule was there, as was Guadagni, Orciani and also Frank Lopez [secretary of the Committee]. We sat down and talked the matter over.

"These were the terms. We were to pay forty thousand dollars for the freedom of both — Sacco and Vanzetti. Of course, we objected and said, 'Where can we get forty thousand dollars?'

"She said, 'We will take an advance of five thousand dollars. You have all summer to collect the rest of it.'

"Mrs. Sproule said, 'And if the money is not raised, will they be convicted?'

" 'Of course, certainly,' said Mrs. DeFalco.

"Moore was of the opinion that, after we had all this down on black and white through the stenographic listening device, we should have Mrs. De-Falco arrested. I didn't want to do that, because after all she had spoken to me in good faith. Finally I had to give in. I went to swear the warrant. Mr. William Callahan, of Brockton, one of the lawyers, was present at the courthouse when I did it. This woman was arrested immediately.

"A few days later we went to court. Judge Michael Murray was the judge on the case. We stayed in court about a week, with all the witnesses, one after another, repeating the story in detail. We produced the list of the license numbers of the cars parked in front of the DeFalco home. But Judge Murray decided that Mrs. DeFalco may have committed a little indiscretion, but was not guilty of a criminal act. We had Katzmann on the witness stand. We had Squires on the witness stand. We had Katzmann's brother on the witness stand.

"It was front-page stuff in the Boston papers day after day. We tried, and we actually did, put the Massachusetts court on trial in a Massachusetts court. That's the thing that Judge Thayer never forgave us for. We sealed, at that trial, the fate of Sacco and Vanzetti. That's my conviction today."

Since the entire incident was abortive and no money was paid to anyone, the only charge that could be brought against Mrs. DeFalco (and Cicchetti as well) was for attempting to solicit law business, not being members of the bar. Samuel L. Bailen (a friend of mine) acted as counsel for the defendants. Fred H. Moore obtained permission to prosecute. Since he was chief counsel for Sacco and Vanzetti, this was a subsidiary bad tactic that tended even further to make Sacco and Vanzetti the targets for the wrath of the authorities incited by the subsequent hearings.

What was in Mr. Moore's mind when he insisted on arresting and prosecuting Mrs. DeFalco? Since the scandalous charges involved the district attorney of Norfolk County, his brother Percy, Mr. Squires, who was the clerk of the Dedham District Court, and two defendants in a first degree murder case, it was bound to bring the whole sordid recital to the front pages of the press. Innocent or guilty, those on whom the suspicion of corruption was cast would be certain to welcome an opportunity to avenge the imputation. As for Fred Katzmann, his resolve to convict Sacco and Vanzetti would almost certainly become unshakable. If the defendants were acquitted, some might believe he had thrown the case, as Mrs. De-Falco reportedly said he might; if they were convicted, he would have proven his incorruptibility. There were only two courses open to Mr. Moore that would not have harmed his clients. He might have retained Messrs. Squires and Percy Katzmann after a fee was agreed upon; or he might have done nothing and said nothing. Instead, he utilized this not very unusual solicitation to make what looked like an attack on the administration of justice in Massachusetts. Mr. Moore disclaimed such a purpose in court, but his rhetorical denial did not change the effect of his action. If his purpose was to discredit Massachusetts justice, the backfire was calamitous. The prosecution of Mrs. DeFalco pilloried in the press people whose good will — or even neutrality — might have helped his clients. The enmity it created was widespread, extending to persons only marginally connected with the Norfolk County courts.

The trial opened in the Boston Municipal Court on January 27, 1921, before Judge Michael J. Murray, and continued until February 3, when the judge announced his finding of not guilty. Mrs. DeFalco was "imprudent and unwise" but had been influenced by older men, "companions of ideas" (meaning, as stated by one of the witnesses, radical or anarchistic views).

Judge Murray was a competent and respected jurist. However, it was too much to expect him to find as a fact what Mrs. DeFalco was quoted as describing as the Norfolk County Ring. The testimony for the prosecution concerning Mrs. DeFalco's talk and actions was overwhelming, but it came from witnesses unlikely to be believed by a conventional judge unfamiliar with people of their type.[1] Those witnesses included Aldino Felicani, Felice Guadagni and Ricardo Orciani; Frank R. Lopez, under order for deportation as an anarchist; and Mrs. Marion Emerson Sproule, Socialist candidate for lieutenant governor and state secretary of the Communist Party, previously convicted of advocating violence. Benjamin Cicchetti, the original contact, the fixer from Providence, was also a defendant with Mrs. De-Falco. Mr. Moore admitted that he had known Mr. Cicchetti previously. Judge Murray's disbelief in these witnesses was deepened when some of

[1] The account of the hearing which follows is taken from the *Boston Herald*, January 28 and 29, 1921, and February 1, 2, 3 and 4, 1921; the *Boston Evening Globe*, January 27 and February 2, 3 and 4; and the *Boston Daily Globe*, January 28 and February 4. No stenographic notes of the hearing are available.

them declined to take the usual oath before testifying and when one of them, Mr. Lopez, stood in silence when asked whether he believed in the government of the United States. Also, during the hearing, Lopez was put in the dock for contempt. Mr. Cicchetti had said he was "a companion of ideas" (viz., anarchy) with Mr. Felicani, and the phrase so impressed Judge Murray that he used it to describe the entire group of prosecution witnesses. Judge Murray's opinion apparently failed to mention the stenographer who testified from the notes she took over "the listening device."

Percy Katzmann and Squires denied that they had ever authorized the use of their names to members of the Defense Committee. Both men admitted that they had occasionally employed Mrs. DeFalco as interpreter — but not nearly to the extent that Mrs. DeFalco was quoted as claiming to Committee members.

District Attorney Fred Katzmann expressed complete ignorance of the DeFalco business and said he never heard her name until she was arrested. He had never seen her before. He denied statements about his relations with Mrs. DeFalco attributed to her by witnesses.

However, Mr. Squires admitted that he had visited the DeFalco home twice, expecting to meet there members of the Defense Committee whom he had been told wanted to retain him as counsel for Sacco and Vanzetti. He also admitted he had received two telephone calls from Mr. Moore.

Samuel Bailen, defense counsel, admitted that one of the cars in front of Mrs. DeFalco's home belonged to Percy Katzmann. However, Katzmann said he had never spoken about the Sacco-Vanzetti case with Mrs. DeFalco until after her arrest. Mrs. DeFalco's testimony did not differ in substance from the prosecution's story, except that she claimed that she was solicited by the Sacco-Vanzetti Defense Committee to enlist the services of Percy Katzmann and Squires, not vice versa, and that Felicani and Guadagni came to her house in Dedham for this purpose.

In telling her version, however, Mrs. DeFalco added some details which seemed to reflect her quite understandable resentment at being "double-crossed." Although police inspector Stephen J. Flaherty testified that Mrs. DeFalco, when arrested, declared she did not know Aldino Felicani and had never been at the Defense Committee's address, she related a different story on the stand. There she told of her horror at seeing in the Sacco-Vanzetti headquarters two posters, one depicting a skeleton labeled *District Attorney Katzmann* and the other showing two men holding the Norfolk district attorney while two others were cutting off his head with big knives. She also stated that Professor Guadagni had said to her, "Don't you know we are anarchist Bolsheviks and that if Sacco and Vanzetti are convicted, Katzmann's head will come off?"

In rebutting her allegations, Felicani and Guadagni brought in a newspaper cartoon feature showing an antiwar picture of a skeleton decorated with a war cross and a soldier's cap. They said that this was the only skeleton's picture in the Committee's room.

On cross-examination, Mrs. DeFalco "developed several lapses of memory" and denied rendering service in a case which Percy Katzmann had admitted in his testimony. Other witnesses contradicted her testimony as to her presence at meetings.

In his opinion, Judge Murray emphatically exonerated District Attorney Katzmann, Mr. Percy Katzmann and Mr. Squires. He also denounced the harm done to society by language which, without warrant, tends to lessen public confidence in those entrusted with the administration of criminal justice.

Judge Murray's reaction to the allegations of the anarchist witnesses is quite understandable and should have been foreseen. He was a member of the Massachusetts judiciary and it should not have been expected that he would make findings at the behest of anarchists that would reflect, even indirectly, upon the integrity of the authorities of the Commonwealth. The outcome of the DeFalco prosecution was a portent of what was to happen later on a much wider scale when the administration of justice in the Commonwealth came under heavy fire because of the allegations of unfairness and the public outcry against wrongdoing in the Sacco-Vanzetti proceedings.

Judge Murray's rather indignant defense of the Norfolk County respectables presaged another development still in the unknown future. He was perhaps justified in finding that the two Katzmanns and Squires were not parties to Mrs. DeFalco's efforts to procure an important case for Mr. Fred Katzmann's brother and the clerk of the Norfolk District Court. And yet there were the curious circumstances that centered around the doings at Mrs. DeFalco's home in Dedham. Judge Murray's rejection of possible unfavorable influences seems to arise from the presumption in favor of the honesty of public officers and their associates.

Had the DeFalco case come some years later Judge Murray might have been more inclined to pry into the possible existence of the alleged arrangements in Norfolk County implied in the claims of Mrs. DeFalco as related by several witnesses. During the decade that followed the DeFalco hearings, the courageous action of some public officials, backed by the courts, brought to light widespread corruption of justice within the Commonwealth. The abuse of power by prosecutors for private gain was found to exist in the highest offices of the State. The district attorneys of Middlesex and Suffolk counties — the two most populous in Massachusetts — were removed from office and disbarred for allegedly collaborating with crooked lawyers.[2] Even an attorney general of the Commonwealth was impeached and disbarred for allegedly using threats of prosecution to compel defendants in civil litigation to pay extortionate amounts to his private clients.[3] Also during the period, a number of the foremost trial lawyers in the State were disbarred for corrupting the administration of justice. The prevalent practice of corruption was shown to have affected humbler members of the so-called "county rings," such as interpreters attached to the Norfolk County courts, including Mrs. DeFalco herself. One such Norfolk county interpreter, Joseph Rossi (or Ross), was sentenced to the house of correction in 1926 after pleading guilty of attempting to bribe a judge.[4] Rossi was the interpreter who proved so unsatisfactory to the defense at the Dedham trial that defense counsel secured another interpreter to watch him. Rossi also acted as chauffeur for Judge Webster Thayer and named a son born during the Sacco-Vanzetti trial Webster Thayer Rossi.[5]

Of course none of this is any proof that the district attorney of Norfolk County, or the men around him, were open to corruption. However, if these events had preceded the DeFalco hearings instead of coming later, Judge Murray might not have relied so confidently on the presumption that office or respectability are necessarily guarantees of integrity. When the proof of corruption seemed credible to the judges before whom these matters were brought, they did not hesitate to cleanse the administration of justice in the Commonwealth.[6] Also, when the abuses became evident,

---

[2] *Attorney General v. Tufts,* 239 Mass. 458 (1921); *Attorney General v. Pelletier,* 240 Mass. 364 (1922).
[3] House of Representatives Resolves, Nos. 1344, 1348, June 1928; In the matter of Arthur K. Reading, Supreme Judicial Court Docket # 26194 Law, 1929.
[4] Vol. V, 5051.   [5] Vol. V, 5051–5052.
[6] The Massachusetts Judiciary itself has had a history singularly free from the suspicion of corruption.

there were members of the Massachusetts bar with the courage to prosecute the powerful wrongdoers, however unpleasant and risky the task might be.

The DeFalco affair is important in two respects. First, it made certain of a resentful attitude on the part of the authorities toward Mr. Moore at the trial court level. Mrs. DeFalco was a Dedham woman with friends in the court circle. Moore was responsible for leading her on and then betraying her confidence. He had spread imputations of corruption in the press concerning powerful figures in the county. Second, Judge Murray's rather angry rejection of the charges was a precursor of the later pattern of reaction in Massachusetts officialdom to the bitter outside criticism of the Dedham trial and subsequent proceedings. Ranks were closed defensively against attacks on the court, however justified they may have been.

12.

The Identifiers — of Vanzetti

Circumstantial evidence against suspects in a criminal prosecution may be divided into two parts for practical purposes (but not for legal classification), as follows: (1) evidence to show consciousness of guilt; (2) physical evidence, known in the law as "real" evidence.

(1) *Evidence to show consciousness of guilt* arouses suspicion of the accused, but falls short of proof of guilt. This would include such matters as motive, opportunity, and conduct of the accused indicating consciousness of guilt. The last would comprise many miscellaneous matters, such as flight; attempts to escape; changes of name, appearance and residence; lies; resisting arrest; carrying lethal weapons; alterations in living standards; and associating with criminals known to have committed similar types of crime. This sort of evidence by itself has little or no validity as proof that suspects committed a particular crime until it can be connected to some positive proof of involvement. Once it can be so related, however, it acquires a potency of its own. Since such indirect evidence needs to attach itself to a more solid body of proof in order to sustain its life, we

may term it "parasitical" evidence. In the Sacco-Vanzetti prosecution there was a considerable amount of such evidence against the accused, consisting of lies told almost immediately after arrest, the carrying of arms, assertions that the defendants attempted to reach weapons when arrested, and alleged suspicious actions around the Johnson house, where they called to get Boda's old Overland. These claims are more fully discussed in other parts of this book. As the trial progressed, the persuasive power of this indirect evidence seemed to push the other parts of the prosecution into a less important position. The presiding judge himself declared as much. Whether there ever was a valid body of direct proof to which this "parasitical" evidence should have become attached is, however, another question.

(2) *Physical or "real" evidence* consists of objects or signs that the accused were present and participating in the crime. There were a number of such items offered by the prosecution in the Sacco-Vanzetti case. Some of these — such as a cap, a revolver, and bullets and shells — and their startling implications will be discussed in subsequent chapters.

Direct evidence such as eyewitness identification is strong proof of guilt, but unless made under favorable conditions is probably the least trustworthy proof that the accused committed the crime. We have already discussed the frailty of this type of evidence in considering its use at the Plymouth trial of Vanzetti. We shall have reason to do so again. In judging the trustworthiness of the testimony of the identifiers of Sacco and Vanzetti at the Dedham trial, we may ask ourselves the following questions, among others: How much of an opportunity did they have to observe the bandits? What was the character or reputation of the identifiers with respect to mental stability, suggestibility, craving for notoriety, vulnerability to pressure and the like? Did they make the identification under conditions which minimized the danger of error? Were they subjected to suggestion or pressure? Was their testimony at the trial consistent with statements made closer to the date when they allegedly had observed the bandits? In the Sacco-Vanzetti case the answers to such questions would seem to make serious consideration a waste of time. For this reason, I have been reluctant to use much space for their alleged identifications. Still, the testimony of these identifiers may not seem as worthless to others as to me and in any case our story would be incomplete without a fairly full discussion of it. Chiefly, however, the development of these identifications of Sacco and Vanzetti, even if hopelessly defective, tells us much about what went on behind the testimony they gave at the Dedham trial.

We do not know whether the prosecutors appreciated the general untrustworthiness of eyewitness identification. Yet such evidence as was available to them was especially unreliable, since it involved the identification of total strangers whom the witnesses had never seen before. Moreover, the bandits and the accused belonged to a racial group foreign and unfamiliar to the eyes of the identifiers. In most instances, the view which the witnesses at South Braintree had of the actual bandits was fleeting. In other instances, the view of alleged participants was quite casual, the identifiers having no knowledge that they were looking at men who had just committed murder or were about to do so. Some of the general descriptions of the bandits might prove useful, but so far as the identification of individuals was concerned, persons familiar with the evaluation of eyewitness recognition would probably have discounted the proposed testimony. And if such experienced men had also known the dubious character of the evidence to be offered by these witnesses, as disclosed later, they would most likely have thrown all of it into the wastebasket.

Nevertheless, it is important to an understanding of the case to examine the process by which the identifications were obtained. Unlike the Plymouth trial, the jury at Dedham may not have rested their verdict so heavily on identification testimony. Despite the fact that much of the prosecution's case consisted of such evidence and Mr. Katzmann in his summation stressed it for many pages, Judge Thayer, in his charge, made scant reference to it. Possibly Judge Thayer perceived the weakness of the eyewitness testimony. Many of the same infirmities also characterized the defense eyewitnesses who testified that neither Sacco nor Vanzetti was one of the bandits they had seen. There was also evidence — damning, I fear — that some of Mr. Moore's efforts to get witnesses to conform their testimony to his ideas of the truth were not above those used for a similar purpose by the prosecution. This must have had a disastrous effect on the credibility of the defense.

Chief Gallivan of the Braintree police, who had worked with the State Police in the early days of the investigation, had his own opinion of the witnesses at the trial. In 1927, before the Governor's Advisory Committee, he told what he thought:

. . . The only thing that took place there that excited my surprise was where all the witnesses were coming from. This is my own private opinion. I don't know whether I have ever expressed it before or not, but it did seem to me that it was dog eat dog there, one crowd would get a big crowd there, and then the other crowd tried to offset them, that's the way it appealed to me. The Government would put on a witness there and then the defense would rush in to offset it, and I guess Katzmann was just as wise, he would dig up one to offset that other one, and then the defense would dig up one to offset him. I may have made that remark before but I do not think I have, but there at the time that's the way the case appeared to me to be drifting along, to strive to see who could get the biggest crowd. In other words to see who could tell the biggest lie.[1]

For purposes of our story, however, a clear distinction should be made between the two sets of witnesses. If we are seeking to determine whether Sacco and Vanzetti were convicted on evidence fairly presented, we are concerned only with the evidence adduced against them by the Commonwealth. If such testimony was produced by questionable tactics, the danger of a miscarriage of justice is not removed if defense counsel sought to offset it by other eyewitness evidence gathered by methods also open to question.

Unlike other evidence in the Sacco-Vanzetti case, the testimony of the prosecution's eyewitnesses at the Dedham trial has been thoroughly analyzed and criticized.[2] Further extensive examination would add or detract little from its weight. This is especially true of some of the able, but very long, cross-examination of the prosecution's eyewitnesses by defense counsel. However, the "evidence behind the evidence" has not been so exhaustively studied. It is part of our story of the case to take a closer look at what

---

[1] Vol. V, 5178.

[2] (a) Article by Professor Morgan in Part I, Chapters II–V, of *The Legacy of Sacco and Vanzetti* by G. Louis Joughin and Edmund M. Morgan (New York: Harcourt, Brace, 1948; Quadrangle, 1964). At the time, the author was professor of evidence at the Harvard Law School. This book is not only a scholarly presentation, but contains an expert appraisal of the evidence.

(b) *The Sacco-Vanzetti Case* by Osmond K. Fraenkel. Mr. Fraenkel's book is a most complete and objective analysis of evidence and should be a source book. He is an experienced and scholarly member of the New York trial bar.

(c) *The Case of Sacco and Vanzetti* by Felix Frankfurter (Sanford, Calif.: Academic Reprints, 1954). This is a reprint of a book published by Atlantic–Little, Brown in 1927, which in turn was a reprint in book form of an article in the *Atlantic Monthly* for January 1927. Although it is a passionate condemnation of the Sacco-Vanzetti proceedings to the date of first publication, its complete accuracy has never been successfully challenged. At the time, the author was professor of law at the Harvard Law School.

apparently went on to prepare these witnesses to make their identifications from the witness stand. Let us begin with the identifiers of Vanzetti. Those who claimed to have seen Vanzetti in the murder car or in South Braintree on April 15, 1920, were:

Michael Levangie, the gate tender at the South Braintree crossing, who claimed that Vanzetti was driving the escaping murder car immediately after the shooting.

Austin T. Reed, a youthful gate tender at Matfield crossing twenty miles away, who said that Vanzetti was then sitting beside the driver in a car assumed to contain the escaping bandits. He made his identification while Vanzetti was still at the police station, two or three days after his arrest on May 5, 1920.[3]

John W. Faulkner, who claimed to recognize Vanzetti as a fellow passenger on a train the morning of April 15, 1920. The passenger got off the train at East Braintree.

It will be recalled that Mr. Katzmann, in 1927, said that there was not enough evidence to charge Vanzetti with murder at the time Sacco was held, viz., May 11, 1920. He further stated that sufficient evidence — from identifying witnesses — did not accumulate in sufficient amount to charge Vanzetti with murder until after his conviction at Plymouth.[4] We must assume that Faulkner was the "accumulation" that persuaded Mr. Katzmann that there was now enough evidence to indict Vanzetti on September 11, 1920. This is confirmed by the fact that Faulkner was the only identifying witness cited by Mr. Katzmann as supplying the allegedly needed additional evidence.[5]

Nine months later, after the trial had begun (on May 31, 1921), the prosecution unexpectedly obtained a fourth witness. Harry E. Dolbeare, a venireman originally summoned for jury duty, was sitting on a front seat in the courtroom on June 2, 1921. Dolbeare never claimed to have seen Vanzetti at the place or time of the crime. However he asserted that when he saw Vanzetti in the dock he immediately recognized him as a man he had seen in the forenoon of April 15, 1920 (over thirteen months before), in an automobile then turning in South Braintree Square, containing a "tough looking bunch" of occupants.[6]

Except for Levangie, none of the four witnesses claimed to have seen the bandits prior to the arrest of Sacco and Vanzetti. None of them except

---

[3] Vol. I, 606–609.   [4] Vol. V, 5078–5079.   [5] Vol. V, 5078.   [6] Vol. I, 490, 495.

Levangie had testified at the inquest or had been mentioned in the reports of H.H., the Pinkerton operative.

1. *Levangie.* As the reconstituted prosecution team of Katzmann, Williams and Stewart projected their case against Vanzetti about the time of his indictment on September 11, 1920, they must have foreseen that he would be an essential witness. Without Levangie, Vanzetti might not even have been indicted. Without Levangie, they would be left with only Faulkner's testimony that he had seen Vanzetti get off a train at East Braintree and Reed's story that he saw him sitting beside the driver of a car at Matfield, about twenty miles from South Braintree, and heard him shouting profanities in clear and unmistakable English. This testimony would be remote, if not entirely unconvincing. (The claim that Vanzetti was carrying Berardelli's revolver when arrested will be considered later. This idea had apparently not yet been born in the minds of the prosecutors by September 11, 1920.) If, however, Levangie would testify that Vanzetti was the driver of the murder car, the case against him might hold fast. At the very least, Levangie's story would force the judge, whoever he might be, to send the case to the jury.

However, serious difficulties, as we shall see, developed with the plan to put Levangie on the stand. Yet, because they had no alternative except perhaps to drop the prosecution of Vanzetti, the Commonwealth decided to run for luck and use Levangie's testimony anyway. The result was to create another Sacco-Vanzetti mystery and produce a tangle of confusion in the State's theory. Fortunately for the prosecution, this apparently escaped the scrutiny of defense counsel. Another result was to move Vanzetti nearer to the electric chair.

Let us first look at what Levangie said just after the shooting on April 15, 1920, three weeks *before* Vanzetti was arrested.

Timothy J. Collins, a newspaper reporter for the *Boston Globe* for the Braintree district, arrived at the scene about twenty minutes after the shooting. He got the following story from Levangie:

. . . I talked to the crossing tender, his name was Levangie. He said he was standing in the railroad crossing lowering the gates and an automobile came up the hill and somebody hollered from the automobile, "Put them up, put them up or we will put a hole through you." He said he did and the car crossed just before the freight train. I asked if he could give me the description of the men. *He said he saw nobody, he was too damn scared to see anyone.* I said, "Didn't you get a glimpse of anyone in the car." He said, "*All I saw was the muzzle of that damn gun and I turned and ran for the shanty and they put a bullet through the shanty.*" [Emphasis added.] [7]

Henry McCarthy of Stoughton was the locomotive fireman on a train that stopped for water at South Braintree at about 3:46 P.M. He saw the crowds and an ambulance in front of Rice and Hutchins. Levangie was at the gate, which was still up. He asked Levangie what was going on:

MCCARTHY. He says "There was a shooting affair going on." I says, "Some one shot?" I says, "Who?" "Some one, a fellow got murdered." I said, "Who did it?" He said he did not know. He said there was some fellows went by in an automobile and he heard the shots, and he started to put down the gates, and as he started to put them down one of them pointed a gun at him and he left the gates alone and ducked in the shanty. I asked him if he knew them. He said, no, he did not. I asked him if he would know them again if he saw them. He said, "No." He said all he could see was the gun and he ducked.[8]

Alexander G. Victorson of South Braintree, freight clerk for the New York, New Haven and Hartford Railroad, overheard Levangie say to a group standing at the crossing about fifteen minutes after the shooting, "It would be hard to identify these men." [9]

Edward Carter of South Braintree was a cutter at Slater and Morrill in the Pearl Street factory. He had known Levangie for fifteen years. He talked with him shortly after the shooting.

Q. (By Mr. Callahan) Did he say anything to you with reference to men in an automobile? A. Well, he didn't say anything to me until I did to him. I asked him who the driver looked like, if he saw the driver of the car, and he said Yes. I asked what he looked like, and he said he was a light man. That is all the talk I had with him.
Q. A light man? A. A *light-complected man*. [Emphasis added.][10]

It seems almost irrational to assume that the four men who reported what Levangie said just after the shooting were lying. They all held responsible positions and were strangers to Vanzetti. Moreover, according to their accounts, Levangie's reaction to the approaching murder car (Shelley Neal saw him "running into the shanty" [11]) was exactly what one would expect. His statement to Carter that the driver was "light-complected" was in line

---

[7] Vol. V, 5004–5005.   [8] Vol. II, 2000.   [9] Vol. II, 1372.   [10] Vol. I, 965.
[11] Supp. Vol., 428.

with what all other witnesses noted. Nevertheless, within a couple of days, Levangie thought he had observed more details of the driver's face. Later, he identified Vanzetti at the Brockton police station "just after they got him" (May 5, 1920).

Let us now look at Levangie's testimony at the Dedham trial. Just as Mr. Harding at the Plymouth trial described Vanzetti's features as those of the bandit whose face he had said he had not seen at Bridgewater just after the attempted holdup, so Levangie at Dedham listed in detail Vanzetti's features as those on the face of the driver of the murder car whom he had said he had not seen at South Braintree. When both Mr. Harding and Mr. Levangie described from the witness stand the man they saw, they were looking at Vanzetti sitting in front of them. Here is Mr. Levangie's testimony at the Dedham trial:

Q. (By Mr. Williams) Now, go ahead and tell us everything that happened from that point on. A. It came right up the hill as far as the gate. Of course, I had my gates down, and the first thing I knew, there was a revolver pointed like that at my head. I looked back at the train to see if I had a chance enough to let them go. I saw there was chance to let them go, and I let them, and I put my gates back again where they belonged.[12]

Thereafter, Levangie's testimony continued:

Q. Did you see anybody in that machine? A. I saw one man.
Q. Where abouts did you see him? A. Driving the machine.
Q. Will you describe the man that you saw as it came across the crossing? A. Dark complected man, with cheek bones sticking out, black hair, heavy brown mustache, slouch hat, and army coat.
Q. What? A. Slouch hat and army coat.
Q. How near were you to that man at any time, — what was the closest? A. I didn't measure it, but I should say it was about 10 or 12 feet.
Q. Have you ever seen that man since? A. Yes, sir.
Q. Where have you seen him since that time? A. Brockton police station.
Q. Have you seen him since then? A. Yes.
Q. Where have you seen him since then? A. Right there.
Q. Where abouts? A. The one with the mustache.
Q. Well, will you point him out? A. Right in the cage.
Q. Which one? A. The one on the left.
Q. With the mustache? A. Yes, sir.
Q. The one that is known as Vanzetti? A. That is the fellow. I didn't know his name, but that is the fellow.
Q. When did you see him in the Brockton police station? A. I ain't got the date. It was just after they got him.[13]

[13] Vol. I, 417–418.

If the record had stopped here, the explanation of Levangie's testimony would seem to be an easy one. Since we can hardly assume that the *Globe* reporter, the locomotive fireman, the freight clerk and the shoe cutter were all liars, it would seem obvious that Mr. Levangie, after he had inspected Vanzetti, then held as a bandit at the police station, began to picture him as the man he had glimpsed at the railroad crossing. It is a pattern of identification with which we are becoming familiar. However, the record does not stop with Levangie's testimony. This is the point where a new mystery develops.

When, on July 21, 1927, at our insistence, Assistant District Attorney Ranney handed to the Governor's Advisory Committee the minutes of the "private" inquest held on April 17, 1920, we were permitted to make a copy. The transcript of Levangie's testimony contains this puzzling section:

Q. (By Mr. Adams) You could not see the driver? A. Yes, I could see him all right. He was in the open end in front.

Q. Could you tell him if you saw him again? A. I could tell him all right.

Q. How did he look? A. *He was dark complexion, dark brown moustache, soft hat and brown coat.*

Q. What color hair? A. I could not see his hair, he had a hat on.

Q. He was at the wheel? A. He was the driver on my side of the car, on the left.

Q. Do you know what kind of car this was? A. No.

Q. Do you know whether Buick or Ford? A. I know it was not a Ford but don't know whether it was a Buick or not.

Q. Before this car went over your crossing did you see another one go along? A. No.

Q. Do you know Slater's car? A. No. That was the only auto I saw coming across.

Q. Didn't you see Slater's car go up before that? A. No, I was inside at that time.

Q. Do you know anything else about this? A. That is all I know and all I saw.

Q. *You are pretty sure you saw a man with a brown moustache that you could tell again?* A. *Yes.* [Emphasis added.][14]

One's first impression is that the foregoing excerpt confirms Levangie's Dedham description of the man he saw. Even if he was mistaken in remembering that the man he described was the driver (as Mr. Katzmann later admitted), it seemed to supply some proof, should it ever be needed, that Levangie had stated prior to the arrest that he had seen a man with a

[14] Supp. Vol., 451.

brown moustache who resembled Vanzetti in the murder car. The opposite is also true. If the minutes had shown that Levangie had testified that he had not seen the occupants of the car, this might, if discovered, constitute proof that he committed perjury at Dedham. And yet reliable and disinterested witnesses swore that Levangie had told them as much almost immediately after the shooting. It is impossible to reconcile what the inquest excerpt shows on April 17, 1920, with what these witnesses reported that he said right after the shooting.

The mystery deepens when we consider some other facts. On April 18, 1920, *only one day after the inquest,* Pinkerton operative H.H. interviewed Levangie. The gate tender gave him a detailed description of the driver but it differed from the description in the excerpt: "48–50 years, 160 lbs., stocky build, black hair, dark complexion, *clean shaven,* and long hooked nose, wearing brown army coat and brown soft hat." (Emphasis added.)

For the moment it is immaterial whether Levangie actually noted these details or imagined them a day or two later. Also, we are not now concerned with the "stocky build" or "long hooked nose," neither of which aptly describes Vanzetti. A dark brown moustache would have been the outstanding feature on the driver's face and it is hardly conceivable that Levangie would have described the driver as "clean shaven" if he had seen it, and yet the minutes cite Mr. Levangie as saying on the previous day that the chauffeur had a "dark brown moustache" and show that the examiner, like a prosecutor, drove that feature home by asking a question which, in retrospect, seemed almost intended to validate Levangie's testimony given later at the Dedham trial: "You are pretty sure you saw a man with a brown moustache that you could tell again?"

Also, how can we explain other differences between the statement to H.H. and the description in the inquest minutes? To H.H., Levangie said the driver was of stocky build with a long hooked nose. In the minutes for the preceding day it is not recorded that he mentioned these features. Nor did he mention them in his testimony at the Dedham trial. Instead, the description given by him at Dedham (except for the "cheek bones sticking out") follows almost exactly the details that appear in the inquest transcript, and in the same order: complexion, moustache, hat and coat. Why should the inquest minutes bear such a close resemblance to what Levangie said at Dedham fourteen months later but differ markedly from what he told the Pinkerton operative on the very next day?

Further, compare the inquest record showing that Levangie had stated that the driver had a dark brown moustache with the official State Police description of the bandits. On April 21, 1920, *four days after the inquest,* the State Police sent out the following description, which was published in the *Boston Herald* on April 22:

Captain Proctor of the State Police yesterday gave out a description of the bandits:
No. 1 — Age 22, 5 feet 5 inches, 125 to 130 pounds, slim, black hair, bald at the temples, probably an Italian.
No. 2 — Age 30, 5 feet 5 inches, 150 pounds, probably an Italian.
No. 3 — Age 30, 5 feet, 9 inches, 150 pounds.
No. 4 — Age 25, 5 feet 7 inches, 130 pounds, light complexion, dimple in cheek, sallow skin.
No. 1 and 3 shot the paymaster and special policeman. No. 3 stood on the sidewalk protecting No. 1 and 2. *No. 4 was the chauffeur. All four are described as smooth shaved.* According to Captain Proctor, only four have been identified as having participated in the affair. [Emphasis added.]

(A fifth stayed on the back seat hidden by the drawn curtains. We shall consider his identity later when we consider the evidence against the Morelli gang.)

Since the inquest into the deaths of Parmenter and Berardelli was held mainly to aid law enforcement officers in their hunt for the guilty parties, we must assume that the descriptions sent out by the State Police were based largely on the inquest testimony. Mr. Levangie had testified at that inquest. If the gate tender at the close-by railroad crossing had said that the murder car chauffeur had a dark moustache, would it not have been extraordinary for the police to have publicized a description of all of the bandits as "smooth shaved"? What is the answer? Was the brown moustache in the original transcript or was it inserted at a later date? Merely to ask such questions would ordinarily appear to stamp the questioner as hopelessly biased. Considering the surrounding facts, however, one wonders. The answer does not affect the believability of Levangie's testimony, which, in any event, was so discredited that even Mr. Katzmann had to disown it in his summation and offer his own speculative theory to explain it. However, the otherwise irreconcilable conflict between Levangie's testimony as recorded in the inquest minutes and what he is quoted as saying to others just before and just after the inquest adds another nagging doubt about the integrity of the prosecution's case.

Later, at the Dedham trial, the minutes of the inquest became the subject of a rather one-sided stipulation between counsel, after the prosecution had finished and the defense had begun. Jeremiah McAnarney, defense counsel, after conference with Mr. Katzmann, reported the following stipulation:

MR. MCANARNEY. If your Honor please, we have here the stenographer who acted for the Commonwealth in the Quincy Court, lower court here [preliminary hearing]. She also is the same stenographer who acted for the Commonwealth at the inquest on this same matter at Quincy. We have agreed here and I will state now that it may be entered in the record that the transcript of the evidence which I have of the hearing in the lower court, and which they have of the hearing at the inquest, is a correct transcript of the evidence given at both of those hearings. We agree to that in order that the stenographer, who is here and has other duties, may not be detained to go through the record. That is correct, is it, Mr. Katzmann?
MR. KATZMANN. Yes.[15]

Ostensibly, the foregoing stipulation was merely the usual agreement to the accuracy of the reporter's transcripts in order to release her from further attendance at the trial. On closer examination, however, it seems to be another example of Mr. Katzmann's skill in outwitting defense counsel by stipulation. (We shall later encounter a number of these instances.) By agreeing that the transcript of the preliminary hearing was correct, Mr. Katzmann conceded nothing. The hearing had been a public one and the minutes were taken by his own stenographer. Except to save time, he had no need for the stipulation. However, he did need an agreement that the inquest minutes were correct, because he wanted to use selected portions in cross-examining defense witnesses, and later did so. On the other hand, Mr. McAnarney gained nothing from the stipulation. The minutes of what Mr. Katzmann termed a "private" inquest remained, undisclosed to defense counsel, in the possession of the district attorney.[16] Even in 1927, six years after the Dedham trial, Mr. Ranney, in order to make the minutes available to us, had to deliver them to the Governor's Advisory Committee, which then permitted us to have copies made. Even if defense counsel had by chance seen the inquest minutes, the timing of the stipulation alone would have made them almost useless for cross-examining the government wit-

---

[15] Vol. II, 1404–1405.
[16] Under Massachusetts law, Mr. Katzmann was under no obligation to show them to defense counsel. 134 Mass. 223, see Chapter 2.

ness. The prosecution had already closed its case when the stipulation was made. However, the record makes it clear that trial counsel for the defense never had a look at the inquest minutes.

I have stated that the decision to use Levangie's testimony resulted in confusion. This is somewhat of an understatement. The prosecutors knew that the driver of the automobile was a thin blond young man. The police had described him as having a "light complexion, sallow skin." Shelley Neal, the expressman, had described him as pale and yellow — like a cigarette fiend. The two witnesses who had the best opportunity to study the driver (but were not called), Louise Hayes and Minnie Kennedy, had told Mr. Katzmann that the chauffeur was a slim blondish young man. They had watched him from a window for about twenty minutes when he was puttering around the car just a few feet in front of them. Practically all of the witnesses of the crime whom the government intended to use would describe him in approximately the same terms. The prosecution therefore knew that Levangie's testimony that the car was driven by the dark-moustachioed Vanzetti would be overwhelmingly controverted, and yet they must have felt that they needed his identification to get the case against Vanzetti off the ground. They tried to solve their dilemma by suggesting that Levangie might be wrong about Vanzetti being the driver, but right about his presence in the car. This also had complications. As we shall see, when the known bandits were accounted for there was no place in the car for Vanzetti. And so Vanzetti was moved around the car in various spots — by Levangie behind the wheel, by Mr. Williams beside the driver, by Mr. Katzmann behind the driver and even, by indirect suggestion, back again to the driver's seat.

It was commonly thought that the Commonwealth opened its case on the theory that Vanzetti drove the car but had to abandon the idea because of the evidence. Even Mr. Thompson and Mr. Ranney mistakenly agreed before the Governor's Advisory Committee that this was so. But Mr. Williams opened the case with the claim that the driver was the rather slight man with an "emaciated yellow face." [17] He anticipated Levangie's expected testimony but forecast it with a difference: "As they came across he noticed *on the front seat* an Italian with a moustache, I believe, with a slouch hat on, whom he identified as the other defendant, Bartolomeo Vanzetti." [18] (Emphasis added.)

[17] Vol. I, 64, 68.   [18] Vol. I, 69.

The idea of putting Vanzetti on the front seat (next to the driver) was not original with Mr. Williams. The prosecution had planned to use this claim for the purpose of reconciling Levangie's identification with all conflicting testimony in the case at least as early as May 7, 1920. At that time Mr. Katzmann had not yet assigned Mr. Williams to the case. Mr. Katzmann must have intended to use this theory that Vanzetti sat beside the driver in his summation to the jury. However, by the time the case ended, the witnesses were unanimous in placing a very different-looking gangster in the seat beside the driver. Since the seat reserved for Vanzetti was occupied by another, Mr. Katzmann in his summation moved Vanzetti to a place *behind* the driver. Here is what he said:

> They find fault, gentlemen, with Levangie, they say that Levangie is wrong in saying that Vanzetti was driving that car. I agree with them, gentlemen. I would not be trying to do justice to these defendants if I pretended that personally so far as you are concerned about my personal belief on that, that Vanzetti drove that car over the crossing. I do not believe any such thing. You must be overwhelmed with the testimony that when the car started it was driven by a light-haired man that showed every indication of being sickly.
>
> We cannot mold the testimony of witnesses, gentlemen. We have got to take them as they testify on their oaths, and we put Levangie on because necessarily he must have been there. He saw something. He described a light-haired man to some of the witnesses. They produced Carter, the first witness they put on, to say that he said the light-haired man, — the driver was a light-haired man. That is true. I believe my brothers will agree with me on that proposition, but he saw the face of Vanzetti in that car, and is his testimony to be rejected if it disagrees with everybody else if you are satisfied he honestly meant to tell the truth? And can't you reconcile it with the possibility, no the likelihood or more than that, the probability that at that time Vanzetti was directly behind the driver in the quick glance this man Levangie had of the car going over when they were going up over the crossing.[19]

The foregoing excerpt is a striking exhibition of Mr. Katzmann's remarkable skill in misleading the jury. He managed to create the impression of complete honesty in that his admission that Vanzetti did not drive the car (he had no choice but to concede it) was made in the interest of "justice to these defendants." He intimated that he had some sort of professional obligation to put in Levangie's testimony despite its infirmities. He had none. Then, omitting the fact that witnesses had quoted Levangie as saying that he saw nothing except "that damn gun," he mentioned the one witness who said that Levangie referred to the driver as "light-complected." This,

[19] Vol. II, 2215.

to Mr. Katzmann, seemed to confirm his statement that he saw "something." Then, with nothing more than a fleeting impression of this blondish face, Mr. Katzmann created an illusion that Levangie saw "the face of Vanzetti in that car"; and then, without any evidence at all, he escalated from the "possibility" to the "likelihood" to the "probability" that Vanzetti was "directly behind the driver." This exercise of Mr. Katzmann's verbal magic at the finish of a long trial contradicted Mr. Williams's statement in his opening five weeks before that Vanzetti was on the front seat. By that time the jury (and probably defense counsel) must have forgotten the opening statement, and so the prosecution successfully explained to them the inexplicable testimony of Mr. Levangie.

Nor apparently was the prosecution troubled by the mathematical problem of getting Vanzetti into the car beside or behind the driver. There were in all only five bandits at the Pearl Street affair. "The contention of the Government, gentlemen," said Mr. Williams, "is that this crime was committed by five men." [20] This accorded with the release of the State Police and most of the testimony. Mr. Williams specified:

> There were two men in the car, the driver and a man we cannot describe, in the back seat. The car crawled up to the scene of the shooting. The two bandits, the man who had shot Berardelli when he was on the ground and the fellow who chased Parmenter when he was across the street, came back, took up the two boxes, and piled them into the car.
> There was some evidence that there was another bandit on the other side of the street over behind the brick pile. A shot was noticed coming from that distance, though I will say now the evidence is rather hazy as to that bandit over there, but there *is evidence that three bandits*, whether it was the man who was over in the brick pile or not, came across the street, and *piled into the car*; there then being *five men* in the car, it proceeded up the street to the crossing. [Emphasis added.] [21]

There were then three bandits who piled in the car from the street. [22] The seat beside the driver as the car moved away was occupied by one of them, sometimes identified as Sacco, but never as anyone who looked like Vanzetti. (In fact, *no* witness other than Levangie identified Vanzetti as a bandit or an occupant of any place in the murder car at South Braintree.) We now have the driver with the emaciated face, the man in the back seat whom "we cannot describe," and the three bandits who jumped in from Pearl Street. This accounts for all five bandits. Where, then, was Vanzetti?

[20] Vol. I, 76.   [21] Vol. I, 68.   [22] Supp. Vol., 420.

Levangie's story had presented the government with a problem, quite unreconcilable with the testimony of all of the other witnesses to the South Braintree crime. The government attempted to solve it by suggesting several untenable solutions — and apparently succeeded. Levangie's testimony had done the job for which it was offered. It supplied essential evidence in the case, however mistaken or absurd, that Vanzetti had been in the murder party, actively aiding his fellow robbers in committing the South Braintree crime. As the court was to say a number of times, "It was for the jury to decide what to believe."

At the time Levangie testified, Mr. Katzmann and the State Police had in their files the descriptions of the driver by Minnie Kennedy and Louise Hayes. The prosecution did not call these witnesses or reveal their existence to the defense. (This later became an issue before the Massachusetts Supreme Judicial Court.) It is quite possible that Mr. Williams did not know of this evidence either, since it was obtained by Mr. Katzmann during the early police investigation of the crime by the State Police, before the arrest of Sacco and Vanzetti and months prior to his being assigned to organize evidence for the trial of the South Braintree case. Nor did Captain Proctor have any responsibility for the State's failure to call these witnesses. He had been removed from his post as chief investigator many months prior to the trial.

Perhaps the story of the confusion created by the intention to use Levangie has not yet been fully told. For some reason I do not understand, Mr. Williams did not quite let go of the idea that Vanzetti was driving the murder car after all. In discussing the guilt of the bandits in the eyes of the law, he said:

You have got two defendants. The Commonwealth has *no evidence* of any eye witness that saw Vanzetti fire any gun. They have *direct evidence* of Sacco shooting at Berardelli, but their evidence connecting Vanzetti with this murder connects him with the gang that perpetrated the murder and puts him in the car, puts him there, and you may fairly ask me if he did not shoot anybody, is he guilty of murder?

The law is this, gentlemen. If two or more conspire to kill and do any joint act looking towards the killing and do kill, one is as guilty as the other. If they in concert aid and assist each other in killing a man, they are both guilty of the killing. You, sir, may hold a man while I shoot him, and you are as guilty as I am. *The man who drove the car up to assist them and was there helping them, bringing them to the scene and taking them away, is just as guilty as the man who fired the shot.* Every one of this group who participated in this hold-up, in this shooting, if they knew that shooting was intended, if there was resistance to the robbery, or if there was not resistance, are guilty of murder as much as if they had actually held the gun. [Emphasis added.][23]

The foregoing statement is remarkable for a singular omission. The only evidence against Vanzetti as Mr. Williams opened the case, according to the above excerpt, was that he was put in the murder car on the front seat as passenger or driver. As the trial progressed, however, the prosecution found a new claim, which, if true, would have been the most crushing evidence against him — that he was carrying in his pocket at his arrest the revolver of the murdered Berardelli! The State had the revolver in its possession for fourteen months before the idea dawned on the prosecutors. This will be discussed in a subsequent chapter.

There is another curious angle to the Levangie affair. It is found in the report of Pinkerton operative H.H. for May 7, 1920. This was after the arrest of Sacco and Vanzetti. At that time, as we saw in our discussion of the Pinkerton reports, H.H. was no longer an active investigator, the companion of Chief Stewart and Officer Brouillard. He apparently was no longer in the confidence of the district attorney's office and made up his reports from what the officials chose to tell him. Hence his daily reports became largely hearsay and were not always correct. For instance, he reported that Orciani was released for want of identification. Actually, there had been several identifications and he was released because of what Mr. Katzmann termed "time clock" alibis. H.H., however, was not so advised.

Operative H.H.'s report for May 7, the third day after the arrest, contained the following (previously quoted) language:

> Levangie, the crossing tender, who also went to Brockton, identified Vanzetti as the driver of the car as it crossed the railroad tracks. Levangie's identification is doubtful as those who saw the chauffeur prior to the holdup and murders, say that Vanzetti was not the man driving the car.
> It must be remembered that Levangie has from the first said that the man driving the car was about 45 years of age and had a moustache, so probably Vanzetti occupied the front seat along with the chauffeur, so Levangie in the excitement, may have gained the impression that Vanzetti was driving.

The second paragraph above seems oddly significant. The sentence beginning "It must be remembered" obviously did not refer to the operative's memory, since his own report for April 18 stated that Levangie told him

[23] Vol. I, 78.

that the driver was smooth-shaven. Those who spoke to the gate tender immediately after the shooting quoted him as saying he did not see anything but "the muzzle of that damn gun," and one said the chauffeur was blond. The balance of the sentence then sets out the opening speculation of the assistant district attorney at the trial fourteen months later that Vanzetti was sitting beside the chauffeur. Does not the entire second paragraph seem like a "handout" from the district attorney's office to prepare the way for Levangie's impossible narrative?

2. *Austin T. Reed* was a young man who had turned up at the Brockton police station in May 1920 shortly after the arrest of Sacco and Vanzetti. He later explained that he was "doing a little detective work on his own." He asked to view the two suspects. This was after newspapers with photographs of the alleged bandits were in his home, but at the trial he denied that he had seen them. His story (as later related in Dedham) was that at about 4:15 P.M. on April 15, 1920, he was on duty at the Matfield crossing (about twenty miles from South Braintree). He stopped a car because a train was just coming and the man beside the driver shouted to him, "What to hell are you holding us up for!" The car crossed the tracks, went up Matfield Street and returned in a few minutes. The same man then repeated the same remark to him. At the trial he described the man as having features like Vanzetti's and a "kind of a stubbed moustache, bushy," and then positively identified Vanzetti.[24]

Apparently, Mr. Reed had pursued his "little detective work" rather diligently. In describing the car he let slip the fact that he had been in Plymouth during Vanzetti's trial for the Bridgewater attempt.[25] This might explain his identification at the Dedham trial. As he watched Vanzetti during the Plymouth trial, the man he saw there could have replaced the fleeting image he saw at Matfield.

However, at the trial Mr. Reed added something which, if Mr. Katzmann and Mr. Williams were aware of at the time when they were preparing the case, should have eliminated Mr. Reed from their consideration of him as an identification witness. The pertinent excerpt from Mr. Reed's testimony follows:

Q. (By Mr. Moore) And his salutation to you in a loud, bold voice, *in the English phraseology* that you saw fit to give, something I believe to the effect "What in hell did you stop us for?" A. Yes, sir.

[24] Vol. I, 597 *et seq.*   [25] Vol. I, 597.

MR. KATZMANN. One minute.
Q. Is that right?
MR. KATZMANN. I object.
THE COURT. You assumed quite a good many things in the question before you got to the conclusion.
Q. Is that what he said to you?
THE COURT. That may stand.
A. Yes.
THE COURT. The rest may be stricken out.
Q. And the voice was loud and full strong back forty feet. Is that right? A. Yes, sir.
Q. What? A. Yes, sir.
Q. With a running motor? A. Yes, sir.
Q. And a train passing, — approaching? A. Yes, sir.
Q. *The quality of the English was unmistakeable and clear?* A. Why, —
Q. Is that right? *Answer yes or no. What?* A. Yes. [Emphasis added.] [26]

In April 1920, Vanzetti could speak little or no English. We do not know whether Mr. Katzmann and Mr. Williams, when preparing the case, knew that Mr. Reed would say that the man whom he thought was Vanzetti used "unmistakeable and clear" English. However, they heard Mr. Reed's testimony at the trial and they then knew that Vanzetti had great difficulty with the English language. Nevertheless, Mr. Katzmann argued that Mr. Reed's identification should be believed by the jury.[27] Strangely enough, Jeremiah McAnarney, counsel for Vanzetti, in arguing that Reed was mistaken, apparently forgot to mention the one part of his testimony that proved conclusively that Vanzetti could not have been the man he saw.[28]

Levangie and Reed were the only witnesses who put Vanzetti in the escape car. Probably Chief Stewart attempted to find other (and more credible) witnesses who could testify to Vanzetti's participation in the South Braintree affair. If so, he failed in the effort. The Dedham trial proceeded without such additional testimony.

However, the prosecution did obtain the two additional witnesses who purported to place Vanzetti in the vicinity.

3. *John W. Faulkner* was apparently discovered by Chief Stewart and Officer Brouillard a couple of days before July 20, 1920.[29] Faulkner said that on April 15, 1920, at 9:23 A.M., he got on a train at Cohasset. There he noticed a man with a black moustache, who looked foreign. This man later got off at East Braintree at about 9:54 A.M., carrying a black bag. Faulkner

[26] Vol. I, 615–616.   [27] Vol. II, 2218–2219.   [28] Vol. II, p. 2173.
[29] Vol. I, 426, 437.

identified the man as Vanzetti. He did not remember that he mentioned this possible identification to anyone in over three months since the incident until two or three days before July 20, when he received a visit from Stewart and Brouillard. Two days later, they took him to the Plymouth jail, where Vanzetti was shown him in a "group" of five. This was apparently the *only lineup* in which either of the defendants was displayed to possible identifiers. Its value may be judged by the fact that Mr. Faulkner had a picture of Vanzetti in his pocket when he was taken to the Plymouth jail and later did not recall whether the others in the lineup were smooth-shaven or had moustaches.[30]

In order to connect the man whom Faulkner saw with the South Braintree crime, the prosecution put forward the hypothesis that Vanzetti came up on the train from Plymouth and got off at East Braintree, where he was met by the other bandits in a motorcar. There was no evidence to this effect. According to Mr. Faulkner, the man had asked at nearly every train stop whether it was East Braintree. Apparently Mr. Faulkner's suspect did not know much about the locality and did not try to remain unnoticed. Mr. Faulkner's description of the car in which he claimed he was riding was contradicted by the conductor of the train,[31] by the ticket agent at East Braintree[32] and later by the assistant trainmaster,[33] and by a letter from the railroad company.[34] The ticket agent at East Braintree testified that he had seen one tall dark man get off at his station on several occasions after April 15 (with a black bag) and that the man was not Vanzetti.[35] The conductor also stated that no cash fares good from Plymouth or neighboring stations to East Braintree, South Braintree or Braintree had been taken on the train on which Faulkner claimed to ride on April 15, 1920.[36] The ticket agents at Plymouth and stations immediately following testified that no tickets had been sold for any such destinations nor had any one of them seen Vanzetti on April 15.[37]

4. *Harry E. Dolbeare* has been previously discussed. He claimed to have recognized Vanzetti in the dock at the courtroom at Dedham as a man he had seen on April 15, 1920, thirteen months before, between ten and twelve o'clock, sitting in an automobile moving in South Braintree Square. He was sitting with a "tough looking bunch," but the only one who at-

[30] Vol. I, 438. [31] Vol. II, 1277. [32] Vol. II, 1305. [33] Vol. V, 5224.
[34] Vol. II, 1350. [35] Vol. II, 1305. [36] Vol. II, 1277–1282.
[37] Vol. II, 1283–1297.

tracted his attention was the one he identified as Vanzetti.[38] Mr. Dolbeare did not connect the car with the Buick except to claim that he had seen Vanzetti. Nor did Dolbeare connect the "tough looking bunch" with the South Braintree bandits.

5. A fifth identifier, *Austin C. Cole,* was the conductor on the trolley car on which both defendants had been arrested the night of May 5, 1920. He stated that during the evening of April 14 or 15, 1920, he had been on the Bridgewater-Brockton run and that on one of these dates (he could not say which) two men whom he claimed were Sacco and Vanzetti had boarded his car at Sunset Avenue about a mile and a half from Elm Square in West Bridgewater. At first he thought the man he said was Vanzetti was a friend of his named Tony whom he had known for a dozen years.[39] Also he could not say positively whether a photograph shown to him by Mr. McAnarney was a picture of the man who got on his car.[40] The picture was of a one Joseph Scavitto who resembled Vanzetti. Even if we assume that Mr. Cole actually remembered seeing someone who looked like Vanzetti, as he said, his testimony is remote from any connection with the South Braintree crime both as to time and place.

The reader may find some interesting similarities between the identifications of Vanzetti in the Bridgewater case and in the South Braintree affair. For instance, Georgina Brooks at Plymouth and Harry E. Dolbeare at Dedham remembered that they had seen Vanzetti on the day of the crime, prior to their being committed, sitting in automobiles with other men. Neither noticed any of the other occupants and could not describe them. And Dolbeare's unexpected recognition of Vanzetti in the dock at Dedham is reminiscent of Harding's instantaneous identification of him in the Brockton police station through a crack in the door.[41]

We have now considered the testimony of *all* of the identifiers of Vanzetti. There was no additional evidence that he was in South Braintree on April 15, 1920. There was no other proof that he was involved with the South Braintree crime in any way except the later claim that he was carrying Berardelli's revolver. This will be considered in a later chapter. It is difficult to conclude that the jury found him guilty on such evidence. There were reasons other than these. Apart from the imponderable atmosphere of the hour, Vanzetti told falsehoods when arrested and was found to be carrying a revolver when searched. These two points formed the warp and

[38] Vol. I, 496.   [39] Vol. I, 737.   [40] Vol. I, 738.   [41] Supp. Vol., 95.

woof of the skein which Mr. Katzmann wove around Vanzetti. He had already deprived his victim of the one source of strength that might have enabled him to struggle to freedom. Had he tried Vanzetti for the South Braintree murders before the Plymouth trial, Vanzetti would have stood before the jury as a hardworking, law-abiding man, never before accused of crime of any sort. This was not the man tried in the Dedham court. There the jury knew full well that the defendant Vanzetti was capable of robbery, if not of murder. The accused in the cage was a felon, a convict from state prison, a robber who had already attempted to hold up a pay truck. For him, the legalistic presumption of innocence was gone. It had been replaced by a realistic presumption of guilt.

13.

The Identifiers — of Sacco

If the new prosecution team of Katzmann, Williams and Stewart had reviewed their evidence of Sacco's identification, they must have felt that something stronger was needed. There were difficulties in his identification.

Sacco certainly could not have been the thin blond chauffeur of the murder car.[1] Testimony at the inquest indicated that of the three bandits on the street, two resembled one another closely in height; all three had similar coloring. Some differences in weight were noted by some witnesses, but hardly enough to permit individual identifications. All had dark hair which, on one of them who was bareheaded, seemed to be retreating at the temples. They looked like thousands of young Italian men — and so did Sacco.

It is not surprising, therefore, that no witness at the preliminary hearing on May 26, 1920, would positively identify Sacco as a South Braintree bandit — nor do we know how many of the inquest witnesses were wanted

[1] Nevertheless, the prosecution did discover a witness, a Mrs. Mabel Hewins, who was ready to identify Sacco as the driver. She was summoned but did not testify, possibly because the prosecution, having put in evidence that Vanzetti was the chauffeur, then that the thin blondish man drove the car, was reluctant to risk the laughter that might follow testimony that Sacco also was the driver.

for this hearing but refused to make even a tentative identification. Of all the inquest witnesses, only Lewis L. Wade was later put on the stand at the trial to identify Sacco. This proved to be a personal misfortune for Mr. Wade.

At the inquest, before the arrest of Sacco and Vanzetti, Mr. Wade had made the following reply when asked whether he could identify any of the bandits if he saw them again: "I probably could, but I would not want to convict an innocent man." [2]

When he viewed Sacco at the police station after his arrest, he had said, "I had a little doubt." [3]

At the preliminary hearing on May 26 in the Quincy court, he testified, "I do not want to make a mistake. This is too damn serious, but he looks like the man." [4]

Nevertheless, the prosecution used Mr. Wade as an identifying witness at the trial thirteen months later. Possibly he had made more positive statements in the interim while the case was being prepared, because Mr. Williams seemed obviously taken aback when the witness said, "Well, I ain't so sure now. I have a little doubt." Pressed to explain his meaning, Mr. Wade said, "Well, the reason why I had a doubt, I have seen a man that resembled him, the man that I saw that day, and that is the reason why I have a little doubt." [5] (Mr. Wade was discharged by Slater and Morrill several weeks after he had testified. He had been an employee of that company for sixteen years.)

In 1927, when I was tracing the connection of the Morelli gang with the South Braintree crime, I visited Mr. Wade's home to have him look over a sheaf of photographs, including some pictures of several of the Providence professionals. His wife was rather apprehensive when I called, but I waited in front of his house for him to return from a Grange meeting. He showed up after midnight. At first he did not wish to see me or look at the pictures, but I sat in his car until he relented. He selected the picture of Joe Morelli — the gang's chief — as "strikingly like the man I saw shooting Berardelli." He also stated that the picture resembled Sacco — as indeed it did. There was no doubt in Mr. Wade's mind as to why he was fired and he was bitter about his treatment.

Another inquest witness, Winfred H. Pierce, had been taken *six* times to

[2] Supp. Vol., 442.   [3] Vol. I, 216.   [4] Vol. I, 216.   [5] Vol. I, 207.

view Vanzetti and *four* times to view Sacco.[6] He had declined to identify either man. When asked at the inquest whether he could identify either of the men on the front seat of the murder car, he had said, "I don't think so. I have had pictures shown me by the State Police and if it was a matter of looking at a million pictures I couldn't say." [7]

He was not called as a witness for the government. The defense, however, put him on the stand. When he testified at the trial, Mr. Pierce, like Mr. Wade, weighed his words. Asked whether the man he saw in the automobile was either one of the defendants in the dock or cage, he answered, "I don't think that it was, but I am not positive, but I don't think so." [8]

Mr. Pierce, also an old employee of Slater and Morrill, was discharged and his place was taken by a juryman. There was no doubt in his mind that his discharge was due to his testifying as a defense witness. He was most reluctant to talk to me about the case. I got the impression that he felt that he had "had it" and did not want any more.

Another identification witness at the preliminary hearing had been Mary E. Splaine, who worked in the Slater and Morrill office at Hampton House. It was Miss Splaine who, on April 19, 1920, filled in Pinkerton operative H.H. with a long recital of gossip and suspicion about various fellow employees, including the murdered Berardelli. Her superintendent, Mr. Fraher, according to the report of H.H. for May 11, 1920, had stated that "no serious attention can be paid to Miss Splaine's stories, because she is one of the most irresponsible persons he ever came in contact with." The operative also reported that on April 22, Miss Splaine selected the photo of Anthony Palmisano ("Tony the Wop") as an excellent likeness of the man she saw. (His picture was also picked out by others who saw the bandits. However, as previously noted, the State Police found that Palmisano had been in a Buffalo jail on April 15.) Looking out of a window at Hampton House, Miss Splaine got a "momentary glimpse" (H.H., April 19) of a man in the escaping automobile, standing between the front and back seats. The shortest distance from the car to the window as it passed up Pearl Street was slightly less than sixty feet.[9] At the preliminary hearing she had said that Sacco bore a striking resemblance to the man she saw, but that she might be mistaken.[10] Like the government witnesses at Plymouth, she

[6] Vol. I, 1047.   [7] Supp. Vol., 466.   [8] Vol. I, 1044.   [9] Vol. I, 233.
[10] Vol. I, 232; Vol. II, 1678.

found her doubts dispelled prior to the trial, at which she was heralded by the press as the "star" witness.

In 1926 I sent John F. Carney, a trained investigator, to show her my sheaf of pictures, which included photos of some of the Morelli gang. He reported that she examined the pictures carefully, stopped at one, grew a trifle excited and exclaimed, "This is a picture of the man who did the shooting! It's a picture of Sacco, isn't it?" She had pulled out a photograph of Joseph Morelli. On being told that the picture was not a likeness of Sacco, she said that her identification of the bandit was based on a three-quarter view and the *very large hand* of the bandit.[11] (She had consistently emphasized the large left hand she saw pressed against the back of the front seat.)

On receiving Mr. Carney's report, I sent Herbert C. Dow, a prominent Boston haberdasher, to the Dedham jail to measure Sacco's hands for gloves. He reported that Sacco had "what men in the glove trade would call small hands." *Sacco's left hand wore comfortably a size 7¾*, the right hand, a size 8.[12]

Mr. Carney reported that his interview with Miss Splaine (by then Mrs. Williams) had been pleasant and amiable. When Miss Splaine's reaction to her error came, it was consistent with her imaginative and excitable temperament. The next day, headlines in the *Boston Traveler* screamed that a mysterious stranger, well-dressed, suave in manner, American-born, had tried to make her alter the testimony she had given at the trial. It stated that a "double guard" had been placed upon her home. The story had come from Miss Splaine and a guard was actually placed on her house.[13]

Pages could be filled with the contradictions and improbabilities in Miss Splaine's testimony, which cross-examination brought out at the trial. However, this would hardly seem to be necessary. Even if she had been a responsible person she would not have been able to make a positive identification of the bandit whom she glimpsed in a fleeing automobile at a distance. Miss Splaine herself realized this in May 1920. How did it happen that by June 1921, she was transformed into the star identifying witness for the prosecution?

Another identifying witness, produced by the prosecution at the preliminary hearing, was Frances Devlin, a friend of Miss Splaine and another bookkeeper in the same office. Both women got their view of the car as it

11 Vol. V, 4471.   12 Vol. V, 4526.   13 Vol. V, 4471.

passed Hampton House from a window on the Pearl Street side. Miss Devlin also saw a bandit standing in the car — his hand on the front seat. At the preliminary hearing, she, like Miss Splaine, declined to make a positive identification of Sacco as the man she saw.[14] As with Miss Splaine, something happened to her in the thirteen months that intervened until the Dedham trial, where she identified, as the bandit she saw, "the man on this side of the cage." [15]

Miss Devlin gave this curious explanation of the doubts she had previously expressed on May 1920:

At the time there I had in my own mind that he was the man, but on account of the immensity of the crime and everything, I hated to say right out and out. I knew he was the man and still I didn't want to say knowing as I knew it would be a deliberate lie, according to my own mind, but still I hated to say right out and out, so I just put it that way.[16]

The immensity of the crime certainly had not grown less between the preliminary hearing and the trial. As in Miss Splaine's case, there were also other unexplainable departures from the May 1920 account.[17] However, again as with Miss Splaine, it would add little to examine her testimony further, since its unreliability is already manifest.

A more useful subject to explore would be the manner in which Miss Splaine and Miss Devlin were led to make their tentative identification of Sacco in the first place. Their opportunity to observe the bandit in South Braintree was far too meager to enable them to recognize the bandit if they ever saw him again. We are indebted to them, however, for giving us the witnesses' own explanation of what went on at the Brockton police station when they were brought in to view Sacco.[18] Their accounts illustrate in some detail the "evolution of identification" previously discussed.

On cross-examination by Mr. Moore, Miss Splaine answered as follows:

Q. (By Mr. Moore) The defendant Sacco that morning did kneel forward in a crouching position in your presence? A. No, sir, he did not.
Q. Did he take and put on his hat or cap? A. He took off his hat.

---

[14] Vol. I, 466, 467.   [15] Vol. I, 464.   [16] Vol. I, 476–477.
[17] Chief Gallivan was present when these witnesses testified at Quincy in May 1920. In 1927, he said to the Governor's Advisory Committee, "I couldn't understand it, how they got stronger in Dedham than they was in Quincy." Vol. V, 5179.
[18] A more detailed recital of the antics which the prisoner was made to perform for witnesses was told by Sacco himself. Vol. II, 1861.

Q. Did he turn around in different positions with the light facing him and in front of him, in back of him and in side of him, as he was directed? A. No sir. I walked around him.

Q. You walked all around him? A. Yes, sir.

Q. With his hat on and with his hat off? A. Yes, sir.

Q. Did he sit down and stand up during part of that examination? A. Yes, sir.

Q. Did you at any time, or anyone else in your presence there, ask him to take any particular position? A. Yes, sir.

Q. Was that at your request? A. No, sir, not at my request.

Q. Whose request was that? A. Miss Devlin.

Q. But, it was in your presence? A. Yes, sir.

Q. And the position that he was requested to take he did take? A. Yes, sir.

Q. Now, you saw him four or five times that day, didn't you? A. I saw him twice that day, — well, three times including when I first saw him at the doorway coming in, but twice when I looked at him afterwards.

Q. All told, the time that you looked him over in these various positions, with his hat on and with his hat off, and walked around him, and so forth, consumed upwards — these various occasions — upwards of a couple of hours, didn't it? A. I don't think so. I saw him while he passed through the room, and while he was in the room I don't think I took more than five minutes to look at him.

Q. You saw him all you wanted to see him? A. Yes, sir.

Q. You saw him in every way and every position that you wanted? A. Yes, sir.

Q. And he also was present in court at the time of the preliminary examination? A. Yes, sir.

Q. And you saw him there for a matter of I suppose three or four hours, at the preliminary examination? A. I couldn't say just how long.

Q. At any rate, when you took the witness stand at the time of the preliminary, you looked right square at the defendant, didn't you? A. Yes, sir.

Q. And you looked at him during the entire period of your twenty-five or thirty pages of testimony? A. Yes, sir.

Q. And you haven't seen the defendant from that time since you saw him in the Brockton jail all that you wanted to see him and the time that you saw him on preliminary, you haven't seen him from the day until you saw him in this courtroom, have you? A. No, sir, I did not.

Q. You availed yourself of every form of opportunity of observation of that young man during the period in the Brockton jail and the police court? A. Not in jail; in that room. I didn't see him in jail.

Q. And you haven't seen him since? A. No, sir.

Q. And it was with all those opportunities of observation, which had not in any wise been supplemented since — They haven't been supplemented since? You haven't had any further opportunities of observation? A. Not since Quincy.

Q. But, it was with those full opportunities of observation to your complete satisfaction that you testified "I don't think my opportunity afforded me the right to say he is the man"? A. I made that answer. . . .[19]

19 Vol. I, 254–255.

Miss Devlin gave even fuller answers to similar questions on cross-examination by Mr. McAnarney.[20]

What apparently happened to the Misses Splaine and Devlin was that the sketchy flash image they had seen in South Braintree became in their minds the much clearer and fuller image they had seen in Brockton. By June 1921 they no longer remembered seeing the bandit they had barely glimpsed in an automobile on Pearl Street, but recalled only the prisoner they had seen in the Brockton police station.

It must have occurred to Mr. Katzmann and Mr. Williams that additional and more positive identification testimony was still needed to convict. Such new eyewitnesses were obtained before the trial began. However, the available supply of fairly reputable witnesses must already have been drained off, because the additional witnesses seemed to come from the residue. The three new witnesses who purported to identify Sacco as one of the bandits were Louis Pelser, a young shoeworker at Rice and Hutchins, who watched the shooting from a window; Mrs. Lola R. Andrews, who was on Pearl Street looking for work on the morning of the fifteenth of April; and Carlos E. Goodridge, who saw the escape car from Magazu's Pool Room as it passed up Pearl Street. They were a sorry trio. Their tangled testimony plus what credible witnesses said about their conflicting previous statements and their lack of opportunity for reliable observation of any bandits should have completely discredited their identifications. Mrs. Andrews had an unsavory past and Goodridge was a crook with a long criminal record. There was no evidence that Pelser had a shady past, but his alternate lies to both prosecution and defense indicated that he lacked the minimum qualifications for truth telling.

All three of these witnesses were treated with pretty rough pulling and hauling by both sides. This went on both before and after the trial. Mr. Moore, after the trial, stepped up the pressure to get them to recant. He even resorted to alleged methods close to blackmail to force Mrs. Andrews and Goodridge to retract. These tactics by Mr. Moore became known to the Supreme Judicial Court and to the Governor's Advisory Committee and, no doubt, deepened further the antagonism against the defendants' cause. It is wrong, but inevitably human, that Mr. Moore's behavior should have affected judgment about his clients. Unlike the prosecution, as we

[20] Vol. I, 474–475.

shall see, the defense did not have Judge Thayer to negate or mitigate indications of misconduct.

Louis Pelser, the young shoeworker, had recently been employed by Rice and Hutchins. He claimed that he looked out of a window and saw a bandit shooting Berardelli. Some writers have assumed that he identified the killer as Sacco. This is not so. After having alternately told different stories to both Moore and the assistant district attorney, he testified at the trial as follows:

Q. You say you wouldn't say it is him, but he is the dead image of him. What do you mean by that? A. Well, he has got the same appearance.
Q. Have you got any question in your own mind, but what he is the man?
(Objection by defense counsel overruled.)
A. I wouldn't say he is the man, but he is the dead image of the man I saw.[21]

Pelser also stated that he saw the escape car as it came up Pearl Street, got the registration number off the front plate and gave it to the police.

After the trial Pelser signed several affidavits which, according to him, indicated that he had been pressured hard by both sides. His retractions and re-retractions were such that even District Attorney Katzmann disowned him in his summation by declaring, "He falsified to the defense. He falsified to the Commonwealth." [22]

As if Pelser's own testimony was not unreliable enough, three fellow employees testified for the defense to the effect that Pelser had not been at the window at the time of the shooting.[23] Two of them were fired shortly after the trial.[24]

On any basis, Pelser's identification of Sacco does not merit serious consideration. Professor Edmund M. Morgan, in his analysis of the evidence at the Sacco-Vanzetti trial, characterized Pelser as "totally untrustworthy." [25]

Worthless as Pelser's testimony was as identification of Sacco, however, it intrigues me for a wholly different reason. He was the only witness who purported to identify Sacco as the bandit who shot Berardelli. He said he first heard three shots and then saw the man put the last shot into Berardelli.[26] He did not see any other person shooting the guard. Other wit-

21 Vol. I, 295.   22 Vol. II, 2212.
23 Brenner, Vol. II, 1122; McCullum, Vol. II, 1149; Constantino, Vol. II, 1166.
24 Russell, *Tragedy in Dedham*, 307.
25 Joughin and Morgan, *The Legacy of Sacco and Vanzetti*, 134.   26 Vol. I, 292.

nesses had also claimed that the murderer of Berardelli fired a succession of shots into him.[27]

Four bullets were extracted from Berardelli's body. Undisputed ballistic evidence was that only *one* of the bullets could have been fired from a Colt, the make of pistol owned by Sacco. The other three had a totally different twist. How then was it possible that only *one* bullet could have come through Sacco's pistol? The bandit who killed him did not fire two pistols at Berardelli, nor were there two bandits pumping bullets into him. Here was another mystery in the Sacco-Vanzetti case which will be considered in a later chapter.

Another new witness was Mrs. Lola R. Andrews. She had been interviewed by Mr. Moore at his home on January 14, 1921, and had given him a statement. At the trial she claimed that sometime after eleven o'clock on April 15 she saw two men near a parked car not far from the Slater and Morrill factory. She was looking for employment. On her way from the plant the darker of the two men had his head and shoulders under the car. As he was getting out from under the car, she spoke to him and asked how to get into the factory of Rice and Hutchins. The man then directed her. This man, she said, was Sacco. Mrs. Andrews was the only witness who claimed to have spoken to Sacco. She made no mention of his having any difficulty in speaking and understanding English, which would have marked Sacco at the time.

Mrs. Andrew's story was controverted by her friend and companion, Mrs. Julia Campbell, who was with her at the time.[28] Also, her testimony created another confusion in the government's identification evidence. She fixed the time when she saw the men at first as between 11:30 and 11:45 A.M.,[29] but on being pressed by Mr. Williams, said between 11 A.M. and 11:30 A.M. However, other government witnesses a few days later claimed to have seen Sacco at approximately the same time in other places. These were William S. Tracey, who said he saw Sacco near South Braintree Square between twenty-five and twenty minutes to twelve,[30] and William J. Heron, who said he saw him in the railroad station just after 12:30 A.M.[31] Officer George W. Fay of the Quincy Police Department testified that Mrs. Andrews had told him that she "did not see the faces of the Braintree men" [32] and Alfred N. LaBrecque, then secretary of the Quincy Chamber

[27] For instance, Wade, Vol. I, 211; Bostock, Vol. I, 189.   [28] Vol. II, 1309.
[29] Vol. I, 333.   [30] Vol. I, 500.   [31] Vol. I, 520.   [32] Vol. II, 1375.

of Commerce, testified that Mrs. Andrews had told him also "that she did not see the faces of the men in Braintree." [33]

Harry Kurlansky, who had run a tailoring business in Quincy since 1909 or 1910, had known Mrs. Andrews for seven or eight years. In the preceding February she had a conversation with him. This is the pertinent part of his testimony:

Q. (By Mr. McAnarney) Now tell us what was said. A. As I sat on my doorstep and as I know her I always spoke to her when she went by. I said to her, "Hello, Lola," and she stopped and she answered me. While she answered me I said, "you look kind of tired." She says, "Yes." She says, "They bothering the life out of me." I says, "What?". She says, "I just come up from jail." I says, "What have you done in jail?". She says, "The Government took me down and want me to recognize those men," she says, "and I don't know a thing about them. I have never seen them and I can't recognize them." She says, "Unfortunately, I have been down there to get a job and I have seen many men that I don't know and I have never paid any attention to any one." [34]

Mr. Katzmann's cross-examination failed to shake Mr. Kurlansky's testimony. However, Judge Thayer intervened to discredit the witness in the eyes of the jury:

THE COURT. Mr. Witness, I would like to ask one question. Did you attempt to find out who this person was who represented the Government who was trying to get her to take and state that which was false?
THE WITNESS. Did I what?
MR. JEREMIAH MCANARNEY. What is that question?
THE COURT. Did you try to find out who it was who represented the Government?
THE WITNESS. No.
THE COURT. Why not?
THE WITNESS. Well, it didn't come into my mind. I wasn't sure, you know. It didn't. . . .
THE COURT. Did you think the public interest was served by anybody representing the Government to try to get a woman. . . .
THE WITNESS. I don't think of anything —
THE COURT. — to identify somebody?
THE WITNESS. I don't think of anything at all.
MR. JEREMIAH MCANARNEY. Keep your voice up.
THE WITNESS. I don't think of anything like that just simply what she tell you.
THE COURT. Don't you think it would be a good idea to find out, if you could?

[33] Vol. II, 1377.   [34] Vol. II, 1378.

THE WITNESS. I think it would be.

THE COURT. I am trying to find out why you didn't do it.[35]

After the trial Mrs. Andrews, like Pelser, gave affidavits repudiating other affidavits she had made. Among these were affidavits that her testimony at the trial was false and affidavits that the statement she had given Moore on January 14, 1921 (which she had practically repudiated), was true. She claimed, in effect, that Mr. Moore had extracted these affidavits from her by threatening to expose certain disgraceful events in her past life. There was some confirmation of this claim. On the other hand, there was the trustworthy evidence that her reputation for veracity was very bad and that she had made false claims to collect insurance.[36]

The shoddy story of Mrs. Andrews as a witness is best dismissed in the words of Professor Morgan: "No rational person would punish a stray dog in reliance upon the word of such a woman." [37]

The third identifying witness produced was Carlos E. Goodridge, who saw the escaping car from Magazu's Pool Room as it moved up Pearl Street. He claimed that Sacco was one of the bandits in the car.[38] His story was impeached by four other men, to all of whom he had made prior contradictory statements.[39]

Goodridge had a long criminal history. He even had a charge of larceny pending in the same court where Sacco and Vanzetti were tried. Prior to testifying Goodridge had pleaded guilty; despite his lengthy criminal record his case had been "filed," and he had been placed on probation. Defendants' counsel tried to get in evidence of this lenient treatment in order to suggest that it biased Goodridge in favor of the prosecution. Judge Thayer excluded the evidence because "filing" the case was not a record of conviction and such a record was necessary in order to impeach Goodridge.[40] However, Mr. McAnarney was not seeking the evidence to impeach Goodridge's character but to show bias. There is a serious question as to whether Judge Thayer's ruling and that of the Supreme Judicial Court which upheld it constituted good law. For our story, however, that question is not the only nor even the most important one. Should we not also ask whether it was ethical for the prosecution, under the circumstances, to use this

---

[35] Vol. II, 1383.   [36] Vol. V, 5157; also Vol. II, 1600.
[37] Joughin and Morgan, *The Legacy of Sacco and Vanzetti*, 132–133.   [38] Vol. I, 545.
[39] Arrogoin, Vol. II, 1353; Magazu, Vol. II, 1356; Manganio, Vol. II, 1404; Damato, Vol. II, 1490.   [40] Vol. III, 2578.

witness to help expedite the defendants to the electric chair and to keep from the jury the knowledge of the extraordinary leniency extended to him by the prosecution?

As in the case of Mrs. Andrews, it is not worth the time to consider Goodridge's testimony seriously. It should be noted, however, that Mr. Moore, after trial, used on Goodridge rough tactics similar to those he had employed against Mrs. Andrews. Armed with Goodridge's very bad record, he went to Maine in the summer of 1922 and had a deputy sheriff take Goodridge to Augusta on a charge of larceny still outstanding in New York. When Moore demanded that Goodridge admit that Mr. Williams had argued, begged and fought with him to identify Sacco, Goodridge said, "You know just how those things is yourself." [41] However, he denied driving a bargain with the district attorney.

Let us dismiss Goodridge also, again in the words of Professor Morgan:

Newly discovered evidence demonstrated that the commission of grand larceny by Goodridge reflected his true character. It tended also to show that no prosecutor with knowledge of the facts and with any regard for the public welfare could have recommended probation. No matter what may be thought of Moore's contemptible treatment of Goodridge in attempting to secure from him a repudiation of his testimony at the trial, the facts remain: Goodridge was using an assumed name; in 1893 he had been sentenced to the reformatory at Elmira, New York, for larceny of two gold watches; in 1908 he had been sent to the Penitentiary at Auburn, New York, for larceny of money; in 1909 he had been divorced by his wife for adultery; in 1911 he had been indicted for further larceny in New York, but had fled; in 1913 he had been implicated in a questionable fire with the obvious intent to defraud an insurance company; he had lived in Vermont under various aliases with a woman not his wife; he had committed perjury to obtain a license to marry the second time; in 1919 he had been divorced by his second wife for cruel and inhuman treatment. In short, he was a confirmed scoundrel, to whom perjury in the hope of escaping a prison sentence would cause no hesitation.[42]

Two other witnesses were found who would claim to identify Sacco as a man they saw near South Braintree Square several hours before the shooting.

William Tracey, who was in the real estate business, saw two men near South Braintree Square before noon on April 15. There was no particular reason for him to notice the two men at the time. Ten months later he saw

[41] Vol. IV, 3885.   [42] Joughin and Morgan, *The Legacy of Sacco and Vanzetti*, 135.

Sacco in jail in the "pit" with two attendants.[43] He felt that his identification of Sacco was "right" but he wouldn't positively say so. As if to confirm the molding of eyewitness identification, Tracey said: "Well, he looks like the man that I have seen so many times, the *four* times that I have seen him. *I have seen him five times now, before I see him in this court room.*" [44] (Emphasis added.)

William Heron, a detective working for the New York, New Haven and Hartford Railroad, had been in the South Braintree railroad station at about twelve thirty on April 15. There were two men sitting in the station. Like Tracey, he had no particular reason to notice the two men. His story of his recognition of Sacco is reminiscent again of Harding's flash recognition of Vanzetti through a crack in the door, and of Dolbeare's identification of Vanzetti in the dock at Dedham as a man he had seen in an automobile. Heron happened to be at the Quincy courthouse when Sacco was brought there for a hearing. That did it apparently. He stated that the moment he saw Sacco, he remarked out loud: "When he got out of the car, I said, I said, 'Gee, that is the fellow I saw down at South Braintree the day of the shooting.' " [45] He thought that Chief Gallivan of South Braintree might have heard him make the remark and that this led to his being interviewed and called as a witness.

If we now follow Sacco's garb as seen by the government's identifying eyewitnesses at South Braintree, we will find that he made several changes of costume, sometimes within seconds.

At 11:20 to 11:35 on the morning of the crime, Sacco was allegedly seen under a car in front of the Rice and Hutchins shoe factory by Lola Andrews. Sacco was then wearing a dark suit.[46] By twenty-five or twenty minutes to twelve, however, Sacco appeared in front of Torrey's Drug Store on the corner of Washington and Pearl streets near South Braintree Square several blocks away, according to the witness Mr. Tracey. Although he had apparently just crawled from under a car on a dusty road, he was then dressed "respectably." [47] He had a soft hat on.[48] At 12:27, Sacco was in the railroad station (near Hampton House), according to Heron, the railroad detective. He was wearing a black soft felt hat[49] and a dark suit.[50] By the time of the shooting, however, at about 3 P.M., Sacco had changed into dark green pants and a brown army shirt, according to the witness Pelser.

[43] Vol. I, 509.   [44] Vol. I, 510.   [45] Vol. I, 538.   [46] Vol. I, 336.
[47] Vol. I, 500–507.   [48] Vol. I, 505.   [49] Vol. I, 519–523.   [50] Vol. I, 524.

As the escape car crossed the tracks and moved up Pearl Street, Miss Mary Splaine glimpsed Sacco standing between the front and rear seats. He was now bareheaded, coatless but wearing a gray woolen shirt.[51] (The prosecution would later forget the black soft felt hat which Sacco had allegedly worn earlier in the day and would claim that he lost a cap at the murder scene. This disappearing hat act parallels the twist in the Plymouth trial, where evidence of the shotgun bandit's soft felt hat was also discarded to make way for testimony to the effect that a bandit supposed to be Vanzetti was wearing his cap.) A few seconds after Miss Splaine saw the light gray shirt on Sacco, the witness Goodridge from Magazu's Pool Room allegedly saw Sacco in the escaping car. Sacco was still bareheaded, but he had now resumed the dark suit seen earlier in the day.[52]

With these transformations we may now leave the eyewitness identification which the prosecution used to convict the defendants of the South Braintree murders and pass on to physical objects or "real" evidence available to the district attorney. The government's proof of the defendants' guilt based on these things will be dealt with in the next and succeeding chapters.

14.

Biography of a Cap

In preparing their case, the prosecution must have reviewed the physical evidence then in their possession or control. They must also have discussed its value as trial evidence and what it might still need to become more convincing proof of the defendants' guilt.

Some of the items of proof available to them had already been used at the Plymouth trial. These would include the Buick car abandoned in the woods off Manley Street, Boda's shed in Bridgewater where the radicals must have secreted the car — along with the ancient Overland — and the shotgun cartridges claimed to have been taken from Vanzetti's pockets on the night of his arrest. However, since the prosecution theory was that both

[51] Vol. I, 229.   [52] Vol. I, 545.

crimes were committed by the same gang, these things could be used again. There would be even less risk in displaying the Buick at the Dedham trial, since there was no doubt that the murder car had been a Buick, whereas at Plymouth there was the evidence, successfully fenced off, that the holdup automobile was a Hudson. The Boda-Coacci shed could be shown even more dramatically to the new jury, since there would now be a buried treasure mystery which could be added to the view. The shotgun shells would present problems, however, because two of them had been surreptitiously opened by the Plymouth jury and no shotgun had been used or even seen for certain at the South Braintree affair. Since the remaining two shells actually were introduced later at the Dedham trial, we may assume that Mr. Katzmann was not baffled by these difficulties. His powers of persuasion had already convinced a jury that Vanzetti had carried the telltale shells in his pocket from the day before Christmas in 1919 to the fifth of May in 1921. He must have felt confident that he would be able to finesse the two remaining shells past the suspicions of defendants' counsel at Dedham. If so, his confidence proved to be justified.

There was also Vanzetti's revolver, which Judge Thayer had admitted at the close of the Plymouth trial. However, in that case it had no relevance other than to suggest that Vanzetti was a dangerous character. With adequate preparation it might be used far more effectively at Dedham.

Physical evidence which had not been used previously included the following: a cap found on Pearl Street in South Braintree after the shooting; six bullets extracted from the bodies of the murdered men; exploded shells ejected by automatic pistols and picked up at the scene of the crime; a clip of a number of cartridges in Sacco's pistol and loose cartridges found in his pocket on his arrest, and fingerprints allegedly lifted from the murder car and compared with fingerprints of Sacco and Vanzetti. Such items belonged to a higher order of evidence than eyewitness identification, which is untrustworthy at best and often subject to crushing refutation. Physical evidence, if genuine and not the subject of debatable opinion, could be proof positive of guilt. For instance, if the cap retrieved at the place of the shooting could be shown to have belonged to Sacco, the jury could hardly avoid finding that he had been at the murder scene and that he was one of the bandits. And if the defendants were convicted, the fact that there was evidence that Sacco had left his cap on the ground during the shooting would be a powerful bar to his obtaining a new trial. The cap, therefore, could become a most important piece of evidence — if it could be shown to have been Sacco's.

In 1927 some facts were revealed which indicated that the government's trial evidence was misleading or false. Thereafter, authorities reviewing the trial and some writers began to regard the cap as unimportant. All of the government's elaborately prepared proof that the cap was Sacco's was shunted aside by asserting that it was not very significant anyway. This, however, was far from the fact.

Prior to the discovery of the falseness of the government's claim, "Sacco's cap" had been a most important factor in molding judicial and public opinion. Of course, we do not know how much effect it had on the jury, although one juror, Alfred Atwood, is reported to have told a friend that what convinced him of Sacco's guilt was the way he tried on the stray cap. Probably the jurors themselves did not know — it was too much an integral part of the whole case to be singled out. Mr. Katzmann made much of it in presenting the evidence and in his summation. Judge Thayer used it in three separate opinions to justify his denial of motions for a new trial.[1] In one of these opinions, he said:

That one Mr. Kelley, Sacco's employers, testified that Sacco wore a cap, that it was similar in some respects to that which was picked up near the dead body of Berardelli; he also testified that Sacco hung his cap upon a nail near the machine where he worked; and, in the lining of that cap there were holes, which the Commonwealth claimed were made by the nail upon which this cap had been hung. Now, the Supreme Judicial Court has said, in the decision of these cases, that that evidence was competent because it tended to prove that that cap belonged to Sacco; and if the Jury should find such to be the fact, then Sacco was present at the time of the shooting.[2]

Although Judge Thayer added from his imagination much more than the Supreme Judicial Court had actually said (it did, however, cite the cap as a part of the evidence which could justify a conviction), the quotation shows the potency of the government's cap evidence on his judgment. Its effect on some lawyers was similar. My friend Max Steuer, Esq., then perhaps the most successful trial lawyer in the United States, made a speech before a bar association denouncing those who questioned the guilt of Sacco and Vanzetti. When I asked him what he knew about the case, he replied, "Wasn't Sacco's cap found at the scene of the murders? That's enough for

[1] Vol. V, 4765, 5555; Vol. IV, 3517.   [2] Vol. V, 4765.

me." Robert H. Montgomery, Esq., indignant defender of all of the Sacco-Vanzetti proceedings, attacked Professor Frankfurter by letter for omitting from his *Atlantic Monthly* article any mention of the supposedly crucial cap evidence. (It was, indeed, omitted, but was later included when the piece was published in book form.)

The complete account of the cap, and how the prosecution used it, has never been told. About all that had been known prior to the present writing about the deceptive use of the cap evidence has been Chief Gallivan's testimony before the Governor's Advisory Committee in 1927. In order to understand what happened, it is necessary to coordinate various bits of evidence from the record, the Pinkerton reports and the press. This I shall now endeavor to do. It may help to clarify the discussion if we divide it into two parts: the first dealing with the actual facts about the cap; and the second, the cap evidence as presented by the prosecution.

In seeking to ascertain the actual facts about the cap, we turn again to what was known *prior to the arrest of Sacco and Vanzetti*. Such material is free from the distortion caused by preconception or from the taint of a determination to convict. It should also assist the reader to follow the story if he knows at this stage that the cap was claimed to have been found by *Fred L. Loring*, an employee of Slater and Morrill, who gave it to *Thomas F. Fraher*, his superintendent, who delivered it to *Jeremiah F. Gallivan*, then chief of the Braintree police in active charge of the investigation, who later turned it over to *John Scott*, an officer of the State Police. Especially is it important to keep an eye on Mr. Loring and Mr. Fraher and to watch the timing of the sequence of events.

At the outset, it should be noted that *no witness at the inquest on April 17 mentioned the finding of any cap on April 15*, the day of the murder. Some of these witnesses had reached the prostrate bodies of Parmenter and Berardelli and had ministered to them almost immediately after the shooting. Others were part of the throng that streamed out of the factories within minutes thereafter. Mr. Fraher testified at the inquest. He did not mention that morning that Mr. Loring had given him a cap. In fact, he stated that he had just talked over the telephone with Mr. Loring, who was then in Boston, and discussed certain suspects with him. When asked if he knew anything further that would help in the detection of the robbers, he told about the telephone talk with Loring, *but nothing about a cap*.[3] From

[3] Supp. Vol., 413.

this alone, it would seem to be manifest that *no cap was found on Pearl Street on April 15, 1920*. It would have been of unestimable value to the defendants if their counsel had seen the minutes of the "private" inquest then resting in Mr. Katzmann's file.

The first mention of any cap being found in South Braintree occurs in the *Boston Herald* for *April 17, 1920*. There we read that an "employee of Slater and Morrill *found a cap in the middle of the road last night* (April 16) *near the factory as he left the building*." (Emphasis added.) He gave it to Mr. Fraher, who gave it to Chief Gallivan.

It is immaterial at this point whether the employee mentioned was Mr. Loring.

This contemporary newspaper account nails down the fact that the cap was found in the street *on the night of the day following the murders*.

We did not know of this newspaper story when Chief Gallivan testified before the Governor's Advisory Committee seven years later. It was only when I checked back through the newspaper files for April 1920 that I stumbled across it.

We meet the cap again in the report of Pinkerton operative H.H. for April 19, 1920. There we read that: "Chief Gallivan showed me the cap. . . . The cap was an old dark color heavy winter cap *about 6⅞ size*." (Emphasis added.)

This is the only reference anywhere to the size number of the Pearl Street cap. Although apparently not a precise measurement, it is an important documentation, as we shall see, since Sacco wore a cap size 7⅛.[4] The size of the Pearl Street cap was never revealed to the jury.

Chief Gallivan, in 1927, told the Governor's Advisory Committee what he did with the cap handed to him by Mr. Fraher. He was being questioned by Mr. Thompson:

[Chief Gallivan] . . . Now, I suppose you want to know something about that cap?

Q. Yes. A. It was Saturday morning when Tom Fraher, Superintendent of Slater & Morrill's factory, called me on the telephone down there.

PRESIDENT LOWELL. When, Saturday morning?

Q. What day was this murder? A. Thursday afternoon.

Q. How do you spell his name? A. Some call him (spelling) F-r-a-y-e-r, some call him (spelling) F-r-a-h-e-r; I think that's the way to spell it. I know him very well; he called me down and says, "Jerry, here's a cap that was picked up there"

4 Vol. II, 1851.

— Now, I understood him to say "last night, last evening," but "*I don't know whether it amounts to anything or not, but I thought you better keep it here.*"

Q. "*Picked up last evening.*" *That would be Friday evening?* A. *Yes, sir.* So I took the cap and looked at it, and if you were to put the cap before me now I wouldn't know it; I haven't seen that cap for seven years. I took it and looked at it and I took it with me in my automobile. Have in mind we had no police headquarters there at that time; my headquarters then was in my house or in any officer's house. I took that cap, not knowing whether it was going to amount to anything or not. I took it and I says, "I may find a name or something inside this cap." Let me say here why I did that. I identified a man that had been dead for over six months by his cap by the name that was on the inside of it, he was a military fellow that was found hanging to a tree, he evidently hung in the fall and he was not found until the following spring, and the only way to identify him was by his cap, and on the inside was marked "Nason" or, "Mason." I won't say which, but as I read it off it was "Nason," but one of the letters in the name on the inside rim had become erased and it made "Nason," and we found out he belonged over here in the Navy Yard. I am just telling you that to let you know why I looked in this cap. I took that cap and made it as small as I could and pulled the inside out, but I couldn't make much headway with it, so I took and ripped that lining right down myself, but there was nothing inside there.

PRESIDENT LOWELL. (Addressing the witness) You ripped the whole lining out?

THE WITNESS. No, not the whole lining, but I tore that, and I think you will find a tear in that lining yet. I haven't seen it for seven years. *That cap was whole when it was given to me, but I am the fellow that tore it.* I tore that hat. I took and kept it in my automobile; there was no other place to keep it as we had no headquarters. Finally I turned it over, possible about ten days or two weeks after, I turned that hat over to John Scott.

Q. John Scott was the State Policeman? A. Yes, sir, and he lived in Braintree I know Scott very well and have known him for a long time.

Q. Where did you keep it in your automobile? A. I kept it underneath the rear seat.

Q. It got a little dirty, didn't it, that way? A. I wouldn't say it had, a great deal.

Q. It would not be a place where you would put clean linen? A. Well, I put food in there.

Q. Some dirt might get on the cap. You put it under there and kept it for two weeks? A. Pretty near two weeks.

Q. Did you ever see that cap again? A. *I saw it in the Dedham Court.*[5]

He later added that he "*saw the cap when it was handed to Tom Fraher, I was there at that time.*" (Emphasis added.)

Chief Gallivan then described how he made the tear in the lining:

JUDGE GRANT. (Addressing the witness) Didn't you say that there was a little hole?

[5] Vol. V, 5169–5170.

THE WITNESS. I said I started to make a little hole to see if I could start it, and I didn't make much headway and I tore it more.

PRESIDENT LOWELL. (Addressing the witness) There was a little hole?

THE WITNESS. No. I started to make a little hole to get onto the inside to see what was between the lining; the lining was sewed onto the hat. If I remember, there was some wool around here (indicating) and I was trying to get that out through the hole that I made myself. There wasn't a hole in the hat, I made a hole, I was trying to get that out through the hole that I made myself. *That lining was perfectly whole when that hat was given to me.* [Emphasis added.][6]

Later, he said:

Q. (By Mr. Thompson) I thought you said you thought he told you it had been picked up the night before but you were not sure of his saying that? A. What I was not sure of is this: Whether he picked it up or some man named Loring; he led me to believe that he picked it up himself, that is the impression I got, that he picked it up himself, and not Loring, the evening before, that would be the Friday before. I don't know whether it amounts to anything or not, but he says, "Oh, you better take it." So I took it. I didn't know anything about the tear. Let me explain that. *The first testimony I heard about the tear was when it was offered as evidence on the stand over a year afterwards, and then when Tom Fraher or anybody else gets on and says that that hat is in identically the same condition as when they handed it to me that is not so because that hat was torn.*

Q. (By Mr. Ranney) Who was the first person you told about having torn it? A. Have you got all through asking me questions or are you going to start over again?

Q. I will ask you some more. Apparently, Mr. Gallivan, you seem to take a hostile attitude towards representatives of the Commonwealth. A. No, I do not. *There's a right and wrong to this thing, that's all there is to it.* [Emphasis added.][7]

We may now summarize the salient features which mark the Pearl Street cap and its discovery:

1. It was found on the evening of April 16, 1920, *which was the next day after the murders.*

2. It was picked up by someone in the *middle of the street.*

3. It was approximately No. 6⅞ size.

4. Its lining was *perfectly whole* when given to Chief Gallivan.

5. The tear in the lining was made by Chief Gallivan looking for identification marks.

6. He kept it in his automobile (under the seat, as he later explained) for about ten days or two weeks.

[6] Vol. V, 5171.   [7] Vol. V, 5183.

7. Neither Mr. Fraher, nor Mr. Loring, nor Chief Gallivan attached any importance to the finding of the cap.

None of the foregoing facts was made known to the judge or jury. Chief Gallivan was not called as a witness, although any proper prosecution required that the history and custody of its exhibits should be traced. It is important to keep in mind the foregoing established facts when we examine the government's presentation of the cap. It is also important to note that at the time the cap was found neither Mr. Fraher, Mr. Loring, nor Chief Gallivan apparently had any thought that the cap found in the street on the night of April 16 might have fallen off the head of a bandit on the afternoon of April 15. Nevertheless, at the Dedham trial, it became Sacco's cap. How was this done?

Now lt us examine the cap evidence as presented by the prosecution.

The Pearl Street cap was introduced into the case by Fred Loring. He testified that he was a shoeworker employed by Slater and Morrill. He was working there on the day of the shooting. He heard "them" speaking about the shooting, looked out of the window and went to the scene of the murders. He saw the body of Berardelli. This is what he said about finding the cap:

Q. (By Mr. Williams) Where was the body of Berardelli lying with reference to the sidewalk, or the street, on that side of the street? A. *Right in the gutter, but on the sidewalk.*

Q. Now, when you arrived at the scene, was there anything which you noticed on the street near the body of Berardelli? A. A cap.

Q. Where was the cap? A. *It was about 18 inches from Berardelli's body, towards the street.*

Q. Did you do anything in regard to that cap? A. *Yes. I picked it up.*

Q. What did you do with it? A. Carried it down to the shop, kept it about an hour, looked it over, and finally carried it in the office *and gave it to Mr. Fraher.*

Q. Is that F-r-a-y-e-r? A. Fraher.

(Mr. Williams hands a bundle to the witness.)

Q. Will you open that bundle, and see if you can tell the jury what it is? A. That is the cap.

Q. Do you mean the cap you found there that day? A. *Found beside the body.*

Q. And gave to Mr. Fraher? A. Yes, sir.

Q. *Can you tell whether it is in the same condition now as when you found it?* A. *Just the same.* [Emphasis added.][8]

[8] Vol. I, 798.

Almost every one of the foregoing statements is contrary to established facts:

1. The cap was found on the evening of April 16, not in the afternoon of April 15.

2. When it was found, it was lying in the middle of the street, not on the sidewalk or "18 inches from Berardelli's body." It was not lying "beside the body." By the time the cap was picked up, there was no body in Pearl Street; it had been removed the day before and the autopsy had already been performed in the undertaker's rooms at Randolph.[9]

3. When offered in evidence at the trial, the cap was definitely *not* in the same condition as when Mr. Loring found it — if he did. As we shall see, the cap now identified by Mr. Loring *at the trial* had a torn lining. This was the tear made by Chief Gallivan *after* Mr. Loring claimed to have found it. At this point in Mr. Loring's testimony, there was no mention of the tear. The purpose of the last question and the false answer was to quietly lay the basis for a later claim that the tear was caused by Sacco's habit of hanging his cap on a nail.

On objection by defendants' counsel, the cap was not yet admitted, for lack of evidence that it belonged to Sacco. It was, however, marked for identification.

On cross-examination, Mr. Loring stated that when he looked out of the window, he saw "a crowd of about forty out there." [10] (Chief Gallivan said that two or three thousand people thronged the streets.)[11]

Mr. Williams later attempted to introduce the Pearl Street cap as evidence. He tried to get the needed link to Sacco through George T. Kelley, Sacco's superintendent at the 3–K shoe factory in Stoughton. He was not very successful. This is what Mr. Kelley said:

Q. What kind of head gear was Sacco accustomed to wear, if you know? A. There were times that he wore a cap. There was other times he wore a hat.

Q. What kind of a cap have you seen him wearing? A. I have seen him wear a dark cap.

Q. Could you describe it any more than that? A. I do not know as I could go into it in detail, outside of knowing that it was a dark cap.

Q. Well, have you in talking it over with anybody, described it in any different terms or more in detail than that? A. I have said of a salt and pepper design.

[9] Supp. Vol., 395.   [10] Vol. I, 801.   [11] Vol. V, 5182.

Q. How was it in regard to anything else? Can you tell us anything further in regard to it that you recall? A. No, sir.

Q. What have you seen in regard to this cap, if anything? A. Nothing more than coming in to work and hanging it up on a nail.

Q. What can you tell us in regard to its condition? As to whether it was old or new clean or dirty? A. Why, I should say it was naturally dirty.

Q. I wish you would look at what has been introduced for identification as No. 11 [the Pearl Street cap], and let me ask you, to the best of your recollection, knowledge and belief, if that cap is alike in appearance to the cap that you have described as being worn by Sacco? A. (Witness examines cap.) The only thing I could say about that cap, Mr. Williams, from hanging up on a nail in the distance, it was similar in color. As far as details are concerned, I could not say it was.

Q. You have been shown that cap before? A. Yes, sir. Of course, you realize that inside there (indicating) the earlappers, and so forth, I never had any way of examining that cap to see if the ear laps were in there. The only method I had of looking at the cap from observation was if it hung on a nail somewhere, just passing by and knowing whether it was black, white or green.

Q. Do you know if anything had happened to Sacco's cap by reason of it being hung up on a nail? A. By reason of what might occur?

Q. Do you know if anything had occurred to his cap by reason of being hung up on a nail? A. No, sir.

Q. Have you examined the lining of this cap? A. I did.

Q. What do you notice to be the condition of the lining? A. Torn.[12]

As he had done at Plymouth to help Mr. Katzmann get another unidentified cap (and the unidentified shotgun shells) into evidence, Judge Thayer intervened to aid the prosecution to better identify the Pearl Street cap with Sacco's cap. He was no more successful than the assistant district attorney (nor was he at Plymouth). But his failure did not prevent him from admitting the cap and having it marked Exhibit 29. He was the judge. This is how the stray cap got admitted into the evidence:

MR. WILLIAMS. If your Honor please, I offer this cap in evidence. It has been marked for identification, and I now offer it as an exhibit.

MR. JEREMIAH MCANARNEY. I object.

THE COURT. I would like to ask the witness one question: whether, — I wish you would ask him, rather, — according to your best judgment, is it your opinion that the cap which Mr. Williams now holds in his hand is like the one that was worn by the defendant Sacco?

MR. MOORE. I object to that question, your Honor.

THE COURT. (To Mr. Williams) Did you put it? I would rather it came from Mr. Williams. Will you put that question?

Q. Mr. Kelley, according to your best judgment, is the cap I show you alike in appearance to the cap worn by Sacco? A. In color only.

[12] Vol. I, 853–854.

THE COURT. That is not responsive to the question. I wish you would answer it, if you can.

THE WITNESS. I can't answer it when I don't know right down in my heart that that is the cap.

THE COURT. I don't want you to. I want you should answer according to what is in your heart.

THE WITNESS. General appearance, that is all I can say. I never saw that cap so close in my life as I do now.

THE COURT. In its general appearance, is it the same?

THE WITNESS. Yes, sir.

MR. MOORE. I object to that last question and answer.

THE COURT. You may put the question so it comes from counsel rather than from the Court.

Q. In its general appearance, is it the same? A. Yes.

MR. WILLIAMS. I now offer the cap, if your Honor please.

THE COURT. Admitted.

MR. MOORE. Save an exception.

MR. JEREMIAH MCANARNEY. Save an exception.

(The cap is admitted in evidence and marked Exhibit 29.)

MR. WILLIAMS. (Passing Exhibit 29 to the jury) Notice the outside and inside. You may inquire.[13]

Up to this point, the Pearl Street cap, Exhibit 29, has been compared only with a description of Sacco's cap. However, the government had in its possession a genuine Sacco cap. As in the Plymouth trial, the police searched the defendant's home without authority and had removed some of his garments, including one of his caps. This cap was used extensively in the trial as "Exhibit 27 for identification," but was not formally admitted as an exhibit until Lieutenant Guerin of the Brockton police identified it, at which time the officer swore that it was *in the same condition as when he obtained it*.[14] Mr. McAnarney and Mr. Moore objected, Mr. Moore stating that it was on the ground of unlawful search and seizure. Judge Thayer nevertheless admitted the cap as Exhibit 43, stating that Mr. Moore had already made many inquiries about the cap from the defendant Sacco and Mrs. Sacco.

Let us now see what the prosecution did with the Pearl Street cap. It seems unlikely that the prosecution did not know that Mr. Loring's testimony about how it was found was anything but the truth. The government's case shows the most thorough preparation and both the district attorney and his assistant were trial lawyers, wise and competent in the use of evidence. Seven years later, before the Governor's Advisory Committee,

[13] Vol. I, 857.   [14] Vol. II, 2093–2094.

Mr. Katzmann claimed that he had no recollection of Chief Gallivan having the cap in his automobile for a week or two and that he had never heard of Gallivan having made the tear inside of it.[15] (At the time neither Mr. Thompson nor I knew the other conclusive facts which would have destroyed the cap as evidence, had defense counsel been aware of them.)

One may well doubt the accuracy of Mr. Katzmann's recollection. Chief Gallivan was an obligatory witness. What reason was there for not calling him to the stand except that the prosecution knew that his testimony would upset their plan to prove by indisputable physical evidence that Sacco was present as one of the murderers in South Braintree?

The cap taken by the police from Sacco's home made its first appearance at the trial during the cross-examination of Sacco.[16] (At that time it was marked Exhibit 27 for identification.)[17] It was on that occasion that Mr. Katzmann made Sacco try on both caps, his own cap that came out of police custody and the cap found in Pearl Street. The examination is revealing. In the excerpt from Sacco's testimony that follows, the cap referred to as Exhibit 29 is the stray cap and the cap called Exhibit 27 is admittedly Sacco's cap.

THE COURT. Will the defendant Sacco please return to the stand.

Q. I show you a cap. Will you look it over, please, and tell me if you know whose cap that is?

MR. MOORE. May —

(Mr. Moore confers with the court.)

MR KATZMANN. Don't answer for a minute.

THE COURT. You may answer the question.

Q. It is all right now. A. It looks like my cap.

Q. Yes. Did you have such a cap as that in your house at the time of your arrest? A. Yes, sir, something like.

Q. You think it is.

MR. KATZMANN. Did you speak, your Honor?

THE COURT. No.

MR. KATZMANN. Oh, I thought you spoke.

THE WITNESS. I said, "something like."

Q. Isn't it your cap? A. I think it is my cap, yes.

Q. Well, wait a minute, please. Look at it carefully, will you? A. (Witness examines cap.) Yes.

Q. There isn't any question but what that is your hat, is there?

THE COURT. "Cap," you mean.

MR. KATZMANN. Cap.

A. No, I think it is my cap.

[15] Vol. V, 5077.   [16] Vol. II, 2093.   [17] Vol. II, 1929.

MR. JEREMIAH MCANARNEY. I don't hear you.

MR. KATZMANN. "No, I think it is my cap."

Q. Will you try that cap on, please, and watch yourself when you put it on, just how you put it on? A. (Witness does so.)

Q. Will you turn around so the jury can see, all the way, please? A. (Witness does so.)

Q. The other side, this side. Is there anything you want to say? Did I catch you as wanting to say something? I thought perhaps you did. A. I don't know. That cap looks too dirty to me because I never wear dirty cap. I think I always have fifty cents to buy a cap, and I don't work with a cap on my head when I work. I always keep clean cap. Right when I go to the factory, take all my clothes off and put overalls and jump. It look to me pretty dirty and too dark. Mine I think was little more light, little more gray.

Q. Is that your hat?

THE COURT. Confine it to cap.

MR. KATZMANN. I beg your pardon.

Q. Is it your cap? I should not say "hat." Cap? A. I think it is. It looks like, but it is probably dirt, — probably dirty after.

Q. When you had it on, was that buttoned or unbuttoned when you just put it on? A. It was buttoned.

Q. Put it on again and keep it buttoned, will you, please? A. Sure. (Doing so.)

Q. On pretty hard? A. No, well, all right.

Q. All right. Now, will you try — A. Not very loose.

Q. Not very loose? A. No.

Q. Will you try Exhibit 29 on, and use the same amount of force in putting it on that you used in putting that hat on? A. Yes. (Doing so) Can't go in.

Q. Can't go in? A. No.

Q. Try and pull it down in back and see if it can't go in? A. *Oh, but it is too tight.*

Q. What is the difference in size between those two hats? A. I don't know, but it looks that is tight to me.

Q. *Is it any tighter than that hat?* A. *Yes, lots.*

Q. *Lots tighter?* A. *Yes.*

Q. You are sure of that? A. I am pretty sure. I can feel it.

Q. You can feel it? A. Yes.

Q. Is there any difference in the weight of material between the one that I now hold in my left hand and the one you have on your head? A. Lots of difference.

Q. Yes. Now, assuming that they are the same head size, would one seem any tighter than the other because of the difference in the weight of material? A. I don't say if it is material.

Q. Look at the hats themselves. Any difference in head size between them? A. It has more material over there inside than this.

MR. KATZMANN. I will offer this hat. I can't offer it now, but I ask it to be marked for identification.

[Sacco's cap marked "Exhibit 27 for identification."]

MR. MOORE. (To the witness) Do you want an interpreter?

THE WITNESS. All right. If you say so, all right.

MR. KATZMANN. I think it would be well to follow his suggestion.

[The testimony of the witness, however, is not given through an interpreter.]

Q. I call your attention to Exhibit 27 for identification, to that in the lining. What is it? A. I never saw that before.

Q. What is it? A. I don't know.

Q. Don't know what that is? A. *It is a hole.*

Q. *It is a hole?* A. *Yes.*

Q. *And you never saw that before?* A. *No.*

Q. *Still you say that is your hat?* A. *Sure. Never saw that before.*

Q. Never saw that before. Was there any hole in your hat when you last saw it? A. Hole, no.

Q. Sure of that? A. Pretty sure.

Q. Where did you hang your hats up? If this is your hat, did you ever wear it to work? A. Yes.

Q. What do you hang it up on? A. On a wall.

Q. On what on the wall? A. On the stake, on two stakes.

Q. Two stakes? A. Yes, sticks.

Q. Sticks of wood? A. One go across and put my jacket, my pants.

Q. Is there a hook there? A. What do you mean, a hook?

Q. A hat hook, or clothes hook? A. Yes, I made myself, for the purpose.

Q. What is it made of? A. Sticks.

Q. That is wood? A. Yes. Then there is a nail through.

Q. *Is it on the nail you hang your hat?* A. *Yes.*

Q. That is something you put up for yourself in the Kelley Shop, wasn't it? A. Yes. [Emphasis added.][18]

We can perhaps understand Sacco's difficulty in trying to pull a 6⅞ size cap with ear flaps over a 7⅛ size head. Even the newspaper cartoonists caught the humor of it and depicted the cap sitting on Sacco's head looking like a perched sparrow. It should also be noted that his own cap showed a hole in the lining *which Sacco claimed he had never seen before. Rose Sacco, Nicola's wife, also testified that she never saw a hole in her husband's cap.*[19] Mr. Katzmann did not cross-examine her about the cap. This paved the way for the talk about hanging his cap on a nail, which it was alleged caused the tear (actually made by Gallivan) in Exhibit 29. This also explains Officer Guerin's testimony that when he appropriated Sacco's cap it was in the same condition as when he identified it. This was intended to forestall Sacco's expected denial that his cap had a tear in it. As with other government exhibits, there apparently was no memorandum made when the item passed into the possession of the police, so that there was no way of checking whether they had tampered with it while they held it in cus-

[18] Vol. II, 1927–1930.   [19] Vol. II, 2065.

tody. Officer Guerin may have told the truth, and Sacco and his wife may have lied, about the cap's condition, but when one recalls that Mr. Loring falsely made the same statement about the condition of the Pearl Street cap when he claimed to have found it next to Berardelli's body, skepticism is justified. The tear in Sacco's cap may have been made by the police to make the jury believe that Exhibit 29 was Sacco's cap because it also had a tear in its lining, supposedly caused by hanging it on a nail in the 3–K factory.

Throughout a substantial part of the trial, the Pearl Street cap was batted back and forth by prosecution and defense like the bird in a badminton game. For us this battle no longer has any relevancy as proof. However, it does indicate the importance which both sides, at the trial, attached to the issue. The significance of this prolonged contest could not have been lost on the jury.

On one occasion, during the running battle over the cap, George Kelley admitted making a remark that must have hurt Sacco a great deal. He had been recalled by the defense to give further testimony by comparing Exhibits 27 and 29. He testified that Exhibit 27 was more like the cap he had in mind as being "Nick's" cap.[20] On cross-examination by Mr. Katzmann, he stated that he and Sacco had visited in each other's homes frequently, that they were intimate friends and he was fond of Sacco.[21] Mr. Katzmann brought this out to show that Mr. Kelley might have been biased in his cap testimony. However, this testimony might have helped Sacco more than it hurt him. Mr. Katzmann also asked Mr. Kelley whether, in giving his initial testimony about the cap, he was moved by fear, to which Mr. Kelley replied, "No." [22] Mr. Katzmann then brought out that a week or so before the opening of the trial Officers Stewart and Brouillard had a conversation with him. (This was the team selected by Mr. Katzmann to prepare the evidence for the prosecution after he had dismissed Captain Proctor and shelved Chief Gallivan.) They pressed Mr. Kelley repeatedly to say whether or not the Pearl Street cap (which they displayed) was or was not Sacco's cap. Mr. Katzmann, with the dramatic sense of the skillful advocate, then brought the jurors to the edge of their seats with the following questions:

MR. KATZMANN. (To the jury) I just want you gentlemen to hear this question. I don't want to speak it out loud. The reason will be obvious.

20 Vol. II, 2004.   21 Vol. II, 2007.   22 Vol. II, 2009.

Q. Did you then say to them, — did they say to you, "Is that Sacco's cap?" referring to the dark cap? A. Yes.

Q. Did you then say, "I have my opinion about the cap, but I don't want to get a bomb up my ass." Did you then say that? "I have my opinion about the cap, but I don't want to get a bomb up my ass." Did you then say that to those officers? A. I might have.

Q. Did you?

MR. JEREMIAH MCANARNEY. That question is objected to, if your Honor please.

THE COURT. Yes.

MR. JEREMIAH MCANARNEY. And exception noted.

Q. Didn't you, Mr. Kelley? A. Sometime during the conversation, but not then.

Q. Sometime during the conversation? A. Yes, sir.

Q. They asked you to give a definite answer, "Is it or is it not his cap?" A. Yes, they asked me.

Q. Didn't you reply on each occasion, "I have my opinion about the cap, but I don't want to get a bomb up my ass"? A. *That part I can't remember.*

Q. Do you say you did not say that? A. *I said the last part there. I might have said it when they drove off, but not at the time when they showed me the cap.*

Q. Was that in reference to the cap? A. Yes.

Q. When you made the remark? A. Yes, surely. [Emphasis added.][23]

It should be observed that the above excerpt shows that Mr. Kelley admitted only the remark about the bomb, and not that he said, "I have my own opinion about the cap," words which Mr. Katzmann incorporated in his question. He also denied that what he said was his reply "on each occasion," or that he made it at the time he was shown the cap, but indicated that he might have said it as Stewart and Brouillard drove off. Even with the qualifications made by Mr. Kelley, however, the part which he admitted saying must have damaged Sacco's defense. The jurors may not have believed that Mr. Kelley's testimony was influenced by fear, but nevertheless the remark about the bomb might have recharged the atmosphere of danger which enveloped the trial from its beginning.

We do not know why Mr. Kelley, the warm friend of Sacco, threw this remark after the policemen as they left. Defense counsel abstained from asking Mr. Kelley any questions about it on re-direct. They probably wanted no more talk about bombs. Did it indicate that Mr. Kelley was restrained by fear from yielding to Chief Stewart's pressure to identify a cap as Sacco's? Or does it suggest that Mr. Kelley was spoofing Chief Stewart,

[23] Vol. II, 2010.

who thought in such sensational terms?[24] Or did he merely want to stop Chief Stewart from badgering him further about the matter by giving an excuse for not talking which he knew was quite in line with Stewart's ideas about anarchists? We will never know. George Kelley died after the trial, but before the case was closed by the execution of his friend Sacco.

So long as we are speculating as to why Mr. Kelley refused to depart from the truth to affirm an untruth, we might also ask what prompted Mr. Loring to switch from facts to fantasy. Could fear be suggested in his case? It would be a different kind of fear, it is true, but a potent one. He could have been afraid of meeting the fate that awaited Lewis Wade and Winfred Pierce (and two employees of Rice and Hutchins) after they failed to cooperate with the prosecution. The fear of losing his job can be a potent influence on the testimony of a workingman.

The prosecution's unfairness about the cap received a fresh impetus in Mr. Katzmann's summation at the close of the trial. Here is how Mr. Katzmann began his argument about the cap:

But that is not all, gentlemen. He has falsified to you before your very faces. When Exhibit 43, his own cap that Lieut. Guerin says he got out of his own house was produced and shown to him before Lieut. Guerin testified he would not admit, gentlemen, that his own cap was his. What is there about that cap, which admittedly was not picked up on the scene of the murder, that would drive him from truth? Do you believe Guerin?

Do you think a man who has risen high enough in the police department in the city of Brockton, a great police department, do you think a lieutenant of that department would on his oath commit the perjurious utterance of saying that was Sacco's cap and that he took it out of his house and that it is in the same condition now as then if that were a fabrication?

And Sacco denied it. Why, gentlemen of the jury? It is too obvious to need argument. The reason he denied it was because this cap that was picked up by — [25]

At this point, Mr. Moore interposed an objection that the record did not support the assertion. Judge Thayer was inclined to agree with Mr. Moore, but cut off further discussion with a favorite judicial formula used when lawyers differ as to testimony: "But it is for you gentlemen [the jury] to determine what the evidence was."

Mr. Katzmann then proceeded to argue that he had correctly interpreted Sacco's testimony to be a denial of his ownership of the cap. He repeated

[24] Mr. McAnarney in his summation assumed it was a joke. Vol. II, 2159.
[25] Vol. II, 2209.

his assertion: "Why, gentlemen, deny the ownership of that cap (indicating)? This (indicating) is the one that was picked up by Loring and handed to Fraher and delivered by Fraher into the court, if I have the history right." [26]

His history was far from "right." Essential links were omitted. The cap was delivered by Loring to Fraher, by Fraher to Chief Gallivan, by Gallivan to State Officer Scott, by Scott (presumably) to Mr. Katzmann, by Mr. Katzmann, during the trial, to Mr. Fraher and (presumably) by Mr. Fraher in a bundle to Mr. Williams for use in examining Mr. Loring.[27]

Mr. Katzmann's allegations that Sacco denied the ownership of the cap was intended to suggest that he was fearful his cap would be compared with the Pearl Street cap, which Katzmann claimed was also Sacco's. Instead of merely excepting to Mr. Katzmann's misstatements, Mr. Moore should have insisted on having the transcript record read to the jury. Since the jury was not permitted to take notes, they had to rely on their memory as to what Sacco said about the cap, a week before, in a mass of other testimony. The unfairness of Mr. Katzmann's flat charge that Sacco denied ownership of his own cap may be judged by referring to the excerpt of his testimony previously quoted in this chapter. This shows that Sacco admitted ownership of the cap. Since the memory of the jury was not refreshed by having Sacco's actual testimony read to them, they were likely to remember only Mr. Katzmann's last-minute assertion that he lied.

Perusal of Mr. Katzmann's argument about the cap reveals a strange omission. After carefully building a basis during the trial for identifying the stray cap as Sacco's on the tear-made-by-a-nail hypothesis, *Mr. Katzmann left the torn lining out entirely in his summation.* Instead, he shifted from what he previously had regarded as a clinching piece of evidence to a different argument founded on a misrepresentation of Sacco's testimony. What caused this switch? It could hardly have occurred unintentionally. We can, however, make a pretty good guess at what happened. As an astute trial lawyer, Mr. Katzmann may have become afraid, at some stage before the close of the trial, to make the torn lining a crucial, or even an important, part of his case. If he had done so, and if evidence that it was a false claim had come to the knowledge of defense counsel, they might then have had a solid reason to demand a new trial. Gallivan was a voluble talker. Before the Governor's Advisory Committee, he said that he had "told lots of offi-

[26] Vol. II, 2210.   [27] Vol. I, 798.

cials" about the torn lining, including Officer Scott of the State Police.[28] His talks were chiefly with the State Police. He had had hardly any interviews with Mr. Katzmann and Mr. Williams. Also, he probably resented the fact that the preparation of a murder case in his own town, which he had investigated, had been turned over to Chief Stewart of Bridgewater. He was more experienced than Stewart. Gallivan had been chief of his hometown police for eleven years; Stewart had been a chief for five years. The scorn which Gallivan expressed in 1927 about the cap performance in court must have been even sharper in 1921 when he saw it happen at the trial. In his talks to State Police officers, he could hardly have failed to refer to the use of the cap as "spurious" evidence. Fear that such talk might reach the ears of defense counsel would have been sufficient reason for Mr. Katzmann to give up his intention to make a crushing argument that the cap was Sacco's because of its torn lining. He did not dare to call Chief Gallivan as a witness, which would have been normal procedure. This is the kind of realistic reasoning easily understood by experienced trial lawyers. At the same time, it offers a key to Mr. Katzmann's abrupt desertion of the cap-torn-on-a-nail theory quite in accord with human nature and with what we know about Mr. Katzmann and Chief Gallivan.

Although Mr. Katzmann's claim that Sacco had denied ownership of his own cap was weaker than the torn-lining argument, its timing was excellent for his purposes. As at the Plymouth trial, where Vanzetti's revolver was displayed to the jury just before they withdrew to consider the evidence, so at the close of the Dedham trial the jury filed out to reach a verdict with Mr. Katzmann's new charge that Sacco had told a guilt-conscious lie ringing in their ears.

15.

The Migratory Revolver

As the prosecutors prepared the case for the Dedham trial, it is clear that they did not then regard the revolver taken from Vanzetti as evidence that he was at the South Braintree crime. Nevertheless, before the trial was over,

[28] Vol. V, 5181–5182.

this gun became transformed into what Judge Thayer later termed "most potent" evidence of his guilt.[1] How and when was this accomplished?

The mere possession of the Harrington and Richardson revolver was not evidence that Vanzetti was present at the scene. The bullets extracted from the bodies of the dead men were the steel-jacketed type fired from automatic pistols, not the lead slugs discharged through revolvers. The exploded shells strewn in Pearl Street had been ejected by automatics, not revolvers. The bullets and shells were all of .32 caliber, whereas Vanzetti's revolver was .38 caliber. Something more was needed to turn the revolver into evidence against Vanzetti.

In his opening, Mr. Williams seemed to recognize the fact that Vanzetti's revolver was not proof that he was involved in the South Braintree affair. As the trial started, he indicated that the prosecution intended to rely solely on the eyewitness identification previously discussed in Chapter 12. Mr. Williams's *only* reference to Vanzetti's revolver was that "Vanzetti [when arrested] had on him a loaded .38 Harrington and Richardson revolver. There were no extra cartridges for the revolver found on Vanzetti." [2]

Before the trial was over, however, the prosecution had evolved a theory which, if sound, would have made Vanzetti's revolver direct and irrefutable proof of complicity in the crime. When Berardelli's body was picked up, no weapon was found in his hand or pocket. It was known that at times he had carried a Harrington and Richardson revolver, probably of .38 caliber. Vanzetti's gun was also a .38 Harrington and Richardson revolver. This apparent coincidence probably suggested a new and startling hypothesis, namely, that Vanzetti's revolver was actually the Berardelli weapon and had been stolen from him by his murderer as he lay dying on the ground.

Vanzetti's revolver had been in the prosecution's possession for fourteen months. It therefore comes as something of a shock to learn that the district attorney did not evolve this idea until the trial was well along. This strange tardiness would be understandable if it were based on new evidence suddenly discovered during the trial. There was no new evidence. Apparently someone for the Commonwealth thought up the idea during the trial and thereafter the prosecution scrounged around for evidence to support it. This process of seeking to confirm a preconception has by now become familiar.

The prosecution never produced the serial number of the gun alleged to

[1] Vol. V, 3514.   [2] Vol. I, 75.

have been carried by Berardelli, although the guard was a special policeman of the town of Braintree, and Parmenter, the paymaster whose gun it was, had been in the employ of Slater and Morrill for fifteen to twenty years and had resided in South Braintree for fifteen or sixteen years.[3]

There is nothing intrinsically implausible about the theory that the gunman who killed Berardelli might have robbed him of his revolver. This would have been a sensible precaution. (It seems irrational, however, to suppose that one of the murderers would carry around in his pocket for weeks telltale evidence of his guilt. This would have been an especially mad act on Vanzetti's part, because he was even then momentarily fearing apprehension by the police as an anarchist.) The chief difficulty with the government's hypothesis is that there was no credible evidence to support it — *either that any bandit took Berardelli's weapon from him, or that the guard was carrying his gun at the time of the robbery, or that Vanzetti's revolver was Berardelli's.* Nevertheless, the prosecution tried to substantiate the hypothesis.

No witness at the inquest or interviewed by the Pinkerton operatives had said that he saw a bandit take anything from Berardelli. Nor did any witness at the trial give such testimony. The prosecution built up its claim from a remark by Peter McCullum (a defense witness), a shoeworker in Rice and Hutchins working before a window facing Pearl Street. This window was opaque to shut off the glare of the sun[4] and had to be opened to give a view of the street. Mr. McCullum heard no shots but a fellow workman told him that some shooting was going on. He opened and shut his window "just as fast as he could," [5] "one of the fastest things he ever did in his life." [6] He said that in that instant he saw one man pushing a box into an automobile holding one gun in his left hand, "revolver type I should say." [7] On cross-examination he stated that the weapon "looked like a white gun," [8] "more of the color of this" (indicating Vanzetti's nickle-plated revolver).[9] Since the killer had fired an automatic, usually dark in color, Mr. Katzmann conjectured that the "white" gun was a different weapon and was Berardelli's revolver. To explain the exchange, Mr. Katzmann imagined that Berardelli's assassin had shoved his own pistol into his pocket, seized Berardelli's revolver[10] (which no one had seen), and held it in his left hand while he used his right to push the money box into the car. Unable to

[3] Supp. Vol., 410.   [4] Vol. II, 1149, 1162.   [5] Vol. II, 1152.   [6] Vol. II, 1158.
[7] Vol. II, 1152.   [8] Vol. II, 1157.   [9] Vol. II, 1163.   [10] Vol. II, 2184.

produce any evidence that a bandit took a weapon from Berardelli, Mr. Katzmann offered to the jury his own speculation instead. Here is what he said in his summation:

Who it was that with a Savage [later shown to be a foreign gun, not a Savage] automatic fired three bullets from a Savage automatic into Berardelli and into Parmenter, we do not know and we have offered no evidence on, except that there was such man, so that the force of my brother's suggestion that Vanzetti were foolish to give up a Savage automatic to take a 38 revolver is of no force in the light of that claim, and I say to you, gentlemen of the jury, it is substantiated on the evidence.

What we do say to you is that we expect you to find upon all the evidence that the 28 [sic] Harrington & Richardson revolver that was found upon the defendant Vanzetti was the 38 Harrington & Richardson revolver that poor Berardelli tried to draw from his pocket to defend himself and before he sunk to his knees with the blood coming out of his mouth dying on that sidewalk that afternoon.

That is what we say to you and we offer it not at all, gentlemen, for the purpose of saying that Vanzetti used it. There were six bullets and every one of them were automatic bullets, and the Harrington & Richardson cannot fire an automatic bullet. We offered that evidence, gentlemen, to show you that some person took that revolver off the person of the dying Berardelli. And that ties up with the other evidence the presence at the scene of the crime and to assist with the defendant Sacco, who we say is the man when Berardelli was sinking down, when they were in a struggle with each other and the defendant Sacco's hands were on the shoulders of Berardelli, took the gun and it eventually came into the possession of his co-defendant Vanzetti.

And as I have got so much to discuss in the way of evidence and so little time really in which to discuss six weeks' evidence in a little over four hours and a half and that I might not forget it, I say to you gentlemen, aside from the Iver-Johnson testimony, that the evidence of a witness produced by the defendants themselves corroborates and clamps down the Commonwealth's claim, and I refer to Peter McCallum [sic], the man working in the "K" department of the Rice & Hutchins factory. He says that when he raised the window in the middle trio and looked out from the second floor, he saw a man whom we have shown and will argue was Sacco, with a gun answering the description, *a bright nickel gun*, gentlemen of the jury, in the left hand of the man putting in the auto a money box. And that is from the lips of the defendant, — from the defendant's own witness, Peter McCallum.

I do not say, gentlemen, that McCallum said that Sacco was the man. If he said anything, he denied it. Whether he said anything or not is for you to say. I do not claim that he said it was Sacco. What I do say is that he says the man who was beside the body of the dying Berardelli putting a box on the left hand of the auto in to it with his right hand, holding in his left hand a gun that answered the description of a bright gun, and it was an automatic that had killed Berardelli. The automatic of the assailant of Berardelli was then in his pocket because he had to use his right hand to put the box into the automobile.

In his left hand he had neither the time nor the opportunity to dispose of the gun that he had just taken from the dying Berardelli. We say that man is the defendant Sacco. [Emphasis added.] [11]

The foregoing speculation represents the entire basis for any claim that a revolver passed from Berardelli to his murderer. It seems likely that Mr. Katzmann anticipated firmer evidence than this from a government witness on which to rest his theorizing. He would hardly have left it to the chance remark of a defense witness. But, the expected testimony did not come. Taking a tip from Mr. Katzmann, we, too, may speculate. We suggest that the witness who failed him was James F. Bostock, a millwright who installed machinery in shoe factories and had visited Slater and Morrill frequently in his work. At least this assumption would explain the following questions and answers in his direct examination of Bostock:

Q. (By Mr. Williams) Now, did you see, during the shooting or just after, any or either of the bandits do anything with their gun? A. I don't get your question.
Q. Did you see any of the men who were doing the shooting do anything with their gun either during the shooting or after, except shoot? A. Why, I should say one of them filled his gun.
Q. Do you know which one that was? A. I should say it was the one that shot at Berardelli. I don't know whether — As he shot his gun, he reached for his pocket, in this direction, slipped something out of his pocket, and acted as though he was slipping it in the gun [apparently inserting another clip of cartridges]. I don't know anything about a gun.
Q. At what stage of the proceedings was that? A. *That was while they were waiting for the car to come up the road.* [Emphasis added.] [12]

However, if Mr. Bostock (or some other prosecution witness) missed his cue, Mr. Katzmann, like an able actor, went ahead with his theory as if nothing happened, using the defense witness McCullum's instant observation as his justification. However, even this frail basis was negated by other testimony. Witness Lewis Wade, who had the best view of all the government witnesses, said that the bandit shooting Berardelli picked up the "box with both hands." [13] Government witness Pelser saw Berardelli's assassin standing two or three feet away from him pumping the last of four bullets into his victim.[14] Mr. Pelser saw the gun being fired by the killer, then held in the right hand. (McCullum had said *left* hand.) He described it very

11 Vol. II, 2183–2184.   12 Vol. I, 194.   13 Supp. Vol., 440.   14 Vol. I, 292.

much as McCullum had done: "It was a bright gun, a brand new gun it looked like, and had a 'whitish' color." [15]

Since we know from the autopsy that the killer had fired steel-jacketed bullets into Berardelli, the gun Pelser glimpsed was necessarily an automatic and not a revolver. Yet both McCullum and Pelser used the word "whitish" to describe the gun they saw through the window. The explanation of the bright color which they thought they saw must lie in the fact that the sun was shining at that time in the windows, as stated by Edward Carter at the inquest[16] and by Mr. Williams in his opening.[17] Sunlight deflected from the metal barrel of the automatic would account for the "bright" appearance of the weapon without resorting to the supposed maneuvers of the bandit conjured up for the jury by Mr. Katzmann. Government witness James E. McGlone was almost in the midst of the fray. He stated that two of the bandits on the street ran with the money boxes and jumped in the car as it moved up. Neither of these two was the one pouring bullets into Berardelli.[18] The gun he saw in the hands of the killer was a black gun that looked like an automatic, flat on both sides.[19]

The prosecution was also hampered by the fact that no inquest witness or any other person could be found who would testify that he saw Berardelli carry a gun on the day of the crime. Some general testimony was available, that it was his custom to carry a weapon, but that was all. The absence of this essential evidence is significant in view of the large number of people who watched the guard carry the payroll box down Pearl Street or witnessed the murder scene.

So much for Mr. Katzmann's reconstruction of the manner in which a bandit got possession of a revolver supposed to have been carried by Berardelli. He then went further, however, and imagined that the robber gave the gun to Vanzetti.

The Commonwealth still had to prove that the revolver taken from Vanzetti was in fact the one that had been Berardelli's. The prosecution had already prepared the way for this claim in its direct case, long before McCullum testified.

Mr. Williams opened the line of government proof about the revolver by calling Mrs. Sarah Berardelli, widow of the murdered guard. After some

[15] Vol. I, 294.   [16] Supp. Vol., 432.   [17] Vol. I, 66.   [18] Vol. I, 269.
[19] Vol. I, 270.

preliminary questions, the direct examination about the revolver proceeded:

(Mr. Williams shows a revolver to the witness.)
Q. I will show you that revolver, which is Exhibit 27 [Vanzetti's gun], and ask you if you have ever seen a gun like that before? A. I think I did.
Q. And where have you see a gun like that? . . . A. I have seen one that my husband carried.
Q. At some time before the shooting, do you know whether or not your husband had done something with the gun which he carried? A. Why, yes, three weeks before he got shot, why, he brought it in the place to have it repaired. [The time is approximately correct.]
Q. Do you know where he took it? . . . A. I forget the name of the place.
Q. You have forgotten the name of the place? A. Yes.
Q. Can you describe to the jury where the place was? A. I think it is on the corner of Washington Street and I don't know what the other street is.
Q. Would you recognize the name if it was told to you? A. Yes, sir.
Q. Was the name Iver Johnson Company? A. Yes, sir.
Q. Now, did anyone go with your husband when he took the gun there? A. Myself.
Q. Do you remember what time of the day it was? A. I know it was in the afternoon; I can't remember the hour.
Q. Do you know what the matter was with the gun that it had to be repaired? . . . A. Yes.
Q. What was it? A. *It was a spring broke.* . . .
Q. Now, when your husband took the gun in there, and you say you were with him — A. Yes, sir.
Q. — what did he do with the gun? A. At that time?
Q. Yes. A. Why, he simply brought it in there to have it repaired.
Q. I mean, did he leave it there? A. Yes, he left it there, of course.
Q. Now, at some time after that did he do anything about getting the gun back? A. No. He returned the check to Mr. Parmenter.
Q. And when you say the "check," what do you mean? A. *The check for the gun he was supposed to take it out. He gave it to Mr. Parmenter to take it out.*
MR. MOORE. I wish you would speak a little louder, please.
Q. He gave the receipt check to Mr. Parmenter? A. Yes, sir. [Emphasis added.] [20]

On cross-examination, Mrs. Berardelli gave more particular testimony:

Q. (By Mr. McAnarney) Do you know where your husband got the revolver that he had? A. That he had? He used to get it from Mr. Parmenter.
Q. He bought it from Mr. Parmenter? A. No, Mr. Parmenter let him take it for all that time.

[20] Vol. I, 806–808.

Q. What? A. Mr. Parmenter let him take it for all that time that he had been there.

Q. Mr. Parmenter let him have the gun all that time that your husband was there? A. Yes, sir.

Q. Didn't your husband have a revolver before he went there? A. No.

Q. Now, what kind of a revolver — You don't know what make it was, your husband's revolver? A. No.

Q. Do you think it had a black handle? A. Yes, sir.

Q. *Now, did you see any broken spring on the revolver?* A. *Yes, sir.*

Q. Whereabouts did you see the spring? A. Why, it was right in between here and the shot —

Q. Where did you see it? Where was the spring when you saw it? A. Where was the spring? Why, I saw it the day he brought it in the repair place, he showed it to me. That is how I know it.

Q. He showed it to a man in the repair place. A. Yes, sir.

Q. And you were with him? A. Yes, sir.

Q. Now, the revolver came back, did it? A. I don't know.

Q. *You don't know whether the revolver ever came back or not?* A. No. [Emphasis added.] [21]

Under cross-examination Mrs. Berardelli got a bit confused about dates, but with help from Mr. Williams straightened them out. Also, when asked on cross-examination what gun her husband had after he took the revolver in for repairs, she unexpectedly threw in a statement that Mr. Parmenter lent him another one exactly like the first. Mr. Williams did not pick up or redirect Mrs. Berardelli's sudden remark about a second revolver, nor did it ever figure in the case again. It may have been an improvisation by a flustered witness and nothing more.

On the other hand, the prosecution may have breathed a sigh of relief that Mrs. Berardelli's answers had not opened up any other new line of thought. Perhaps they had learned what she had said to her friend Mrs. Aldeah Florence, who lived next door to Mrs. Berardelli prior to her husband's death and afterwards became her landlady. It might be helpful to get ahead of our story and quote from Mrs. Florence's testimony when the defense put her on the stand. Her direct examination follows:

Q. (By Mr. Jeremiah McAnarney) What is your full name? A. Aldeah Florence.

Q. You live in Quincy? A. Yes, sir.

Q. Are you a married woman? A. Yes, sir.

Q. Where do you live? A. I live 121 Water Street.

Q. You know Mrs. Berardelli? A. I knew her when I was living on Phipps Street.

[21] Vol. I, 808–809.

Q. Did she live in a tenement house belonging to you? A. No. She lived in a house next to mine.

Q. Did she at one time live with you? A. She boarded with me for four months.

Q. When was the time she boarded with you? A. After her husband was dead.

Q. How soon after the death of her husband did she? A. Right away.

Q. You say "right away." How many days or weeks? When was it? A. When she came back from the funeral she came and lived at my house.

Q. She lived with you for five weeks? A. For four months.

Q. Anytime after his death did she say anything about his revolver? A. Yes, she did —

Q. Before you answer that, let me ask you another question. Before his death had she talked with you anything about her husband and a revolver? You may answer that yes or no? A. Yes.

Q. Had she? A. Yes, sir.

Q. How long before his death was that? A. I couldn't tell you just the time, but I know one day she spoke about his revolver. I couldn't tell you just how long it was though.

Q. What did she say about the revolver? A. She said, — she was talking about his job. She said what a particular job he had. I asked her if he carried—

THE COURT. Suppose it appears a little more clearly when this conversation was, before Berardelli's death or afterward, because I understood her to say she had two different conversations.

MR. JEREMIAH MCANARNEY. Very well, your Honor.

Q. Now, this conversation you are just giving us now, tell us as well as you can when that occurred. In the first place, perhaps I will help you. Was it before or after his death, that first conversation? A. Before. One was before his death and one after his death.

Q. Now, the conversation before his death, I want that. What was said then? A. *She said how he had a revolver and that he never carried it, and that it was broken, and she was going to have it taken into Boston to have it fixed.*

Q. Did you see the revolver? A. Yes, she showed it to me.

Q. After his death, did you have a conversation with her? A. Yes.

Q. What did she say then? I mean, anything that was said about the revolver? A. Well, three or four days after she came back from the funeral she said, "Oh, dear," she says, "If he had taken my advice and taken the revolver out of the shop he would not be, maybe he would not be in the same condition he is to-day."

Q. Get the revolver out of the shop? A. Out of the repair shop.

Q. Will you repeat that answer? I did not get the middle of it. A. She said, "Oh, dear, if he had taken my advice and taken the revolver out of the repair shop, maybe he would not be in the same condition he is in to-day."

Q. And that, you think, was three or four days after his death? A. Three or four days after he was buried. [Emphasis added.] [22]

[22] Vol. II, 1686–1687.

Mr. Katzmann cross-examined Mrs. Florence, but could not shake her story. In fact, he drove it in deeper as the following excerpt will show:

Q. (By Mr. Katzmann) Would you mind repeating it again? A. The conversation I had with her?

Q. Before Alessandro Berardelli died. A. One day I was there. We were talking about what kind of particular job he had, and she said, — I said to her, I said, "Does he carry anything?" She said, "No," *but she says, "I have a revolver and I will have it fixed for him and make him carry it, but I should take it in and have it repaired first." She says, "Do you want to see it?" She took me upstairs and showed it to me.*

Q. You never met this woman before October, 1919, had you? A. No. I never seen her before.

Q. When did you first remember this conversation? A. I don't remember just the time.

Q. Don't remember that? A. No.

Q. Did you have many conversations with her? A. Well, I was quite an intimate friend of hers after I got acquainted with her, but I never been to talk any more about that conversation.

Q. You had another talk about the revolver? A. After his death, yes.

Q. Did she show you the revolver then? A. Before he died?

Q. No. After he died? A. No.

Q. Did she say anything about having the revolver in the house then? A. No, she had it in the shop then.

Q. She had it in the shop? A. She had it in the shop, repair shop at that time.

Q. She told you that? A. Yes.

Q. Did she tell you she had taken it in alone? A. She told me she had taken it in.

Q. Alone? A. She did not say whether she took it in alone, no, but she told me she took the revolver in herself.

Q. It was still in the repair shop? A. And she had never taken it out.

Q. And she had never taken it out? A. And she had never taken it out.

Q. Did you infer her husband had not taken it out? A. I never come to that conversation about asking her.

Q. Did she say it was still in the shop? A. Yes, but I did not ask if her husband took it out.

Q. *I am asking you if after her husband's death she said that the revolver was still in the shop where it had been taken for repair?* A. Yes, sir.

MR. KATZMANN. That is all. [Emphasis added.] [23]

Mr. Katzmann never recalled Mrs. Berardelli to deny what her friend had testified Mrs. Berardelli had told her. In his summation, however, he tried to counter the effect of Mrs. Florence's story, which he had failed to shake or refute. This he did in a single paragraph which is worth a moment

[23] Vol. II, 1688–1689.

of study as a condensed sample of Mr. Katzmann's type of argumentation. Here is how he met Mrs. Florence's uncontradicted testimony:

. . . before I pass away from that 38 Harrington and Richardson, I want to call your attention to the lady who was described by my genial friends as that good looking young lady from Quincy. She was good looking, Mrs. Florence, and was produced to contradict Mrs. Berardelli.[24]

The foregoing two sentences show again Mr. Katzmann's resort to sarcasm when other courses failed him. Also, as such, it misquotes Mr. McAnarney's characterization of Mrs. Florence. Actually he had said that she was "that clean, wholesome, honorable looking woman," [25] and had not argued that comeliness sponsored veracity. However, this sidelong snipe at Mrs. Florence heightened the contrast with the picture of Mrs. Berardelli which he sketched in his next sentence. The statement that Mrs. Florence was produced to contradict Mrs. Berardelli was untrue. Mrs. Berardelli had never said that the gun came back from the repair shop. Nor did Mrs. Florence's testimony contradict Mrs. Berardelli's in relating what the widow had told her. In this manner, nevertheless, Mr. Katzmann covered up his own failure, or inability, to contradict Mrs. Florence. The district attorney's next sentence was even more illustrative of his skill in avoiding a confrontation with facts inconsistent with his hypotheses:

Mrs. Berardelli, a woman who said she could not read or tell the calendars, a poor beknighted [sic] widow, when after she has been made the widow, the defendants are trying to make a perjurer out of her now.[26]

Here, Mr. Katzmann sought to exploit the jury's natural sympathy with Mrs. Berardelli, again as a cover-up for his failure to get her to deny Mrs. Florence's testimony. He then attacked the defendants for "trying to make a perjurer" out of Mrs. Berardelli. This he justified as follows:

They produced Mrs. Florence to testify that poor Mrs. Berardelli said three or four days after the funeral [again the exploitation of Mrs. Berardelli's grief], "If he only carried his gun or done what I told him or got it back from the shop perhaps he would not be in the condition he is in now"; that prior to his death she is quoted as saying that he did carry a gun but she had taken it in and was going to have it fixed, if he had only gotten it out perhaps he would not be in the condition he was then in, dead.[27]

[24] Vol. II, 2230.   [25] Vol. II, 2169.   [26] Vol. II, 2230.   [27] Vol. II, 2230.

There was nothing inconsistent in this paraphrase of Mrs. Florence's testimony with anything Mrs. Berardelli had said. In fact, it tended to confirm her testimony. Mr. Katzmann never asked Mrs. Berardelli about her conversation with Mrs. Florence but, as he so often had done, substituted his own loose talk for proof.

Mr. Katzmann then turned to a seemingly sounder line of attack upon Mrs. Florence's testimony. He cited the statement of a government witness, James Bostock, who had said in direct examination that Berardelli had shown him his revolver on the Saturday before the murder. Mr. Bostock's testimony will be considered later in the context of other evidence offered by the Commonwealth, bearing on the missing Berardelli revolver.

The next government witness after Mrs. Berardelli was Hattie B. Parmenter, widow of the dead paymaster.[28] She was asked how her husband was dressed on the morning of April 15 and whether she had ever before seen the cap found in Pearl Street. That was all. This failure to ask any really pertinent questions seems extraordinary. She was not asked about her husband's gun (or guns), nor whether he was armed when he left home, nor whether she had seen or had any memorandum of the serial number of her husband's gun, nor whether she ever found the claim check from the Iver Johnson Company, which Mrs. Berardelli said had been given to Mr. Parmenter.

Why had the prosecution put her on the stand and then asked her no significant question? Did they feel they *had* to produce her, but were fearful of opening up something unfavorable to their thesis? Defense counsel wisely did not cross-examine Mrs. Parmenter. It is an axiom of trial practice to abstain from cross-examining a witness whose testimony has done no harm, unless counsel knows of some helpful testimony the witness is willing to give.

The next witness in the government's chain of proof was Lincoln Wadsworth.[29] In March 1920 he had been in charge of the pistols and repairs to firearms for the Iver Johnson Sporting Goods Company, a well-known and long-established firm with headquarters in Boston. He stated that he had received for repairs a .38 Harrington and Richardson revolver, property of Alex Berardelli, and that he had "sent [it] up to the shop on March 20, 1920." [30] Mr. Williams offered to put in evidence the store record of the receipt of the gun, but on Mr. McAnarney's objection, it was excluded by

[28] Vol. I, 811.   [29] Vol. I, 813.   [30] Vol. I, 814.

Judge Thayer. As it turned out, defense counsel's objection was a mistake, but Mr. McAnarney did not then know that the entry would not have been harmful. The debate over the admission of the record before the jury injured the defendants' cause. It made the receipt for Berardelli's revolver look like a vital matter that threatened the defense and it evoked questions from the bench and answers by Mr. Williams that made it appear that the government could prove that the "revolver in front of the witness" (Vanzetti's) "was the same revolver that Berardelli had at the time of the alleged shooting." [31]

Moreover, the exclusion of the record did not serve its purpose anyway. Mr. Wadsworth was permitted to testify to its contents, using the entry to "refresh" his recollection. This testimony was incomplete. For instance, it did not include the job number, an important gap in the government's chain.

Mr. Wadsworth was shown Vanzetti's gun. He stated that it was a .38 Harrington and Richardson revolver. Its particular name was "Auto," *referring to its automatic extractors.* He stated that the revolver brought in was of "the same type and calibre" as the one shown him. He was then asked by Mr. Williams:

Q. Will you tell us whether or not that revolver answers the description of the revolver brought in that day. A. It does.

The above question and answer were objected to and excluded as leading. However, the damage was done. As we shall see, this testimony weighed on Mr. Wadsworth's conscience for over six years. Neither Mr. Wadsworth nor any other witness testified that the company had any receipt or other record showing delivery of the revolver to its owner after the repairs were made.

If this had been all of the testimony about the revolver left at the Iver Johnson Company, it would have offered a complete explanation of the missing Berardelli gun consistent with the testimony of Mrs. Berardelli, Mrs. Florence and the routine of Iver Johnson. It would have shown that: (1) Mr. and Mrs. Berardelli brought the gun in for repairs about three weeks before April 15, 1920; (2) the gun had a broken spring; (3) it was sent to the repair shop on March 20, 1920; (4) Mr. Berardelli gave the

[31] Vol. I, 815.

claim check to Mr. Parmenter. Mr. Parmenter and Berardelli were slain on April 15, 1920. If the gun had been redelivered to Mr. Parmenter prior to his death, a company of the standing of Iver Johnson would normally have had a receipt for its delivery, or the returned claim check, or some other record. *It had nothing* to show that Mr. Parmenter or anyone else had picked it up. Nor was there any such evidence following Mr. Parmenter's death. He had received the claim check but could no longer use it to retrieve the weapon. The Berardelli gun in all probability must have remained uncalled for until it was disposed of with other unclaimed repair jobs, or possibly until some employee, knowing that its owner would never call for it and not foreseeing its quite unexpected trial significance, removed it personally.

The foregoing simple explanation of the missing revolver, did not, however, fit into the government's thesis that one of the bandits, alleged to be Sacco, had robbed Berardelli of his weapon and given it to Vanzetti. The prosecution, therefore, proceeded to throw the defense off this direct track to an obvious conclusion. In this they succeeded. To accomplish this feat, the government relied on several witnesses.

The evidence on which Mr. Katzmann leaned most heavily was the testimony of James Bostock.[32] In the course of his direct examination, which was primarily concerned with his own unusual and close view of the crime, he had said that he knew that Berardelli had a revolver and had joshed him about it a number of times.[33] Then followed this:

Q. (By Mr. Williams) How long before the shooting had you last seen the revolver in Berardelli's possession? A. I think the Saturday night before the shooting.
Q. And when was the shooting? A. Thursday.
Q. That is, you saw it the previous Saturday? A. Yes, the previous Saturday.
Q. What kind of a revolver was it, do you know? A. No, I couldn't tell you the make of it. I don't know anything about revolvers. It was a 38 calibre revolver, that is all I can tell you. I don't know. I never owned one.
Q. What did it look like? A. It was a nickel-plated revolver.
Q. It was 38 caliber? A. Yes, sir.
Q. And you saw him have it the Saturday before the shooting? A. Yes, sir.
Q. How long, to your knowledge, had he possessed that revolver? A. I couldn't tell you. I have seen it with him a number of times. I couldn't tell you how long he had it.
Q. Just roughly? A. Probably a month or two. Ever since I worked at the

[32] Vol. I, 185, 196–200, 826–831.   [33] Vol. I, 196.

factory. I had been working at the factory there at that time probably two months.

Q. You had known Berardelli during that time? A. Yes, sir.[34]

On being shown Vanzetti's revolver, Mr. Bostock said that the gun he saw was "similar to that, yes; that kind of a revolver."

Mr. Bostock's answers on cross-examination were most unusual. He did not merely correct his testimony on direct — *he ignored it completely*. It may be noted that his account on cross-examination of necessity excluded his first story about seeing the gun the Saturday night before the murder.

He was asked by Mr. McAnarney, "When did he [Berardelli] show you this revolver?" to which he replied, "*I couldn't tell you exactly when it was, but one morning right at the elevator.*" (Emphasis added.)[35]

Mr. McAnarney then pursued the episode at the elevator. The following is an excerpt from his testimony on cross-examination:

Q. (By Mr. McAnarney) Any other time did you ask him about his revolver? A. Yes, a number of times, — because I joshed him on his gun. I was fooling with him, carrying a gun at the factory.[36]

Omitting a number of questions and answers, the cross-examination continued:

Q. When you asked him if he had the revolver, you couldn't say when you asked him? A. No.
Q. And he did not take it out? A. No, sir.
Q. *On none of the occasions when you asked him if he had the revolver did he take it out?* A. Yes, sir, on one occasion he took it out.
Q. *When was that?* A. *I think that was the first time. I asked him if he carried a gun.*
Q. You knew he carried one? A. Yes, sir.
Q. You were joshing him? A. I was joshing him.
Q. I think you told me the first time that he said he did, and that was all that transpired? A. Yes, sir.
Q. Was there more than that transpired the first time? A. No, sir.
Q. Well, I now ask you did he any of these times take the revolver out? A. *One time he took the revolver out.*
Q. Which time? A. *The first time I asked him.*
Q. Very well. The first time you asked him did he carry a revolver? A. Yes, sir.
Q. What did he say to you? A. Why, he showed it to me.
Q. Did he say anything? A. No, sir.

[34] Vol. I, 196–197.　　[35] Vol. I, 198.　　[36] Vol. I, 199.

Q. Then he never said anything to you. He took it out of his pocket, or did he have it in his hand? A. He took it out of his pocket.

Q. What did he do? A. He showed it to me, that is all.

Q. Did he show it to you? A. Yes, sir.

Q. Did he hold it in his hand, or lay it on a desk or any place? A. *I had it in my hand.*

Q. You took the gun out of his hand? A. No, I did not take the gun out of his hand. He showed it to me. He handed it to me. I had the gun Berardelli carried in my hand.

Q. He took it out of his pocket in his hand? A. Yes.

Q. And you took it out of his hand? A. No; he passed it to me.

Q. From his hand into your hand it went? A. That is where it went, from his hand into my own. He passed it to me.

Q. What did you do then? A. *I looked at it.*

Q. Did you really? A. Yes, sir.

Q. Have you a distinct recollection of anything on that revolver? A. No, sir, not one particularly. I couldn't tell it if I saw it again.

Q. And that is the only time you saw it? A. Yes, sir. I have seen it a number of times in his possession.

Q. But you couldn't tell it again? A. No, sir.

Q. And you don't know whether this is the revolver [referring to Vanzetti's]? A. No, sir. [Emphasis added.] [37]

Mr. McAnarney moved to strike out Bostock's revolver testimony on the ground that the witness could not "tell the revolver if he saw it again." Judge Thayer then ruled as follows:

THE COURT. The answer to that is that he testified to the best of his judgment and belief that was the revolver that he saw the Saturday night before. In cross-examination *he has testified differently.* I won't say differently. That is a question for the jury. *The courts have said where a witness testified one way on direct and then a different way on cross, it is a question of fact for the jury which testimony they believe to be the true testimony.* It seems to me I am obliged to allow it to be heard by the jury. Its weight is for them, entirely for them. If they believe that is the same, then it is competent. [Emphasis added.] [38]

Whether Judge Thayer's ruling was right or not, it must have confused the jury with respect to the more crucial issue as to whether Bostock had seen *any* revolver on the Saturday night before the murder. On this issue, the direct testimony was not on a par with the cross. Mr. Bostock himself had thrown away his earlier statement, yet the jury was instructed that they could select which version they chose to believe. In addition to Mr.

[37] Vol. I, 200.   [38] Vol. I, 831.

Bostock's cross-examination answers, it was improbable in any event that he could have recalled the exact date and time of day of a casual incident after a time lag of fourteen months. The *first* of the several times he "joshed" Berardelli *might easily have been prior to March 20, 1920,* and probably was. In any event, his entirely different story about the time had made it too indefinite to constitute the proof for which his testimony was first offered.

The testimony which Mr. Bostock discarded, however, was reinstated by Mr. Katzmann to support his continued attack on Mrs. Aldeah Florence. In his summation, Mr. Katzmann baldly asserted that: ". . . James Bostock takes care of the evidence of Mrs. Florence, because he says on the Saturday before the murder he saw Berardelli show the gun, the man whom they say is a fine witness." [39]

Mr. Moore objected to this alleged statement of the evidence, but solely on the basis that Bostock did not identify the gun, not that his testimony showed that Mr. Katzmann's assertion about Bostock seeing the gun on Saturday, as he left it after the cross-examination, was incorrect. Judge Thayer again ended the discussion by telling the jury to use their own recollection. After listening to weeks of testimony, without notes, this was a futile exhortation. The jury was most likely to remember what the district attorney said was claimed by Mr. Bostock, not his actual testimony. Here again was a glaring example of Mr. Moore's lack of judgment — or skill as a trial lawyer. By basing his protest on the sole ground that Bostock had not identified the gun as Vanzetti's, *he admitted by inference* that Bostock's testimony had shown that he had seen the revolver on the Saturday before the murders. As if this was not bad enough, Mr. Moore failed to remind the jury, when given this opportunity by Mr. Katzmann, that Mr. McAnarney's able cross-examination had brought out Bostock's now uncontradicted story about the time when he had last seen Berardelli's revolver. This might also have indicated that Katzmann was again being unfair in his assertions about the evidence. A good trial lawyer seizes every chance to argue his case. In this respect, Mr. Moore was no match for Mr. Katzmann, who understood and used this tactic of advocacy repeatedly.

The prosecution then attempted to prove that the Berardelli gun had been redelivered by the Iver Johnson Company. Since this could not be done by the usual direct evidence, such as a receipt, the claim check, or any witness, Mr. Williams attempted to prove its delivery by the absence of any

[39] Vol. II, 2230.

record. He called one James H. Jones, sales manager of the firearms department for the Iver Johnson Company.[40]

Mr. Jones was queried about a gun having a repair job, "No. 94765," alleged to have been the Berardelli gun. He was then asked:

Q. (By Mr. Williams) Can you tell the jury whether or not the gun was re-delivered? A. To the best of my knowledge it was delivered.
Q. And how can you tell the jury then that, to the best of your knowledge, it was delivered? A. Because the gun is not in our place of business now.[41]

At this point, Mr. McAnarney objected and asked that the testimony be stricken out. Then followed a long session between counsel and judge, in and out of the presence of the jury. At the end, Judge Thayer ruled that he would strike the question and answer out of the record and did so in the presence of the jury.[42]

However, with some questioning by the judge as well as Mr. Williams, it was brought out by Mr. Jones that the gun was not in the possession of Iver Johnson, that repair jobs not called for were kept until the first of the year when they were sold, that the company kept a record of such sales and that there had been such a sale in February 1921, that it had no record of the sale of "this revolver" or of *"this revolver" being sold at that time.*[43] (The witness had no personal knowledge that it was not sold.)

Here we have a most curious proof that the particular gun was delivered. It seems to rest on evidence that it was *not* delivered, as follows: (1) The Iver Johnson usual and routine records did not show the redelivery of the repaired Berardelli revolver to anyone;[44] this must have been because such records were in some instances defective. (2) The Iver Johnson records on the sale of abandoned repair jobs did not list a sale of the repaired Berardelli revolver, but, since these records were infallibly complete and correct, the revolver must have been redelivered.

We do not know what the jury made of this circuitous and improbable method of proof. Probably, after having listened to the gunsmith from Iver Johnson, referred to below, they were so confused that they did not know what to think.

The prosecution put on the stand George F. Fitzemeyer to prove that Vanzetti's gun was the Berardelli revolver. Mr. Fitzemeyer had been a gun-

[40] Vol. I, 823.　　[41] Vol. I, 824.　　[42] Vol. I, 833.　　[43] Vol. I, 833–835.
[44] Vol. I, 824.

smith at the Iver Johnson Company for thirty years or more and was the foreman of its gun shop.[45] Except for his testimony, the course of the Berardelli revolver at the company would appear fairly well outlined. Mr. Fitzemeyer, however, brought chaos out of order.

Before viewing the chaos, let us look at the order: (1) The Berardelli revolver had a *broken spring*. On this point Mrs. Berardelli was explicit and clear. She had even pointed out to the jury the location of the broken spring. (2) Mr. and Mrs. Berardelli had left the revolver with Mr. Wadsworth at Iver Johnson, after showing him the broken spring. (3) Mr. Wadsworth's record showed that a "38 Harrington & Richardson revolver, property of Alex Berardelli, was brought in for repairs and sent to the shop in March 20, 1920." [46] He gave it job number 94765.[47] (4) Mr. Wadsworth also gave Mr. Berardelli a claim check which was then given to Mr. Parmenter. (5) Iver Johnson could not locate any kind of record to show that the revolver had ever been redelivered to its owner or anyone else. (6) Mr. Jones, the sales manager, stated that uncalled for repair jobs were sold after the following January 1. The only such sale after March 20, 1920, was in February 1921. Mr. Jones stated he could not find a record of the sale of the Berardelli revolver. From this he speculated that it must have been redelivered to someone. (7) Mrs. Berardelli did not know whether the revolver ever came back or not.[48]

The only way to grasp the ensuing confusion created by Mr. Fitzemeyer's testimony is to read it. He had testified that if a gun was left in the afternoon, he would receive it at about quarter to nine the next morning or a little earlier. This followed:

Q. (By Mr. Williams) Now, referring to any records you may have of March 21, 1920, will you tell us whether or not you received any Harrington & Richardson revolver on that date for repairs? A. March 19 I received —
Q. Not the 19th. The 21st, I think. A. Do you want the number of the repair job, the ticket?
Q. No. I am referring to the 21st of March. A. My record is the 19th.
Q. No; I am referring to the 21st. A. 21st? Anything on the 20th?
Q. Anything on the 20th? A. It may be that I entered this on the 20th. I may have repaired this next morning, for all I know. I have it marked in with the 19th. Yes, I guess it is the 20th, — between the 22nd and the 19th.
Q. You received a Harrington & Richardson revolver? A. Yes, sir. "H & R," I call it.

[45] Vol. I, 816. [46] Vol. I, 814. [47] Vol. I, 819. [48] Vol. I, 809.

Q. How many did you receive during that time? A. It is pretty hard telling. I never counted them up. Probably thirty-five to forty.

Q. No, Harrington & Richardson, I am asking you. Did you receive more than one Harrington & Richardson revolver during that time for repairs? A. *Two.*

Q. Now, on what dates did you receive them? A. Well, I couldn't say. I have put the "19th"; I couldn't say whether it came up on the 19th or went down on the 19th.

Q. Have you the record of any Harrington & Richardson revolver being received on the 20th?

MR. MCANARNEY. Wait. I object.

A. No. I haven't any record between the 19th — only the 19th to the 22nd. I have got one between the 22nd and the 19th. That probably didn't go downstairs until the day afterwards.

THE COURT. Do you insist upon the objection after the answer?

MR. MCANARNEY. Not in view of the answer, no, if your Honor please.

MR. WILLIAMS. What was that answer, please?

(The answer is read.)

Q. Well, hasn't your attention been called, Mr. Fitzemeyer, before going on the stand, to repairs made on a certain Harrington & Richardson revolver? A. Yes, sir.

Q. And haven't you found a record of that particular revolver? A. Yes, sir.

Q. Have you the record before you? A. Yes, sir.

Q. Now, will you tell the jury, referring to your record to refresh your recollection, when that revolver was received, what was done upon it, and what was done with it?

MR. MCANARNEY. To that I object.

A. My book shows the 19th —

THE COURT. Just a minute. I suppose you claim this was the Berardelli revolver?

MR. WILLIAMS. Yes, if your Honor please. I am trying to trace it from this record to the record of the witness.

THE COURT. Of course, it isn't competent unless that fact is established.

MR. WILLIAMS. I appreciate that.

THE COURT. With that assurance, you may proceed.

MR. MCANARNEY. Your Honor will save an exception.

MR. MOORE. Exception.

THE COURT. Certainly.

Q. All right, Mr. Fitzemeyer, will you go ahead? A. *H & R revolver 32, new hammer, half an hour.*

MR. MCANARNEY. Not so fast. Say it again, please. A. H & R revolver, 32 calibre, new hammer, repairing, half an hour.

Q. On what date? A. Mine is marked the 19th.

THE COURT. What is that about a hammer? A. New hammer.

Q. 19th? A. It may be the 19th. It is between the 22nd and the 19th.

Q. You say it is marked between the 22nd and the 19th? A. Yes. I haven't any record of the 20th at all.

Q. What do you mean to say, — that it was between the 19th and the 22nd?

A. That job was done — I have "19th" and then marked "22nd," starting over marking the record again. I don't put down every morning when I start in.

Q. You mean your 19th record covers the days up to the 22nd, is that what you mean? A. Yes, sir, that is what I mean.

Q. What have you to connect that job with the Harrington & Richardson which came in downstairs on the 20th?

MR. MCANARNEY. I object.

THE COURT. You must ask him if he can, and then he can refresh his recollection. The difficulty is —

MR. WILLIAMS. I will put it that way.

Q. Can you identify that particular revolver which you are now testifying about, and that job upon it, with the Harrington & Richardson revolver received downstairs on the 20th? A. *No, sir, I cannot.*

Q. Well, now, you say there were two Harrington & Richardson jobs done or received by you or received by you during that interval between the 19th and the 22nd? A. Yes, sir.

Q. What was the other one? A. There was two of them marked together, *two H & R revolvers tied together, that is, two in one repair job.* "New main spring, new friction spring, repairs, an hour and a half on two."

Q. What calibre guns are those? A. I didn't make a record.

Q. Well, can you tell us — Is there any number on either which will help us to check up with any record they may have downstairs? A. Yes, sir, my repair number.

Q. Would that repair number be on the books downstairs? A. Yes, sir.

Q. What is your number of your 32 Harrison & Richardson job? A. 94765.

(Mr. Williams shows a book to the witness.)

Q. Now, I wish you would look at the record downstairs, and see if you can identify the job with that? A. 94765. [Emphasis added.] [49]

If we analyze the foregoing testimony carefully, we learn that Mr. Fitzemeyer was insisting that he was talking about a job which he marked as received on *March 19, not March 21,* and that it was *a .32 caliber, not a .38,* and that on the nineteenth he had repaired the gun by putting in a *new hammer, not a new spring.* This gun was received and repaired with a new hammer before the Berardellis came in. However, it bore the job number, when produced in court, assigned by Mr. Wadsworth on the next day to the Berardelli .38 with the broken spring. As to the date he did the work, Mr. Fitzemeyer said that it might have been from March 19 to March 22, since his record shows that he had marked "22nd" over his original date, March 19. However, he started the record on the nineteenth. How did it happen that *the number for the Berardelli .38, left for a new spring, found itself, at the trial, attached to another weapon?* Was the job ticket as migra-

[49] Vol. I, 817–819.

tory as the revolver itself? Despite the identical job number, however, Mr. Fitzemeyer stated he *could not identify* the job with the Harrington and Richardson revolver received on the twentieth.

The testimony shows that there was one other Harrington and Richardson job received between the nineteenth and twenty-second. This consisted of two H & R revolvers *tied together in one repair job* for which he made a new main spring and a new friction spring. This could not have been the Berardelli repair job, which covered only one revolver, nor was it claimed to be. Mr. Fitzemeyer said he made no record of the caliber of these two guns but that he had a repair number for the job — which, however, was never produced.

One can only sympathize with Mr. Williams in his attempt to apply Mr. Fitzemeyer's testimony to the Berardelli job. He then tried to jump the gap to Vanzetti by showing to the witness Vanzetti's gun, Exhibit 27. He asked the witness whether, in his opinion, any "repairs have been made to that revolver recently":

A. (By Mr. Fitzemeyer) Well, a new hammer I should call it, a new hammer.
Q. And how can you tell a new hammer has been put in there? A. Well, the firing pin does not show of ever being struck.
Q. What? A. The firing pin does not show of ever being struck. There isn't any burnt mark or powder mark or anything on it.[50]

Two well-known ballistic experts, called by the defense later, denied that Vanzetti's gun had been fitted with a new hammer.[51] In view of the fact that the Commonwealth had never shown that a new hammer for Berardelli's gun had been fitted in his weapon, or even ordered by the customer, or any record at all showing what repairs, if any, had been made to Berardelli's gun, one wonders whether the defense, bewildered by the Fitzemeyer testimony, had not been driven to hunt butterflies with spears.

Mr. Williams made another effort to retrieve something from the wreckage left by Mr. Fitzemeyer's testimony. He elicited some testimony from the witness ostensibly to show that it was easy to mistake a .38 Harrington and Richardson for a .32. The try should have backfired. He could hardly claim that Mr. Wadsworth had made the error. Apart from Wadsworth's wide knowledge of firearms, this would have destroyed the government's claim. The entry by Wadsworth that Berardelli had left a .38 Harrington

[50] Vol. I, 822.   [51] Vol. II, 1418, James E. Burns; Vol. II, 1465, J. Henry Fitzgerald.

and Richardson was the *only* reliable evidence the prosecution had that the guard's weapon was in fact of the same caliber as Vanzetti's. Therefore, the prosecution was compelled to intimate that Mr. Fitzemeyer may have erred, since he did all the revolver repair work himself.[52] This certainly was an unlikely mistake to have been made by a man who had been a gunsmith for thirty years. However, this did not deter Mr. Williams. His examination proceeded as follows:

Q. (By Mr. Williams) What, if any, distinctions are there between a 32 and 38 Harrington & Richardson revolvers?
(Objections)
A. No difference. It is a larger frame.
Q. What is a larger frame? A. Larger frame, one shot more and one calibre.
Q. Which is the one shot more? A. One shot less in the 38.
Q. The 38 has how many shots? A. Five.
Q. And the 32? A. Six.
THE COURT. 32 has one shot more? A. Yes, one shot more.[53]

This testimony that a .38 had a larger frame than the .32, and one less chamber, radically reduced the possibility of a mistake. Nevertheless, after getting Mr. Fitzemeyer to say there "isn't much difference" in the size of the two frames, Mr. Williams dismissed the witness.

During the recess which followed, however, Mr. Williams apparently tried to get Mr. Fitzemeyer to improve his testimony for the prosecution. Mr. Fitzemeyer was recalled and this followed:

Q. (By Mr. Williams) Mr. Fitzemeyer, is there any part of your testimony which you gave a few minutes ago which you desire to correct? A. Yes, there is.
Q. What is it? A. On the size of the frames. 38 and 32 are the same size frame in an ejector — hand ejector. The other model is a Premier and it is a smaller frame.
Q. On the Premier the frame is smaller? A. On the Premier, smaller on the 38 and 32. On this style there, the same size frame.
Q. That is, on the style you now hold in your hand [Vanzetti's revolver]? A. Yes, sir.
Q. The same size in the 32 and 38? A. Yes.
MR. WILLIAMS. And the Premier is smaller. (No answer)

Then on redirect, the examination continued:

Q. (By Mr. Williams) What is that particular model, so that we may have that in the record? A. That is what we call a police model, 38 police model.

[52] Vol. I, 822.   [53] Vol. I, 821–822.

Q. 38 police model? A. A break-open hand ejector. Break-open ejector; break-open — there(indicating) is your ejector.

MR. WILLIAMS. I get you.[54]

Mr. Fitzemeyer's attempt to correct his earlier testimony by now identifying Vanzetti's gun as a hand ejector (and therefore with a frame of the same size as a .32) only added to the shambles of the firearms testimony. Mr. Wadsworth had already described the *Vanzetti revolver as exactly the opposite,* as follows:

Q. (By Mr. Williams) Will you tell the jury what type and calibre that revolver is? I now show you, and I am referring to Exhibit 27.

(Mr. Williams hands a revolver to the witness.)

A. That is a 38 Harrington & Richardson auto. *"Auto" refers to automatic extractors. That is the particular name of that revolver.* [Emphasis added.] [55]

Apart from worse confounding the confusion, this tail-end examination of Mr. Fitzemeyer still contains the unlikely implication that the gunsmith could not tell the difference between a six-shooter and a five-shooter.

Despite the fact that the prosecution's attempt to prove that Vanzetti's revolver was the Berardelli gun had collapsed, defense counsel took the claim seriously. Vanzetti testified that he had bought his revolver for five dollars "at Falzini's house" [56] two or three months before. (On the morning after his arrest he had told Mr. Katzmann that he had bought it for nineteen dollars in Hanover Street, Boston, several years before.[57] He explained his falsehood as he had explained other lies told by him that morning — namely, since he had thought he was arrested as part of the drive against radicals, he did not want to say anything that might lead to identifying his fellow anarchists.)

Defense counsel produced testimony far beyond the call of the prosecution's proof (or failure of proof) to trace the lineage of the Vanzetti revolver:

Rexford Slater came down from Dexter, Maine, to testify that Exhibit 27 had belonged to his mother-in-law, Mrs. Mogridge, about three and a half years earlier. She had sold it to him when they both lived in Norwood, Massachusetts, for four dollars. He later sold it to Ricardo Orciani.[58]

Eldridge Atwater also came down from Dexter, Maine, to testify that he

[54] Vol. I, 823.   [55] Vol. I, 815.   [56] Vol. II, 1715.   [57] Vol. II, 1750.
[58] Vol. II, 1635.

had fired the gun when it belonged to his father-in-law, Mr. Mogridge. The last time he had seen the revolver it was in possession of Mrs. Mogridge, following the death of her husband.[59]

Luigi Falzini testified that he had bought the gun from Orciani and later sold it to Vanzetti in January or February 1920 for five dollars.[60]

Mr. Katzmann cross-examined these witnesses chiefly to attack their identification of the Vanzetti revolver as the gun about which they were testifying. It would add little to extend our story with a recital of this testimony. It is perhaps a significant commentary on the fear felt by defendants' counsel at the way the trial was going that they went to such lengths to meet a claim which the prosecution had failed to prove.

The defense did not produce Orciani to confirm Falzini's statement that he had bought the revolver from him. Mr. Katzmann used the absence of Orciani from the witness stand to discredit Falzini's testimony.[61] Orciani had been around the courthouse for some time and had been Mr. Moore's chauffeur. Despite what Mr. Katzmann had called Orciani's time clock alibis and Mr. Williams's frank admission that he could not place him (or Boda either) in South Braintree on April 15, 1920, Mr. Katzmann and Chief Stewart believed that he was guilty. Their belief became courtroom gossip. Francis Russell in his book *Tragedy in Dedham* quotes Chief Stewart as stating that the last time Orciani showed up Mr. Katzmann pointed a finger at Orciani and accused him of taking Berardelli's gun from the guard's dead body and giving it to Vanzetti.[62] Chief Stewart mistakenly places the incident during the cross-examination of Vanzetti. Whether it occurred or not, however, it is symbolic of the government's threatening posture toward Orciani. At any rate, Orciani did not take the stand, and, like Boda, disappeared from the view of the authorities.

According to the prosecution's hypothesis, the Berardelli revolver had been left at Iver Johnson for repairs; had gone into the repair shop, where it was listed as a .32 caliber instead of a .38 and had a new hammer inserted instead of a new spring; had then been delivered to some unknown person who had failed to present a missing claim check which Berardelli had given to Parmenter; had then been given by someone to Berardelli; had been carried by Berardelli, unbeknownst to anyone, on his walk with Parmenter with the payroll boxes down Pearl Street; had been seized by Sacco, who

[59] Vol. II, 1556.   [60] Vol. II, 1629.   [61] Vol. II, 2187, 2229.
[62] Russell, *Tragedy in Dedham*, 19.

pumped bullets into Berardelli and then grabbed the payroll box and shoved it into the murder car; had been given by one of the active bandits to their fellow highwayman Vanzetti; had then been carried by Vanzetti from April 15, 1920, to May 5, when he was arrested with the dead man's gun in his pocket.

Such was the prosecution's chart of the migration of Berardelli's revolver. If, however, the district attorney and his assistants had kept their minds and ears open, the supposed travels of the Berardelli gun would have reached a dead end in the Iver Johnson shop.

In 1926, during the course of my investigation, I had learned that Mr. Wadsworth had been a special agent of the Department of Justice. This fact might show his bias against anarchists. It was not much, but we were seeking anything that might possibly help Sacco and Vanzetti. Therefore, I called on him at the Iver Johnson store. I received a great surprise.

There was no difficulty in persuading Mr. Wadsworth to give me an affidavit that he had been a special agent. However, he seemed reluctant to let me leave. He then began to talk about his testimony at the trial. He appeared to be a greatly troubled man. When I returned with a draft affidavit, he continued to talk about his trial testimony. The result was that we asked him to testify before the Governor's Advisory Committee. He came.

Mr. Wadsworth had been the man "in charge of pistols and repairs to firearms." [63] He was not in specialized work like Mr. Fitzemeyer, but served in an overall capacity. Probably more than any other man, he knew the system of record-keeping at Iver Johnson and its deficiencies. But what he told to the Committee was not only pretty authoritative about the Berardelli revolver, but most instructive as to the manner in which the prosecution prepared to try the defendants for their lives.

Mr. Wadsworth was more troubled by the impression his testimony created in the context of the trial than by the bare words he had spoken. Of this he said in part:

. . . Although I certainly tried to give a fair and unbiased testimony at that trial and under these circumstances, but I felt very prejudiced in a good many ways at things that were said to me by the District Attorney. I cannot mention anything specific, but I felt an atmosphere of prejudice.
Q. (By Mr. Thompson) What were the things that were said to you? A. *By the way the questions were asked* of me at the time of the trial, when they found out what I was testifying to and they asked me questions; I cannot say anything

[63] Vol. I, 813.

of any sentence or any statement that was made, but it was just that feeling, and it was more of a mental state than anything else. There was nothing that was wrong or deliberate falsehoods, or anything like that, but it was just that atmosphere that I felt, and it certainly was broadcast at that time.[64]

Mr. Wadsworth's fears — that his testimony would be taken to mean more than a mere recital of make and caliber — were fully justified. Unimportant in itself, his testimony became integrated by Mr. Katzmann and Judge Thayer into Mr. Fitzemeyer's proofless recital. The combination was then viewed as evidence identifying Vanzetti's revolver as the Berardelli weapon. Judge Thayer used the unproven claim as a reason for denying a motion for a new trial,[65] and the Massachusetts Supreme Judicial Court gave Mr. Wadsworth's testimony the effect which he feared it would receive.

Although we do not know what the court would have said if it had known what lay behind Mr. Wadsworth's trial testimony, let us close this chapter with Mr. Wadsworth's testimony before the Governor's Advisory Committee:

THE WITNESS. I had not seen the newspapers for several months and I knew nothing of the case, so I came down here [from New Hampshire] absolutely unbiased and had a talk with the District Attorney, Mr. Katzmann, at that time, and I was shown this exhibit which was supposed to have been brought into our place to be repaired. Well, our records showed that a Berardelli, either himself or somebody for him in his name, had brought in a certain pistol to be repaired, a revolver, and what my part was supposed to be was to try to prove that this pistol, the exhibit, the one that had been brought into our shop, was this exhibit that was in court, and part of my testimony was to that effect, and I testified that the records on our books could have covered this pistol, and, as a matter of fact, it could have covered thousands of others just like it; and our records were very incomplete, in fact according to our records, which I had no control of at that time, I had left the employ of the company, they showed that the pistol had never been delivered; but that is just simply a possibility, it might have and it might not have.

Q. (By Judge Grant) Who showed? You said, "they showed." A. The records, such as we had in court, showed that it never had been delivered, the last space never had been filled out. But that is a very common mistake, some of the boys might not have checked it off. But what disturbed my conscience was this thing later that developed. I was under the impression, from hearsay and reports, that I had testified or had given the impression that the pistol in court was the pistol that came into our shop. I had nothing to do with the repairing of the pistol, but I had charge of all the records and handled them at that time,

[64] Vol. V, 5237–5238.   [65] Vol. V, 4764.

coming in, but I had nothing to do with their going out, — with the records going out. And I heard from several different sources that that testimony was quite important. Of course, a lot of this is hearsay.

Q. (By Mr. Thompson) You can go ahead and give the hearsay and everything else. A. But I have felt that I had created the impression that there was a possibility that that was the pistol. Well, that is just a possibility. There are a number of possibilities, and that is a possibility. *There is just the one possibility in the number of pistols a factory of that kind happens to make.* There was no distinguishing number so that you could tell that that was the pistol. Of course, every revolver has a serial number, but there was no record of this serial number in court. There was nobody had the number in their possession; nobody knew it, and for that reason that pistol had just a very slim chance that that is the one. That is all I can think of on that.

Q. Did you make an effort to say something more? A. Yes, before I went into the court room at all, — I don't know whether it was the first or the second interview that I had, it is so long ago my memory fails me on that, — I tried to say that there was, just the same way I do now, that there was just a very slim possibility. But the attorney was insistent there, and he seemed —

Q. You will have to speak a little louder. A. Mr. Williams did not seem to want to have that at all, so that I just let be on it. And then in the court room I felt sure I would have a chance to say the same thing that I have said here, but when the time came to be cross-examined I simply was not, that was all, and I went down on the records, as I thought, and still think, that while not a direct statement that that was the pistol, it might lead to the impression that it was the pistol. In fact, it was brought to my notice later that it had very strongly, by a number of people. That was what bothered me.

Q. *What is your belief today, judging from your records and all that you have personal knowledge of, what is your belief as to whether that was or was not Berardelli's pistol?* A. Well, there are thousands of times more chances that it was not than that it was, because there is only one, and just that one pistol, and there are just as many other chances as they had made pistols before that time — I don't know how long they have been in business, but probably thirty or forty years — *that it was not.*" [Emphasis added.] [66]

Mr. Wadsworth's positive opinion that Vanzetti's revolver was not Berardelli's was not heard at the trial. This fact, however, should not diminish the magnitude of Mr. Katzmann's accomplishment. Without any proof that Berardelli's revolver had been released to anyone by the repair shop, but with considerable evidence that it had not, he had nevertheless convinced judge and jury that it had been redelivered by the Iver Johnson Company. This was a forensic tour de force, believable only because it succeeded.

[66] Vol. V, 5234–5235.

16.

The Consistent Bullet and the Anonymous Shell

The last pieces of "real" evidence that might be used to prove that either of the defendants was a South Braintree murderer consisted of six bullets (four removed from the body of Berardelli and two from Parmenter); three or four exploded .32 caliber cartridge cases allegedly picked up on Pearl Street after the shooting on April 15; Sacco's Colt automatic, .32 caliber; and thirty-odd unexploded cartridges of the same caliber, taken from him at the time of his arrest. It was the misleading character of the testimony by the government's ballistic experts about some of these items at the Dedham trial which later brought almost universal condemnation from responsible sources of the tactics employed by the prosecution.

It may come as a surprise to persons familiar with cases of homicide by firearms that no claim was made by the prosecution that Sacco's pistol had fired any of the recovered bullets or shells until *after the Dedham trial had been underway for nearly three weeks*. By that time the government had been in possession of the items for more than thirteen months. Far from making such a claim, Mr. Katzmann, until after June 18, 1921, had stipulated with Mr. Moore that he would *not* claim that any bullet had been fired by any particular gun. As with the claim that Vanzetti was carrying Berardelli's revolver, the claim ultimately made by the prosecution that Sacco's gun had fired one of the bullets (mortal bullet No. III) and one of the exploded shells (Fraher shell F4) was not originally part of the government's case against Sacco. In fact, it was the last important claim to be entered by the Commonwealth. It was put forward in the middle of the Dedham trial.

This claim has been kept alive, or rather revived, by several writers who have accepted as infallible certain off-the-record ballistic tests made many years after the trial by volunteer experts on one of the bullets, marked III, and one of the exploded shells, referred to as F4. These writers assumed that the items examined by the latter-day experts were authentic originals or at least were the same exhibits as were the subjects of expert testimony at the trial. As we shall see, there is much doubt as to the validity of such assumptions.

In the field of crime detection, marks left on bullets and shells discharged by firearms rank almost as high as fingerprints in the order of convincing proofs. If any bullets and shells can be connected with weapons carried by the defendants, this will constitute important proof of guilt. To do this, however, requires ballistic opinions by experts and these are necessarily subject to error, because they depend on the skill, experience and judgment of the expert witnesses, on the condition of the exhibits, and on manipulation of apparatus. For this reason, such evidence often lacks the satisfactory positiveness of certain other physical objects. Expert ballistic testimony at its best deals only with the question of whether the subject bullet was fired through a particular gun. It does not determine whether the bullet examined was in fact the genuine original and this lack often widens the area for mistakes and controversy.

If we thread our way backward from testimony before the Governor's Advisory Committee, through the affidavits and testimony that accompanied motions for a new trial based on ballistic evidence, through Mr. Katzmann's arguments, the trial and other evidence, we can pretty well reconstruct what went on in the district attorney's office in connection with the preparation of firearms evidence for the Dedham trial and the later proceedings.

At the outset, a review of the prosecution's handling of the bullet and shell evidence reveals a rather unusual phenomenon. The claim that Sacco's pistol had been used to fire shots at South Braintree was not made *until after the defense had requested and obtained permission to make tests with the weapon. Thereafter, the government's evidence that Sacco's pistol had been used seemed to grow in positiveness in response to moves by the defense.* Its positions may be stated as follows:

First period, from May 5, 1920, date of arrest, until June 5, 1921, fifth day of trial. It was during this period that Mr. Katzmann stipulated that he would make no claim that any particular bullet was fired by any particular gun.

Second period, from June 5, 1921, when defense counsel requested and obtained permission to make tests with Sacco's gun, to the close of the Dedham trial. After the tests, the real opinion (unknown to the defense) of one of the State's experts (Captain Proctor) was that the bullet III had not passed through Sacco's pistol. The prosecution's second expert (Captain Van Amburgh) merely was 'inclined to think" that it had. Neither expert stated an opinion that shell F4 had been so fired.

Third period. This began on November 5, 1923, when defense counsel filed motions for new trial based on affidavits from new ballistic experts containing opinions that neither bullet III nor shell F4 had been fired in Sacco's pistol. Captain Proctor was no longer a government expert. Captain Van Amburgh, however, was now *positive* that the mortal bullet III was fired in Sacco's pistol. He also gave an opinion that Fraher shell F4 had been fired in Sacco's pistol.[1] A second expert (new), Merton A. Robinson, was "satisfied" that bullet III and shell F4 were fired in Sacco's pistol.[2]

The details concerning the government's handling of the bullet and shell evidence will be discussed later in this chapter.

Sacco's pistol was a Colt .32 caliber automatic. Since the bullets and shells were fired through .32 automatics, his gun was naturally immediately suspect as the murder weapon. (They might also have been discharged by pistols of 7.65 millimeter, the designation of guns produced by foreign makers, equal to our .32 caliber.)[3] The evidence makes it seem unlikely that the district attorney's office was then aware of this possibility. Prior to trial, however, the prosecution had failed in its efforts to obtain expert testimony to sustain a claim that Sacco's pistol had been fired at South Braintree.

The Commonwealth was more or less compelled to look to Captain Proctor for expert advice about whether Sacco's automatic had been used. It was well known that Proctor was the State's leading ballistics authority. Writers who have focused on ballistics as proof of Sacco's guilt have, of necessity, belittled his skill as an expert. However that may be, he had examined bullets, cartridges, pistols and revolvers for over twenty years and had testified in over one hundred capital cases. More particularly, he had made examinations of bullets he had passed through barrels to obtain the difference in the rifling shown on bullets.[4] Captain Proctor had held the South Braintree bullets and shells in his department for over a year and had made extensive tests upon them.[5] These tests may seem crude today in the light of later improvements, but they had then been used as the basis for firearms identification in capital cases. If expert testimony became essential

[1] Vol. IV, 3666–3667.   [2] Vol. IV, 3676–3677.   [3] Vol. II, 1415.   [4] Vol. I, 886.
[5] Vol. I, 902.

and it had appeared that the prosecution had not used its leading expert, the government's case. The omission would have had a high visibility and the defense would have rightly suspected that something was wrong with could not have been buried as the fingerprint evidence had been.

Of the six bullets extracted from the bodies of the murder victims, Captain Proctor immediately eliminated five. These five bullets showed marks of a right twist or spiral, whereas the twist in a Colt automatic barrel was to the left.[6] *Only one bullet alleged to have been removed from Berardelli's body showed marks of a left twist which could have been made by a Colt.* This bullet was fatal to Berardelli. It was identified as bullet No. III.

Captain Proctor, after using every means known to him to form an opinion, advised Mr. Katzmann and Mr. Williams that if they asked him whether in his opinion the No. III bullet was fired from Sacco's Colt he would be obliged to answer in the negative.[7] He probably went even further. Since, as we learned after his death, in his opinion, the fatal bullet *had not* been fired in Sacco's pistol, it seems unlikely that he did not so inform the district attorney. It is significant that Mr. Katzmann, when questioned about the matter in 1927, could not deny that Captain Proctor had expressed to him the opinion that Sacco and Vanzetti had not committed the crime.[8]

The prosecution was not entirely satisfied with Captain Proctor's advice. Accordingly, they brought in the second expert, Captain Charles J. Van Amburgh, then an assistant in the ballistics department of the Remington Union Metallic Cartridge Company in Bridgeport, Connecticut.[9] Captain Van Amburgh was requested specifically to consider the No. III bullet.[10] He first began his examination in December 1920. We have no documentary proof that Captain Van Amburgh then reported to the district attorney that he found nothing on which to base an opinion that the No. III bullet had been fired in Sacco's gun. However, it is a fairly safe inference that such was his opinion, for it was during the period including Captain Van Amburgh's examinations that Mr. Katzmann entered into the oral stipulation with Mr. Moore that *he would make no claim and intended to offer no proof to the effect that any particular bullet came from any particu-*

---

[6] Vol. I, 892–893. There were also at least 14 other makes of automatics with a left-hand twist, but apparently this was not known by the government experts.
[7] Vol. IV, 3642.   [8] Vol. V, 5084.
[9] Vol. I, 911. However, "ballistics" as used at Remington did not mean "identification" as used in forensics.   [10] Vol. I, 923.

lar gun.[11] He would not have made such an agreement if one of his experts had intimated that he had found any evidence that Sacco's gun had fired bullet No. III.

The stipulation remained in effect *until June 21, 1921, the eighteenth day of the trial,* following the test shooting at Lowell, Massachusetts, on June 18. The circumstances surrounding Mr. Katzmann's revocation of the agreement will be considered later. The prosecution's stipulation had contained the implicit admission that such examinations and tests as were made by both Proctor and Van Amburgh had yielded no evidence whatever that Sacco's automatic had been fired at South Braintree. It is arguable that these examinations were not conclusive. This could be so. However, these experts *were retained by the State* and they would hardly have made the report on which the district attorney's stipulation was based if they had found anything at all which created a doubt in their minds.

Mr. Katzmann's stipulation has not received the attention it deserves. It should hold a key place in any discussion about the No. III bullet, the subsequent testimony about it and the authenticity of any bullet or shell subjected to later examinations.

The trial record shows that Mr. Katzmann, in preparing his case, seized upon everything, no matter how flimsy, ephemeral or dubious, which might be made to prove, or even suggest, the guilt of the defendants. *Nevertheless, prior to the trial, after consulting his two experts, he abandoned any claim that Sacco's pistol had fired any particular bullet.* Later, at the trial and in motions thereafter, he reversed his position entirely and claimed that Sacco's Colt had killed Berardelli. What caused such a drastic change in Mr. Katzmann's position? And is it possible that the physical evidence itself also underwent a change?

According to Mr. Katzmann, his switch was the result of test shots fired at Lowell on June 18, 1921. The tests had their origin in something that happened on June 6, the fifth day of the Dedham trial, before the prosecution had opened its case. To understand what happened we must jump ahead in our story and listen to what Judge McAnarney said to the Governor's Advisory Committee in 1927.

Q. (By Mr. Thompson) Mr. McAnarney, I forgot to ask you one question, you reminded me of it when I telephoned to you yesterday. Was there any conversation with Sacco about the experimentation with his pistol, was his permis-

[11] Vol. V, 5319.

sion asked, tell us about that. A. That question came up as to making experiments with Sacco's automatic.

Q. Who was to make the experiments? A. Well, this expert Burns [Defense Expert], and I don't know whether it was Captain Proctor or not.

JUDGE GRANT. Fitzgerald.

THE WITNESS. No, Mr. Burns, who I think lived in Lowell, had a place of business there, and in all probability, somebody from the Government would accompany him to make the experiments. The question came up. Mr. Moore came to me about it, and I said, "Why, Sacco has protested his innocence. He says it is not his gun, he was not there, and therefore the bullet could not have come from his gun. There's Sacco sitting in the cage, you go and explain to him" —

PRESIDENT LOWELL. Who did you say this to?

THE WITNESS. Mr. Moore. "You go and explain to Mr. Sacco that it is now proposed to take his pistol or automatic and make certain experiments." Of course, if he was not there his gun was not there; no harm could result to him. Mr. Moore had a talk of perhaps ten or fifteen minutes with him. He came back to me and Sacco was not unwilling but consented that they should experiment all they wished. I said, "If that is so I have nothing to say about it." Even at that stage of the proceedings I could see that it might invite a controversy of experts. It was not something ordinarily that you would approve of.

Q. Did Sacco understand that scientific methods would be employed by the experts to see whether the bullet went through that pistol? A. I explained to him the different things that the experts had talked about, that the experts could determine from an examination of the bullets with reasonable certainty whether it came through a certain pistol or not.

Q. Now that you are here I am going to put another question to you.

PRESIDENT LOWELL. Let me ask you what the bearing of all this is?

MR. THOMPSON. Sacco was not afraid, when put to the test in court, to have his pistol experimented with.

PRESIDENT LOWELL. No. *That is what you are after.* I supposed that the Government had a right to make experiments.

THE WITNESS. I question that very much.

PRESIDENT LOWELL. However, that is all right. It was his pistol?

THE WITNESS. Sacco's automatic; it was to be experimented with.

MR. THOMPSON. You cannot experiment with exhibits without the consent of the other side.

THE WITNESS. The point Mr. Thompson has in mind and what he brought me up here for was to *make it clear that Sacco understood.* [Emphasis added.][12]

The foregoing excerpt is important as showing that Sacco, an accused murderer, was willing that his attorney should request that firearms experts make ballistic experiments with his pistol. This should have been striking evidence of consciousness of innocence. It is also a dismal illustration of the attitude of President Lowell toward the defendants. When Mr. Thompson

[12] Vol. V, 5185–5186.

pointed out that Sacco's assent showed that he was not afraid to have his pistol tested, Mr. Lowell flatly denied it, adding a sneer at Mr. Thompson for his saying so as *merely something that he "was after."* He "supposed" that the government could have made the experiments anyway. In this he was contradicted by Judge McAnarney and Mr. Thompson. Mr. Ranney remained silent. Even more significantly, Mr. Lowell passed over the fact that the government, through Mr. Katzmann's stipulation, had, in effect, already disavowed *any intention of requesting experimentation* with Sacco's pistol. (We shall later examine in detail Mr. Lowell's whole approach to the Sacco-Vanzetti evidence.) Nor did Judge Thayer see in Sacco's voluntary submission to test firing any proof of his consciousness of innocence. To the judge, it simply indicated that the defense regarded the matter as important.[13]

After obtaining his clients' permission, defendants' counsel then presented their motion to the court. The record shows the following:

(Conference at Bench between Court and Counsel)
THE COURT. Sheriff Capen, I have made an order here, and I wish you would come around, because you are going to be custodian of the weapons and also the bullets, and they are to be kept in your possession and not to be taken from your possession by anybody. *Counsel for the defendants have made a motion to that effect, that they be given an opportunity to have the bullets and weapons examined by their expert.* I have granted that motion. I have insisted that they remain in the custody of yourself.
(Sheriff Capen joins Court and Counsel at Bench.)
And therefore, you will not allow them to go out of your custody. They can, in your immediate presence, have them for examination, and after their experts have examined them sufficiently, then you will return them to Captain Proctor. That is the order of the Court. Under no circumstances allow them to go out of your possession. They are to be used, as I understand, for purposes of evidence later in the trial of these cases, so they may examine them. The request of the counsel for the defendants for an opportunity to have an expert or experts to examine the weapons is a reasonable one and is granted. They will be put in your possession, and they will be, in your presence, examined by experts of the defendants, but they are to leave your custody under no circumstances whatsoever. And so that they must remain exactly as they are at the present time, there must be no change in them, and I cannot conceive of anybody thinking of changing the condition of either of the weapons or the bullets. That goes with the orders, Sheriff, so bear that in mind. [Emphasis added.][14]

It was a bold stroke by Mr. Moore and should have resulted in a powerful argument for the innocence of his client. Having made the request for

13 Vol. V, 5551.   14 Vol. I, 50.

the experiments, Mr. Moore should have followed it through. It was one of those situations which demanded that he kill the quarry, not merely wound it. He may not be blamed for not realizing that he had actually won the battle of the tests (as we shall see later), but how can we justify his judgment in belittling the importance of the experiment itself and so, in effect, disowning his own child.[15] Since Mr. Moore was not prepared to drive home to the jury the full meaning of his requesting the tests, he should have been satisfied with Mr. Katzmann's agreement. It is an axiom of trial practice never to challenge a favorable decision unless it is not good enough. Young advocates are advised to pick up their papers immediately when they get what they want and leave the courtroom as quickly as possible. They should never try to paint the lily.

Apparently Mr. Moore did not fully appreciate the danger of not letting well enough alone. Having obtained a critical concession on behalf of his clients, he sought to turn this most effective shield into a sword (but then failed to wield it). Mr. Katzmann's account of the affair was set out by him in his reply to Mr. Moore's argument that the verdict was against the weight of the evidence.

Here is what Mr. Katzmann told the court:

MR. KATZMANN. [Quoting Mr. Moore as having said] "And I think I may be permitted further to say that at that time, collateral to the issue, I understood that there would be no claim made that the bullet did come, or any particular bullet did come from any particular gun."

Then Katzmann goes on, saying:

That is true, but that is only part of the story, if your Honor please. I told Mr. Moore myself before the Lowell experiment on that Sacco gun in private conversation when he asked me if we made the claim and intended to offer any proof to the effect that any particular bullet came from any particular gun before the Lowell experiments, and I said, "No, Mr. Moore." But that is not the whole story. Then, as he says, at the request of the defendants, and if your Honor please, as a practical matter may I suggest to you that it was after he had that assurance from the District Attorney that the request came for an opportunity to fire the Sacco gun afterwards, and my good friend will not contradict me when I go outside of the record, as did he, in making that statement, when I say to your Honor in all seriousness that after the Lowell experiments I went to Mr. Moore before Van Amburgh took the stand and said, "Mr. Moore, in the light of the result of the experiments at Lowell I withdraw the statement that I made

15 Vol. II, 2147.

to you the other day in regard in making no claim that any particular bullet was fired from any particular gun." [16]

Mr. Moore's request to fire Sacco's gun must have upset the district attorney's office. Apparently the prosecutors had reconciled themselves to their lack of expert testimony to support a claim that Sacco's gun was used. They could leave out the expert testimony entirely and still let the jury draw its own conclusions from the other evidence in the case. However, when Mr. Moore declined to accept Mr. Katzmann's assurance and wanted his own experts to make tests, Mr. Katzmann faced a different situation. The defense experts might *prove* that Sacco fired no shots. This would be contrary to the government claim so carefully prepared for the trial. The prosecution's case might then collapse under the impact of the experts' ballistic opinions based on the shooting tests. This fear must have practically forced Mr. Katzmann to find evidence quickly that bullet No. III (the mortal bullet) was fired in Sacco's gun. Mr. Williams had opened the case for the prosecution without mentioning any clai mthat bullet No. III, or any exploded shell, had been fired in Sacco's pistol. (He did state, however, that one of the bullets had been fired from a .32 Colt automatic and that Sacco had such a weapon.)[17] *Yet, these were crucial claims.* No testimony to support bullet or shell evidence entered the case until after Mr. Katzmann had revoked the stipulation, some three weeks after the trial had begun. It was perhaps the hurried preparation by the prosecution to counter the ballistic testimony which they feared Moore might obtain which led to the State's own ambiguous expert testimony for which the entire trial has been so often condemned. Before we examine the testimony itself, however, it is necessary to see how the bullets and shells came to be admitted as evidence. This is the foundation of all of the ballistic testimony. The recital is disquieting, to put it mildly.

When Sacco was searched by Brockton Police Officer Merle A. Spear, after his arrest, there were taken from him a .32 Colt automatic, containing one cartridge in the barrel, a clip of eight cartridges and a number of loose .32 caliber bullets. As to the number of loose cartridges Officer Spear said he *"later counted twenty-three."* [18] *The cartridges were never identified* [19] *or made the subject of a memorandum when taken from Sacco. There was no way of verifying the identity of the loose cartridges or even their number.* There might have been more than twenty-three originally taken from

16 Vol. V, 5319.   17 Vol. I, 77.   18 Vol. I, 781.   19 Vol. I, 783.

Sacco's pocket for all the record shows. Those in the pistol and from his pocket were turned over to Officer Scott of the State Police in the presence of Captain Proctor, along with the automatic pistol. Cartridges from the gun and those from Sacco's pocket were mixed together and, according to Captain Proctor, handed to Officer Scott in the Brockton police station and by Officer Scott to Proctor.[20] At the trial Captain Proctor was shown an envelope of cartridges and asked to identify them. He identified the envelope and said the cartridges had been in his possession until delivered to the sheriff. The makes of the cartridges were sixteen Peters, three Remingtons, seven United States Cartridge Company and six Winchesters.[21] Mr. Williams offered the cartridges in evidence and Mr. McAnarney objected. Judge Thayer asked a question similar to one he had asked at Plymouth about the shotgun cartridges, namely, whether the police officer (Spear) handed the cartridges to Officer Scott in Proctor's presence. On receiving an affirmative answer he admitted the pistol cartridges as Exhibit 31. Again, it is difficult to see how the answer to Judge Thayer's question rendered admissible cartridges never identified by the officer who took them from Sacco. Mr. Williams also offered in evidence the revolver and cartridges taken from Vanzetti. Mr. McAnarney then explained his objection and exception: "As to the revolver [Exhibit 27] or the pistol [Exhibit 28], there is no question there as to identity, but as to the identity of *some of these unmarked shells I would not waive any rights there*." [22] (Emphasis added).

Mr. McAnarney's objection seems to have been sound, but it did him no good. The revolver cartridges (as well as the pistol cartridges) were also admitted as Exhibit 32. We have no way of knowing whether the cartridges offered as being those removed from Sacco's pocket included all of the cartridges taken by the police.

Four exploded shells, ejected by automatics, found their way into the "real" evidence offered at the trial. They were in an envelope shown to Captain Proctor, who testified that they were given to him by Mr. Fraher of the Slater and Morrill factory.[23] Over Mr. McAnarney's objection they were admitted in evidence as Exhibit 30. The following is their history:

The government witness James E. Bostock had testified as follows:

Q. (By Mr. Williams) Did you pick up any shells there? A. Yes, I picked up some shells.

[20] Vol. I, 887. [21] Vol. I, 888. [22] Vol. I, 889. [23] Vol. I, 885.

Q. Where abouts did you pick them up? A. *I picked them up just close to where the shooting was, about two or three feet from the shooting.*
Q. What did you do with them? A. I think Mr. Fraher had them.
Q. Mr. Fraher? A. I left them in Slater & Morrill's office.
Q. How many did you pick up? A. *Three or four.*
Q. You turned them over to Mr. Fraher? A. No. I left them in the office of Slater & Morrill, in one of the desks.
Q. Is that all you found there? A. That is all. I saw some others picked up. I saw some others had some others, but that is all I picked up. [Emphasis added.] [24]

The significant answer in the foregoing testimony was the addition of the words "or four." *There were no identifying marks on the exploded pistol shells left by Mr. Bostock.*[25] Neither Mr. Bostock nor Mr. Fraher was asked to identify any of the shells. Three of these shells could not have been fired in Sacco's pistol. The fourth shell, however, might have been so fired.

Did Bostock pick up only three shells? It was the first number he mentioned. Surely he knew how many he found. Also, Bostock had testified that he picked them up "about two or three feet from the shooting." Since the fourth shell, if authentic, must have been fired by a second bandit with a different weapon, how did it happen that it had been ejected into the midst of the other shells? Skepticism grows on studying the facts. Was he persuaded (before trial) that there might have been a fourth? We know that he apparently tried to help the prosecution by stating on direct examination that he remembered that Berardelli had shown him a nickel-plated revolver on the Saturday night before the murders. Then on cross-examination, Bostock paid no attention whatever to his own original story, but gave voluntarily far more likely testimony indicating that Berardelli had shown the revolver in the morning at some indefinite time quite a while before the crime. Possibly Mr. Bostock had merely tried to be accommodating and reasonably truthful at the same time. He certainly was not friendly to the defense. I found that out in 1927 when I wanted him to look at my sheaf of photographs including some of the Morelli gang. At first he absolutely refused even to talk to us. However, when my companion, Mr. Carney, gave him a lodge password, he changed his attitude precipitately and granted us an interview.

Thomas F. Fraher, superintendent of Slater and Morrill, stated that Mr. Bostock "delivered" to him "four empty shells" which he gave to Captain

24 Vol. I, 195.   25 Vol. I, 882.

Proctor.[26] (Bostock had said that he left them in a desk in the office.) However, Mr. Fraher was hardly a disinterested witness. The record suggests that he was an active aide to the prosecution, and it was Mr. Fraher's assistant, Fred Loring, who told of finding a cap next to Berardelli's body just after the killing and giving it to Mr. Fraher. Not only Mr. Loring, but Mr. Fraher himself must have known that this testimony was false.

So we have no way of knowing whether the unmarked shells left by Mr. Bostock numbered three or four. The number might have been either but it seems unlikely that he would not have remembered the true one. Since later expert testimony indicates that only one of the four shells (Fraher Winchester shell F4) could have been fired through Sacco's pistol, one wonders. Mr. Fraher's testimony about shell F4 was intended to lay a basis for the later claim that it had passed through Sacco's pistol. Was this as spurious as the story used to get the Pearl Street cap into evidence? Such wonder may be increased by the fact that neither government expert at the trial testified to an opinion that shell F4 had been fired in Sacco's gun. There is still another striking coincidence. Three of the shells were of a manufacture different from that of the No. III bullet. The fourth, however, supposedly also picked up from among those strewn in Pearl Street, was the *only one of the four that was a W.R.A. Winchester, claimed to be of the same manufacture as the slug that killed Berardelli.* By these chances, the assistant district attorney was enabled to insinuate that the fourth shell matched *the fatal bullet* and so formed the single cartridge alleged to have been fired through Sacco's gun. It is all quite reminiscent of the shotgun shells claimed to have been found in Vanzetti's pocket, where the fourth cartridge also turned out to be a Winchester to match the exploded shell found in the street.

Four bullets were extracted from the body of Berardelli and two from Parmenter. The surgeon who performed the autopsies was Dr. George Burgess Magrath, medical examiner for Suffolk County. Dr. Magrath described his procedure in the Berardelli autopsy as follows:

As my operating proceeded and I came upon a bullet, the location of this bullet and its location and character were noted and described *and the bullet marked on its base with the point of a needle, a numeral, a Roman numeral, in the order in which it was taken out.* Thus, the first bullet recovered was marked "I," a small scratch on the base. Succeeding bullets as taken out as they were come upon were similarly and appropriately marked. Two was marked — the second

[26] Vol. I, 882.

was marked with a Roman II and three with a Roman III, and the fourth with the Roman IIII or four vertical lines. [Emphasis added.] [27]

Two features of Dr. Magrath's testimony should be noted. *The slugs were marked seriatim as extracted*, and they were identified with *small scratches made with the point of a needle*. Therefore, all of the bullets should have exhibited scratches made by the same hand with the point of the same needle. As we shall see later, the mark on the base of the bullet with Roman numeral III cut into its base, when examined in 1927, bore the clear aspect of having been made by a clumsier hand and a duller instrument than the others. When photographed in 1960 for Mr. Russell's book, the III had the appearance of a gouge rather than a fine scratch. The bullet marked III by Dr. Magrath was the one which killed Berardelli and was claimed to have been fired in Sacco's gun.

The unusual manner in which the bullets were handled as evidence excluded any comparison at the trial of the identifying marks on the base of the four bullets. Each bullet was placed in its own separate envelope and so produced at the trial. Dr. Magrath was then handed an envelope, and asked to take the bullet out and see if he could identify it as a bullet he had removed. As he identified each bullet by the scratch he had placed on its base, he was asked to replace it in its envelope and take up the next envelope. In this manner he identified the bullets without ever comparing the base marks with one another. They were then admitted in evidence and the exhibit numbers put on the separate envelopes, not on the bullets. The envelope holding the No. III bullet was labeled Exhibit 18.[28]

The custody of the bullets from autopsy to trial was never traced. Nor do we know just how the envelopes were handled after they were marked as exhibits. Mr. Katzmann told Judge Thayer that he left some exhibits with the clerk but kept others. Judge Thayer then remarked, "I think all the exhibits ought to be left with the stenographer or with the Clerk." [29] Even if left with the clerk, however, there were no adequate safeguards if parties connected with the case wished to inspect or use the exhibits. Bullet III, especially, was handled frequently by various persons. The clerk could check the numbers on the envelopes but would have no way of knowing whether they contained the same bullets when returned to him. Any of the bullets may have become mixed during the handling, or accidentally

[27] Vol. I, 112–113.   [28] Vol. I, 118–119.   [29] Vol. I, 904.

dropped, or removed as souvenirs or for other purposes, or lost, and the replacement would not have been scrutinized or recognized.

Such occurrences to ballistic exhibits were not infrequent. In *State v. Civitan* (Hudson County, N.J., 1932), after the prosecution had closed its case, it was found that the bullet admitted in evidence was not the bullet removed from the victim. The prosecution had to reopen the case and submit the correct bullet. Shelley Braverman relates that in a case involving international repercussions, with armed guards supposedly guarding the custody of the evidence, he found the evidence bullet one evening still in the microscope chuck after the guards had left. Something of the sort may have happened to throw off Captain Van Amburgh's opinion in another case,[30] and Major Calvin Goddard, about whom we shall hear later, blamed a confusion of bullets for a grievous blunder in giving *his* expert opinion, also in another case.[31] We do not know how much of this went on during the various stages of the Sacco-Vanzetti proceedings. We do know that there were a number of mishaps to the exhibits. At one place the record shows the following brief interlude:

Defense expert James Burns had taken Vanzetti's revolver to the window to examine its hammer in better light. The Record then interrupts itself:

(A bullet falls to the floor.)
MR. KATZMANN. What is it, do you know?
MR. JEREMIAH MCANARNEY. Put your glass on that. What is the mark?
THE WITNESS. Search me. That is your —
MR. KATZMANN. I do not know whether it is mine or not.
MR. JEREMIAH MCANARNEY. What is the marking on it?
MR. KATZMANN. He says to search him.
MR. JEREMIAH MCANARNEY. It is one of those three. [Meaning three test bullets fired by Captain Van Amburgh, which had been placed in an envelope and marked Exhibit 35.[32]] I will show it to Captain Van Amburgh. It is his exhibit, so that he may — is that one of yours? [The Record does not indicate any answer.][33]

The foregoing excerpt is curiously indefinite. It does not tell us who was handling the bullet when it dropped, how the accident happened, who picked it up, how it was marked, or whether Captain Van Amburgh identi-

---

[30] *State v. Israel,* Criminal Court, Fairfield County, Conn., 1924.
[31] Arthur Warner, "A Sacco Revolver Expert Revealed," *Nation,* December 7, 1927.
[32] Vol. I, 897.   [33] Vol. II, 1463.

fied it. Apparently, however, the bullet had been in Van Amburgh's custody. Three years later Captain Van Amburgh found himself as a ballistic expert in a mix-up which nearly cost the life of one Harold Israel. Among other things, *the case involved finding an extra shell*. The accused was cleared and his life was saved only by the conscientious industry of Homer S. Cummings, Esq., then State's attorney, later United States Attorney General. Captain Van Amburgh's professional conduct came under severe criticism in the Israel case. Nevertheless, he was later appointed head of the ballistics laboratory of the Massachusetts Department of Public Safety.

Yet the bullets with the Roman numerals had more to identify them than some other exhibits, such as the thirty-two cartridges taken from Sacco, the four empty .32 shells, and the shotgun cartridges allegedly taken from Vanzetti. Francis Russell, in *Tragedy in Dedham*, quotes Lieutenant John Collins, in charge of the ballistic laboratory for the Massachusetts State Police in 1960, as saying, "The way they handled these exhibits from the beginning makes my hair stand on end." [34]

The failure to take adequate precautions to protect the integrity of the physical exhibits tends to vitiate conclusions based on them.[35] Ordinarily, one would assume that they were authentic and free from tampering. Especially would this be so in a capital case. There is little indication that defense counsel at the trial at Plymouth or Dedham suspected the integrity of the government's use of the exhibits. It was apparently this reliance on the good faith of the prosecution that kept them from challenging the authenticity of the trial exhibits. By the time Sacco and Vanzetti were executed, however, enough had already been revealed about the methods used by the prosecution in preparing its case to shake both professional and public confidence in its integrity. We know now that much more went wrong behind the trial curtain than was supposed at that time. Some of these things we have already considered. Let us now examine the manner in which Captain Proctor and Captain Van Amburgh came to give their expert testimony about the mortal bullet.

The test shootings at Lowell were held on June 18, 1921, and those who participated were Captain Proctor and Captain Van Amburgh for the prosecution, and James E. Burns, ballistic engineer at the United States

---

[34] Russell, *Tragedy in Dedham*, 316. At present writing, Collins is a captain.
[35] I am advised by Mr. Braverman that in New York City experts attend the autopsies to get the bullets personally.

Cartridge Company, for the defense. (Another defense expert, J. Henry Fitzgerald, in charge of the testing room at the Colt Patent Firearms Company, testified about the results of the tests but apparently did not attend the Lowell experiments.) According to Captain Proctor: "We fired the automatic pistol in the case [Sacco's Colt] into sawdust and recovered the bullets themselves, that sprung from the pistol. I got six empty shells that I picked up that came from the pistol. . . . Van Amburgh fired six and Mr. Burns fired eight." [36]

The recovered bullets and shells were then compared by Captains Proctor and Van Amburgh with the six bullets extracted in the autopsies and with the four so-called Fraher shells. The two experts then reported their opinions to the district attorneys. Captain Proctor found nothing to indicate that Sacco's pistol had been used at South Braintree. Captain Van Amburgh expressed a tentative and rather tepid opinion to the contrary. There were repeated conferences between the two experts in which Captain Van Amburgh pointed to a scratch or scratches on which he based his opinion, but to Captain Proctor these were entirely unconvincing.[37]

The prosecution now had problems. They might have refrained from putting one or both of their experts on the stand. However, they probably felt obliged to produce them as witnesses, since the district attorney had sent them to the Lowell test shootings. If so, then how should their expert opinions be presented to judge and jury? A simple solution would have been to have asked for their opinions without seeking in any way to shape the answers or to load the questions against the defendants. It is a lamentable fact that this course was not followed.

What took place between Proctor and the prosecution in the district attorney's office is best told by the principal himself. In the affidavit which he gave to Mr. Thompson in October 1923, he said:

My name is William H. Proctor. I live in Swampscott, Mass., and I am Captain in the Department of Public Safety, in charge of the Division of State Police. I have been Captain for sixteen years and in the State Police Department for thirty-six years. My office is at the State House in Boston. I am making this affidavit in my own office and at the request of Mr. William G. Thompson, who I understood is now one of the counsel for one of the defendants in the above entitled case. I was associated with the prosecution of the defendants in this case and I had in my custody for a considerable time the Colt automatic pistol taken from the defendant Sacco at the time of his arrest, the cartridges taken from him at the same time, the so-called Fraher shells picked up on the ground at the time of the murder and some other exhibits in the case not material for the purpose which I understand from Mr. Thompson is the subject matter of this statement.

I also had in my custody and made examination of from time to time, with great care, the bullets said to have been taken from the body of Berardelli, all except one of which were, as I testified at the trial, fired from a pistol which was not a Colt automatic pistol. One of them was, as I then testified and still believe, fired from a Colt automatic pistol of 32 calibre.

During the preparation for the trial, my attention was repeatedly called by the District Attorney and his assistants to the question: whether I could find any evidence which would justify the opinion that the particular bullet taken from the body of Berardelli, which came from a Colt automatic pistol, came from the particular Colt automatic pistol taken from Sacco. I used every means available to me for forming an opinion on this subject. I conducted, with Captain Van Amberg, certain tests at Lowell, about which I testified, consisting in firing certain cartridges through Sacco's pistol. At no time was I able to find any evidence whatever which tended to convince me that the particular mortal bullet found in Berardelli's body, which came from a Colt automatic pistol, which I think was numbered 3 and had some other exhibit number, came from Sacco's pistol and *I so informed the District Attorney and his assistant before the trial.* This bullet was what is commonly called a full metalpatch bullet and although I repeatedly talked over with Captain Van Amberg the scratch or scratches which he claimed tended to identify this bullet as one that must have gone through Sacco's pistol, his statements concerning the identifying marks seemed to me entirely unconvincing.

At the trial, the District Attorney did not ask me whether I had found any evidence that the so-called mortal bullet which I have referred to as number 3 passed through Sacco's pistol, nor was I asked that question on cross-examination. *The District Attorney desired to ask me that question, but I had repeatedly told him that if he did I should be obliged to answer in the negative;* consequently, he put to me this question: Q. Have you an opinion as to whether bullet No. 3 was fired from the Colt automatic which is in evidence? To which I answered, "I have." He then proceeded. Q. And what is your opinion? A. My opinion is that it is consistent with being fired by that pistol.

That is still my opinion for the reason that bullet number 3, in my judgment, passed through some Colt automatic pistol, but I do not intend by that answer to imply that I had found any evidence that the so-called mortal bullet had passed through this particular Colt automatic pistol and *the District Attorney well knew that I did not so intend and framed his question accordingly. Had I been asked the direct question: whether I had found any affirmative evidence whatever that this so-called mortal bullet had passed through this particular Sacco's pistol, I should have answered then, as I do now without hesitation, in the negative.* [Emphasis added.][38]

---

[38] Vol. IV, 3641–3643. Mr. Thompson said later that if he had known that Captain Proctor had a positive opinion that the mortal bullet had *not* been fired by Sacco's gun, the affidavit would have been far stronger.

Mr. Katzmann's reply affidavit, dated October 31, 1923, reads as follows:

I, Frederick G. Katzmann, being first duly sworn, on oath, depose and say, that I have read the affidavit of Capt. William H. Proctor dated October 20, 1923; that the said Captain Proctor examined the four bullets which had been recovered from the body of Berardelli, and the Sacco pistol, in the summer and fall of 1920, and he informed me that three of the said bullets were, in his opinion, fired from a 32 calibre Savage automatic pistol, and that the fourth of said bullets had been fired from a 32 calibre Colt automatic pistol; that later, and prior to his testifying, Captain Proctor told me that he was prepared to testify that the mortal bullet was consistent with having been fired from the Sacco pistol; that I did not repeatedly ask him whether he had found any evidence that the mortal bullet had passed through the Sacco pistol, nor did he repeatedly tell me that if I did ask him that question he would be obliged to reply in the negative.[39]

Mr. Williams's reply affidavit, dated October 30, reads as follows:

I, Harold P. Williams, being first duly sworn, on oath depose and say: I first met Captain William H. Proctor during the trial of these cases at Dedham. I knew that he had made an examination of the bullets taken from the body of Berardelli and asked him what this examination had disclosed. He told me that he had compared these bullets with bullets in his possession which had been pushed by him through various types of pistols, and which had taken the rifling marks of these pistols. He said such comparisons showed that the mortal bullet (later exh. 18) had been fired in a Colt automatic and the other three in a Savage automatic. I asked him if he could tell in what pistol this so-called mortal bullet was fired and he said that he could not although the marks upon it were consistent with its having been fired in the Sacco pistol. He said that all he could do was to determine the width of the landmarks upon the bullet. His attention was not repeatedly called to the question, whether he could find any evidence which would justify the opinion that this bullet came from the Sacco pistol. I conducted the direct examination of Captain Proctor at the trial and asked him the question quoted in his affidavit, "Have you an opinion as to whether bullet number 3 was fired from the Colt automatic which is in evidence?"

This question was suggested by Captain Proctor himself as best calculated to give him an opportunity to tell what opinion he had respecting the mortal bullet and its connection with the Sacco pistol. His answer in court was the same answer he had given me personally before.

From the foregoing two affidavits it appears that the only Proctor allegation that was specifically denied was that he had been *"repeatedly"* asked whether he had found any evidence that the mortal bullet had passed through the Sacco pistol and that he had *"repeatedly"* told Mr. Katzmann

[39] Vol. IV, 3681.

that if he was asked the question he would be obliged to reply in the negative. It was this fact, more than any other, that stung Felix Frankfurter with a sense of outrage and drove him to further investigation of the trial evidence. What he discovered resulted in the publication, in January 1927, of his article in the *Atlantic Monthly*, "The Case of Sacco and Vanzetti."

The significance of the Proctor episode was not whether his real opinion was well founded or not. We do not know now, and probably never will, whether his judgment was correct on the physical evidence he then examined. What is indisputable, however, is that his testimony misled the judge[40] and defense counsel [41] as to *his* true opinion. If these men were deceived, we may be sure that the twelve amateurs on the jury listening to the prosecution expert never even dreamed that Captain Proctor's *real opinion was that he had found nothing to indicate that the mortal bullet had passed through Sacco's pistol.*

Judge Thayer charged the jury in the following language:

> Now, the Commonwealth claims that there are several distinct pieces of testimony that must be considered upon the question of personal identification. Let us see what they are. First, that the fatal Winchester bullet, marked Exhibit 3, which killed Berardelli, was fired through the barrel of the Colt Automatic pistol found upon the defendant Sacco at the time of his arrest. If that is true, that is evidence tending to corroborate the testimony of the witnesses of the Commonwealth that the defendant Sacco was at South Braintree on the 15th day of April, 1920, and it was his pistol that fired the bullet that caused the death of Berardelli. To this effect the Commonwealth introduced the testimony of two witnesses, Messrs. Proctor and Van Amburgh. And on the other hand, the defendants offered testimony of two experts, Messrs. Burns and Fitzgerald, to the effect that the Sacco pistol did not fire the bullet that caused the death of Berardelli.[42]

Since Judge Thayer, over three years later, attempted to shrug off his own understanding of the meaning of Proctor's testimony,[43] it should be noted that at the trial he charged the jury that Proctor (and Van Amburgh) had testified "to the effect" that the fatal Winchester bullet marked Exhibit 3,

---

[40] Vol. III, 3422; Vol. II, 2254.   [41] Vol. V, 5054, 5188.   [42] Vol. III, 3422.
[43] Vol. IV, 3702. For a complete, if partisan, analysis of Judge Thayer's confusing and largely irrelevant "Decision" to avoid drawing the plain conclusion from the affidavits, see discussion in defendants' brief in support of amended Bill of Exceptions, Vol. IV, 4119 et seq. The Supreme Judicial Court declined to disturb Judge Thayer's findings of fact on the Proctor motion, again affirming its own rule that the "question of granting a new trial even in a capital case, ordinarily rests in the sound discretion of the court." Vol. IV, 4356–4357; *Commonwealth v. Sacco*, 255 Mass. 456–457.

which killed Berardelli, was fired through the barrel of the Colt automatic pistol found on Sacco.

A close study of the direct examination of Captain Proctor concerning the mortal bullet seems to indicate that his *answers* strove to keep his definition of the word "consistent" within the technical meaning he had intended it to convey, whereas the *questions* put to him tried to impart the impression that by employing the expression "consistent," Captain Proctor had a positive opinion that the No. III bullet passed through Sacco's gun.

After Captain Proctor had testified that at the Lowell tests he had recovered the bullets he and Captain Van Amburgh had fired and six empty shells, the examination continued:

Q. (Continued) What make of cartridges did you and Captain Van Amberg [*sic*] fire? A. There were three W.R.A. and three Peters.
Q. When you say "W.R.A." do you mean Winchester Repeating Arms? A. Winchester.
Q. What kind of a bullet would you say bullet No. 3 was? A. W.R.A., Winchester Repeating Arms Company.
Q. Now, will you examine for a moment the four shells received from Mr. Fraher? Have you an opinion as to how many weapons were used to fire the four shells which you received from Mr. Fraher? A. I think two.
Q. And can you tell us, in your opinion, how many of those shells and which shells were fired from one and how many and which were fired from the other? A. I think there were three fired from one and one from the other.
Q. Will you tell us which, in your opinion, were fired from one? A. From the right.
Q. Well, can you describe it? I want to show it to the jury. A. It is a W.R.A., Winchester.
Q. What are the other three? A. Two are Peters and one U.M.C.
Q. The W.R.A. was fired from one gun, and the other three, in your opinion, from another? A. It is.
Q. And on what do you base your opinion? A. Well, the looks of the hole in the primer that the firing pin struck that exploded the cartridge.
(Mr. Williams shows the shells to the jury.)
MR. WILLIAMS. Gentlemen, the one in my right hand is the one that he says, in his opinion, was fired from one, and the other three in my left fired from the other.[44]

Up to this point, Captain Proctor had simply given his opinion that of the four Fraher shells, *three had been fired from one weapon and the fourth from another. He did not state that any of them had been fired through Sacco's gun.* (To distinguish the fourth shell from the other three,

[44] Vol. I, 894–895.

let us designate it "Fraher Winchester." It was later designated "F4.") He made the distinction by the looks of the hole in the primer.

We now come to the first appearance of the word "consistent." *It is used by Mr. Williams, not Captain Proctor.*

Here is the question:

Q. Now, will you examine that W.R.A., that we will call for the minute the Fraher shell, and compare it with the six shells fired by you and Captain Van Amberg [*sic*], of which, I understand, three are W.R.A. and three are Peters, and ask you if, in your opinion, the marks on those seven shells are *consistent* with being fired from the same weapon? [Emphasis added.] [45]

Captain Proctor declined to accept the implied positive meaning of the word "consistent," which here would have included the Fraher shell F4, and limited his opinion as follows:

A. I think so, *the same make of weapon.* [Emphasis added.] [46]

Captain Proctor then stated that he based his opinion (that the shells were fired by the same make of weapon) on the similarity "in the looks of the hole in the primer which does not exist with the other three." Captain Proctor was not asked whether this similarity went further than to indicate the same *type* of weapon.

We now come to Captain Proctor's use of the word "consistent" in the prearranged question and answer pertaining to the No. III bullet.

Q. Captain Proctor, have you an opinion as to whether bullets Nos. 1, 2, 5, and 6 were fired from the same weapon? A. I have not.
Q. Have you an opinion as to whether bullet 3 was fired from the Colt automatic which is in evidence?
MR. MCANARNEY. Will you please repeat that question?
Q. Have you an opinion as to whether bullet 3 was fired from the Colt Automatic which is in evidence? A. I have.
Q. And what is your opinion? A. *My opinion is that it is consistent with being fired by that pistol.* [Emphasis added.] [47]

From the affidavits we know that Captain Proctor's use of the word "consistent" was intended as an opinion that bullet III might have been fired in Sacco's gun. The *immediate* continuation of the examination, however, then went on to define the word "consistent" just used by Captain Proctor as meaning a positive opinion. This followed:

[45] Vol. I, 895.   [46] Vol. I, 895.   [47] Vol. I, 896.

Q. Is there anything different in the appearance of the other five bullets —
A. Yes.

Q. Just a minute, I had not completed. — the other five bullets to which I have just referred, which would indicate to you that they were fired from more than one weapon? A. There is not.

Q. Are the appearance of those bullets *consistent* with being fired with the same weapon? A. *As far as I can see.*

Q. *Captain, did you understand my question when I asked you if you had an opinion as to whether the five bullets which you say were fired from an automatic type of pistol were fired from the same gun?* A. *I would not say positively.*

Q. Well, have you an opinion? A. *I have.*

Q. Well, that is what I asked you before. *I thought possibly you didn't understand. What is your opinion as to the gun from which those four [five?] were fired?* A. *My opinion is, all five were fired from the same pistol.* [Emphasis added.] [48]

The foregoing brief exchange is significant. Captain Proctor *twice* refused to answer a question incorporating the word "consistent" in a context implying that he had a positive opinion. After being twice pushed hard by the examiner, to "understand the question," he finally capitulated and allowed the word "consistent" used by Mr. Williams as applied to the five bullets to seem equivalent to a positive opinion. Proctor's real opinion that he found no indication that bullet III had passed through Sacco's pistol was well screened from the jury.

The prosecution had better luck with Captain Van Amburgh after the Lowell tests. As stated by Captain Proctor, Van Amburgh pointed out a scratch or scratches on the bullet which seemed to him to be some evidence that the No. III bullet had been fired in Sacco's gun. This bullet in his view was a Winchester, because it bore a small "W" on the metal. He noted that the indentation of the firing pin was slightly off-center in the Fraher Winchester shell and the other Winchesters fired at Lowell and *that the principle* distinguishing mark was their same diameter. He also mentioned a slight setback as a common feature, meaning a flowing back of metal around the firing pin.[49] He gave no opinion that these features were peculiar to the Sacco gun and to no other. *Van Amburgh was not asked whether in his opinion the Fraher Winchester was fired by Sacco's pistol.* This would seem to indicate that he had advised the prosecutors that he had no opinion, or no favorable opinion, on this subject.

[48] Vol. I, 896–897.   [49] Vol. I, 919.

Nevertheless, this is the wording of the questions put to Van Amburgh concerning his expert opinion about bullet No. III.

Q. Now, Captain, *having in mind the similarities of the shells of those cartridges,* having in mind your examination of No. 3, your examination of the six bullets fired by you and Captain Proctor at Lowell, have you formed an opinion as to whether or not the No. 3 bullet was fired from the Colt automatic gun which you specifically have in front of you? A. Will you just state that question again, please? I don't quite get it all.

Q. You may strike that out, please. Have you formed an opinion, Captain, as to whether or not No. 3 bullet was fired from that particular Colt automatic? A. I have an opinion.

Q. And what is your opinion? A. I am inclined to believe that it was fired, No. 3 bullet was fired, from this Colt automatic pistol.[50]

From the above it will be noted that the inclusion of the words "similarity of the shells of those cartridges" carries a strong implication that the Fraher Winchester, like the Lowell Winchesters, was fired in Sacco's gun. There was no such evidence. However, by the question's making reference to "similarities of the shells," the Fraher Winchester shell was now joined to bullet No. III, supposedly to form one original cartridge fired in Sacco's pistol. Whether intended or not, the coincidence of allegedly finding a single exploded Winchester shell to match the bullet No. III, also of Winchester make, had now accomplished an important purpose for the prosecution.

Captain Van Amburgh's statement that he was merely "inclined to believe" that bullet No. III had been fired from Sacco's gun suggests that he had doubts. He had been brought in from Connecticut to strengthen the prosecution's case and would have put it more strongly had he had a positive opinion. He gave no opinion as to whether the Fraher Winchester shell had been used in Sacco's automatic. Nevertheless, Mr. Katzmann, in his summation, again misstated the evidence. Throughout his closing argument the district attorney assumed that Van Amburgh had given a positive opinion that bullet No. III and the Fraher Winchester cartridge case had been fired in Sacco's pistol. No doubt the jury believed that Mr. Katzmann's misquotations were correct.

At the close of the Dedham trial there occurred a most unusual and rather poignant episode. It is related by the *Brockton Enterprise* in its issue for July 15, 1921:

[50] Vol. I, 920.

About ten minutes after the verdict, the courtroom was cleared of all but a few. Williams (the assistant to Katzmann) walked through the room, his head bent. One of the attorneys for the defense met him, extended his hand and said, "Congratulations on a brilliant victory." With tears streaming down his face Williams replied, "For God's sake, don't rub it in. This is the saddest thing that ever happened to me in my life." With tears still streaming, he walked through the courtroom.

In *The Legacy of Sacco and Vanzetti*, Professor G. Louis Joughin reprints the above report of this remarkable scene and then adds his own interpretation of it:

The *Enterprise* considers this "typical of the manner in which Katzmann and his assistants took the verdict;" in other words, their humanity was moved by the result arrived at in the performance of their painful duty. An entirely different explanation can be had by calling to mind the fact that it was Mr. Williams who had been deeply involved in the framing of Captain Proctor's testimony.

To those of us who knew Harold Williams, either or both of these interpretations could be correct. I know that the Sacco-Vanzetti case was on his mind. Years after the executions, when Mr. Williams was a Superior Court judge, I had occasion to be in his courtroom. The court messenger brought word to me that the judge wanted to see me in chambers after the session. When I entered, he shook hands with me warmly and said: "Herbert, I simply wanted to say to you that I know you are sincere in believing that Sacco and Vanzetti were innocent. I want you to believe that I am just as sincere in believing that they were guilty."

Mr. Williams was later appointed a justice of the Supreme Judicial Court. During his long service on the bench he was widely respected as a fair and conscientious judge. He is another of the puzzles in the Sacco-Vanzetti case.

Two experts of high standing testified for the defense, James Burns, ballistic engineer for the United States Cartridge Company,[51] and J. Henry Fitzgerald, in charge of the testing room at Colt Patent Firearms Company.[52] Mr. Burns gave a positive opinion that No. III bullet had not been fired from Sacco's gun.[53] He also disagreed with Captain Van Amburgh's technical explanation concerning supposed similarities in the exploded shells. Mr. Fitzgerald, too, gave a positive opinion that No. III bullet was

[51] Vol. II, 1405 *et seq.*   [52] Vol. II, 1464 *et seq.*   [53] Vol. II, 1414.

not fired from Sacco's gun.[54] Like Mr. Burns, he differed with Captain Van Amburgh concerning the significance of alleged characteristics of the exploded shells.

With respect to the bullets, all four of the experts relied chiefly on measurements of the "lands" and "grooves" inside the barrel and on their reverse imprints on the bullets as they passed through the barrels. The lands are raised-up spirals and the grooves are the lowered portions between the lands. These spirals are referred to as "rifling" and give the bullet a spin when it passes through the barrel which makes the bullet go straighter. The rifling in some makes of pistols twists to the right and in others to the left. If the rifling twists in one way and the impression on the subject bullet in the other, the suspected pistol may be immediately eliminated from consideration. If they both twist in the same direction, further study by experts is required to determine what pistol fired the bullet. At the time of the Sacco-Vanzetti case, ballistic experts believed that by fine measurements of the space between the marks of the lands and grooves on the bullet they could tell what make of pistol had fired it. Since there were occasionally slight variations in such measurements and flaws due to the effects of rust and other causes, even in the same makes of pistols, they thought that they might also indicate whether a particular pistol had fired a particular bullet. This method of identifying suspect bullets with guns has since been discredited as unreliable, but at the time of the trial was still used by some experts.

The identification of exploded shells with a particular gun involved various technical considerations, such as measuring the exact location and size of the firing pin indentation on the base of the suspect shell, the flowback of metal around the spot, and scratches on the base left by tool marks on the firing pin as it struck the cartridge. Identification of shells has also been improved since the trial.

Since the experts at the trial could not agree on what they measured in the exhibits or on the things they claimed were significant, it is difficult to see how the jury of amateurs could decide among them. Nevertheless, Mr. Katzmann argued at length to the jury that they could determine many of the points of difference with a microscope or even with their bare eyes,[55] and Judge Thayer thought the same. The jury sent for and received an ordinary microscope.[56]

[54] Vol. II, 1466.   [55] Vol. II, 2225–2226.   [56] Vol. II, 2265.

If we review the opinions of the experts as they stood at the close of the Dedham trial, we find the following:

1. Captain Proctor, the chief expert for the prosecution, had given an equivocal opinion as to bullet No. III, meaning that it *might* have been fired in Sacco's gun, but if he had been cross-examined he would have been a defense witness.

2. Captain Van Amburgh was only "inclined to believe" that No. III bullet had been fired in Sacco's pistol. Coming from a government expert, this language was vulnerable to sharp attack in argument.

3. Two defense experts, with impressive credentials as to competence, had testified that the No. III bullet had *not* been fired in Sacco's pistol.

With respect to Fraher shell F4, *there was no opinion from any expert that it had been fired in Sacco's pistol:*

1. Captain Proctor was not asked for his opinion.

2. Captain Van Amburgh discussed certain similarities with a test shell, but did not state that in his opinion the shell F4 had been fired in Sacco's pistol.

3. The two defense experts testified that the shell had *not* been fired in Sacco's pistol.

(There was an even graver lack in the evidential worth of Fraher shell F4. Apparently unperceived by defense counsel, there *was no testimony nor any mark identifying this exhibit as a shell found at the site of the shooting.*)

If we consider the ballistic testimony at the trial, therefore, may we not safely conclude that if the jury had known the real meaning of this evidence they could not have found that the prosecution had proved that Sacco's gun had been used at South Braintree? This, however, would have required a careful analysis of the testimony which did not occur. The way had been opened for Mr. Moore to dramatize Sacco's voluntary request for test firing as a supreme gesture of an innocent man and then to hurl the favorable ballistic testimony at the jury proving that Sacco's faith was fully justified. Incredible as it may seem to an experienced trial lawyer, Mr. Moore brushed aside the ballistic testimony as if it did not really matter. The following is the sum total of what he said to the jury about it:

Gentlemen, if the time has come when a microscope must be used to determine whether a human life is going to continue to function or not and when the users of the microscope themselves can't agree, when experts called by the Commonwealth and experts called by the defense are sharply defined in their disagreements, then I take it that ordinary men such as you and I should well hesitate to take a human life.[57]

To a jury awaiting a massive attack on the government's expert testimony, the foregoing must have had all the bang of a wet firecracker. Mr. Moore may have been quite right in the sentiment which he expressed, but in the circumstances of the case, where he himself had requested the test firing, it was forensic suicide.

Mr. Katzmann made the most of Mr. Moore's failure to discuss the expert testimony. Affirming the infallibility of a microscope or a magnifying glass in the hands of a skilled user, he launched into an extensive argument based on the various opinions of the experts.[58] He skillfully created the impression that he was a master of the technicalities. This must have swept the jury along with his presentation of the ballistic evidence. It probably passed unnoticed, however, that in an argument that covers over four pages of the printed record, *he never once mentioned the name of Captain Proctor or his opinion.* Nevertheless, Mr. Katzmann could not silence the outcry that arose when the knowledge of the prosecution's handling of his testimony became public.

The close of the trial did not end the ballistics questions. Subsequent testimony and experiments tended to shore up what we now know in retrospect to have been an actual collapse of the government's case at the trial with respect to Sacco's gun. This will be examined in the next chapter.

17.

The Expert Opinions Escalate

In 1923 Mr. Moore reopened the matter of ballistic evidence on a motion for a new trial based on alleged new evidence. This stimulated the prosecution to find stronger evidence than it presented at the trial to counter the proof offered by the defense. The issue was supposed to be decided on affidavits, not witness stand testimony, but some (unreported) oral testi-

[57] Vol. II, 2147.   [58] Vol. II, 2223 *et seq.*

mony crept in during argument.[1] The defense experts now included Albert H. Hamilton, a well-known freelance expert who had testified in 165 homicide cases. Mr. Hamilton was tremendously resourceful but his reputation among fellow experts was not high, partly because he claimed to be an expert in so many diverse fields. Like Captain Van Amburgh and Major Goddard, he had given a grievously erroneous opinion in a homicide case. Associated with him was Augustus H. Gill, professor of technical chemical analysis at the Massachusetts Institute of Technology. He was proficient in micrometer measurements. The prosecution countered with affidavits by Captain Van Amburgh and Merton A. Robinson, ballistic engineer and supervisor of the ballistic department at the Winchester Repeating Arms Company. The defense experts found that the mortal bullet III had not been fired through Sacco's pistol and the prosecution's affiants claimed that it had. All of the affidavits were based principally on micrometer measurements. Captain Van Amburgh's opinion was far stronger than at the Ded-

---

[1] On November 8, 1923, the last day of the oral hearings, the defendants' expert, Mr. Hamilton, illustrated his argument by comparing the Sacco pistol with two new Colt automatics of the same caliber which he had previously filed with the clerk. For this purpose, he disassembled the parts of the three weapons, and, when he finished his explanation, reassembled them. The three pistols were then returned to the clerk.

On or about February 13, 1924, District Attorney Williams informed the court that Captain Van Amburgh had told him that the barrel then in Sacco's reassembled pistol was not the rusty foul barrel that belonged in it. This led to a protracted judicial inquiry. Mr. Hamilton admitted that the barrel in Sacco's pistol came from one of his own new automatics, but disputed Van Amburgh's assertion that the old foul barrel, now in one of the new pistols, was the original Sacco's foul barrel. The prosecution claimed that the switch was made by Mr. Hamilton for the purpose of securing a new trial when the substitution was discovered, as it was bound to be sooner or later. Defense counsel claimed that the switch was made by someone representing the prosecution to defeat a fresh series of test firings as requested by Mr. Thompson. (The request was not granted.)

In a document filed by Judge Thayer in the Superior Court at Dedham, but not made part of the official record, the judge found that the rusty foul barrel was the original Sacco barrel and that the new barrel in Sacco's automatic belonged to one of Hamilton's new pistols. He made no finding concerning the party responsible for the switch or whether it was intentional. Nevertheless, Judge Thayer obviously believed that Mr. Hamilton was the responsible party. Certainly Hamilton's unconvincing explanations in answer to the court's questions would seem to justify such a conclusion. If Judge Thayer believed that Hamilton had perpetrated such a trick, he could hardly have taken seriously the carefully documented affidavits filed by Hamilton as the basis for a new trial. (It is surprising that the defense, in accusing the prosecution of switching the barrels, did not voice the suspicion that it was done by Van Amburgh to destroy the effect of Hamilton's affidavits which he was then trying to controvert.)

Judge Thayer's findings and decision are far too extensive to be reproduced here. Fortunately, Professor Edmund M. Morgan has included them in Joughin and Morgan, *The Legacy of Sacco and Vanzetti*, 160–173.

ham trial. Where he had previously only been "inclined to believe" he now was "positive" that the No. III bullet had been fired through Sacco's pistol. Where he had not expressed any opinion at the trial about Fraher shell F4, he now was "absolutely certain." He explained this difference by asserting that his 1923 opinion was arrived at by using a more powerful microscope.[2]

The prosecution filed no affidavit from Captain Proctor. The defense, however, filed a motion based on Captain Proctor's affidavit concerning the prearrangement between him and the district attorney for him to use the word "consistent" in giving his opinion at the trial about the mortal bullet. Judge Thayer denied both motions.

Since I am not qualified to discuss the conflicting claims of the experts disclosed in the affidavits and accompanying photographs, I shall not attempt to do so. Instead I shall quote the conclusion reached by Jack Desbrow Gunther and Charles O. Gunther in their extensive analysis of the testimony by experts in the Sacco-Vanzetti case. Their book, *The Identification of Firearms*,[3] was widely regarded as the standard work on the subject.

After severely criticizing all of the experts for incompetence both as to their qualifications and methods, the Gunthers set out their own evaluation of the ballistic testimony as follows:

The inevitable conclusion is that the defendants did not receive a fair trial on this all important issue. The jurors were not properly equipped to make an

2 Vol. IV, 3666–3667. Later apparently, Captain Van Amburgh relied on a similarity of lines appearing on photographs of the shell tops (bases). Possibly this was due to the growing influence of the Goddard technique, hereinafter discussed. The photographs were made under the direction of Captain Van Amburgh.

I have a copy of a letter from Dr. Magrath, dated March 29, 1932, answering an inquiry from Mrs. Katharine Codman (Mrs. Ernest A. Codman) concerning the history of certain photographs of shell tops which he had been using in his lectures about the Sacco-Vanzetti case.

After tracing the shells (somewhat erroneously) into the hands of the District Attorney, Dr. Magrath stated that the shells and bullets were conserved by the government until the hearings on the motions for a new trial were instituted. At that time the shells were placed in the temporary custody of Captain Van Amburgh (spelled Amberg) who had the shell tops photographed in the laboratory of photography at the Massachusetts Institute of Technology. Dr. Magrath was present while this was being done. Later, a photograph of the top of a test shell, admittedly fired through Sacco's pistol, was compared with the photograph of the top of the shell allegedly picked up at the murder scene (Fraher shell F4). Whatever these comparisons may be said to show, our basic difficulty still remains — lack of proof of the authenticity of the shell with which the test shell was being compared.

3 New York: John Wiley and Sons, Inc., 1935.

intelligent determination. They had to rely upon incompetent expert testimony which was not, within the narrow limits of information set by the experts, either intelligently or fairly explained during the presentation and summary; and the observable data which the jurors were advised to consider had but little, if any, significance to them. [Emphasis added.] [4]

The Gunthers then turned to the motions for a new trial and made the following comment on Judge Thayer's opinion:

And from a reading of the affidavits, which contained remarkable disagreements in measurements as between those of the various experts and between the measurements of a single expert, Judge Thayer, like any other reasonable person, should have realized *the weakness in the State's proof upon the identity of bullet III and the W.R.A. Fraher cartridge case.* He should have appreciated the doubt shadowing the prosecution's testimony, and, on the basis of this doubt, granted a new trial. [Emphasis added.] [5]

On the issue raised by the Proctor affidavit and the reply affidavits by Mr. Katzmann and Mr. Williams, the Gunthers commented:

However, aside from the affidavits and the acts of misconduct set forth therein, the whole Record bristles with circumstances which negate the possibility that the District Attorney and his assistants were ignorant of the deceptive nature of Proctor's testimony. If they knew his entire opinion, they were guilty of misconduct which should be far beyond the bounds of the discretionary power of the trial judge to conceal, permit or condone. [6]

The decision of Judge Thayer on the defendants' motion based on new ballistic evidence should have put an end to further expert opinion. This it failed to do. Nearly four years later the issue was again raised — this time by the prosecution. In view of the timing, it was unfortunate for the defendants. The governor had just begun to consider our petition for commutation or clemency when Dudley P. Ranney, then assistant district attorney, requested that we join him in cosponsoring an experiment on the bullet and shell exhibits by Major Calvin Goddard, an expert in firearms identification. The experiment, which was supposed to be voluntary and off the record, was for the purpose of enabling Major Goddard to demonstrate the use of the comparison microscope, then a relatively new instrument, in firearms identification. We declined his request when we learned that Major Goddard had already expressed an opinion that bullet III and the

4 Ibid., 214.   5 Ibid., 245.   6 Ibid., 218–219.

Fraher shell F4 had been fired through Sacco's pistol. We did not want to be a party to this injection of any extrajudicial opinion by a committed expert at a most crucial moment in our clients' lives. Mr. Ranney then stated that he was going to conduct the experiment anyway and suggested that we might attend as guest observers. Neither Mr. Thompson nor I had the qualifications or preparation to act as counsel or participants. I accepted his invitation to attend as an observer only.

Probably Major Goddard's demonstration did not affect the governor's ultimate decision, but had we anticipated the importance which some writers in afteryears would attach to his experiment, we might have insisted on the presence of an expert who knew the limitations of the comparison microscope, and had we known then what I know today about the exhibits, we would have probed deeply into the question of the authenticity of the objects which Major Goddard proposed to examine.

I had a special reason for wanting to inspect the exhibits. In reading witnesses' testimony describing the shooting, I had noticed an apparent conflict between the testimony and the government's claim that Sacco had fired bullet III. Most of the witnesses at the trial had described Berardelli's assassin as firing a number of bullets into his victim, and then chasing Parmenter across Pearl Street and shooting him also. (There was also some testimony that a bandit had fired a single shot at Berardelli's prostrate body from the escaping automobile.[7]) The prosecution claimed that bullet No. III was fired by a bandit standing over Berardelli as he was sinking to the ground. To prove that this killer was Sacco, Pelser's uncertain testimony was offered. The other government witness expected to identify Sacco as this assassin was Wade, but he too declined to be positive about it. Both Pelser and Wade pictured the bandit standing over Berardelli as firing several shots into him at close range. So also did other witnesses such as Bostock, but they did not intimate that the bandit was Sacco. However, the ballistic testimony showed that No. III slug had a left twist, whereas the other three bullets in Berardelli's body had a right twist as did the two extracted from Parmenter. Since no witness had seen the bandit bending over Berardelli as firing two pistols, I had concluded that something was wrong with the bullet No. III or with the purported identification of Sacco as the killer who fired several bullets into him. Because of this confusion as

[7] McGlone, Supp. Vol., 421; Vol. I, 269.

to who was shooting whom and with what, I wanted to look at the identifying numerals on the base of the bullets during the Goddard experiment.

However, I did not allow for the incautious faith occasionally placed in mechanical instruments as diviners of the truth. As with most new devices, the impression had gone out that the comparison microscope was an infallible means of making firearms identification. This is not so. As will be seen, its use cannot exclude the chances of error. Experts using the instrument have been known to differ.[8] Errors occur in the use of the comparison microscope, as in the use of other devices or methods once regarded as infallible. There have been numerous such instances. A recent example involving the assumed infallibility of a fingerprint expert may be found in *Stopelli v. United States*.[9] Stopelli was convicted on the testimony of a government fingerprint expert so willing that he had to be cautioned by the court. The conviction was affirmed on appeal. Chief Judge Denman, however, dissented, and in his opinion issued the following caveat against relying on a supposed bit of infallible evidence to convict an accused: "*A single circumstance, standing alone, within the realm of the possible can usually be accounted for upon an innocent basis.*" Judge Denman's judgment was later vindicated. With the help of the FBI and others, Stopelli was cleared and eventually pardoned by President Truman. Judge Denman's warning would seem to apply to the conclusion sometimes voiced that Sacco's guilt may be presumed because of an expert's opinion based on a voluntary ballistic test. In any out-of-court demonstration of this sort the possibility of error, always present, is vastly increased by the lack of the usual safeguards provided by judicial procedures or positive proof of authenticity of the object examined. If the "single circumstance" does not integrate easily into the entire case or into the known probabilities, one may rightly suspect that something was wrong with the test.

One well-known example involving the comparison microscope was a bad blunder by Major Goddard himself a few months after his experiment with the Sacco-Vanzetti exhibits. The story is told by Arthur Warner in the *Nation*, issue of December 7, 1927, in an article entitled "A Sacco Revolver Expert Revealed." It reads in part as follows:

[8] According to Shelley Braverman, this happened at the trial of *People v. Hoffman*, Indictment 33 (1927), Richmond County, N.Y. Sup. Ct., May 6, 1929. See also Braverman's "Forensic Ballistic Errors," 1966 *Guns Digest*.
[9] 9th Cir., California S. Div., August 2, 1950. 183 F. 2nd 391.

On October 8, last, a bootlegger by the name of Ernest J. Yorkell was murdered in Cleveland. A few weeks later Frank Milazzo was arrested with a revolver in his possession. A detective sergeant who was instructed to trace the history of the revolver reported his belief that the weapon was the one used in the killing of Yorkell. The revolver was thereupon sent to an expert in New York City together with bullets taken from the dead man. The expert found that the bullets had been fired from the revolver, upon learning which the Cleveland police charged Milazzo with the murder of Yorkell.

Milazzo presumably would have gone to trial and might have been convicted, but the *Cleveland News* suddenly confounded the police with the information that the revolver in question had not been sold until November 3, nearly a month after the murder. This statement was confirmed by the records of the manufacturer and the retail dealer, the murder charge against Milazzo was dropped, and an inquiry was ordered into the work of the detective sergeant who had incorrectly reported the history of the revolver.

The article then adds the following about the "expert" involved:

He is Major Calvin H. Goddard, a former military man, who last summer announced that he had determined by new and positive tests the guilt of Nicola Sacco.

Major Goddard attributed his mistake in the Milazzo matter to a possible confusion of bullets. The Cleveland officials denied the possibility. Whatever the explanation, the Milazzo episode illustrates the danger of accepting any tests as infallible. Especially is such a conclusion to be distrusted where it does not fit in with other known data or circumstances.

The demonstration was held on June 3, 1927. Major Goddard confirmed his opinion that had been reported to us, namely, that the bullet and shell had been shot in the Sacco pistol. However, he complained about the dirt that obscured the markings. The experiment was witnessed by several persons in addition to Assistant District Attorney Ranney and myself, including Frank W. Buxton, managing editor of the *Boston Herald*, Thomas Carens, special writer for the *Boston Herald*, and Dr. Augustus H. Gill, the micrometer expert who had testified for the defense with Mr. Hamilton in the 1923 proceedings. Dr. Gill was listed as representing the defendants, but to my recollection neither Mr. Thompson nor I authorized him to do so. He acted as a sort of assistant to Major Goddard and asked questions intended, apparently, to bring out more clearly the major's opinion. By his remarks, he seemed to be much impressed by what Major Goddard pointed out, but the demonstration did not seem conclusive to Mr. Buxton or Mr. Carens or to me. According to Francis Russell, Major Goddard had already demonstrated the use of the comparison microscope to Dr. Gill, who had then announced beforehand that he would abide by the result of the experiment. To my recollection this was not revealed to Mr. Thompson or to me. Russell also stated that Dr. Gill told Mr. Thompson that he now doubted his own original findings (made in 1923). He quoted Dr. Gill as saying to Mr. Thompson that he wished to sever all connection with the case.[10] At the time of the Goddard experiment, however, Dr. Gill had had no connection with the case for years.

None of us had the technical ballistic knowledge which would have been necessary to ask intelligent, probing questions of Major Goddard. Nor did we have the general background with which we would have been armed if he had conducted his experiment at a trial. None of us knew enough even to question Goddard's statement *that the Colt was the only American automatic with a left twist.*[11] Neither his experience nor his opinion nor the exhibits that he examined nor his use of the new instrument were subjected to the safeguarding checks of trial procedure that our jurisprudence deems vital in the quest for the truth. So far as I was concerned, I could follow to some extent what Major Goddard claimed were "matches" on the base of the shell, but not the several patches on the bullet which he asserted were proof of his thesis. Major Goddard later sent a written opinion to Mr. Ranney. We were assured that it would not go to the governor or the Advisory Committee, but we were not so naive as to believe that his conclusions would be kept secret.

However, when I examined the roman numeral marks I, II, III and IIII on the bases of the four bullets allegedly extracted from Berardelli's body, I felt that my presence at the Goddard experiment was rewarded. (There was no point to looking at the Fraher shell, since it had never been identified as a shell found on the scene.) The numerals on the bases of the bullets I, II and IIII were fine parallel scratches, as if made with the point of a needle, exactly as Dr. Magrath had stated, whereas the numeral III looked as if it had been gouged into the base of the bullet and the lines that formed it were not straight, but wobbly. I called Major Goddard's attention to this difference. He saw it immediately, but passed it off with the remark that it

---

[10] *Tragedy in Dedham,* 376.
[11] The statement may have been correct as to *American-made* pistols only, but it was misleading. Mr. Braverman reports that in 1927 there were at least *fourteen* left-twist pistols with land and groove dimensions consistent with No. III. Berardelli may have been shot with any of them.

might be due to difference in the alloy or distortion in the bullet.[12]

On June 6, 1927, however, when we had a conference in Mr. Thompson's office, Major Goddard took a somewhat different view of the peculiar looks of the roman numeral III. He said that the edges of the marking on No. III were considerably more ragged than the others, but that he could not say what was the cause of the difference. Mr. Crawford said that he had never excluded from his mind the possibility of a substitution. Both he and Goddard readily agreed that there was nothing in the conduct of the trial which would lead one to place any great confidence in the authenticity of the exhibits. Major Goddard thought that the peculiar markings on the No. III bullet were a fact deserving of attention.[13]

I then asked Wilbur F. Turner, handwriting expert and criminologist, to look at the markings on the base of the bullets. (He had made the enlarged photographs to accompany the Hamilton affidavit.) He testified before the Governor's Advisory Committee about the numerals on the bullets: "There was a tremendous difference in the marking, as though they were made with a different tool or scratched with a different instrument." [14]

In his book *Tragedy in Dedham*, Russell quotes Lieutenant John Collins, in charge of the ballistics laboratory of the Massachusetts State Police, as asking him: "You think that this Number III might have been switched from the one they cut out of Berardelli?" and then, as he cupped the bullet in his hand, "The markings on the base do look somewhat different." [15]

Fortunately, Mr. Russell in his book reproduced photographs of the bases of bullets I, II, III and IIII. Although the pictures are rather dark and the scratches quite old, one can still see plainly that the numeral III looks very different from the others.

Mr. Russell's photographs figured importantly in an article by Shelley Braverman entitled "Were Sacco and Vanzetti Framed?" [16] In addition to reproducing the photographs, Mr. Braverman added a new feature. Dr.

---

[12] Francis Russell in *Tragedy in Dedham*, 376–377, quotes me as remarking that the scratches on the base of bullet III were "irregular and almost indecipherable." I made no such statement. He also quotes Major Goddard as "agreeing" that the scratches on bullet III were "less clear" than the others. He made no such statement. The scratches were clear enough — too clear to still doubts about their origin.

[13] From contemporaneous memoranda by Thompson and Ehrmann on June 6 and June 9, 1927.

[14] Vol. V, 5225.   [15] *Tragedy in Dedham*, 317.

[16] *Guns Magazine*, May 1963, 16. Mr. Braverman is a firearms consultant whose expert testimony has been accepted by courts in Canada, Central America and throughout the United States. See the bibliography.

Magrath had stated that the III bullet which he had extracted had come to rest against the left hipbone and was "slightly" flattened. This, it has been claimed, proves that it is the original mortal bullet. It may prove the opposite. The bullet which we saw in 1927 was markedly "flattened," and to my eyes there seemed nothing "slight" about it.[17] Mr. Braverman produced almost a replica of the marked flattening of this III bullet by the simple expedient of firing a "W"-type bullet through a one-inch board. A photograph of the base of this bullet is also published in his article, so that its strikingly similar distortion in comparison with the Russell picture of III is instantly obvious.

The ragged mark III on the bullet examined in June 1927 in and of itself makes it seem unlikely that it was one of the four slugs scratched on their bases with the point of a needle by Dr. Magrath on April 15, 1920. When its different appearance is considered against the background of the descriptions of the shooting by witnesses, the prosecution's presentation of evidence including other physical exhibits and the recurring one-in-four coincidences, doubt approaches conviction. However, if there was a substitution, when did it occur?

So far as we know, the *first* comparison of the numeral marks was made in June 1927 during the Goddard experiment. We get no help from the trial record. Each of the four bullets had been put in a separate envelope and each envelope had been opened at different moments of the trial. No witness had been asked to compare the base marks on the several bullets. Between the date of the autopsy in April 1920 and the Goddard examination in June 1927, the bullets and shells had been accessible to a number of people and were handled on several occasions by various persons.

Thirty-four years after the execution of Sacco and Vanzetti there was another voluntary experiment on the bullets and shells. Francis Russell located these items in private hands, where they had apparently been the subject of some unauthorized tests, and had them returned to the Department of Public Safety. In preparation for writing his book, Mr. Russell retained two ballistic experts to make new examinations. For this he obtained Jac Weller and Colonel Frank Jury. It was a questionable choice since these gentlemen, *without making any examination of the bullets and*

---

[17] Government expert Merton Robinson described it as *"badly deformed."* Vol. IV, 3674.

shells, had already published their joint opinion that bullet III had been fired in Sacco's pistol.[18] Nevertheless, they went ahead with their examinations through a comparison microscope, using separate instruments and comparing their separate observations, and found that they were right the first time. There was another weakness that affected the value of their findings. The experts themselves stated that the bullets and shells were corroded and that the rust on the inside of the barrel of Sacco's pistol had to be blasted out by firing preliminary shots before "test" shots could be fired.[19] These conditions made any definitive examination extremely difficult.[20]

We have now traced the evolution of the claim that Sacco's pistol fired the bullet that killed Berardelli. It began with a stipulation by the district attorney before trial (unknown to the jury) that he would offer no evidence that any particular bullet was fired by any particular gun. It ended in 1923, after the trial, with the positive testimony of two government ballistic experts that Sacco's pistol had fired a bullet alleged to be No. III removed from Berardelli's body and also that it had discharged an unidentified and unmarked shell assumed to be one picked up at the murder scene.

The escalation of this evidence has raised disturbing questions to which answers can no longer be given. The only certainty in the course of our study is that the jury never heard the opinion which Captain Proctor, its chief expert at the trial, had given to the district attorney, namely, that he had found no evidence that bullet III had passed through Sacco's gun. Nor did the jury or any court ever learn that Captain Proctor (who knew the case from its beginning) had later stated that his real opinion was that bullet III had *not* been fired in Sacco's pistol. Nor did the jury or trial counsel for the defense know that the form of opinion which Captain Proctor gave on the witness stand had been prearranged in the district attorney's office. The record shows that the judge and defense counsel had been misled by this testimony. The bullet and shell evidence seems to suffer from a taint as to its integrity similar to that which afflicted the government's handling of the other physical evidence. Indeed, its conduct in this respect appears to fit into a pattern common to most of the prosecution's case.

---

[18] Julian S. Hatcher, Frank J. Jury and Jac Weller, *Firearms Investigation, Identification, and Evidence* (Harrisburg: Stackpole, 1957), 466.
[19] Russell, "Sacco Guilty, Vanzetti Innocent?", *American Heritage*, June 1962, 5, 110.
[20] Shelley Braverman, in a personal conference, August 1966, in Brunswick, Maine.

The history of the bullet and shell evidence offered in the Sacco-Vanzetti case may serve as a striking lesson to us in the futility of trying to decide the issue of the guilt of the accused apart from considering the question of the fairness of the government's case. If the prosecution's production or presentation of evidence is untrustworthy, then a judgment based on any part of it must necessarily be equally untrustworthy.

In recent decisions the United States Supreme Court has affirmed this principle that integrity of the government's case is essential to the pursuit of justice in the criminal law. This has not always been understood, even by lawyers, in regard to cases where the irregularities consisted wholly in disregarding the safeguards of proper procedure. However, in the Sacco-Vanzetti case, the violations of the principle seem clear. They were not limited to departures from procedural protections. They struck at the very heart of justice itself.

18.

Cross-Examination of Vanzetti

Q. (By *District Attorney Katzmann*) You were going to advise in a public meeting men who had gone to war? Are you that man?

A. (By *Vanzetti*) Yes, Sir. I am that man, not the man you want me, but I am that man.

Holt Record, Vol. II, 1778

In the preceding chapters we have examined practically all of the positive evidence offered by the prosecution to establish the guilt of the defendants. However, the Commonwealth did not rely exclusively on this direct proof. It made much of indirect evidence, such as the alleged inability of Sacco and Vanzetti to explain satisfactorily the lies told by them on their arrest and other conduct claimed to be suspicious, and their alleged failure to establish convincing alibis. This sort of proof may be regarded as purely ancillary to the main case, since by itself it is meaningless, but acquires significance only as support for positive evidence of guilt already in the case.

In the Sacco-Vanzetti trial this ancillary evidence was made into a principal part of the prosecution's case. The Commonwealth may have been weak in its direct evidence, but it had in its arsenal a very effective weapon in Mr. Katzmann's great skill as a cross-examiner and his willingness to use it ruthlessly. This was apparent at the earlier trial of Vanzetti. There he was able to make the simple Italian folk of Plymouth appear like perjurers who had connived with one another to secure the acquittal of a highwayman in their midst. At Dedham, however, Mr. Katzmann had a far wider scope for the exercise of his talent for rousing prejudice and creating suspicion.

Mr. Katzmann's opportunity lay in the fact that at Dedham the defendants took the witness stand. Once Sacco and Vanzetti testified in their own behalf, they were practically compelled to explain why they told lies on the night of their arrest and the next morning, and why they tried to obtain Boda's broken-down Overland from the Johnson garage. If they had not told their story in their own way Mr. Katzmann would have dragged it out of them, which would have been worse. Since the explanation of their falsehoods and other suspected conduct was that they thought they were arrested in the drive against anarchists, radicalism was bound to enter the trial evidence.

Before we consider these cross-examinations let us briefly look at their legitimate purpose. Sacco and Vanzetti had ascribed their falsehoods and other suspicious actions to the fear of being apprehended and perhaps mistreated in the drive against anarchists and other radicals. They also feared to involve their radical friends. In addition, they feared their arrest for evading the draft. It was therefore proper for Mr. Katzmann to show that these fears either did not really exist, or if they did, that they did not constitute an adequate explanation of their falsehoods and other behavior thought to be indicative of guilt.

A few background items may be helpful. We already know that the United States Attorney General's drive against radicals was a fact. This was not only notorious but had even been judicially determined in the celebrated case of Colyer v. Skeffington[1] in which Judge Anderson denounced the lawless raids on supposed radicals under the direction of the Attorney General. At one stage in the cross-examination of Sacco, it seemed as if Judge Thayer was going to require proof of this condition,[2] but it was not seriously controverted by Mr. Katzmann. Neither was it disputed that anarchists Elia and Salsedo were held for weeks by the Department of Justice,

[1] D. Mass. 265 F. 17 (1920).   [2] Vol. II, 1873.

nor that anarchists including Sacco and Vanzetti were collecting money for their defense, nor that Salsedo's body was found crushed to a pulp on May 3, 1920, at the base of the Department's building in New York. It was the news of Salsedo's violent death which Sacco and Vanzetti claimed speeded their attempt to collect the radical literature which they had been distributing.

Throughout the trial record there are indications that the prosecutors and Judge Thayer did not think that arrest and deportation were eventualities serious enough to have aroused the fears alleged as an explanation of the defendants' falsehoods told on their arrest. To the judge and Katzmann deportation meant only a free trip to Europe and was nothing to fear. This view is perhaps understandable in native Americans safely integrated in their country. It is the product of a lack of imagination. They might have thought otherwise had they been able to put themselves in the position of members of a group of Italian anarchists, traditionally in dread of the police, who found themselves a hated and hunted minority in an alien land. We got a glimpse of the other view through the eyes of Mrs. Sacco as she testified before the Governor's Advisory Committee in 1927:

Q. (By Mr. Thompson) Now just before your husband was arrested did you hear any talk about radicals, reds? Did you hear? A. Oh, yes, more than once.

Q. Well, when they talked about their ideas and used the word deportation, what did he mean? A. Well, there was talk that they might kill them, or get them on the boat and kill them. That it was terrible to be deported, you know, many different things they could do to you if they caught you. And they were afraid to be deported, they were very much afraid. They would just go around collecting the papers. He was afraid he would be killed or injured in some way. That is what.

Q. Did you hear of any talk in your house about Massachusetts law? Did you hear any talk in your house about arresting a man in Massachusetts for being radicals? A. Yes, I have heard them, especially of Salsedo. He was thrown or jumped from a high window.

Q. (By President Lowell) In New York? A. Oh, yes, that was it.[3]

It will also be helpful to keep in mind the fact that Mr. Katzmann knew quite well that Sacco and Vanzetti were telling the truth when they claimed to be in danger of arrest and deportation as undesirable radicals. He knew that the defendants were caught in the first place in Chief Stewart's trap because they were anarchists and that the examination of the men

[3] Vol. V, 4952–4953.

at the Brockton police station on the very night of the arrest dealt mainly with their radical associations. Mr. Katzmann himself had made a deal with the Department of Justice to put a spy in Sacco's cell in the hope of getting information about the Wall Street bombing. At the Plymouth trial he had cross-examined some of Vanzetti's alibi witnesses about Vanzetti's radical views. Nevertheless, when in 1927 Mr. Thompson asked Mr. Katzmann concerning his knowledge of the defendants' radicalism, he got evasive answers. For instance:

Q. (By Mr. Thompson) You knew before you started that trial that they were men holding radical opinions of some sort? A. I do not know how much I knew about that.

Q. I am asking you whether it was not a fact before you started trying that case that you knew you were dealing with men who held radical opinions? A. It was a *fact perfectly well known* that these men were radicals. *From the newspapers I knew that very well.* [Emphasis added.] [4]

It is interesting to note that it was well-known "from the newspapers" that the defendants were radicals, since this again makes nonsense of the claim that Sacco and Vanzetti "brought radicalism into the case." But why was Mr. Katzmann so unwilling to admit his own quite intimate knowledge of the defendants' radicalism? Was it because much of his most damaging cross-examination had no excuse unless it was for the purpose of probing the sincerity of the defendants' claim that they were hunted radicals — a claim which Mr. Katzmann already knew was absolutely sincere? The reader must judge.

Some of Mr. Katzmann's questions, especially those asked of Vanzetti, were for the legitimate purpose of showing that certain falsehoods served no apparent purpose in shielding the defendants or their friends from identification as undesirable radicals. Here again some background knowledge is important. Immediately following their arrest, Sacco and Vanzetti, for the protection of themselves and friends, had to decide on the spot, without counsel and without being advised of the reasons for being in custody, what questions were dangerous or, if not dangerous, would lead to further questions which might be dangerous. In such a case, the only safe course was to avoid all truthful answers touching on their conduct. A similar dilemma is often faced by defendants and witnesses who refuse to answer questions on

[4] Vol. V, 5040.

William G. Thompson, Herbert B. Ehrmann, and Thomas O'Connor leaving the
State House, Boston, July 21, 1927. (Courtesy of Brandeis University Library)

Nicola Sacco

Sacco as he looked shortly after his arrest on May 5, 1920.

Joseph Morelli

This rogues' gallery photograph, taken after one of Joe Morelli's various arrests, underscores the extraordinary facial resemblance between Sacco and Morelli.

Bartolomeo Vanzetti

This rogues' gallery photograph shows Vanzetti as he looked shortly after his arrest on May 5, 1920, and at the Plymouth trial in June of that year. Note particularly Vanzetti's long, bushy moustache.

Sacco and Vanzetti under police escort

This undated photograph shows the accused men being taken back to jail from Dedham courthouse. (Courtesy of *Boston Globe/Boston Post*)

The arrow #1 points to a foreign ejector cut .12″ long. The arrow #2 points to a foreign ejector cut .04″ wide.

The arrow points to a foreign ejector cut .12″ long.

The arrow #1 points to a foreign ejector cut .12″ long. The arrow #2 points to a foreign ejector mark .04″ wide.

The "Fraher shells"

These shells were picked up at the scene of the crime in South Braintree. The ejector cuts indicate that they were fired through a foreign automatic. See Chapter 24 for a full account of their significance.

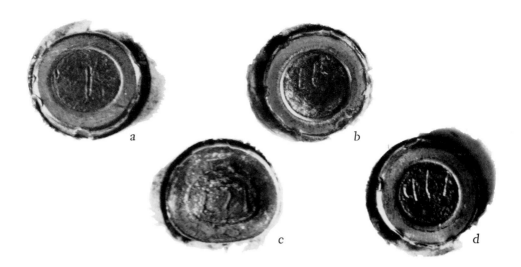

The bases of four bullets alleged to have been removed from the body of Berardelli on April 15, 1920. (These photographs were taken in 1961.)

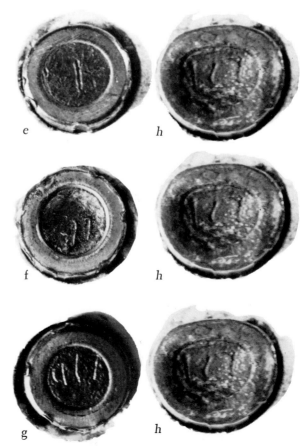

The Alleged Mortal Bullet

The prosecution claimed that the bullet marked III was fired by Sacco. It was also alleged to have been the bullet that caused the death of Berardelli. This was the *only* bullet that could possibly have been fired from Sacco's pistol.

Dr. Magrath, who performed the autopsy, testified that he had scratched a numeral with the point of a needle on the base of each bullet, seriatim, as he removed it, to indicate its place in the order of extraction. In these photographs the appearance of the marks on bullet III is separately compared with the scratches on the other three bullets. See Chapter 16 for a full discussion of these critical exhibits.

(Photographs through the courtesy of Francis Russell and *American Heritage*.)

FRED H
MOORE
COUNSEL FOR
SACCO

I WEAR
A 7¼

SACCO CONTEMPTUOUSLY TRIES
ON THE "BANDIT" FUR LINED CAP

The Pearl Street cap

This cartoonist's impression of how the stray cap found in Pearl Street fitted Sacco's head appeared in the *Boston Herald* on July 6, 1921. A Pinkerton agent was shown the cap by Chief Gallivan and reported that it was about size 6⅞. At the trial, it was agreed that Sacco's hat size was 7⅛ (see Chapter 14).

Although the prosecution sought to prove that the cap was found by a Slater and Morrill employee on the afternoon of April 15, 1920, Chief Gallivan's testimony before the Governor's Advisory Committee almost exactly confirmed this account in the *Boston Herald* dated April 17, 1920. By the *Herald*'s — and Gallivan's — account, the cap was found on the evening of April 16, more than twenty-four hours after the shooting.

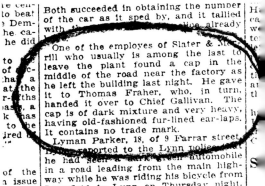

Both succeeded in obtaining the number of the car as it sped by, and it tallied with the ......

One of the employes of Slater & Morrill who usually is among the last to leave the plant found a cap in the middle of the road near the factory as he left the building last night. He gave it to Thomas Fraher, who, in turn, handed it over to Chief Gallivan. The cap is of dark mixture and very heavy, having old-fashioned fur-lined ear-laps. It contains no trade mark.

Lyman Parker, 18, of 9 Farrar street, ... reported to the Lynn police ... he had seen a dark green automobile in a road leading from the main highway while he was riding his bicycle from Lynnfield to Lynn on Thursday night. ...the car bore the number 49,782.

LA NOTIZIA — VENERDI' 16 APRILE 1920

BOSTON E DE

The "banchetto" for Commander Williams

This circled excerpt from the April 16, 1920, issue of *La Notizia* describes the banquet tendered to Commander Williams by Italians in Boston's North End. It was this event that helped witnesses to Sacco's alibi to fix the day when he came to Boston as April 15. Subsequently, President Lowell attempted to prove that the banquet did not take place on April 15. His failure to do so is discussed in Chapter 21.

In lieu of signing each page of this book shipper has signed the agreement on the inside front cover.

AMERICAN EXPRESS COMPANY at _____ BOSTON, MASS.

RECEIVED FROM_____ **CORSO & CANNIZZO CO.** the shipments, hereinafter listed, subject to the classifications and tariffs in effect on date hereof, which shipments the Company agrees to carry upon the terms and conditions of the uniform express receipt in effect on date of shipment. **NOT NEGOTIABLE.**

DATE	DESCRIPTION AND CONTENTS	VALUE HEREIN DECLARED BY SHIPPER TO BE	CONSIGNED TO	DESTINATION.	FOR THE COMPANY
DEC 20 1919	1 Bbl	140	Angelo Vinci	Rome N.Y.	
DEC 20 1919			C. O. D. # 21 and charges		
DEC 20 1919	1 Bbl	40	B. Vanzetti	Plymouth Mass	

entering shipments forwarded C. O. D. always use two lines. Receipts must give on both lines once for the shipment and once for the C. O. D.

American Express Company receipt

This receipt was found by Aldino Felicani and the author after a frantic canvass of all fish dealers on Boston's Atlantic Avenue and at South Boston Fish Pier. The successful search was precipitated by a reported remark by Governor Fuller that no proof had been offered at the Plymouth trial that Vanzetti had received any eels for delivery on December 24, 1920. The peculiar effect the discovery of this receipt had on the Governor's thinking is discussed in Chapter 30.

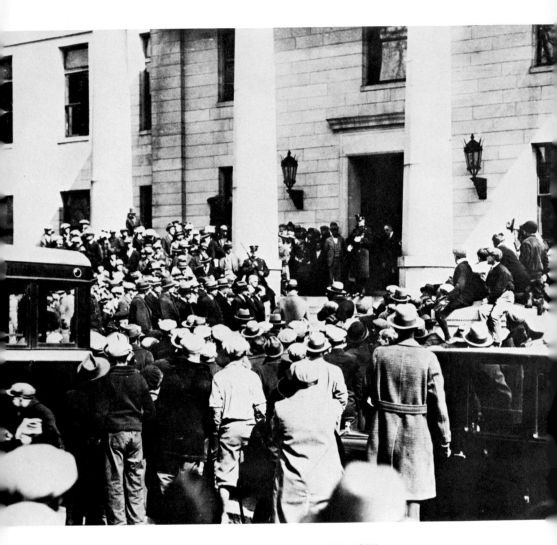

The sentencing, April 9, 1927
(Courtesy of Boston Globe/Boston Post)

the ground that the answers might incriminate them. Frequently they will state their names and addresses but nothing more. They are fearful that further answers to the most innocent-appearing queries might lead them into unknown morasses. It is also helpful to hold in mind that at the Dedham trial Sacco and Vanzetti readily admitted that answers given on May 5 and 6, 1920, were falsehoods. Nor is there much doubt but that they answered the same questions truthfully at the cross-examinations in July 1921.

With these preliminaries, let us now turn to the cross-examinations of Sacco and Vanzetti.

Although Vanzetti took the stand before his companion, Mr. Katzmann saved his more savage examination for use against Sacco. This may have been because Vanzetti's answers disclosed a keener perception of the examiner's objectives, a greater capacity for precise responses and more restraint under the goadings of the prosecutor. There may have been a more purposeful reason, however, which explains why Mr. Katzmann postponed his more massive assault until Sacco took the stand. This we shall explore in the next chapter. Nevertheless, Mr. Katzmann opened his cross-examination of Vanzetti by what is sometimes called "a lunge for the jugular." Only in this instance, the jugular was not, as you would expect, the South Braintree crime, but something quite alien to it. The vital vein which Mr. Katzmann went for was Vanzetti's act in going to Mexico to avoid military service in World War I. Vanzetti had told about this in his answers to Mr. McAnarney. The excerpt from the transcript of the direct examination on this point shows how Mr. Katzmann had already begun to wind up for his initial blow at Vanzetti. It reads as follows:

Q. (By Mr. McAnarney) During the year of registration, 1917, you went away? A. (By Vanzetti) Yes.
Q. How long were you away [viz., from Plymouth]? A. How far, you mean?
Q. No, how long? When did you come back from — You went away then. Now, when did you come back? A. I should say a year or a year and a half after.
Q. Why did you go away? A. *I go away for not to be a soldier.*
MR. KATZMANN. *"Go away for"* —
THE WITNESS. *Not to make a soldier, not to go to the war.*
Q. Where did you go?
MR. KATZMANN. *May I get that exact answer?*
THE COURT. *"I go away"* —
THE WITNESS. *I go away for not to go to the war as a soldier.*

> Q. Where did you go to? A. At first time I went to Mexico.
> Q. How long did you remain in Mexico? A. Three or four months, or five months. [Emphasis added.] [5]

A trial lawyer will quickly detect that Mr. Katzmann was using the trial lawyer's device of getting a witness to repeat testimony which he regarded as extremely damaging to the other side. Here it worked most successfully. The result of Mr. Katzmann's interruptions was that Vanzetti, in four successive statements, told the jury that he went to Mexico to avoid military service.

A short time after Vanzetti gave the foregoing testimony on direct examination, Mr. Katzmann started the cross-examination. He struck the prepared blow in his opening question, if it may be called a question. Here is how he began:

> Q. (By Mr. Katzmann) So you left Plymouth, Mr. Vanzetti, in May, 1917, to dodge the draft, did you? A. Yes, sir.
> Q. And you stayed away, did you not, until the class in which men of your age came had all been drawn in the draft? Is that true? A. Not exactly.
> Q. What part of it isn't true? A. It isn't true because men of my condition were never compelled to be a soldier.
> Q. No men of your condition were compelled to be soldiers? A. Yes, sir.
> Q. Were you physically unable to be a soldier? A. I don't speak of the physical condition. I speak of civil condition. [He was an alien.]
> Q. Were you physically sound? A. I hope so.
> Q. Do you know? A. I ought to be.
> Q. Did you believe you were? A. Yes, sir.
> Q. Physically sound as you were, and after you had been in this country since 1908? A. Yes, sir.
> Q. When this country was at war, you ran away so you would not have to fight as a soldier? A. Yes.
> Q. Is that true? A. It is true. [6]

What legitimate purpose did Mr. Katzmann's opening questions serve? Vanzetti was charged with murder, not draft dodging. They had not the remotest bearing on whether Vanzetti had committed murder. Nor were they intended to show that Vanzetti had lied in his direct examination. On the contrary, the questions were so worded as to inflame the sensitive area of patriotic public emotion by rubbing in the fact that Vanzetti *had told the truth,* unreservedly and harmful as it might be to his defense.

After the opening questions, Mr. Katzmann stopped referring to Van-

[5] Vol. II, 1727.   [6] Vol. II, 1737.

zetti's draft dodging and devoted himself to trying to show that Vanzetti's lies on being arrested were not logically due to his fears as a radical or of arrest as a draft evader and that his explanation for trying to borrow Boda's car was not true. There was, however, still an occasional sounding of the patriotic note.

Vanzetti had testified that the false answers he gave just after his arrest were for the purpose of concealing the names and addresses of friends who had literature and because they had gone together to Mexico to avoid conscription or registration.[7] Mr. Katzmann then asked:

Q. Well, has the fact you told me an untruth about how long you knew Nick Sacco anything to do with your evasion of the draft? A. Yes.
Q. What has it to do with your evasion of the draft? A. It has to do because me and Nick we go, we go to Mexico together.
Q. Oh, did Sacco go with you, too? A. Yes, sir. [This was the first time testimony as to Sacco's draft evasion entered the case.]
Q. For the same purpose, Mr. Vanzetti? A. Yes, sir.[8]

Mr. Katzmann then took another swing at Vanzetti's disloyalty:

Q. And are you that man, Mr. Vanzetti, that on May 9th was going to address a meeting down at Brockton to your fellow citizens, saying: "You have fought in the wars, and you have worked for capitalists, and tried their ways?" Are you the man, sir, that was going to address the returned soldiers? A. Yes, sir.
Q. You were going to advise in a public meeting men who had gone to war? Are you that man? A. Yes, sir, I am that man, not the man you want me, but I am that man.[9]

Mr. Katzmann's questions were apparently not intended to elicit answers, but rather were declaimed for the purpose of condemning Vanzetti for conduct hateful in the eyes of the jurymen.

Mr. Katzmann asked Vanzetti about many questions which he claimed to have asked him at the Brockton police station and about Vanzetti's answers to them. Vanzetti readily admitted most of the questions and answers, did not remember others and denied some of them. Vanzetti also admitted that many of his answers had been falsehoods. He stated further that he might have given certain answers which he did not recall, but some of them could have been mistakes of memory, not lies. He claimed that Mr. Katzmann asked other questions which he answered, but this was contro-

[7] Vol. II, 1777.   [8] Vol. II, 1777–1778.   [9] Vol. II, 1778.

verted by the prosecutor. Mr. Katzmann held in his hand an alleged transcript of the interrogation but did not offer it (except in one instance) to prove its accuracy.

Vanzetti ascribed many of his falsehoods to fear of giving leads to the identity of his friends, some of whom had incendiary anarchist literature.[10] Since Vanzetti admitted that many of his answers at the police station were falsehoods, no lengthy recital is needed to show that he lied. Vanzetti also admitted that in some instances his falsehoods had no direct bearing on his fears for himself and friends as radicals because of the inciting literature which had been distributed. However, he endeavored to make a reasonable connection between his falsehoods and his fears.

For instance, Vanzetti said in Brockton that he had purchased his revolver for nineteen dollars at a store in Hanover Street, Boston. In Dedham, he stated that this was untrue, that he had bought it (fully loaded) two or three months before from his friend Falzini.[11] He conceded that there was no reason connected with collecting literature that made him falsify, but said that "what I tell you about revolver has the same report as literature" [12] (viz. he did not want to involve his friends), referring to his lie that he had bought the revolver cartridges in Hanover Street and fired them off on the beach. Mr. Katzmann asked him:

Q. Was that helping you to conceal the names and addresses, Mr. Vanzetti?
A. I don't say I bought that by Falzini.[13]

If it was true, as Vanzetti claimed, that he bought his revolver from Falzini, then his telling a false story about how he acquired it was quite consistent with his stated motive to protect his friends from police investigation and harassment. If at the time of his arrest he had admitted that he had bought the revolver from Falzini instead of naming some fictitious retail store, the police would certainly have interviewed his friend, with unforeseeable consequences.

This was not, however, how the matter appeared to Judge Thayer. In his "Decision" on defendants' motion for a new trial in 1926, the judge undertook to justify Mr. Katzmann's type of cross-examination of the defendants on the ground that the prosecutor's *sole purpose* "was to show that there was no logical connection between their falsehoods and incriminating conduct on the one side and radicalism on the other." With respect to Vanzetti,

[10] Vol. II, 1758 *et seq*.   [11] Vol. II, 1715.   [12] Vol. II, 1751.   [13] Vol. II, 1799.

Judge Thayer selected as his only example Mr. Katzmann's cross-examination about the false story of the revolver purchase. In making his point, however, the judge apparently *forgot entirely that Vanzetti, in answering Mr. Katzmann, had stated a quite simple connection between his lies and his radicalism.* Instead of testing Vanzetti's story on the basis of his claim that he wanted to protect Falzini, the judge built on his own conviction that Vanzetti sought to conceal the fact that he was carrying Berardelli's revolver. This is how he reasoned: "Now, let me give an illustration of Mr. Katzmann's cross-examination of Mr. Vanzetti with the same purpose in view. Mr. Katzmann asked Vanzetti at his interview after arrest, when he got his Harrington and Richardson revolver; his answer was, 'Four years before.' He said he bought it on Hanover Street, Boston, that he paid $18.00 or $19.00 for it, that the revolver had six chambers in it. And yet, on the witness stand, he admitted that he lied to Mr. Katzmann, and that the fact was that he had bought the revolver about three months before he was arrested, that he only paid $5.00 for it and that it had five chambers instead of six."

Judge Thayer then made an assertion which, in the context of the argument he was then making, conveyed a totally wrong impression. He said, "The jury had a right to say there was no reason, in answering these questions at the time of the interview, why Vanzetti should not have told the truth."

Judge Thayer went on to give his own explanation of why Vanzetti had lied:

. . . and they [the jury] had a right to find, also, that if Vanzetti had stuck to this story, it could have been established that this revolver could not have been purchased on Hanover Street, Boston, because the law at that time provided that certain records must have been kept. The jury had a right to say that he changed his story about the cost of the revolver because it developed that the market value of a Harrington and Richardson revolver was only $5.00; and on this particular question the jury had a right to say that if a man could not get within nearly four times of the market value of this Harrington and Richardson revolver then he did not probably buy it, and if he did not buy it, it was consistent with the claim of the Commonwealth that it belonged to Berardelli.[14]

Although Mr. Katzmann's cross-examination of Vanzetti was replete with questions intended to show that there was no logical link between

[14] Vol. V, 4770–4771.

Vanzetti's lies and his fears as a radical, Judge Thayer's selection of the revolver subject as his solitary example of the achievement of this purpose would appear to be something less than convincing.

Asked whether he had denied that he had slept in Boston more than once, Vanzetti said that if he had so stated it was untrue. "It was the same thing for the books and for the revolver. I don't want to tell." [15]

On another occasion he explained why he had claimed to have given a wrong name at the time when he bought his revolver on Hanover Street: "When I say the first thing false, I have to say everything false." [16]

Vanzetti may not have known the old adage about the tangled web of deceit, but he knew its underlying truth.

The cross-examination includes a curious colloquy between Katzmann and Vanzetti about the shotgun cartridges allegedly taken from Vanzetti upon his arrest. In an earlier chapter dealing with the shells at the Plymouth trial where Vanzetti did not take the stand, we were compelled to look forward to the Dedham trial testimony for the defendant's explanation of his possession of the cartridges. There we learned that Sacco stated that a friend who had visited him to do a little hunting had left three unused shells from the lot he had brought with him. These Mrs. Sacco had placed on a shelf and Vanzetti had taken them, as he said, to sell "for the cause." On direct examination Vanzetti, when asked whether anything was given to him when Mrs. Sacco was packing things for the trip to Italy, had replied, "Yes, before we go away I take three gun shells." [17]

In the earlier chapter we noted that Officer Michael J. Connolly had said that he had taken four shotgun cartridges from Vanzetti, but he did not identify the shells put into evidence as the same ones alleged to have been so taken. We also noted the coincidence that *three* of the Connolly shells were of Peters manufacture and the fourth was a Winchester. Dr. Murphy had found an exploded Winchester in the Bridgewater street and Mr. Katzmann had argued to Judge Thayer that the Winchester allegedly found on Vanzetti was "the same size and type of shell that Dr. Murphy picked up in the vicinity of the shooting and immediately afterwards." [18] (However, it contained buckshot whereas the Murphy shell had held # 10 shot, very much smaller pellets, a fact not known to defense counsel.) We have also noted that of the four pistol shells (Fraher shells) introduced at the Dedham trial (Mr. Bostock, who found the shells, had said "three or

[15] Vol. II, 1753.   [16] Vol. II, 1797.   [17] Vol. II, 1714–1715.   [18] Supp. Vol., 145.

four"), one turned out to be of Winchester manufacture and therefore matched the only Winchester bullet among the four slugs extracted from Berardelli's body, and that this Winchester bullet and shell were the only ones claimed to have been fired in Sacco's pistol.

It was partly because of these singular coincidences, and the uncertainties surrounding the origin of the Winchester shotgun cartridge at the Plymouth trial, that I raised a question as to whether this unidentified Winchester allegedly taken from Vanzetti was not actually a fourth shell which had never been in his possession. If so, then Sacco and Vanzetti were correct in stating that there were only three shells at the Sacco house. However, no such question was raised at the Plymouth or the Dedham trials. Indeed, at Dedham, no such claim could have arisen, since no discharged shotgun shell had been found in South Braintree. Whatever significance the number of shotgun shells taken from Vanzetti might have had in the Bridgewater case, it had no bearing on the South Braintree crime. If the presence of shotgun cartridges in Vanzetti's pocket constituted proof that he had been in South Braintree (practically nil in any event), three would have had the same probative value as four. Against this background Mr. Katzmann's cross-examination of Vanzetti about the shotgun shells is peculiar. He seemed to be obsessed with a determination to make Vanzetti admit there were four shotgun cartridges, not three. This seemed to be a rather unimportant matter to Vanzetti. It apparently had no significance for Mr. McAnarney either. He opened his examination of Mrs. Sacco about the shells by stating: "I call your attention to three or four shells . . ." [19]

Not so for Mr. Katzmann. To him Vanzetti's statement that he was given three cartridges seemed to have some crucial significance unknown to the defense and never revealed during the trial. This is how he began the subject with Vanzetti:

Q. Mr. Vanzetti, when Mr. McAnarney was examining you this morning, do you remember that you said you took three gun shells off a shelf in the Sacco kitchen? A. Yes, sir.
Q. Did you mean to emphasize the word "three"? Did you mean to bear with force on the word "three"? "I took three shells." Did you mean that? A. No, I don't, — I never say I took *three* shells. I say I took three shells.
Q. Did you take four shells? A. I am not sure.
Q. Aren't you sure, Mr. Vanzetti? Aren't you sure? A. If I am sure? No, I am not sure. Mr. McAnarney has asked me this morning if I took three shells. I say yes, I took three shells.

[19] Vol. II, 2057.

Q. Mr. McAnarney did not ask you if you took three shells. He asked you if you took any shells, didn't he? A. I should say he asked me if I took three shells. [Both Vanzetti and Katzmann were in error.]

Q. Well, I will ask you now if you took four shells? A. I don't remember. I believe that I took three shells.

Q. You believe you took three? A. Yes.

Q. Do you remember this question and this answer that I asked of you at the Brockton police station:

"Q. Did you have anything else that could be shot in your pocket?"
And your answer:

"A. I have four of that thing to go hunting."
Did you say that at Brockton? A. I don't remember.

Q. Will you say you did not say it? A. Oh, no, I don't say that.

Q. And did I then follow up with this question:

"Q. Shells, you mean? What did you take those for?"
And your reply:

"A. I took that because Nick gave it to me, gave them to me." A. Yes.

Q. And do you remember what you said this morning, how you got those shells? A. Yes.

Q. What did you say this morning? A. I say I see that on a board against the wall and I asked if he used it. He say he don't use it. I say, "Give to me that I bring to my friends of Plymouth, some men who go to hunt, and I give to him."

Q. Did you say anything else? Did you say anything this morning about his wife giving you those shells? A. I don't remember if his wife —

Q. Will you say you did not? A. I don't remember if his wife give me or Nick give me.

Q. Which one gave you? A. I don't remember, I told you.

Q. Now, having read those questions and those answers to you that were asked at the Brockton police station, how many shells did you get, no matter how you got them, how many did you get? A. Well, I don't know if I got three or four. I don't remember if I got three or four. I don't remember exactly. I don't want to insist at all about it.

Q. Were they shown to you at the Brockton police station? A. I can't remember. It was shown in some other place, but I do not in the Brockton police station.

Q. Will you say, Mr. Vanzetti, you did not get four shells at the Sacco house? A. I say I don't at all insist. I don't remember exactly.

Q. You won't say it isn't four, will you? A. No.[20]

Mr. Katzmann was apparently not yet satisfied that he had made Vanzetti admit that the cartridges were four in number. After a long further cross-examination on other matters, he returned to the subject. Although ostensibly inquiring into the day of the week when Vanzetti received the

[20] Vol. II, 1747–1748.

shells, he incorporated the words "four shells" three times in a page and a half of the record by the following dialogue:

Q. (By Mr. Katzmann) Do you remember my asking you this question:
  "Q. What day did Nick give you those *four* shells? A. Well, I do not know if it was yesterday morning or the day before."
Do you remember that question and that answer? A. No, I do not remember.
  Q. Will you say that I did not ask it of you and you did not make that answer? A. No, it is right. I think I answered like that.
  Q. Then on Thursday, May 6th, is it not the fact you could not remember whether you got those *four* shells from Nick on Tuesday or Wednesday, two or one day before I asked you? [Emphasis added.] [21]

A few questions later Mr. Katzmann again loaded his question with the number four:

Q. All right. Then going back in your memory to the *four* shells, let me ask you if you remember this question and this answer . . . [Emphasis added.] [22]

The examination had contained numerous questions concerning what he said fifteen months before about the shells. Vanzetti's answers indicate that he was getting tired of this type of question and his testimony on shells ended as follows:

Q. About the shells, when Nick gave you the shells, when I was asking you on Thursday? A. Only what I remember is that I was asked about those shells, but I don't remember anything else.
  Q. I am asking you now if you remember that you made those answers to those questions I have read to you? A. I don't remember. I remember I was called about those shells, but I don't remember everything I was called about.[23]

What was in Mr. Katzmann's mind that he made such a strenuous effort to force Vanzetti to concede that he had *four* shotgun cartridges in his possession and not *three*? No one was then suggesting that the Winchester cartridge might have been added to the three Peters cartridges alleged by the defendants to have been left over by Sacco's friend after the shooting. So far as I know it is being suggested for the first time in this book as a result of careful analysis of the record. Since such a claim would not even have been relevant to any issue in the Dedham trial, Mr. Katzmann's bear-

[21] Vol. II, 1771.   [22] Vol. II, 1772.   [23] Vol. II, 1773.

ing down so heavily on "four shells" must remain another mystery among the many in the Sacco-Vanzetti case. Did it have a Freudian implication?

Much of the cross-examination was devoted to an attack on Vanzetti's explanation of the reason for his call at the Johnson home in West Bridgewater on May 5, 1920. This has been referred to in a previous chapter. On direct examination Vanzetti had said that he, Boda, Orciani and Sacco had made the call to get Boda's Overland car. Here is an excerpt from the record:

Q. What were you going to get the automobile for? A. We were going to take the automobile for to carry books and newspapers.

Q. I did not get the first part of your answer. I repeat the question. What were you going to get the automobile for? A. For to take out literature, books and newspapers, from the house and the homes.

Q. What house and homes did you want to take the books and literature from? A. From any house and from any house in five or six places, five or six towns. Three, five or six people have plenty of literature, and we want, we intend to take that out and put that in the proper place.

Q. What do you mean by a "proper place"? A. By a proper place I mean in a place not subject to policemen go in and call for, see the literature, see the papers, see the books, as in that time they went through in the house of many men who were active in the Radical movement and Socialist and labor movement, and go there and take letters and take books and take newspapers, and put men in jail and deport many.

MR. KATZMANN. I ask it be stricken out.

THE WITNESS. I say that in that time —

MR. KATZMANN. Wait one moment.

THE WITNESS. And deported many, many, many have been misused in jail, and so on.

Q. Where were you going that night if you could have got the automobile? A. I intended to go to Plymouth and speak to some of my friends of Plymouth who is owner of the house.

Q. And do what? A. And if they are willing to receive such literature and newspapers in his house.

Q. Now, where were you going to take these papers and literature you were going to take from these houses? What were you going to do with them? Suppose you had got the automobile that night and you had gone down to Plymouth to these houses? What were you going to do with the papers you would pick up here? A. Before to pick the paper, I want to find the place and ask if my friend in Plymouth, if he was willing that we bring the paper in his house.

Q. I see. You were going to some friend and ask him if he would receive the things? A. Yes, if he was willing to receive such papers and such books in his house.

Q. Now, whether or not this going around to get these papers was as a result of what you learned when you went to New York? A. Yes. What we read in newspapers, too [Salsedo's death].[24]

He also said on direct examination:

Q. (By Mr. McAnarney) Now, I had asked you what you were going to do if you had got the automobile up at Elm Square that night. You have told me about going to pick up this literature, these books and tracts, and things. Was there anything else you were going to do? A. Well, I was to pass in Bridgewater and if possible to find Pappi.

Q. What for? A. To tell him we will have a meeting, we will have a speech in Brockton the next Sunday, to come and to tell the Italians to come, and then we go. We come, we planned to go to Plymouth from the place we put the literature.

MR. KATZMANN. I did not hear that.

MR. JEREMIAH MCANARNEY. I did not either. Kindly repeat the answer.

THE WITNESS. Yes. To go to Pappi and tell to Pappi that next Sunday we will have a speech in Brockton somewhere, in Brockton Hall somewhere, to tell to the friends in Bridgewater to come down, to the Italians to come down to Brockton next Sunday, and if he will, if we will be able to find him, after speaking with him we intend to go to Plymouth and speak with my friend, if he was willing to accept the literature in his house.

Q. Now, in talking to Officer Spear and to any other official, District Attorney or others, did you at any time tell them what you have now told us, that you were going to get any of this literature, or anything of that sort? A. No, I don't tell them that thing.

Q. You withheld that from him. You never told that to them before? A. No.

Q. Why not? A. Because in that time there, there was the deportation and the reaction was more vivid than now and more mad than now.

Q. The action? A. The reaction. What you call "reaction." It mean the authority of this country and every country in the world was more against the Socialist element in that time than before the war and after the war. There were exceptional times.

MR. KATZMANN. If your Honor please, may I have the stenographer read that last thing? [25]

After a long and argumentative cross-examination Vanzetti's story remained unshaken. He gave further testimony on the same subject as follows:

Q. (By Mr. McAnarney) Any one time you mentioned that you were afraid, what did you mean by that? A. I mean I was afraid, for I know that my friends

[24] Vol. II, 1721–1722.   [25] Vol. II, 1726.

there in New York have jumped down from the jail in the street and killed himself. The papers say that he jump down, but we don't know.

Q. You now allude to who? Who is that man? A. Salsedo.

Q. When did you learn of Salsedo's death? A. On the day, in the day, 4th, of May.[26]

Vanzetti then told of his trip to New York on May 2. Mr. McAnarney then inquired:

Q. (By Mr. McAnarney) What you learned in New York, how did that affect your actions and why did you do what you did? Was it in consequence of what you learned in New York? A. Yes, it was.

Q. In what way? A. In what way with what I hear in New York, what I learned in New York, was —

Q. What did you hear in New York? What did you learn? A. I learned that most probably for the May 1st there will be many arrest of Radicals and I was set wise if I have literature and correspondence, something, papers in the home, to bring away, and to tell to my friends to clean them up the house, because the literature will not be found if the policemen go to the house.

Q. And was it in consequence of that that you were there that night, May 5th, to get this car? A. Yes, not only for that, not necessarily for that, — we want to go to Bridgewater to speak to Pappi for the conference, for the speech, too.

Q. Well, the two things? A. *The principal purpose is to go to Plymouth, suggest a place where we can put the literature and then bring around the literature to that place.*

Q. Now, assuming you had got the Boda car as you had planned, were you going to Plymouth that night? A. Yes.

Q. What were you going to do? A. To see if I found friend that he will be, that will agree that will accept the responsibility to take such literature in his house.

Q. So that at the time, then, that night, May 5th, you had not arranged with any one to receive or to keep or to hide this literature? A. No, we don't know yet on that night nor if we take the literature out where we are to put it. We don't agree yet on the place. We don't know yet the place. [Emphasis added.] [27]

Mr. Katzmann made no serious effort to controvert the basic facts underlying Vanzetti's story of the events which led to the call at the Johnson house. Instead he devoted many questions to trying to show that Vanzetti's explanation was not logical. Were not some of Vanzetti's actions inconsistent with his explanation? How would truthful answers to some of Katzmann's questions on May 6, 1920, have given his friends away? Why did Vanzetti answer some questions truthfully but not others? Why couldn't

26 Vol. II, 1808.   27 Vol. II, 1810–1811.

Vanzetti have accomplished his mission in some other way? Wouldn't Orciani's motorcycle have done as well as Boda's Overland? [28] Was it necessary for Vanzetti to go along with Boda? [29] Couldn't Boda have gotten his car from the Johnson garage without Vanzetti's help? [30] Couldn't Boda have gone to Plymouth instead of Vanzetti? [31] And couldn't Vanzetti have met Boda (for the West Bridgewater visit) in the morning as well as at night? [32]

What was Mr. Katzmann trying to prove by this type of cross-examination? He did not attack the facts that underlay Vanzetti's explanation of the visit to Elm Square. He introduced no evidence to controvert the testimony that Vanzetti had been sent to New York on May 2, that he had been warned of renewed danger for his group in Massachusetts, that he received advice from the New York committee to reclaim the radical literature previously distributed and that Vanzetti had transmitted the information to the Boston committee.

Vanzetti's explanation of the reason for wanting to take out the Overland was consistent with the known facts. If it was not the truth, then what did the Commonwealth claim was the real reason? It had the burden of proving that the defendants were guilty beyond a reasonable doubt. *And yet Mr. Katzmann made no claim that there was any other particular reason for the call for the Overland.* He went no further than to turn on a barrage of questions designed to arouse vague suspicions that there was some other unnamed purpose. This he did by simply phrasing his interrogatories in such form as to intimate that Vanzetti's account was improbable and inconsistent.

Nevertheless, it was the unspoken theory of the prosecution that Vanzetti and his companions wanted the old jalopy as a conveyance for robbery purposes. Mr. Katzmann stated to Judge Thayer that he would show that the car was wanted for a purpose different from that given by Vanzetti,[33] but failed to do so. Before the Governor's Advisory Committee, Mr. Thompson pressed Mr. Katzmann to state what he claimed to be the purpose of the defendants in calling for the Overland. Here Mr. Katzmann let slip what had really been in his mind:

Q. (By Mr. Thompson) What did you try to show the jury, — what Sacco's purpose was in going to Johnson's house and trying to get the car? A. I cannot remember. I don't believe, as a matter of recollection, that we were trying to

[28] Vol. II, 1745.   [29] Vol. II, 1746.   [30] Vol. II, 1746.   [31] Vol. II, 1746.
[32] Vol. II, 1746.   [33] Vol. II, 1815.

show any definite purpose, for instance, that they were going to commit another crime.[34]

What Chief Stewart thought is perhaps also indicative of the kind of thinking in the district attorney's office. He was in charge of the preparation of evidence for the trial. As late as September 15, 1962, he was interviewed by Judge Musmanno and Clement A. Norton at his home in Scituate. Judge Musmanno quotes Chief Stewart as telling them then that Sacco and Vanzetti wanted the Overland for a holdup the next day and could not use the Buick, since "the police had it." [35] (The police had not deprived the robbers of the Buick, — it had been voluntarily abandoned by them on the night after the crime as a tactic typical of professionals.) Defense counsel had no means of refuting this sort of whispered and mysterious evidence, which was rife at the Dedham trial. Mr. Katzmann, therefore, was wise in not putting forward a claim which he could not prove. In such a situation, pure speculation, devoid of evidence but fed by rumor, is more persuasive than vulnerable testimony.

This completes the discussion of Mr. Katzmann's cross-examination of Vanzetti except as to the alibi testimony, which will be considered later.

We now turn to the cross-examination of Sacco — surely one of the most extraordinary cross-examinations in a capital case that ever took place in a modern courtroom.

19.

Cross-Examination of Sacco

It was a bitter cross-examination, a cruel one, but not beyond the bounds that our laws have set down for such cross-examination.
ASSISTANT DISTRICT ATTORNEY RANNEY, July 25, 1927
Holt Record, Vol. V, 5340

Mr. Katzmann opened his cross-examination of Sacco exactly as he had done with Vanzetti — by an attack upon him as a draft dodger. This time the pretext was an almost parenthetical statement made by Sacco in telling

[34] Vol. V, 5041.   [35] Musmanno, memorandum of visit with Stewart.

of his emigrating to America. Mr. Moore was asking him for the usual kind of introductory information preliminary to direct examination. Among his questions was the following:

Q. (By Mr. Moore) And how did you happen to come here? What was the occasion for your coming here? Who did you come with? A. Well, my father got some friend here when he was young. This friend he baptize most of the people in the family, so my brother, — who is Sabeno — he was in army three years and he served in the army about thirty six months.
Q. In the Italian Army? A. Yes, so he came back. My father's friend live in Milford and he like very much to see my brother, so my brother when he came back from the army, he desired to come to this country, so I was crazy to come to this country, because I was liked a free country, call a free country. I desire to come with him.
Q. So you two came together, did you? A. Yes.
Q. How old were you at that time? A. Seventeen years old.
Q. Do you know what port you landed? Where did you come into the United States, at what city? A. Milford [where Sacco first settled].[1]

Embedded in the foregoing dialogue was Sacco's comment that he "liked a free country." There was nothing unique about this explanation. It was a motive that moved millions to cross the Atlantic. Nevertheless, Mr. Katzmann used it as a lever to pry open the latent prejudices in the jurors' minds. As he did with Vanzetti, Mr. Katzmann began with an assault on Sacco's patriotism. The attack on Sacco, however, lasted for about thirteen pages of the printed record. This part of the cross-examination was justified by Mr. Katzmann in these words: "Well, he stated in his direct examination yesterday that he loved a free country, and I offer it to attack that statement made in his examination by his own counsel." [2]

It will be observed that in Mr. Katzmann's cross-examination of Sacco on this subject, which follows, he changed Sacco's remark that he *liked a free country* into a protestation that he *loved the United States*. Sacco's conduct and answers were quite consistent with what he had actually said. By assuming that Sacco had said something quite different, Mr. Katzmann made him appear as a liar and a hypocrite. Defense counsel apparently did not notice this substitution of the meaning of Sacco's remark and did not protect him from its consequences. So Sacco, with his own meager knowledge of the connotation of English words, was left a helpless victim of Mr. Katzmann's masterful ridicule and innuendos. The cross-examination began and proceeded as follows:

[1] Vol. II, 1818.   [2] Vol. II, 1875.

Q. (By Mr. Katzmann) Did you say yesterday you love a free country? A. Yes, sir.

Q. Did you love this country in the month of May, 1917? A. I did not say, — I don't want to say I did not love this country.

Q. Did you love this country in the month of 1917? A. If you can, Mr. Katzmann, if you give me that, — I could explain —

Q. Do you understand that question? A. Yes.

Q. Then will you please answer it? A. I can't answer in one word.

Q. You can't say whether you loved the United States of America one week before the day you enlisted for the first draft? A. I can't say in one word, Mr. Katzmann.

Q. You can't tell this jury whether you loved the country or not?

MR. MOORE. I object to that.

A. I could explain that, yes, if I loved —

Q. What? A. I could explain that, yes, if I loved, if you give me a chance.

Q. I ask you first to answer that question. Did you love this United States of America in May, 1917? A. I can't answer in one word.

Q. Don't you know whether you did or not?

MR. MOORE. I object, your Honor.

THE COURT. What say?

MR. MOORE. I object to the repetition of this question without giving the young man an opportunity to explain his attitude.

THE COURT. That is not the usual method that prevails. Where the question can be categorically answered by yes or no, it should be answered. The explanation comes later. Then you can make any inquiry to the effect of giving the witness an opportunity of making whatever explanation at that time he sees fit to make, but under cross-examination counsel is entitled to get an answer either yes or no, when the question can be so answered. You may proceed, please.

Q. Did you love this country in the last week of May, 1917? A. That is pretty hard for me to say in one word, Mr. Katzmann.

Q. There are two words you can use, Mr. Sacco, yes or no. Which one is it? A. Yes.

Q. And in order to show your love for this United States of America when she was about to call upon you to become a soldier you ran away to Mexico?

MR. JEREMIAH MCANARNEY. Wait.

THE COURT. Did you?

Q. Did you run away to Mexico?

THE COURT. He has not said he ran away to Mexico. Did you go?

Q. Did you go to Mexico to avoid being a soldier for this country that you loved? A. Yes.

Q. You went under an assumed name? A. No.

Q. Didn't you take the name of Mosmacotelli? A. Yes.

Q. That is not your name, is it? A. No.

Q. How long did you remain under the name of Mosmacotelli? A. Until I got a job over to Mr. Kelley's.

Q. When was that? A. The armistice.

Q. After the war was practically over? A. Yes, sir.

Q. Then, for the first time, after May, 1917, did you become known as Sacco again? A. Yes, sir.

Q. Was it for the reason that you desired to avoid service that when you came back in four months you went to Cambridge instead of to Milford? A. For the reason for not to get in the army.

Q. So as to avoid getting in the army. A. Another reason why, I did not want no chance to get arrested and one year in prison.

Q. Did not want to get arrested and spend one year in prison for dodging the draft. Is that it? A. Yes.

Q. Did you love your country when you came back from Mexico? A. The first time?

THE COURT. Which country did you say? You said —

Q. United States of America, your adopted country? A. I did not say already.

Q. When you came back, I asked you. That was before you went. A. I don't think I could change my opinion in three months.

Q. You still loved America, did you? A. I should say yes.

Q. And is that your idea of showing your love for this Country? A. (Witness hesitates.)

Q. Is that your idea of showing your love for America? A. Yes.

Q. And would it be your idea of showing your love for your wife that when she needed you you ran away from her? A. I did not run away from her.

MR. MOORE. I object.

THE WITNESS. I was going to come after if I need her.

THE COURT. He may answer. Simply on the question of credibility, that is all.

Q. Would it be your idea of love for your wife that you were to run away from her when she needed you?

MR. JEREMIAH MCANARNEY. Pardon me. I ask for an exception on that.

THE COURT. Excluded. One may not run away. He has not admitted he ran away.

Q. Then I will ask you, didn't you run away from Milford so as to avoid being a soldier for the United States? A. I did not run away.

Q. You mean you walked away? A. Yes.

Q. You don't understand me when I say "run away," do you? A. That is vulgar.

Q. That is vulgar? A. You can say a little intelligent, Mr. Katzmann.

Q. Don't you think going away from your country is a vulgar thing to do when she needs you? A. I don't believe in war.

Q. You don't believe in war? A. No, sir.

Q. Do you think it is a cowardly thing to do what you did? A. No, sir.

Q. Do you think it is a brave thing to do what you did? A. Yes, sir.

Q. Do you think it would be a brave thing to go away from your own wife? A. No.

Q. When she needed you? A. No.

Q. What wages did you first earn in this country? A. Wage?

Q. Wages, money, pay? A. I used to get before I leave?

Q. When you first came to this country? A. $1.15.

Q. Per day? A. Yes.

Q. What were you getting at the 3–K factory when you got through? A. Sometimes sixty, fifty, seventy, eighty, forty, thirty, twenty-five, thirty-five. Depends on how much work was.

Q. That was within eight years after you first came to this country, isn't it? A. After seven years, — no, after twelve years.

Q. 1908. I beg your pardon. That is my mistake, Mr. Sacco. I did not mean that. That is within thirteen years? A. Yes, sir.

Q. From the time you came to this country? A. Yes.

Q. From $1.15 a day to $5 a day or better? A. Yes.

Q. And your child was born in this country, wasn't it? A. Yes.

Q. And your marriage took place in this country? A. Yes.

Q. Is Italy a free country? Is it a republic? A. Republic, yes.

Q. You love free countries, don't you? A. I should say yes.

Q. Why didn't you stay down in Mexico? A. Well, first thing, I could not get my trade over there. I had to do any other job.

Q. Don't they work with a pick and shovel in Mexico? A. Yes.

Q. Haven't you worked with a pick and shovel in this country? A. I did.

Q. Why didn't you stay there, down there in that free country and work with a pick and shovel? A. I don't think I did sacrifice to learn a job to go to pick and shovel in Mexico.

Q. Is it because, — is your love for the United States of America commensurate with the amount of money you can get in this country per week? A. Better conditions, yes.

Q. Better country to make money, isn't it? A. Yes.

Q. Mr. Sacco, that is the extent of your love for this country, isn't it, measured in dollars and cents?

MR. JEREMIAH MCANARNEY. If your Honor please, I object to this particular question.

THE COURT. You opened up this whole subject.

MR. JEREMIAH MCANARNEY. If your Honor please, I object to this question. That is my objection.

THE COURT. The form of it?

MR. JEREMIAH MCANARNEY. To the substance and form.

MR. KATZMANN. I will change the form, if your Honor please.

THE COURT. Better change that.

Q. Is your love for this country measured by the amount of money you can earn here?

MR. JEREMIAH MCANARNEY. To that question I object.

THE COURT. Now, you may answer. A. I never loved money.

MR. JEREMIAH MCANARNEY. Save my exception.

THE COURT. Certainly.

Q. What is the reason then? —

THE COURT. I allow this on the ground that the defendants opened it up. [Sacco had said he "liked a free country."]

Q. What is the reason you came back?

MR. JEREMIAH MCANARNEY. My exception lies just the same.

THE COURT. Certainly.

MR. MOORE. Both defendants.

THE COURT. Certainly.

Q. What is the reason you came back from Mexico if you did not love money, then? A. The first reason is all against my nature, is all different food over there, different nature, anyway.

Q. That is the first reason. It is against your nature. The food isn't right. A. Food, and many other things.

Q. You stood it for four months, didn't you? A. Three months.

Q. Three months? A. Yes.

Q. You came back all right physically, didn't you? A. I should say yes.

Q. And you had Italian food there, didn't you? A. Yes, made by ourselves.

Q. You could have had it all the time if you sent for it, couldn't you? A. Not all the time. I don't know.

Q. Did you fail to have it at any time in the three months you were there? A. Yes, sir. Different.

Q. What is the difference about it? A. Oh, different food that we did not like.

Q. It was Italian food, wasn't it? A. No, sir.

Q. Didn't you say it was? A. Sometimes after.

Q. You could have had it all the time if you sent for it, couldn't you? A. Could have had beans sometimes and any other vegetable.

MR. KATZMANN. I ask that be stricken out and the witness required to answer the question.

Q. Could you have had it by sending for it? A. Could not get it all the time.

Q. Why couldn't you get it in Mexico the same as you get it here? A. I suppose Mexico is not very much industries as in this country.

Q. Couldn't you send to Boston to get Italian food sent to Monterey, Mexico? A. If I was a D. Rockefeller I will.

Q. Then, I take it, you came back to the United States first to get something to eat. Is that right? Something that you liked? A. No, not just for eat.

Q. Didn't you say that was the first reason? A. The first reason —

Q. Didn't you say that was the first reason? A. Yes.

Q. All right. That wasn't a reason of the heart, was it? A. The heart?

Q. Yes. A. No.

Q. That was a reason of the stomach, wasn't it? A. Not just for the stomach, but any other reason.

Q. I am talking first about the first reason. So, the first reason your love of America is founded upon is pleasing your stomach. Is that right? A. I will not say yes.

Q. Haven't you said so? A. Not for the stomach. I don't think it is a satisfaction just for the stomach.

Q. What is your second reason? A. The second reason is strange for me, the language.

Q. Strange language? A. Yes.

Q. Were you in an Italian colony there? A. If I got them? I can't get that, Mr. Katzmann.

Q. Pardon me. Were you in a group of Italians there? A. Yes.

Q. When you came to America in 1908, did you understand English? A. No.

Q. A strange language here, wasn't it? A. Yes.

Q. What is the third reason, if there is one? A. A third reason, I was far away from my wife and boy.

Q. Couldn't you have sent for your wife and your boy? A. I wouldn't send for my wife and boy over there, because it was the idea to come back here.

Q. I know that. You are back here. My question is, couldn't you have sent for Mrs. Sacco and your boy? A. Extreme condition, it would be bad. I could not go back in this United States, why I would get my wife and my boy.

Q. Your answer means, does it not, you could have had Mrs. Sacco and the boy come down there to live with you? A. Yes.

Q. You preferred to come back to this country? A. Yes.

Q. But you preferred to remain under the name of Mosmacotelli until the armistice was signed, didn't you? A. Yes.

Q. Now, is there any other besides those three reasons why you loved the United States of America? A. Well, I couldn't say. Over here there is more accommodation for the working class, I suppose, than any other people, a chance to be more industrious, and more industry. Can have a chance to get anything he wants.

Q. You mean to earn more money, don't you? A. No, no, money, never loved money.

Q. Never loved money? A. No, money never satisfaction to me.

Q. Money never a satisfaction to you? A. No.

Q. What was the industrial condition that pleased you so much here if it wasn't a chance to earn bigger money? A. A man, Mr. Katzmann, has no satisfaction all through the money, for the belly.

Q. For the what? A. For the stomach, I mean.

Q. We got away from the stomach. Now, I am talking about money. A. There is lots of things.

Q. Well, let us have them all. I want to know why you loved America so that after you got to the haven of Mexico when the United States was at war you came back here? A. Yes.

Q. I want all the reasons why you came back? A. I think I did tell you already.

Q. Are those all? A. Yes. Industry makes lots of things different.

Q. Then there is food, that is one? A. Yes.

Q. Foreign language is two? A. Yes.

Q. Your wife and child is three? A. Yes.

Q. And better industrial conditions? A. Yes.

Q. Is that all? A. That is all.

Q. Among those four reasons, Mr. Katzmann, then, do you find any one that is called love of country? Have you named that reason?

MR. MOORE. I object to that question. The others are reasons, I take it.

THE COURT. Read it, please.

(The question is read.)

THE COURT. That last remark does not belong in your question.

MR. KATZMANN. "Have you named them?" No, I suppose not.

THE COURT. Leave that off, and you may ask it.

MR. KATZMANN. All right.

Q. Did you find love of country among those four reasons? A. Yes, sir.

Q. Which one is love of country? A. All together.

Q. All together? A. Yes, sir.

Q. Food, wife, language, industry? A. Yes.

Q. That is love of country, is it? A. Yes.

Q. Is standing by a country when she needs a soldier evidence of love of country?

MR. JEREMIAH MCANARNEY. That I object to, if your Honor please.

Mr. McAnarney then added: "And I might state now I want my objection to go to this whole line of interrogation." [3]

This general objection had a surprising effect on Judge Thayer. He suddenly took over from Mr. Katzmann a part of the cross-examination on the patriotic theme. Six times he demanded to know whether Mr. McAnarney claimed that the collection of the literature and the books was in the interest of the United States. This was a switch from Mr. Katzmann's line of questioning, but was probably more effective. Vanzetti had already told in considerable detail of the events that had led to the decision to collect the anarchist material. The purpose, he said, was to remove evidence of anarchism which might cause the arrest and deportation of its possessors. Fear that the literature would be discovered was also the reason he gave for not telling the truth to Chief Stewart about his friends on the night of his arrest.[4] The jurymen had heard all of this testimony. Therefore, they knew that the claim of the defendants was that they had planned to secrete or destroy evidence in order to frustrate the attempts of the United States to identify and arrest them and their friends as anarchists. This was so manifestly against the interest of the United States that the repetition of Judge Thayer's demand on Mr. McAnarney could only constitute an ironic judicial reminder of that fact. This is how the judge interjected his own cross-examination of Sacco, using Mr. McAnarney as a conduit, following his objection to Mr. Katzmann's questions:

THE COURT. I think you opened it up [viz. by Sacco saying he "liked a free country"].

MR. JEREMIAH MCANARNEY. No, if your Honor please, I have not.

THE COURT. It seems to me you have. Are you going to claim much of all the collection of the literature and the books was really in the interest of the United States as well as these people and therefore it has opened up the credibility of

[3] Vol. II, 1867–1873.   [4] Vol. II, 1731.

the defendant when he claims that all that work was done really for the interest of the United States in getting this literature out of the way?

MR. JEREMIAH MCANARNEY. That claim is not presented in anything tantamount to the language just used by the Court, and in view of the record as it stands at this time I object to this line of inquiry.

THE COURT. Is that not your claim, that the defendant, as a reason that he has given for going to the Johnson house, that they wanted the automobile to prevent people from being deported and to get this literature all out of the way? Does he not claim that that was done in the interest of the United States, to prevent violation of the law by the distribution of this literature? I understood that was the —

MR. JEREMIAH MCANARNEY. Are you asking that as a question to me?

THE COURT. Yes.

MR. JEREMIAH MCANARNEY. Absolutely we have taken no such position as that, and the evidence at this time does not warrant the assumption of that question.[5]

At this point there occurred a rather strange interlude in Judge Thayer's even stranger questions about collecting the literature.

THE COURT. Then you are not going to make that claim?

MR. JEREMIAH MCANARNEY. I am going to make whatever claim is legitimate.

THE COURT. I want to know what that is. You are going to claim in argument —

MR. JEREMIAH MCANARNEY. I am going to claim this man and Vanzetti were of that class called Socialists. I am going to claim that riot was running a year ago last April, that men were being deported, that twelve to fifteen hundred were seized in Massachusetts.

THE COURT. Do you mean to say you are going to offer evidence on that?

MR. JEREMIAH MCANARNEY. I am going to claim —

THE COURT. I am asking the claim. You must know when I ask the claim I mean a claim that is founded on fact, evidence introduced in the case, and not upon anything else.

MR. JEREMIAH MCANARNEY. We have not concluded the evidence, if your Honor please.

THE COURT. Do you say you are going to introduce evidence to that effect?

MR. JEREMIAH MCANARNEY. We have witnesses which we may introduce here. I do not know whether we will introduce them or not.

Mr. McAnarney's statement about the perilous position of Socialists in Massachusetts in April 1920 was an excellent summary. After demanding and getting the statement, however, Judge Thayer's reaction was again somewhat peculiar. In a rather belligerent manner he demanded to know whether the defense planned to introduce evidence to prove it and then

[5] Vol. II, 1873.

asserted that he could not "pass judgement as to the competency of something that may not be introduced and never come before me for consideration." This rebuke was uncalled for. Mr. McAnarney had not asked the judge to pass on the competency of anything. However, the defense closed the case without offering evidence on which to base Mr. McAnarney's proposed claim, although there was abundant proof available.[6] Some of it, including the U.S. District Court (Mass.) decision in *Colyer v. Skeffington*, may have been known to Judge Thayer — or should have been.

The interlude about conditions in Massachusetts in 1920 having been concluded, Judge Thayer then returned to his own cross-examination of Mr. McAnarney about the collection of the literature.

MR. JEREMIAH MCANARNEY. Your Honor now sees the competency of my remarks, when I said to your Honor that I objected to the question in the present state of the evidence?

THE COURT. Are you going to claim that what the defendant did was in the interest of the United States?

MR. JEREMIAH MCANARNEY. Your Honor please, I now object to your Honor's statement as prejudicial to the rights of the defendants and ask that this statement be withdrawn from the jury.

THE COURT. There is no prejudicial remark made that I know of, and none were intended. I simply asked you, sir, whether you propose to offer evidence as to what you said to me.

MR. JEREMIAH MCANARNEY. If your Honor please, the remarks made with reference to the country and whether the acts that he was doing were for the benefit of the country. I can see no other inference to be drawn from those except prejudicial to the defendants.

THE COURT. Do you intend to make that claim?

MR. JEREMIAH MCANARNEY. What claim, please?

THE COURT. The one that I am suggesting.

MR. JEREMIAH MCANARNEY. When this evidence is closed, if your Honor please, I shall argue what is legitimate in the case.

THE COURT. All I ask is this one question, and it will simplify matters very much. Is it your claim that in the collection of the literature and the books and papers that that was done in the interest of the United States?

MR. JEREMIAH MCANARNEY. No, I make no such broad claim as that.

THE COURT. Then I will hear you, Mr. Katzmann, on the competency of this testimony.

MR. KATZMANN. I am sorry I did not hear what Mr. McAnarney said.

THE COURT. Mr. McAnarney says it is not his claim, as I got it, he does not propose to make the claim that the collection and distribution of this literature was any matter to be done by either or both of the defendants in the interest of the United States.

[6] See, for instance, Joughin and Morgan, *The Legacy of Sacco and Vanzetti*, 208 *et seq.*

MR. KATZMANN. Then, if your Honor please, I offer the line of cross-examination I have started upon as tending to attack the credibility of this man as a witness.

THE COURT. As to what part of his testimony?

MR. KATZMANN. As to any part of his testimony to affect his credibility as a witness *in toto*.

THE COURT. You can't attack a witness's credibility *in toto* excepting concerning some subject matter about which he has testified.

MR. KATZMANN. Well, he stated in his direct examination yesterday that he loved a free country, and I offer it to attack that statement made in his examination by his own counsel.

THE COURT. That is what I supposed, and that is what I supposed that remark meant when it was introduced in this cross-examination, but counsel now say they don't make that claim.

MR. KATZMANN. They say they don't make the claim that gathering up the literature on May 5th at West Bridgewater was for the purpose of helping the country, but that is a different matter, not related to May 5th.

THE COURT. I will let you inquire further first as to what he meant by the expression.[7]

At this point Mr. Moore, who had remained silent during the Thayer-McAnarney altercation, reserved an exception to all the questions "with reference to the issue of love of country." Judge Thayer then sought to kill the exception by exhorting the jury in effect to pay no attention to what he had said.[8]

The adjuration accomplished Judge Thayer's purpose. The Supreme Judicial Court ruled later that it repaired whatever damage had been caused by the court's previous remarks. Yet this concept of cure by exhortation is a legal fiction. In a trial like the Sacco-Vanzetti case the verdict would depend on which set of witnesses the jury would believe. If the jurors believed the defendants and their witnesses they would vote for acquittal, but if they had been led to distrust their testimony, whether fairly or foully, they would believe the case of the Commonwealth and find the defendants guilty. If a judge, during the trial, shows his distrust of a witness, the jury, especially a new one as in the Dedham trial, is apt also to distrust the testimony. When this happens, it is futile to urge the jurymen to ignore the judge and form their own judgment of the witnesses' veracity. They are more likely to interpret the judge's ex post facto remarks as a verbal wink.

Upon Judge Thayer's nod to proceed, Mr. Katzmann resumed his inquiry into Sacco's views:

[7] Vol. II, 1874–1875.   [8] Vol. II, 1875.

Q. (By Mr. Katzmann) What did you mean when you said yesterday you loved a free country? A. First thing I came in this country —

Q. No, pardon me. What did you mean when you said yesterday you loved a free country? A. Give me a chance to explain.

Q. I am asking you to explain now.

Sacco welcomed this invitation to expound his views to the courtroom. Almost every one of the words he uttered about our country struck at some cherished belief of his auditors. The fact that they were spoken by a foreign-born agitator, ungrateful for the blessings of America, would deepen their resentment. What Sacco naively believed to be an opportunity to win over the jury to his ideas was illusory, but for Mr. Katzmann the chance to exploit their offensive character was very real indeed. Sacco walked unsuspectingly into the trap and Mr. Katzmann closed it firmly upon him.

When I was in Italy, a boy [Sacco began], I was a Republican, so I always thinking Republican has more chance to manage education, develop, to build some day his family, to raise the child and education, if you could. But that was my opinion; so when I came to this country I saw there was not what I was thinking before, but there was all the difference, because I been working in Italy not so hard as I been work in this country. I could live free there just as well. Work in the same condition, but not so hard, about seven or eight hours a day, better food. I mean genuine. Of course, over here is good food, because it is bigger country, to any those who got money to spend, not for the working and laboring class, and in Italy is more opportunity to laborer to eat vegetable, more fresh, and I came in this country. When I been started work here very hard and been work thirteen years, hard worker, I could not been afford much a family the way I did have the idea before. I could not put any money in the bank. I could no push my boy some to go to school and other things. I teach over here men who is with me. The free idea gives any man a chance to profess his own idea, not the supreme idea, not to give any person, not to be like Spain in position, yes, about twenty centuries ago, but to give a chance to print and education, literature, free speech, that I see it was all wrong. I could see the best men, intelligent, education, they been arrested and sent to prison and died in prison for years and years without getting them out, and Debs, one of the great men in his country, he is in prison, still away in prison, because he is a Socialist. He wanted the laboring class to have better conditions and better living, more education, give a push his son if he could have a chance some day, but they put him in prison. Why? Because the capitalist class, they know, they are against that, because the capitalist class, they don't want our child to go to high school or to college or Harvard College. There would not be no chance, there would not be no, — they don't want the working class educationed; they want the working class to be a low all the times, be underfoot, and not to be up with the head. So, sometimes, you see, the Rockefellers, Morgans, they give fifty, — mean they give five hundred thousand dollars to Harvard College, they give a million dollars for another school. Everybody say, "Well, D. Rockefeller is a great man, the best in the country." I want to ask him who is going to Harvard College? What benefit the working class they will get by those million dollars they give by Rockefeller, D. Rockefellers. They won't get, the poor class, they won't have no chance to go to Harvard College because men who is getting $21 a week or $30 a week, I don't care if he gets $80 a week, if he gets a family of five children he can't live and send his child and go to Harvard College if he wants to eat anything nature will give him. If he wants to eat like a cow, and that is the best thing, but I want men to live like men. I like to get everything that nature will give best, because they belong, — we are not the friend of any other place, but we are belong to nations. So that is why my idea has been changed. So that is why I love people who labor and work and see better conditions every day develop, makes no more war. We no want fight by the gun, and we don't want to destroy young men. The mother been suffering for building the young man. Some day need a little more bread, so when the time the mother get some bread or profit out of that boy, the Rockefellers, Morgans, and some of the peoples, high class, they send to war. Why? What is war? The war is not shoots like Abraham Lincoln's and Abe Jefferson, to fight for the free country, for the better education, to give chance to any other peoples, not the white people but the black and the others, because they believe and know they are mens like the rest, but they are war for the great millionaire. No war for the civilization of men. They are war for business, million dollars come on the side. What right we have to kill each other? I been work for the Irish, I have been working with the German fellow, with the French, many other peoples. I love them people just as I could love my wife, and my people for that did receive me. Why should I go kill them men? What he done to me? He never done anything, so I don't believe in no war. I want to destroy those guns. All I can say, the Government put the literature, give us educations. I remember in Italy, a long time ago, about sixty years ago, I should say, yes, about sixty years ago, the Government they could not control very much these two, — devilment went on, and robbery, so one of the government in the cabinet he says, "If you want to destroy those devilments, if you want to take off all those criminals, you ought to give a chance to Socialist literature, education of people, emancipation. That is why I destroy governments, boys." That is why my idea I love Socialists. That is why I like people who want education and living, building, who is good, just as much as they could. That is all.[9]

Using Sacco's discourse as a text, Mr. Katzmann then engaged the man whom he was prosecuting for murder in a lively debate over the advantages and disadvantages of life in these United States. The argument covered such subjects as Harvard's policy in granting scholarships, free public school education, district nursing and whether the fruits and vegetables in Italy were fresher than in the United States.[10] The debate closed with Mr. Katzmann's assertion that a hundred thousand children attended the Boston

[9] Vol. II, 1876–1877.   [10] Vol. II, 1877–1881.

public schools and Sacco's reply that millions did not. Mr. Katzmann then turned to other subjects.

Much of the succeeding cross-examination followed the pattern of Mr. Katzmann's cross-examination of Vanzetti. Sacco's falsehoods to Chief Stewart and Mr. Katzmann in the Brockton police station on May 4 and 5 again figured prominently, as well as the arguments over whether the alleged fears of the defendant were logical explanations of his lies and suspicious actions. Other parts of the cross-examination, such as those dealing with physical exhibits and the carrying of the pistol and cartridges, have been considered in earlier chapters. The alibi testimony will be considered later. There is, however, one subject inquired into by Mr. Katzmann which mystified the defense for over five years. It related to one Fruzetti, a resident of Bridgewater who, according to Sacco, had been deported for his ideas and opinions.[11] The deportation had occurred about a year before the arrest of Sacco and Vanzetti.[12]

For a long time Mr. Katzmann's questions about Fruzetti presented a puzzle. They seemed to be simply a bold attempt to prejudice the jury against Sacco without relevance or legal justification. This would still seem to be a valid objection, but a review of the entire record brings to light a very different objective. Mr. Katzmann began:

Q. Did you know Fruzetti, of Bridgewater, who was deported you said. A. Yes.
Q. Did you know him personally? A. Yes, sir.
Q. Been to his house? A. I met him lots of times.
Q. In Boston? A. In conference.
Q. Talked with him about anarchy, haven't you? A. Certainly.
Q. Did you know his views on anarchy?
MR. JEREMIAH MCANARNEY. I object.
A. His words?
MR. KATZMANN. Wait a minute. It wasn't "words."
Q. Was his "views." Don't answer.
THE COURT. Supposing he should say he was a constitutionalist or something of that kind. Doesn't that tend to attack his credibility that one of the reasons why there was to be a disposition to be made of these papers was on the ground this man had been deported, among others? [13]

Judge Thayer had naturally assumed that Mr. Katzmann's purpose was to attack Sacco's credibility. However, it soon appeared from the subsequent questions that Mr. Katzmann had no such intention. They indicate

[11] Vol. II, 1888. [12] Vol. II, 1807. [13] Vol. II, 1885.

that Mr. Katzmann *knew that Sacco was telling the truth and that he intended to attack him for that very reason, namely, that his friend Fruzetti was an anarchist.* But Mr. Katzmann did not tell Judge Thayer that he was *not* attacking Sacco's credibility or that he intended to prove that he was an anarchist. He let the judge continue in the belief that the cross-examination had in some as yet undisclosed way the reason stated by the judge. When the examination was finished it was too late to remedy the damage caused by it. However, as we shall see, his chief purpose in this instance was probably not to injure Sacco before the Dedham jury, although this may have been a desirable, if collateral, result. Before we consider what Mr. Katzmann was really seeking to accomplish by his examination about Fruzetti, let us set down the rest of the interrogation itself. After Judge Thayer had supposed that Fruzetti might have been a "constitutionalist," Mr. McAnarney stated his objection and the examination continued by Mr. Katzmann.

Q. Were your views with respect to anarchy substantially the same as Fruzetti's?

MR. JEREMIAH MCANARNEY. That is the same objection.

A. I could not say if I do.

MR. JEREMIAH MCANARNEY. I do dislike to be getting up.

THE COURT. I would rather you make an objection and then we will know where we stand on each question.

Q. What is your answer?

THE COURT. You may answer.

A. I could not see as far as he could.

Q. *As far as you could see, did you go along the same path with him? Did you have the same views, as far as you could see them?* A. Men never, — men can see far to last —

MR. KATZMANN. I don't understand. Mr. Ross [the interpreter], please, unless you object to him. I want to make sure we have your answer.

Q. The question, perhaps, — do you understand the question? A. Yes.

Q. All right. What is the answer? A. (Through the interpreter) A man, in order to be of the same opinion and to have the same ideas, he should read the books what anarchists means.

(The witness talks to the interpreter, after saying "No.")

THE WITNESS. (Through the interpreter) A man must read his books to the extreme, the extreme, the foundation of those books, then to know what anarchist means.

MR. KATZMANN. I ask that be stricken out, if your Honor please, as not being responsive.

Q. Now, will you please pay attention to my question.

THE COURT. The defendant Vanzetti wants to speak to one of his counsel.

MR. KATZMANN. Shall I suspend, your Honor?

THE COURT. You better, for a minute. Shall we proceed, Mr. Moore? All right.

MR. KATZMANN. Yes?

The question is this: as far as you understood Fruzetti's views, were yours the same?

MR. JEREMIAH MCANARNEY. To that I object.

THE COURT. You may inquire.

MR. JEREMIAH MCANARNEY. Save an exception.

THE COURT. Certainly.

Q. Answer, please. A. (Through the interpreter) I cannot say yes or no.

Q. *Is it because you can't or because you don't want to?* A. (Through the interpreter) *Because it is a very delicate question.*

Q. *It is very delicate, isn't it, because he was deported for his views?*

MR. JEREMIAH MCANARNEY. I object.

MR. KATZMANN. I withdraw it.

Q. *Was Fruzetti deported for his views?*

MR. JEREMIAH MCANARNEY. To that I object, too.

THE COURT. Didn't you bring out the fact that Fruzetti was deported?

MR. JEREMIAH MCANARNEY. Yes, if your Honor please.

THE COURT. Now, is he limited to that so that he cannot make inquiry with reference to Fruzetti, about this deportation about which you have inquired?

MR. JEREMIAH MCANARNEY. No.

THE COURT. For instance, supposing it should turn out that he had no views, anarchistic or anything of that kind, as bearing on the credibility of the witness, because that is one of the reasons that I understand caused the collection of the literature, because he was one of the men who had been deported.

MR. JEREMIAH MCANARNEY. Fruzetti may have been deported for having one of these periodicals in his house. He may have been deported for many things —

THE COURT. See if he knows the reason.

MR. JEREMIAH MCANARNEY. (Continuing) — that have not appeared.

Q. *Do you know why Fruzetti was deported?* A. (Through the interpreter) Yes.

Q. *Was it because he was of anarchistic opinions?*

THE INTERPRETER. He says he understands it now.

Q. *Was it because Fruzetti entertained anarchistic opinions?* A. One reason, he was an anarchist. Another reason, Fruzetti been writing all the time on the newspapers, and I am not sure why the reason he been deported.

Q. You do not know which of the two it was? A. Yes.

Q. You did not read that in your paper? A. Probably I forget. Probably I miss that, I don't know.

Q. *Wasn't it the fact on record, — on consideration isn't it the fact that he was deported because he held and entertained anarchistic views?* A. Yes.

MR. JEREMIAH MCANARNEY. That I object to.

THE COURT. You are referring to a record now. Of course, he can't testify as to what the record was.

Q. Who was the other man? Oh, pardon me. *Was Fruzetti, before deportation, a subscriber to the same papers that you had in your house on May 5th?* A. Probably he is.

MR. JEREMIAH MCANARNEY. I object, if your Honor please.

THE COURT. Is that of much consequence? He already stated why Fruzetti was deported.

MR. KATZMANN. Perhaps it isn't. Yes, I think that is correct.

Q. Who was the other man that you said was deported from Bridgewater? A. I did not say; I am sure there is another man been deported, but I do not know the name.

Q. See if I can refresh your recollection. Was it Ferruccio Coacci? A. He is one. There is another one.

Q. Who was the other man? A. I do not remember the name.

Q. Now, you said, did you not, this morning, the first thing when recalled to the stand, that it was your plan to go to Brockton that night, May 5th, and warn your friends to have these books, circulars and papers in the valise ready to be taken out? A. Yes.

Q. Yes. *Were those persons to whom you intended to go that Wednesday night, subscribers to the same paper that you were, same papers?* A. Have got any literature?

Q. Have you seen the literature they had? A. Men love an idea, socialist or anarchist, any other thing they had.

Q. You believed they had that night? A. Sure.

Q. You believed they had books similar to yours, too, did you not? A. Because some —

Q. Pardon me. Answer that question. Did you believe that they had in their homes books similar to the ones you had in your house? A. Yes.

Q. *And the books which you intended to collect were books relating, to anarchy, weren't they?* A. Not all of them.

Q. How many of them? A. Well, all together. We are Socialists, democratic, any other socialistic information, Socialists, Syndicalists, Anarchists, any paper.

Q. Bolshevist? A. I do not know what Bolshevism means.

Q. Soviet? A. I do not know what Soviet means.

Q. Communism? A. Yes. I got some on astronomy, too.

Q. I did not ask you what you had. You weren't afraid the books of astronomy were going to be taken by anybody, were you? A. No.

Q. You knew I did not mean that, didn't you? You understood I didn't mean that, didn't you? Will you answer that? A. Yes, sir.

Q. Nor any books you had on arithmetic or spelling, either. Did you expect the officers of the law were going to seize your wife's cook book? A. No, sir.

Q. Were you afraid to have those books and those papers in your house? A. At that time.

Q. In that time. On May 5th. A. Well, all the rest.

Q. All during the reaction? A. Yes.

Q. Then you mean before May 5th, don't you? A. Yes, at the time.

Q. How long before May 5th? A. I should say a couple of weeks. Three weeks, a month.

Q. You never made a move to take them out of your house, did you? A. We never heard before.

Q. You heard on May 2nd, didn't you? A. Yes. [Emphasis added.][14]

Obviously his interrogation about Fruzetti's views and literature was not intended (as Judge Thayer mistakenly assumed) to prove that Sacco was lying when he said he feared deportation. He kept pounding Sacco to admit that Fruzetti was deported because he was an anarchist and that Sacco held the same views as Fruzetti. He seemed to be determined to show that Sacco's fears of being deported were fully justified. Why did he do it? In an earlier chapter we had occasion to discuss affidavits showing the cooperation of Mr. Katzmann's office with the agents of the Department of Justice in Boston in connection with the prosecution of Sacco and Vanzetti. This went even to the extent of placing the spy Carbone in the cell next to Sacco. Among the affidavits obtained by Mr. Thompson was one from Fred J. Weyand, who had been special agent of the Department during the entire administration of Mitchell Palmer. In this Mr. Weyand had stated in part:

The understanding in this case between the agents of the Department of Justice in Boston and the District Attorney followed the usual custom, that the Department of Justice would help the District Attorney to secure a conviction, and that he in turn would help the agents of the Department of Justice to secure information that they might desire. This would include the turning over of any pertinent information by the Department of Justice to the District Attorney. Sacco and Vanzetti were, at least in the opinion of the Boston agents of the Department of Justice not liable to deportation as draft dodgers, but only as anarchists, and could not be deported as anarchists unless it could be shown that they were believers in anarchy, which is always a difficult thing to show. It usually can only be shown by self-incrimination. The Boston agents believed that these men were anarchists, and hoped to be able to secure the necessary evidence against them from their testimony at their trial for murder, to be used in case they were not convicted of murder. There is correspondence between Mr. Katzmann and Mr. West on file in the Boston office of the Department. *Mr. West [agent in the Boston office] furnished Mr. Katzmann information about the Radical activities of Sacco and Vanzetti to be used in their cross-examination.* [Emphasis added.][15]

Mr. Weyand's sworn statement was partially corroborated by the affidavit of another agent, Lawrence Letherman. He said in part:

[14] Vol. II, 1887–1890.   [15] Vol. V, 4503–4504.

The Department of Justice in Boston was anxious to get sufficient evidence against Sacco and Vanzetti to deport them, but never succeeded in getting the kind and amount of evidence required for that purpose. It was the opinion of the Department agents here that a conviction of Sacco and Vanzetti for murder would be one way of disposing of these two men. It was also the general opinion of such of the agents in Boston as had any actual knowledge of the Sacco-Vanzetti case, that Sacco and Vanzetti, although anarchists and agitators, were not highway robbers, and had nothing to do with the South Braintree crime. My opinion, and the opinion of most of the older men in the Government service, has always been that the South Braintree crime was the work of professionals.

The Boston agents of the Department of Justice assigned certain men to attend the trial of Sacco and Vanzetti, including Mr. Weyand. Mr. West also attended the trial. . . . [Emphasis added.][16]

We now know from Department of Justice agents themselves why Mr. Katzmann sought to get Sacco to admit that he was a deportable anarchist in a cross-examination permitted for the purpose of proving that he was *not* such a radical. In asking the Fruzetti questions Mr. Katzmann was not acting as the district attorney of Norfolk County prosecuting a murder case but as agent for the Department of Justice attempting to secure admissions for a federal case. We also may surmise why Mr. Katzmann spared Vanzetti this type of cross-examination. The Department of Justice could not have been much interested in getting evidence of Vanzetti's anarchy, since he was already serving a long sentence in state prison on the Plymouth conviction.

Mr. Katzmann himself did not specifically state that he was trying to test the sincerity of Sacco's claim that he was a radical. He had a talent for creating the impression he wanted by loose talk and he used it well on Judge Thayer. We have just seen how, in the cross-examination about Fruzetti, Judge Thayer twice admitted the questions because they might show that Fruzetti was not a radical at all, much less an anarchist. Mr. Katzmann, for good reason, made no such argument. He remained silent and left it to the judge to find a purpose which Mr. Katzmann knew was not the real one. Nevertheless, the reason assigned by Judge Thayer remained in the case until the end.

In his decision on the so-called Gould motion, Judge Thayer explained the primary reason for his admitting the questions as follows:

In other words, the defendants having introduced the subject of radicalism to show fear of deportation or some other punishment because of the falsehood he

16 Vol. V, 4506.

had told, then the Commonwealth had a right to cross-examine for the purpose of showing that his or their *beliefs, acts, conduct and the character of the literature they possessed were not of such a character or nature that would subject either of them to deportation or to any other punishment whatsoever.* . . . [Emphasis added.]

(The foregoing justification by Judge Thayer for allowing the questions was written before the proof was laid in front of him that Mr. Katzmann not only knew all about Sacco's radicalism, but was acting in close cooperation with the agents of the Department of Justice because of it. Later, after he had the affidavits of the agents of the Department, he repudiated his own explanation. This will be considered later.)

The district attorney's office in its brief on the appeal argued that the reason for admitting the questions was the same as stated by Judge Thayer. It should be stated, however, that the district attorney and his assistants who wrote the brief were not the men in office when Mr. Katzmann cross-examined Sacco. Nor should it be presumed that they had knowledge of the secret cooperation between former District Attorney Katzmann and the Department of Justice. Their justification for the cross-examination, offered to the Supreme Judicial Court, contains the following statement:

Radicalism, socialism, radical literature, evasion of the selective service draft, were all subjects which, if connected with Sacco, might prejudice him in the eyes of the jury. But his own counsel opened up this subject for the purpose of rebutting the natural inferences of guilt which must have arisen from his falsehoods. Under such conditions, the presiding judge could do no more than to give the District Attorney full opportunity and latitude to develop this field of inquiry to see whether Sacco's radical views and radical actions were real or feigned to meet this serious inference of guilt which arose from his falsehoods.[17]

Let us now consider Judge Thayer's repudiation of his own stated reason for permitting the cross-examination after Mr. Thompson had assailed Mr. Katzmann's alleged justification for it as false.

In his "Decision" on the motion for a new trial (mentioned in the preceding chapter in connection with his ruling on the cross-examination of Vanzetti) Judge Thayer now explained:

Much severe criticism by counsel for the defendants was made of District Attorney Katzmann because of a reply that he made to the Court when he said he wanted to go into this subject of radicalism in cross-examination for the

[17] Vol. IV, 4224.

purpose of testing the credibility of their claim. Severe criticism was made of him because he wanted to ascertain in cross-examination whether or not these men were radicals *when he had already been informed by the agents of the Federal Department that they were radicals. This was not Mr. Katzmann's purpose at all.* It was not necessary for him to cross-examine these defendants for this purpose, because before his cross-examination began, the defendants, in direct examination, told everything that they desired about their radical views and activities and their fear of punishment and deportation. *Mr. Katzmann cross-examined with one view in mind* and that was, to show there was no logical connections between their falsehoods and incriminating conduct on the one side and radicalism on the other. In other words, the cross-examination by Mr. Katzmann was carried on with a view of proving to that Jury that the evidence of their consciousness of guilt was more consistent with the murder of these two defendants than it was with radicalism.

Let me give an illustration of just what is meant by Mr. Katzmann's purpose in cross-examination, by taking one illustration in each case. Mr. Sacco said that he feared punishment, that he was afraid of deportation, that he did not want to go back to Italy, that he had told all these falsehoods because of this fear. Mr. Katzmann, in his cross-examination, brought out all these facts and then asked this question: "Mr. Sacco, you say you feared deportation and that is why you told all these lies and why you did what you did?" and Mr. Sacco said "Yes." Then came the next question: "Mr. Sacco, at the very time when you were telling these lies, you had already secured a passport for Italy on which you, your wife, and two children were to sail two days after the night of your arrest?" and the answer was "Yes." Mr. Katzmann, on this same line, asked many other questions and forced Sacco, as well as Vanzetti, to admit that they could see no logical connection between the falsehoods told and radicalism. [Emphasis added.][18]

Many of Mr. Katzmann's questions were indeed intended to show that there was no logical connection between the falsehoods told and radicalism. *However, those were not the questions which brought "severe criticism" from Mr. Thompson.*

The reference in the above quotation to "the murder of these two defendants" was of course a slip, although there may be those who would like to think of it as prophetic. The passage, however, does contain a most significant misstatement by the judge. The question and answer above quoted to illustrate Mr. Katzmann's successful achievement of the purpose ascribed to him by the judge *have no existence anywhere in the trial record.* Moreover, at the time, Sacco had only one child.

The fact that Judge Thayer recalled a question and answer which never occurred is another example of the manner in which his fixation on the

[18] Vol. V, 4770–4771.

assumed guilt of the defendants forced his memory to confirm it.[19] The thought behind the false quotation is also another expression of Judge Thayer's inability to disassociate his mind from his assumption that Sacco and Vanzetti should have reasoned like secure Yankee natives to whom deportation apparently meant a free trip to Italy.

In any event, the fact that Sacco and Vanzetti told falsehoods on their arrest seems to have been accorded an importance far greater than it deserved. Sacco and Vanzetti, as hunted radicals, had good reason to fear the police questionings. This has already been considered in great detail. However, so powerful was the effect on Judge Thayer's mind of the defendants' falsehoods that in his charge to the jury he devoted most of his emphasis to this rather ambiguous and indirect type of proof and played down the direct case offered by the Commonwealth, such as identification, ballistics and physical evidence. Later he stated that "the evidence that convicted these defendants was circumstantial and was evidence that is known in the law as consciousness of guilt." [20] He repeatedly reemphasized this same thought in his various "Decisions" on motions before him.

In its report issued in the summer of 1927 the Governor's Advisory Committee explained at some length that Mr. Katzmann's cross-examination of Sacco was justified as an attempt to find out whether he was a real or false radical. Ignoring the fact that the judge himself had later declared that "this was not Mr. Katzmann's purpose at all" and omitting mention of the evidence (then known to the Committee) that Mr. Katzmann had been briefed on the defendants' radicalism by the agents of the Department of Justice, the report on this subject concluded:

For these reasons [lack of evidence that Sacco was a radical!] Mr. Katzmann was justified in subjecting Mr. Sacco to a rigorous cross-examination to determine whether his profession that he and his friends were radicals liable to deportation was true, *or was merely assumed for the purpose of the defense.* The exceptions taken to his questions were not sustained by the Supreme Court. [Emphasis added.] [21]

Later we shall examine other conlcusions of the Advisory Committee's report.

[19] Even as imagined, the recollection was in error — Sacco did not have "two children" at the time.
[20] Vol. IV, 3514.
[21] Vol. V, 5378 K. The report also overlooked Mr. Katzmann's admission before the Committee that he had known very well that the defendants were radicals "from the newspapers." Vol. V, 5040.

The Supreme Judicial Court denied Sacco's exceptions to the cross-examination on the ground that it was in the exclusive control of the trial judge's discretion to test the defendant's accuracy, veracity or credibility, or to shake his credit by injuring his character. This was the Massachusetts rule and was not invented for the Sacco-Vanzetti case. The harshness of the opinion resulted from the court's definition of "abuse of discretion," namely, that no conscientious judge acting intelligently could have honestly taken the view expressed by the trial judge. In effect this made the trial judge's discretionary rulings irreversible.

In his summation before the Governor's Advisory Committee Mr. Thompson made the following comments on the Massachusetts doctrine of discretion. Although he was then counsel for the defendants, his learning and his long experience as a leader of the bar make the statement well worth pondering:

The Supreme Court followed the usual custom of overruling that motion [for a new trial based on abuse of discretion]. They have never granted a motion on that ground since that court was established. They have always said that they could, but they never have. I suppose it would require proof of actual insanity in the technical sense of the term, or of utter depravity, to get them to do it. The courts are so linked up together that you can hardly expect our Supreme Court to find a lower court judge guilty of abuse of discretion. Judge Loring once said in another case which unfortunately came out of our office, that to find "abuse of discretion" is equivalent to finding that the judge is unfit for his office.[22]

Professor Edmund M. Morgan made the following comment on the doctrine of discretion as used in the Sacco-Vanzetti case:

Had the material demonstrating his settled prejudice against defendants, which was later put before the Advisory Committee, been presented to the Supreme Judicial Court, it would have had a harder task. In its first opinion, in order to sustain the rulings of the judge at the trial, it had to resort to the doctrine of discretion on at least sixteen different occasions covering nine distinct points; and to sustain his denial of the new trial on each of the five points raised, it had to rely on the same doctrine. In its second opinion, all the really important questions raised were determined solely on the basis of the exercise of an honest discretion. Had the record been such as to have compelled a finding of his prejudice, it is almost inconceivable that the Supreme Judicial Court could have solemnly relied upon the pious fiction that such a judge had honestly and intelligently exercised his discretion against the defendants on practically every occasion at every stage of the proceedings. On the record as it stood, however, these defendants received the kind of treatment then usually accorded appellants in the Supreme Judicial Court of Massachusetts.[23]

[22] Vol. V, 5274.   [23] Joughin and Morgan, *The Legacy of Sacco and Vanzetti*, 151.

With respect to Mr. Thompson's argument that Mr. Katzmann's purpose was not to test the credibility of Sacco, the opinion of the Supreme Judicial Court said:

The argument is pressed that the purpose of the District Attorney's questions obviously was not the purpose declared by him and accepted by the trial judge, namely to affect the credibility of Sacco, but was to excite and intensify prejudice against him. But we must follow the record, and a careful reading of it does not sustain this contention.[24]

Again, it should be noted that when this opinion was written, the Supreme Judicial Court did not know of the affidavits from the agents of the Department of Justice indicating that the district attorney, on their behalf, was actually trying to prove that Sacco was an anarchist and that his fear of deportation was justified.

The opinion on this aspect of the case then closes with a quote of Judge Thayer's exhortation to the jury to be fair. This was cited to indicate that whatever injuries Sacco may have suffered from Mr. Katzmann's exploitation of the jury's hostile emotions and Judge Thayer's prejudicial intrusions had been healed by the following rhetoric at the close of the trial:

Furthermore, the judge specifically instructed the jury:". . . the radical as well as the conservative, the foreign-born as well as the native-born, are entitled to and should receive in all trials under our laws the same rights, privileges and consideration as the logic of law, reason, sound judgment, justice and common sense demand. I therefore beseech you not to allow the fact that the defendants are Italians to influence or prejudice you in the least degree. They are entitled, under the law, to the same rights and considerations as though their ancestors came over in the Mayflower.[25]

The idea that the foregoing words of caution to avoid prejudice delivered at the close of a long trial would cure the injurious consequences of the cross-examination was a wholly unrealistic concept. There was not one thing in the pious generalities of Judge Thayer's words to suggest that he was referring to possible prejudice aroused by Mr. Katzmann's cross-examination. In fact, Judge Thayer had obviously favored Mr. Katzmann's cross-examination and had, in effect, joined in this cross-examination himself by numerous ironical intrusions of his own concerning the collection of literature. It is also unlikely that the jurymen were conscious of the influence of any

[24] Commonwealth v. Sacco, 255 Mass. 369; Record, Vol. V, 4339–4340.   [25] Ibid.

prejudice in their thinking. They must have thought their verdict was based on the acceptance of the evidence offered by the Commonwealth and on their rejection of that introduced by the defense. They were probably unaware of the subtle imponderable factors that produced this faith in the prosecution and this distrust of the defense. And once they arrived at the belief that the defendants were guilty, they could easily find reasons of their own to rationalize it. The operation of prejudice on the human mind is not always understood. Those who are aware of its presence will themselves nullify its influence, while those who believe that they are not prejudiced will remain unconscious of its effect upon their thinking.

It was not only unfortunate for Sacco and Vanzetti that Mr. Katzmann's cross-examination was not reproved by the Supreme Judicial Court. The reputation of the Massachusetts courts for earnestly seeking to maintain the highest standards of justice was injured, perhaps irreparably, by the court's declared inability to recognize and to act upon so patent an abuse of the right of cross-examination, especially in a capital case. In the context of the times, Mr. Katzmann's dissection and demonstration of Sacco's views and the sneers at his cherished beliefs could not help but stir up animosity against him. The brief of the Commonwealth admitted as much, although it blamed the injury on the inherent nature of the matters necessarily the subject of inquiry by the district attorney. This, however, was beside the point. It was not the inquiry into Sacco's radicalism that made the cross-examination unfair, but *Mr. Katzmann's prejudicial exploitation of it.* And does not the description of the cross-examination as "unfair" seem like an understatement when we realize that its alleged justification was a hoax which fooled the judge at the trial, the Governor's Advisory Committee and even Mr. Katzmann's successors in the district attorney's office?

20.

Alibi of Vanzetti

The Cloth and the Fisherman

Vanzetti's mode of life in Plymouth knew no calendar. He had no regular employment. He peddled fish when he could obtain a supply, he worked on outside construction when he could get the job, he dug clams when the tide was out. When he was doing none of these things, he loafed, and when he loafed, he occupied himself with talk. He liked people of all ages and loved to swap comments with them and to expound his ideas about how best to cure the ills of society. He also read much — chiefly books on philosophical or historical subjects. Living this sort of existence, there was no reason why he should have been able to answer sudden spot questions as to what he had been doing on any particular dates. Even when he had time to reflect, he still had problems. If April 15, 1920, fell during a time when he was living in Plymouth, as he said he was, there was nothing in retrospect to enable him to disentangle his memory of events on that day from, let us say, happenings on April 16 or April 17. This was Vanzetti's predicament when he finally realized that his life might depend on his finding proof that he was not in South Braintree on April 15, 1920.

Before discussing Vanzetti's alibi in detail, let us pause for a moment to consider the nature of an alibi. The word means that the accused was in some place other than the place of the crime when it occurred. If evidence to this effect is believed, the alibi is an absolute defense. The jury need not accept all of the alibi evidence offered by the defense in order to acquit the defendant. It does not matter if it is skeptical about most of the alibi testimony. If it believes that a single piece of evidence proves that the accused was not present when the crime was committed, it must find a not guilty verdict. By its very nature, therefore, there is no such thing as a generally "weak" alibi. Such a defense is no weaker than its strongest link. Also, because the prosecution is supposed to have the burden of proving its case beyond a reasonable doubt, an accused cannot be convicted (in theory) even if the proffered alibi meets total disbelief. For instance, the Plymouth jury might have been persuaded by Mr. Katzmann that Vanzetti's neighbors in the town had conspired with "those Italians up there" to concoct an alibi for him and yet find that the Commonwealth's identifying witnesses were mistaken. If so, Vanzetti should have been acquitted. Such a result, however, would have been extremely unlikely. The same facts that caused them to reject the testimony of nearly a score of reputable Italians would (and did) lead them to accept as true the identification by native Yankee witnesses, despite its manifest improbability. Prejudice ordinarily does not impel the jurors directly to find a defendant guilty or not guilty. It does, however, condition them to believe or disbelieve particular evidence and, by this process, to reach a verdict. They may feel that they arrived at their conclusion by weighing the evidence, but they are often quite unconscious of what it was that tipped the scales one way or the other.

An accused may be innocent and yet find it difficult to establish an alibi. Such a defense may be comparatively easy for a person who has a daily routine, especially where it involves contact with other people or written records of his whereabouts. For example, it compelled the State to release Orciani because of his "time clock alibis" on both December 24, 1919, and April 15, 1920, despite the district attorney's belief that he was one of the criminals. Or proof of it may be readily available because some unusual event in the life of the suspect fixes the place and time of the alibi. Such was Vanzetti's alibi at the Plymouth trial. It so happened that the highway robbery attempt in Bridgewater occurred on the day before Christmas, the traditional "day of remembrance," when Vanzetti's Italian customers in Plymouth received delivery of the eels which they had ordered from him.

On the other hand, an accused person lacking any daily routine or any special reason to be elsewhere than the scene of the crime might find it extremely difficult to prove an alibi. To reconstruct his whereabouts or movements on the date of the crime he would have to search his uncertain memory, review particular day's doings with his family and friends, and consult all persons with whom he might have had contact around the time of the crime. And if he found some prospective alibi witnesses, they also would have to scour their recollections to uncover some event associated with their seeing the accused which would fix the time and place of the encounter. Under such circumstances, the possibility of error as to details through defective or overimaginative recollection, even by honest witnesses, is considerable. When mistakes are discovered, the entire alibi may be discredited. This is an understandable but not necessarily a sound conclusion.

Mr. Katzmann never asked Vanzetti directly where he was on April 15, 1920, but approached the date by a circuitous route which Vanzetti had difficulty in following. Later, at the trial in Dedham in July 1921, he cross-examined Vanzetti on this subject and especially about the questions he had asked him on May 6, 1920, in the Brockton police station:

Q. Mr. Vanzetti, do you remember this question and this answer at the Brockton police station that I made of you, and which you gave in reply:

"Q. Well, do you remember the holiday we had in April, the 19th of April, they call it Patriots' Day, the middle of April? A. Yes. I heard that before, but I did not remember that was in April."
Do you remember saying that to me at Brockton? A. What holiday?

Q. The 19th of April? A. What holiday it is?

Q. Patriots' Day? A. Patriot?

Q. Patriots' Day. A. Oh, patriotics day.

Q. Yes, do you remember my asking you that question and your making that reply? A. No, I don't; I don't remember.

Q. Will you say you did not make that reply to that question? A. No, I don't say that I didn't.

Q. Do you remember the next question:

"Q. This year it came on a Monday."
You remember the answer:

"A. I don't remember."
Did you make that reply? A. No, I don't remember.

Q. Will you say you did not make it? A. Well, maybe I did. I might have, yes.

Q. Do you remember this question and this answer:

"Q. You don't know where you were the Thursday before that Monday, do you? A. No."
Do you remember that answer to that question? A. Oh, yes, I answered some other thing no, that I don't remember in that time, but I remember it now, not only this.

Q. On May 6th, 1920? A. Yes.

Q. You did not remember where you were on the 15th of April, did you? A. More probable, yes.

Q. But after waiting months and months and months you then remembered, did you? A. Not months and months and months, but three or four weeks after I see that I have to be careful and to remember well if I want to save my life.

Q. That four weeks after the date you could not remember, but seven or eight weeks after you could. Is that right? A. I say that after three or four weeks after my arrest I understand enough to see that I have to be very careful to save my life and my liberty and I have to remember.

Q. Weren't you careful, sir, when you were making your reply to that question? A. Yes, but I never know in that time on the day 15th and the day 24th it was the day of the assault at South Braintree and Bridgewater. I don't know in that time.

Q. Didn't you intend to tell me the truth where you were on any day that I asked you? A. I intend to tell you the truth, but I never can dream that you will say that on the 15th and the 24th I went to steal and kill a man.

Q. Then if you could not dream that you were to be charged with murder on the 15th of April, how was it you were so certain that you could not remember where you were on the 15th of April? A. Because in the 15th of April is a day common to every other day to me. I peddled fish.

Q. Didn't I fix it, Mr. Vanzetti, by the holiday, the 19th of April, when I talked with you? A. Yes, but probably I don't make any speculation on that patriotics day, you see.[1]

Later, at the end of the Dedham trial, Mr. Katzmann, by agreement, put into the record three of the foregoing questions and answers as a correct transcript of what Vanzetti had said at Brockton. However, the stipulation stated that the questions *were denied by Vanzetti as having been made at the Brockton police station.*[2] Even a quick glance at the excerpt of the record above quoted will show that Vanzetti *had not denied the questions. He had simply said that he did not remember them.* This was not the only occasion when Mr. Katzmann caught defendants' counsel napping by getting them to "stipulate" something false or misleading. Some of these loaded stipulations were deadly.

By the time Vanzetti testified at the Dedham trial, however, he was able to reconstruct some of his movements on April 15. Mr. Katzmann used this refreshed recollection to assail Vanzetti's veracity because in the Brockton police station, the morning after his arrest, he had been unable to remember what he had done on "the Thursday before that Monday" that was "Patriots' Day."

At the trial Vanzetti stated that on April 15, 1920, he had remained in Plymouth, peddling fish part of the day. He sold fish from the first week in March to the middle of April. He produced an express receipt showing that on April 8, 1920, he received a shipment of 488 pounds of fish which took him three days to sell. Thereafter he got some fish from a local dealer, Antonio Carbone, and continued to peddle fish until about noon on April 15, when his supply of fish had been sold. He did not remember the particular customers to whom he sold the fish.

There were only two episodes on April 15 that he was able to recall. The first incident concerned his purchase of a piece of cloth from a peddler

[1] Vol. II, 1802–1803.   [2] Vol. II, 2117.

(Joseph Rosen) and the other, a social chat with a fisherman named Melvin Corl. The meagerness of these remembered incidents has been cited as indicating a "weak" alibi, but it may also be a voucher for its honesty. One would expect that a synthetic alibi, fabricated for the occasion as claimed by Mr. Katzmann, would have more content and much more definition than the story related by Vanzetti and his witnesses at Dedham. Here is Vanzetti's account of what he did on April 15, 1920:

A. On the 15th, I have a few, not very many, fish in the morning of the 15th, and I peddled in Cherry Street, Standish Avenue and Cherry Court, down Suosso's Lane, around that place, around that centre. Castle Street is the last place I sell fish on the day of the 15th.

Q. Now, tell us anything else that you did on the day of the 15th. A. On the day of the 15th, when I was going by Suosso's Lane, from Suosso's Lane I reached Court Street and then I turned towards Plymouth, toward south, and I was intentioning to go in Castle Street. Almost on the corner of Castle Street I met this man that go around with cloths.

Q. Yes. A. And he asked me, — I can't say that.

Q. You met that man with the cloths? A. Yes.

Q. Did you do anything with him? A. Yes. He stopped me. He says something to me.

Q. Very good. You are not going to give the conversation. That is right. Now, you talked, I assume. He talked, too. Did you do anything? A. Yes, I buy a piece of cloth from him.

Q. Yes. Now, what was done with the cloth? A. He sold me a piece of the cloth and I told him I don't know nothing about the cloth.

MR. KATZMANN. One moment.

Q. You are telling us now what you said. You talked about the cloth, didn't you?

THE COURT. In consequence of that, what did you do?

Q. Good. A. I bring him to the Brini house. I knew that the Brini wife was in the house, and I know she worked in the woolen mill and she know the cloth.

Q. You brought this man to Brini's house? A. Yes.

Q. You knew she had worked in the woolen mill? A. Yes.

Q. Did she look at the cloth? A. Yes.

Q. I can't ask you what she said, but after she examined the cloth, looked it over, did you or did you not buy it? A. Not in the house of Mrs. Brini.

Q. Then you went out after she looked at the cloth, and you had your conversation, you and the man went out? A. Yes, he went out alone and I went out a little after him.

Q. After you had got out, what happened then? A. I go around my cart, the fish cart, with the fish in, and I found that man wait for me, and he say, "If you want" —

Q. Now, again be careful, what he said. After you had, — when he said what he did and you did what talk you wanted to do, did you, yes or no, buy the cloth? A. Yes, I buy the cloth.

Q. What did you pay for it? A. I should say something like twelve dollars, but I don't remember exactly. Not twelve dollars, not twelve dollars, but $12.75 or something like that. I give him fifty cents after to buy because he say he lost.

Q. What time in the day was that, about what time? A. Near one o'clock, about half past eleven, something like that, half past twelve, about one o'clock.

Q. Now, you say then you had your fish about all sold? A. Yes. Then I went to Castle Street and I finished my fish.

Q. Where did you go then? A. Then I took my cart and I went in Ocean Street in front of Mr. Corl's house.

Q. All right. Now, what did you do when you got down in front of Corl's house? A. I left my cart there and I went down to the shore. I have finished the fish. I went down to the shore.

Q. When you got down to the shore, who did you see there? A. I saw on my left side near the house where they build the boat I saw Mr. Corl in the boat, in his boat. The boat was on the sand.

Q. The boat was on the sand? A. On the shore.

Q. What was he doing? A. I went there and I saw he was painting the boat.

Q. Again I can't ask you what you said or what he said. Did you have a conversation with him? A. A long conversation.

Q. About how long were you there with him? A. More than an hour, anyhow.

Q. And do you remember whether any one else came while you were there near Mr. Corl while he was working on his boat? Do you remember whether any one else came there? A. Yes, two men came.

Q. Two men. Were they strangers to you or men you knew? A. I know them.

Q. Who were the men that came there? A. I think it was Mr. Jesse.

Q. Mr. who? A. Mr. Jesse.

Q. Jesse? A. Jesse.

Q. Is he a man you knew? A. Yes, I know him. He is a boat builder there in Seaside.

Q. Who was the other man who came? A. The other man is Mr. Holmes, but he don't stay long. He say two or three words and then go away.

Q. What is Mr. Holmes's business? What does he do? A. He worked for the lumber yard, in the office of the lumber yard. I do not know if he is boss, if he is owner or not.

Q. Whose lumber yard does he work in? A. I call that lumber yard. I do not know if he is owner or if he is employee there.

Q. You do not know the name, whose lumber yard it is? A. No, I do not know.

Q. How near is this lumber yard to where Corl was working on his boat? A. It is a little back toward Plymouth. It is a street without a house but I do not know the name.

Q. Can you see the lumber wharf or the lumber yard from where Corl was working on his boat? Do you know whether you can see it or not? A. I can't tell you for sure because it is very easy to see that, but my opinion is the building where Jesse worked to build the boats were in front of his, and so we can't see that, but I can't tell sure.

Q. After you left Corl there at the boat, where did you go? A. I came back and took the cart in the street, then go home.

Q. Where do you keep the fish cart, the cart you sell fish in? A. I keep my fish cart in the yard of Mr. Fortini, where I board.

Q. Did you bring the fish cart home? A. Yes.

Q. You say you came to what house? A. I don't came from no house. I left the fish cart in front of Corl's house when I go to the shore, and when I left Corl to the shore I came back into Ocean Street, and I take the cart and I go home.

THE COURT. We will have the morning recess, now.

(Short recess.)

Q. Now, you brought the fish cart home to your own house. What did you do then? A. Then I changed the clothes.

Q. All right. After you changed your clothes, what did you do? A. Made supper.

Q. You had your supper? A. Yes.

Q. You eat. After you had your meal, what did you do then the rest of the day? A. I went out of the home, but I don't remember where I go.

Q. About what time did you get your supper? A. Six o'clock.

Q. Did you stay in Plymouth that night? A. Yes.[3]

Mr. Katzmann did not cross-examine Vanzetti concerning his testimony as to what he did on April 15, 1920, in Plymouth except as to one item. He wanted to know Vanzetti's whereabouts at 12:13 P.M. on that day. Probably this was for the purpose of discrediting the testimony of Angelo Guidobone, who had testified that he had bought fish from Vanzetti on that day at about thirteen minutes past twelve or quarter past twelve. Vanzetti answered that he had been at or near the Brini house between twelve and one o'clock, probably nearer one o'clock, since the people were going back to work at the cordage plant, which resumed operations at one o'clock.[4] However, Mr. Katzmann cross-examined Vanzetti concerning what he said he had done on days other than April 15 and, as we have seen, attacked him because, on the witness stand, he had recalled various matters, whereas he had said that he had no memory when questioned the morning after his arrest.

The testimony of the following witnesses corroborated, to some extent, Vanzetti's story of what he had done on April 15:

Antonio Carbone, a Plymouth fish dealer, testified that he had sold fish to Vanzetti in April, either in the evening of the thirteenth or the morning of the fourteenth. Mr. Katzmann did not cross-examine him.[5]

Salvatore Boya, a Boston fish dealer, testified that he sold 425 pounds of

[3] Vol. II, 1701–1703.   [4] Vol. II, 1791.   [5] Vol. II, 1625.

fish to Carbone on April 12, 1920. On cross-examination, he said he did not know to whom the Plymouth dealer resold the fish or when.[6]

Angelo Guidobone, of Suosso's Lane, Plymouth, was the only one of Vanzetti's customers who told of buying fish on the morning of April 15. He testified (through an interpreter) that he had bought some codfish from him in Suosso's Lane at about quarter past twelve as he was going to dinner.[7] He remembered the date because he had an appendicitis operation on April 19. He had a pain on Saturday the seventeenth, and was examined that day and told that "he had to go and have an operation right away." This was an odd association to assist him to remember the date when he bought the fish and Mr. Katzmann did his best to make it seem ridiculous. The witness handed the sarcasm back to Mr. Katzmann in a spirited fashion. At the end, Mr. Katzmann inadvertently brought out what may have been the association in Guidobone's mind. For it was the witness's custom to buy fish on Thursday to eat on Friday, and the Thursday before he went to the hospital was April 15.

Joseph Rosen of Boston was the cloth peddler whom Vanzetti said he had brought to the Brini house between noon and one o'clock. He told of meeting Vanzetti on the street in Plymouth. Vanzetti had his pushcart and was selling fish. Rosen approached Vanzetti, who selected a piece of material, "just enough to make for himself a suit." Vanzetti then took him to a house about two blocks away to show the cloth to a lady "whether it was good material or not." [8] There was also a younger lady present. They came out of the house, returned to Vanzetti's pushcart and bargained to reach a price. Vanzetti bought the cloth. It was about noontime when he first met Vanzetti. He placed the time by the blowing of the whistles in the cordage plant and people just going home to get their dinner. He remained in Plymouth until 6:10, when he took the last train for Whitman. He stopped that night at Litchfield's rooming house and worked in Whitman the next day.[9]

In his cross-examination of Rosen, Mr. Katzmann adverted to his favorite device of questioning the witness about where he was and what he did on dates that he had had no opportunity to check.[10] This sort of examination continued for sometime, until Mr. Katzmann wore out even Judge Thayer's patience which had been considerable. When Mr. Katzmann

[6] Vol. II, 1626.   [7] Vol. II, 1587.   [8] Vol. II, 1496.   [9] Vol. II, 1498.
[10] Vol. II, 1499ff.

asked: "Where were you last Wednesday?" the judge interjected: "Haven't you tested him on recollection sufficiently?" to which Mr. Katzmann replied, "Very likely, your honor." [11]

Indeed, Mr. Katzmann had done just that. Many other Massachusetts judges would have stopped Mr. Katzmann in this and other cross-examinations long before Judge Thayer did. However, the prosecutor could not resist making a few sarcastic comments phrased as "questions." In doing so, he asked one too many "questions," as follows:

Q. (By Mr. Katzmann) It is pretty hard to remember any day except the 15th day of April, isn't it? A. Well, I remember that, yes.
Q. Yes. That is an easy day to remember, isn't it? A. I got reasons for that to remember.
Q. Is it any easier than any other day? A. Yes.
Q. To you? A. Yes, sir.[12]

Mr. Katzmann did not ask Mr. Rosen his reasons for remembering that it was April 15 when he had been in Plymouth. However, one can picture defense counsel suddenly coming to attention and exclaiming, "My God! How did we forget!" On redirect, associate counsel Callahan retrieved what could have been a crucial oversight.

Q. (By Mr. Callahan) You told Mr. Katzmann you had some reason why you remembered it was April 15, 1920, that you were at Plymouth. Will you say what those reasons are? A. When I reached the town of Whitman, the town was all excited. It was all boiling about the South Braintree murder, and I was talking also in town around the people, around the restaurant, and they were talking about it, about the murder at South Braintree and that is what reminds me when that particular day, April 15th, I had been in Plymouth and by going with the 6:10 train from Whitman. It is a neighboring town around South Braintree, so they were talking about the crime, and I sold Vanzetti that particular day at noon time a piece of cloth, a dark blue, with a hole in it, a damage. I made him a bargain with him. I asked him if the piece of cloth — [13]

Rosen had stated that he spent the night of April 15 at Litchfield's rooming house at Whitman. He was followed on the witness stand by Miss Lillian Shuler, who had been a waitress at Litchfield's, and had been on duty from four o'clock in the afternoon until midnight on April 15. Refreshing her recollection from her own personal memorandum in a journal kept by Litchfield's, she stated that while on duty that day she had rented

[11] Vol. II, 1515–1516.   [12] Vol. II, 1513.   [13] Vol. II, 1517–1518.

one room, but only one room. She was not asked whether she knew the name of the roomer, nor if she could identify Rosen. Mr. Katzmann did not cross-examine her.[14]

Before leaving Rosen's story about the bargain he had given Vanzetti because of the holes in the cloth, it would add to the continuity if we looked at the place in the record where the cloth itself was introduced in evidence during the examination of Vanzetti. The transcript follows:

Q. (By Mr. McAnarney) I show you this piece of cloth (indicating). Will you examine that and state whether or not that is the piece? A. Well, as far as I can answer honestly it looks the same color, and I found the hole to-day. I look in this (examining cloth). That time I saw some small hole, and some one big hole, but I can't see the small hole there. It is too dark.

Q. You run it all off. A. Here —

Q. You hold that a minute (a piece of cloth). Is that the, — you say there was a hole. Well, now, tell us about that hole. You haven't told us anything about that. A. Yes. I asked the lady, — I can't say what —

Q. First, we have got to get that conversation again. Well, was there any conversation with the peddler about this cloth? A. Yes, a conversation about the stuff above the hole.

MR. KATZMANN. One moment.

Q. What you said I don't ask. After your talk with the peddler you and the peddler went up to Mrs. Brini's? A. Yes.

Q. And whether or not this cloth was shown to her? A. Yes, it was.

Q. Is this the piece of cloth? A. Yes.

Q. Whether or not that hole was in the cloth? A. Yes, it was. Some other little damage that I can't see now.

MR. JEREMIAH MCANARNEY (Showing cloth to the jury) I do not know that you gentlemen see the hole in the material. You see it on the back. I will put my finger against it so you will get it. I suppose I might offer that in evidence, if your Honor please.

I am going to offer this as an exhibit, Mr. Katzmann.

MR KATZMANN. I haven't seen it yet.

(Mr. Jeremiah McAnarney shows cloth to Mr. Katzmann.)

(The cloth is admitted in evidence and marked "Exhibit N.")[15]

The holes in the cloth have some significance in the light of the corroborative testimony about them. The mention of the holes was a homely detail remembered by the witness, but not likely to be contrived in order to fortify a false alibi. However, as we shall see, it gave Mr. Katzmann an opportunity to practice his gift of ridicule on Mrs. Brini (who had to use an interpreter to understand his questions) and to jeer at Rosen, Mrs. Brini

[14] Vol. II, 1520–1522.   [15] Vol. II, 1731.

and her daughter LeFavre as a trio of liars.[16] (The availability of the cloth suggests that Vanzetti's arrest ended his plan to have a suit made of it.)

Mr. Rosen also recalled that before he left home on the morning of April 15, he had reminded his wife that "the man was going to come around" to collect his poll tax. He left the money with her to pay the bill. He produced as evidence a poll tax warrant receipt dated April 15, 1920, for "4.40 in full payment of 1918 poll tax and costs." It became Exhibit K.

Mrs. Alfonsini Brini of Plymouth, testifying through an interpreter, corroborated Vanzetti and Rosen with respect to the piece of cloth shown her by Vanzetti. Her daughter LeFavre also was present. She said that she did not recall having ever seen Rosen before that day, but on cross-examination said she might have. She stated that she had not bought cloth herself from Rosen, although the peddler had said that he sold the lady a piece about two months before. Mrs. Brini placed the time of the incident between half past eleven and twelve o'clock, somewhat earlier than the hour stated by Vanzetti. She recalled that it was April 15, because "that was my first week that I came home from the hospital." [17]

As he had done at Plymouth, Mr. Katzmann brought out that Vanzetti was on intimate terms with the Brini family. On direct examination Mrs. Brini had stated that there were one or two small holes in the middle of the piece of cloth. Mr. Katzmann persisted in assuming that Mrs. Brini had stated that she remembered the date "because you saw the two holes." This was untrue. Apparently the witness was unable to understand Mr. Katzmann's questions and thought that he was really interested in learning how she remembered the date. A pertinent excerpt follows:

Q. (By Mr. Katzmann) Is there anything about the fact that there is two holes in a piece of cloth that enables you to fix any date? A. Well, I remember that I saw the cloth and I saw the holes.

Q. Well, I will grant that. Assuming you did see the cloth and the holes in it, is there anything about that fact that enables you to fix any date thereby? A. I remember that the day before on the 14th my sickness was getting worse.

THE INTERPRETER. She wants to say some more.

MR. KATZMANN. If your Honor please, I submit that is not responsive to the question. Wait just a minute.

THE COURT. Let her start in again. Put the question.

Q. What is there about two holes in a piece of cloth that enables you to know the date you saw it?

MR. CALLAHAN. I pray your Honor's judgment. She has not said that. She said

[16] Vol. II, 2196.   [17] Vol. II, 1523.

that she remembered two holes in the cloth, but not related to the 15th of April.

MR. KATZMANN. Then I will put a new question.

Q. Is there anything about two holes in a piece of cloth that enables you to fix any date from that fact that there were holes in the cloth? A. Yes, sir.

Q. What is it? A. Why, that very morning I got somebody to call up my husband, and that was the morning that I went out of my house.

Q. I am asking you if there is anything about the fact that there are two holes in a piece of cloth that enables you to fix the date when you saw those holes? A. Yes, sir.

Q. What is it about the holes in the cloth that fixes the date or helps you to fix the date? A. I remember that was the 15th day of April because the day before, on the 14th, my illness was getting worse.

MR. KATZMANN. I ask that be stricken out, if your Honor please, as not being responsive.

THE COURT. That may be. Just tell her, Mr. Interpreter, to pay attention to the question and answer that.

(The Interpreter talks to the witness.)

Q. Mrs. Brini, is there anything about the fact of your seeing two holes in a piece of cloth that enables you to say it was a date certain because you saw those holes? A. Why, yes. I remember that that morning I had a visit from a person that came up to visit me in regard to my sickness that very morning.

Q. What has that got to do with the two holes in the cloth? A. I remember because that was the day that this man came over with Mr. Vanzetti in my house with the piece of cloth. Q. That is the way you remember, is it? A. And my condition.[18]

Mr. Katzmann may have been unable to shake Mrs. Brini's sworn testimony, but he knew how to destroy its credibility in another way. There was a conference at the bench followed by a suspension of the cross-examination.[19] On the next day, the cross-examination purported to be "resumed," but instead it appears that Mr. Katzmann merely wanted to put on record another deceptive "stipulation." Here it is:

MR. JEREMIAH MCANARNEY. If your Honor please, it is agreed by counsel for the Commonwealth and counsel for the defendant as follows: that the witness — I will change that to "this" —

MR. KATZMANN. "This."

MR. JEREMIAH MCANARNEY. — that this witness —

THE COURT. Give her name, so it will be in the record.

MR. KATZMANN. Alphonsin [sic] Brini.

MR. JEREMIAH MCANARNEY. Alphonsin Brini has, in another case, testified on behalf of the defendant Vanzetti as to his whereabouts different from the date set forth in that case.

MR. KATZMANN. Different from the place.

18 Vol. II, 1525–1526.   19 Vol. II, 1555.

MR. JEREMIAH MCANARNEY. Different from the place set forth in that case.

MR. KATZMANN. I would like to have that read as finally agreed.

(The agreement is read as follows: — "It is agreed by counsel for the Commonwealth and counsel for the defendant as follows: that this witness, Alphonson Brini has, in another case, testified on behalf of the defendant Vanzetti as to his whereabouts different from the place set forth in that case.")

THE COURT. Now, you are through with the witness?

MR. KATZMANN. Yes.[20]

The foregoing alleged statement of fact was false. Here again Vanzetti suffered because his counsel at Dedham had not been his lawyer at Plymouth. Mrs. Brini had *not* testified that Vanzetti was in some place other than set out in "another case." The attempted payroll robbery in Bridgewater had occurred at seven-thirty on the morning of December 24. Mrs. Brini had given no testimony concerning Vanzetti's whereabouts on December 24 prior to eight o'clock in the evening. She had testified that Vanzetti had spent Christmas Eve in her home from eight P.M. until a late hour.[21] In his summation, Mr. Katzmann made effective use of the stipulation, driving home to the jury its false innuendo. Here is how he wiped out what should have been a convincing alibi at the Dedham trial:

Mrs. Brini, it is agreed in another case when another date was alleged, testified to the whereabouts of this same Vanzetti on that other date there involved, *a stock, convenient and ready witness* as well as friend of the defendant Vanzetti. [Emphasis added.] [22]

No doubt defense counsel at Dedham were persuaded to make these stipulations (and one infinitely worse, as we shall see later) in the belief that they would shield Vanzetti from the introduction of the record of his prior conviction. If so, the price was exorbitant and the protection illusory. If, by virtue of some miracle, the jurors did not already know or remember that Vanzetti was a convicted highwayman, the stipulation itself advised them of the fact.

Miss LeFavre Brini, daughter of Alfonsini, was the young lady mentioned by Rosen as being present at the cloth episode. At the time of the Dedham trial she was fifteen years old. She corroborated her mother's story. She fixed the time as about noon, because she was then "setting the table for dinner." She remembered that it was April 15, because "it was just one week after I left my work to take care of my mother who came home

20 Vol. II, 1555.   21 Supp. Vol., 305. See Chapter 9.   22 Vol. II, 2192.

from the hospital," and "because that morning my father called the nurse for my mother" and "because the day before the 15th my mother was sick and called the doctor."

As he had done with LeFavre's little brother at Plymouth, Mr. Katzmann examined LeFavre rather extensively on the number of times she had discussed her story with her mother. Mr. Katzmann cross-examined and re-cross-examined her. Before he started the second cross-examination, someone must have informed him that there was a prior date when Mrs. Brini had been taken to the hospital. He made good use of it. Without any preliminaries about the earlier date, he skillfully eased in "March 18," with apparent casualness. This part of the re-cross-examination follows:

Q. (By Mr. Katzmann) Two months before that date daytimes were you working at the Gorton-Pew Fisheries? A. Yes.

Q. So you were not home daytimes at all except when your mother was ill, were you? A. Yes.

Q. That is true, isn't it? And how long before that had you been working for the Gorton-Pew Fisheries? How long before your mother became ill? A. I worked there all summer.

Q. All what summer? A. All that summer.

Q. Well, I say before March 18th? A. March 18th?

Q. Yes. A. How do you fix March 18th?

Q. Don't you fix March 18th? Doesn't that date mean anything to you, March 18, 1920? Doesn't that date mean to you, Miss Brini? A. (Witness hesitates.) Why should it?

Q. Is that your answer to me? Do you love your mother, Miss Brini? A. Yes.

Q. Don't you know that was the day that she says she went to the hospital? A. Yes.

Q. And that date didn't mean anything to you? A. Why, Yes.

Q. Well, why didn't you remember it when I asked you? A. (Witness hesitates.)

Q. Excuse me for raising my voice to you, I didn't mean to frighten you. Why didn't you remember it, Miss Brini, when I told you that day? A. I did not know what you meant by that.

Q. You know what March means, don't you? A. Yes.

Q. You know what 18th means, don't you? A. Yes.

Q. You know March 18th is a date, don't you? A. Yes.

Q. When I asked you about March 18th, you did not remember, did you, that that was the day your mother was taken out to the hospital — was taken out of the house to the Jordan Hospital did you?

MR. CALLAHAN. Wait a minute. I pray your Honor's judgment.

Q. That your mother went to the Jordan Hospital? A. (Witness hesitates.)

Q. You did not remember that, did you, Miss Brini? A. (Witness hesitates.)

Q. Is that too hard to answer? A. No.

Q. Will you please answer it? A. (Witness hesitates.)

THE COURT. I wish you would please answer it if you can.

THE WITNESS. I did not remember when you first asked me.

Q. You did not. And that is why you said to me, "Why should I remember March 18th?" A. Yes.

Q. Don't you think you should have remembered March 18th more than April 15th? A. (Witness hesitates.)

THE COURT. Won't you please answer the questions so we can go along?

MR. KATZMANN. I won't press it, your Honor.[23]

This was not the only instance where Mr. Katzmann's tests of the witness's memory seemed to bewilder her. On direct examination she had said that Vanzetti had delivered fish to her house at ten or ten thirty on the morning of April 15 (when she was keeping house). Mr. Katzmann asked her when Vanzetti first began selling fish to her family. She did not know, but said it was more than a year. Mr. Katzmann then demanded to know whether the date when Vanzetti first began to sell fish to her family was not more important than a single day when he left fish in her sink (April 15, 1920). He repeated this question many times as LeFavre puzzled over it and hesitated. At an early stage of these queries, he asked, "Is that too hard for you to answer?" On Mr. Callahan's objection, he explained that he was just being solicitous. "I am seeking to be gentle with the child. Do you object to that?"

Counsel on both sides concluded LeFavre's examination with the customary, "That is all." [24] Nevertheless, both counsel must have assumed that her examination had merely been suspended, and she showed up the next day when the examination of Alfonsini was resumed in order to introduce the stipulation. However, when Mr. McAnarney offered LeFavre for further examination, Mr. Katzmann waved her aside:

"In view of that agreement made of the matter, as a matter of evidence, I don't care for the daughter to remain."

This remark again exhibited Mr. Katzmann's prowess as a trial lawyer. It plainly told the jury that LeFavre, and possibly the entire alibi, was no longer of concern to Mr. Katzmann since the stipulation, by inference, conceded that Mrs. Brini was a utility witness who would swear to anything to help Vanzetti. This apparently was the end of the Vanzetti-Rosen-Alfonsini-LeFavre alibi which, if believed, would have resulted in Vanzetti's acquittal.

[23] Vol. II, 1546–1547.   [24] Vol. II, 1547.

Two final notes should be mentioned. Ella M. Urquhart, a nurse from the Plymouth Cordage Company, brought in her records of the Nurses' Department for the month of April 1920. She made the record herself. It was the original record, written out from what the attending nurse reported to her. Judge Thayer excluded the evidence, stating that it might have been admitted in a civil suit but not in a criminal case. He directed Mr. Callahan to bring in the party who had personal knowledge of what was done by the nurse at the place, "that is the important thing." [25] Mr. Callahan then put Gertrude Mary Matthews on the stand. She was the nurse from the Plymouth Cordage Company who attended Mrs. Brini. She testified that she made several calls on Mrs. Brini in April 1920, probably between the fifteenth and the twenty-fifth of the month. However, she could not recall the date when she made the first call at the Brini home. She was not asked to refresh her recollection by looking at the dates in the record reported by her to Miss Urquhart.

A second note to the Rosen episode is the fact that the peddler himself appeared before the Governor's Advisory Committee in 1927. Apparently he had come voluntarily to see the governor because he thought that Mr. Katzmann was not being "fair" with him. He told the Committee substantially the same story that he had related on the witness stand. He added, however, the fact that he first learned about Vanzetti's arrest by seeing his picture in the newspaper. At the time he did not know Vanzetti's name but did know that he was the only fish peddler in Plymouth. When he next went to Plymouth he went to the Brini house and discussed the matter with LeFavre Brini.[26]

The other episode which Vanzetti had recalled to trace his movements in Plymouth on April 15th was his talk on the beach with Melvin Corl, the fisherman. It was an inconsequential incident in an idle afternoon. There was no tie-in with the date of any other happening, nor was there any written record to mark the occasion. The only evidence of the date available to the defense was the groping memory of witnesses trying to recall something which had made little impression on them at the time. The Corl story was therefore easy for Mr. Katzmann to attack on the ground of indefinite proof as to time.

Corl stated that he had known Vanzetti since 1915 and had sold him fish during the fall of 1919. On April 15, 1920, he was on Plymouth Bay beach

25 Vol. II, 1582–1583.   26 Vol. V, 5254–5255.

from 7 A.M. to 5 P.M. painting his boat. On direct examination he told the following story:

Q. (By Mr. Callahan) Do you recall seeing him on the 15th of April, last year? A. I do.

Q. Where was he and where were you when you saw him? A. I was painting my boat and he came down the shore and stopped and talked with me.

Q. What time of the day was it that he was talking with you? A. Around 2 o'clock he arrived there.

Q. How long did he remain talking with you? A. About one hour and a half, I should say.

Q. How was he dressed? A. As if he had been working. He had on working clothes, I should say. He was not dressed up at all.

Q. Was anybody with him? A. No, sir, he was alone when he came up there.

Q. Did he have anything with him? A. Well, he had something on his arm, a coat or jumper or something, I did not notice particularly what it was.

Q. How do you fix it as being the 15th of April? A. He came along and he said he was going to Mr. Sampson's to look for a job.

MR. KATZMANN. I object.

Q. You can't tell what he said to you. A. On account of painting my boat, and I was going to put it in the following day, but it was not completed and I put it in on the 17th, my wife's birthday.

Q. Whether or not that was the first day you had started painting your boat? A. No, I was painting, — I had been working on it practically the whole week.

Q. When did you put the boat in the water? A. April 17.

Q. Does that date mean anything to you? A. It was my wife's birthday; and I also towed a boat from Duxbury on that date.

Q. Is there any other thing you have in mind that enables you to fix the day as being April 15th last year? A. Nothing that I can remember of.

Q. Do you recall anybody else being there while you and Vanzetti were having a talk? A. Yes, sir. Mr. Jesse.

Q. And do you recall overhearing a conversation between Mr. Vanzetti and Mr. Jesse? A. Yes, sir.

Q. Was it about an automobile? A. It was.

MR. CALLAHAN. Your witness.[27]

The foregoing testimony, though brief, is quite rich in detail. Later, on redirect, Mr. Corl added a few further particulars.[28]

On cross-examination, Mr. Katzmann again "tested" the memory of the witness by "taking him over the hurdles." He asked him where he was on a large number of dates and days of the week. The dates, mostly in 1921, had nothing to do with the Corl incident and the witness himself had had no previous opportunity to search his memory for answers. To many of them

[27] Vol. II, 1549.   [28] Vol. II, 1554.

Corl replied, "I couldn't say," but observed occasionally that he could "figure back" or "figure it up." He was quite clear, however, about the dates and days of the week around April 15, 1920, to which he had directed his memory:

> Q. What day of the week did the 17th of April 1920 fall on? A. On Saturday.
> Q. Then what day of the week was the 15th? A. Thursday.
> Q. Yes. How do you remember it was the 17th that fell on a Saturday? A. On account of my wife's birthday and going to Duxbury.[29]

Mrs. Melvin Corl, wife of the fisherman, testified that her husband was getting his boat painted during the week of April 17, 1920. She wasn't at the shore while he was painting, but saw the boat, with fresh paint, "a couple of nights or so before the seventeenth of April." On cross-examination, she became more positive about the night she saw the boat, stating that it was "Thursday" (April 15), and that she was sure that it was *not* Friday, since on that night (on Fridays) she either stayed home or went to the moving pictures. Mrs. Corl gave additional and exact corroboration of her husband which started when Mr. Katzmann asked:

> Q. Did he tell you about a Duxbury tow on Saturday? A. Yes, he did.

The slip, if it was a slip, enabled Mr. Callahan to spell it out on redirect:

> Q. What did he tell you about the Duxbury tow? A. That he had to go to Duxbury Saturday afternoon to tow a boat from Duxbury to Plymouth for Mr. Morey.[30]

Frank Jesse, the Plymouth boatbuilder, was the man who had joined Corl and Vanzetti during their talk on the beach as Corl was painting. He testified that he had known both Corl and Vanzetti three or four years. He recalled seeing Corl painting his boat "right in his [boat] yard" last year (1920). He had a talk with Vanzetti about an automobile. This was in the spring of the year, but he could not remember the month or the day. The last time he saw Vanzetti was at the time he was talking to Corl as he was painting his boat.[31] Mr. Katzmann did not cross-examine Mr. Jesse.

Joseph Morey, a cloth inspector at the Puritan Mills in Plymouth, testified that Corl had towed a boat for him from South Duxbury to Frank

[29] Vol. II, 1553.   [30] Vol. II, 1674.   [31] Vol. II, 1586.

Jesse's boatyard at Plymouth. This was on Saturday, April 17. Corl's boat had been newly painted. On cross-examination, Morey said the boat stayed in his boatyard about six weeks until it was sold sometime in May. The first time his attention was called to the date when Corl towed his boat was on his way to court that morning in response to a summons. He and Mrs. Corl talked it over "on the way up." It is worthwhile to see the exact answers to Mr. Katzmann's questions made by Mr. Morey:

Q. (By Mr. Katzmann) Did you remember it right off? A. No, I did not.
Q. Did someone tell you what it was? A. Yes.
Q. Who told you? A. Mrs. Corl and I talked it over.
MR. KATZMANN. That is all.
THE WITNESS. And decided that was the date.
Q. You decided that was the date? A. We weren't sure of it.
Q. You weren't sure? A. She wasn't sure.
Q. She wasn't sure? A. Yes.
MR. KATZMANN. That is all.[32]

To most people, Mr. Morey's frank statement above would seem to indicate that he and Mrs. Corl had been honest with one another. That is not how Mr. Katzmann presented it to the jury two weeks later. In his summation, he attacked Mrs. Corl's integrity, as he had assailed Mrs. Brini's — *for testimony which she had not given*. This time, however, he supplied the false basis himself without a stipulation. Here is how he did it:

Of course the good lady had a birthday on the 17th of April. Nobody disputes it, but the lady herself and her recollection that it was on the 15th that her husband was down there than [*semble*, that] Vanzetti was there talking that afternoon . . .

A quick reference to Mrs. Corl's testimony shows that she said nothing whatever *about her husband talking with Vanzetti at any time*.[33]

Then referring to Morey's statement above quoted, that Mrs. Corl wasn't sure of the date when her husband towed his boat, Mr. Katzmann continued:

And she was the woman who had just left the stand and had testified under oath as to her means of recollection that she was sure.

The transcript of Mrs. Corl's testimony shows that she had never *testified that "she was sure." It was Mr. Katzmann himself who incorporated*

[32] Vol. II, 1676.   [33] Vol. II, 2195.

the date in his own question when he asked her whether her husband had told her about a "Duxbury tow." Her affirmative answer did not even involve her own knowledge (as Mr. Katzmann inferred), but only what her husband had told her. But Mr. Katzmann was not yet through with his denunciation of Mrs. Corl:

> She not only was sure of it, but she was seeking for some purpose best known to herself to make young More [*semble*, Morey] fabricate the story that it was on the 17th two days before [*semble*, after?] it was alleged that Vanzetti was over talking with him that his boat was towed by Corl.

Thus, on his own fabrication of testimony, Mr. Katzmann accused the fisherman's wife of perjury and seeking to suborn perjury.

The testimony of the witnesses with respect to the Corl incident may have failed to prove with certainty that it happened on April 15, but there can be little doubt that it did take place in the same week. It occurred during the period when Corl was painting his boat. This job must have been finished when the boat was put into the water at the end of the week. If it is conceivable that Vanzetti left Plymouth on Thursday, the fifteenth, to commit murder and robbery in South Braintree, it is hard to visualize him "shooting the breeze" on the Plymouth beach with the fisherman Corl a day or two before or after the crime. The idea is comparable to the one (voiced even by Governor Fuller in 1927) that Vanzetti was delivering eels in Plymouth on the days immediately preceding Christmas in 1919 but suspended his deliveries just long enough to attempt highway robbery in Bridgewater, twenty-odd miles away. The Sacco-Vanzetti case is replete with such bizarre concepts accredited by the prosecution.

21.

Alibi of Sacco

The Oversized Picture and the Banchetto

On April 15, 1920, at about noon, the Italian newspapermen of Boston gave a *banchetto* to honor Commander James T. Williams, Jr., the editor (from 1912 to 1925) of the *Boston Evening Transcript*. Williams had just been decorated with the Order of the Crown by the king of Italy for the attitude of his newspaper in favor of Italy during the First World War.[1] The luncheon took place at the Convent of the Franciscan Fathers on North Bennet Street in the midst of the Italian settlement in Boston's "North End." It began just three hours before the murders and robbery in South Braintree. There was no connection between the two events, yet the *banchetto* later developed into a pivotal feature of Sacco's alibi. Although Sacco himself did not attend the affair, it was an event by which witnesses at the trial were able to fix his presence in Boston at a time when the murders were being committed many miles away. Later, in the summer of 1927, it acquired new significance. Quite unexpectedly, it then exposed the slipshod methods of the Governor's Advisory Committee and reduced to an absurdity its claim to objectivity.

Sacco's alibi actually began with the receipt of a black-bordered letter on March 23 or 24 from his brother Sabeno in Italy. It carried the news that his mother had died on March 7, 1920.[2] The letter itself became Exhibit S in the record.[3] Attached to the letter on another page was a personal message from his sister.[4]

The letter arrived at his home about eleven o'clock, but Mrs. Sacco did not let him read it until he had finished his dinner (lunch). She did not want to disturb him.[5] The news upset him so much that he became "disabled" and was unable to work the rest of the day.[6] Sacco went back to the factory, but returned in half an hour after a talk with George T. Kelley, his superintendent. Mr. Kelley testified that Sacco was so overcome that he did not work.[7] Sacco also showed the black-bordered letter to Michael F. Kelley, George's father and the owner of the 3–K shoe factory. He told him that his mother had died.[8] Mr. Kelley did not read the whole letter.

Prior to his mother's death, Sacco had been hoping to visit his home in Italy. This was confirmed by Mrs. Sacco.[9]

George Kelley also quoted Sacco to this effect:

He told me that his mother had died, and that he was very sorry to think that he wasn't at home when she died, that they had wanted him to come home previous to her death and that he thought now that as long as he had an opportunity, that he would go home while his father was still alive and on that ac-

---

[1] Vol. II, 2025.   [2] Vol. II, 1964.   [3] Vol. II, 1976.   [4] Vol. II, 2047.
[5] Vol. II, 2053.   [6] Vol. II, 1976.   [7] Vol. I, 859.   [8] Vol. II, 1607.
[9] Vol. II, 2067–2068.

count that was the reason that he gave me for going home at that particular time that he had tried to make arrangements for, to see his father while he was alive.[10]

Shortly after receiving Sabeno's letter, Sacco received a letter from his father which apparently precipitated his plans to make the trip to Italy. Sacco had already made inquiries concerning getting a passport about the middle or last of March.[11] He learned then that he would need a photograph.

George Kelley, called as a government witness, testified that on or about Monday or Tuesday (April 12 and 13 respectively) Sacco spoke to him about taking a day off as follows:

He said he would like to have one day off that week to go in to see the consul in regard to passports. I told him at that time that if he was caught up he may have the day off. At that time, there was no mention of the day. It went along about Wednesday, and he came to me and said he was going in tomorrow. That would be Thursday, and if possible, would be back again to his work Thursday, to which I said, "Very well." Now, Friday morning, I went to him —
Q. (By Mr. McAnarney) Just a minute, please. A. Yes, sir.
Q. You say he did not work Thursday? A. He did not work Thursday, no, sir.
Q. Did he come back any time during the day? A. No, sir, not at the factory.
Q. That is what I mean. A. Yes. Do you want me to go about Friday?
Q. Yes. A. Then Friday morning I went to him early and asked him how he got along and he told me that he was trying to get back Thursday but on account of the crowd that was there waiting for passports, it was impossible for him to come out so he could get up to work Thursday afternoon. I said, "All right," and there was nothing more then said about why he was not to work or anything about it. I took the excuse as being all right.
Q. Now, was he away from his work any other day or any part of a day that week? A. No, sir.
Q. Now, about Tuesday, did he work all day Tuesday? A. You mean the previous Tuesday?
Q. Yes. I mean, that would be the 13th. A. Oh, he was there every day. Now, whether or not he went out in the afternoon, say three or four o'clock, that I couldn't say, but he was to work every day.[12]

Mr. Kelley also stated the following in cross-examination:

Q. (By Mr. McAnarney) Now, recalling to your mind, did not Sacco tell you that he wouldn't take the day off until he got this man [a new edge trimmer "broken in" by Sacco] so he could do the work? A. I couldn't say as to that, no. The understanding was that the work would be caught up or he would not go.

10 Vol. I, 859.   11 Vol. II, 1823.   12 Vol. I, 853.

Q. I see. A. And when it was caught up, I was willing that he should go.

Q. And that was the fact and that was what did take place, wasn't it? A. Yes.

Q. When he got the work caught up, he took that day? A. Yes.[13]

Mr. Kelley's testimony is interesting in view of the prosecution's claim that Sacco really took the time off to commit a couple of murders and a payroll robbery. From this supposition it would follow that the South Braintree crime, involving the execution of detailed and coordinated plans, the synchronized use of two automobiles and cooperation among at least six confederates was, as it were, held in abeyance until Mr. Kelley gave Sacco permission to suspend his steady work for a day — provided he was at his bench in the 3–K factory early the next morning. As difficult as it is for reason to accept this concept, it becomes even more so when one realizes that further integration of the time factors would have been required. The day off had to fall on Thursday, April 15, the only day in the week when the Slater and Morrill payroll would be carried down Pearl Street. Indeed, but for this presumed perfect timing, there would never have been a Sacco-Vanzetti case.

Sacco testified that on April 15 he went to Boston for the purpose he had stated to Mr. Kelley. His testimony about his doings on that day follows:

Q. (By Mr. Moore) Mr. Sacco, where were you on April 15th, Mr. Sacco? A. I was in Boston.

Q. What hour that day? Or, first, I will ask you what you went to Boston for? A. To get my passport.

Q. Now, at any previous time before that time, had you made any effort to get a passport? A. Yes, I did.

Q. How long before? A. Sometime in the middle of March, I should say the middle or last of March.

MR. KATZMANN. I don't get it.

THE WITNESS. I should say the middle or last of March.

Q. Did you at that time, — what occurred, did you make an application for a passport?

MR. KATZMANN. One moment, if your Honor please. I object. Too leading.

Q. Did you make an application for a passport? A. I went to see why I could not get my passport, what way I could get it. You know, I did not know what way I could get information.

Q. Now, on April 15th, what did you go into Boston for? A. To get my passport.

Q. What time did you leave Stoughton that day? A. I leave Stoughton on the 8:56 train.

[13] Vol. I, 869.

Q. Are you absolutely sure of that hour or about that hour or what? A. I am sure.

Q. And went into Boston? A. Yes, sir.

Q. And where did you go on arrival in Boston? A. I left the South Station. I went in the North End. I went buy a paper, *La Notizia*.

Q. You went to the North End? A. Yes.

Q. Did you get a paper? A. Yes.

Q. Where did you get it? A. Prince Street.

Q. Prince Street? A. Yes.

Q. Near where? A. Between Hanover and Prince, between Hanover and North Square. I suppose Hanover like that, Prince cross like that, and North Square right back, — sort of finish in North Square, passed through Hanover.

Q. What did you do then? A. Oh, I stayed over there about fifteen minutes, I guess. I read a little. So then I take a walk, and I went on Hanover Street.

Q. What else did you do that forenoon?

MR. KATZMANN. Mr. Moore, we would like to hear what this witness is saying.

MR. MOORE. (To the witness) Speak up so that everybody can hear clearly what you say.

MR. KATZMANN. You asked him how long he remained after buying the paper. A. About fifteen minutes. I don't know exactly.

Q. Suppose you speak as though you were talking to me. A. All right.

Q. What did you do then? A. I turned a corner on Hanover Street.

Q. Where did you go? A. I started to walk, and I met a friend.

Q. Do you know who that was? A. Sure.

Q. A. Monello, — Angelo Monello.

Q. And did you have a talk with him? A. Yes.

Q. Then where did you go? A. We walked until Washington Street, and I go back again, so I stopped in the stores and been looking at a straw hat, some suits, — a price, you know. Then I go back. I have my mind to go in the afternoon and get my passport. I say probably I go to get my dinner first, so I have a little time and I go there, so I went over to Boni's restaurant.

Q. And who did you see there? A. I met Mr. — Professor Guadenagi [*sic*].

Q. Who else, if any one? A. That is the first one I met, before I go into the restaurant.

MR. KATZMANN. Mr. Moore, we cannot hear this witness.

MR. MOORE. Keep your voice up, Mr. Sacco.

Q. Who did you meet outside of the restaurant? A. Professor Guadenagi.

Q. Any one else after going in?

THE COURT. How do you spell that name, please?

THE WITNESS. It is so hard. I could write it.

Q. Now, do you remember who else you met there, if any one? A. Yes. Mr. Williams.

Q. Any one else? A. Mr. Bosco.

Q. Is there any one else? Well, how long were you in the restaurant? A. I should say about an hour and fifteen minutes, — fifteen or twenty minutes.

Q. Do you know about what time you left there? A. Yes.

Q. And then where did you go? At what hour did you leave there? A. Twenty minutes past one; twenty minutes past one.

Q. Where did you go then? A. I went right straight to the consul's, — Italian consul.

Q. About what hour, if you know, Mr. Sacco, did you get to the Italian consul? A. It was about two o'clock.

Q. And what occurred on your going into the consulate? Who did you talk with there and what happened? A. I went in and meet in the office, and I got near the, — when I went in the office there is a bank just like this (indicating). I went in and a man came around.

Q. You went up to the railing? A. Yes.

Q. And then a gentleman the other side came up to his side of the railing? A. Yes.

Q. Then you talked together? A. Yes.

Q. Now, what did you say and what did he say? A. I said, "I like to get my passport for my whole family." He asked me, — he said, "You bring the picture?" I said, "Yes," so I gave it to him, see, a big picture. He says, "Well, I am sorry. This picture is too big." "Well," I says, "can you cut, and make him small?" "No," he said, "the picture we cannot use, because it goes too big." I says, "Can you cut?" He says, "No, no use, because got to make a photograph just for the purpose for the passport, small, very small," — so I did.

Q. Now, I call your attention to the photograph marked "B" attached to the depositions in this case.

MR. MOORE. You gentlemen have seen this, I believe.

MR. KATZMANN. Yes.

Q. Is that a duplicate of the photograph that you showed the gentleman there that day? A. Yes, sir.

MR. MOORE. (Showing the picture to the jury) I imagine you gentlemen have all seen this.

Q. How long were you in the consulate, to your best recollection? A. Ten or fifteen minutes, I should say, about ten minutes.

Q. Then what did you do? A. I go back to buy my stuff, groceries, so before I got my groceries, I went to get coffee in a coffee store in the North End near the Boni restaurant.

Q. About what time did you get to the cafe, or coffee house? A. It was a little before three o'clock.

Q. How long were you in there, if you remember? A. I don't remember certain what time I remained there.

Q. About? A. About twenty minutes, — twenty.

Q. Twenty minutes. And did you see any one while you were there? A. Yes.

Q. Who? A. Professor Guadenagi.

Q. Any one else, if you know? A. Yes. Professor Dentamore.

Q. Then where did you go? A. I went to buy grocery.

Q. Do you remember where? A. Yes. I do not remember the name of the store, but I remember the street, the same street in the North End, about fifteen minutes, — about fifty steps from, well, I should say about one hundred steps from the cafe.

Q. From the cafe? A. Yes.

Q. And on what street, on the North Square there?

MR. KATZMANN. One moment.

A. North End.

MR. KATZMANN. Wait a minute.

THE COURT. Leading.

Q. What street was it on? A. North End.

Q. How long were you there? A. I should say a half hour, pretty near.

Q. Was there anything else you did? A. I am not sure, but twenty or twenty-five minutes, anyway.

Q. What did you do from there? Where did you go? A. Home.

Q. You mean to Stoughton? A. Yes.

Q. Do you know about what hour you left for Stoughton that night, that afternoon? A. I should say about twelve minutes past four.

Q. And you went immediately back to Stoughton and then to your home? A. Yes.

MR. KATZMANN. One moment, if your Honor please.

THE COURT. Leading.

Q. What did you do on arrival at Stoughton?

MR. KATZMANN. One moment. I object.

Q. Did you take a train to Stoughton? A. Yes.

Q. All right. What did you do when you got there? A. I went and buy elixir for physic.

Q. Then what did you do? A. I went home, walking home.

Q. Do you know about what time you got there? A. Around six o'clock, I should say. I don't remember exactly, but around six o'clock, anyway.

Q. Now, that afternoon or that day in Boston, do you remember any other particular thing or special thing that occurred during this morning or afternoon? A. In the afternoon, yes.

Q. What? A. I met Afa and pay him $15 for bill.

Q. Are you sure about any of these spellings, or are you just spelling by your ear? A. I know him sure. I think Afa is the way you spell it. I don't know for sure.

Q. At any time, Mr. Sacco, on April 15, 1920, were you at South Braintree, Massachusetts? A. No, sir. What do you mean, working?

Q. Doing anything? A. Any day?

Q. No. Were you at any time, on April 15, 1920, at South Braintree? A. No, sir.

Q. You have heard certain testimony placing you in the railroad station at South Braintree during the hours about noon hour of that day? A. Never.

Q. Is that statement false or true? A. True.

MR. KATZMANN. One moment, if your Honor please.

Q. Were you in that station at any time that day? A. South Braintree station? No, sir.

Q. You have also heard certain testimony referring to you as being at or near the corner of Pearl and Hancock Street sometime around about the noon hour of that day leaning up against a window there. At any time, either at that hour or any other hour — A. Never.

Q. — on April 15th, were you in South Braintree? A. No, sir.[14]

14 Vol. II, 1823–1827.

Mr. Katzmann's cross-examination of Sacco after he gave the foregoing testimony followed a pattern similar to the type of cross-examination that he gave Vanzetti after he had told of his movements on April 15, 1920. It was chiefly concerned with Sacco's lies or misstatements made on May 6, 1920, when questioned by Mr. Katzmann in the Brockton police station. During part of the examination Sacco called for an interpreter, because of dissatisfaction with Joseph Ross's translating. (By this time, Ross was now supplemented by Felix Forte, Esq., assisting the defense, and by a third interpreter, Mr. Minimi.) Sacco readily admitted that many of his earlier answers were untrue. He had stated that on April 16 he had read about the South Braintree crime in the newspaper and had discussed the affair with fellow workmen. Katzmann had questioned him as to whether he had worked all day on the day before. To this question Sacco had given answers that seemed to fluctuate between saying that he did not remember, or that he was sure that he had worked the whole day, or half a day. At the Dedham trial, he explained that he simply did not remember when asked on May 6, 1920,[15] and that if he said he had worked it was because he was not sure.[16] He also explained to Mr. Katzmann: "There was not interest to me very close to find out the date I have been out." Mr. Katzmann commented:

Q. After thirty people, strangers, had looked at you? A. No, because I did not think it was going on.[17]
Q. After I had asked you if you ever worked in Braintree? A. What of it?
Q. After I had asked if you ever tried to get work in Braintree? What do you say to that, Mr. Sacco? A. I don't say no fault.
Q. After I asked you if you knew Berardelli or who Berardelli was, did you see anything about that? A. Well, yes, I could see.
Q. After I asked, you could see then, couldn't you? A. Yes.
Q. That was before I asked if you knew something had happened in Braintree the month before I was talking with you? A. I did not remember when you mentioned the name Berardelli.[18]

Although Mr. Katzmann's hints as to the purpose of his questions were somewhat closer to the South Braintree affair than his cross-examination of Vanzetti, he did not at any time make it clear, but left it to the prisoner to figure it out. Sacco's mind had already been set in a different direction by Chief Stewart's prior inquiries into his radical affiliations.

On redirect examination, Mr. Moore asked Sacco:

[15] Vol. II, 1948.   [16] Vol. II, 1948.   [17] Vol. II, 1948.   [18] Vol. II, 1948–1949.

Q. Mr. Sacco, in the discussion with Mr. Katzmann, in the Brockton police station, was there at any time that Mr. Katzmann told you fully and definitely that you were being held on suspicion or on charge of being involved in the South Braintree murder? A. Never. You mean on the 6th day of May?

Q. Yes, on the 6th day of May. A. Never.[19]

Nor did Mr. Katzmann ever offer anything to contradict Sacco's flat statement that he was not told why he was being held or questioned.

Mr. Katzmann had mentioned the fact that Sacco had denied working in South Braintree. At the trial, Sacco had testified that he had worked there briefly under his mother's maiden name, Mosmacotelli.[20] He gave this explanation of his denial:

Q. (By Mr. Moore) Why did you tell Mr. Katzmann at Brockton that you had not worked at South Braintree? A. Because, if I give Mr. Katzmann my name, Nicola Sacco, he would go to South Braintree and not find my name. Then, of course, Mr. Katzmann would come back and he would say to me, "Why you told me a lie," and after I would have to tell him the reason. I would have to tell him that my name was Nicola Sacco, Nicola Mosmacotelli, because I was a slacker. Well, I did not want to get arrested in order to be a slacker.

Q. Mr. Sacco, what was the actual — what is your best recollection, the actual number of days you worked at Rice and Hutchins? A. My best that I could tell, my best that I could tell, I don't think there was two weeks that I worked there. The most, I think, was eight, nine or ten days, eight or nine days.

Q. What month or year was that? A. The middle of October, I think the middle of October, 1917.[21]

At one stage of the cross-examination, Mr. McAnarney protested Mr. Katzmann's reiteration that Sacco had intentionally lied about working on April 15. Mr. McAnarney's protest was upheld.[22]

Previously, Sacco had also tried to explain the distinction between an intentional falsehood and a statement that was not true:

Q. (By Mr. Katzmann) And do you remember this question and this answer:
"Q. Worked all day?"
That is the question. The answer:
"A. Yes, sir."
Did you say that to me at Brockton? A. I don't remember if I said it. If I said it, that wasn't true. I told a lie.

Q. And you now claim that that day you were at the consul's office, don't you? A. On the 15th of April?

Q. Yes. A. Yes, sir.

[19] Vol. II, 1964.   [20] Vol. II, 1821.   [21] Vol. II, 1968–1969.   [22] Vol. II, 1954.

Q. Was there any reason why you should have told me a falsehood about that? A. *No reason other than that I did not remember.*

Q. Is a failure to remember a lie, Mr. Sacco?

MR. KATZMANN. He has just used the word "lie." He said, "I lied to you about that." I am asking him now, "Is a failure to remember a lie?" Use his word.

A. *I did not tell you a lie. I did not tell it in bad faith.* [Emphasis added.][23]

Under conditions which would have assured a considered reply to Katzmann's 1920 questions and against a different background of the entire case, a statement by Sacco that he believed he had worked on April 15 might have had some significance. Even so, however, the inference that such an answer was an intentional cover-up for murder would have involved the assumption that Sacco was a fool, since he knew that a mere telephone call to Mr. Kelley would have revealed its falsity. As we have seen, Sacco was far from being a fool. Also, as a matter of police experience, a criminal, conscious of having committed murder and robbery at a particular time, would most likely have been ready with a plausible and tenable story to explain his whereabouts on the day of the crime.

If we now turn back to the account of Sacco's movements on April 15, as told by him on the witness stand at Dedham, we find a surprising amount of credible confirmation by a variety of witnesses. In order to disbelieve it, we must necessarily assume that a number of ostensibly honorable people concocted several false stories to secure the acquittal of a suspected murderer. Some of these witnesses did not even know Sacco. It is not difficult, however, to understand the jury making such an improbable assumption. It was subjected to the spell of the Dedham courtroom atmosphere and to Mr. Katzmann's persuasive innuendos. However, there were others later who were not under such influences. They also saw Sacco's alibi witnesses as a bunch of criminal-protecting perjurers. This requires special explanations. First, however, let us see who these witnesses were and what they said. As an incidental dividend, they give us a composite picture of Sacco's sociable personality.

If we follow Sacco's account of his Boston trip, we learn that the first person he mentioned was one Angelo Monello. They walked and talked.

Angelo Monello, called by the defense, testified that he had been a contractor for thirteen years and resided in Roxbury (Boston). He said he had first met Sacco a couple of months prior to his arrest at Maverick Square

[23] Vol. II, 1950–1951.

Hall in East Boston. There were dramatic people there at the time. Monello was an amateur actor himself.[24] Monello said he saw Sacco on April 15, 1920, at about eleven o'clock near the corner of Washington and Hanover streets. This is the reason he gave for remembering that it was April 15:

Q. (By Mr. Callahan) How do you fix it was the 15th of April last year you met him at Hanover Street? A. How I fix it?
Q. Yes. A. Of course, you know the next Sunday, April 18th, was a play by a great artist from New York. His name is Mimi Aguglia.
Q. What nationality, do you say? A. Italian.
Q. An Italian artist? A. Yes. One of the greatest artists of the world.
Q. And you were going to say where the play was? A. The play at Tremont Theatre, *Madame X*.
Q. Is that the name of the play? A. Yes.
MR. KATZMANN. *Madame X*.
Q. Did you go to the play? A. Yes.
Q. Did you talk with Sacco about the play? A. Yes, I just —
MR. KATZMANN. One moment, one moment.
THE COURT. Did you have any conversation with him about the play?
THE WITNESS. Yes.[25]

On redirect examination, Mr. Monello added that his conversation with Sacco also included talk about a passport and about the consul's office.

Monello never saw Sacco again after the chance meeting on Hanover Street until he saw him in the courtroom.

On cross-examination, Mr. Katzmann was unable to discredit Monello's testimony except by the tactics with which we are now quite familiar. He asked the witness whom he had talked with about the play on about a dozen dates, chosen at random. Monello responded, simply, "I do not remember." [26]

The next person mentioned by Sacco was Professor Guadenagi (sometimes spelled Guadagni).

Felice Guadenagi testified that he had lived in Boston for seven years and that his business was "journalist and literature." (He was a graduate of the Institution of Naples and had been a professor of Italian and Latin). He met Sacco in front of Boni's restaurant in North Square at half past eleven on April 15, 1920. They went into the restaurant to have dinner together. In the restaurant he introduced Sacco to two of his friends, Albert

---

[24] So also were Sacco and Rosina in Stoughton.
[25] Vol. II, 1668–1669.   [26] Vol. II, 1669–1670.

Bosco[27] and John D. Williams[28] (no connection with James T. Williams, Jr., editor of the *Boston Evening Transcript*). They left Boni's at about half past one and separated outside on the square. Later that day he met Sacco again about three o'clock at Joe Giordano's coffeehouse.[29]

Mr. Guadenagi placed the date when he met Sacco in Boston as April 15 for the following reason:

Q. (By Mr. McAnarney) Now, how is it, Mr. Guadenagi, that you say that you saw him on the 15th day of April; how do you know that? A. I first recalled that it was the 15th, because in that I had some discussion about a banquet which was given to Mr. Williams, the editor of the *Boston Transcript*, and I had some discussion about that banquet with Bosco first and Professor Dentamore afterwards in the coffee house. I was invited to that banquet.
Q. When was the banquet to be? A. The night of the 15th.[30]

It was Guadenagi's mention of the banquet to Mr. Williams that later found its way into the proceedings of the Governor's Advisory Committee.

Mr. Guadenagi also testified that he had had a conversation with Sacco "about his going to Italy" and about his passport. At the coffeehouse later he talked with Sacco again about his passport.[31]

Mr. Guadenagi testified further on direct that he saw Sacco next at the police station in Brockton. Following a talk he had with Mrs. Sacco, he made some investigation at the Italian consulate four or five days after Sacco's arrest. He talked with the acting consul, the vice consul and a member of the staff named Andrower. He discussed with Andrower what occurred at the Consulate on April 15.

On cross-examination, Guadenagi stated that he was called by the title "Professor" and that he was a member of the Defense Committee. In talking with Andrower at the consulate he first showed a photograph of Sacco. Prior to April 15, he had met Sacco in a hall in East Boston where weekly meetings were held. He last saw Sacco, prior to April 15, in March, but could not fix the date because "I have nothing of importance on that date." He agreed with Mr. Katzmann that April 15 was the only date he could remember and that this did not become important to him until after Sacco was arrested.[32]

Albert Bosco was one of Guadenagi's friends who was introduced to

[27] Vol. II, 1662.   [28] Vol. II, 1645.   [29] Vol. II, 1993.
[30] Vol. II, 1993. Mr. Guadenagi's recollection was in error — the banquet was at noon, not at night!   [31] Vol. II, 1994–1995.   [32] Vol. II, 1997.

Sacco in Boni's restaurant. He testified that he was one of the editors of *La Notizia*, the leading Italian daily newspaper in Boston, with a circulation of about twenty thousand. He lived in East Boston. Testifying through an interpreter, Bosco said that he had been dining in Boni's restaurant when Sacco and Professor Guadenagi came in. When Guadenagi introduced Sacco, he said, "This is the man that is going to Italy." There was some conversation about passports and the consul's office. This was the first time he met Sacco. The next occasion was on the morning he was testifying. After the witness read about the shooting at South Braintree and saw pictures published in the papers, he changed his mind with reference to the date on which he met Sacco. He fixed the date as follows:

Q. (By Mr. McAnarney) Was there anything that transpired on the day of your meeting Sacco that enabled you to in any way to check that date up? A. Yes. sir.
Q. What was it? A. Well, from the conversation that I had with Mr. Guadenagi that we were giving a banquet to the director of, — Mr. Williams.
Q. Who is Mr. Williams? A. He is the director of the *Transcript*.
Q. *Boston Transcript?* A. Yes, sir, the *Boston Transcript*.
Q. What were you giving to him? A. A banquet.
Q. When was that banquet held? A. The evening of the 15th.
Q. Well, how do you know that it was the 15th day of April that you saw Sacco? A. When I saw the picture in the paper and Mr. Guadenagi spoke to me about it. *I went and looked back to the paper and I discovered that that was the evening of the banquet.*
MR. JEREMIAH MCANARNEY. That is all. [Emphasis added.][33]

On cross-examination, Mr. Katzmann brought out that for about a year the witness had been eating at Boni's restaurant and used to meet Guadenagi there frequently. Mr. Bosco also stated that the Defense Committee had had an office upstairs in the building where *La Notizia* was located. The witness himself had never been in the Defense Committee's rooms or attended any of its meetings.[34] He said he thought Guadenagi was a member of the Defense Committee, but had seen him very few times in the building since the previous September. Guadenagi was an employee of the *Gazzetta del Massachusetts*.[35]

[33] Vol. II, 1663–1664. Mr. Bosco was also mistaken in stating that the banquet was in the evening, instead of at noon.
[34] He was not a member of the Defense Committee.
[35] A weekly Italian newspaper of extremely conservative outlook.

John D. Williams was Guadenagi's other friend whom he said he introduced to Sacco in Boni's restaurant. Williams was an advertising agent
specializing in obtaining advertising in foreign language newspapers. He
said he entered the restaurant between 1:15 and 1:30 P.M. on April 15,
1920, and saw Professor Gaudenagi sitting at a table with a stranger, who
was introduced to him as Mr. Sacco.[36] They had finished dinner, but remained for about fifteen or twenty minutes. There was some talk about
passports. Williams never saw Sacco again until "just now."

Early in May (1920) his attention was called to Sacco's arrest by Felicani,[37] a compositor on the Italian paper *La Notizia*. This was the first he
knew of the arrest. Felicani showed him newspapers and pictures. Because
Mr. Katzmann in cross-examination had asked about Felicani calling Mr.
Williams's attention to April 15, Judge Thayer allowed Mr. McAnarney to
inquire further:

Q. (By Mr. McAnarney) Now, Mr. Williams, kindly tell us what conversa-
tion did take place between you and Felicani. A. I can only give it in substance.
Q. In substance, I mean. A. He asked me if I recollected taking dinner with
Professor Guadenagi and Sacco and I said "yes." He said, "Do you know that is
the date that the occurrence is said to have taken place in Braintree or South
Braintree?" I said, "I did not know that." "Well," he says, "it is. Do you recol-
lect the time?" I told him. "Well," he said, "that fixes Sacco."
Q. What did you tell him? A. I told him between 1:15 and 1:30, around
about.
Q. Of what date? A. April 15. I took pains to find out about it and I saw him
again afterwards. He says, "Then that fixes Mr. Sacco in Boston instead of
South Braintree." I said, "All right, so it does."

A few questions thereafter his testimony added the following, which perhaps indicates that Mr. Williams was trying to be exact:

Q. I ask you this question: if when he was speaking about, you and Felicani
speaking about the day he was in there, you and he mentioned the fact of his
going to the Consul's office? A. I mentioned that is what they had told me he
was going to do.[38]

Mr. Williams had testified that he had checked his memory by looking at
his advertising order book,[39] but he did not have it with him when he testi-

---

[36] Vol. II, 1645.
[37] Aldino Felicani, treasurer of the Sacco-Vanzetti Defense Committee.
[38] Vol. II, 1656–1657.   [39] Vol. II, 1646.

fied. He did bring with him a copy of an advertisement for help by the Washington Knitting Mills, bearing his "O.K.," which he said he obtained on April 15, 1920. In cross-examination, the following questions and answers occurred:

Q. (By Mr. Katzmann) Is there any connection in your mind between the Washington Knitting Company, Knitting Mills "ad," and the defendant Nicola Sacco? A. You mean that they have any relationship to each other?
Q. Yes. A. None whatever that I know of.
Q. There was no mental process through which you went to connect them? A. Not at all.[40]

The foregoing answers seemed to impair the weight of Mr. Williams's testimony. On redirect, however, Mr. McAnarney brought out that Mr. Williams had understood Mr. Katzmann's questions to mean "whether Mr. Nicola Sacco had any connection with the Washington Knitting Mills." After Mr. McAnarney explained what Mr. Katzmann really meant, the following cleared up the previous testimony:

Q. How does the fact of that order [from Washington Knitting Mills] place you with Nicola Sacco on April 15th, and what it is that enables you to place Nicola Sacco on the 15th of April? A. That order there ran on the dates 17th, 18th, and 19th, and it would be secured for running the latter part of the week, and Sunday, Monday, and the fact that Thursday was the day regularly on which I went in the North End, and the fact I secured this order and the fact I met this young man down there, and the fact that he was said to be going for his passports; all of these things brought a sequence of events back to me, and I recalled the incident very easily.[41]

Previously, on direct examination, Mr. Williams had told why he knew he had taken the order on Thursday, April 15. During the inquiry, he had blurted out one of those inadmissible answers that often tell more than a properly responsive reply. Here it is:

Q. So you took an order to run the 17th, 18th and 19th of April 1920? A. Yes, sir.
Q. Now, I believe you have informed us that it was Thursdays that you made that route once a week? A. Yes.
Q. How do you know this is April 15th and not April 8th? A. *Why, no employment manager could tell over a week ahead what his wants would be in the help wanted line. We could not possibly get them to advertise a week before.*

40 Vol. II, 1655.   41 Vol. II, 1655.

MR. KATZMANN. I ask that be stricken out, if your Honor please. [Emphasis added.][42]

Mr. Williams also recalled that on the same day he "took the dinner there," he made a visit to the office of a Dr. Gibbs, who was treating him for asthma. He stated on cross-examination that during March, April and May 1920 he visited Dr. Gibbs, on an average, once a week, "after I had an attack." Asked when he visited Dr. Gibbs before and after April 15, he stated that he could not recollect "off hand" without consulting the doctor's records. When Mr. Katzmann said, "I am consulting your memory," Mr. Williams replied, "I can't tell you."

Dr. Howard A. Gibbs then testified that he had treated Mr. Williams for two or three different ailments. Turning to his card records to refresh his recollection, he stated that he had treated him one day in April 1920, recorded as April 15, but on no other day that April. On cross-examination, he stated that he had also treated Mr. Williams on four days in March, one day in May and three in June. The treatment on April 15 was for asthma. Mr. Williams had seen Dr. Gibbs's records on one occasion in "April or May of this year." [43]

Sacco had stated that at about one twenty he went to the Italian consulate. The large photograph that he had said he carried with him had been taken by a Brockton photographer named Neville. Nicola, Rose and their son Dante had gone to Brockton late in February (1920) to have their picture taken. He wanted it "to send to my mother because she is very sick." It arrived in March. "Probably my mother is died when I have the photograph all ready to send; she was dead already, probably." [44] The photograph was introduced as an exhibit.[45]

Sacco's visit to the consulate was confirmed by Guiseppe Andrower, formerly a clerk in the Italian consulate. In a deposition taken in Rome on April 13, 1921, he stated that in April 1920 he was on the staff of the Italian consulate in Boston, charged with the routine duty of advising or interviewing of people who desired to procure passports for Italy.

Mr. Andrower stated that when Professor Guadagni (Guadenagi) asked him whether he remembered that Mr. Sacco had applied for a passport on April 15, 1920, he answered that he did not remember who Mr. Sacco was. On being shown a group photograph, he then recalled seeing the photograph and the man shown in the group. The man had called at his office on

[42] Vol. II, 1647–1648.   [43] Vol. II, 1662.   [44] Vol. II, 1934.   [45] Vol. II, 1976.

April 15 about securing a passport for himself and his family. A copy of the photograph was annexed to the deposition marked B.

Since interrogatories in a deposition are necessarily (and endlessly) repetitive, I have omitted them. I have, however, set out Andrower's responses in full:

I first saw the photograph marked "B" on April 15, 1920, in the office of the Royal Italian Consulate at Boston, Massachusetts. . . . Yes, I know the name of the man whose likeness appears on the photograph. . . . It was on Thursday, April 15, 1920, at about two or quarter past two in the afternoon that I saw the photograph marked "B." . . . The photograph marked "B" was first exhibited to me by Mr. Sacco. . . . Early in April Mr. Sacco came to the Royal Italian Consulate for information how to get a passport for Italy. I gave him the information and told him that he should bring two photographs, one to be attached to the passport and the other for the records of the office. He then left and on April 15, 1920, as I have stated before, he returned with a photograph the same as exhibit "B." I told him that this photograph was too large for use on a *foglio di via* or an Italian passport. He left saying that he would return with smaller photographs but I never saw him again. . . . April 15, 1920, was a very quiet day in the Royal Italian Consulate and since such a large photograph had never been before presented for use on a passport I took it in and showed it to the Secretary of the Consulate. We laughed and talked over the incident. I remember observing the date in the office of the Secretary on a large pad calendar while we were discussing the photograph. The hour was around two or a quarter after two as I remember about a half an hour later I locked the door of the office for the day. . . . This day made a special impression upon me as there was much less business than on the previous and following days. There were only about thirty or forty people in the office applying for passports that day and we usually had about two hundred. . . . Mr. Sacco objected to going to the expense of having other photographs made and asked if I could not cut the pictures down to suit the forms. I told him this was not possible because the space covered by the persons in the group was too large for use. He then left without any further discussion in the matter. . . . I told him that the photograph was too large to be used on a passport or a *foglio di via*.[46]

It does not appear that the prosecution propounded any counterinterrogatories to Mr. Andrower.

Following Mr. Andrower's advice, Sacco had a proper passport photograph taken by Edward Maertens of Stoughton[47] and on May 4, 1920, obtained from the consulate a *foglio di via* — a less expensive type of passport used by Italians returning to Italy.[48]

Sacco had said that after leaving the consulate he "went to get coffee in a

46 Vol. II, 2266b–2266d.   47 Vol. II, 1979–1980. Marked Exhibit 42, 1979 and 2091.
48 Vol. II, 1857.

coffee store . . . near the Boni restaurant." This was the cafe referred to by Professor Guadenagi as Joe Giordano's coffeehouse. He had mentioned meeting there a Professor Dentamore and, for a second time, Professor Guadenagi.

The next witness, Antonio Dentamore, at the time he testified was in charge of foreign exchange at the Haymarket National Bank. His testimony confirmed both Sacco and Guadenagi. He was the only witness who actually attended the banquet to Editor Williams. He also was the only witness who stated the correct hour, namely, noontime. Dentamore was a "solid citizen" and Mr. Katzmann was unable to impeach him with his usual innuendos suggesting some sort of bias in favor of Sacco. (It later came out before the Governor's Advisory Committee that he was a Catholic priest.) His testimony was an extraordinarily strong link in Sacco's alibi.

Unable to shake Mr. Dentamore's direct testimony that the banquet was held at noon, Mr. Katzmann resorted again to his much-used device of "memory testing." The business of asking the witness to recall irrelevancies must have struck Mr. Dentamore as absurd, since shortly after it started he responded rather relevantly, "I am not a fortune teller." However, this sort of cross-examination must have had some effect on the jury, because had they believed Dentamore, they would have been compelled to find Sacco not guilty.

Mr. Katzmann's cross-examination as to dates proved unproductive. He therefore then attempted to establish some kind of sympathetic relation between Sacco and Dentamore:

Q. You say that banquet to Mr. Williams was at noon time on the 15th? A. Noontime.

Q. You did not hear Guadenagi testify, did you? A. No.

Q. Are you connected with the Italian Naturalization Club in Maverick Square, East Boston? A. No.

Q. Are you connected with the Defense Committee? A. No.

Q. Were you in the Boni restaurant at noontime — A. No.

Q. — of the 15th of April? A. No.

Q. Do you ever eat in the Boni restaurant? A. No.

Q. Have you never eaten there? A. Never? Sometimes.

Q. And when is the last time you ate there? A. Oh, about a year ago.

Q. About a year ago. Where did you eat twenty-two days ago to-day, the noon lunch hour? A. Well, I am practically having my lunch hour at home, because I live near the bank.

Q. I am asking you where you had your lunch twenty-two days ago to-day? A. I can't say now.

Q. Do you have your lunch every day at home? A. Yes, practically.
Q. What? A. Practically.
Q. I asked you if every day you had lunch at home? A. Not every day.
Q. Not every day. Then you can't tell me where you had it twenty-two days ago to-day? A. It is very seldom when I don't eat —
Q. No. Can you tell me where you had your lunch twenty-two days ago to-day? A. No.
Q. What time was that banquet due to start? A. Twelve o'clock.
Q. Twelve o'clock. How long did it last? A. Oh, a couple of hours.
Q. Two hours. Got through at two o'clock? A. Not exactly.
Q. Well about? A. About two.
Q. When was the first time that day you saw Guadenagi? A. Just about quarter of three.
Q. Down in the Giordani coffee house? A. In the Giordani coffee house.
MR. KATZMANN. That is all. [Emphasis added.] [49]

Mr. McAnarney and Mr. Moore both sought to bring out from Mr. Dentamore that he had asked Sacco to take a message to a Mr. Mucci, a mutual friend in Italy, then a member of the Italian Assembly. Mr. Mucci had once practiced law in Boston. In talking with Sacco, Mr. Dentamore had learned that both Sacco and himself came from the same district in Italy and that Sacco's family home, to which he was going, was near to Mr. Mucci's residence. The pertinent questions were excluded.[50]

Before we consider the surprising turn taken by the *Banchetto* evidence in the hearings, six years later before the Governor's Advisory Committee, we should mention several other alibi witnesses.

Sacco had mentioned that he had met a man named "Afa" in the afternoon and had paid him a bill of fifteen dollars. Carlos M. Affe, through an interpreter, testified that he was a dealer in groceries and that he had sold Sacco some goods on March 20, 1920, at 180 North Street, Boston. It was Sacco's first purchase from him. The bill was for $15.67. The bill was unpaid until April 15, when he met Sacco between three and four o'clock. Sacco paid him $15.50. Affe used penciled memoranda in one of his own notebooks to refresh his recollection. On cross-examination, Mr. Affe stated that he sometimes put down the dates of sales and payment and sometimes did not. He did so in this instance because it was his first sale to Sacco and he wanted to see how good a customer he was and the length of time that it took him to pay.[51] Mr. Affe's direct testimony does not appear to have been much shaken by cross-examination. However, Mr. Katzmann offered a handwriting experiment. He dictated a number of the memoranda in the

[49] Vol. II, 2026–2029.   [50] Vol. II, 2029–2032.   [51] Vol. II, 2037.

book for the witness to write down. We have no way of judging the effect of this. Mr. McAnarney called the jury's attention to alleged similarities in the appearance of certain letters and figures.[52] Mr. Katzmann, in his summation, pointed out alleged dissimilarities and other differences.[53] The specimens were not reproduced in the record, but even if they had appeared, a layman's judgment would not be worth much. No handwriting expert was called to give an opinion.

An alibi witness not mentioned by Sacco was Dominic Ricci, a Needham carpenter. He stated that in April 1920 he was living in Stoughton, where he was putting up some beaverboard on a piazza ceiling for a Mr. Monohan, whose home was right in back of Michael Kelley's, about two hundred yards from the 3–K factory. He claimed to have met Sacco on the morning of the fifteenth, on the platform of the Stoughton railroad station, and to have talked with him about a passport and the consul's office. He also said he saw Sacco the next morning at the 3–K factory and talked with him about the holdup and murder in South Braintree. The next time he saw Sacco was about 11:15 A.M. on May 5 in front of the Stoughton Trust Company. He walked a bit with Sacco and talked with him about a passport.

Mr. Ricci's testimony seems entirely too pat. He seems always to have seen Sacco at the right times and to have talked with him about the right things. He was made to order for Mr. Katzmann. On cross-examination he was asked whether he was putting up the beaverboard on April 18 (a Sunday, but not so stated to the witness) and on a string of forty successive dates at weekly intervals thereafter. Instead of admitting the fact that he did not remember, as the other witnesses had done, he readily stated that he had worked on all of them. The cross-examination was then concluded by Mr. Katzmann: "I have got to the end of my calendar. You worked every Sunday, didn't you, from then on? That is all." [54]

It is quite understandable that Mr. Callahan asked this witness no questions in redirect examination and that neither Mr. Moore nor Mr. McAnarney mentioned Mr. Ricci's testimony in their summations.

A far more impressive witness was James Matthews Hayes. He had been a resident of Stoughton for about thirty-three years. Mr. Hayes was a mason and contractor and had held the post of highway surveyor in his town for three years until March 1920. He was a rather unusual alibi witness in that

[52] Vol. II, 2046.   [53] Vol. II, 2232.   [54] Vol. II, 1682–1683.

he did not remember seeing Sacco at all on April 15, 1920. He did not know Sacco and had never met him.[55] Contrary to the government witnesses who had purported to identify Sacco, it was, in this instance, Sacco who identified the witness. This came about in a rather dramatic fashion.

During the early days of the Dedham trial, Mr. Hayes had visited the courtroom to meet a Mr. Woodbury, an investigator for the defense. He had not known Mr. Woodbury and had never met him.[56] However, Mr. Woodbury sought information from him as to the address of a Stoughton laborer, Wilson O. Dorr, wanted as a defense witness. They met by prearrangement at the courthouse. Mr. Hayes remained for a couple of days to watch the trial. On his fourth visit to the courthouse he was called on by Mr. McAnarney. This was on July 6, 1921. While there he received a summons to appear in court the next day.[57]

As the result of his talk with Mr. McAnarney (he was not allowed to give the conversation), he went home and made an investigation to try to find out if he could place himself on the fifteenth of April 1920.[58] What had happened was that Sacco had recognized Mr. Hayes as a man who had returned to Stoughton on the same train and in the same car with him.

Mr. Hayes's report of his investigation was as follows:

Q. (By Mr. McAnarney) What investigation did you make? A. I found that on the 15th of April I had gone to Boston.

Q. Tell us how you remember that you went to Boston on the 15th of April? A. I remembered that by a perusal of my time books and by other incidents that happened previous to that.

Q. Well, take up the point where you first got your connection as to your movements April 15th or 14th or 13th. What first set you on the track? A. Well, I see by my time book I had received some money the 15th from my brother.

Q. Have you got your time book with you? A. Yes, sir.

Q. You may confer, look at that, if it refreshes your recollection. A. And another thing, the 11th day of April, one of my children had a birthday. In talking, looking this up, of course, I spoke to my wife about it. She called my attention to that.

MR. KATZMANN. I ask that be stricken out, if your Honor please.

MR. JEREMIAH MCANARNEY. What your wife said, I don't care.

THE COURT. It may be stricken out.

Q. On the 11th of April, one of your children had a birthday? A. Yes, sir. And of course I remembered giving the child a little time. The next day, Monday, I worked in the forenoon at, — that is, excavating over at Meade's factory. At noontime, coming home from my father's place I sprained my instep or

55 Vol. II, 2016.   56 Vol. II, 2024.   57 Vol. II, 2017.   58 Vol. II, 2014.

strained my instep, which made it impossible for me to work, do my work for a couple of days.

Q. Now, what did you do? A. I had my Ford automobile, so the rear end was grinding, that is, needed taking down and needed repairing, and I took that down, that rear end down.

Q. When did you take that down? A. I took that down Tuesday and Wednesday and a couple of hours Thursday morning, and then I needed some things, grease, and one thing and another, a grease gun in order to put that back again. And, another thing, previous to that I had joined what they call the Montgomery-Brooks, taking some profit-sharing stock in that Montgomery-Brooks concern, and the 27th day of March I had paid, that is, the 25th day of March I had paid $126 on that, and before I paid any more I made up my mind I would go and look the concern over and see whether it was worth going through with it or whether I would drop it. So I took the day off. However, I could not work very well at my own work, and also was to make some of these purchases, and I went into Boston a little after twelve, took a little after twelve train and went into Boston, and I went down to this Montgomery-Brooks place and bought the stuff and had the opportunity to look this thing over.

Q. You say you bought your automobile supplies? A. Yes, sir.

Q. What time did you come out from Boston? Strike that out. About what time did you arrive in Stoughton, if you remember, definitely? A. Between five and six.

Q. That is on the 15th day of April? A. Yes, sir.

Q. Did you know Sacco? A. No, I never knew Sacco. Never met him.

Q. And until I spoke to you and asked you to try and place yourself on April 15th, had you ever given it a thought as to where you were? A. No, sir, I never had any occasion to.

Q. Whether Sacco was on that train or not you don't know? A. I don't know.

Q. But you came out on that train? A. Yes, sir.

MR. JEREMIAH MCANARNEY. That is all.[59]

On cross-examination, Mr. Katzmann could not do anything to discredit Mr. Hayes's testimony. He threw a few of his memory-testing questions at the witness, but was told by Mr. Hayes that he could not tell him where he worked without looking it up in his time book.[60] Mr. Katzmann then set a trap for him, but it caught the prosecutor instead of the witness. This is how it happened:

Mr. Hayes had not been in the courtroom when Sacco testified. Therefore, he was not dismissed until Sacco could be recalled to identify him. Sacco then gave the following testimony:

Q. (By Mr. Jeremiah McAnarney) Mr. Sacco, where did you see this man [Mr. Hayes]? A. I remember that I might have seen him in the — (The witness

[59] Vol. II, 2015–2016.   [60] Vol. II, 2018.

talks to the interpreter.) I remember that I have seen him the 15th day of April in Boston.

Q. Well, where did you see him? A. I saw him on the train coming home to my house.

MR. JEREMIAH MCANARNEY. Now, Mr. Ross, that there be no mistake, he did not say, "I might have seen him." You used the word "might." The witness did not use that.

MR. ROSS. Well, the words —

(The interpreter talks to the witness.)

MR. ROSS. — said, "I saw him," said that, "I saw him in Boston."

MR. JEREMIAH MCANARNEY. That "I saw him in Boston"?

MR. ROSS. Yes.

Q. Do you mean in Boston or on the train? There is some confusion here.

MR. KATZMANN. One moment.

THE COURT. Leading.

Q. Did you see him in Boston or — wait a minute,

MR. ROSS. Did you see him in Boston or on the train, which? A. On the train.

Q. And from that time that you saw him on the train, when did you next see this man? A. I saw him in court last week.

Q. And what did you do when you saw this man in court? A. I looked at him for several times, for quite some time, to make sure. Then I called you. Pardon me, I called the lawyer.

Q. Well, meaning me. Not that I am the only lawyer. A. Mr. McAnarney.

MR. ROSS. He said "I called the lawyer." I did not want to say he called you.

MR. JEREMIAH MCANARNEY. That is all.[61]

(Mr. Ross's error in interpreting Sacco's testimony illustrates the reason why defense counsel had retained the help of Felix Forte, Esq., to check his work.)

Mr. Hayes was then apparently temporarily excused from the courtroom during Mr. Katzmann's re-cross-examination of Sacco. In the transcript which follows, emphasis has been added to call special attention to certain replies:

Q. (By Mr. Katzmann) What car did you ride out in? A. I don't remember.

Q. At what stations did that train stop? A. I don't remember about which stations that train did stop, but I remember that that train stopped at Canton Junction and several other stops after that.

Q. Is there — A. Before I arrived to Stoughton.

Q. Is there any train that runs to Stoughton on the Providence Division and that stops at Stoughton that does not stop at Canton Junction? A. That they go where?

[61] Vol. II, 2021–2022.

Q. Is there any train that runs from Boston to Stoughton by way of the Providence Division that stops at Stoughton that does not stop at Canton Junction? A. I don't know.

Q. Did you ever ride out on the Providence Division from Boston to Stoughton on a train that did not stop at Canton Junction? A. My best recollection, I remember that when I went from Boston to Stoughton I always stopped at Canton Junction.

Q. "I always stopped" — A. The train.

Q. I understood. The train stopped. Were you in the first car back of the engine? A. I cannot say.

Q. How many cars were there on the train? A. I don't know.

Q. On what side of the coach did you sit? A. *I remember that I sat on my right, as you go to Stoughton.*

Q. In what part of the coach? A. What do you mean, what part?

Q. I mean, how far from the front or how far from the rear. Locate the seat. A. *About the centre.*

Q. Where did this man sit you are now speaking of? A. *On the left, right aside of me.*

Q. On the aisle side of the seat? That is, next to the aisle? A. *Near the aisle, on the side.*

Q. And where were you sitting? Next to the aisle or next to the window in your seat? A. *I was sitting near the aisle.*

Q. Was there anybody sitting in the seat with you, *to your right?* A. Yes, there was a man.

Q. Who was he? A. I don't remember. I don't know him.

Q. What did he look like? A. *I don't remember.*

Q. Did he ride out all the way from Boston to Stoughton with you? A. Yes, sir. He did not get off in Stoughton. I got off and I saw him remain.

Q. Did you have a newspaper with you? A. I don't remember, but every time I have a newspaper to read something.

Q. I did not get that answer. A. I don't remember. I always have a newspaper to read something.

Q. Does that mean you don't remember every time you have a newspaper, or does it mean you do have a paper every time? A. I don't remember whether I had, that I had it that day, but when I go away on the train I always have something to read.

Q. Was there any particular occasion for you to look at the man who was seated at your left on this particular trip? A. Nothing, no occasion, well —

MR. JEREMIAH MCANARNEY. Mr. Sacco, will you please talk louder. We cannot hear you.

THE WITNESS. No, there wasn't any occasion, but he got off at the same place where I did, and I noticed his face and I remember faces.

Q. Was there anybody else who got off at the Stoughton depot besides yourself? A. Yes, sir, there were others.

Q. How many? A. I don't remember.

Q. Describe what any other person looked like who got off at the Stoughton station that day. A. I cannot do it, because I don't remember.

MR. KATZMANN. That is all.

MR. JEREMIAH MCANARNEY. That is all. Tell the officer to bring Mr. Hayes back for one question.[62]

Mr. Hayes was then brought into the courtroom for Mr. Katzmann to cross-examine him.

Q. (By Mr. Katzmann) Do you remember, Mr. Hayes, and if you do not hear me just let me know. I am trying to raise my voice. Do you remember, Mr. Hayes, in what coach you came out? A. It seems to me I came out along in the middle of the train.
Q. How many coaches were there on the train? A. I should say six or seven.
Q. Well, in coming out from Boston to Stoughton, on which side of the coach were you seated, left or right? A. *I was seated on the left.*
Q. And whereabouts in the car? A. *About midway in the car.*
Q. And on which side of the seat? A. On the inside of the seat.
Q. That is, next to the window or next to the aisle? A. *Next to the aisle.*
Q. Have you talked this over with Mr. Sacco before he took the stand? A. No, sir.
Q. Or his counsel? A. No, sir.
Q. Has anybody asked you before I asked you in which part of the coach you were seated? A. No.
Q. Or which part of the seat? A. No, sir. . . . [Emphasis added.][63]

The foregoing testimony would seem to be entitled to unusual weight, because the direct examinations of both witnesses had been concluded without Mr. McAnarney touching on the subject of their seats in the car. The fact that Sacco was correct in placing Mr. Hayes was brought out by Mr. Katzmann in his unexpected re-cross-examination.

Sacco's wife Rose (Rosina) testified that it was April 15 when her husband went to Boston with the large picture of the family. He brought the picture back and told her that the consul said it was too large. Asked how she placed the date as April 15, she said: "I remember that because I had company that day in the house from Milford." [64]

Mr. Katzmann did not cross-examine Mrs. Sacco about the guest from Milford. Instead he built his cross-examination on these other statements by Mrs. Sacco:

Q. (By Mr. Katzmann) No. What is the date of the letter from Sabeno? A. The mother died on the 7th of March and I suppose Sabeno write the letter a few days after or probably the day after the mother died. It reached here sometime the 23rd or 24th of March.[65]

[62] Vol. II, 2022–2023.   [63] Vol. II, 2023–2024.   [64] Vol. II, 2054.
[65] Vol. II, 2068.

After some uncertainty in the witness's mind about the meaning of Mr. Katzmann's questions, she said that Sacco went into Boston thirteen or fourteen days later and took the picture with him that day.[66] However, she stuck to her story that the day when he took in the picture was April 15. Through the interpreter she then said, "A person could make a mistake, because I have a lot of sorrow," and, "Well, you count up from the 23rd or 24th of March and going to the fifteenth, I say thirteen or fourteen days, and I don't think it is much different, because it is over a year he is in prison and I don't remember everything."

It could well be that Mrs. Sacco had forgotten that Sacco had made an earlier trip to the consulate at the time he was informed that a photograph was required. Sacco had placed the time of this first trip after he had heard of his mother's death but before the end of March.[67]

Although defense counsel did not attempt to explain Mrs. Sacco's arithmetic, he did offer convincing evidence that she had the guests from Milford on April 15, 1920, which had enabled her to fix the date. Mention has been made of the fact that Sacco was attempting to secure another edge trimmer to take his place in the 3–K Factory when he went to Italy. The proposed replacement was Henry Iacovelli, of Milford. Iacovelli had been Sacco's instructor in shoemaking at the Milford Shoe Company in 1912 or earlier.[68] Michael Kelley, owner of the 3–K shoe factory, identified a copy of a letter dated April 8, 1920, which he had sent to Mr. Iacovelli. The letter offered Mr. Iacovelli an opportunity to work in his plant. The copy was marked Exhibit X. Mr. Kelley next introduced the original reply, dated April 9, 1920, expressing his interest. This letter became Exhibit Y. Mr. Kelley then produced his own reply dated April 12, 1920, requesting Mr. Iacovelli to come to Stoughton on Thursday, April 15.[69] The chain of communication being complete, Mr. Iacovelli took the witness stand. He testified that he came to Stoughton on Thursday, April 15, and entered the shop at a quarter to twelve. There he had a conversation with George Kelley. After his conference at the factory, he went over to Sacco's home. While there he had a conversation about Nicola and his passport. He said they talked about where Nicola was and his whereabouts that day. He was not permitted to give the conversation.[70] Mr. McAnarney also tried to get in the

[66] Vol. II, 2068.
[67] Vol. II, 1936–1937. It could have been a little later, since George Kelley thought he had been out about a week before April 15, 1920. [68] Vol. II, 1627.
[69] Vol. II, 2075. [70] Vol. II, 2076.

witness's conversation with George Kelley about Sacco, but his questions were excluded.[71] Thus, although the defense counsel were unable to prove through any witnesses that Sacco had gone to Boston that day, they did confirm that the event with which Mrs. Sacco had connected the date of his visit to the consulate had occurred exactly as she had stated.

This completes the evidence corroborative of Sacco's alibi. When the characters of the various witnesses are considered and their separate accounts are synthesized, the result seems very impressive indeed. Even Lawrence Lowell said it made a very serious alibi. He said this, however, when he thought he had destroyed it. How he happened to say this and what he said after he found that he was mistaken are the subject of the next chapter.

22.

Tragedy of Errors

President Lowell Destroys a "Serious Alibi"

Sacco's alibi came to play a revealing role in the proceedings before the Governor's Advisory Committee. Although this did not happen until July 1927, it would seem best to relate the occurrence while the evidence concerning Sacco's alibi is still fresh in the reader's mind.

By early in 1927, some of the most distinguished citizens in the Commonwealth had become troubled by growing doubts about the conduct of the trial and the guilt of the accused. At their suggestions, Governor Alvan T. Fuller appointed an Advisory Committee consisting of Robert Grant, a former judge of the Probate Court, Abbott Lawrence Lowell, president of Harvard, and Samuel W. Stratton, president of the Massachusetts Institute of Technology. The personnel of this committee will be considered in a later chapter dealing more fully with the hearings before it and its report to the governor. For the present, it is perhaps sufficient to say that no member

71 Vol. II, 2076.

of the Committee had the essential sophistication that comes with experience in the trial of criminal cases, or any familiarity with the ways of criminals, or, to our knowledge, any understanding of rudimentary precautions in crime detection and prosecution generally regarded as essential to avoid mistakes. The high positions in the community held by the members of the Committee obscured the fact that they were not really qualified to perform the difficult task assigned to them. On the contrary — the announcement of their distinguished names reassured the leaders of Massachusetts that a thorough and impartial investigation would be made. The news of the appointment of the Committee was released on June 1, 1927; hearings were begun on July 11 and continued until July 21; arguments were made by counsel on July 25; and the report of the Committee was dated July 27.

On the fourth day of the Committee hearings, Mr. Thompson and I were returning from lunch to resume the taking of testimony when we noticed two strangers waiting in the anteroom. We soon learned that they were Felice Guadagni (or Guadenagi) and Albert Bosco, both of whom had been alibi witnesses at the trial. We did not know either of them. They had been summoned as witnesses to appear before the Committee on that day, but had not been told for what purpose. Nor had Mr. Thompson or I been advised that the Committee wanted their presence or why. It would have been protocol for the Committee, as impartial investigators, to have explained to us beforehand what they had in mind. Judging from what took place on that summer afternoon, we must assume that the Committee members intended to catch us unawares with the news that they had unearthed proof that Guadagni and Bosco had perjured themselves at the trial, or, at best, were indisputably mistaken in their testimony about meeting Sacco in Boston on April 15. Apparently, the Committee was afraid to trust us with advance information. Had they so advised us, we could have saved them from a humiliation so great that in their report they sought to hide it from public knowledge.

Mr. Lowell acted as chairman, or rather, as it appeared to us, as prosecutor. He began by getting Mr. Guadagni to restate that he had met Sacco on April 15, 1920, first at Boni's restaurant and then afterwards in the coffeehouse. He repeated that he knew it was April 15 when he saw Sacco because it was the day of the banquet to Mr. Williams of the *Transcript*. Mr. Lowell then asked: "Why did it make such an impression on your mind then, because you had to write it up for your paper [the weekly *Gazzetta del Massachusetts,* on which Guadagni was an editor]?" [1]

In asking this question, Mr. Lowell was not seeking information. On the contrary, he wanted to prove that Professor Guadagni was a liar. Unbeknownst to the witness, or to Mr. Thompson or to me, *Mr. Lowell had already consulted the files of the* Gazzetta del Massachusetts *and knew that it contained no account of the banquet to Mr. Williams.*

However, the professor did not accept Mr. Lowell's suggestion. Instead, his answer was: "The impression, because I was invited. An Italian newspapermen's banquet. It was in a church." [2]

Professor Gaudagni stated that he had not written up the account of the banquet for the *Gazzetta del Massachusetts.* Mr. Lowell then lighted the fuse to the bomb.

Q. (By Mr. Lowell) Now let me ask you this: The *Gazetta de Massachusetts* would give a correct account of the banquet, wouldn't it? A. Oh certainly.

Q. Certainly? A. Yes certainly.

Q. The *Gazetta de Massachusetts* on the 14th day of May said this: Do you recognize this (showing a paper to the witness)?

(The witness looks at the newspaper.)

Q. That is from the *Gazetta de Massachusetts.* And the *Transcript* [*Boston Evening Transcript*]. I suppose, you would think the *Transcript* would know when the dinner took place? A. Yes. [Mr. Lowell did not read, or show to us, the *Gazzetta* article.]

Q. Now the *Transcript* of May 14th says that the dinner took place the night before. Can you explain that? A. [Although Professor Guadagni was obviously getting confused, he still clung to his story.] Yes, certainly. I speak about the banquet, I was invited with a friend of mine, Orlandini, and somebody mistaken in the day, *but I remember Sacco at the coffee house,* he ask me, "Why you don't come to the banquet," and I say, "You know I don't come to any banquet." The banquet was in a place, in a church house.

Q. But you remembered that it was the day of the banquet that you met Sacco?

JUDGE GRANT. (Addressing witness) You said so, didn't you?

THE WITNESS. *There must be some mistake.* I recollect the banquet in this place and this talk with Sacco, because we spoke about the banquet with another man who was a friend of Sacco. [Emphasis added.] [3]

Professor Guadagni tried to give additional reasons why he knew it was on April 15 that he saw Sacco, but Mr. Lowell pressed him. Mr. Thompson

[1] Vol. V, 5086. In this part of the record, both *Gazette* and *Gazetta* are used as the name. In the trial testimony, the newspaper name is given as *Gazetta della Massachusetts.*
[2] Vol. V, 5086.   [3] Vol. V, 5087.

and I had been growing more apprehensive with each answer. Guadagni began to flounder, although he still remembered the coffeehouse scene.

Q. (By Mr. Lowell) But you do not explain how you happen to have stated that that was the day of the banquet when it was not? A. I was not careful, I don't talk, I do not know that something of that kind comes up. I had in my mind, in my conscience, that Sacco was there when I spoke about the banquet to Williams. *I was there with Sacco in the coffee house, and some friends were there.*
Q. You did not take pains to look up the date of that banquet before you testified? A. No. [Emphasis added.] [4]

In answer to later questions, Professor Guadagni said that he verified the date, April 15, by asking Dentamore, who had attended the luncheon.[5]
Mr. Lowell — having, as he believed, wrecked Guadagni — turned him over to Mr. Thompson with the air of a prosecutor who had pulled off a coup. He granted to Mr. Thompson carte blanche to attempt what he obviously thought was the hopeless task of rehabilitating the witness.

PRESIDENT LOWELL. That is all I have. You may ask any questions you wish.

The witness, however, added in a low voice, "I was so sure of that day."
Mr. Thompson and I were taken by surprise without any opportunity to check the particular unexpected point sprung by Mr. Lowell. We were therefore inclined to accept without much question his dogmatic assertions. Had this not been so, we might have realized at the time of the hearing that there was already implicit in Mr. Lowell's confrontation of Guadagni an almost incredible carelessness. Three different witnesses on different days had testified that they remembered that when they spoke with Sacco in Boston at Boni's or Giordani's, the banquet to Mr. Williams on that same day had been a topic of conversation.[6] Not only the date, but even the place of the banquet was specified, namely, the Franciscan Friars Convent on North Bennet Street in the North End. The thoroughness of the investigation by the district attorney's office in all other respects precluded the possibility that it had not verified the date and place of this affair, which formed a key association for three alibi witnesses. And, had the Committee

[4] Vol. V, 5089.   [5] Vol. V, 5100.
[6] Bosco, Vol. II, 1662, on June 30, 1921; Guadagni, Vol. II, 1991, on July 9, 1921; Dentamore, Vol. II, 2024, on July 11, 1921.

read the record carefully, they would have known that *Mr. Katzmann himself had conceded that there had been the banquet to Mr. Williams on April 15*. In his summation to the jury, he had said: "Do you suppose that there wasn't a banquet to Mr. Williams of the *Transcript* on the 15th? *You know better. You know there was such a banquet.*" [7] (Emphasis added.)

Mr. Lowell had stated that he knew that the banquet had been on May 13 (when Sacco and Vanzetti were in jail), because he had consulted the files of the *Boston Evening Transcript* (the daily bible for old Boston) and an Italian-language weekly, *Gazzetta del Massachusetts*. No witness, however, had claimed that the April 15 affair had been mentioned in either of these papers. However, the most widely circulated Italian daily in Boston was *La Notizia*. One witness, Albert Bosco, had testified (through an interpreter) that he was an editor of that paper. He had said that he checked the date by looking back "to the paper." Apparently the committee had not consulted *La Notizia*.[8]

Mr. Thompson and I believed that Professor Guadagni was trying to tell the truth. Mr. Thompson sought an explanation from the witness, but this only resulted in more confusion, probably because Professor Guadagni himself had become badly muddled by Mr. Lowell's newspaper proof that what he believed to be true was now claimed to be indubitably false.

After some further comments and questions, Mr. Lowell observed:

This man testified it occurred at night and another one testified it occurred at noon, and I looked it up and found it occurred in the evening of the 13th of May. Moreover, Mr. Williams informs us by telegram that that is the only banquet he attended. [He later stated it was a telephone talk, not a telegram.] That is the point I want to make. This gentleman told the jury that he knew this happened on the 15th because that was the day they discussed the banquet.[9]

At some stage of the examination, Mr. Thompson and I had a brief private conference near a window. We concluded that there could be only one explanation which would solve the apparent contradictions. Despite the alleged telegram from Mr. Williams, there probably had been two banquets. Mr. Thompson then said to the Committee: "There must be some reason. *There must have been two banquets.*" (Emphasis added.)

At this, Mr. Lowell intimated his distrust of Mr. Thompson's integrity.

[7] Vol. II, 2194.   [8] Vol. V, 5103.   [9] Vol. V, 5095.

PRESIDENT LOWELL. I don't know whether you are trying to reach the truth or not. I assume, of course, that you are, and that, I think, is a fair assumption.[10]

This stunned Mr. Thompson like a sudden slap in the face. It took a moment or two before he could fully absorb the full connotation of Mr. Lowell's remark. A few questions later, however, when Mr. Lowell again intimated doubt of Mr. Thompson's sincerity in putting a question to Professor Guadagni, Mr .Thompson burst out: "I am not going to put any questions to this witness or to any other witness in this case unless it is assumed by the Commission that I am not here to deceive this Commission. There has been a good deal of imputation and it is very painful to me." [11]

Later, when Mr. Thompson was trying to get from Professor Guadagni an explanation for his testifying to something which was apparently untrue, he said:

MR. THOMPSON. If it was deliberate I do not think you would see me around here very much longer, in spite of the fact that I have been charged with putting up things on this Committee.

PRESIDENT LOWELL. No, No, No, Mr. Thompson.[12]

MR. THOMPSON. If I did not think these men were innocent I should not be fooling away my time.

PRESIDENT LOWELL. Of course not, Mr. Thompson.

MR. THOMPSON. And I would not resort to any means to justify an end, just because I was convinced these men were innocent, any more than if I thought they were guilty.

The dialogue was coming to a boil and Assistant District Attorney Dudley Ranney hastened to cool it off.

DISTRICT ATTORNEY RANNEY. I wonder if we could get along any better if we had an interpreter. I must confess I have had very great difficulty in understanding him.[13]

Mr. Ranney, of course, referred to Professor Guadagni and the Committee. However, he might just as well have applied the remark to Mr. Thompson and Mr. Lowell. Both spoke English, but they did not understand one another.

---

10 Vol. V, 5096.   11 Vol. V, 5096.

12 It is related that Sigmund Freud, on receiving the same triple-no answer to a question, gave his visitor the shortest psychoanalysis on record by dryly observing, "One no would have been enough."

13 Vol. V, 5098–5099.

As a veteran trial lawyer, Mr. Thompson was accustomed to occasional aspersions, in court proceedings, on his character. He was not unduly sensitive. He did not even resent it very much when Judge Thayer disposed of his argument about the collaboration of Mr. Katzmann with the Department of Justice by charging him with suffering from some form of mental disease. This was because he had only contempt for Judge Thayer, whom he regarded as a half-educated politician with rather a low order of intelligence. Lawrence Lowell's opinion of him, however, held a very different place in his esteem. At the time of the hearings, Mr. Thompson still shared some of the reverence for Lawrence Lowell so prevalent in his own group. Largely for this reason, he accepted without reservation Mr. Lowell's repeated assertions that his own investigation was infallibly correct and that he knew positively that there had been only the one banquet on May 13, 1920. This is what Mr. Thompson said to Guadagni, one of Sacco's chief alibi witnesses, by way of starting a very effective cross-examination:

Now, listen a minute. I am going to try go find out how this thing happened. You can believe what Mr. Lowell tells you because he has looked it up and he knows that that banquet did not take place until after Sacco was arrested and in the Dedham jail. What Mr. Lowell says is true, so Sacco could not have been in Boston the day before or the day after or that day. We will take that for granted. Nobody is trying to deceive you, nobody is accusing you of telling what is not so . . .[14]

Mr. Thompson then tried to show that the three witnesses, in discussing when they saw Sacco, must have proceeded by some sort of reciprocal suggestion that the banquet must have been on April 15. Although Guadagni finally agreed with Mr. Thompson, a reading of all of his testimony indicates that his heart was not in it. Students of the administration of justice will be interested in seeing how a very skillful trial lawyer, earnestly believing that a witness is wrong, can get him finally to admit that the truth which he told was in fact a falsehood.

Mr. Thompson then unexpectedly brought out a fact about Dentamore. After summarizing in detail Dentamore's testimony, the following took place:

Q. (By Mr. Thompson) . . . Is Dentamore a reliable man? A. He is a Catholic Priest.

PRESIDENT LOWELL. He is not a Red then.[15]

14 Vol. V, 5097.   15 Vol V, 5100.

After Guadagni left the hearing room there was some discussion between counsel and members of the Committee. Mr. Lowell repeated the story of his discovery that the banquet to Mr. Williams had occurred on May 13, 1920, when Sacco was in jail. He gave the impression of patting himself on the back for his cleverness in consulting the *Boston Evening Transcript* and the *Gazzetta del Massachusetts*. As he paced back and forth across the floor, he remarked once or twice, "A serious alibi has been destroyed."

Albert Bosco was then brought in from the anteroom. Mr. Lowell, now apparently confident that he had indisputably established the fact that the dinner to Mr. Williams had taken place on May 13, opened by addressing Mr. Thompson: "I am going to let you ask him questions." [16]

Mr. Thompson then began to examine Mr. Bosco about how he happened to testify that he saw Sacco in Boston on April 15. Unlike Guadagni, Mr. Bosco could not be shaken in his insistence that this was the day of the party to Editor Williams.

Q. (By Mr. Thompson) How do you know that was the time you saw Sacco, on April 15th? A. When Sacco and Vanzetti were arrested, some weeks after when I see a countryman and they show me a paper with a picture and he ask me, "Did you remember the day I introduce you to Sacco?" And so that day was the day that somebody gives a party to the editor of the *Transcript*, to Mr. Williams —

Q. How do you know that? A. Because I put it in my paper where I was working, *La Notizia.*

Q. You put it in on the 15th? A. Yes, sir; the day after.

Q. Did you look it up? A. Yes.

PRESIDENT LOWELL. *It is perfectly obvious that is not so.*

Q. Can you send for that paper? A. Yes.

Q. As a matter of fact, that banquet did not happen until after Sacco and Vanzetti were arrested, it did not happen in April, it happened in May? A. When they were arrested I see in *La Notizia*, I see the 16th of April, the day after, because the newspaper come out in the morning, and the same newspaper says about Williams, and I recall the fact it was the same day I was introduced to Sacco.

Q. When did you think the banquet was? A. The 15th.

Q. Of what month? A. April.

Q. No, it was not, it was in May. A. No, it was April.

Q. No, you are wrong. A. No, it was the 15th of April.

Q. No, Mr. Lowell has looked it up and he finds it was not until the 15th of May, and that is right. A. Well —

Q. (By President Lowell) Do you know the *Gazetta?* A. Yes.

[16] Vol. V, 5102.

Q. (Showing a paper to witness) I am going to show you something that was copied from the *Gazetta*. Where was that banquet held? A. I don't know.

Q. (Indicating) Can you read that? That is copied from the *Gazetta No. 18 de Massachusetts* of the 14th of May. A. *But this is something that the Italians give to Mr. Williams. I think it was another dinner.* [Emphasis added.] [17]

Mr. Bosco would not even concede tentatively the possibility that this had not taken place on April 15.

Q. (By President Lowell) And if it did not occur on the 15th of April then that was not the day that you saw Sacco in Boston? A. No, it was that day.

Q. The day of the banquet? A. The day of the banquet.

Q. Supposing the banquet did not occur on the 15th of April then the day you saw Sacco was not on the 15th of April? A. Because I got another recollection. I had a lot of discussion with Guadagni at that time to be sure of the date that I was introduced to Sacco.

Q. You know it was the day of the banquet? A. Yes. Another thing, in *La Notizia* the fact of the South Braintree I wrote myself.

Q. You know the banquet took place at that time? A. I translate that fact the day after; it must be on the 16th, and the day before I see Sacco.

Q. The day before the banquet? A. No; the day before I translate the fact, the day before Mr. Guadagni introduce me.

MR. THOMPSON. (Addressing the witness) Your have got to bring up the *La Notizia* for the 14th, 15th and 16th of April. (Addressing the Committee) This man is perfectly sincere.

Q. (By Mr. Thompson) Were there two banquets? A. No, one.

Q. One? A. Yes. Maybe they give another one.

PRESIDENT LOWELL. Mr. Williams says they gave him only one.

MR. THOMPSON. *I am beginning to suspect that there were two banquets*, only one to Williams, and another one in honor of Williams which he did not attend.

Q. Do you know anything about there being two banquets, one which he did go to and another one which he did not go to? A. I don't know.

MR. THOMPSON. (Addressing the witness) What is the use of your telling us about a banquet to Mr. Williams on the 15th when Mr. Lowell has investigated and he has found out that there was not any banquet on April 15th that Mr. Williams attended. Mr. Lowell knows that there was not any banquet which Mr. Williams attended on the 15th because there was not any such banquet. That is so because Mr. Lowell has found it to be so. You can trust Mr. Lowell for that, he has investigated it, he knows, there was no banquet on the 15th, and Mr. Lowell is right.

PRESIDENT LOWELL. (Addressing the witness) You come here at eleven o'clock tomorrow morning. [Emphasis added.] [18]

The examination then ended with Mr. Bosco still insisting that he had checked the files of *La Notizia*, Mr. Thompson again suggesting that there

[17] Vol. V, 5103–5104.   [18] Vol. V, 5104–5105.

must have been two banquets, and Mr. Lowell again flatly asserting: "It cannot be so."

Mr. Lowell then dismissed Mr. Bosco as follows: "You bring up your paper here at eleven o'clock tomorrow for the 16th of April and the 13th of May, 1920."

As Mr. Thompson and I followed Mr. Bosco through the anteroom, I asked him to get the files of *La Notizia* immediately and bring them to Mr. Thompson's office. Tensely silent, we then walked down Beacon Hill to Mr. Thompson's office, there to await Mr. Bosco and his files. Both of us were too apprehensive to say much to one another. After what seemed to us an interminable time, Mr. Bosco and an assistant arrived bearing a huge tome containing bound copies of *La Notizia* for the year 1920. Mr. Bosco laid the volume on the table and opened it to the issue for April 16. There he pointed out an article which, as translated, read:

IN HONOUR OF THE EDITOR OF THE BOSTON TRANSCRIPT

Yesterday the Franciscan Fathers of North Bennett St. gave a banquet in honour of the new Commandante Williams, editor of the *Boston Evening Transcript*.

At the table of honour, which was all decorated with Italian and American flags, were seated, beside Comm. Williams, the Acting Consul [?], Cavaliere Melano Rossi, and the patriotic Reverend Antonio Castellano.

Among the guests we observed Lieutenant Joseph A. Langone of the State Militia [?] and the representatives of the press. During dessert, the Reverend Castellano read an address of homage to which Comm. Williams replied in moving terms. After the banquet Comm. Williams visited the flourishing parochial school. The girls recited in his honour poems and dialogues in English and Italian.

Comm. Williams will very soon be honoured with a banquet by the [Italian] colony, for the success of which a committee is actively working. [Emphasis added.] [19]

It is not easy to recapture the lift to our hopes wrought by the little item in *La Notizia*. Apparently the Committee's thinking had been influenced by the conviction that Guadagni, Bosco and Dentamore were liars. As honorable men, they would now regret their erroneous assumptions and rectify their thinking accordingly. Or so we assumed. However, as happened after we had discovered the express company recepit for shipment of eels to Vanzetti, our hopes were destined to fade under a pall of disillusionment.

The volume of *La Notizia* was produced at the opening of the hearings

[19] Vol. V, 5256g.

on the next morning, July 15, before the full committee. Mr. Bosco offered to furnish a translation of the article, but Mr. Lowell said that he understood Italian and could read it for himself. He then read the article and announced that a mistake had been made. Bosco and Guadagni, at the request of the Committee, withdrew and the members of the Committee conferred together.

Mr. Lowell then approached us and said that there must have been two dinners, and that Mr. Williams must have misinformed the Committee. He said that he had received the information from Mr. Williams through Mr. Stratton. He asked Mr. Stratton to telephone Mr. Williams at Washington, where Mr. Williams was head of the Universal Service. This Mr. Stratton immediately did, in our presence. He reported that his telephone call had reached Mr. Williams when he was in a barber's chair and that he now remembered that there was only one dinner, and that it was on April 15. Mr. Lowell then said that Mr. Williams had made another mistake in forgetting the second dinner.

Mr. Lowell resumed his habit of walking to and fro in the room, and had a conference with Judge Grant and another one with Mr. Stratton; but what was said was not heard by us.

Mr. Thompson then reminded Mr. Lowell that he had said on the previous day that a serious alibi had been destroyed, and suggested that as the alibi had now been rehabilitated it must again be regarded as serious. He asked why the Committee had not looked at *La Notizia* instead of the *Transcript* and *Gazzetta del Massachusetts*. So far as we could remember no reply was made to this inquiry.

Mr. Thompson then further suggested that the effect of the proceedings on the day before had been to cast a serious imputation upon the honesty and good faith of Messrs. Guadagni and Bosco, who now turned out to have been perfectly honest in their testimony at the trial as in their testimony before the Committee. Mr. Thompson added that he felt that it was not fair to them to dismiss them leaving the matter as it then stood. Mr. Lowell hesitated a moment and then approached Bosco and Guadagni, offered his hand, which each of them took, and told them that he believed them to be honest men and that he regretted his mistake. I remember that his words were in substance as follows:

"Gentlemen, you remember that last night I intimated that I thought you were not telling the truth. I based this upon an examination which I had caused to be made in the files of the *Transcript* and the *Gazzetta del Massachusetts*. I find that I was in error, and that the dinner which you testified to as having taken place on April 15, 1920, actually did take place on that day, as you testified. I wish to apologize to you and to express my regret for the mistake that has been made."

Mr. Thompson then said that he thought something still remained for consideration, namely, what effect the testimony of these men and of Dentamore, which the Committee now saw was perfectly honest, had upon the case of Sacco and Vanzetti, and whether it did not raise a reasonable doubt of their guilt, as the Committee now believed the witnesses to have been perfectly honest in their testimony. Mr. Lowell made no answer to this question, but Judge Grant said, "You are just back where you were before." Mr. Stratton said nothing. Mr. Thompson expressed dissatisfaction with the attitude of the Committee, but was unable to obtain any further statement on the subject from any of the members.

Before Mr. Bosco and Mr. Guadagni left, Bosco asked Mr. Lowell whether he might have permission to publish a brief statement of what had occurred in his paper, *La Notizia*. Mr. Lowell declined to give him this permission, and told him that he must publish nothing on the subject of what had occurred.

Mr. Thompson also called the attention of the Committee to the fact that the strong assertions of Mr. Lowell had almost led him not only into the position of distrusting the three important alibi witnesses, but also of distrusting the whole case of his clients, and he protested against the making of such strong assertions without more careful investigation.

Later, when we received the minutes of the proceedings for the morning when Mr. Bosco brought in the files of *La Notizia*, we were dumbfounded to find that *there was no record whatever of what had occurred, except the following notation*:

> Executive Chamber, State House, Boston,
> Friday, July 15, 1927, 10:30 A.M.
> Investigation Resumed with all the Members of the Committee present.
> [The witness Bosco who was on the stand yesterday afternoon again appeared, with the editions of the paper *La Notizia*, requested by the Committee, and the Committee, all counsel present, and the witness look in the books produced by the witness.] [20]

[20] Vol. V, 5109.

When we called the court reporter's attention to the serious omission in his transcript, he replied that *he had not taken any notes of what had been said or of any part of the episode, because Mr. Lowell had instructed him not to take "colloquies."*

From this it would appear the official record of the Bosco-Guadagni examination was left in such an amputated condition that it ended with Mr. Lowell accusing the two men of lying and Sacco's own counsel doubting the truth of their testimony. Also, the culpable carelessness of the Committee's investigation in a matter of life and death, and their gross error that ensued, was covered over by silence.

An effort was made to set out the facts in Mr. Thompson's argument before the Committee, and again in our brief, but the minds of the Committee members remained crystallized. Nevertheless, both Mr. Thompson and I still expected that the Committee report would, of necessity, deal with Sacco's alibi, once called "serious" by Mr. Lowell when he thought he had destroyed it. How the Committee disposed of the alibi evidence will be considered in the chapter analyzing its report.

Sacco and Vanzetti had been dead for more than fifteen months before Mr. Lowell made a record admission of his blunder in the matter of the Bosco-Guadagni episode. In November 1928, Mr. Lowell, Mr. Thompson and I received the following letter from two very distinguished lawyers:

President A. Lawrence Lowell,
Cambridge, Massachusetts.

William G. Thompson, Esq.,
Boston, Massachusetts.

Herbert B. Ehrmann, Esq.,
Boston, Massachusetts.

Dear Sirs: —

In the preparation of the proof for the record of the Sacco-Vanzetti case, a question has come up with regard to the testimony of Messrs. Bosco and Guadagni, the banquet to Mr. Williams and the newspaper *La Notizia*, which makes it necessary for the sponsors of the record to appeal to you.

The stenographic minutes of the hearings before the Advisory Committee on July 14, 1927, among other statements concerning the banquet to Mr. Williams, contain the following:

"MR. THOMPSON. There must have been two banquets.
PRESIDENT LOWELL. It cannot be so. He said he went and looked in his paper, therefore if it is not in his paper he did not go and look in his paper.

(Addressing the witness) You bring up your paper here at eleven o'clock tomorrow for the 16th of April and the 13th of May,1920."

The minutes for the next day contain the following:

"(The witness Bosco who was on the stand yesterday afternoon again appeared with the editions of the paper *La Notizia*, requested by the Committee, and the Committee, all counsel present, and the witness looked in the books produced by the witness.)"

The last-quoted statement seems meaningless unless there is added something to indicate what the Committee, the counsel and the witness found on looking in the books containing the files of *La Notizia*. We are writing you therefore to ask you whether you will be so good as to let us have a statement as to what the Committee, the counsel and the witness found in the files of the paper.

Awaiting the favor of your reply, we are,

Yours very truly,

BERNARD FLEXNER
CHARLES C. BURLINGHAM[21]

Mr. Thompson and I replied by briefly stating most of the facts set out in this chapter.

Under the date of December 8, 1928, Mr. Lowell answered as follows:

Dear Sir:

On the day following the testimony of Guadagni, Bosco produced before the committee the files of the *Notizia*, by which it appears that there was a luncheon given for Mr. Williams on April 15 (the date of the murder) at an Italian priory in the North End. The committee, in their subsequent deliberations, assumed it to be a fact that besides the larger public dinner, given to Mr. Williams on May 13, this luncheon took place on April 15.

Yours very sincerely,

A. LAWRENCE LOWELL[22]

Mr. Lowell's letter immediately evoked in my mind the painful memory of the exchange between Mr. Thompson and Mr. Lowell when Sacco was still living:

MR. THOMPSON. . . . There must have been two banquets.
PRESIDENT LOWELL. I don't know whether you are trying to reach the truth or not. . . .

[21] Vol. V, 5256a.   [22] Vol. V, 5256b.

23.

Missing Evidence

The Dedham trial started on May 31, 1921, and ended on July 14, 1921. Its beginning was marked by the tears of Mrs. Sacco when the McAnarneys failed in their attempt to induce Mr. Moore to yield to Mr. Thompson his place as chief defense counsel. The trial record closes with this agonized cry from her husband:

DEFENDANT SACCO. They kill an innocent man. They kill two innocent men.

The jurors retired to "deliberate" in midafternoon on July 14, and returned their verdicts on the same day after dinner. It appears to be manifest, from the brevity of their deliberations, that the jurors had concluded that Sacco and Vanzetti were guilty "beyond a reasonable doubt" even before they spent any time to ascertain whether there were any doubts, reasonable or otherwise. The jury may well be criticized for their failure to thresh out the evidence before reaching a verdict. It is a common experience that a juryman, even if he starts with a strong opinion, may change his mind when a thorough discussion shows that his assumed premise is mistaken. This is true not only of the main issues raised by a mass of conflicting testimony which require thorough sifting and understanding, but also of some details "discovered" by a juryman which he thinks may solve the entire case. For instance, Alfred L. Atwood, a juror, according to one of his friends, later stated that he was convinced of Sacco's guilt by the way he tried on the Pearl Street cap. Other jurors might have questioned his observation and its significance in any event. Juror Dever based his opinion, as we shall see, on a misremembered bit of testimony given by defense expert Burns that the mortal bullet was "obsolete." Others might have had a different recollection or called for a check of the record. The great advantage of the jury is that the number of individuals who compose it can, and often do, prevent a decision on a single juror's faith in assumptions which may be wrong, whereas no such corrective process exists where the decision is made by one judge alone.

It may therefore be said with some justice that the Sacco-Vanzetti jury did not adequately perform the duty assigned to it by the law. That the evaluation of the evidence which confronted them was a most difficult task has been confirmed by most competent jurists who have reviewed the record. Even Dudley P. Ranney, Esq., who handled the case for the district attorney's office in its later stages, told me that had he been on the jury he would have concluded, in the language of the Scotch verdict, "Not proven."

However, except for their failure to probe the evidence sufficiently, the jury in the Sacco-Vanzetti case should not be blamed for reaching a guilty verdict. They had to decide on the evidence presented to them and they knew nothing of the "evidence behind the evidence." We must assume that they were conscientious men who earnestly wanted to reach a just verdict.

Let us now look at the defendants as they must have appeared to the jury in the summer of 1921. We have already seen that they must have been viewed through the poisonous smog of fear and suspicion which enveloped the courthouse. During the trial they were compelled to sit in a cagelike enclosure in the center of the room — a fixture prevalent in Massachusetts courts, used to prevent escape or delivery. If one assumed that the prisoners were criminals, they would certainly have looked it, even if they had actually been angels with their wings concealed.

There was, however, a condition graver than atmosphere and iron restraint which dominated the jury's view of the prisoners as they watched them during the trial. And this was Mr. Katzmann's astonishing capacity to distort and control the testimony at nearly every point in the proceedings. For instance, when Officer Connolly, who arrested Vanzetti, testified that his prisoner put his hand in his hip pocket (a claim not made by him at the Plymouth trial), Vanzetti burst out: "You are a liar." [1]

Here is how Mr. Katzmann built up this interjection by Vanzetti after making it appear that he had intended to murder the police officer:

But it fell to the man Vanzetti, the man who showed the gruff voice because he could not control himself because again he was facing his natural enemy, a

[1] Vol. I, 752.

police officer [the police in Plymouth thought well of Vanzetti], Connolly, when he was on the stand, and he showed that same quality of gruff voice that he shows under emotion and excitement that Austin Reed told you about, the crossing tender at Matfield, when he wanted to know why in "H" they were holding him up [in clear and unmistakable English!], when Connolly got to that part of his testimony when he said, "When I came in the car, Vanzetti made a move to his pocket."

Will you ever forget the uncontrollable outburst of the defendant Vanzetti, keen enough to realize that condemned any consciousness of guilt theory of a minor offence, of which the authorities had no proof whatever. "You are a liar" burst from his lips when Connolly told about that move.[2]

Sacco, in telling of his trip to Boston on April 15, 1920, had claimed that he had overstayed his expected time in the city because he felt like taking off a few extra hours for personal diversions, such as shopping and gossiping. He explained his failure to return to the factory in the afternoon to George Kelley by telling him that he had been delayed because the consulate was crowded. He said that his work was covered anyway for the day. Ordinarily, one would have said that his excuse to Mr. Kelley was simply a "white lie." Mr. Katzmann, however, made it appear like a disloyal fabrication to his good friend Kelley to conceal the fact that he had actually spent the few extra hours in robbing and murdering. Here is Mr. Katzmann's interpretation:

That is not all, gentlemen, upon consciousness of guilt. There is something more telling than that, gentlemen, more convincing than anything I have yet said to you. You have seen enough of George Kelley, you have seen enough of George Kelley to feel, I should judge, that you know him. Been on the stand at least three times, if not more. He first appeared as a witness for the Commonwealth, and he appeared twice, I think, thereafter as a witness for the defense. I mean called by the defense. Will you remember what he finally said on the final — I don't mean there was any difficulty in eliciting it from him, he was frank about it — that he knew Sacco very well, that they were real friends, that Sacco lived next house to him, that he had eaten many times at his house and that similarly the defendant Sacco had been in his, George Kelley's house. They were intimate friends over a period of two or three years. Apparently they were about of the same age, and they come from rather a small settlement in Stoughton [South] where the 3–K factory is; men of the same age, living near together, it is but natural and proper that they should be friends.

This man, Kelley, who [*semble*, whose] father had employed Sacco, who had entrusted him with the keys to his factory to keep the fires up during the first winter that he was there? And my brother would have you believe from that that everybody who is entrusted with the keys of a factory, a night watchman, is a man of superlative integrity and could do no wrong. Why, he was the one man

2 Vol. II, 2207–2208.

in the factory that if anything was missed it could not have been taken by anybody but Sacco in there as a night watchman. No particular difficulty in detecting that. No particular trust or confidence in him.

But they were on intimate terms of friendship, and this man George Kelley was the one who had arranged for Sacco to go to Boston some time after the defendant Sacco showed him a letter, and don't lose sight of the juggling that Sacco tried to do in that letter, and I will call your attention to it very soon. He talked with him on the Friday before the Thursday of April 15th, George Kelley said, and about again about Tuesday when he spoke to him about his work, being out. All Kelley knows about Sacco's whereabout that day is that he did not work all that day.

And when he came back he told him that the consulate was so crowded that he had to stay there or that he could not get his passport — the inference being that he stayed there from the time he went in until too late to get the noon train and that is why he did not come back to work — and George Kelley uttered a significant remark in his original examination, either in direct or cross, "I accepted that as being the excuse."

If you find, gentlemen, as I suggest common sense and logic must force you to find that this is a suspicious alibi that Sacco has built up around himself about being into Boni's restaurant and meeting people, talking with them, who do not remember the date and truly because of the time of the banquet, or remembering it logically who are friends and associates of his, some of them associated with his very defense here now, and Williams associated in a business way with those friends, if you do not believe that, gentlemen of the jury, don't you see that when he falsified again — and he admits that he lied to his friend George Kelley — that he was falsifying again from consciousness of guilt of the crime that had happened but the day before. It must have been something substantial it strikes me, that would make him falsify to the man who had been as good to him as George Kelley had.[3]

To the jury, Vanzetti necessarily appeared as a known bandit and Sacco as his close friend and associate in crime.

Vanzetti was supposed to be protected by a stipulation against the use of his Plymouth conviction to impeach him, but as we have seen, Mr. Katzmann managed to remind the jury of it anyway. Moreover, there was a genuine legal question as to whether Mr. Katzmann could have impeached Vanzetti with a record of his Plymouth conviction, since that case was not then concluded. There was a pending Bill of Exceptions which kept the judgment from becoming final. However, defence counsel might have been afraid to take a chance lest Judge Thayer permit Mr. Katzmann to throw open the doors to another wide-roaming and crushing cross-examination should they put in evidence of Vanzetti's good reputation.

As Mr. Katzmann put it to the Governor's Advisory Committee in 1927:

[3] Vol. II, 2208–2209.

A. (By Mr. Katzmann) Because if witnesses were produced as to the good character of a man who had been convicted of another offense it would have opened the way to cross-examination upon the Plymouth trial, which neither I nor the Court, nor the defense wanted opened.

Q. (By Mr. Thompson) Did that apply to Sacco? A. No, and Sacco had witnesses of good character.[4]

In some way, however, Mr. Katzmann utilized defense counsel's fear of Vanzetti's conviction coming out to obliterate proof of Sacco's good reputation as well. Michael Kelley, proprietor of the 3–K shoe company, where Sacco worked, testified as follows:

Q. (By Mr. McAnarney) What have you to say with reference to his reputation for being a peaceful and law-abiding citizen?

THE COURT. He may answer.

A. I have to say this: I never saw a man that was more attentive to his family.

MR. KATZMANN. One moment.

THE COURT. Mr. Kelley, you pay attention to the question, will you, please, and answer that and nothing else.

THE WITNESS. I did not understand it.

THE COURT. Then don't answer it until you understand it. Repeat it so the witness may get it, and then there will be no objection.

(The question is read.)

THE COURT. That means whether it is good or bad.

THE WITNESS. *It is the best, — good.*

Q. What did you observe of his habits there around the factory? Do you hear me? A. Yes. I hear what you say. You say "with reference —"

Q. To his habits. A. Yes.

Q. What have you to say? A. Nothing to say.

THE COURT. What do you mean by that? Working habits?

MR. JEREMIAH MCANARNEY. Yes; how he conducted himself with reference to his work.

THE WITNESS. *Oh, the best.*

Q. How steady did he work? A. Every day.

Q. Did he occupy any position of responsibility or trust there with you? Do you hear me? A. Yes, I hear you.

Q. I only want to know you hear me. A. In reference to his night watchman's work there?

Q. Yes. A. Yes, he had keys to our factory and the whole thing was in his hands there in the evening after everybody had gone home. [Emphasis added.][5] [Mr. Kelley *also stated that it was customary in his plant for the night watchman to carry a revolver on his nocturnal inspection and that he knew that Sacco was carrying such a weapon.*][6]

4 Vol. V, 5081.   5 Vol. II, 1606.   6 Vol. II, 1608.

Leon Kelley, one of Michael's sons, who worked in the factory with his father, after stating that he had known Sacco for seven years, testified as follows:

THE COURT. Kindly pay attention to just the questions that Mr. McAnarney asks you, and answer them.
Q. The question is, do you know what his reputation is for being — A. Yes.
Q. — being a peaceful and law-abiding citizen? A. Yes.
Q. Now, what is it? Is it good or bad? A. I should say —
MR. KATZMANN. One moment, Mr. McAnarney.
THE WITNESS. Good.
MR. JEREMIAH MCANARNEY. You don't want him to say the other, do you?
THE WITNESS. I said, "Good." [7]

John J. Millick had known Sacco for eight years and testified as follows:

Q. (By Mr. Jeremiah McAnarney) What is your name? A. John J. Millick.
Q. What business are you engaged in? A. Shoe business.
Q. How long have you been in that business? A. Fifty years.
Q. Do you know the defendant Nicola Sacco? A. Yes.
Q. When did you first get acquainted with him? A. Got acquainted with him about eight years ago.
Q. Where? A. Milford Shoe Company.
Q. You have known him since? A. Yes.
Q. In what capacity did you become acquainted with him? A. Well, I was foreman of the bottoming department, and he came in looking for a job.
Q. In what factory was that? A. The Milford Shoe Company.
Q. Did he procure employment? A. Yes, I gave him a job, — edge trimmer.
Q. How long did he work for you? A. Oh, he worked for me four years.
Q. Do you know what his reputation for being a peaceful and law-abiding citizen is? Do you know it? A. Yes.
Q. What is it? A. Good.
Q. With reference to his habits of employment, whether or not he was a steady workman or otherwise? A. Steady workman. He worked for me four years and never lost a day in that time.[8]

From the foregoing testimony (and also from Sacco's relations with George Kelley) it would appear that Sacco's good reputation was fairly well established. It was, however, about to be destroyed. The defense made the mistake of calling Joseph W. Schilling, a Plymouth police officer, to testify to Vanzetti's reputation in that town. This must have been a violation of the stipulation with Mr. Katzmann, who seems to have promptly punished defense counsel (and Sacco) most severely.

[7] Vol. II, 1612.   [8] Vol. II, 1617.

Q. (By Mr. Callahan) What is your name? A. Joseph W. Shilling.
Q. Where do you live? A. Plymouth.
Q. What is your occupation? A. Police officer.
Q. How long have you been a police officer? A. Ten years and a few months.
Q. Do you know the defendant Vanzetti? A. I do.
Q. How long have you known him? A. I have known him about a year.
Q. Do you know what his reputation is in Plymouth for being a law-abiding, peaceful citizen? A. Yes.
Q. What is it? A. Good.
MR. CALLAHAN. You may inquire.
MR. KATZMANN. (To Mr. Callahan) Step up to the bench, will you, please?
(Conference at bench between Court and counsel)
THE COURT. Take a recess of five minutes.
(Short recess)
(Conference between Court and counsel continued)
THE COURT. Suspend on this witness.[9]

We do not know what was said at the bench conference. A fair inference would be that Mr. Katzmann brandished the threat of cross-examining Vanzetti on the Plymouth conviction opened up by Officer Shilling's answer. He extracted from the defense a stipulation which stripped Sacco, as well as Vanzetti, of their good reputations. What was perhaps even more damaging, however, was the form of words used in the new stipulation. Although literally correct, the language nevertheless implied strongly that the defendants had *bad* reputations. Here is how it read:

MR. KATZMANN. If your Honor please, I desire to read to the jury, after the conference that was had with counsel for the defendants the following agreement: The Commonwealth *assents to the request* of both of the defendants that all evidence heretofore offered in the course of this trial to the effect that either or both of said defendants bore the reputation of being peaceful and law-abiding citizens be stricken from the record of this trial, and that such evidence heretofore offered be entirely disregarded by the jury, so that as a result of striking the same from the record *there is no evidence before the jury that either or both of said defendants bore the reputation of being a peaceful and law-abiding citizen.* [Emphasis added.] [10]

What did the foregoing language connote to the jury? Could one blame them if they understood it to mean that the prosecution had discovered that both men bore very bad reputations indeed, and that the Kelleys and Mr. Millick had probably lied to protect Sacco? In this manner was the adversary method of trying cases utilized by Mr. Katzmann as a game to

[9] Vol. II, 1618–1619.   [10] Vol. II, 1629.

deprive a defendant on trial for his life of the reputation which he had rightfully earned by honesty and hard work. Instead, the evidence which he had produced to prove it was now made to hurt him far more than if he had never offered it in the first place. Since Mr. Katzmann knew that Sacco actually had a good reputation as a law-abiding person, the new stipulation, as in other instances, must have been intended to mislead the jury. It may have been a successful coup by Mr. Katzmann, but lawyers may well ask whether a prosecutor should manipulate the rules of evidence to achieve an unjust end.

The picture of the defendants as desperate criminals covering their tracks was highlighted by Judge Thayer in his charge to the jury.

There was also important evidence favoring the defendants which the jury never heard. We already know that Minnie Kennedy and Louise Hayes had the best opportunity to study the driver of the car. They were the young ladies who watched the dapper chauffeur for at least twenty minutes from a front window of Slater and Morrill only a few feet from the waiting car. Prior to the arrest of the defendants, Mr. Katzmann had interviewed them and had requested and received written reports from them. (In 1927 Mr. Ranney conceded that such reports had been received by the district attorney, but stated that he could not find them.[11]) He even spoke of re-opening the inquest to get their testimony. However, they were not called as witnesses; nor were defense counsel told of these important witnesses.

Absent also was one Roy E. Gould, the person who had the closest view of the man beside the driver who was identified at the trial as Sacco by Mary Splaine and Frances Devlin. This bandit had fired at Mr. Gould as the murder car started to move up Pearl Street and had put a shot through his coat at a range of between five and ten feet.

There was a contemporaneous voucher for the authenticity of Mr. Gould's close call from the killer's bullet. In March 1923 Officer John J. Heaney of the Braintree police force deposed:

. . . on April 15, 1920, in the absence of Chief of Police Galvin [*semble*, Galli-van], he took charge of the situation at and about the scene of the shooting of Berardelli and Parmenter, that within a very short time of said shooting he interviewed a man who was near to the gate tender's shanty at the railroad crossing near the shooting, and took his name, address and what he saw of the shooting and the occupants of the so-called Bandit Car, and this information *was given*

11 Vol. V, 4367.

to the police department of Braintree and the State Police: that the man's name was Roy Emerson Gould. [Emphasis added.] [12]

In June 1927, before the Advisory Committee, Chief Gallivan of Braintree confirmed Officer Heaney's story. Gallivan had been away chasing the murder car to Holbrook and back to South Braintree while Heaney was making his on-the-spot investigation. On his return, Gallivan joined a conference in the Rice and Hutchins office, where there was a gathering of State Police, Quincy police, Weymouth police and citizens. This is what he said:

. . . whilst I was there John Heaney, my man, come in to me and he says: "Jerry, there's a fellow outside here that I am holding and he's willing to stay but he wants to get away as soon as he can; I have kept him for two hours; his name is Gould, and he was shot through the coat." I says, "Well, John, we are kind of busy in here now but I will take it up with the State Police." I called [State Police Officer] Scott over and told Scott and Scott said, "We'll be out in a few minutes." . . . Well, that few minutes drifted into half an hour, and when we all went out, Gould had gone. That was about all we done.[13]

Chief Gallivan stated that Heaney had not given him Gould's address. Apparently both Gallivan and Captain Scott must have dropped the matter, since the Commonwealth made no real effort to locate this man who might have become a "star" witness.

Prior to the trial, however, one Frank J. Burke picked up the clue while talking to an acquaintance in the Norris Hotel in Brockton. Mr. Burke immediately relayed the information to Mr. Moore, who referred him to Robert Reid, one of his investigators. Therefore, several people, including Reid, Mr. Burke and his brother, attempted to locate Mr. Gould, but without success until November 2, 1921, four months after the close of the Dedham trial.

On November 6, 1921, Mr. Gould was interviewed by Mr. Moore in Portland, and on November 10 he came into Boston to view the defendants. He first looked at photographs of Sacco and Vanzetti. He was positive that none of the photographs was a likeness of the man he saw. He later was confronted with Sacco in the Dedham jail and observed him for more than ten minutes while Moore and Sacco conversed together. He was positive that was not the man he had seen on April 15, 1920, seated beside the driver.[14]

[12] Vol. IV, 3508–3509.   [13] Vol. V, 5168–5169.   [14] Vol. IV, 3504–3505.

On March 17, 1922, Mr. Gould gave Mr. Moore an affidavit which was made the basis for the second supplementary motion for a new trial of Sacco filed on May 4, 1922. Mr. Gould's affidavit not only contained his positive statement that Sacco was not the man he saw, but also gave an interesting account of his experience on the afternoon of April 15, 1920.

His testimony clearly marks the man Mr. Gould saw as the same individual glimpsed by Miss Splaine and Miss Devlin, and it further indicated that Mr. Gould was under the impression that he had reported his observations to Chief Gallivan, whereas he actually spoke to Officer Heaney, who was then in charge. This led to a counteraffidavit by Chief Gallivan denying that he had ever spoken to a man by the name of Roy E. Gould or ever heard of him until before he filed his affidavit.[15] Mr. Gould executed a second affidavit correcting his error at the same time that Officer Heaney signed the affidavit stating that he (and not Gallivan) had talked with Gould.[16] This seemed to have refreshed Chief Gallivan's mind about the episode.

Mr. Thompson argued that the failure of the prosecution to locate Gould was intentional. The record, however, would seem to indicate that it was more likely due to sloppy police work. Judge Thayer's decision on the Gould motion is interesting. He first stated that "the public have rights in these verdicts that equal those of the defendants, rights that must be as safely guarded as those of the defendants." [17] This is strange doctrine to govern a decision on a motion for a new trial. If a trial judge believes that the new evidence might result in a different verdict, it is his duty to grant the motion. If he thinks that it would not change the previous verdict, he should deny the motion. Judge Thayer's talk about the "rights" of the public to retain the verdicts is surely irrelevant.

The judge then gave a proper juridical reason for denying the motion: "In the first place, this evidence only means the addition of one more eye witness to the passing of the bandit automobile . . . and in my judgment, would have no effect whatever upon the verdicts." [18]

It was true that there were other witnesses who had said that Sacco was not the man they saw. Their testimony was not worth much, since their opportunity to make trustworthy observations was as defective as that of the government witnesses who purported to identify Sacco.

However, in the usual criminal case the trial judge would probably have

[15] Vol. IV, 3507.   [16] Vol. IV, 3508.   [17] Vol. IV, 3513–3514.   [18] Vol. IV, 3514.

considered seriously whether Mr. Gould's testimony had a unique importance making it desirable for a new jury to hear it. After all, if the jury believed the testimony of Mr. Gould, it would make no difference what they thought of other identification testimony — practically all of it was worthless in any event. Judge Thayer did not weigh the special conditions, if any, marking Mr. Gould's evidence.

Instead, for fourteen printed pages of the Holt Record, he argued almost the entire case of the prosecution. After briefly referring to the evidence "tending to prove that the mortal bullet" was fired through Sacco's Colt, he discussed at great length (under the heading "Berardelli's Revolver") the claim that Vanzetti had the dead guard's revolver, which, even if there had been any substance to it, had no bearing on whether Sacco had been wrongly identified; the cap found in Pearl Street, under the heading "Sacco's Cap"; the abandoned car found in the Manley woods on April 19, 1920, "not far remote" from where Sacco and Vanzetti were arrested on May 5 in a streetcar; the armed condition of both defendants and their alleged attempts to draw weapons on their arrest as consciousness of guilt of the South Braintree murders; Sacco's falsehoods and a rather extended dissertation on the subject of the defendants' claim that their lies and other conduct was due to their fear of arrest and deportation because they were radicals; the importance of personal observation of witnesses in criminal trials; the failure of Vanzetti's counsel to mention Vanzetti's alibi in his opening statement (which had no bearing on whether Sacco was mistakenly identified). Judge Thayer then concluded: "Therefore, for the reasons herein given, and others not herein specifically mentioned, the motion of the defendants for a new trial, *based on the Gould affidavit*, should be and the same is herein and hereby denied." [19] (Emphasis added.)

"The reasons herein given" surely constitute an extraordinary basis for denying the motion for a new trial grounded on a possible mistaken identification of Sacco. Possibly Judge Thayer was trying to preconvince the Supreme Judicial Court (or himself) that the evidence against Sacco was so massive that a future jury's verdict would not be affected by Mr. Gould's testimony. His decision on the motion may have been right, and yet the "reasons herein given" could have been wrong. These "reasons" were hotly contested issues. If ever a jury would find that the identification of Sacco was mistaken, they could easily dispose of the reasons mentioned by finding

[19] Vol. IV, 3527.

that "Sacco's cap" was not Sacco's cap, that "Berardelli's revolver" was not Berardelli's revolver, that the alibi witnesses told the truth, that the conduct of the defendants showed consciousness of innocence of the South Braintree crime rather than of guilt, and that the falsehoods told by the defendants were more consistent with the undisputed fact that they were hunted radicals than with the hypothetical assumption that they had committed murder and robbery. It is doubtful, however, whether Mr. Gould's testimony would have changed the verdict rendered in July 1921. In this respect, Judge Thayer was probably right. This particular jury was apparently impervious to everything that favored the defendants — or even to giving it any thought after the close of the evidence. Whether it would have affected the judgment of a second jury, hearing the case under different circumstances at another point in time, is another question.

Entirely missing at the trial, also, were the fingerprints previously mentioned as having been lifted from the murder car and the comparison made of them with fingerprints of Sacco and Vanzetti. Nothing further was heard of them after the press had reported a high-level conference in the district attorney's office. No one knows to this day what the official-expert report showed.

In 1967, John Nicholas Beffel, author and journalist, recalled that he had mentioned the fingerprints in a book published in 1924. Until then he had forgotten his own reference. This is what he wrote:

Consider the Sacco-Vanzetti case, tried at Dedham, Massachusetts, in 1921. Nicola Sacco and Bartolomeo Vanzetti were accused of the alleged murder of a payroll guard and were convicted. Before the trial the prosecution's investigators photographed the finger-prints found on the automobile used by the bandits, but no finger-impression evidence was introduced in court. Demand was made repeatedly by counsel for the defense for permission to examine the prints discovered on the murder-car, but District Attorney Frederick Katzmann refused to grant this permission. In this position the prosecutor may have been supported by law, but certainly not by the dictates of right and justice.[20]

Whether or not defense counsel had a legal right to obtain the prints, they made no attempt of record to get them. However, they had Captain Proctor on the stand under cross-examination and could have brought out that the witness had taken fingerprints off the murder car and had com-

[20] Albert Wehde and John Nicholas Beffel, *Finger Prints Can Be Forged* (Chicago: Tremonia Publishing Company, 1924), 92.

pared them with prints taken from Sacco and Vanzetti. Had the prosecution then refused to produce the prints, the effect would have been most damaging to their case.

Nor did the jury have knowledge of the contents of the "private inquest" held on the second day following the murders, nor of the existence of reports by the Pinkerton detective agency. We have already seen that much of the case presented by the prosecution diverges from the material contained in these documents. However, one of the most significant gaps between the inquest and trial testimony still remains to be considered.

In the second chapter of this book, the inquest testimony of Shelley Neal was set out in full. Mr. Neal was the expressman who carried the payroll money from the train into Hampton House on the morning of April 15, 1920. He told a rather colorful story of seeing two automobiles before the entrance and two chauffeurs apparently cooperating with one another. He also identified one of the automobiles as the murder car on Pearl Street in the afternoon. To the jury in Dedham, however, he told of seeing only *one* car in the morning — the one used in the crime. In fact, his testimony seemed to emphasize that he had seen only one car. We can only speculate why Mr. Neal omitted such an important part of his inquest testimony. We may be sure, however, that the strategists of the prosecution had an impelling reason for not wanting the jury to know that the bandits had used two good automobiles and at least two drivers. Possibly the district attorney feared that this information would weaken the jury's readiness to believe that such well-prepared robbers would have any need for Boda's obsolete Overland to accomplish some dark, but unspecified, criminal purpose. Or perhaps the revelation that two cars were cooperatively involved might have suggested a tactic of professional criminals to defense counsel and started them on an explorative diversion. We can only surmise. It is hardly likely, however, that the district attorney and his assistants, or anyone else, foresaw at that time that the suppressed portion of Mr. Neal's story would eventually become a crucial element in the proof that the South Braintree murders were the work of a notorious gang of professional criminals from Providence.

The theory that two automobiles had been employed in the crime remained hidden from defense counsel for five years after the Dedham trial. Our first knowledge of it came on November 19, 1925, when Mr. Thompson interviewed Celestino F. Madeiros in the Dedham jail.[21] Madeiros was the young gunman who had just confessed to being one of the robber team in the murder car at South Braintree. He stated that a Buick had been used at the scene of the crime, but that the occupants with their loot had switched to a Hudson, waiting for them in a wood about two miles away. He repeated this account in an affidavit dated May 29, 1926,[22] and again in substantial detail in his very extensive deposition taken on June 28, 1926.[23] As we shall see in a later chapter, we were able to piece out some confirmation of the Madeiros two-car account by comparison of the descriptions of the alleged bandit car, or cars, seen by various witnesses along the escape route. This was impressive, but not conclusive.

In June 1927, we persuaded Mr. Ranney to send a copy of the minutes of the "private" inquest[24] in the district attorney's possession to the Governor's Advisory Committee and this won for us permission to make copies. We then learned to our astonishment that more than five years before Mr. Thompson's interview with Madeiros, Shelley Neal had given sworn testimony in the Quincy District Court that on the morning of April 15, 1920, he had seen two automobiles parked in front of Hampton House, their chauffeurs apparently watching for, and checking on, the arrival of the payroll money by train. The unchallenged theory throughout the trial had been that only one automobile had been used. Madeiros's story about the two cars had added an entirely new feature to the account of the robbery as it had been related in the courtroom five years earlier. His description of the switch of cars so close to the place of robbery (to throw off pursuit as soon as possible) had a special significance, since it marked the affair as a professional job. The missing part of Shelley Neal's narrative had now become powerful proof that Madeiros had personal knowledge of what had actually occurred.[25]

We have now considered substantially the entire government case against Sacco and Vanzetti — what was presented and what was omitted. Before proceeding further, we should perhaps pause to note certain changes in counsel that occurred after the close of the Dedham trial.

The district attorney's staff was simply reshuffled. Harold Williams had

[21] Vol. V, 4543.   [22] Vol. V, 4416–4417.   [23] Vol. V, 4615.   [24] Vol. I, 1064.
[25] For Robert Noah, in his drama *The Advocate* (and for others as well), Madeiros's account of the two cars was conclusive proof of its truth.

become district attorney, but since Mr. Katzmann was appointed assistant to Mr. Williams (on March 9, 1923) the team continued as before. However, primary responsibility for carrying on the post-trial proceedings for the Commonwealth now passed to Mr. Williams.

The shift in defense counsel began on March 16, 1923, when William G. Thompson and Arthur D. Hill filed a special appearance to argue the first supplementary motion for a new trial based on the alleged misconduct of foreman Ripley and others.[26] From then on, the dissatisfaction with Mr. Moore continued to grow. Sacco had not wanted Mr. Moore from the start, but by the summer of 1924 the relationship between the two men, never friendly, had become so strained that Sacco sent Moore a letter denouncing him for selfishly exploiting his case and for not getting out as he had promised. Contrary to his usual polite and considerate nature, Sacco signed it "Your implacable enemy, now and forever, Nick Sacco." [27] Meanwhile, Mr. Moore's relations with the Defense Committee had also reached the breaking point. Moore then began to form his own defense group and to raise funds for it himself. Although he had been retained by the Committee, he refused their request to withdraw as counsel. Finally the Committee appealed to Elizabeth Gurley Flynn (who had originally sent Mr. Moore to them) to help them to get rid of the lawyer whom nobody wanted. This proved effective, and on November 8, 1924, Mr. Moore stepped out of the Sacco-Vanzetti case. On November 25, 1924, Mr. Thompson entered his appearance as general counsel for the defense. The McAnarneys withdrew their appearances for Vanzetti on December 9, 1924, relieved, no doubt, that Mr. Thompson, their original choice as trial counsel, was now taking over the defense. My own appearance as associate counsel was not entered until May 1926, just after the Supreme Judicial Court had overruled all of the defendants' exceptions to Judge Thayer's denial of the motions for a new trial.

For Mr. Moore, his removal from the case was a bitter blow and he reportedly brooded over it in mounting resentment.[28] It was not merely a

---

[26] Mr. Hill withdrew his appearance on October 23, 1924, and was replaced by his partner, Richard H. Wiswall. Mr. Hill later took over the defense in the last desperate days of 1927.

[27] *The Letters of Sacco and Vanzetti* (New York: Viking Press, 1928), 21 (August 18, 1924).

[28] Moore's resentment may be the explanation of a statement attributed to him many years later by Upton Sinclair, who was writing a novel based on the Sacco-Vanzetti case. He quoted Moore as saying that in his opinion, Sacco was probably guilty, Vanzetti possi-

hurt to his pride. It took away from him something of transcendent importance that he felt was rightfully his. In a sense, the case actually was his own creation. Through his radical connections he had remade the criminal case of *Commonwealth v. Sacco and Vanzetti* into a symbol of the oppression of workingmen in a capitalistic society. This work was not yet finished. There still had remained the many exceptions to be argued in the Supreme Judicial Court. His forced withdrawal deprived him of this opportunity and threw him abruptly out of the limelight into the surrounding obscurity.

For Sacco and Vanzetti, however, Mr. Moore's dismissal had come much too late. His representation of them as trial counsel had been marked by a succession of calamitous mistakes of judgment and the case was now beyond repair. A number of his blunders have already been noted and considered. If some of them were tactical errors which any counsel may commit in the heat of trial, this is definitely not true of his failing to prepare his defense adequately. Although he spent many thousands of dollars on wide-roaming investigators, he neglected his own "homework." A careful reading of the daily papers for several days following April 15, 1920, would have enabled him to punch holes in some of the prosecution's principal claims. An analysis of the transcript of the Plymouth trial of Vanzetti would have helped him to avoid pitfalls at Dedham. The reports of the Pinkerton detective agency on the Bridgewater and South Braintree crimes would

---

bly. Moore added that he had not received the slightest hint from Sacco or Vanzetti to justify the opinion. Nor had Moore given any hint of such an opinion to those associated in the defense. His former wife, who had worked with him on the case throughout, felt that bitterness at being dropped as counsel had poisoned his mind — a view shared by Aldino Felicani and a number of close associates. Moore's words, however, were reportedly repeated by others, including his friend Carlo Tresca, an anarchist leader (and husband of Elizabeth Gurley Flynn), in a hurried — and interrupted — reply to a question by Max Eastman, the writer. In an article in the *National Review* for October 21, 1961 (long after Tresca's death), Mr. Eastman quoted Tresca as saying that Sacco was guilty, but Vanzetti was not. Tresca's assassination prevented any check on the accuracy of the quote or any further questions concerning its basis. The hearsay comment, however, was sufficient to give currency to the theory that Sacco was a guilty criminal, but the twice-convicted Vanzetti was innocent. It has gained little acceptance among those who were convinced that both men were guilty, since it implied that Massachusetts had executed an innocent man. To many who believed that neither defendant was involved in the robbery and murder at South Braintree, the split-guilt theory did not seem to fit anywhere in the case. This view was presented by Judge Musmanno in an article in the *New Republic* for March 2, 1963. A similar opinion was held by Upton Sinclair, to whom Moore had made the original remark. Vanzetti, in the death house, a few hours before his electrocution, assured Mr. Thompson that Sacco, as well as himself, was innocent of the South Braintree crime.

have been invaluable aids to his cross-examination of government witnesses, but apparently his investigation never discovered their existence. (Although Mr. Moore cannot be blamed for not securing the transcript of the inquest in view of a Massachusetts decision that such minutes belonged to the district attorney, there is no record of any efforts by him to get them, or some of their contents.) Such sources of information would not only have strengthened the defense immeasurably, but would have told Mr. Moore what really happened at South Braintree. Without this knowledge, Mr. Moore's own grasp of the case was incomplete and uncertain.

It would not be fair to Mr. Moore to blame the outcome of the trial on his ineptitude. This may have played an important role, but, if so, it was only one of a number of factors combined by a cruel fate to send Sacco and Vanzetti to the chair.

24.

Madeiros and the Morellis

In retrospect things originally disregarded often take on great significance when some event occurs that relates them to one another. In the Sacco-Vanzetti case there were a number of such features. One by one they were passed over without notice, because the authorities made it clear that they were convinced that they had arrested the guilty men. Pursuit of clues that led elsewhere were dropped and signals that warned of a mistake were ignored. Then, in May 1925, there began a series of incidents which culminated in knitting together these loose ends and making a sensible whole of them.

On November 1, 1924, there was an attempted robbery of the First National Bank at Wrentham, Massachusetts, in which the elderly cashier was shot and killed by Celestino F. Madeiros, a young gunman. Others in the affair were James F. Weeks and Fred Bedard. Weeks and Bedard pleaded guilty and were given life imprisonment. The State refused to make any deal with Madeiros and he was sent to the Dedham jail on November 8, 1924, pending trial for murder.

During Madeiros's trial in May, Madeiros was assigned a cell next to one occupied by Sacco. On several occasions he suggested to Sacco that he send for a boy named Thomas in Randolph. He later explained that Thomas lived on Oak Street in Randolph and that he might have seen the bandit car go past his home and recognized the occupants. (Thomas later said that it was his mother who saw the car, but she was now dead.) Madeiros was convicted of the Wrentham murder, but his counsel filed a Bill of Exceptions to obtain a new trial. Subsequently, he sent Sacco a plan of Oak Street in Randolph on a yellow sheet of paper, with the residence of Thomas marked with a cross. In this way, Sacco's friends would be led to make their own investigation and relieve Madeiros of an unprofessional confession. Sacco, however, paid no attention to Madeiros and destroyed the plan. He knew that the State, in cooperation with the federal government, had placed a spy in the cell next to his and thereafter distrusted all efforts by inmates to communicate with him. Madeiros was moved to a cell on the lower tier directly below Sacco. On several occasions, in the bathroom and while exercising in the corridor below Sacco's cell, Madeiros would say to Sacco, "Nick, I know who did the South Braintree job." Sacco, still unbelieving, ignored him, except for one occasion when he notified Albert C. Crocker, the night officer. The incident was recalled by Mr. Crocker in his affidavit filed by the prosecution in 1926. Mr. Crocker's statements added that Sacco reported that Madeiros had said, "I was the one that done the job." [1] During this period, Madeiros was awaiting the outcome of his appeal to the Supreme Judicial Court.

After all his efforts to communicate orally with Sacco had failed, Madeiros, on November 16, 1925, wrote the following statement: "I hearby confess to being in the shoe company crime at South Braintree on April 15, 1920 and that Sacco and Vanzetti was not there."

He put the paper in an envelope addressed to the *Boston American*. The envelope reached Deputy Sheriff Curtis that same afternoon but got no further. Mr. Curtis later filed an affidavit stating that he received the envelope thirty or forty minutes after Edward Miller, a trusty, had obtained from him a financial report of the Sacco-Vanzetti Defense Committee and delivered it to Madeiros.[2] Later, in his deposition, Madeiros insisted at

[1] Vol. V, 585.
[2] Vol. V, 4574. Mr. Curtis did not state how it happened that he had the report in his possession.

some length that the delivery to him of the Committee report was *after* not *before* he wrote his confession to the *Boston American*.[3]

Madeiros did not give up, however. When he learned that his communication to the *Boston American* had never left the jail, he wrote substantially the same message on a slip of paper and sent it to Sacco. The story is told by Edward Miller, the trusty who took it to Sacco.[4]

This time the slip of paper reached Mr. Thompson, who immediately obtained permission to interview Madeiros and did so in the open rotunda of the Dedham jail. For the moral effect, Sacco also sat at the table where he entreated Madeiros to tell the truth "for Jesus sake." This is the story he told Mr. Thompson on November 19, 1925:

On April 15, 1920, I was picked up at about 4 A.M. at my boarding house,[5] 181 North Main Street, Providence, by four Italians[6] who came in a Hudson five passenger open touring car. The landlord of my boarding house was a Jew whose name I do not remember. One of my sisters lived at the same place. She was then a widow and her name was Mary Bover. She has since been married, and now lives at 735 Bellville Avenue, New Bedford. There was also living there at the same time a man named Arthur Tatro, who afterward committed suicide in the New Bedford House of Correction. He was Captain and I was a Lieutenant in the American Rescue League at that time. Two or three privates in the League also lived there, whose names I do not remember.

We went from Providence to Randolph, where we changed to a Buick car brought there by another Italian. We left the Hudson car in the woods and took it again after we did the job, leaving the Buick in the woods in charge of one man, who drove it off to another part of the woods, as I understood.

After we did the job at South Braintree and changed back into the Hudson car at Randolph, we drove very fast through Randolph, and were seen by a boy named Thomas and his sister. His father lives on a street that I think is called Oak Street, and is in the window metal business or something of that kind. I became acquainted with him four years later when I went to live in Randolph with Weeks on the same street. Thomas told me one day in conversation that he saw the car that did the South Braintree job going through Randolph very fast.

When we started we went from Providence first to Boston and then back to Providence, and then back to South Braintree, getting there about noon. We spent some time in a "speak easy" in South Braintree two or three miles from the place of the crime, leaving the car in the yard of the house. When we went to

---

[3] Vol. V, 4662–4663.   [4] Vol. V, 4496–4497.

[5] Later he said the meeting place was across the street from his boardinghouse, at a barroom — "figure that's the same thing."

[6] Later Madeiros said this was an error, as one of the four, the driver of the car, was a Pole or Finn.

Boston we went to South Boston and stopped in Andrews Square. I stayed in the car. The others went into a saloon to get information, as they told me, about the money that was to be sent to South Braintree.[7]

I had never been to South Braintree before. These four men persuaded me to go with them two or three nights before when I was talking with them in a saloon in Providence. The saloon was also a pool-room near my boarding house. They talked like professionals. They said they had done lots of jobs of this kind. They had been engaged in robbing freight cars in Providence. Two were young men from 20 to 25 years old, one was about 40, the other about 35. All wore caps. I was then 18 years old. I do not remember whether they were shaved or not. Two of them did the shooting — the oldest one and another. They were left on the street. The arrangement was that they should meet me in a Providence saloon the next night to divide the money. I went there but they did not come.

I sat on the back seat of the automobile. I had a Colt .38 calibre automatic but did not use it. I was told that I was there to help hold back the crowd in case they made a rush. The curtains on the car were flapping. I do not remember whether there was any shotgun or rifle in the car or not.

These men talked a lot about New York. As soon as I got enough money I went to New York and also to Chicago hoping to find them in cabarets spending the money, but I never found them.

They had been stealing silk, shoes, cotton, etc., from freight cars and sending it to New York. Two of them lived on South Main Street and two on North Main Street, in lodging houses.[8] I had known them three or four months. The old man was called Mike. Another one was called Williams or Bill. I don't remember what the others were called.[9]

The money that they took from the men in South Braintree was in a black bag, I think.

I was scared to death when I heard the shooting begin.

Both cars had Massachusetts numbers.

The names of these men don't amount to anything. They change them whenever they want to. When they are driven out of New York they come to Providence. I haven't any idea where they are now. I have never seen any of them since.

Sacco and Vanzetti had nothing to do with this job, and neither did Gerald Chapman. It was entirely put up by the oldest of the Italians in Providence.[10]

Was Madeiros "the man whom we cannot describe" in the back seat of the murder car as it moved up after the shooting to take on the bandits and the payroll boxes? Was the barrel of his .38 caliber automatic what the

---

[7] Madeiros was hazy as to the movements of the car after leaving Andrews Square until the exchange in Randolph woods.

[8] Madeiros later admitted that these addresses were false.

[9] Madeiros later admitted that "the names of the men wasn't true"; that he knew the right names of the members of the gang but refused to tell.

[10] Vol. V, 4416–4418.

witnesses glimpsed protruding from the opening in the rear curtain? This question may be answered later in this chapter.

Later Madeiros did a little "talking off the record" to Mr. Thompson. He admitted that some of the details in his first account were intentionally misstated, such as the names and addresses of the gang members. He also corrected his statement that all four of his companions were Italians, saying that one of them was a Pole or Finn.

The Madeiros account differed from the trial evidence in two important particulars. The trial testimony told of only *one* automobile in the bandit party and of a *continuous* flight, at high speed, of the escaping murder car. Madeiros, however, told of the presence of *two* bandit cars in South Braintree on April 15, 1920. Also, he had added to the getaway a delay in the woods off Oak Street in Randolph. This would have been required to permit the change of cars, passengers and loot and the time for precautions necessary to accomplish this switch in safety. It was not until months after the interview in the rotunda of the Dedham jail that we found the startling truth that *Madeiros was right on both counts and that the trial record was wrong.*

Both Mr. Thompson and Mr. Ranney agreed that nothing further should be done about the confession until after final disposition of the Wrentham murder charge against Madeiros. It was felt, with obvious cause, that Madeiros's defense might be prejudiced if it became known that he had implicated himself in another murder. On March 31, 1926, the Supreme Judicial Court reversed the conviction of Madeiros, thereby reinforcing the reason for postponing further action on his story, since he was then facing a second trial. Legally, Madeiros was then innocent until proven guilty. At no time, however, did Madeiros waver in his claim that he was one of the robbers in South Braintree. The second trial of Madeiros began on May 15, 1926, almost immediately after my conference with Mr. Thompson. Both of us attended the trial. Madeiros was defended by Francis J. Squires, Esq., the same lawyer who had defended the anarchist Zagroff and who had been mentioned in the DeFalco story as being available to defend Sacco and Vanzetti along with Percy Katzmann. My first impression of Madeiros came when I saw him in the Dedham courtroom. At that time, as he sat hunched over on the bench, inside the cage, he appeared to me almost like an anthropoid ape. This impression changed materially as I came to know him as a human being. At the trial, however, he appeared to be imperturbable, even when his mother fell from the witness stand in a violent epileptic fit and had to be carried from the courtroom.

Madeiros was convicted for a second time on May 20, 1926. Two days later Mr. Thompson and I began our investigation of the Madeiros story.

Mr. Thompson was most desirous of making the investigation jointly with the district attorney's office so that it would "not degenerate into a contest of affidavits." The attorney general approved of the suggestion, but Winfield M. Wilbar, then district attorney of Norfolk County, rejected his request.[11] As it turned out, the district attorney's office made no investigation of its own either, but merely gathered a few affidavits supposed to discredit Madeiros. Mr. Ranney later declared in open court that the policy of his office was to "answer, but not investigate." [12] And so Mr. Thompson and I were left to make our search alone. We were a couple of amateurs, not only without help from the power of the Commonwealth, but actually in the face of its opposition. That so much factual corroboration of the Madeiros story could be obtained under such conditions would seem to be an additional voucher for its truth.

Although refusing to join us in the investigation (or to make any of its own), the district attorney's office finally agreed to our taking the deposition of Madeiros. Mr. Ranney cross-examined Madeiros. The deposition affirmed in great detail the original story and brought out clearly that Madeiros's shuffling of names and addresses and refusals to answer certain questions were due to his attempt to "shield a crowd." In this he did not succeed. The deposition was taken on June 28, 1926, at a time when the Supreme Judicial Court was considering his appeal from his second conviction.[13] Since it is sometimes stated that Madeiros made a "death house" confession, it should be noted that *from the time of his early approaches to Sacco during his first trial to his reaffirmation of his confession in the deposition, Madeiros was never finally adjudged guilty of the Wrentham job.*

However, I have gone a little ahead of my story. Returning to the conference in the rotunda of the Dedham jail, we find that the key information imparted by Madeiros to Mr. Thompson was that his companions in the South Braintree crime were Italians from Providence who had been robbing freight cars in that city of shoes, silk and cotton textiles and that they talked like professionals. Although he had not identified his confederates by name, this was more than enough to identify the gang — if it existed. Al-

11 Vol. V, 4536–4537.   12 Vol. V, 4390.   13 Vol. V, 4368.

most immediately upon his second conviction I took to the road, skepticism in my mind, hope in my heart.[14]

On my way to Providence I stopped at the Blue Bird Inn at Seekonk, where Madeiros had been employed as a "bouncer" prior to his feud with Barney Monterio, proprietor of the roadhouse. There I learned many things about Madeiros from Barney's handsome blonde wife who, it was rumored, had been the reason for the quarrel. Important was the information that in January 1921, after a few months' sojourn in jail for a minor offense, Madeiros had made a trip throughout the United States and to Mexico with a circus girl as a companion and twenty-eight hundred dollars in his pocket. Twenty-eight hundred dollars! Where had the money come from? I began to wonder.

The most anxious moment of my entire investigation came when I arrived at the Providence police headquarters on Fountain Street. I expected that the Madeiros story would end with the answer to my first questions. Chief Inspector Connors was on duty and he, an inspector in uniform and another officer listened skeptically to my story. Their attitude of doubt was not disconcerting, however, since I shared it.

There were three questions to which an affirmative answer was vital. If Madeiros had told us an imaginary yarn, this would become evident with the first negative answer.

Was there a group of criminals in 1919 or 1920 who were engaged in robbing freight cars of shoes and textiles? Chief Connors's answer took us over the first hurdle at a bound. There had been such a group engaged in freight robberies. They were known as the "Morrell gang" because several of the Morrell brothers belonged to it.

"Were they Italians?" I interrupted anxiously.

"American-born Italians."

We were over the second hurdle. There was still a third, however — the highest of all. The Morrells (or Morellis, as they were generally known) had to be at liberty when the South Braintree crime occurred. The time element was the heart of my inquiry. I feared the worst.

"Were they at liberty on April 15, 1920?"

The effort to answer this question kept me on the rack for half an hour. The trial for the freight car robberies had been in May. After considerable

14 The complete story of my investigation is related in *The Untried Case*. The evidence unearthed as told in this chapter has been pared to manifest essentials.

searching and attempting to refresh one another's recollection, the officers finally concluded that most of the gang had been out on bail during the month of April 1920. (We learned later that Joseph Morelli, oldest of the brothers, had given new bail on March 15, 1920, and that Frank Morelli was bailed on April 5, 1920. Of two younger brothers, Pasquale was out on bail and Fred was committed in default, but neither was ever implicated by our evidence in the South Braintree affair. Michael lived in New Bedford and was not indicted for the freight car robberies, but was the brother mentioned in Inspector Ellsworth Jacobs's notebook as driving the new-looking Buick in New Bedford last seen in the late afternoon of April 15, 1920.) We had taken the third hurdle in stride. I was elated. I could hardly wait to telephone to Mr. Thompson that the Madeiros story still lived.

My visit to the dingy Fountain Street station yielded several extra dividends. The news that the date of the South Braintree robbery was just several weeks before the trial of the Morellis began in the Federal Court at Providence was in line with the professional criminals' practical ways of raising money when the expenses of a serious trial had to be financed. Chief Connors also gave me a number of leads to other police sources of information. Two of these proved to be of great value. One was to General John J. Richards, who had been United States marshal at the time of the federal prosecution of the gang, and the other was to Captain Ralph Pieracini, chief of police in New Bedford, the home of Mike Morelli.

Seekonk and Providence proved to be the first stops on an odyssey which took me to many places, including New York, New Bedford, the federal penitentiary at Leavenworth, Kansas, and the state prison at Auburn, New York. Meanwhile, Mr. Thompson was actively engaged in getting additional information from sources in the vicinity of Boston, including persons living in South Braintree and on Oak Street in Randolph, from pals of Madeiros then "doing time" at Charleston State Prison and from Madeiros himself.

A fairly extensive sketch of Madeiros will be found in The Untried Case. As part of the story of the Sacco-Vanzetti case it is important only to note that his brief life was marked by crime and violence. One facet of his character, however, made our investigation more difficult than it might otherwise have been. This was his faithfulness to the code of the gangster which led him to try to shield the identity of his associates. To that extent he was an unwilling witness. He wanted to tell enough to save Sacco, because he "felt sorry for Mrs. Sacco and the kids," [15] but he tried to avoid directly naming or identifying his associates. "If I cannot save Sacco and Vanzetti by my own confession, why should I bring four or five others into it?" [16]

We have already seen that the gang implicated by Madeiros as his confederates had the requisite criminal capacity, that they answered the witnesses' description of the physical appearance of the bandits and that they were at liberty on the day of the crime. The Italian members were American-born and could speak English that was "unmistakable and clear." Facing a long and expensive federal trial, they had an urgent need for cash. It might be possible for an invented story to lead to finding such a gang, in fact, but this hypothesis taxes one's credulity.

But can we further assume that it could be mere coincidence between fancy and reality that Madeiros said he sat on the back seat of the escape car and that Mr. Williams, in his lengthy opening, had made a passing reference to a man in that position whom he could not describe? Possibly, perhaps — but again we find ourselves approaching the outermost bound of rational supposition.

When we consider the further extrinsic proofs we seem to pass entirely out of the realm of possible coincidence into the zone of truth. For instance, let us consider the New Bedford angle, previously referred to. I had gone to New Bedford at the suggestion of Chief Connors merely to inquire about Mike Morelli of that city. A friend accompanied me for the ride into the pleasant countryside. When I told Captain Pieracini that the Madeiros story had implicated the Morellis as the South Braintree criminals, he became visibly excited. "Jake," he called, "come here and listen to this." The big sergeant came in and almost immediately wheeled out of the room. "You'll see something," the captain said. We certainly did. I can hardly describe the impact on me when Sergeant Jacobs returned with his notebook and told of his seeing Mike Morelli driving a new-looking Buick just before April 15, 1920, of seeing it again on the late afternoon of the day of the crime, of its disappearance thereafter, of his seeing the number plate he had originally noted on the Buick a few days later on Joe Morelli's Cole 8 in

---

[15] Mrs. Sacco was a young woman of considerable charm and refinement. In happier days she had acted with her husband in amateur benefit performances. The beauty of their two children, Dante and Inez (born after Nicola's arrest), was a continuous subject of comment by all who saw them.

[16] *The Untried Case*, 30–33.

front of Fiore's restaurant, and of the tense scene when he went inside to investigate. It brought an almost instant realization that Madeiros, in his cell at Dedham, could never have falsely invented a story implicating as his guilty confederates this group of professionals *who had actually been under police surveillance in April 1920 as prime suspects.*

Immediately on my return to my home in Brookline, I telephoned to Mr. Ranney. I had expected him, as assistant district attorney, to become excitedly interested in the narrative of the New Bedford police. Disillusionment struck fast again. On my suggesting that the news might lead to his "nolprossing" (dropping) the case against Sacco and Vanzetti, he answered, "Over my dead body." I could hardly believe that I had heard him right. At that time my connection with the case was rather fresh and I did not realize the relentlessness of the official policy to keep Sacco and Vanzetti convicted.

The importance of the New Bedford revelation to professional crime detectors was confirmed to me many years later by one of the most knowledgeable police heads in the Commonwealth. Captain John F. Stokes of the State Police (later Massachusetts commissioner of public safety) was stunned when he read the New Bedford story in *The Untried Case.*

"I am a policeman," he said to me, "and what shook me was that Madeiros in 1925 pointed the finger at a gang of professional criminals suspected by the New Bedford police in 1920."

Another discovery which defies explanation by coincidence came on my second visit to Providence. On that occasion, Mrs. Ehrmann accompanied me and I asked her to check the indictments at the federal courthouse while I talked with Daniel E. Geary, Esq., who had been defense counsel for the Morellis at their trial for having in their possession merchandise stolen from the freight cars.

I wanted to learn from Mr. Geary how the Morellis knew what freight cars to "crack" in the Providence yards, since their business with "fences" was largely confined to shoes and textiles. Obviously they could not afford the time to rummage haphazardly through freight cars looking for their stock in trade. Mr. Geary said that the trial testimony indicated that they had "spotters" at the points of origin who noted the numbers on the cars into which their special merchandise was loaded.

Later, the Commonwealth admitted that railroad policeman Karnes had been taken by Joe Morelli to Taunton and Attleboro for the purpose of identifying places at which goods stolen by Morelli or members of his gang had been "spotted" and from which they had been shipped.[17]

When Mrs. Ehrmann met me after I returned from Mr. Geary's office, she was blazing with excitement. She held in her hands some notes on the indictments which she had found. This is what I read:

INDICTMENT	United States
	v.
NO. 563	Joseph Morelli et als.
FIRST COUNT	. . . two hundred and twenty-eight pairs of ladies shoes from Rice and Hutchins, at South Braintree in the Commonwealth of Massachusetts . . .
SECOND COUNT	. . . one hundred and fifty-one pairs of ladies shoes from Rice and Hutchins, at South Braintree, in the Commonwealth of Massachusetts . . .
THIRD COUNT	. . . one hundred and twenty-seven pairs of ladies shoes from Rice and Hutchins, at South Braintree, in the Commonwealth of Massachusetts . . .
FOURTH COUNT	. . . one hundred and five pairs of ladies shoes from Rice and Hutchins at South Braintree, in the Commonwealth of Massachusetts . . .
EIGHTH COUNT	. . . seventy-eight pairs of men's shoes, from Slater and Morrill, Inc., at South Braintree, in the Commonwealth of Massachusetts . . .

Of nine indictments for stolen shoe shipments *five had been loaded at the South Braintree station! The shoes were shipped by Rice and Hutchins and Slater and Morrill, before whose plants Berardelli and Parmenter had been murdered as they were carrying the payroll to Slater and Morrill.*

A glance at a plan of the neighborhood of the crime[18] will show that the position of a spotter watching shoe cases being loaded on the freight car would enable him to observe many other things that later became features of the robbery itself. He would know the day of the week and the train on which the consignment of payroll money usually arrived at the South Braintree station, he would see the expressman and his guards take it into Hampton House, he would note the approximate time when Parmenter and Berardelli emerged with the containers after the payrolls had been sorted, he would watch the two men walk with the boxes down Pearl Street

[17] Vol. V, 4366. The government denied and the defendants contended that Morelli had also taken Karnes to South Braintree.
[18] See Fraenkel, *The Sacco-Vanzetti Case.*

toward the two factories. He would also note whether either of the men carried a pistol or revolver in his free hand. The thoughts which this scene would engender in the mind of a watching criminal should not be hard to guess.

The story told by Madeiros, therefore, not only led to the discovery of the indictments which connected the Morelli gang with the South Braintree factories, but also explained the almost faultless execution of the crime itself as told by witnesses at the trial.

By what chance could the epileptic youth in the Dedham jail fabricate a story that would bring his alleged confederates almost to the exact spot where Parmenter and Berardelli were slain and the Slater and Morrill payroll seized? One in a hundred? One in a million? One in infinity? Or do we need a computer? Or shall we dismiss the evidence of the indictments and also Sergeant Jacobs's notebook as inexplicable "coincidences" and then forget them? *It was done.*

We have seen that it was Madeiros who first brought to our attention the fact that two automobiles were involved in the South Braintree crime. The trial went on the theory that only one car was involved. The presence of a second car, known to the prosecution, was intentionally kept from the jury. It was not until July 21, 1927, one month before the electrocutions, that Mr. Ranney handed the minutes of the "private" inquest to the Governor's Advisory Committee,[19] and we first learned that Shelley Neal had told of seeing the *two* automobiles and their drivers before Hampton House apparently checking the arrival of the payroll money. This foreknowledge was essential if the robbers were later to hold up the paymaster.

The bare statement of Madeiros that two cars had been used would not, standing by itself, necessarily prove that he was telling the truth. It was one of the techniques used by professionals for escape after committing a crime. Madeiros, as shown by his deposition, knew these devices well. However, the statement did not stand alone. It was now confirmed by the minutes of the inquest held in the secret possession of the district attorney for over seven years. As part of his detailed and largely unrefuted account, this new contribution to the story of the crime takes on a crucial significance.[20]

[19] Vol. V, 5251–5252. Before releasing the minutes, President Lowell removed five pages containing evidence given by Mr. Katzmann secretly to the Committee. We never saw this testimony.
[20] The importance of the Madeiros inquest testimony was more fully disclosed in Chapter 23.

Madeiros's story of the car exchange led to further proof that he was telling the truth. This came as the result of the work of James E. King, then an editor of the *Boston Evening Transcript*. Neither Mr. Thompson nor I had thought of it. I had never met Mr. King before the summer afternoon in 1927 when he came to my office. His color was dead white and he was trembling with emotion. He told me that he had not slept for several nights, and that his conscience was torturing him. The *Transcript* had assigned him to investigate the Sacco-Vanzetti case for the purpose of dissipating the rising doubts as to their guilt. At the end he had concluded that the convicted men were innocent. Mr. King noted that a New York, New Haven and Hartford Railroad train had passed through South Braintree at the time of the crime and that somewhat later, the gate tender at Matfield crossing had held up the escaping car to allow a train to pass. The time of each passing could be fixed by railroad records and the distance between the two points over the escape route definitely established. Mr. King made the study and out of it another original contribution by Madeiros was proved to be true, namely, that there had been a considerable delay in the Oak Street woods while contents and occupants were switched to another waiting automobile in order to throw off pursuit. Mr. King set out his findings in a letter to Lowell dated July 19, 1927. Part of it read:

If you will bear with me, it seems that I have duty to address you.

On Wednesday, April 13, fully presuming a strong Commonwealth case, and acting, at the time, upon an editorial purpose highly adverse to the defendants, I began, in regard to the grave matters which your honorable board now is considering, a study which conscience and circumstances have impelled me ever since to continue, night and day, for more than three months.

This investigation — to my own astonishment no less than to that of competent and conservative persons in Boston and New York, whose names I would be glad to supply to you — has established certain facts, never before disclosed, which seem to possess great importance. *These facts tend to prove, in my opinion they do prove, that the State's case concerning the escape of the South Braintree murderers leads to a categoric impossibility. This impossibility, moreover, can only be resolved if one will take into account the confession of the convict Madeiros.*

The sources from which I have secured these facts are the New York, New Haven & Hartford's train-sheets for April 15, 1920, two odometer and six chartometer readings of the length of the roads of escape, and a precise study of all statements made by witnesses as to the times when they observed the fleeing criminals and as to the speed at which the fugitives then were proceeding.

The facts thus established show that upon the State's theory of a continuous flight the *murderers could only have travelled at an average speed of between*

*14.65 and 16.21 miles per hour, whereas all the witnesses, as you know, declare
that the fugitives were travelling at high speed.*

I earnestly ask an opportunity to undertake to present to your honorable
board the data so procured, together with all, or any such part as you may wish
to receive, of the large fund of carefully detailed material, maps and graphical
charts which I have prepared in the course of this study. [Emphasis added.]

Prior to learning of Mr. King's study, Mr. Thompson and I had examined carefully the statements of witnesses alleged to have seen the flight of
the murder car. Their descriptions of the automobile varied considerably as
to its condition (from shiny but dusty to very dirty and old-looking), the
number of occupants (from one to five or six) and the time when they saw
it. This data was not nearly as reliable as Mr. King's study, since some
discrepancies could be expected even if the witnesses were actually observing the same car. On the other hand, if they saw different cars, there would
be no need to ascribe all of the differences to errors of observation. The
data were not certain enough to admit positive conclusions. Nevertheless, a
large number of inquest and trial witnesses who saw the murder car in
South Braintree described it as "newly painted," or "shiny," or "with paint
in good condition" (with some dust on it), whereas most of the witnesses
who saw it beyond the Oak Street woods do not use such phrases, but call it
"old" or "dirty." One of the cars which Shelley Neal had described as
standing in front of Hampton House (and later in South Braintree) was
either a new car or newly varnished and the other was either dirty color or
had not been washed.[21]

One trial witness, Mrs. Alta Baker, said that "around three o'clock" she
saw a large dirty car coming out of South Braintree going at an awful rate of
speed (fifty miles per hour) past her home on Pond (North) Street just
before the turnoff into Oak Street in Randolph. She saw a light-haired
man on the right side of the front seat, but could not see the driver. She
saw no one on the back seat.[22] Mrs. Baker's home was at least a mile and a
half from South Braintree Square. If three o'clock was even approximately
correct, the car she saw could not possibly have been the automobile that
picked up the murderers and the money boxes on Pearl Street shortly *after*
three o'clock, went off toward Holbrook, doubled back into South Braintree and left by Pond Street toward Randolph. The description of the car
fits the second car described by Mr. Neal. Did Mrs. Baker see a car which

[21] Supp. Vol., 426–427.　　[22] Vol. I, 564.

dashed out of South Braintree when its driver heard a signal shot fired by one of the bandits to notify him that the payroll containers had been secured? Was it then speeding to the rendezvous off Oak Street, as Madeiros had described it, to provide the robbers with a different escape car? If so, then the second car carried two occupants, which might have been the case, since a number of witnesses described two strangers (one blond and the other dark) hanging around South Braintree before the shooting.

The testimony of another witness to the escape car may be sufficient to give added support to Madeiros's claim of an exchange of cars in Randolph. The State put on the stand a fourteen- or fifteen-year-old schoolgirl named Julia Kelliher, who said that on the day of the crime she was walking home from school in Brockton. School had let out at three thirty and she had almost reached her home in Brockton Heights. Before four o'clock she saw an automobile coming over the hill at a high rate of speed raising a lot of dust, with the number plate all spattered with mud. She said that she noted four digits on the number plate from a combination of the front and back plates, "*most of it from the back.*" [23] These were four of five digits allegedly seen by Mr. Pelser on the escaping Buick in South Braintree. Miss Kelliher further stated that she had written the numbers "in the sand." Since Miss Kelliher knew nothing of the happenings in South Braintree, there was no reason for her to pay any attention to the numbers and certainly not to write them in the sand. However, the State put on this schoolgirl with her weird story in order to establish the escape route of the murder car.

If Madeiros's story had been told at the Dedham trial, Miss Kelliher's testimony would have tended to confirm his claim of the prior switch in the Oak Street woods before reaching Brockton. We may well doubt Miss Kelliher's tale of the digit details and of her sand scribbles, but *if she saw any rear number plate at all she saw something that was not on the escaping car as it moved out of South Braintree.* Three different people ran into Pearl Street behind the departing automobile expressly to read the number plate. *Each of them reported that there was no rear license plate on the car.*[24] Mr. Pelser himself, who was credited with obtaining the registration number off the escaping car, claimed that he got it from *"the front part of the car."* [25] Therefore, if Miss Kelliher saw an escaping bandit car, as the State claimed,

23 Vol. I, 591.
24 Devlin, Vol. I, 472; Knipps, Supp. Vol., 458; Greenlaw, Pinkerton South Braintree report, April 19, 1920.   25 Vol. I, 296.

it had to be the exchange vehicle described by Madeiros or, if it was the Buick, a number plate had been hung on its rear end *after* it had left South Braintree. Either way, the road points back to the Oak Street woods.

But let us return to the young convict in the Dedham jail. We have seen how the gang implicated by him as his confederates turned out to be the robbers who had been looting freight cars of shoe shipments consigned by Slater and Morrill and Rice and Hutchins at South Braintree; how his story had led us to discover that the police of New Bedford, with good reason, had suspected the Morelli gang of being the Slater and Morrill payroll bandits; and how his account of the presence of two automobiles was confirmed by the original inquest evidence which had been withheld from the trial testimony in 1921. Since these matters are proven facts, and not hypotheses, they cannot be rationally explained singly, and certainly not in combination, as "coincidences." If we cannot conclude from these things that Madeiros must have told the truth, we have no explanation whatsoever except perhaps that Madeiros was a clairvoyant, able to see from his cell in Dedham the pertinent records in the files of the United States District Court at Providence, the old notebook of Sergeant Jacobs in his locker at the New Bedford police station and the minutes of the "private" inquest in the office of the district attorney of Norfolk County.

This gift of divination would have had to go even farther, however. If Madeiros was not telling the truth, he would have had to perform the equally incredible feat of selecting and reading the record in the district attorney's office in New York concerning the murder of one Alberto Alterio on Mulberry Street in New York City on February 10, 1921. In order to grasp the full significance of this record, we must revert to some of the ballistic testimony given in the Sacco-Vanzetti case.

There were produced at the trial six bullets claimed to have been extracted from the bodies of the murdered men and four exploded shells alleged to have been found at the scene of the crime. Only one bullet and one shell, however, were claimed to have been fired by Sacco and none by Vanzetti. No theory was advanced as to who fired the other bullets and shells. Nevertheless, the evidence as to these exhibits is most interesting. State expert Captain Proctor thought that the three shells had been fired by a single weapon, as had the five bullets. It was his opinion that the bullets had been fired through a Savage automatic, but on cross-examination he admitted he had never even heard of a Steyr pistol, one of the best-known foreign automatics. He gave no opinion as to the type of weapon used to fire the shells.

State expert Captain Van Amburgh thought the bullets "consistent" with having been fired through a Savage, but it was later learned that the technical meaning of consistent was simply "might have." He believed they were all fired from the same weapon. Captain Van Amburgh gave no opinion as to what weapon had fired the shells. On cross-examination he admitted his unfamiliarity with "foreign guns." Apparently, in 1921, foreign pistols with metric measurements were rather uncommon.

Defense expert Burns, ballistic engineer for the United States Cartridge Company, however, *was positive that the five bullets had been fired through a foreign automatic of 7.65-millimeter caliber and designated the "Steyr" make.* Such a weapon will take .32 caliber cartridges. He added that the bullets might have been fired through a Savage, Steyr or Walther, made in Germany.

Defense expert Fitzgerald did not testify as to these bullets and shells.

At the trial, therefore, it appeared that the State experts believed the bullets to have been fired through a Savage, but disclosed unfamiliarity with foreign makes. Mr. Burns, with knowledge of both foreign and domestic pistols, unhesitatingly selected the foreign 7.65-millimeter. After the trial, defense expert Hamilton studied the exhibits with the aid of powerful microscopic instruments and greatly enlarged photographs. He came to the conclusion that the bullets had not been fired through a Savage, and also that their markings were completely matched *by no American weapon,* although the Harrington and Richardson automatic corresponded in some particulars. Then Mr. Hamilton turned his attention to the shells, apparently as the first expert to make deductions as to the type of weapon from the shells, since the others had considered the bullets only. Mr. Hamilton easily eliminated the Savage as a possibility by pointing out that the photographs *"reveal upon the side of the shell an ejector or claw mark utterly unknown to a shell ejected from a Savage pistol and impossible to be made by the Savage mechanism."* (Emphasis added.) He then examined other American possibilities and concluded: "From all of the above the affiant gives it as his unqualified expert opinion, with no reservations, that Fraher shells F1, F2, and F3, appearing on page one of the album and the same shells appearing again on page thirteen of the album, *were not fired from*

any American-made automatic pistol, but were of necessity fired from some
automatic pistol of foreign manufacture."

Although the State experts filed many affidavits contesting other findings
of Mr. Hamilton concerning the so-called "mortal bullet" and shell, none
controverted his conclusions as to these other exhibits that no American
weapon completely matched the bullet markings and that the shells had
been fired through a foreign automatic. Indeed, as to the shells, the evidence, when pointed out, was quite obvious and conclusive.

From the foregoing summary, it is apparent that the State experts, in the
end, did not seriously contest that five bullets and three shells had been
fired through a 7.65 foreign automatic. At the time of the trial and in subsequent proceedings the type of weapon that discharged the five bullets and
three shells was not a vital issue, because the prosecution did not claim that
Sacco or Vanzetti had fired any of them. In 1926, however, the foreign
make and offbeat caliber of the pistol became another important link connecting the Morelli mob with the South Braintree murders. When this
occurred, the State no longer claimed that the murder weapon had been a
Savage,[26] but practically conceded that it had been a foreign gun, 7.65-
millimeter caliber.

From General Richards and the police in Providence, I had learned that
Anthony Mancini had been one of the important members of the Morelli
group. He was known as one of their "big job" associates, and a cool killer.
Some of my informants thought that Joe Morelli would not have engaged
in the South Braintree affair unless Mancini had joined in the venture. It
was Tony Mancini who calmly killed Alterio on Mulberry Street within
pitching distance of the New York police headquarters. When General
Richards and I visited Joe Morelli at Leavenworth Penitentiary, he denied
at first that he knew Mancini. However, later, when I mentioned the words
"Sacco and Vanzetti," he exclaimed, "Sacco? Sacco? See Mancini about
that." I took his advice.

My interview with Mancini at Auburn State Prison was a fascinating
experience. It is told in some detail in *The Untried Case.* He was quite
familiar with the Sacco-Vanzetti trial, volunteered a comment that the

[26] Captain Proctor's opinion at the trial that a Savage had fired the bullets and shells
may have been suggested in part by Chief Stewart's report that he had found a diagram
of a Savage in Coacci's dresser drawer after he had been deported.

State had not treated the men squarely in putting Captain Proctor on to mislead the jury as to his real opinion about the mortal bullet. He also observed that the Department of Justice should have kept out of it, and that Sacco and Vanzetti were not the type who would be in a stickup. At first he gave a sort of tacit acceptance to Madeiros's story, but said that Freddy Morelli would not have been in it. (Mancini was right.) Later, as he read on in the affidavits I handed him that his own name was also mentioned, he became (understandably) more critical. He would not admit his own participation, but, unlike Joe Morelli at Leavenworth, he limited his denials to essentials.

The next day found me in New York City at the office of an old friend, Henry Epstein, a young lawyer, then assistant attorney general of New York. I asked Mr. Epstein to look up the crime for which Mancini had been sentenced, with special reference to the type of weapon used by him. I rather expected to find that the weapon had not been discovered, or that the record of its character had not been preserved. If Mr. Epstein should be successful, however, I felt that no person could really believe that mere coincidence, starting with a slip of paper in the Dedham jail, could reach back five years to Mulberry Street, New York, and kill Mancini's victim with the same peculiar weapon which ten months before had slain Parmenter and Berardelli in South Braintree.

In a few days, I received the report from Mr. Epstein. It read as follows:

The automatic pistol with which the murder was committed to which Mancini pleaded guilty and which was taken by Detective Dugan who made the arrest was a "Star Automatic Pistol," of the calibre 7.65; the pistol No. 70480. There were found on the scene of the murder two discharged cartridges from said pistol and in the magazine seven undischarged cartridges. This pistol it is reported by Mr. Foster of the Colt Arms Co. is found in two calibres, the smaller calibre corresponding to the twenty-five calibre automatics and the kind with which the murder was committed, namely, 7.65; corresponds to the thirty-two calibre automatics. This pistol is not manufactured in America and the only known agent is reported to be Adolf Frank, Hamburg, Germany.[27]

The report also indicated that Mancini had carried the pistol in Providence before the time of the murder.

It is easy to picture our excitement on receiving this dramatic news. I immediately telephoned Mr. Epstein and asked him to offer a reward for

[27] Vol. V, 4557.

the production of Mancini's pistol or bullets or cartridges. These items, however, had disappeared completely. Time had done its work, leaving only the record in the office of the district attorney to speak in the face of Mancini's silence. We attempted to paint the lily by suggesting "Star" in the file was a mistake for "Steyr." Such an error was at least possible. State expert Van Amburgh filed an affidavit alleging that a "Star" automatic was not a "Steyr," that neither was of American manufacture, but that both accommodated American-made cartridges as well as those of foreign manufacture. He made no further reference to his trial testimony that the bullets were "consistent" with having been fired through a Savage. It did not matter much, however, since we had landed Mancini with a foreign automatic, 7.65 caliber. For even Captain Van Amburgh no longer denied the basic fact that there was present in South Braintree, at 3 P.M. on April 15, 1920, a weapon of this peculiar description, spitting its message of death and dropping shells marked by the telltale foreign ejector claw.

The discovery that Mancini owned and used a foreign automatic 7.65-millimeter caliber automatic marked him as the one member of the Morelli mob who could have fired at least five of the six slugs extracted from the bodies of Parmenter and Berardelli. (The Morellis themselves owned Colt automatics.) In general appearance, Joseph Morelli, Frank Morelli and Anthony Mancini were of the same type — dark, medium-sized or short, and Italian. They could easily answer the description of the three men seen on the street by inquest and trial witnesses and described in Captain Proctor's press release.

Joseph Morelli and Tony Mancini, especially, correspond to Mr. Williams's description of the two men leaning against the fence in front of the Slater and Morrill factory: "Two short men perhaps five feet six or seven . . . between 140 and 160 . . . of apparent Italian lineage." The Providence police records show that Joseph Morelli was five feet six inches and weighed 147 pounds, and the New York police records gave Mancini's height as five feet five inches and his weight as 148. Mancini was an inch shorter than Joe and a pound heavier. He might have been the bandit who appeared to be stockier or stouter than the two others. The 1920 photograph that I had of him showed rather heavy jowls, but when I saw him at Auburn in 1926 they were not obvious. Was Mancini the "short, heavy set man with a wide square face who reached for his hip pocket when Sergeant

Jacobs approached his table in Joseph Fiore's Restaurant in New Bedford"?[28] Witnesses identified pictures of both Joe and Mancini (in different positions) as a man they saw, but this sort of identification is not worth much except to supplement other evidence more trustworthy. Since there was such other evidence, Joe Morelli and Tony Mancini seemed indicated as two members of the bandit party.

We were not able to secure a photograph of Frank Morelli. By description, he was somewhat taller than his brothers. It will be recalled that the police had described the "No. 3" bandit as taller than the other two who did the shooting and placed him on the sidewalk protecting "No. 1" and "No. 2." It was Frank who faced up to Sergeant Jacobs in Fiore's restaurant and demanded to know what the policeman wanted in a tense scene where Jacobs feared for his life. I learned that in Providence Frank was regarded as the most dangerous of the Morelli brothers. One of the gang's local "fences," through whom they disposed of stolen merchandise, told me that he feared Frank more than any of the others. According to James Weeks, friend and companion of Madeiros in the Wrentham crime, Madeiros had stated that the Morelli brothers participating in the South Braintree holdup were Joe, Butsy and Mike.[29] Frank was somewhat younger than Joe, but considerably older than Mike. He qualified for a place in Madeiros's description of the party at South Braintree.

Madeiros placed himself on the back seat. His assigned function was to stop pursuers by shooting at them, if necessary, through the opening in the back curtain. That left the pale, sickly-looking chauffeur, described by Shelley Neal as a Pole or a Finn. Madeiros had identified the driver as a Pole or a Swede. After considering all available data, we finally surmised that Madeiros's young friend Steve Benkoski had been the driver. His photograph was also identified. Much of our information came from several of Madeiros's youthful associates. We found that in the early 1920's there had been a group of youthful criminals to which Madeiros belonged, including Weeks, Pacheco, Mingo, McDevit and Benkoski. Apparently they were the first crop of prohibition criminals in the Providence area. We learned that Madeiros had told some of them that he was running with the Morelli mob. "Jimmie" Weeks was especially helpful. He was serving life in state

---

[28] Vol. V, 4420.
[29] Weeks mistakenly assumed that "Butsy" was Fred, but the record was corrected to show that this nickname belonged to Frank, not Fred. This was agreed to. Vol. V, 4375.

prison for participating with Madeiros in the attempted robbery of the Wrentham bank. Madeiros, Benkoski, Joseph and Frank Morelli and Mancini would add up to the five occupants of the Buick on Pearl Street in South Braintree. (Mike Morelli was described by Sergeant Jacobs as about five feet four and one-half inches, dark, smooth-shaven, with bright snappy eyes, a chin that was rather long and stuck out and cheeks that were inclined to be sunken.[30])

Mike Morelli, whom Sergeant Jacobs had seen driving the Buick, would be indicated as the accomplice who brought that car from New Bedford to meet the party arriving from Providence in the Hudson, took charge of the Hudson until after the job was done and then redelivered the Hudson to the bandits in the Oak Street woods so that they could return to Providence with the payroll in a car never seen in South Braintree. This ruse, as described by Madeiros, precluded the discovery of any association by the Providence Morellis with the actual murder car and kept it far from their home city. On the other hand, the presence of a new-looking Buick in New Bedford would ordinarily not have aroused suspicions. It was only the alertness of Sergeant Jacobs in noting that the Morellis' Cole 8 in front of Joe Fiore's restaurant bore the same Rhode Island number plate as the Buick Mike had been driving that linked the Providence professionals to the South Braintree crime.

The Madeiros story was not only confirmed by our major discoveries, but also by a number of "fringe" data which might have been explicable on the grounds of coincidence had they stood alone. For instance, we quite unexpectedly ran into the fact that a number of trial witnesses, for the State as well as the defense, selected a photograph of Joseph Morelli from my sheaf as a likeness of Nicola Sacco. Taking a second look ourselves, we found that there were indeed striking resemblances. We have already noted that the Morellis, American-born, could speak unmistakable English, attributed by the witnesses to the escaping robbers. The thorough scouting, planning and execution of the South Braintree job reflected the same foresight and assignment of functions shown in the operation of the freight car robberies. That plan was so well projected that it continued to function with its "fences" for a time after the first arrest of the principals.[31]

[30] Vol. V, 4421.

[31] Apparently Joseph Morelli was not the only brother with executive ability. At recent hearings in Washington on organized crime, it was stated that Frank Morelli had been New England head of Cosa Nostra, preceding Raymond Patriarca.

True to their declared belief that they had found the truth and that nothing else mattered, the Norfolk County authorities made no attempt to deal with the evidence uncovered by our investigation. They did not meet the crucial points in the Madeiros narrative or the extrinsic facts that confirmed it. They filed a few affidavits disputing some peripheral allegations of Madeiros such as related to his whereabouts in New Bedford and Providence prior to April 15, 1920.

Their main effort was directed at obtaining denials from members of the Morelli gang. This produced an abundance of evidence of their "consciousness of guilt" but little else. On June 4, 1926, Winfield Wilbar, then district attorney, and his assistant Dudley Ranney interviewed Frank, Pasquale and Fred Morelli in the presence of their attorney, Joseph H. Kiernan.[32] (Our evidence had not implicated Pasquale, and as for Fred, he had been in jail on April 15, 1920.) They assured the Norfolk County authorities that they had nothing to do with the murders and robbery at South Braintree and that they did not know where South Braintree was. Frank stated that he had been in Providence the entire month of April 1920. (*Sergeant Jacobs had questioned him in Fiore's restaurant in New Bedford; his own lawyer, Daniel E. Geary, had said he was in New Bedford*[33]; *and Frank himself, at his trial for the freight car thefts, had stated that he had been in New Bedford for three or four months.*[34]) Relying upon an affidavit given to the district attorneys by the warden of the state prison in Rhode Island, the three Morellis then assured their interviewers that Joseph Morelli had been in jail during the month of April 1920. (*Subsequently it was discovered that the warden's affidavit was in error and that Joe Morelli was bailed on March 15, 1920.*[35])

Mr. Ranney then asked each of the Morellis to sign and swear to a statement setting forth the "said facts," but "each of said persons refused to do so, saying that he feared for his personal safety."

Later Pasquale overcame his fears and signed an affidavit stating that he saw his brother Joseph every night and every morning and almost hourly from June 1919 until May 1920.[36] Frank, the only one of the trio implicated by our evidence, gave no sworn or written statement. However, he must have later outgrown his timidity in order to rise to the exposed position of reputed head of Cosa Nostra of New England.

[32] Vol. V, 4582.   [33] Vol. V, 4487.   [34] Vol. V, 4551.   [35] Vol. V, 4410, 4462.
[36] Vol. V, 4605.

Joseph Morelli was questioned by Massachusetts detective Joseph F. Ferrari at Leavenworth Penitentiary. To questions which might incriminate him, his answers were either indefinite or flat denials. To the classical query "Where were you on April 15, 1920?" he replied: "I went from my home to my lawyer's office, then to Jones Restaurant, hung around and then drive home." [37]

The final affidavit in the alibi series was by Pauline Gray, Joseph's "housekeeper," an unfortunate woman with a long record for streetwalking and kindred offenses. She swore that Joseph was home every night during said month of April before twelve o'clock and that he did not leave the house on any night during April until ten o'clock the following morning, adding that "I was in a position to know." Pauline either forgot or never knew that Joe had testified at his trial that he had stayed out all night until "sometimes five or seven" o'clock. (The federal prosecutor had contended he was stealing, but Joe maintained that he was merely gambling.)

The affidavits of both Pasquale and Pauline were taken on the same day by Mr. Kiernan, the Morellis' lawyer. None of the Morellis was cross-examined nor were their statements checked by the authorities.

(There was additional collateral evidence of consciousness of guilt on the part of the Morellis, including an alleged attempt by Joseph Morelli [while in the federal penitentiary at Atlanta] to fashion a false alibi for himself covering April 15, 1920. Some of this is related in *The Untried Case*.[38])

The government also filed affidavits from two psychiatrists who examined Madeiros in April 1926 (without notice to defendants' counsel). Although their justification for the visit was to determine Madeiros's sanity, they cross-examined him apparently to shake his confession. Madeiros later said that he could not see what right they had to question him and told them the first things that came into his head, whether true or not. The notes of these doctors on the interview show that Madeiros had some real or feigned losses of memory about dates, and lied about the time when he learned that Sacco and Vanzetti were accused of the South Braintree crime. Nevertheless, he told them substantially the same story he had related to Mr. Thompson. The two psychiatrists then tried to get him to retract, with adverse results:

Q. Why did you want to make a statement of that kind? A. I rather not talk about it.

37 Vol. V, 4604.   38 Vol. V, 4468. See *The Untried Case*, 105–106.

Q. You must have had some purpose one way or the other for giving out that information. A. May be it is true.

Q. Would you want to go further and say maybe or that it *is* true? A. Yes. Q. It is true? A. Yes.[39]

Instead of attacking the extrinsic evidence implicating the Morelli gang, which no longer depended on the Madeiros story, Mr. Ranney devoted himself to an endeavor to discredit Madeiros's claim that he was at South Braintree by pointing out alleged internal contradictions and inability to remember certain details of the crime.

In presenting his arguments, however, Mr. Ranney failed to deal with the proof that Madeiros was telling the true story. In addition to his original contributions, which were not brought out at the trial, but which on investigation proved to be correct, Madeiros's description of the crime, *as it would have appeared from his position as the occupant of the back seat, shut in by curtains,* was almost perfect. Nor are any allowances for memory lapses necessary. Among other things, Madeiros accurately gave the number of bandits on the street and in the car at the scene, placed them all correctly (including his own post at the rear window with a weapon to halt pursuers), described the other bandits as including three Italians and the blond driver, mentioned that the automobile curtains were down but not fastened at the bottom (to allow easy ingress and egress), and gave the sequence of events — including the wait in the car near the factories, the throwing of the money container into the car while it was moving, followed by the boarding of the moving vehicle, and certain events along the escape route not related by any witnesses at the trial. He corrected the assistant district attorney's attempt to mislead him, including an inaccurate suggestion as to the grade of the street. Moreover, his own plan to rob the Wrentham bank, during which crime he shot the cashier, was patterned on the South Braintree job. He even stated that he wanted a Hudson car for the getaway in his own robbery, because he had had enough of the Buick in the South Braintree job. On checking the record, we found that a number of witnesses at the inquest and at least one at the trial had noted that the Buick at South Braintree was not in good running order. Apparently Mr. Ranney could not fit any of the foregoing facts into his theory that Madeiros lied. Like Sergeant Jacob's notebook, the docket entries in the Federal Court at Providence and Mancini's pistol, they were passed over in silence.

[39] Vol. V, 4576.

A number of persons sought to get a statement regarding the South Braintree crime from Joe Morelli, with occasionally suggestive, but inconclusive, results. Among these was Morris Ernst, Esq., a noted lawyer in New York. Mr. Ernst took Joe to his home overnight. While denying his own participation, Joe admitted that his gang had done the job. However, he put a high price on his story which, if paid, would have destroyed its credibility. Another, a Providence reporter named Bagdikian (now a well-known journalist), obtained a promise through Joe Morelli's lawyer that Joe would send for him when he was ready to talk. The summons finally came when Joe was dying, but by the time Mr. Bagdikian got into the sickroom, Joe Morelli had passed into the terminal coma of cancer.

A most intriguing contribution to the Madeiros-Morelli literature was made recently by Francis Russell in *Tragedy in Dedham*. Toward the end of the book, he discusses a statement purporting to be a summary of what Joe Morelli said about the affair in an autobiographical manuscript. Mr. Russell gave me a copy of the memorandum soon after he received the information. Joe Morelli first eliminates himself as a participant in the robbery and murder by stating that the "South Braintree hold-up was committed by Sacco, Vanzetti, Orciani, Boda and Coacci, Coacci was the driver of the car." The memorandum then proceeds with this astounding self-implication:

The hold-up was Joe Morelli's original idea. For months before he had gone over the ground and planned all the details. Berardelli was his confederate within Slater and Morrill's. Joe had planned the hold-up for April 22 with the above group. But the others had decided to double-cross him. That was why they had to kill Berardelli, because he would have recognized them and the double-cross at once. That was why they so deliberately killed him.

And then the statement adds at the end: "For a long time Joe had been stealing truckloads of shoes from Rice and Hutchins with the help of Coacci working from inside." (On my copy "Rice and Hutchins" is stricken out and "a South Braintree fac [*sic*]" inserted.) I have quoted the crucial parts of the statement verbatim because Mr. Russell's paraphrase is not quite accurate.

Apparently Mr. Russell is unable to grasp the damning, incriminating force of the statement. Given the background of the other evidence implicating the Morelli gang, its effect in a courtroom would have been deadly. Apart from the inherent improbability of professional criminals plotting murder and robbery with the men named, the trial record refutes Joe's alleged claim. Assistant District Attorney Williams admitted in open court that the prosecution could not place Coacci, Boda and Orciani in South Braintree on the day of the crime, and the driver of the murder car was established by the evidence as a thin, blond, sickly-looking man in no way resembling the dark, stocky Coacci. However, the statement that Coacci "from the inside" had helped Joe Morelli to steal shoes could have been true, since Joe was then in the business of stealing shoes and would have used the services of any dishonest employee. Also, Joe's thieving operations around the South Braintree factories suggest that the robbers had ample opportunity to acquire intimate knowledge of the routine followed in receiving, sorting and delivering the payrolls.

No one would expect the truth from Joe Morelli. Even his pride of authorship as the brain that planned the crime would be suspect, in and of itself, if the statement were merely a boast to impress fellow criminals. However, it was not bravado. It was intended to tell his own story — without, of course, imperiling himself. He knew from my talk with him in Leavenworth that he was a prime suspect as the author of the South Braintree crime. He had read and annotated Fraenkel's book, which detailed some of the record evidence against him and his mob. I had sent to him, through his lawyer, a galley proof of *The Untried Case* with a promise to print his comments if he cared to make any. If, with the knowledge that he was seriously suspected of the crime, Joe Morelli admitted that he had been stealing truckloads of shoes from South Braintree factories for a long time, that the holdup was his original idea, that for months he had "gone over the ground and planned all the details," and if this admission integrates itself easily into all the evidence against the Morellis, then it has the unmistakable ring of truth.

Mr. Russell mentions Morelli's statement that Berardelli, the guard, was his contact within Slater and Morrill, but again completely overlooks its implications. Yet this may be the most significant part of Morelli's story next to his admission that he planned the robbery in all its details. No objective mind could fail to connect this statement with Morelli's further statement that Berardelli was deliberately killed because he would have recognized the robbers.

The reference to Berardelli's death stirred my memory of the record, and I looked again at the transcript of the inquest into the causes of the deaths of Parmenter and Berardelli. The testimony of witnesses at the inquest was fresh, free of the influence of suggestion that operated on the trial witnesses and not artificially selected as would be the case when lawyers have the object of presenting only their side of the case. The testimony of a number of witnesses at the inquest makes it clear that the robbers were determined to kill Berardelli. Annie F. Nichols, the only witness who saw the crime from beginning to end, stated that the murderer of Berardelli spoke to him just before the shooting. I further found that the witness Lewis Wade gave this testimony (previously quoted) at the inquest:

A. . . . I think the reason Berardelli was killed, I think he knew him.
Q. What leads you to that belief? A. I think so and will always think so. It looks as though this fellow wanted him out of the way.
Q. They followed Parmenter and did their best to get him out of the way. A. He held onto his bag. Berardelli didn't hold onto his box. Parmenter held onto his box and they fired at him back to. Berardelli was on the ground and why should this fellow want to turn around and want to kill him when the money box was on the ground? I think they knew each other.

Joe Morelli's explanation of the relentless shooting of Berardelli confirms the impression of witnesses at the inquest. The transcript of the inquest was unknown to him and his statement would therefore seem to be based on personal knowledge. But whom did Berardelli recognize a few seconds before he was murdered? Was it Boda, Orciani or Coacci, none of whom could be placed in South Braintree on the day of the crime? Was it Vanzetti, the fish peddler from Plymouth, or Sacco, the shoemaker from Stoughton? Or was Berardelli slain because he would have identified Morelli, who had "gone over the ground" around South Braintree for months and admitted that he knew Berardelli even to the extent of claiming a confidential relationship with him?

There was also something a bit characteristic and reminiscent about the Morelli account — even in the rather entertaining touch that he took a group of scared radicals into his confidence on the planning of murder and robbery and that they then double-crossed him and his hard-boiled gang of crooks. Thirty-four years before Mr. Russell obtained the Joe Morelli version, Madeiros had predicted that Joe would deny everything and try to throw the blame on others, that his habit was to throw the blame for his misdeeds on others.[40] Mancini in 1926 explained to me the course to be

[40] Vol. V, 4666.

followed by criminals who would not tell the whole truth, but only a half-truth. I had told him of the Madeiros confession and how he had sought to withhold the identity of the Morellis. "But if you're going to tell, why not tell the whole truth? Why didn't Madeiros tell a whole-story instead of a half-story?" Mancini commented, "He might as well come clean if he started." The half-truth could have been Joe Morelli's formula also, when he wrote of the role he played in the South Braintree robbery and murder. If he was telling a "half-truth," which half is the truth and which half is Joe Morelli's fanciful invention?

25.

Judicial End of the Morelli Evidence

What happened to the obviously strong prima facie case against the Morellis? Why did it not get further in the courts? Outside of the courtrooms of Massachusetts, leading jurists who examined the evidence concluded that the case against them was at least as strong, if not stronger, than the case against Sacco and Vanzetti. This comparison was necessarily based on the evidence against Sacco and Vanzetti presented by the prosecution at the trial. Had the real weaknesses of the government's case been known as we have reviewed it, such opinions might have been phrased in much stronger terms.

Coupled with the confession of a self-alleged participant in the South Braintree crime (totally lacking in the case against Sacco and Vanzetti) and a mass of what may be called "fringe" confirmatory evidence, there were solid indisputable facts to prove that Madeiros told the truth.

That the Commonwealth could make no answer to the evidence against the Morellis is shown by the fact that none was offered. Instead, the prosecution devoted its attention to an endeavor to prove the now almost by-passed claim, namely, that the statement of Madeiros contained lies or errors. Even this effort was rather unsuccessful except as to matters which Madeiros freely conceded were intentionally misstated. Although Mr. Ranney put in evidence the financial report of the Sacco-Vanzetti Defense Committee sent for by Madeiros, he made no argument based on this fact.

Nor did Mr. Ranney ascribe any particular motive to Madeiros's telling a false story other than that he was a "psychopathic personality." [1] (Would psychic have been a more apposite characterization?)

This being so, we have every reason to ask why the Madeiros-Morelli evidence never resulted in a new trial for Sacco and Vanzetti. By now, the explanation may be familiar to the reader. Under Massachusetts law, all motions for a new trial based on newly discovered evidence had to be submitted to the discretion of the trial judge, and the Supreme Judicial Court would not reverse his decision unless the defense could prove that no conscientious judge, acting intelligently, could honestly have reached the same conclusion. Between these two doctrines, the Madeiros-Morelli evidence was whipsawed to death. This will be examined more fully later in this chapter.

Mr. Thompson argued the motion for a new trial during the better part of four days, from September 13 to September 17, 1926. The courtroom was crowded. His presentation was powerful and, as it seemed to his biased junior, irresistible.

Another basis for the motion for a new trial was the cooperation of the district attorney with the Department of Justice. Mr. Ranney was driven by the policy of his office into defending positions which he may have inwardly deplored. In attacking the affidavits of Department of Justice agents Letherman and Weyand, he insinuated that they had acted dishonorably in revealing government "secrets." This roused Mr. Thompson to exclaim:

What are these secrets which they admit? They have then admitted secrets, have they? There are secrets, are there? I thought there were from the fact that it was not denied or contradicted. And I will say to your Honor that a government which has come to value its own secrets more than it does the lives of its citizens, has become a tyranny, whether you call it a republic, a monarchy or anything else. Secrets! Secrets! [2]

It was during this hearing that Mr. Ranney declared that the Commonwealth had found the truth and that it would not investigate the Madeiros-Morelli evidence. In answer to Mr. Thompson's criticism that Mr. Katzmann had put the untrustworthy Levangie on the stand to identify Vanzetti as the driver of the murder car, but failed to call the two ladies who, he knew, had observed the slim blond chauffeur for quite a time in front of their window (or to reveal their existence to the defense), Mr. Ranney

[1] Vol. V, 4369.   [2] Vol. V, 4385.

wondered "if Mr. Thompson has not an exaggerated and too ethical a no-
tion of the functions of a District Attorney." [3]

Judge Thayer listened impassively throughout the long argument. It
might be an overstatement to say that Mr. Thompson and I expected a
favorable decision from Judge Thayer, but we were tentatively optimistic.
At least, we expected a serious and careful review of the material which we
had submitted with our motion. Instead, on October 23, we received a long
"Decision" [4] filled with emotion and self-justification, and so jumbled up
with misstatements that it was a difficult task for us to untangle the snarls
created by the opinion. It is still a problem.

In a sense, Mr. Thompson and I provided the occasion for addition to
the confusion. By making the intervention of the Department of Justice a
part of the same motion for a new trial, we tempted Judge Thayer into long
dissertations to argue that the defendants' guilt was proven by evidence
with which the Department of Justice had nothing to do. Some of this
found its way into his discussion of the Madeiros-Morelli evidence as well.
In his effort to align behind his "Decision" opinions of the Supreme Judicial
Court, Judge Thayer misstated the legal import of that court's actions on an
earlier Bill of Exceptions. These motions, however, are no longer important
to our story, except perhaps to indicate the judge's rather chaotic state of
mind. Legal students will find them discussed in defendants' brief, reprinted
in the record.[5]

Like Mr. Ranney, Judge Thayer ignored the independent extrinsic evidence of the Morellis' guilt and, also like him, he devoted himself almost
entirely to an attack on Madeiros and some details of his story.

Here are the principal reasons stated in his "Decision" for denying the
motion: "Madeiros is, without doubt, a crook, a thief, a robber, a liar, a
rum-runner, a 'bouncer' in a house of ill-fame, a smuggler, and a man who
has been convicted and sentenced to death for the murder of one Carpenter,
who was cashier of the Wrentham Bank."

From this, Judge Thayer concluded that an "affidavit from a man of this
type must be examined and scrutinized with the greatest possible care, caution and judgment before the *verdict of a jury approved by the Supreme*

[3] Vol. V, 4371.
[4] Hereafter in this chapter, the judge's title of the document as "Decision" will be
carried in quotation marks as in the opinion of the Supreme Judicial Court. Vol. V, 4880.
259 Mass. 128.
[5] Vol. V, 4816.

Judicial Court of this Commonwealth is set aside." [6] (Empsasis added.)

The judge's characterization of Madeiros reads like a recommendation to the Morellis to use the services of this young man. Certainly a recruit for a dangerous mission, to be acceptable to these professionals, would have had to be tough and experienced in crime. Nor could one differ from the judge's observation that an affidavit from a man of his type should be examined with the greatest care.

The judge might have added, however, that "a man of this type" (or any man) would not be apt to confess to robbery or murder unless it was true, or unless there was some impelling motive for him to lie about his participation in such a crime. As we have seen, Mr. Thompson and Mr. Ranney agreed to do nothing about Madeiros's confession because knowledge of it could only injure him in his trial for the murder of Mr. Carpenter. Madeiros had tried to get his story to Sacco as early as his first trial. Perhaps it should also be mentioned that his confession about the Wrentham killing was used as the truth by the prosecution in the trial for that crime. The further statement by the judge that the Supreme Judicial Court had "approved" the jury's verdict (repeated in various forms in other parts of the "Decision") was not correct. The court had simply overruled the defendants' exceptions to Judge Thayer's judicial actions. It did not purport to deal with the verdict of the jury.

Although the judge said nothing in his "Decision" about the extrinsic evidence corroborating Madeiros, or about the many internal indications that his story was true, he mentioned numerous details of Madeiros's story which apparently proved to him that the confession was a lie. An examination of some of these other reasons may convey some idea of the workings of the judge's mind.

For instance, Madeiros did not remember certain features of the landscape in South Braintree. However, if he was on the back seat, behind curtains, he would not have noticed them. *Such things as he would have observed from that position, he described fully and accurately.* The "Decision" did not mention this feat of memory.

Madeiros did not remember correctly the caliber of the automatics used by his associates. Why should he have? This, and his failure to recall the South Braintree landscape, would seem to indicate that he had no familiarity with the testimony at the trial. (Judge Thayer intimated that he was

[6] Vol. V, 4726–4727.

trying to fit his story into the trial evidence, although, as we have seen, many of his most important contributions were not mentioned at the trial.)

Madeiros had said that one of the gang had told him that his share would be between four and five thousand dollars, whereas one-sixth of the actual amount stolen would be $2,621.44. The judge then asked if the Morelli gang would have been apt to pay Madeiros such a bonus. However, the robbers expected that the Rice and Hutchins payroll would also be carried by the paymaster. It was only by a mischance that it did not arrive that day on the same train as the Slater and Morrill money. The judge apparently did not observe that the sum he calculated as Madeiros's one-sixth share approximated the amount which was waiting for Madeiros (twenty-eight hundred dollars) when he emerged from a short jail sentence and traveled over the United States and Mexico with his girl friend from the circus.

Madeiros had said that the money was in a "black bag" covered over with a blanket and so was taken to Providence. The judge then made a series of assumptions to prove that Madeiros was a liar. "But if the money was counted at Providence so that one of the gang could fix his share [the loose estimate of four to five thousand dollars had now, in the judge's mind, become a share "fixed" by actual count] then he must have seen the two metal boxes, if he was there." [7]

The judge then proceeded to assume that the boxes were opened en route and so never reached Providence. He based his argument on the fact that "about sixty cents was found on the front seat of the abandoned Buick car in the Manley Woods." [8] Then followed another series of assumptions.

Now let us inquire where in all probability that money came from? Is it not more reasonable to presume from all the circumstances that it came from the payroll boxes and was probably dropped in the haste of the murderers to get the money and probably to get rid of the boxes (which if found in their possession in the Buick or the Hudson would be almost conclusive evidence of their guilt)? If the money came from the payroll (as would seem to be quite likely) then Madeiros, if he was there, must have known the payroll was not in a black bag, but in two metal boxes.

How far Judge Thayer's chain of "probabilities" may be from the facts can be judged by the testimony of Margaret Mahoney, paymistress at Slater and Morrill, describing the manner in which the payroll was put up on April 15, 1920:

[7] Vol. V, 4735.   [8] Vol. V, 4735.

A. . . . I placed it in two steel cases.
Q. In what shape was it inside the cases? A. In two wooden boxes.
Q. What was it inside the boxes? A. In pay envelopes.
Q. That is, there was a pay envelope for each employee? A. Yes, sir.
Q. And was the exact amount due the employee at that time in cash? A. Yes.[9]

Every male car driver knows that loose change in his trousers pocket frequently spills onto the seat if he slouches. That Judge Thayer did not assume that this had occurred may perhaps be due to his unfamiliarity with driving a car. However, his own explanation of the presence of sixty cents on the front seat is illustrative of the sort of naïve theorizing that had plagued the Sacco-Vanzetti case from the beginning. Were the subject not tragic, one could enjoy the imaginary spectacle of the escaping robbers, after a successful holdup and two murders, feverishly opening the steel cases en route, taking out the wooden boxes within, and then tearing open hundreds of payroll envelopes so hastily that they spill sixty cents in change on the front seat.

The judge also attacked the Madeiros story because Madeiros said the money was in a "black bag." The steel containers, black or brown in color, were "about 2 feet long, about 1 foot high, and about 8 inches wide," [10] shaped and fitted with handles like suitcases, often called "bags." Mr. Thompson, in argument on the Madeiros motion, had called Judge Thayer's attention to the fact that McGlone — one of the government witnesses at the trial — referred on redirect examination to the property taken from Parmenter and Berardelli as a "black bag" and in substance repeated this description on his cross-examination, adopting the designation "two black bags." [11] Unfortunately, at the time of the argument, neither Mr. Thompson nor Judge Thayer (to our knowledge) had seen the minutes of the "private" inquest. Had this been available at the time, there would have been no attempt to discredit Madeiros on the ground that he had described the money container as a "black bag." At that hearing, the witness Nichols had also described it as a "black bag" [12]; the witness Colbert spoke of "black boxes," but the district attorney examining him used the word "bags" [13]; the witness Carter called them "boxes or bags" [14]; the witness Wade, both

[9] Vol. I, 168–169.   [10] Vol. I, 169.
[11] Vol. V, 4376. McGlone's actual words were, "The next thing I saw two fellows running with a black bag . . ."   [12] Supp. Vol., 397.   [13] Supp. Vol., 416–417, 419.
[14] Supp. Vol., 432.

"bag" and "box."[15] Even the inquest judge referred to the container as a "bag."[16] If the full facts had been known, Madeiros's use of the phrase "black bag" would have been proof that he had been at South Braintree, since he described the money box he saw in practically the same terms used by every witness who had characterized it.

Judge Thayer also urged as proof that Madeiros had lied the alleged fact that: "The evidence at the trial overwhelmingly contradicted the statement of Madeiros that *immediately after the murder* the Buick car was turned over to one Italian alone and that the five *immediately left for Providence* in the Hudson car."[17] (Emphasis added.)

Madeiros never made such a statement. This misrepresentation is indicative of the judge's state of mind, since in just the second preceding paragraph he had quoted Madeiros (correctly) as stating the contrary.[18] This was then followed by reference to Madeiros's statements (again correctly quoted) about the exchange in the Randolph woods (Oak Street woods), which the judge estimated would have taken about ten minutes.

How can we explain the judge's false paraphrase of what Madeiros said following almost immediately after he had correctly restated the testimony to the contrary? Could it have been due to any cause other than a mind in turmoil?

Nor was the statement of Madeiros that the robbers left the Oak Street woods in a Hudson "overwhelmingly" (or to any extent) contradicted by evidence at the trial. If we review the testimony of the pertinent witnesses, we find that five of them, Mr. and Mrs. Albert Farmer, Wilson O. Dorr, Francis Clark and Miss Julia Kelliher, do not contradict, but tend to support Madeiros's account of the escape of the bandits from the Oak Street woods in a different car from the one used in South Braintree.[19] Except for Clark and Reed, there is no testimony that the car was a Buick, and the descriptions differ one with the other.[20] This evidence has been reviewed in a previous chapter.

Judge Thayer did not know that there was testimony in the minutes of the "'private" inquest proving that two cooperating cars were involved in the South Braintree crime, as Madeiros had stated. Nor did we know it at

---

[15] Supp. Vol., 444.   [16] Supp. Vol., 397.   [17] Vol. V, 4730.   [18] Vol. V, 4729.
[19] Vol. II, 1334 *et seq.*; Vol. II, 1359 *et seq.*; Vol. II, 1365; Vol. I, 585; Vol. I, 581.
[20] Vol. I, 597; Vol. I, 587 *et seq.*

the time we wrote our brief supporting our motion for a new trial based on the Madeiros-Morelli evidence. Nor did Mr. Thompson know anything about it when he argued the motion. No one immediately concerned, perhaps not even Mr. Ranney, knew of its existence until he handed the minutes to the Governor's Advisory Committee just one month before the electrocutions.[21]

There was another ground stated by the judge for claiming that Madeiros lied: "He does not recall there was a shotgun in the car, yet evidence at the trial showed that the barrel of a gun stuck out from the rear window that had been removed from the Buick car." [22]

Since Madeiros said he was the gunman on the back seat assigned the job of shooting pursuers, if necessary, it is understandable that he did not see a "shotgun." If the barrel of any gun stuck out a few inches through the opening in the back curtain[23] it was probably the barrel of Madeiros's own revolver. There was no testimony that the protruding weapon was a shotgun beyond the statement of one of several witnesses who said that it was a "rifle or a shotgun." Pursuing his thought further, Judge Thayer then proceeded to weave a number of misstatements into a single chaotic sentence: "At the trial two shotgun cartridges were in evidence that were found in the possession of one of the defendants; and this same defendant testified he understood they were to be used for small birds; and yet when these cartridges were opened at some time during the trial it was found that they contained buckshot." [24]

The foregoing sentence illustrates the writer's problem in trying to unscramble Judge Thayer's attempted refutation of the Madeiros-Morelli evidence. The shotgun cartridges he referred to were supposed to be two of a total of four introduced at the Plymouth trial of Vanzetti. The peculiar circumstances attending their use as exhibits have been discussed in two earlier chapters.

If we now look at the sentence quoted above, we find that it contains the following misstatements:

1. That two cartridges were identified as shells found in Vanzetti's possession.

2. Vanzetti never said that they were to be used for "small birds." He gave no testimony as to their use.

[21] Vol. V, 5251.   [22] Vol. V, 4736–4737.   [23] Vol. I, 284.   [24] Vol. V, 4737.

3. *The two cartridges mentioned by the judge were not opened "at some time during the trial."* In fact, *they were never opened at any time. They were never found to contain buckshot.*

4. Judge Thayer's mind had obviously merged the Plymouth trial with the Dedham trial. This resulted in a hopelessly confused recollection. However, the statement was not even true of the incident at Plymouth, which the judge now thought had occurred at Dedham. *No shells were opened at that trial either.* What happened there was that two of four cartridges allegedly taken from Vanzetti (but not identified as such) were opened surreptitiously by the jury after the evidence was closed.

5. The statement, with all its misleading and erroneous inferences, was phrased as if it rested on facts proven at the trial. The truth was exactly the opposite. The opening of the cartridges by the jury (with subsidiary questions) was never raised in either trial and so had never been the subject of an open inquiry by counsel or the court. Unfortunately, when Judge Thayer learned of the episode at Plymouth, he did not bring it into the light by judicial order. Instead, he allowed it to remain where he found it — in the dark. When the Supreme Judicial Court later reviewed Judge Thayer's "Decision," it could hardly avoid the conclusion from this flat assertion of the trial judge that Vanzetti had been proven to be a perjurer and the wielder of a gun loaded with lethal shot. Such a belief in the minds of the justices must have resulted in grievous harm to Vanzetti's claim that he was innocent. From what we know about the trial judge's attitude toward the defendants, this may have been precisely what he intended.[25]

The "Decision" contained the first intimation that Madeiros had some motive for making his confession other than the one he stated, namely, that he felt sorry for Mrs. Sacco and the kids. As a basis, the judge relied on Deputy Sheriff Curtis's statement that Madeiros had requested a copy of the financial report of the Sacco-Vanzetti Defense Committee and that a half hour after he got it, he sent to Curtis the envelope containing his note dated November 16, 1925.

By the time Judge Thayer penned his "Decision," there had been accumulated a mass of evidence, extrinsic and intrinsic, indicating that the Morelli gang were the perpetrators of the South Braintree crime and that Madeiros

[25] In our long brief, we made a rather casual reference to the fact that Vanzetti had not made the statement about "small birds." We did not, however, then examine the judge's assertion in its relation to Vanzetti's trial for the Bridgewater affair and to the secret happenings in the jury room at Plymouth.

was in the murder party. This being so, one would assume that the principal inquiry should have been to ascertain whether this mass of incriminating material was authentic or not. If it were found that the data were genuine, then Madeiros's motive in talking, whether good, bad or irrational, would be immaterial. On the other hand, if investigation revealed that the evidence pointing to the participation of the Morelli gang was false, or could be explained by other proven facts, then Madeiros's motive in lying might become helpful in dispelling the doubts created by his confession. In the matter of our motion for a new trial, the factual data submitted to the court were indisputable and were not controverted by other established facts. Therefore it made no difference what motive Madeiros might have had in telling his story. Nevertheless, Judge Thayer paid little attention to what could not be disproved, but concerned himself with extensive speculation concerning his motive. In this speculative endeavor he was later followed by the Governor's Advisory Committee and by the governor, although no explanation agreed with the other, not even with Mr. Ranney's — that Madeiros was a psychopathic personality.

However, Judge Thayer's speculation furnished him with an opportunity to again assail the defense for disreputable conduct. This is what he said in part, referring to Madeiros's message to the *Boston American* of November 16, 1925:

Madeiros says he sent for this report out of curiosity. But, the important question would seem to be, Who pumped this curiosity into him? It did not come to him by intuition, but rather by the acquisition of knowledge conveyed to him by somebody else who was interested in the defense of these defendants. Was Madeiros given to understand that he would receive the same aid if he had the power of this organization behind him? Would not that report show to him that there was such an organization? . . .[26]

We do not know whether the judge was charging this attempt to corrupt justice to Mr. Thompson or to some member of the Defense Committee, possibly to Francis Squires, counsel for Madeiros, who was asked to attend every conference that Mr. Thompson had with him. The slur was expressly negatived in the Bill of Exceptions (agreed to by Mr. Ranney and signed by the judge), which stated the following:

No evidence was introduced tending to show why or how the Financial Report of the Sacco-Vanzetti Defense Committee was at the Dedham jail in the

[26] Vol. V, 4745–4746.

possession of Mr. Curtis, who sent it there, or how long it had been there. No evidence was introduced that anything had been said to Madeiros by anybody about the sum of money raised by the Sacco-Vanzetti Defense Committee; or that any aid of any description had been promised to Madeiros by the Sacco-Vanzetti Defense Committee, or anyone representing Sacco and Vanzetti.[27]

The judge's speculation that Madeiros's statement resulted from his perusal of the financial report was also refuted by evidence that he had made similar statements before he sent for the report and had made earlier efforts to tell his story while in jail. This was expressly confirmed by the affidavit of Albert C. Crocker, the night officer in the jail referred to in the previous chapter.[28]

Since this occurred before Madeiros addressed his letter to the *Boston American* on November 16, when Mr. Curtis said he permitted Miller to take the financial report to Madeiros, the financial report, even if it could have had the significance Judge Thayer attached to it, could not have inspired Madeiros to make a false confession.

The judge asserted further that at the time of making his confession there was in Madeiros's mind the expectation that he would then get a respite, or series of respites (together with aid from the Committee), so that he might testify at the new trial of Sacco and Vanzetti if it were granted.[29] Judge Thayer cites as proof of what "was in Madeiros' mind" the stipulation previously mentioned in his "Decision."

One would be tempted to dismiss this part of Judge Thayer's opinion with the comment, "What of it!" The course recommended in the alleged stipulation would seem to have been proper in any event. However, the quotation from the "Decision" is important as indicating the state of Judge Thayer's mind, rather than that of Madeiros.

The paper referred to by the judge was not a stipulation nor was it signed by defendants' counsel. It was a letter from Mr. Ranney to Mr. Thompson setting out certain conditions under which the government agreed to taking the deposition of Madeiros.[30]

Not only did the judge misstate the nature of the paper, *but he failed to show that it was dated June 10, 1926, seven months after the date of Madeiros's confession* addressed to the *Boston American.*

According to Judge Thayer, therefore, "what was in Madeiros' mind" on November 16, 1925, was shown by a letter signed by the assistant district

[27] Vol. V, 4376.   [28] Vol. V, 4584–4585.   [29] Vol. V, 4746.
[30] Vol. V, 4717, and also Vol. V, 4826.

attorney on June 10, 1926. This was so, the judge reasoned, because: "One's intentions may be ascertained from subsequent acts." [31]

We recognize the soundness of this generality and also the possibility that a convict under a death sentence might confess to another crime in order to delay his execution. However, neither can be fitted into the framework of the Madeiros-Morelli evidence without drastically changing the factual context — which Judge Thayer accomplished.

Before leaving Judge Thayer's stated reasons for rejecting the Madeiros-Morelli evidence, we should mention his own original contribution. This consisted of an argument based upon a confusion of the names assigned to members of the Morelli mob.[32]

We had claimed that the evidence showed that the Buick murder car contained five persons, including two Morelli brothers (Joe and Frank), and that a third brother (Mike) had brought this car from New Bedford to South Braintree, where he met the others who had come up from Providence in the Hudson. There the Providence group switched to the Buick and put Mike in charge of the Hudson. After the robbery, according to Madeiros, the cars were again exchanged (in the Oak Street woods, just out of South Braintree) and the gang escaped in the Hudson while Mike returned in the now-empty Buick to New Bedford. To us, this seemed to be a simple explanation of what took place, was based on such evidence as we had and on known professional tactics. To Judge Thayer, however, our explanation proved that Madeiros was a liar. He based his contention on Weeks's mistake in saying that "Butsy" was the nickname for Fred Morelli. Weeks had quoted Madeiros as saying that "Mike, Joe, Bill and Butsy" were in the South Braintree job. Judge Thayer ignored the proven fact that "Butsy" was the nickname for Frank. This enabled him to make two Morellis out of one, viz.: Fred and Frank. The judge then substituted his own words "in the murder car" for Weeks's language "in that job," and this assumption produced a total of eight bandits in the Buick — five Morellis plus Madeiros, Mancini and the blond chauffeur. Since there were only five bandits in the murder car and Fred was in jail, the judge then claimed that his reasoning proved the falsity of the Madeiros account.[33]

The judge not only expanded one Morelli into two, but also contracted

---

[31] Vol. V, 4746.   [32] Vol. V, 4727 *et seq.*

[33] The judge's analysis is discussed at greater length in *The Untried Case*, 170–174, where it is referred to as "the test of the multiplying Italians."

two into one. This he did by accepting at face value Madeiros's original statement that the leader of the gang who planned and directed the job was the oldest, called "Mike." However, Madeiros said at the time that the names did not amount to anything; later he admitted that they were wrong, that Joe was older than Mike, and that he had been trying to "shield a crowd." [34] Nevertheless, by assuming that the name "Mike" assigned by Madeiros originally to the boss of the gang was meant by him to designate Mike Morelli, the obscure car thief from New Bedford, the judge was again enabled to attack Madeiros as a liar. Obviously, "Mike" could not have directed the escape to Providence if, as we claimed, he was driving the Buick in New Bedford. The judge concluded, "If Madeiros' affidavits and deposition are true, it would seem as tho Sergeant Jacobs has established a pretty good alibi for Mike since that officer had seen Mike in New Bedford on April 15, 1920, between 5 and 5:30 o'clock." [35] (Except for this reference to Sergeant Jacobs, the judge made no further use of the New Bedford episode.)

Thus, by citing as fact what was admittedly error and omitting what was admittedly correct, the judge disposed of the Madeiros account of the crime.

Perhaps the most self-revealing portion of the judge's "Decision" occurred in that part which purported to discuss the cooperation between the district attorney and the Department of Justice. He began with a personal attack on Mr. Thompson, questioning his mental responsibility.

Since the trial before the Jury of these cases, a new type of disease would seem to have developed. It might be called "lego-psychic neuroses" or "hysteria" which means: "a belief in the existence of something which in fact and truth has no such existence." This disease would seem to have reached a very dangerous condition, from the argument of counsel, upon the present Motion, when he charges Mr. Sargent, Attorney-General of the United States and his subordinates, and subordinates of Former-Attorney-General of the United States Mr. Palmer and Mr. Katzmann and the District Attorney of Norfolk County, with being in a conspiracy to send these two defendants to the electric chair, not because they are murderers but because they are radicals. From the insinuations made in the argument it seems as if the present District Attorney and his assistants must be included, from the following statement: —

"I do not believe they would indict 'Joe' in this case if two angels from heaven

---

[34] Switching of names among criminals is a well-known device to confuse the police. Madeiros himself, when arrested, said that he was "Fred Bedard," one of his accomplices in the Wrentham job.
[35] Vol. V, 4734.

came down with an affidavit in each hand saying they saw him commit the murder."

This charge was made notwithstanding the decision of the Supreme Judicial Court of this Commonwealth which affirmed the verdicts of "Guilty" in these cases. . . .[36]

The decision referred to by Judge Thayer had not "affirmed the verdicts of 'Guilty.'" It had simply overruled exceptions to Judge Thayer's actions at the trial and to his denial of motions for a new trial. Nor did the Supreme Judicial Court's decision have any bearing whatever on Mr. Thompson's remarks about the angelic affidavits accusing "Joe" of murder. At the time of the decision referred to, the Supreme Court justices had not even heard of the evidence implicating the Morelli gang.

The slur against Mr. Thompson that he was suffering from some deep-seated mental disease derived from Judge Thayer's claim that defendants' counsel had referred to the cooperation between the Department of Justice and the district attorney as "conspiracy," "fraudulent conspiracy" or "fraudulent co-operation." The charge was repeated twelve times or more in the "Decision." It was, however, another of the judge's misstatements. The Bills of Exceptions, agreed to by Mr. Ranney and signed by the judge, expressly contradicted it: "Defendants' counsel did not use the words 'conspiracy,' 'Fraudulent conspiracy,' or 'fraudulent cooperation' in reference to any United States official, or to the former or the present District Attorney of Norfolk County." [37]

Apparently the judge thought that the following argument by Mr. Thompson was equivalent to charging a "fraudulent conspiracy":

And I do not care if the evidence [referring to the correspondence between Mr. Katzmann and the Boston office of the Department of Justice], when disclosed, would be entirely neutral, would not help them at all; the mere fact that the lives of men are to be endangered, are going to be taken from them, by a Government which will not let the truth come out whether that truth helps or hurts, is enough to warrant the granting of this motion.[38]

It would have been within Judge Thayer's judicial province had he found that there was nothing improper or prejudicial in the conduct of the federal and county authorities. Others might not agree with such a conclusion, but it would not have been an unjudicial treatment of the issue. What Judge

[36] Vol. V, 4748–4749.   [37] Vol. V, 4377.   [38] Vol. V, 4750–4751.

Thayer did, however, was to question Mr. Thompson's sanity, to set up a man of straw by attributing to him abusive epithets which he did not use, and then to frame an elaborate defense of the Attorney General and Mr. Katzmann, not against the real accusation, but against accusations that existed only in the imagination of the judge. Since Judge Thayer could find no evidence proving a "fraudulent conspiracy," he denied defendants' motion for a new trial based on this nonexistent claim.

The "Decision" then went further and made the fictitious charge of "conspiracy" an excuse for Judge Thayer to hammer home the evidence which he believed justified the verdict of guilty. (It will be recalled that he used a similar device in his charge so as to restate the evidence for the Commonwealth.)

The "Decision" then restated (and occasionally misstated) the evidence which he deemed important, with many a reference to the Supreme Judicial Court as supposed added authority. It included: (1) the defendants' possession of loaded guns; (2) their alleged attempts to reach for their guns; (3) the lies told by the defendants on their arrest; (4) evidence purporting to prove that Vanzetti was carrying Berardelli's revolver; (5) the cap found in Pearl Street with all the falsehoods purporting to prove it was lost by Sacco; (6) the Fraher Winchester shell; (7) the mortal bullet; (8) the identification testimony.

We have already considered in detail the validity of the foregoing claims of the prosecution.

The "Decision" then detoured into a long discussion of the defense of "radicalism." He began by setting up another straw man: "Now, the Court desires to take up this question of 'radicalism' that has been the bone of contention since the Jury returned their verdict of 'Guilty.' " [39]

The "Decision" then dilated on the undisputed fact that it was the defendants who had introduced the subject of radicalism.

As we have seen, it was not radicalism that was the "bone of contention." It was the exploitation of it by Mr. Katzmann and the judge so as to arouse the hatred of the jury, and the abuse of it by the prosecutor to serve the purposes of the federal government. It was in his discussion of this subject that Judge Thayer forgot that he had allowed Mr. Katzmann's cross-examination of Sacco as to his defense of radicalism on the ground that he was attacking his "credibility."

[39] Vol. V, 4768.

This justification for permitting Mr. Katzmann's cross-examination was repeated by the judge in several different forms. Now, however, confronted with the affidavits proving that Mr. Katzmann was actually acting as agent of the Department of Justice concerning the defendants' "radicalism," and therefore knew all about the defendants' "radicalism" without testing his "credibility," he repudiated his own ruling at the trial: "This was not Mr. Katzmann's purpose at all. . . . Mr. Katzmann cross-examined with *one view in mind* and that was, to show there was no logical connection between their falsehoods and incriminating conduct on the one side and radicalism on the other." [40] (Emphasis added.)

Even as to this justification, as we have seen, the judge chose unfortunate illustrations. He imagined questions he supposed had been asked by Mr. Katzmann and answers by Sacco *which did not exist*.[41] He also stated, in effect, that Vanzetti gave no reason for lying about the purchase of his revolver, whereas Vanzetti had given a very logical reason: he did not want to bring his friend, Falzini, to the attention of the police.

The rest of the "Decision" was largely devoted to the theme he had dwelt upon in talking to the reporters during the trial — his fairness in conducting the trial. He quoted the remark occurring in Jeremiah McAnarney's summation (which Judge Thomas McAnarney said that Judge Thayer had solicited), "that everything has been done as Massachusetts takes pride in doing, granting to any man, however lowly his station, the fullest rights to our Massachusetts laws." [42] He quoted excerpts from his charge exhorting the jury to be fair. However, he omitted the opening of his charge comparing the jurymen to true soldiers, responding to the call to render their service in the *spirit of supreme American loyalty*.[43] In quoting what he designated as the "concluding words," he left out the actual concluding words: "Gentlemen, be just and fear not. Let all the end thou aimest at be thy country's, thy God's and truth's." [44]

He omitted any analysis of the body of his charge which, as we have seen, was a wholly unbalanced presentation calculated to produce the intended verdict of guilty. In this respect, the "Decision" would seem to be even more unfair than the charge.

Toward the end of the "Decision," the judge inserted a couple of statements that would again suggest a confused state of mind. He said: "Why,

[40] Vol. V, 4770. [41] Vol. V, 4771. [42] Vol. V, 4772. [43] Vol. II, 2239.
[44] Vol. II, 2264.

then, if the Supreme Judicial Court has affirmed these verdicts [here is the misstatement again] does it become necessary for this Court to defend that Jury against the charge of unfairness?" [45]

Why indeed? We had made no charge of unfairness against the *jury*. There was no occasion for Judge Thayer to defend the jury against that, or against any other charge. Their verdict had been based on evidence presented to them. Our motion for a new trial was based on evidence never before the Dedham jury. We were seeking a new trial for the very purpose of presenting this evidence before a jury. The judge then answered his own question. "It [his purported defense of the jury] is done solely for the purpose of having a correct statement made as to the actual proceedings before this court according to the record."

What does this assertion mean? Except for the Madeiros-Morelli evidence and the intervention of the agents of the Department of Justice, there was already in existence a correct record of the "actual proceedings before this court." Even if Judge Thayer's restatement of the trial testimony had been correct, it would not have refuted the mass of evidence pointing to the gang of professionals implicated by Madeiros. Nor could there be any explanation for the judge's excursion into the Dedham trial except a continuing psychological need to reassure himself constantly that he had been fair and that the men he was so determined to convict were in fact guilty? At any rate, Judge Thayer's "Decision" gives us his reasons for denying the motion based on the Madeiros-Morelli evidence.

Writing in the *Atlantic Monthly* in 1927, Felix Frankfurter had this to say of Judge Thayer's "Decision":

. . . I assert with deep regret, but without the slightest fear of disproof, that certainly in modern times Judge Thayer's opinion stands unmatched, happily, for discrepancies between what the record discloses and what the opinion conveys. His 25,000-word document cannot accurately be described otherwise than as a farrago of misquotations, misrepresentations, suppressions and mutilations. The disinterested inquirer could not possibly derive from it a true knowledge of the new evidence that was submitted to him as the basis for a new trial. The opinion is literally honeycombed with demonstrable errors, and confused with a spirit alien to judicial utterance.[46]

Judge Thayer denied our motion for a new trial on October 23, 1926, and we argued the appeal before the Supreme Judicial Court on January 27 and

[45] Vol. V, 4772.   [46] "The Case of Sacco and Vanzetti."

28, 1927. During the recess on the first day, Mr. Thompson suddenly asked me to continue the argument which he had begun, saying that he was tired. Undoubtedly he was tired, but it would have been characteristic of him to ask me, as his young junior, to share in our last courtroom opportunity to save our clients. My personal involvement with the Madeiros-Morelli evidence made the task an easy one. I thought that both our arguments had been received with deep and sympathetic interest. Apparently this was due to my inexperience in reading the expressions of the judges.

After the close of the hearing, Mr. Thompson and I went to his office to exchange impressions. Mr. Thompson sensed my optimism and tried to sustain it. He called attention to what he said appeared to be favorable reactions on the part of several judges whom he named. I departed in a rather confident mood. However, I had left my brief bag in his office and returned unexpectedly to pick it up. Mr. Thompson was standing behind his desk. His usual erect posture was gone, his great frame seemed slack and somewhat stooped. I thought he was looking down at something on his desk. He did not raise his eyes when I entered, but apparently mistook my tread for the step of his partner, George Mears.

"There is no hope, Mr. Mears," he said in a husky voice, broken with emotion. "There is no hope."

When he saw that it was not his partner but his junior in the Sacco-Vanzetti case who stood before him, there was a moment of troubled embarrassment, but nothing further was said by either of us concerning his inadvertent disclosure of deep despair.

The decision of the Supreme Judicial Court overruling all exceptions to Judge Thayer's denial of our motions for a new trial came down on April 5, 1927. On the fourth day thereafter, Judge Thayer sentenced Sacco and Vanzetti to death by electrocution. Mr. Thompson's premonition was fully justified.

26.

Sentencing of Sacco and Vanzetti

COMMONWEALTH OF MASSACHUSETTS.

Norfolk, ss.   Superior Criminal Court
Nos. 5545 and 5546   Thayer, J.

COMMONWEALTH

v.

NICOLA SACCO

and

BARTOLOMEO VANZETTI

Present:

    Winfield M. Wilbar, DISTRICT ATTORNEY
    Wm. P. Kelly, ASS'T. DISTRICT ATTORNEY
    Dudley P. Ranney, ASS'T. DISTRICT ATTORNEY
    for the Commonwealth.

    William G. Thompson, Esq.,
    Herbert B. Ehrmann, Esq.,
    for the Defendants.

DEDHAM, MASSACHUSETTS,
Saturday, April 9, 1927.
10 A.M.

MR. WILBAR. May it please the Court, the matter under consideration at this session is indictments Nos. 5545 and 5546, Commonwealth vs. Nicola Sacco and Bartolomeo Vanzetti.

At this time I would like to move the Court to have an interpreter sworn.

(An interpreter is sworn by Clerk of Court Worthington.)

MR. WILBAR. It appears by the record of this Court, if your Honor please, that on indictment No. 5545, Commonwealth vs. Nicola Sacco and Bartolomeo Vanzetti that these defendants stand convicted of murder in the first degree. The records are clear at the present time, and I therefore move the Court for the imposition of sentence. The statute allows the Court some discretion as to the time within which this sentence may be imposed. Having that in mind, and at the request of the defendants' counsel, to which the Commonwealth readily assents, I would suggest that the sentence to be imposed shall be executed some time during the week beginning Sunday, July 10 next.

CLERK WORTHINGTON. Nicola Sacco, have you anything to say why sentence of death should not be passed upon you?

Statement by Nicola Sacco

Yes, sir. I am not an orator. It is not very familiar with me the English language, and as I know, as my friend has told me, my comrade Vanzetti will speak more long, so I thought to give him the chance.

I never know, never heard, even read in history anything so cruel as this Court. After seven years prosecuting they still consider us guilty. And these gentle people here are arrayed with us in this court today.

I know the sentence will be between two class, the oppressed class and the rich class, and there will be always collision between one and the other. We fraternize the people with the books, with the literature. You persecute the people, tyrannize over them and kill them. We try the education of people always. You try to put a path between us and some other nationality that hates each other. That is why I am here today on this bench, for having been the oppressed class. Well, you are the oppressor.

You know it, Judge Thayer, — you know all my life, you know why I have been here, and after seven years that you have been persecuting me and my poor wife, and you still today sentence us to death. I would like to tell all my life, but what is the use? You know all about what I say before, and my friend — that is, my comrade — will be talking, because he is more familiar with the language, and I will give him a chance. My comrade, the man kind, the kind man to all the children, you sentence him two times in the Bridgewater case and the Dedham case, connected with me, and you know he is innocent. You forget all the population that has been with us for seven years, to sympathize and give us all their energy and all their kindness. You do not care for them. Among that peoples and the comrades and the working class there is a big legion of intellectual people which have been with us for seven years, but to not commit the iniquitous sentence, but still the Court goes ahead. And I think I thank you all, you peoples, my comrades who have been with me for seven years, with the Sacco-Vanzetti case, and I will give my friend a chance.

I forget one thing which my comrade remember me. As I said before, Judge Thayer know all my life, and he know that I am never been guilty, never, — not yesterday nor today nor forever.

CLERK WORTHINGTON. Bartolomeo Vanzetti, have you anything to say why sentence of death should not be passed upon you?

Statement by Bartolomeo Vanzetti

Yes. What I say is that I am innocent, not only of the Braintree crime, but also of the Bridgewater crime. That I am not only innocent of these two crimes, but in all my life I have never stole and I have never killed and I have never spilled blood. That is what I want to say. And it is not all. Not only am I innocent of these two crimes, not only in all my life I have never stole, never killed, never spilled blood, but I have struggled all my life, since I began to reason, to eliminate crime from the earth.

Everybody that knows these two arms knows very well that I did not need to go in between the street and kill a man to take the money. I can live with my two arms and live well. But besides that, I can live even without work with my arm for other people. I have had plenty of chance to live independently and to live what the world conceives to be a higher life than not to gain our bread with the sweat of our brow.

My father in Italy is in a good condition. I could have come back in Italy and he would have welcomed me every time with open arms. Even if I come back there with not a cent in my pocket, my father could have give me a possession, not to work but to make business, or to oversee upon the land that he owns. He has wrote me many letters in that sense, and other well to do relatives have wrote me many letters in that sense that I can produce.

Well, it may be a boast. My father and my uncle can boast themselves and say things that people may not be compelled to believe. People may say they may be poor when I say that they are to consider to give me a position every time that I want to settle down and form a family and start a settled life. Well, but there are people maybe in this same court that could testify to what I have say and what my father and my uncle have say to me is not a lie, that really they have the means to give me position every time that I want.

Well, I want to reach a little point farther, and it is this, — that not only have I not been trying to steal in Bridgewater, not only have I not been in Braintree to steal and kill and have never steal or kill or spilt blood in all my life, not only have I struggled hard against crimes, but I have refused myself the commodity or glory of life, the pride of life of a good position, because in my consideration it is not right to exploit man. I have refused to go in business because I understand that business is a speculation on profit upon certain people that must depend upon the business man, and I do not consider that that is right and therefore I refuse to do that.

Now, I should say that I am not only innocent of all these things, not only have I never committed a real crime in my life — though some sins but not crimes — not only have I struggled all my life to eliminate crimes, the crimes that the official law and the official moral condemns, but also the crime that the official moral and the official law sanctions and sanctifies, — the exploitation and the oppression of the man by the man, and if there is a reason why I am here as a guilty man, if there is a reason why you in a few minutes can doom me, it is this reason and none else.

I beg your pardon. (Referring to paper) There is the more good man I ever cast my eyes upon since I lived, a man that will last and will grow always more near and more dear to the people, as far as into the heart of the people, so long as admiration for goodness and for sacrifice will last. I mean Eugene Debs. I will say that even a dog that killed the chickens would not have found an American jury to convict it with the proof that the Commonwealth produced against us. That man was not with me in Plymouth or with Sacco where he was on the day of the crime. You can say that it is arbitrary, what we are saying, that he is good and he applied to the other his own goodness, that he is incapable of crime, and he believed that everybody is incapable of crime.

Well, it may be like that but it is not, it could be like that but it is not, and that man has a real experience of court, of prison and of jury. Just because he want the world a little better he was persecuted and slandered from his boyhood to his old age, and indeed he was murdered by the prison. He know, and not only he but every man of understanding in the world, not only in this country but also in the other countries, men that we have provided a certain amount of a record of the times, they all still stick with us, the flower of mankind of Europe, the better writers, the greatest thinkers of Europe, have pleaded in our favor. The scientists, the greatest scientists, the greatest statesmen of Europe, have pleaded in our favor. The people of foreign nations have pleaded in our favor.

Is it possible that only a few on the jury, only two or three men, who would condemn their mother for worldly honor and for earthly fortune; is it possible that they are right against what the world, the whole world has say it is wrong and that I know that it is wrong? If there is one that I should know it, if it is right or if it is wrong, it is I and this man. You see it is seven years that we are in jail. What we have suffered during these seven years no human tongue can say, and yet you see me before you, not trembling, you see me looking you in your eyes straight, not blushing, not changing color, not ashamed or in fear.

Eugene Debs say that not even a dog — something like that — not even a dog that kill the chickens would have been found guilty by American jury with the evidence that the Commonwealth have produced against us. I say that not even a leprous dog would have his appeal refused two times by the Supreme Court of Massachusetts — not even a leprous dog.

They have given a new trial to Madeiros for the reason that the Judge had either forgot or omitted to tell the jury that they should consider the man innocent until found guilty in the court, or something of that sort. That man has confessed. The man was tried and has confessed, and the court give him another trial. We have proved that there could not have been another Judge on the face of the earth more prejudiced and more cruel than you have been against us. We have proven that. Still they refuse the new trial. We know, and you know in your heart, that you have been against us from the very beginning, before you see us. Before you see us you already know that we were radicals, that we were underdogs, that we were the enemy of the institution that you can believe in good faith in their goodness — I don't want to condemn that — and that it was easy on the time of the first trial to get a verdict of guiltiness.

We know that you have spoke yourself and have spoke your hostility against us, and your despisement against us with friends of yours on the train, at the University Club of Boston, on the Golf Club of Worcester, Massachusetts. I am sure that if the people who know all what you say against us would have the civil courage to take the stand, maybe your Honor — I am sorry to say this because you are an old man, and I have an old father — but maybe you would be beside us in good justice at this time.

When you sentenced me at the Plymouth trial you say, to the best of my memory, of my good faith, that crimes were in accordance with my principle, — something of that sort, — and you take off one charge, if I remember it exactly, from the jury. The jury was so violent against me that they found me guilty of both charges, because there were only two. But they would have found me guilty of a dozen of charges against your Honor's instructions. Of course I remember that you told them that there was no reason to believe that if I were the bandit I have intention to kill somebody, so that they will take off the indictment of attempt to murder. Well, they found me guilty of what? And if I am right, you take out that and sentence me only for attempt to rob with arms, — something like that. But, Judge Thayer, you give more to me for that attempt of robbery than all the 448 men that were in Charlestown, all of those that attempted to rob, all those that have robbed, they have not such a sentence as you gave me for an attempt at robbery.

I am willing that everybody that does believe me that they can make commission, they can go over there, and I am very willing that the people should go over there and see whether it is true or not. There are people in Charlestown who are professional robbers, who have been in half the prisons of the United States, that they are steal, or hurt the man, shoot him. By chance he got better, he did not die. Well, the most of them guilty without trial, by self-confession, and by asking the aid of their own partner, and they got 8 to 10, 8 to 12, 10 to 15. None of them has 12 to 15, as you gave me for an attempt at robbery. And besides that, you know that I was not guilty. You know that my life, my private and public life in Plymouth, and wherever I have been, was so exemplary that one of the worst fears of our prosecutor Katzmann was to introduce proof of our life and of our conduct. He has taken it off with all his might and he has succeeded.

You know if we would have Mr. Thompson, or even the brother McAnarney, in the first trial in Plymouth, you know that no jury would have found me guilty. My first lawyer has been a partner of Mr. Katzmann, as he is still now. My first lawyer of the defense, Mr. Vahey, has not defended me, has sold me for thirty golden money like Judas sold Jesus Christ. If that man has not told to you or to Mr. Katzmann that he know that I was guilty, it is because he know that I was not guilty. That man has done everything indirectly to hurt us. He has made long speech with the jury about things that do matter nothing, and on the point of essence to the trial he has passed over with few words or with complete silence. This was a premeditation in order to give to the jury the impression that my own defender has nothing good to say, has nothing good to urge in defense of myself, and therefore go around the bush on little things that amount to nothing and let pass the essential points either in silence or with a very weakly resistance.

We were tried during a time that has now passed into history. I mean by that, a time when there was a hysteria of resentment and hate against the people of our principles, against the foreigner, against slackers, and it seems to me — rather, I am positive of it, that both you and Mr. Katzmann has done all what it were in your power in order to work out, in order to agitate still more the passion of the juror, the prejudice of the juror, against us.

I remember that Mr. Katzmann has introduced a witness against us, a certain Ricci. Well, I have heard that witness. It seems that he has nothing to say. It seemed that it was foolishness to produce a witness that has nothing to say. And it seemed if he were called by the Commonwealth to tell the jury that he was the foreman of that laborer that was near the scene of the crime and who claimed, and it was testified in our behalf, that we were not the men and that this man, the witness Ricci, was his foreman, and he has tried to keep the man on the job instead of going to see what was happening so as to give the impression that it was not true that the man went towards the street to see what happened. But that was not very important. The real importance is that that man say that it was not true. That a certain witness that was the water boy of the gang of the laborers testified that he take a pail and go to a certain spring, a water spring, to take water for the gang — it was not true that he go to that spring, and therefore it was not true that he see the bandit, and therefore it was not true that he can tell that neither I nor Sacco were the men. But it was introduced to show that it was not true that that man go to that spring, because they know that the Germans has poisoned the water in that spring. That is what he say on that stand over there. Now, in the world chronicle of the time there is not a single happening of that nature. Nobody in America — we have read plenty things bad that the Germans have done in Europe during the war, but nobody can prove and nobody will say that the Germans are bad enough to poison the spring water in this country during the war.

Now, this, it seems, has nothing to do with us directly. It seems to be a thing by incident on the stand between the other thing that is the essence here. But the jury were hating us because we were against the war, and the jury don't know that it makes any difference between a man that is against the war because he believes that the war is unjust, because he hate no country, because he is a cosmopolitan, and a man that is against the war because he is in favor of the other country that fights against the country in which he is, and therefore a spy, and he commits any crime in the country in which he is in behalf of the other country in order to scrve the other country. We are not men of that kind. Katzmann know very well that. Katzmann know that we were against the war because we did not believe in the purpose for which they say that the war was done. We believe it that the war is wrong, and we believe this more now after ten years that we understood it day by day, — the consequences and the result of the after war. We believe more now than ever that the war was wrong, and we are against war more now than ever, and I am glad to be on the doomed scaffold if I can say to mankind, "Look out; you are in a catacomb of the flower of mankind. For what? All that they say to you, all that they have promised to you — it was a lie, it was an illusion, it was a cheat, it was a fraud, it was a crime. They promised you liberty. Where is liberty? They promised you prosperity. Where is prosperity? They have promised you elevation. Where is the elevation?

From the day that I went in Charlestown, the misfortune, the population of Charlestown has doubled in number. Where is the moral good that the War has given to the world? Where is the spiritual progress that we have achieved from the War? Where are the security of life, the security of the things that we possess for our necessity? Where are the respect for human life? Where are the respect and the admiration for the good characteristics and the good of the human nature? Never as now before the war there have been so many crimes, so many corruptions, so many degeneration as there is now.

In the best of my recollection and of my good faith, during the trial Katzmann has told to the jury that a certain Coacci has brought in Italy the money that, according to the State theory, I and Sacco have stole in Braintree. We never steal that money. But Katzmann, when he told that to the jury, he know already that that was not true. He know already that that man was deported in Italy with the Federal policeman after our arrest. I remember well that the

Federal policeman with him in their possession — that the Federal policeman has taken away the trunks from the very boarding where he was, and bring the trunks over here and look them over and found not a single money.

Now, I call that murder, to tell to the jury that a friend or comrade or a relative or acquaintance of the charged man, of the indicted man, has carried the money to Italy, when he knows it is not true. I can call that nothing else but a murder, a plain murder.

But Katzmann has told something else also against us that was not true. If I understand well, there have been agreement of counsel during the trial in which the counsel of defense shall not produce any evidence of my good conduct in Plymouth and the counsel of the prosecution would not have let the jury know that I was tried and convicted another time before in Plymouth. Well, I call that a one-sided agreement. In fact, even the telephone poles knew at the time of this trial at Dedham that I was tried and convicted in Plymouth; the jurymen knew that even when they slept. On the other side the jury have never seen I or Sacco and I think they have the right to incline to believe that the jury have never approached before the trial anyone that was sufficiently intimate with me and Sacco to be able to give them a description of our personal conduct. The jury don't know nothing about us. They have never seen us. The only thing that they know is the bad things that the newspaper have say when we were arrested and the bad story that the newspaper have say on the Plymouth trial.

I don't know why the defense counsel have made such an agreement, but I know very well why Katzmann has made such agreement, because he know that half of the population of Plymouth would have been willing to come over here and say that in seven years that I was living amongst them that I was never seen drunk, that I was known as the most strong and steadfast worker of the community. As a matter of fact I was called a mule and the people that know a little better the condition of my father and that I was a single man, much wondered at me and say, "Why you work like a mad man in that way when you have no children and no wife to care about?"

Well, Katzmann should have been satisfied on that agreement. He could have thanked his God and estimate himself a lucky man. But he was not satisfied with that. He broke his word and he tell to the jury that I was tried before in this very court. I don't know if that is right in the record, if that was take off or not, but I hear with my ear. When two or three women from Plymouth come to take the stand, the woman reach that point where this gentleman sit down over there, the jury were sit down in their place, and Katzmann asked this woman if they have not testified before for Vanzetti, and they say, yes, and he tell to them, "You cannot testify." They left the room. After that they testified just the same. But in the meanwhile he tell to the jury that I have been tried before. That I think is not to make justice to the man who is looking after the true, and it is a frameup with which he has split my life and doomed me.

It was also said that the defense has put every obstacle to the handling of this case in order to delay the case. That sound weak for us, and I think it is injurious because it is not true. If we consider that the prosecution, the State, has employed one entire year to prosecute us, that is, one of the five years that the case has last was taken by the prosecution to begin our trial, our first trial. Then the defense make an appeal to you and you waited, or I think that you were resolute, that you had the resolute in your heart when the trial finished that you will refuse every appeal that we will put up to you. You waited a month or a month and a half and just lay down your decision on the eve of Christmas — just on the evening of Christmas. We do not believe in the fable of the evening of Christmas, neither in the historical way nor in the church way. You know some of our folks still believe in that, and because we do not believe in that, it don't mean that we are not human. We are human, and Christmas is sweet to the heart of every man. I think that you have done that, to hand down your decision on the evening of Christmas; to poison the heart of our family and of our beloved. I am sorry to be compelled to say this, but everything that was said on your side has confirmed my suspicion until that suspicion has changed to certitude. So that you see that one year it has taken before trying us.

Then the defense, in presenting the new appeal, has not taken more time that you have taken in answer to that. Then there came the second appeal, and now I am not sure whether it is the second appeal or the third appeal where you wait eleven months or one year without an answer to us, and I am sure that you have decide to refuse us a new trial before the hearing for the new appeal began. You take one year to answer it, or eleven months, — something like that. So that you see that out of the five years, two were taken by the State from the day of our arrest to the trial, and then one year to wait for your answer on the second or the third appeal.

Then on another occasion that I don't remember exactly now, Mr. Williams was sick and the things were delayed not for fault of the defense but on account of the fault of the prosecution. So that I am positive that if a man take a pencil in his hand and compute the time taken by the prosecution in prosecuting the case, and the time that was taken by the defence to defend this case, the prosecution has taken more time than the defense, and there is a great consideration that must be taken in this point, and it is that my first lawyer betrayed us, — the whole American population were against us. We have the misfortune to take a man from California, and he came here, and he was ostracized by you and by every authority, even by the jury, and is so much so that no part of Massachusetts is immune from what I would call the prejudice, — that is, to believe that each people in each place of the world, they believe to be the better of the world, and they believe that all the other are not so good as they. So of course the man that came from California into Massachusetts to defend two of us, he must be licked if it is possible, and he was licked all right. And we have our part too.

What I want to say is this: Everybody ought to understand that the first of the defense has been terrible. My first lawyer did not stick to defend us. He has made no work to collect witnesses and evidence in our favor. The record in the Plymouth Court is a pity. I am told that they are almost one-half lost. So the defense had a tremendous work to do in order to collect some evidence, to collect some testimony to offset and to learn what the testimony of the State has done. And in this consideration it must be said that even if the defense take double time of the State without delay, double time that they delay the case it would have been reasonable, whereas it took less than the State.

Well, I have already say that I not only am not guilty of these two crimes, but I never commit a crime in my life, — I have never steal and I have never kill and

I have never spilt blood, and I have fought against the crime, and I have fought and I have sacrified myself even to eliminate the crimes that the law and the church legitimate and sanctify.

This is what I say: I would not wish to a dog or to a snake, to the most low and misfortunate creature of the earth — I would not wish to any of them what I have had to suffer for things that I am not guilty of. But my conviction is that I have suffered for things that I am guilty of. I am suffering because I am a radical and indeed I am a radical; I have suffered because I was an Italian, and indeed I am an Italian; I have suffered more for my family and for my beloved than for myself; but I am so convinced to be right that if you could execute me two times, and if I could be reborn two other times, I would live again to do what I have done already.

I have finished. Thank you.

THE COURT. Under the law of Massachusetts the jury says whether a defendant is guilty or innocent. The Court has absolutely nothing to do with that question. The law of Massachusetts provides that a Judge cannot deal in any way with the facts. As far as he can go under our law is to state the evidence.

During the trial many exceptions were taken. Those exceptions were taken to the Supreme Judicial Court. That Court, after examining the entire record, after examining all the exceptions, — that Court in its final words said, "The verdicts of the jury should stand; exceptions overruled." That being true, there is only one thing that this Court can do. It is not a matter of discretion. It is a matter of statutory requirement, and that being true there is only one duty that now devolves upon this Court, and that is to pronounce the sentences.

First the Court pronounces sentence upon Nicola Sacco. It is considered and ordered by the Court that you, Nicola Sacco, suffer the punishment of death by the passage of a current of electricity through your body within the week beginning on Sunday, the tenth day of July, in the year of our Lord, one thousand, nine hundred and twenty-seven. This is the sentence of the law.

It is considered and ordered by the Court that you, Bartolomeo Vanzetti —

MR. VANZETTI. Wait a minute, please, your Honor. May I speak for a minute with my lawyer, Mr. Thompson?

MR. THOMPSON. I do not know what he wants to say.

THE COURT. I think I should pronounce the sentence. — Bartolomeo Vanzetti, suffer the punishment of death —

MR. SACCO. You know I am innocent. That is the same words I pronounced seven years ago. You condemn two innocent men.

THE COURT. — by the passage of a current of electricity through your body within the week beginning on Sunday, the tenth day of July, in the year of our Lord, one thousand nine hundred and twenty-seven. This is the sentence of the law.

We will now take a recess.

(At 11:00 A.M., the Court adjourned without day.)

The next day Vanzetti handed to friends the notes of what he had wished to say further to Judge Thayer when he interrupted the pronouncement of sentence. Included in those notes was this estimate of Sacco:

I have talk a great deal of myself but I even forgot to name Sacco. Sacco too is a worker from his boyhood, a skilled worker lover of work, with a good job and pay, a bank account, a good and lovely wife, two beautiful children and a neat little home at the verge of a wood, near a brook. Sacco is a heart, a faith, a character, a man; a man lover of nature and of mankind. A man who gave all, who sacrifice all to the cause of Liberty and to his love for mankind; money, rest, mundain ambitions, his own wife, his children, himself and his own life. Sacco has never dreamt to steal, never to assassinate. He and I have never brought a morsel of bread to our mouths, from our childhood to to-day — which has not been gained by the sweat of our brows. Never. His people also are in good position and of good reputation.

Oh, yes, I may be more witful, as some have put it, I am a better babbler than he is, but many, many times in hearing his heartful voice ringing a faith sublime, in considering his supreme sacrifice, remembering his heroism I felt small small at the presence of his greatness and found myself compelled to fight back from my eyes the tears, and quanch my heart trobling to my throat to not weep before him — this man called thief and assassin and doomed. But Sacco's name will live in the hearts of the people and in their gratitude when Katzmann's and yours bones will be dispersed by time, when your name, his name, your laws, institutions, and your false god are but a *deem rememoring of a cursed past in which man was wolf to the man.* . . .

27.

Judge with a Mission

Did you see what I did with those anarchistic bastards the other day?
JUDGE WEBSTER THAYER, to PROFESSOR
JAMES P. RICHARDSON at DARTMOUTH
Holt Record, Vol. V, p. 5065

Of all the "ifs" that might have changed the ending of the Sacco-Vanzetti case, perhaps the one with the highest degree of visibility is the personality of the trial judge himself. Of course, it is not possible to state positively that the final result would have been different if another judge had been chosen for the task. However, a lawyer familiar with the personnel of the bench in 1921 could say with some assurance that the trials, especially the murder case at Dedham, would have been conducted quite differently. Most, if not all, of the other judges would have shown a far more scrupulous regard for fairness toward the accused.

Judge Thayer was unique among the judges in that it is now obvious that from the start he was determined to secure a conviction. Although much of what we know about Judge Thayer's mind and his intentions comes from his own talk off the bench and from his conduct of the trial and rulings thereafter, there were premonitory signals even before he began to preside over the trials, as for instance his tirade against the jury for acquitting the anarchist Zagroff in April 1920.

It was pure chance that, not many weeks after the Zagroff episode, Judge Thayer donned his judicial robes at Plymouth to preside over Vanzetti's trial in 1920. In Massachusetts, the Superior Court justices are statewide judges, but are designated by the Chief Justice to sit in the various counties for the trial of cases arising in the respective jurisdictions.

The situation in June 1921, however, was different. In the spring of 1920, Judge Thayer was the designated judge to sit at the jury session in Norfolk County. When the tentative schedule of sittings was made up in July 1920 for the next twelve months, Judge Thayer was designated to sit at the jury session in Fitchburg in June 1921. However, when the special session to try Sacco and Vanzetti opened on May 31, 1921, it found Judge Thayer presiding in Dedham. Reportedly, Judge Thayer requested Chief Justice Aiken to assign him to the Dedham trial for the South Braintree murders. In his book *Tragedy in Dedham*,[1] Francis Russell states that Judge Thayer wrote his fellow Dartmouth alumnus Chief Justice Aiken requesting that he be assigned to preside at the special session in Dedham to try Sacco and Vanzetti. I had previously received advice that there was such a letter among Judge Aiken's papers in Northampton, but did not receive a copy.

It is rather surprising that Judge Aiken acceded to this request, especially since Judge Thayer had been the trial justice at Plymouth. Defense counsel Thomas McAnarney later stated his opinion that it was impossible for Judge Thayer to be fair after he had been the judge in the Plymouth trial. It is unlikely, however, that Judge Aiken, who was a good judge, had

[1] P. 127.

any idea that Judge Thayer's purpose was to make sure, so far as possible, that Sacco and Vanzetti would be convicted.

It has been said in Judge Thayer's defense that his attitude toward the defendants was the normal judicial reaction to a belief that the defendants were guilty. This, however, was not the result of any evidence presented at Dedham. We shall see that he indicated his belief at the start of the trial before the prosecution had proceeded very far and prior to any defense testimony. Possibly he formed his opinion as a result of the Plymouth trial, not merely from the verdict and testimony in that case, but also from Mr. Katzmann's insinuations about Boda, the Buick, shotgun shells, the supposedly mysterious doings around the Johnson home and loose claims to evidence which he never produced. If so, it would be confirmation of Judge McAnarney's opinion, given to the Governor's Advisory Committee, that Judge Thayer could not be fair at Dedham because he had been the trial judge at Plymouth.

During and after the trial, Judge Thayer talked freely about the case off the bench to various persons. This was highly improper and most Massachusetts judges would have eschewed all such talk with anyone outside of the courtroom. Judge Thayer's violation of judicial standards in this respect was another abnormality in the Sacco-Vanzetti case — although history owes a debt to Judge Thayer for this self-exposure of his thoughts and purposes.

Let us now turn to some of Judge Thayer's talk during the trial.

John Nicholas Beffel was a journalist who attended the trial as correspondent for the Federated Press. On April 28, 1927, he deposed (in part) as follows:

On or about the fourth morning of the trial, Marquis A. Ferrante, Italian consul at Boston, was present in court as a spectator. At the close of that session, I went over to where the consul was seated and talked with him. He asked me to take down a brief statement which he wished to give out to the press, and requested me to pass it on to all the reporters at the trial. The statement was this: "The Italian authorities are deeply interested in the case of Sacco and Vanzetti, and this trial will be closely followed by them. They have complete confidence that the trial will be conducted solely as a criminal proceeding, without reference to the political or social beliefs of anyone involved."

Immediately afterward I typed this statement, making several carbon copies. Then I walked down to the Dedham Inn, and entered the private dining-room in which Judge Webster Thayer and the reporters usually ate their lunches. I sat down with several of the other newspapermen and gave them copies of the consul's utterance. Judge Thayer was sitting in another corner of the room, at his own table. When the judge got up to leave the room Jack English of the *Boston American* showed him Marquis Ferrante's statement and asked him what he thought of it. Judge Thayer made a gesture of anger.

"Why," he said, "that fellow came clear out to my home in Worcester and assured me that the Italian government had no interest in this case."

This was uttered in the presence of several newspapermen including Jack English, Frank P. Sibley of the *Boston Globe*, Jack Harding of the Associated Press, and I think Charles Folsom of the *Boston Herald*.

Other questions were then asked by the reporters. One of the questions had to do with Fred H. Moore, of counsel for the defense. Mention of Moore's name aroused signs of hostility from Judge Thayer. (This was on the day when the special venire of 175 extra talesmen had been gathered in, and all morning the defense had strenuously opposed the use of any of these talesmen as jurors, on the ground that they had been summoned not from the highways and by-ways as required by law, but from special places such as a Masonic meeting.)

Referring to Attorney Moore's objections to this special venire, Judge Thayer said: "And what do you suppose that fellow wanted me to ask those veniremen? 'Are you a member of a labor union? Are you opposed to union labor? Are you a member of a secret society?' "

The judge made another gesture of anger, and went on, addressing the newspapermen in general: "Did you ever see a case in which so many leaflets and circulars have been spread broadcast saying that people couldn't get a fair trial in the State of Massachusetts?"

There was no mistaking that Judge Thayer was thoroughly angry. His remarks were uttered in a high voice and his face was flushed.

He was now near the doorway leading out into the hall of the inn. At this point I stepped forward and tried to explain to him that I had given the other reporters Consul Ferrante's statement at the consul's express request. But the judge would not listen to my explanation. He brushed me aside, and as he turned to leave the room he shook his fist and said to the other newspapermen: *"You wait till I give my charge to the jury. I'll show 'em!"*

Immediately after Judge Thayer left, there was a consultation among the newspapermen as to what they ought to write about the incident. This discussion lasted until we were all back in the courtroom. Harding of the Associated Press looked upon the occurrence as controversial matter, quite apart from the issues involved in the trial, and the policy of his organization was to keep clear of controversies. Sibley of the *Boston Globe* was of like opinion, and said: "Let's all agree that we won't say anything about it." This was agreed to, and none of the newspapers nor press associations mentioned the incident. It has never yet been made public. [Emphasis added.][2]

According to this statement by Mr. Beffel, Judge Thayer, *even before the jury was impaneled*, was voicing a threat to the reporters concerning what he would do to the defendants in his charge. Since Mr. Beffel later aided the defense as an investigator, the truth of his statement might be subject to

[2] Vol. V, 4929–4930.

doubt *were it not for the fact that Judge Thayer's expressed attitude toward the defendants was fully confirmed by others.* Judge Thayer must have imparted his attitude to the McAnarneys, since it was at this time that John McAnarney telephoned to Mr. Thompson at night, getting him out of bed, with his S.O.S. call for help the next morning at Dedham.

Mr. Beffel's statement contains other interesting information. Apparently Judge Thayer had discussed international aspects of the case with the Italian consul, who visited him at his home in Worcester for this purpose. This was indeed a strange dialogue between a Massachusetts judge presiding at a murder trial and an accredited diplomatic representative of a foreign country. For a special reason, I believe the conference between Judge Thayer and Ferrante occurred. On July 20, 1927, Marquis Agostino Ferrante appeared before the Governor's Advisory Committee and made an eloquent, if unofficial, plea on behalf of Sacco and Vanzetti, "on my own personality," [3] as he put it. He said he had a talk with Judge Thayer at the beginning of the trial, "But he was sure that those two men were guilty, he was absolutely confirmed in his soul that those two men were guilty, and this feeling of his was evident all through the trial." He explained that Judge Thayer made his belief obvious, not by words which can be read in the record, but by his manner and inflection of voice when he was ostensibly putting questions, or answering counsel or making rulings.[4]

Marquis Ferrante attended the trial almost every day. He was not only critical of Judge Thayer's attitude on the bench, but also of Katzmann's harping on socialism and communism, which created a feeling that the defendants were "bad men" because they were Reds. He said the evidence against the men was not sufficient "in my conscience." In effect, the consul's appraisal of the government's case was "not proven" — the same opinion voiced by Assistant District Attorney Ranney. Marquis Ferrante could not see how twelve men who heard the same evidence could declare a man guilty in "a very short time." He disliked Moore, because he had asked him to do something he did not consider right. (The marquis did not specify what this was. We can only surmise.) He thought Moore had done more to "hurt these two men than anything else." [5]

As Marquis Ferrante left the hearing room, Mr. Lowell exclaimed reverently, "The finest type of Italian gentleman." The governor's secretary, Herman MacDonald, then went to lunch with Marquis Ferrante at the

[3] Vol. V, 5251.   [4] Vol. V, 5245.   [5] Vol. V, 5250.

consul's invitation. Perhaps the marquis wanted to send the same word to the governor that he had conveyed to Judge Thayer, namely, that (despite his plea) his government had no interest in the outcome of the case. As Mr. Thompson and I watched this bit of byplay, we looked at one another. We understood the marquis's problem and were willing to concede that he was a gentleman. However, the same thought passed through both our minds. It concerned Mr. Lowell's views, not those of the marquis. By this time we had been advised, and noted for ourselves, that Mr. Lowell saw Vanzetti as a robber and a murderer. For us, who had come to know well the quality of Vanzetti's spirit under a mental torture so great it had even temporarily unhinged his mind, it was the humble fish peddler who more nearly approached "the finest type of Italian gentleman."

Frank Sibley, ace reporter of the *Boston Globe*, confirmed to the Governor's Advisory Committee the impression that Judge Thayer was determined to secure a conviction. Sibley had been a reporter for thirty-five years, on the *Boston Globe* for twenty-five years. He was highly respected as the dean of all Boston reporters.

What affected me more than anything else was his manner. It is nothing that you can read in the record. In my thirty-five years I never saw anything like it. . . . His whole manner, attitude seemed to be that the jurors were there to convict these men. . . .[6]

His method of conducting this case was something I had never seen before. The rulings against the defendants were done with the air of prejudice and scorn.[7]

Mr. Sibley told how Judge Thayer would approach the reporters' table at lunchtime at the Dedham Inn and talk about the case. On one of these occasions the judge admonished the reporters: "I think I am entitled to have printed in the newspapers a statement that this trial is being fairly and impartially conducted."

When this was followed by silence, Judge Thayer turned to Sibley and said: "Sibley, you are the oldest, don't you think this trial is being fairly and impartially conducted?"

To this, Sibley replied: "Well, I don't know whether to express their opinion, but of course we have talked it over, and I think I can say we have never seen anything like it." [8]

[6] Vol. V, 4956.   [7] Vol. V, 4957.   [8] Vol. V, 4955.

Mr. Sibley reported that at the very beginning of the case, Judge Thayer "referred to Moore to me as 'a long haired anarchist from California.' " [9]

After a while Sibley quit being with Judge Thayer because it was improper for a judge to discuss the case with a reporter.[10]

Mr. Sibley called attention to a number of instances of Judge Thayer's unprecedented conduct. One of these occurred when he happened to pass close to the bench as the lawyers stepped up to have a conference. The court reporter, as was the customary procedure, approached with his notebook to take down what was said. When Judge Thayer saw this he waved him away with the remark: "Get the hell out of here, who called you up here?" [11]

On another occasion, the judge charged Sibley with printing a false story reporting the judge's questions to McAnarney about whether the lawyer would claim that Sacco was acting in the interest of the United States in seeking to collect radical literature. He showed Sibley a sheet supposed to be a typewritten excerpt from the record. The phrase did not appear on the sheet. (Actually, Judge Thayer had interjected the question at least six times.)

Mr. Sibley stated that "the unfairness of the whole thing" impressed him so strongly that six months after the trial he wrote a letter to Attorney General J. Weston Allen urging him to look into the matter with a view to removing Judge Thayer from the bench. Mr. Allen never replied, but at a casual encounter on the street, he said there was nothing in Mr. Sibley's charges. Asked by Mr. Thompson whether he thought that Mr. Allen really believed that his charges were unfounded, Mr. Sibley replied, "I would rather not answer that question." [12]

Lois B. Rantoul represented the Boston Federation of Churches. Except for one afternoon, she was present during the entire trial.[13] Mrs. Rantoul filed an affidavit in the case, dated June 10, 1926, to which was attached a copy of her report on the trial written at its conclusion. She also testified in

---

[9] Vol. V, 4957.   [10] Vol. V, 4960.   [11] Vol. V, 4956.   [12] Vol. V, 4958–4959.
[13] Mrs. Rantoul was one of a group of wellborn New England women who actively supported the cause of Sacco and Vanzetti. Many of them attended the trial faithfully. Some made the facts about the case known through their published writings and oral reports. Some of them taught English to Sacco and Vanzetti, one of them for six years. Others brightened the prisoners' hours with lively and thoughtful correspondence. Some of these letters were published in *The Letters of Sacco and Vanzetti*. Their sustained, keen interest in the cause of Sacco and Vanzetti became one of the features of the proceedings.

person before the Governor's Advisory Committee.[14] These three statements are substantially in accord on the attitude of Judge Thayer.

She said (in part) that the judge had interviewed her in his lobby at his request at the end of the government's case and asked her how she thought the trial was going. When she replied that she had not yet heard sufficient evidence to convince her that the defendants were guilty, he expressed vigorous dissatisfaction and said that "after hearing both arguments and his charge, I would come to him feeling differently." Judge Thayer interviewed her a second time in his lobby while the case for the defense was going in and again asked for her opinion. She replied that she thought the testimony of George Kelley, Sacco's employer, was important. Kelley had praised Sacco's steady character. To this the judge had replied that Kelley did not mean what he said, "because he [Judge Thayer] had heard that on the outside Kelley had said that Sacco was an anarchist and that he couldn't do anything with him." In her report, Mrs. Rantoul added that "through the district attorney to whom I spoke, I found the hearsay statement of Judge Thayer to be untrue." [15]

We get our first intimation of Judge Thayer's sense of mission in the testimony of George U. Crocker before the Governor's Advisory Committee. Mr. Crocker was a prominent Boston citizen, a former city treasurer and a lawyer of long standing. In the autumn of 1926 he first volunteered some information to Mr. Thompson about his experience with Judge Thayer but refused to sign an affidavit for personal reasons. The unsigned affidavit is in the record.[16] However, he drew up a memorandum to preserve his memory for use by the governor or the attorney general.[17] Then on July 11, 1927, he appeared personally before the Governor's Advisory Committee. Part of Mr. Crocker's testimony follows:

Q. (By Mr. Thompson) Oh, yes. Do you recollect while the trial of the Sacco case was going on, being approached by Judge Thayer in the University Club? A. I do.
Q. Now, will you state in your own words what you recollect about that matter? Please state as fully and carefully as you can. A. Well, the first time, one evening, this gentleman approached me, called me by name and I didn't recollect having met him before, but he began talking to me and *told me how we must protect ourselves against reds, then he began to talk about this Sacco —* Sacco and Vanzetti case. I finally realized he was the presiding judge in the case

14 Vol. V, 4932, 4943, 5023.   15 Vol. V, 4944.   16 Vol. V, 5411–5413.
17 Vol. V, 4947.

and he talked to me a great deal about it until I got away. He told me a good deal about their being reds and anarchists and how we must protect —

Q. (By President Stratton) What did he say? A. I cannot remember exactly the words he used, but to the effect that *we must protect ourselves against them, there were so many reds in the country, and he had a couple of them up in the trial at which he was presiding.*

Q. (By President Lowell) How far along was the trial? A. I don't know. Why perhaps halfways through the trial. I don't know.

(By President Lowell) It lasted seven weeks.

Q. (By Judge Grant) You mean the trial? A. It took seven weeks.

(By Mr. Crocker) And he talked to me several times along the same lines. He told me about the evidence somewhat, and I got away from him as soon as I could. One morning at breakfast, it was on the morning when he delivered his charge, he was living at the University Club at that time. He either signalled me to come over to his table, or I was at breakfast and he came in and sat down, and he began to talk again about this trial and it went in one ear and out, because I didn't want to have anything to do with him. In part he talked about the counsel for the defense in the argument for the defense, and I don't know what it was. I didn't like to listen to it. Then he pulled out of his pocket a paper which he said was part of his charge and he said "Now Moore said so and so yesterday in his argument to the jury and I want to read you part of the charge I am going to deliver. That will hold him," etc.

Q. (By President Lowell) It would what "hold him"? A. Hold him.

Q. (By President Lowell) Hold him.

Q. (By Judge Grant) Where? A. It would hold him. It was an answer to his argument, McAnarney's argument and he talked and I was very uncomfortable and I got away as soon as I could, and I avoided in the future all talk with him about the case. In fact, I spoke to the head waiter or stewart [*semble*, steward] at the Club "For Heaven's sake, don't put me with that man." Of course I can't remember all he said, but the circumstances impressed it upon my memory, but I can't remember any definite language that he used, except that matter of McAnarney's argument and his answer to him and didn't I think it would hold him. [Emphasis added.][18]

It came with a special kind of shock to learn from Mr. Crocker that at least part of Judge Thayer's talk was in the presence of Judge Crosby, then a justice of the Supreme Judicial Court of Massachusetts.[19] This is what he said:

Q. (By Mr. Thompson) Now, can you describe in words what might be called the attitude of Judge Thayer in these conversations towards these two

---

[18] Vol. V, 4968–4969.

[19] It does not appear, however, that Mr. Justice Crosby participated in the hearings on defendants' first appeal, 255 Mass. 369, Holt Record, Vol. IV, 4269 (1926), but his name is listed in Massachusetts Reports as present at the second appeal, 259 Mass. 124, Holt Record, Vol. V, 4880 (1927).

defendants in any more words than you have already used? Can you give us a
description of the impression produced on your mind by his conversations in
reference to his partiality? A. I felt that he was bound to convict these men
because they were reds. That was the impression I got. He was very excited,
especially the last morning when he read parts of his [*semble,* answer to]
McAnarney.

Q. Do you recollect if he showed his charge to Judge Crosby of the Supreme
Judicial Court? Do you remember when Judge Crosby was there that he took
out his charge? A. No. I don't remember.

Q. *Did he talk with Judge Crosby?* A. *I know that he and Judge Crosby — he
talked to Judge Crosby much the same as he did to me.*

Q. Yes. *Judge Crosby a member of the Supreme Judicial Court?* A. I don't
know anything about his knowing Judge Crosby. *I have heard him talk to Judge
Crosby about the case and also —*

Q. (By Judge Grant) One of the times? The third you were talking together?
A. I think so.

Q. How many times in all? A. *Well, I should say three or four times. He was
under my shoulder a good many times.* [Emphasis added.][20]

On cross-examination by Mr. Ranney, he was a bit more specific:

Q. (By Mr. Ranney) Well, what did he say? A. Well, he said — *he started in
with a talk about protecting our courts against anarchists.* Then he talked about
this case in the Dedham court. I have heard him discuss the evidence in a way
no judge should while the case is going on. [Emphasis added.][21]

That Judge Thayer regarded himself as a heroic defender of the bench
against pressure and threats by radicals received unexpected confirmation
from a distinguished source. Robert Benchley, the noted humorist, had
been watching the ominous progress of the Sacco-Vanzetti case and by
spring of 1927 could no longer withhold making public information which
he had previously only mentioned in private conversation. Like Mr.
Crocker, he finally decided that justice was more important than the amen-
ities. On March 25, 1927, Mr. Benchley, on his own initiative, executed the
following affidavit:

My name is Robert Benchley. I reside in the City of New York. I am Dramatic Editor of "Life." I was brought up in the City of Worcester, Massachusetts, and am acquainted with many people there, among others with Mr. Loring Coes, with whom I have been on friendly terms for many years. In the year
1921, during the trial of Sacco and Vanzetti before Judge Webster Thayer in
the Superior Court at Dedham, Mrs. Benchley and I were visiting Mr. and Mrs.
Loring Coes in Worcester. During this visit, on a day which I think must have

[20] Vol. V, 4970–4971.   [21] Vol. V, 4972.

been a Saturday or Sunday, I was sitting in an automobile with Mrs. Benchley and Mrs. Coes outside the Worcester Golf Club waiting for Mr. Coes to come out. When Mr. Coes came out and got into the automobile he told us what Judge Thayer, who was in the club, had just said in his presence and in the presence of several others about Sacco and Vanzetti. The account by Mr. Coes of these remarks of Judge Thayer made a vivid impression upon my mind, and I remember them with considerable distinctness. Mr. Coes told us that Judge Thayer, whom he referred to as "Web," *had just been telling what he Judge Thayer intended to do to Sacco and Vanzetti, whom Judge Thayer referred to as "those bastards down there."* Mr. Coes said that Judge Thayer had referred to Sacco and Vanzetti as bolsheviki who were "trying to intimidate him," and had said that "he would get them good and proper." Mr. Coes said that Judge Thayer had told him and the other men that a "bunch of parlor radicals were trying to get these guys off and trying to bring pressure to bear on the Bench," and that he "would show them and would get those guys hanged," and that he, Judge Thayer, "would also like to hang a few dozen of the radicals." Mr. Coes said that Judge Thayer added that "no bolsheviki could intimidate Web Thayer," and that he added in substance that Worcester would be proud of having such a defender as Judge Thayer. I am informed and believe and therefore allege that Mr. Coes has within a few days been requested by Mr. Thompson, counsel for Sacco and Vanzetti, to make an affidavit as to the remarks of Judge Thayer which I have mentioned and has refused to do so on the ground that it is difficult for him to remember that happened so long ago, and that he is disinclined to make the effort because Judge Thayer is an old friend of himself and his family. I am also informed and believe and therefore allege that in October, 1926, Mr. Coes was thrown from his horse and sustained a injury from which he has not yet entirely recovered. [Emphasis added.] [22]

When the *Boston Evening Transcript* on May 5, 1927, printed the Benchley affidavit, it was offset in the same issue with a purported statement from Mr. Coes.[23] In the article Mr. Coes was quoted as denying substantially everything Mr. Benchley had said in the affidavit. Here is what the *Transcript* printed as being Mr. Coes's oral statement to the reporter:

I flatly deny the truth of Mr. Benchley's statement that I told him that Judge Thayer had referred to those two men as "bastards," [24] that Judge Thayer said he would like to hang a few more of such radicals, or any of the other statements which Mr. Benchley alleges I told him the Judge made.

I do not recall any such incident as Mr. Benchley describes in his affidavit. My wife, who is mentioned by Mr. Benchley as being one of the party to whom I repeated the Judge's language, denies any recollection of the entire episode.

I have known Judge Thayer since 1908. I have never heard him use language

22 Vol. V, 4928.
23 The *Transcript* was vehemently hostile to the cause of Sacco and Vanzetti and their supporters.
24 The *Transcript* was rather prim in 1927 and used a blank for the word "bastards."

that he could not repeat in mixed company and I have played golf with him.

Had Judge Thayer, in my hearing, made the statement which Mr. Benchley charges me with repeating to him, I should have remembered it.

I am particularly annoyed with Mr. Benchley's closing statement that I was thrown from my horse and sustained an injury from which I have not completely recovered, insinuating that my memory has been affected. My memory is not affected. Mr. Benchley makes the further statement that I was requested by Mr. Thompson, counsel for the two men, to make an affidavit as to the incident and that I declined to do so because of difficulty in remembering and also because of my friendship with Judge Thayer. I was not requested to make an affidavit. Mr. Thompson telephoned me and asked if I recalled telling Mr. Benchley something Judge Thayer had said. I informed him that I did not remember. He did not say what it was that I was supposed to have heard Judge Thayer say. Had he told me that I was supposed to have heard the judge call these two men "bastards" or that he "would like to hang a few dozen of these radicals" . . . I should have been glad to give him affidavit that such was not the truth, had he cared for such an affidavit . . . And I could have done this, for any such statements of Judge Thayer would have remained in my memory. However, Mr. Thompson did not ask me if I remembered any specific statements.

I was also telephoned by a Boston newspaperman who said he had a copy of an affidavit by Mr. Benchley and if I had anything to say about it. When I invited him to read it, he declined. Naturally I had nothing to say.[25]

Mr. Benchley testified in person before the Governor's Advisory Committee on July 13, 1927, and repeated what he had said in his affidavit. He fixed the time of the Coes incident as early in July 1921, when the trial was going on. He also stated that Mrs. Coes was visiting the Benchleys when Mr. Thompson tried unsuccessfully to get an affidavit from her husband and reported that Mr. Coes was very angry that Mr. Benchley had "dragged him into it." [26] Mr. Benchley also said that neither Mrs. Benchley nor Mrs. Coes could hear what the men were saying on the front seat.

Mr. Ranney cross-examined Mr. Benchley without impairing his original account of what Mr. Coes had said.

For me, the scene while Benchley testified brought back personal memories. The three of us, "Bob" Benchley, "Dud" Ranney and I were fellow members of the Harvard class of 1912. We knew each other at college, although we were then engaged in quite different activities. Benchley was our beloved class humorist, and editor of The Lampoon; Ranney was a successful distance runner on the varsity track squad; I rowed on minor

[25] As printed in Robert H. Montgomery's book Sacco-Vanzetti: The Murder and the Myth, 297–298.
[26] Vol. V, 5020.

college crews and battled for Harvard against Yale on the debating team. It was a strange circumstance that a murder case should have brought us together in July 1927, — three classmates, one the assistant district attorney, one a voluntary witness impelled to speak out of conscience and one of counsel for the defendants. I was proud of Benchley's moral courage. As for Ranney, although I regretted that he felt compelled to uphold what (to me) seemed like an indefensible course of action, it is gratifying for me to state that he was always fair to Mr. Thompson and me in performing what he conceived to be his duty.

There can be little doubt that Mr. Coes made the remarks to Mr. Benchley as he emerged from the Worcester Golf Club. That part of Mr. Benchley's affidavit is not hearsay. He stated he heard Mr. Coes himself — not that someone told him that Coes had said it. The only question, therefore, on this aspect of his statement is whether Mr. Benchley told the truth in relating what he heard him say, not whether Mr. Coes told the truth about Judge Thayer's outburst. Every probability indicates that Mr. Benchley reported correctly what Mr. Coes had said. Otherwise, there is no sensible explanation for his quoting his friend's purported remarks. On the contrary, there would have been powerful reasons to restrain him from volunteering to make a false affidavit. By speaking out as he did, he violated the mores of his own group and alienated an old friend. The purported denial by Mr. Coes, on the other hand, is understandably suspect. It was not an affidavit nor even an unsworn statement, but only a reporter's account of what Mr. Coes had told him.

A different question is whether "Web" Thayer actually made the remarks reported by Coes. Since Benchley did not hear Judge Thayer himself, he could only state what Coes had told him, ordinarily inadmissible as "hearsay."

However, we are not here concerned with a question as to whether Coes's report of Judge Thayer's remarks would be admissible at a trial. Hearsay or not, the Coes account bears the stamp of truth, because of collateral circumstance. *The speech that Mr. Coes so enthusiastically related to Mr. Benchley was of a piece with other reported utterances by Judge Thayer to other auditors.*

More than three years after the Coes incident, James P. Richardson, Parker professor of law and political science at Dartmouth College, had a conversation with Judge Webster Thayer, a Dartmouth alumnus, at a football game on the college athletic field in Hanover, New Hampshire. This was in November 1924, a short time after the judge had denied various motions for a new trial in the Sacco-Vanzetti case. Judge Thayer insisted on talking with Professor Richardson about the action which he had taken.

Like Robert Benchley and George U. Crocker, Professor Richardson did nothing about the incident until it became evident that Sacco and Vanzetti were headed for the electric chair. Then, on April 19, 1927, ten days after the men had been sentenced to death, he wrote a letter to Governor Alvan T. Fuller, containing the following:

> *I know of my own personal knowledge that Judge Thayer's mental attitude during the progress of this case was such as to make him liable to pre-judge it in many of its later stages. I had a personal conversation with him in Hanover at a date which was either in the fall of 1924 or in the fall of 1925,* (I regret that I cannot place it more accurately) *in which it was very evident that Judge Thayer regarded these men with a feeling which can only fairly be described as abhorrence.* [Emphasis added.] [27]

Mr. Thompson and I knew nothing about the Richardson incident until after news of his letter became public. We also learned that Dartmouth alumni had telegraphed President Ernest M. Hopkins that they would contribute ten thousand dollars to the college if he would discharge Professor Richardson. We did not succeed in getting an affidavit from Professor Richardson, but he appeared in person before the Governor's Advisory Committee on July 12, 1927. He testified in part as follows:

A. Judge Thayer met [me] on the field with a group about. He spoke to me by name. He has known me for a long time. He immediately went into the subject of the Sacco-Vanzetti case; he referred at once to the motions which had been pending before him, and which he within a short time disposed of. My recollection is, I don't know, but Mr. Ranney is probably correct, would have been that some of these motions had been decided on shortly before this conversation.

Q. (By Mr. Ranney) That is right, all decided. A. (By Prof. Richardson) All had been decided, probably a short time before. Judge Thayer said as near as I can remember, *"Did you see what I did with those anarchistic bastards the other day. I guess that will hold them for a while."*

Q. (By Mr. Thompson) Yes? A. *Let them go to the Supreme Court now and see what they can get out of them."*

Q. Yes? A. There was more of the same sort.

Q. Yes? A. Well, there was more of the same sort. My recollection is fairly accurate.

[27] Vol. V, 5067–5068.

Q. Yes, he used a word that is commonly used to describe born out of marriage? A. My recollection is that he did. I think he used the words "*sons of bitches.*"

Q. That is not an uncommon expression of his? A. I don't know.

Q. Did he refer to their political views? A. As I have stated he called them anarchists and commented on the matter as such to the best of my recollection. He said "They wouldn't get very far in my court."

Q. Yes? Got up some feeling against the anarchists or socialists? A. No question about that, sir. [Emphasis added.] [28]

Professor Richardson also described Judge Thayer's attitude while talking about Sacco and Vanzetti:

Q. (By Mr. Thompson) His attitude on the occasion you refer to, did he discuss it calmly, or was he excited over Sacco and Vanzetti? A. At both times, Mr. Thompson, he was violent.

Q. (By Judge Grant) He was what? A. Violent in his methods of expression.

Q. I think that is all.

Even before some of the motions referred to by Professor Richardson had been heard, Judge Thayer had indicated his determination to deny them. The motions were based on the Proctor and Ripley affidavits and were being argued in June or July 1923.[29] Apparently he regarded the motions as assaults upon the courts and thought of himself as the rather heroic judicial defender. Judge Thayer revealed his thoughts to Miss Elizabeth Rintels (now Mrs. Bernkopf), then a recent Smith College graduate, who was there reporting the hearings for the International News Service. She told her story in person to the Governor's Advisory Committee on July 11, 1927.[30] She stated that she went by train to Dedham practically every morning while certain motions were being argued and that Judge Thayer took the same train and sat beside her practically always. He talked freely about the Sacco-Vanzetti case. This is part of what she told the Committee:

Q. (Mr. Thompson) Will you please state if you are able to, giving his words, if you can remember them? A. I think it's practically impossible after this length of time to give them. I know what his impression was at the time, and I know he conducted himself as no judge should; that he talked continually about the case and the impression he gave was that he was decidedly antagonistic toward the defense. He referred to Moore as "that long-haired anarchist from the West," and that he couldn't come into his court and run

[28] Vol. V, 5065–5066.   [29] Vol. V, 4966.   [30] Vol. V, 4964–4965.

things as he pleased, and that he might be able to get away with that sort of thing in the court of California, but he was going to find out that he couldn't be intimidated by Moore or anybody. The conversation was along that tenor entirely.

Q. (Pres. Lowell) Anything about McAnarney? A. No.

Q. (Mr. Thompson) About Moore? A. Always about Moore.

Q. (Judge Grant) What year was that in. A. 1923.

Q. What month? A. June, I believe.

Q. (Mr. Thompson) Did he say anything about the defense lawyers? A. He said they would see how far they got with him.

Q. Just what did you understand him to mean by that? A. They wouldn't get very far and the inference was very strongly that he was protecting the integrity of the Massachusetts courts.

Q. Did he say that any appeal to the Supreme Court would be of no avail? A. That was my impression.

Trial lawyers who had cases before Judge Thayer were being continually called into his chambers to listen to talks about the Sacco-Vanzetti case. Judge Thayer may not have succeeded in convincing these lawyers of his fairness, but quite unintentionally he did convince some of them of very different traits in his character. A vivid impression of the judge as he lectured about the case to captive lawyers has been left for us by Joseph N. Welch, Esq., one of Boston's ablest and most experienced trial lawyers:

I also knew Judge Webster Thayer. I have tried cases before him. I have sat in his lobby and heard him discuss the Sacco and Vanzetti case. It is clear he believed Sacco and Vanzetti to be guilty. It is also clear that this was not merely an intellectual conclusion on his part, but a passionate dedication to the proposition that the two of them were to die. It was unfortunate that under Massachusetts law one man and only one man could grant Sacco and Vanzetti a new trial. That man was Judge Thayer. After the jury verdict, Judge Thayer's rulings on the various motions for a new trial were as fatal and as conclusive as was throwing the switch at their execution. But Judge Thayer was beyond persuasion. He was not to be moved by reason. He was, in this case, incapable of showing mercy. This is not to say he was wrong. It is only to describe him.

I have always thought that the great tragedy of the Sacco-Vanzetti case was that it happened to be assigned to Judge Thayer. I think almost any other judge would have granted a new trial.[31]

Judge Thayer's constant craving for public recognition of his fairness presents a fascinating psychological problem. Here was a judge who con-

[31] Joseph N. Welch, Esq., in the foreword to *The Untried Case*, 1960 edition, iii–iv. Mr. Welch was the lawyer most responsible for destroying Senator Joseph McCarthy's public image at the Senate hearings on his conduct. Toward the end of his life, Mr. Welch made a smash hit as the judge in the motion picture *Anatomy of a Murder*. It was his first venture as a professional actor.

fessedly set about to secure the conviction of the defendants from the beginning and yet felt that he was entitled to be regarded as a fair judge.

Judge Thayer again expressed his persistent craving for public recognition of his fairness, on April 9, 1927, within minutes after he had sentenced the two defendants to "suffer the punishment of death by the passage of a current of electricity through your body . . ." Reporters were waiting for the judge in his retiring room. My wife, Sara R. Ehrmann, happened to catch a few snatches of his remarks and made a written note on the same day of what she heard. Here is a copy of her note:

After the sentencing of Sacco & Vanzetti, Mr. Gardner Jackson & I were awaiting the sheriff at the Court House in Dedham.

We saw Judge Thayer standing with a group of men in a small room the door of which was open. We overheard some of the remarks the judge was making to these men — Following are the remarks which we overheard:

Judge Thayer said to two newspaper reporters "Goodbye boys, don't forget me —" They shook hands. The reporters said the judge needn't worry about anything they might say. "I've never had a reporter go back on me yet."

"I am not ashamed of anything I have done. I've done my duty as God gave the power to see it.

I want to be through with their case. I want to drop out altogether. Anybody else can do what he wants. I want to have the happiness of life to which I am entitled.

This is all propaganda.

I hope it will go to the Supreme Court of U.S."

Judge Thayer's reported remarks to the reporters would seem to indicate that his first concern was for favorable publicity. The episode affected Mrs. Ehrmann profoundly.[32]

The judge did not succeed in persuading the press to pay a tribute to his fairness on this or any other occasion. However, he induced defense counsel Jeremiah McAnarney to insert something at the end of the trial in his summation which could be so construed. This is how Mr. McAnarney complied with the request:

. . . I say it to those men [Sacco and Vanzetti] and to their friends, that they have had every opportunity there, they have had every patience, every consideration. I want them to know that we have done — that everything has been done as Massachusetts takes pride in doing, granting to any man, however lowly his station, the fullest rights to our Massachusetts Commonwealth laws.[33]

[32] Due largely to her contacts with the Sacco-Vanzetti proceedings, Mrs. Ehrmann later became a leader in the fight to abolish the death penalty both in Massachusetts and throughout the nation.
[33] Vol. II, 2175–2176.

Although Mr. McAnarney had spoken carefully and made no direct reference to Judge Thayer, but only to rights and consideration, the *Boston Herald* naturally interpreted the remark to mean "fairness and impartiality." And so, Judge Thayer got the desired notice of his "fairness" in the press.

It is quite usual for counsel, in summation, to say something pleasing to the judge in the hope of a favorable, or at least a fair, charge by the court to the jury. The need to do this in a capital case would be felt especially by defense lawyers. For a local attorney like Jeremiah McAnarney, there could hardly have been any choice when Judge Thayer requested a tribute from him. Whatever his own thoughts, he had no alternative to compliance.[34]

It would seem to be unnecessary to question whether Judge Thayer's attitude and conduct of the trial influenced the jury. The judge himself had stated at the start of the trial that he had intended to do it and after the verdict had boasted that he had accomplished his project. No doubt the jurymen believed that he was fair. Had they thought otherwise, they might have resented his favoring the prosecution and this would have helped the defendants. However, the case was tried before a "green" jury, assembled for this particular trial. The jurors had no standard acquired from experience with which to measure the trial judge's fairness. This was intimated to me by juror Dever at our conference in 1927. They naturally took for granted that Judge Thayer's conduct of the trial was in accord with proper judicial standards.

No doubt, Judge Thayer's rulings on questions of law seemed to be fair.

[34] Judge Thomas F. McAnarney told the Governor's Advisory Committee about Judge Thayer's request for the tribute, but when in 1929 we looked for his testimony in the Holt Record we did not find it. Apparently it had been cut out of the reporter's transcript of the hearings like the vindication of Bosco and Guadagni. Only in this instance, the Holt Record had already been published when we discovered the omission. Mr. Thompson, Mr. Ranney and I had a clear memory of it, however.

In a letter to Judge Grant dated January 7, 1935, Mr. Thompson referred to the omissions from the records of the Governor's Advisory Committee:

"The record of the hearing is unreliable, both in the matter of testimony and in the matter of colloquies. It omits the important statement of Judge McAnarney in response to a question of your own, that the reason why his brother in his closing argument commended Judge Thayer's conduct of the case was that, before the argument, Judge Thayer asked him to make such a statement in his closing argument. It also omits the important colloquy following the discovery of Mr. Lowell's error in dealing with the Bosco-Guadagni matter, in which Mr. Lowell retracted his accusation that the testimony of these two important alibi witnesses was false."

Judge Grant made no response to Mr. Thompson's impeachment of the record. There is no evidence, however, that Judge Grant was responsible for the excisions.

It was his expressed intention to forestall any reversal of a guilty verdict because of error on his part. In this respect he was successful. The Supreme Judicial Court sustained the judge on all matters of law, although in the view of some juristic authorities, the law was occasionally stretched a bit to cover his possible mistakes.

It was in the area of "discretionary" acts and decisions that Judge Thayer's purpose to convict the defendants found its widest scope. Like Mr. Thompson, Judge Thayer knew that no Massachusetts judge had ever been found to have abused his "discretion." Under the Massachusetts definition of what constituted abuse, the Supreme Judicial Court would have had to find Judge Thayer either "corrupt or crazy." This impossible rule provided the judge with a sanctuary from which he could safely destroy the defense. He seems to have used it well.

Edmund M. Morgan made an adequate note of Judge Thayer's actions in this respect by calling attention to the fact that the Supreme Judicial Court, "In its first opinion, in order to sustain the rulings of the judge at the trial, had to resort to the doctrine of discretion on at least sixteen different occasions, covering nine distinct points." [35] Further, in stating his conviction that "these defendants were the victims of a tragic miscarriage of justice," he concludes, "The fault lies chiefly, however, with the Commonwealth in that it placed in judgment over these men a trial judge whose prejudices made him overlook misconduct of the prosecutor, made him determine every discretionary matter against the accused, and permeated the proceedings from the beginning to end with its vicious influence. The defendants had a trial according to all the forms of law, but it was not a fair trial." [36]

However, the rule of discretion was not the only weapon used by Judge Thayer to defend the integrity of the courts and to overcome his anarchistic enemies. He had other opportunities to accomplish his purpose. As to these, he had no need to rely on any legal authority. His position as presiding judge gave him power to work against the defendants without even attracting attention to what he was doing. One of these opportunities was the right to charge the jury. If he was careful to explain the law correctly and did not misstate the evidence (which Judge Thayer, however, did in several instances), he might shape the jury's opinion without restricting

[35] Joughin and Morgan, *The Legacy of Sacco and Vanzetti,* 151.   [36] Ibid., 157.

himself unduly and without fear of running a substantial risk of reversal by the Supreme Judicial Court.

Even before we examine Judge Thayer's presentation to the jury of his version of the trial evidence, we find that he sounded a preliminary note with which we are now familiar. The charge begins with a reminder to the jury of the virtues of loyalty and patriotism.[37] This was the same theme with which Judge Thayer opened the trial in his first address to jurymen — patriotism, courage and devotion, the soldier boy who answered the call of the Commonwealth, the battlefields of France and the supreme sacrifice.[38]

In the usual criminal trial, this stirring up of the emotions of patriotism might not have harmed defendants of a different type, but in the Sacco-Vanzetti case it could only arouse the loathing of the jurors against the two draft dodgers and alien detractors of our country, sitting so heavily guarded in the cage.

The judge's references to the patriotism of the soldier boys was one of the things selected as showing his unfairness by some who attended the trial.[39] Just as Mr. Katzmann, in his cross-examinations of Sacco and Vanzetti, began by immediately pouncing upon their draft dodging, so Judge Thayer, at the start of his charge, began by reminding the jury indirectly of their disloyalty. At least Judge Thayer and Mr. Katzmann must have thought that such an opening was effective.

Now let us turn to Judge Thayer's presentation of his version of the evidence to the jury. In his charge, Judge Thayer, consciously or unconsciously, used a device customarily employed by magicians when they wish to make a person or article apparently disappear. The method is to focus the attention of the audience on something else while the prestidigitator slips the object of his magic from view. This is exactly what Judge Thayer did in his charge. The diversion that he used was a lengthy and detailed recital of what he said was "evidence of consciousness of guilt." Under this cover, all reference to the defendants' specific alibi evidence disappeared, unobserved, from the judge's charge. The unfairness of this unbalanced presentation may be appraised by recalling that the "consciousness of guilt" evidence, at best, was only secondary proof of the defendants' supposed guilt, even if its ambiguities were resolved most unfavorably to them. On the other hand, the testimony of the alibi witnesses needed no interpretation and was direct proof of the defendants' innocence. If we take a brief

[37] Vol. II, 2239.   [38] Vol. I, 15.   [39] Vol. V, 5026, 5410.

look at the charge, we may see how Judge Thayer accomplished his feat.

The charge first takes up the matter of identification. This he discusses generally as an abstract proposition for about a page and a half of the printed record.[40] He then devotes a single short paragraph to "the fatal Winchester bullet, marked Exhibit 3." Even this brief reference, however, shows that he misunderstood Captain Proctor's testimony. Then follows a discussion of the government's claim that the revolver "found or taken from the defendant Vanzetti, was taken by him at the time of the killing of Berardelli." This consumes about three-quarters of a printed page.[41] Two short paragraphs then deal with the claim that the cap "found near the body of Berardelli" belonged to Sacco.

In discussing the foregoing claims about the evidence introduced by the Commonwealth, Judge Thayer necessarily relied on the trial testimony as he understood it. He knew nothing of the realities that lay behind the production of these items.

The charge then moved on to an overshadowing diversion as Judge Thayer discussed "consciousness of guilt." It consumes almost seven whole pages of the printed record,[42] running to twenty-seven paragraphs of varying lengths. This afforded the judge an opportunity to remind the jury of most of the prosecution's claims about the supposedly incriminating conduct of the defendants. For instance, he repeated in great detail the alleged suspicious activities at the Johnson house on May 5, 1920. However, he did not call attention to the failure of the prosecution to suggest any explanation of the defendants' purpose in seeking to take out Boda's ancient Overland, other than that offered by the defendants. He omitted mention of the defense claim that they wanted the old car to use for the collection of radical literature previously distributed. This was, at least, consistent with other testimony, whereas the government's silence as to their supposed purpose was consistent with nothing. Again, Judge Thayer developed (somewhat inaccurately) in detail for a page and a half alleged movements of Sacco and Vanzetti to draw weapons, as told by the arresting officer, Connolly. In a series of questions, he asked what was in the defendants' minds when, as testified by the officers, they supposedly made such movements. He answered his questions by asking another: "If they did make such movements, did they, the two defendants, or either of them, intend by what they did to use the revolvers, or did they make the movement for the purpose of

[40] Vol. II, 2252–2254.   [41] Vol. II, 2255.   [42] Vol. II, 2256–2262.

reaching for their revolvers for the purpose of protecting themselves against the officers?" [43]

Judge Thayer brushed off the defendants' testimony rebutting Officer Connolly's story by stating simply that "they denied it." (As I have noted earlier, Officer Connolly, at the Plymouth trial, had given no testimony about "movements" by either Vanzetti or Sacco. Although Judge Thayer had presided over that trial, he probably had forgotten this fact.)

Judge Thayer then dwelt upon the falsehoods told by the defendants to Chief Stewart and Mr. Katzmann at the time of their arrest and the following morning. Again he asked a series of questions touching on consciousness of the guilt of murder. In this instance, however, he restated the claim of the defendants that they had lied "to protect themselves and their friends from some kind of punishment, either by way of deportation because they were radicals, or because of their activities in the radical movement, or because of radical literature that they then had possession of." [44]

Now, after having implanted in the jurors' minds almost the entire case of the prosecution, fairness would have imposed upon the judge an obligation to discuss with equal consideration evidence that favored the defendants. For instance there was no reference to their conduct which showed consciousness of *innocence* — nor to the fact that some of their falsehoods were consistent with fear for their safety as hunted radicals; and also could have had no logical connection to the claim that they had committed murder.

The grossest unfairness, however, lay in the omission from the charge of any consideration of the extensive and credible alibi evidence presented by the defense. The alibis were the most important positive defense, since, if the jury believed them, they would have necessarily found the defendants not guilty. Early in his charge, Judge Thayer had promised to "consider that matter more in detail later." [45] He never did. The alibi evidence which defense counsel had so laboriously collected and the testimony of the many alibi witnesses received no specific mention whatever from Judge Thayer. He sank all of the alibi evidence in six printed lines:

An alibi is always a question of fact. Therefore, all testimony which tends to show that the defendants were in another place at the time the murders were committed tends also to rebut the evidence that they were present at time and place the murders were committed. If the evidence of an alibi rebuts evidence of

[43] Vol. II, 2260.   [44] Vol. II, 2262.   [45] Vol. II, 2254.

the Commonwealth to such an extent that it leaves reasonable doubt in your minds as to the commission of the murders charged against these defendants then you will return a verdict of not guilty.[46]

Apparently, Judge Thayer feared that even this empty reference to the defendants' alibi might possibly be taken seriously by the jury, because he hastily added:

On the other hand, if you find the defendants or either of them committed the murders and the Commonwealth has satisfied you of such fact beyond reasonable doubt from all the evidence in these cases, including the evidence of an alibi, then you will return a verdict of guilty against both defendants or against such defendants as you may find guilty of such murders.[47]

It may be doubted whether the jury even noticed Judge Thayer's miniscule reference to the alibi evidence, buried as it was in his otherwise lengthy and detailed charge. If they had, they must have forgotten it before they filed into the jury room. If the presiding judge had given the same serious and painstaking review of the alibi testimony as he had of the "evidence of consciousness of guilt," it is hardly likely that the jury would have jumped to a guilty verdict without any real examination of the case for the defendants.

As he had threatened to do, Judge Thayer had effectively used his power to charge the jury to assure a conviction. He had done this by concentrating so heavily and dramatically on the prosecution's claims that the defendants' evidence, which might have saved them, vanished imperceptibly from the minds of the jurors.

Reliable proof of Judge Thayer's violent and active prejudice against the defendants and their chief counsel came out for the first time in the hearings before the Governor's Advisory Committee. How the Committee disposed of it will be considered in a later chapter dealing with their report. Meanwhile, legal steps were being taken to obtain a new trial grounded on the evidence of "prejudice."

A motion for a new trial based on Judge Thayer's unfitness as revealed in his talks off the bench was filed on behalf of the defendants on August 6, 1927. On that date, Mr. Thompson and I withdrew as counsel and Arthur D. Hill, Esq., entered his appearance for the defendants. All of us knew

[46] Vol. II, 2263.   [47] Vol. II, 2263.

that our cause was desperate, but after the governor had rejected the petition for clemency Mr. Thompson and I felt that fresh minds and a change of faces might possibly improve the chances of getting judicial or executive relief. It was gallant of Mr. Hill to take on the defense in an almost hopeless hour. He was soon joined by a number of associates, including Elias Field and Richard G. Evarts of the Boston bar. A young lawyer from Pittsburgh, Michael A. Musmanno, was sent by the Sons of Italy to aid the defense. The case so affected Musmanno that his interest carried him past the execution of Sacco and Vanzetti and over all the years since that day. He has written one of the most appealing books on the case and many articles. Even today he continues to fight for the vindication of Sacco and Vanzetti.

On August 6, 1927, Mr. Hill appeared before the Honorable Walter Perley Hall, then Chief Justice of the Superior Court, and requested that he assign some judge other than Thayer to hear the motion based on Judge Thayer's prejudice. The Chief Justice refused to grant this request and directed that the motion be presented before the trial judge, Webster Thayer. On August 8, defense counsel appeared before Judge Thayer. They again objected to the motion being heard by Thayer and requested the judge to withdraw so that another judge could be appointed to hear it. Judge Thayer declined to withdraw and then denied the motion based on his alleged prejudice and also on a procedural point.[48]

"With reference to the question of prejudice," Judge Thayer is reported by Judge Musmanno as saying, "there is not any now and never was at any time." [49] No doubt Judge Thayer believed this "finding of fact" to be true. However, he did not then, or at any other time, publicly deny the massive proof of his prejudice, disclosed in his own words in the affidavits on which the motion rested. Defendants filed a Bill of Exceptions to Judge Thayer's action and this was heard by the Supreme Judicial Court (together with related matters) on August 16, 1927. On August 19, 1927, the court overruled the exceptions on the ground that a motion for a new trial in a capital case is made too late if made after sentence has been pronounced.[50] The motion for revocation of sentence (to remove this obstacle) was also denied as coming too late. The court declined to discuss Judge Thayer's con-

---

[48] Vol. V, 5528–5529.   [49] *After Twelve Years*, 294.
[50] The time limit for motions for a new trial in criminal cases was removed by Chapter 82 of Acts of 1964 (Mass. G.L. Ch. 278, sec. 29).

duct in hearing and deciding the motion based on his own alleged prejudice, "because neither the judge nor any of his associates had jurisdiction to entertain the motion." At the same time, other moves to secure judicial reviews based on Judge Thayer's prejudice were denied for procedural reasons.[51]

In this manner Arthur Hill and his colleagues were frustrated by an impenetrable maze of technicalities in their efforts to save the lives of their clients and to preserve the reputation of the Commonwealth for judicial justice.

Meanwhile the group of defense lawyers was seeking relief from the United States courts by way of various applications for writs of certiorari and habeas corpus.[52] Their pursuit of federal intervention continued until the day before the electrocutions. Always they found the road blocked by the doctrine, then strongly held, that the federal courts had no power to intervene in a state court case unless the proceedings there were actually void.[53] Application was first made to Mr. Justice Holmes, who declined jurisdiction. This tolled the bell on similar applications to other judges, all of whom followed Mr. Justice Holmes.

Although the various legal issues so faithfully raised by counsel during the last days of Sacco and Vanzetti might have received different treatment by the Supreme Court today, they are not an integral part of our story. They are mentioned here more to indicate the ultimate fate of indisputable evidence of the trial judge's mental and emotional attitude during and after the trial. For many lawyers, however, the shunting aside of Judge Thayer's virulent hatred of the defendants in 1927 might offer a justification for the current expansion of federal jurisdiction where the states ignore fundamental human rights.

[51] Vol. V, 5500; 1927 AS, 1711, *Commonwealth v. Sacco.*
[52] Vol. V, 5505.
[53] Vol. V, 5516, 5532. Mr. Justice Brandeis disqualified himself because he had permitted Mrs. Sacco and her son Dante to reside in his Dedham home during the trial.

28.

A Witness Well Worth Considering

If I am wrong, I will say I am wrong.
LOTTIE TATTILO *in reply to*
PRESIDENT LOWELL, July 15, 1927
Holt Record, Vol. V, 5117

The announcement of the appointment of the Governor's Advisory Committee was greeted with relief throughout the Commonwealth and the nation. The consciences of thousands were assuaged by the thought that at last there would be a fair and impartial review of the Sacco-Vanzetti proceedings. John F. Moors, a member of the Harvard Corporation and a close friend of Lawrence Lowell, was jubilant. "Now we can sleep nights," he said to me, "in the thought that the president of Harvard is on the Committee!"

Mr. Thompson and I were, however, not very happy with the personnel of the Committee. We could learn very little about Mr. Stratton. We were told that he would probably follow the lead of Mr. Lowell — which he **did**, unfortunately. Judge Grant was altogether unsatisfactory. Not only did we feel that he had a black-tie class concept of life around him, but it was reported to us that he had expressed himself violently against Sacco and Vanzetti to some congenial spirits in his club. Mr. Moors protested the appointment of Judge Grant, but he failed to change Governor Fuller's decision. Later, during the hearings before the Committee, Judge Grant indignantly denied that he had ever spoken against the two defendants. He asserted that he had only criticized Professor Frankfurter for writing the *Atlantic Monthly* article while the appeal was pending. This may have been true of the words he spoke, but the violence of his emotion was more consonant with a deep-seated feeling against the accused.

Yet even if the members of the Committee had been fully qualified and had not been handicapped (as we saw in the Bosco-Guadagni incident) by the preconception that Sacco and Vanzetti were guilty, the time allowed for their investigation was wholly inadequate. During the month of June, when the record had to be read and digested, the two college presidents had their commencement activities. Hearings began on July 11, 1927, and continued until July 21. During this period they received entirely new documents, such as the Pinkerton reports on the Bridgewater attempted holdup, the minutes of the "private" inquest into the deaths of Parmenter and Berardelli, and the transcript of the Plymouth trial. This material, if understood, would have shaken the Committee's complacent acceptance of the State's case as presented at the trial and would have lent support to the defense evidence.

On July 23, 1927, we handed the Committee our brief. At that time we ourselves had not yet had an opportunity to digest the new material, although we did call attention to certain features, such as the testimony which Shelley Neal omitted at the trial and why it would have confirmed the Madeiros account. The Committee's report was dated July 27, 1927. On such a time schedule the ablest Committee could not possibly have reached a considered conclusion.

However, the Governor's Advisory Committee did not even require the few days at their disposal. Like the jury at Dedham, they knew the answers before their deliberations began: Sacco and Vanzetti were guilty. Mr. Thompson and I sensed this a short time after the hearing got under way. The Committee members gave us the impression that they regarded themselves as prosecutors, whose duty it was to expose or discredit anything pointing to the innocence of the men. The attempt to destroy Sacco's alibi on the basis of their own investigation, their aggressive attempt to make the witnesses Bosco and Guadagni admit to perjury and their insinuation that Mr. Thompson was not interested in the truth occurred on the fourth day of the hearings. At about the same time our impression received additional confirmation from a State House attendant who overheard the three members discussing the case. Although the hearings had hardly begun, he reported that their talk assumed that they would find both men guilty. Mr. Thompson and I then became convinced that we were captive actors in a tragic farce. We became unwilling to lend a spurious appearance of fairness to such a proceeding and decided to withdraw from the hearings. We were deterred, however, by Professor Frankfurter and Judge Mack, at a private dinner at the Harvard Club. Both of them said that President Lowell was not entirely hopeless and that we should continue on the chance that we might get through to him. They also emphasized that our withdrawal might be taken as an indication that we had lost faith in the innocence of our clients. And so we were persuaded to continue with the hearings, despite our strong sense of preordained hopelessness.

The procedure adopted by the Committee was another factor in beclouding their investigation. We were not permitted to be present when the Committee examined Judge Thayer or eleven of the Dedham jurors and during part of Mr. Katzmann's testimony, nor were we told what they said. We were also excluded from their questioning of the Honorable Walter Perley Hall, and from some views of different premises which the Committee had reportedly taken. In Anglo-American jurisprudence, it is universally recognized that the truth is more apt to be found in so-called adversary proceedings than in the secrecy of the star chamber. Justice is better served where counsel for both sides are permitted to bring out from witnesses what they deem important to correct errors in testimony, due to mistake, omissions, faulty judgment or perjury. The process may lead to some abuses, but has justified itself as essential in our system of the administration of justice.

As for examining the jurors seen by the Committee, it would have been most important for us to have been present. Ordinarily, inquiry into why jurors reached their decision is prohibited, but here they were turned into witnesses by the Committee and, as we later read in the report, apparently influenced the Committee greatly by their opinions. It may seem childish to us that the Committee found that the jury were not prejudiced against the defendants because the jurors said so, since we know that this is not evidence at all. The Dedham jurors interviewed by the Committee were honest and fairly intelligent men and I believe that a few questions by Mr. Thompson or myself might have led to a thoughtful reassessment of their attitude.

When we learned of secret investigations by the Committee, as in the Bosco-Guadagni episode, we were able to head off mistakes. However, for the most part, we did not know of the Committee's "off-the-record" investigations until we read about them in the report. By then, it was too late for any correction.

In the early stages of the Committee hearings, the testimony was recorded by Mr. Lowell's secretary and by State House stenographers. However, none of these helpers was a court reporter and it soon became apparent that their work was so full of errors and blanks that it was quite unreliable. Mr. Ranney joined with us in requesting court reporters and these were later supplied. Even this, however, did not assure us of a correct transcript, since Mr. Lowell, without informing us, occasionally intervened to tell them what to omit.

After the Committee's private hunt for evidence to destroy Sacco's alibi had turned into a fiasco, Mr. Thompson and I did not anticipate that there could be another attempt by the Committee to develop new proof, outside of the record, that our clients were guilty. Yet the Committee made a number of such efforts, some of which we learned about only after reading them in their report to the governor. Implicit in these forays into untrodden fields was the assumption that they were able to discover critical evidence which Mr. Katzmann had overlooked or even to prove that the district attorney misstated his own case. We certainly were not prepared, however, for the production of Carlotta T. Tattilo, sometimes referred to in the record as Carlotta Packard, her maiden name, or Mrs. Charmock, the surname of her first husband. She was a well-known character in the South Braintree community, where she was usually called Lottie Packard.

In every publicized murder case there are almost invariably people who imagine that they have important knowledge of the crime. Mary Splaine, Lola Andrews and Georgina Brooks, previously discussed, were apparently of this type. Lottie Packard's trouble seems to have been more deep-seated than mere susceptibility to suggestion. She certainly believed that she had seen and heard things of vital importance. Although she told her story (with variations) to a number of people, including the police, none seem to have credited it. She was interviewed by Mr. Moore on November 10, 1920, about six months after the arrest of Sacco and Vanzetti. Nothing came of this either, except that Mrs. Tattilo later claimed that Mr. Moore had offered her five hundred dollars to leave the state prior to the trial and Mr. Moore's stenographic transcript of the conference indicated that she came to him to get money for her "expenses" if she made herself unavailable as a witness.[1] Mr. Lowell, however, had already concluded that Mr. Moore had tried to bribe her and Lowell said that that "*bears upon the preparation of the case.*" [2] (Emphasis added.) He reminded us that Lola Andrews had also claimed that Mr. Moore tried to bribe her. By his comment, Mr. Lowell revealed his conviction that the defense was fraudulently prepared by Mr. Moore.

[1] Vol. V, 5155.   [2] Vol. V, 5114.

Mrs. Tattilo was regarded as mentally irresponsible in her hometown. We thought that she fully justified this reputation by her testimony before the Governor's Advisory Committee. While she was testifying even Mr. Ranney looked meaningfully at me and made circles around his temples with his fingers to indicate that she was "batty." However, the Committee sought to prove by her testimony that she had known Sacco and had seen him in South Braintree on April 15, 1920. This is how it went:

Q. (By President Lowell) What was your maiden name? A. Packard, Carlotta T.

Q. Your name now is? A. Tattilo. (Spelling) T-a-t-t-i-l-o.

Q. You worked in the Rice & Hutchins factory? A. Yes; for twenty-one years.

Q. Do you remember Sacco's working there? A. Yes, sir; he worked there in 1908.

Q. *Did you know his name at that time, that his name was Sacco?* A. Why, everybody that worked in the factory knew him because there was a strike there at that time, because I was very young, and I can trace that back; I am forty years old now and I was young at the time and I was working there at the time of the strike, and, of course, young and child-aged at that time, young, and we worked all during the strike, but we were protected, there were detectives there, I don't who they were, but this Sacco worked there in the lasting room.

Q. He was working there during the strike? A. Yes. I think, I don't say that he caused the strike, but I think he was implicated in the strike.

Q. He was working there during the strike? A. He was out during the strike.

Q. He was out during the strike? A. Out on the railroad tracks he was and around the factory.

Q. He was not working in the factory during the strike? A. He was working in the factory up to the time the strike commenced and then after that he left.

Q. And then he left? A. Yes, sir.

Q. How did you know his name was Sacco? A. Because I heard the people in there telling it.

Q. *He was not registered under that name, was he?* A. I couldn't tell you.

Q. When he came to the factory *before the strike what was he called?* A. Sacco, or whatever he is.

Q. *He was called Sacco then?* A. Yes, sir.

Q. How long did he work there, do you know, before the strike? A. I couldn't tell you.

Q. He did not come back after the strike? A. I don't know.

Q. You did not see him come back? A. No, sir.

Q. How long do you think it was that he was working there? A. I couldn't tell you. I don't know anything about the man before or after. I have a faint remembrance and I must have a pretty good brain to remember away back to 1908.

Q. You could not tell whether it was a week or a month or what it was? A. No, I could not. . . .

Q. Did you see him on the day of the murder? A. I don't say I saw him, I will never say I saw him, and I don't think it was him now.

Q. You don't think it was him now? A. No, I don't think so. And anybody that has written down the statement that said that I said I saw him they are lying, and I don't care who it is, whether it's Governor Fuller or anybody else. [Emphasis added.] [3]

It seemed quite obvious that the year "1908" made no sense. That was the year when the seventeen-year-old boy Sacco landed in the United States. His first job was that of a waterboy at Milford for six or seven months. He then got a job with the foundry of the Draper Company at Hopedale, where he remained for about a year. He then started to learn the craft of edge-trimming, after which he got a job in a shoe factory at Webster. After six or seven months he took a job at the Milford Shoe Company in Milford which he held until 1917, when he left for Mexico.[4] Mr. Moore's stenographic report of his talk with Lottie Packard in 1920 indicates that at that time, seven years earlier, she had put the year as "1915." However, she now denied that she had said it, and repeated over and over again that it was "1908." On cross-examination, Mr. Lowell tried to make her story credible, as to the date, by offering his own explanations, but the witness would have none of it.

Q. (By Mr. Thompson) How sure are you that the year was 1908? A. I know it was 1908. It is in the records. That's the year the strike was there. I have worked there since I was eighteen years old, and if I am the bad woman that you say I am —

JUDGE GRANT. Mrs. Charmock, please answer the question.

PRESIDENT LOWELL. *That is obviously a slip.*

THE WITNESS. *1908. If I am wrong I will say I am wrong.*

MR. THOMPSON. Sacco only came to this Country in 1908.

MR. RANNEY. He was seventeen years old at the time he came here on the White Star Line.

MR. EHRMANN. She said she remembered it and she was a little girl when she saw him.

THE WITNESS. I am forty years old. I was born in 1887. Now figure that up.

Q. You are perfectly sure that the year you first saw Sacco was 1908? A. Yes, when we had the strike.

Q. And no other year at all? A. No, not that I remember of. I can't remember everything, and you don't. If you do you are a pretty smart man, both of you over there. [Emphasis added.] [5]

Possibly it was also a "slip" by Mr. Lowell to call the witness's testimony as to the date a "slip." This revealed that he already believed her story, but

[3] Vol. V, 5109–5110.   [4] Vol. II, 1818–1820.   [5] Vol. V, 5117.

that she had merely by inadvertence misstated the true year. However, the witness continued to claim that 1908 was correct.

It is also to be noted in the short excerpt above that Mr. Lowell was quite concerned with the name by which Sacco was known at the time when Mrs. Tattilo said he was working at Rice and Hutchins. The reason for this was that Rice and Hutchins had found no record of Sacco working at the factory. When testifying at the trial, Sacco had stated that he worked for about a week at the plant in October 1917, after he returned from Mexico, but under his mother's name, Mosmacotelli. To Mr. Lowell this seemed at first to lend some kind of support to Mrs. Tattilo's story, provided that 1908 could be corrected to 1917 [6] and that she would say she knew him as Mosmacotelli. However, the witness upset these possibilities by insisting that the year was 1908 and that she and everybody at the factory knew Sacco as "Sacco." Balked again, Mr. Lowell then turned to another possibility. He quoted Mr. Katzmann as telling the Committee that there were two years when the Rice and Hutchins records were burned in a fire. Maybe Sacco had worked at that time under his right name. If so, and if the date were properly adjusted, Mrs. Tattilo might have known him as "Sacco" during that period. Mr. Lowell speculated: "Moreover, we have no reason to suppose that Sacco worked under the name of Mascatelli [sic] as early as 1918 [1908?]. If he worked as early as that, he probably worked under his own name." [7] Apparently Mrs. Tattilo's story had to conform to what Mr. Lowell wanted even if this required him to substitute his own testimony for that of the witness.

It should also be noted that the excerpt shows that the witness said she *no longer thought that the man she saw on the day of the murder was Sacco*.[8] This was confirmed later to the Committee in the testimony of Jeremiah Gallivan and John W. Moran, Jr., both of whom talked with her when she was waiting in the State House to see the governor.

The witness's direct examination continued:

Q. What did you see? A. I came out of the factory at half past eleven the same as I always did when I worked there, — and in my beginning of the story, anyway, I want to try to tell the same that I have told the Government, — that morning of that murder I had it dated the 20th, and you see I am way off because that is not the date, Governor Fuller told me the date, and I don't know whether he should have or not, but that is not so far off, that that morning there

[6] Vol. V, 5119.   [7] Vol. V, 5120.   [8] Vol. V, 5110.

was, the morning of that affair, gentlemen, there was a machine out front, it was not in front of the shop, the Rice & Hutchins' Shop —

Q. What day was this? This was the day of the shooting? A. Yes, sir. Rice & Hutchins shop is by the crossing, the first building at the right, and this machine was over the crossing, this side, just a little above that little black shanty, I don't know whether any of you gentlemen have been there —

Q. Yes, we have all seen it. A. It's just a little above that black shanty, that machine was right up above that, at the first pole, there are two electric poles, so it was between those two poles, just a little the other side of the pole; I don't remember what the machine looked like; I don't even remember the number, but all that morning we young girls, every time we would go by the window the machine was out there and we were saying among ourselves, "I wonder who the first person is to get out and see what those people are doing," never thinking anything so terrible was going to happen. I always came up on the left-hand side, and I went up at half past eleven, and when I got to that little Hottentot, it was on the side by the American Express, and there was a gentleman standing there —

Q. By the American Express? A. Yes.

Q. That is way beyond the tracks? A. That is not so far up. There is a large building up there that Mr. Slater had it for a shoe factory, it is one story, I always called it a Hotentot, and this gentleman was standing there —

Q. That was below this machine? A. It was opposite the machine. (Illustrating) The machine was about like where that gentleman is there, and this fellow was standing there, (indicating), and I went right along about my own business. Mr. Parmenter was standing there, I knew him personally, and he was a mighty fine man, and Mr. Tracey was in back of Mr. Parmenter and I was in back of Mr. Tracey, and this fellow still stood there. Well, I began to think and think and think, and I said to myself, "That fellow looks familiar." But I did not speak to him, I went right on my own business, you know, and I said, "Well, I wonder where did I see that fellow?" Well, then, it dawned on me, and I said, "Oh, goodness, I think that's the fellow that worked here in 1908, during the strike." So when I went back to work that noontime I spoke to Frank Jackson, I mentioned his name when I was in here before —

Q.   That is Frank Jackson — A. The superintendent now of the Braintree Shoe.

Q. What was he then? A. He was superintendent of Rice & Hutchins. In fact, I know he has been in here to verify my statement.

Q. You see, we have not seen him. . . .

Q. And that is all you know? A. That's all I know. *I don't say Mr. Sacco done it. I do not say it was him I saw that day.*

Q. You have told us all that you know? A. Yes, sir. If you wish to ask me anything that was offered to me seven years ago, if you know anything about it, I am willing to tell you, and if not my lips are closed. [Emphasis added.] [9]

When the witness finished her direct examination, Mr. Thompson and I thought that her testimony was so obviously irresponsible that it would be a

[9] Vol. V, 5110–5112.

waste of everybody's time to cross-examine. Mr. Thompson asked: "Is it worthwhile for me to cross-examine?"

To his dismay, Mr. Lowell said: "That is for you to decide."

Mr. Thompson then explained:

It puts me in a little difficult position. Sometimes the court says they do not think it is necessary to cross-examine after a witness has made a statement or told a story in direct, and that they do not wish to go any farther. If you leave it to me that means that you do take some stock in this woman.

JUDGE GRANT. I am not saying what stock we take in it.

A couple of minutes later, we could have discerned precisely what "stock" was taken in Mrs. Tattilo's testimony, had our attention not been focused on another aspect of the testimony. What we missed was almost a confession of prejudgment by Mr. Lowell. Impossible as the idea was for us to accept (and, I believe, also for Mr. Ranney), the Committee not only took "stock" in Mrs. Tattilo's wild and whirling tale, *but believed it to be truth, even before cross-examination or further evidence.* Here is the revealing dialogue:

PRESIDENT LOWELL. *This* [Lottie Tattilo] *is the only person in South Braintree who had seen Sacco before the murder.*

MR. THOMPSON. I don't think she ever saw Sacco before the murder.

THE WITNESS. You don't, ha? Then I'll tell you.

Here Mr. Lowell tried to bail out of his commitment to her story, but in doing so fell into a confirmation of it:

PRESIDENT LOWELL. Well, the only woman who claims she did. She had the best opportunity to see him, on the Government side, together with Lola Andrews.

Mr. Lowell then went on to insinuate darkly about charges which the report might contain against Mr. Moore for allegedly attempting to bribe Mrs. Tattilo and Lola Andrews.[10] Mr. Lowell's belief that the defense had been corruptly fashioned by Mr. Moore was apparently justified to himself by allegations from the two most disreputable witnesses in the case (excepting Carlos Goodridge, the crook). Mr. Lowell's conviction that Mr. Moore had corruptly sought to secure defense evidence may partially explain his aggressive attempts to destroy it.

If Mrs. Tattilo's testimony seemed weird during direct examination, it

10 Vol. V, 5114.

became fantastic as Mr. Thompson attempted to cross-examine her. She seemed to regard him as her arch persecutor, determined to drag her character in the dirt. Apparently this was caused by his seeking to introduce documents relating to her divorce and to questions based on Mr. Moore's transcript of her conference with him in November 1920. Mr. Thompson showed her a memorandum in her own handwriting dated August 31, 1920:

. . ."On the 15th day of April, 1920, at 11:30 A.M. I saw Mike Sacco standing in front of the express stable. Vanzetti on right-hand side of street talking of selling clams, and chauffeur working at machine as though something were wrong with" —

PRESIDENT LOWELL. (Handing the paper to the witness) Perhaps you can read your own writing. "As if something were" — will you tell me what that is (indicating)? I know I cannot always read my own handwriting.

THE WITNESS. (Indicating on the paper) Well, that word down there does not look as though it was my writing. I can't make it out myself. It might mean, "wrong with the machine."

Q. Does this refresh your recollection, now that you have heard this read, so that you now remember that you saw Vanzetti there talking of selling clams? A. Mr. Thompson, I can answer you that if you will give me permission.

Q. I would like to have you answer my question. If you do not understand it, tell me and I will put it to you again. Will you please listen to my question. All that you are doing here is to answer questions. Are you able to say now, having heard this read to you, and it being in your own handwriting, that you now remember that you not only saw Mike Sacco standing in front of the express stable, but you saw Vanzetti also, and heard him talking about selling clams? . . . A. No, I did not know it was Vanzetti until Mr. Moore showed me the picture and asked me if I had seen the man. I was shown Vanzetti's picture, and I said, "That's the picture that was with Sacco. That's the man that was with Sacco, he had a slouch hat on, and he —

Q. Tell us a little more what you remember about Vanzetti selling clams. A. When I came up Sacco, whatever you call him, was on the other side, and this man was across the street; I didn't know who the other man was until I was confronted with his picture, and then I identified the picture. Who was under the machine I couldn't say, he was laying flat under the machine.

Q. I haven't asked you that. A. I know what you asked.[11]

Mr. Thompson then went on to examine Mrs. Tattilo on the basis of Mr. Moore's transcript of her statements in November 1920. This part of her testimony was studded with denunciations of Mr. Moore and his stenographers as crooks and with occasional outbursts against Mr. Thompson. She stuck to her statement that when she returned to Rice and Hutchins after the noon hour on April 15, 1920, she told Mr. Jackson (her superin-

[11] Vol. V, 5120–5121.

tendent) before the murders were committed that she had seen Sacco that morning in front of the factory:

Q. (By Mr. Ranney) Who was the first person that you saw after the crime that took place? A. After the murder?
Q. Yes. A. Mr. Frank Jackson.
Q. When was that? A. That was after noon-time. *Before the murder was committed I said I saw Sacco.*
Q. That was before anything happened? A. Yes, sir. [Emphasis added.] [12]

She then stated that the first person she spoke to *after* the murder was James Reynolds, the paymaster.

Mrs. Tattilo had previously replied to a question by Judge Grant: "You will find him at the Braintree Shoe, Frank Jackson, and he will verify my statement word for word, what I have told him on that day." [13]

Although Mrs. Tattilo's story was well known to the police and the prosecution, Mr. Katzmann did not put her on the stand. Apparently, Mr. Katzmann, without our knowledge, had given the Committee his own explanation as to why he had not called her. Mr. Ranney had no personal knowledge, but stated: "I am talking on events which are mostly hearsay and may be unreliable, but *I was told* that the reason this woman was not produced was because a search of the records was made [of Rice and Hutchins] but how far back it went I do not know." [14] (Emphasis added.)

Mr. Ranney also added another reason: ". . . there was some question of immorality and Mr. Katzmann did not want to put her on the stand." [15]

After the close of the hearing, however, *when Mrs. Tattilo had left,* he added what appears to be the real reason. It was *certainly not* based on hearsay: ". . . *and it is quite obvious from her conduct here why we did not put her on, — she would be almost uncontrollable in the courtroom.*" [16] (Emphasis added.)

Mr. Thompson and I did not think that "uncontrollable" was precisely the word for her style of testifying, but we got his point.

Mr. Ranney put on the stand Frank W. Jackson, Mrs. Tattilo's superintendent, who, she said, would confirm her story. Mr. Jackson did relate that Mrs. Tattilo had told him that she had seen Sacco the day of the crime on the street (and talked with him) but said that *this was after Sacco and Vanzetti had been arrested in Brockton,* as follows:

[12] Vol. V, 5139.   [13] Vol. V, 5113.   [14] Vol. V, 5119.   [15] Vol. V, 5119.
[16] Vol. V, 5145.

Q. (By President Lowell) She did not tell you that until after the arrest? A. Not until after the arrest, no, sir. That is the best of my opinion, that it was after the arrest. I am pretty sure nobody knew anything about anybody until after the arrest.

Apparently Mrs. Tattilo embroidered her tale in telling Mr. Jackson about the matter. To him she mentioned a relationship with Sacco beyond the casual incident of his throwing a last at a boy in the distant past. She told Mr. Jackson that she had been out with Sacco "when he worked there," which Mr. Jackson took to mean that she meant she had been "on a party" with him.[17]

Q. What impression did she give you as to her degree of intimacy with Sacco? A. She gave me the impression that she was very intimate with him.

This seemed to interest Mr. Lowell:

Q. (By President Lowell) When did she give you that impression? A. When she talked with me at the time of the story.
Q. And not before? A. No; because none of us knew of it before the story.[18]

At the hearing, when Jeremiah Gallivan, formerly chief of police of Braintree, told the Committee about his tearing a hole in the Pearl Street cap, Mr. Thompson asked some questions about Lottie Tattilo. I should state that Chief Gallivan had refused to talk with me or Mr. Thompson before the hearing. Here is what he said about Mrs. Tattilo:

Q. (By Mr. Thompson) I want to ask you another question. Do you know a woman out there in Quincy — I don't mean in Quincy — in South Braintree named Packard, Lottie Packard? A. Yes.
Q. Tell us frankly, Mr. Gallivan, is there anything the matter with that woman? What is the matter with that woman? . . . A. Well, my honest and frank opinion, to be frank and honest and candid with you, is that that girl is a nut, and I have known her since she was born. She ought to be out in the Brookline Psychopathic Hospital. She is a nut. She is crazy, and she has been that way for years. She imagines things. She has pipe dreams, and that has been her makeup for years. She told me something about Sacco and Vanzetti. I don't know what she testified to here before this Commission the other day at all, but she said here the other day, and there was a man sitting on the right of me, he knew me but I didn't know him. He said, "Where are you from, Brookline?" I said, "No." I didn't have no more to say to him, but he said to me afterwards,

"That girl has made some awful statements there." I said, "Don't be surprised at anything from Lottie for you don't know anything about her." He said, "That's an awful statement she made about Moore." I said, "I don't pay no attention to her, she talks that way for years." I am going to tell you what she did say: I am not interested in Sacco and Vanzetti, I don't know whether they are guilty or not if anybody asked me my opinion. There's lots of things in their favor and there's lots of things that ain't in their favor in this case. The Governor asked me the other day what did I think, and I told him just what I thought, that there's some things in their favor and I thought there was lots of things against them in this case. I talked with Lottie Packard shortly after that murder and she told me then that she passed Sacco on the road, that she was on one side of the street and he was on the other. She said, "I seen him." Well, I thought then that that was funny, that she should make such a remark as that after Sacco and Vanzetti was arrested, because, and I'll tell you the reason why I thought that: There was a murder committed in Braintree. Vanzetti and Sacco were under arrest, they were looking up all strangers, the State Police was looking up strangers, looking up everybody; you can take that for granted anyway. So why didn't Lottie Packard say, "I saw Sacco in Braintree that day?" Why didn't she say that before Sacco was arrested? But after he was arrested Lottie Packard said, "I saw Sacco," after he was arrested. Why didn't we hear that before then? That's the time you are trying to get track of everybody that moves. You keep track of all strangers. That is how Gould was taken in. Why didn't Lottie Packard tell that information at that time, that she saw Sacco in Braintree that day, so he could be looked up? That information never came out until after Sacco had been arrested.

Q. Does she have delusions, is that what you mean? A. I don't know what she has. Lottie Packard as a girl was a girl that associated with men ever since she was a little girl, and she was a mighty pretty girl, a pretty girl, and if there was any records kept by the Board of Health in Braintree you will find that there's lots of young men that visited doctors on account of Lottie Packard . . .[19]

Q. (By Mr. Thompson) What did Lottie say about this? A. She drifted on with this case, as I say, and about her work, and about Moore, and she says, "Do you know, Mr. Gallivan," she says, *do you know I have realized I have made an awful mistake?*" I says, "What do you mean?" She said, "Do you know Colatto's brother was in South Braintree?" I said "Yes." She says, "He looks an awful lot like Sacco." I says, "I don't know; I know Colatto." She says, "*I feel now that the man I saw in South Braintree was not Sacco.*" I said, "That's up to you." I says, "Where did you see him?" She says, "We was walking up the street, Mr. Tracey ahead of me, and we passed by him." I says, "Another brain storm. That's just the way," I says, "She saw that man." I said right there to that man, you have just told me his name, I haven't seen him since; but as she went out he said, "She has made some pretty broad statements." I says, "I don't take any stock in her at all." That's just the words she said, it was Colatto's brother. She says, "This Colatto looked so much like Sacco that they called him Sacco." They called him Sacco; I don't know the fellow. [Emphasis added.] [20]

[19] Vol. V, 5172–5174.   [20] Vol. V, 5180–5181.

Mr. Moore's transcript of his conference in 1920 with Lottie indicates that on that occasion she mentioned a possible confusion between Sacco and one Collette[21] (sic, Colatto), because of an obvious resemblance. She did not then admit outright that she had made a mistake as she did to Chief Gallivan and to the next witness, Mr. Moran. However, at that time, according to the transcript, she was trying to get expense money from Moore to leave the state, in which case she would not have wanted to weaken supposed value to the defense of getting rid of her alleged identification of Sacco.

And finally we produced John W. Moran, Jr., who was the man sitting with Chief Gallivan outside of the governor's office. Here is his testimony before the Committee:

Q. (By Mr. Thompson) Mr. Moran, you are a reporter on the *Boston Traveler*? A. Yes, sir.

Q. Were you up here a little while ago when Lottie Packard was up here? A. I think it was Friday, July 2nd.

Q. Did you hear her talking about Sacco and Vanzetti? What did you hear her say? A. Among other things I heard her say that at the time the crime was committed that she had made the statement that the man who stood near the automobile was Sacco, but on that day, Friday, July 2nd, she would say it was not Sacco. She said, among other things, to me, that Moore had offered her $500 to get out of the Commonwealth, and then she talked about some man, some male witness who had been given money to get out of the Commonwealth, and she ranted on about how she had a very fine opportunity to see the man who did it, and she felt confident it was not Sacco. When she went out I asked Chief Gallivan what her name was and he said her name had been Lottie Packard and that she was now living over in Quincy, and was now married. I asked him if she had been a witness at the trial, and he said, "No", and he said, if she was a witness you couldn't believe her or that anything she was telling was the truth, that she was a confirmed liar. She said that while her husband was an Italian that there never had been anybody approach either she or her husband with a view to having her give any help to either Sacco or Vanzetti. I heard her say nothing whatever about Vanzetti; she spoke principally about Sacco.

Q. You did not hear her say anything about her having said that she heard Vanzetti say to Sacco he wished he would hurry up because he had an engagement to dig clams at half past three? A. No. She and Chief Gallivan were here in the room when I came in here.

On cross-examination, Mr. Ranney asked:

Q. *Do I understand you that she said the man she had seen that day was not Sacco?* A. *Yes, sir.* [Emphasis added.] [22]

21 Vol. V, 5153–5154.   22 Vol. V, 5184–5185.

The Tattilo appearance before the Committee has a significant place in the history of the Sacco-Vanzetti case. It is not presented here because she is an interesting sample of the kind of witness who frequently disrupts police investigations with fanciful tales. If that were all it meant, then Lottie Tattilo's testimony itself could be dismissed with a smile. Its importance lies not in what she said, but in how the Committee received it. This is essential to a full-length view of the course of the Sacco-Vanzetti case. Here were three men, presumably of superior intelligence and education, who had just listened to fanciful and self-contradictory ravings by an individual obviously suffering from severe mental disorder. If they had any question of her irresponsibility, the undisputed opinion of those who knew her should have settled it. When she had concluded, Mr. Thompson and I wrote her off as a serious witness, even as Mr. Katzmann had done. At that time we had not yet fully realized the finality of the Commmittee's commitment to a belief in the guilt of our clients.

The governor released the report of the Committee on August 6, 1927. We shall shortly consider some of their findings. These contained much that seemed incredible, but nothing, perhaps, more than their reference to Mrs. Tattilo's testimony. This is what we read:

> The other witness is Mrs. Tattoni [*semble*, Tattilo] formerly Lottie Packard, who claims to have known Sacco when he was working in the factory of Rice and Hutchins where she also worked and to have seen him at South Braintree on the morning of April 15 on Pearl Street. The woman is eccentric, not unimpeachable in conduct; *but the Committee believe that in this case her testimony is well worth consideration.* [Emphasis added.] [23]

The statement ignored the fact that Mrs. Tattilo had told the Committee that she did not believe that it was Sacco whom she saw[24] and had said the same thing to Chief Gallivan and to Mr. Moran in the State House corridor. However, this did not disturb us overmuch. We had become somewhat immune to half-truths, misstatements and omissions in summaries of the prosecution's evidence. What really shook us was the frank admission that "*in this case*" testimony from irresponsible witnesses became worthy of consideration so long as it was against Sacco and Vanzetti. At the beginning of this book we had occasion to discuss the shambles in the human mind wrought by a firmly held preconviction.[25] The treatment of Lot-

---

23 Vol. V, 53780.   24 Vol. V, 5110, 5112.
25 See also Ehrmann, "The Magnetic Point," *Harvard Law Review*, Vol. 29, No. 8 (January 1966).

tie Tattilo's ravings is a good example. However, we are not yet through with the Committee's process of latching on to anything that might make Sacco and Vanzetti appear to be the murderers and robbers at South Braintree. It even went so far as to twist the law itself to make a special case against Sacco and Vanzetti. This we shall examine in the next chapter.

29.

The Document That Ended Hope

Report of the Governor's Advisory Committee

All possibility of saving the lives of our clients centered on the forthcoming report of the Governor's Advisory Committee. The final power rested with Governor Fuller (with the advice of the executive council), but if the report was favorable, or expressed doubt, it was practically certain that he would recommend clemency. On the other hand, it was just as certain that he would do nothing to stop the march to the chair if the Committee sent to him a unanimous opinion that the defendants were guilty.

Therefore, in order to understand how the last barrier in the path to the chair was toppled, it becomes necessary to examine the Committee's report to the governor. It is obviously impracticable to measure this report against all that we know about the Sacco-Vanzetti proceedings. We can, however, obtain some idea of the reliability of the report, and of its fairness, by setting out some of its more important findings and commenting upon them. The comments to some extent represent my personal views, but they are largely based on the material contained in the preceding chapters of this book.

The summary which follows does not attempt to deal with the Committee's general conclusions, such as that the trial was fair, that the judge endeavored successfully to secure a fair trial, that the district attorney was not in any way guilty of unprofessional behavior, and so forth. As to these generalities, the facts speak for themselves and the reader is in a better position than the Committee to grasp their meaning.

Let us now examine some of the Committee's specific findings.

1. Cross-examination of Sacco

Report:

The cross-examination by Katzmann of the defendant, Sacco, on the subject of his political and social views seems at first unnecessarily harsh, and designed rather to prejudice the jury against him than for the legitimate purpose of testing the sincerity of his statements thereon; . . .

For these reasons [lack of evidence as to Sacco's radical activities and affiliations], Mr. Katzmann was justified in subjecting Mr. Sacco to a rigorous cross-examination to determine whether his profession that he and his friends were radicals liable to deportation was true, or was merely assumed for the purpose of the defense.[1]

Comment:

The foregoing justification of Mr. Katzmann's cross-examination had already been denied by Judge Thayer himself, as shown in Chapter 25.

2. Judge Thayer's "Prejudice"

Report:

Affidavits were presented to the Committee and witnesses were heard to the effect that the Judge, during and after the trial, had expressed his opinion of guilt in vigorous terms. Prejudice means an opinion or sentiment before the trial. That a judge should form an opinion as the evidence comes in is inevitable. . . .[2]

Comment:

The foregoing would make it appear that the judge merely expressed an "opinion of guilt" and that he formed it quite naturally in the course of the trial "as the evidence came in." This was *not* the testimony "presented to the Committee." The witnesses had shown that Judge Thayer's expressions of "opinion" began at the very start of the trial and preceded the submission of defense testimony. The words "prejudice" and "opinion" create a wrong impression. What the judge said indicated not merely a prejudgment, but intense hostility against the defendants and a determination to use his power as a judge to obtain a conviction.

Report:

. . . and [the Judge's opinion is] not prejudicial if not in any way brought to the notice of the jury as we are convinced was true in this case.

1 Vol. V, 5378j–5378k.   2 Vol. V, 5378l.

Comment:

Since we were not permitted to be present when the Committee interviewed the jurymen, I can make no comment on what it was that "convinced" the Committee. If the jurors simply stated that they were unaware
of the judge's views, we would like to have asked them about a few specific
indications of his attitude toward the defense. In any event, the communication to the jury of a judge's prejudice was not the main question. While
this might hurt the accused defendants with "green" jurors, it might even
help them with the more sophisticated. Where Judge Thayer's prejudice
could operate with deadly effectiveness would be in ways not easily perceived by the jury, such as in his numerous "discretionary" rulings, his admission of unauthenticated exhibits, his interventions injurious to the defense, his unconscious misstatements of the evidence and his lopsided
charge. As we have seen, this is what actually occurred. The Committee,
however, knowing little or nothing about the trial of cases, assured the
governor that Judge Thayer's "prejudice" was quite natural and did no
harm to the defendants' cause, because the jury was unaware of it.

Report:

From all that has come to us we are forced to conclude that the judge was
indiscreet in conversation with outsiders during the trial. He ought not to have
talked about the case off the bench, and doing so *was a grave breach of official
decorum.* But we do not believe that he used some of the expressions attributed
to him, and we think that there is exaggeration in what the persons to whom he
spoke remember. Furthermore, we believe that such indiscretions in conversation did not affect his conduct at the trial or the opinions of the jury, who
indeed, so stated to the Committee. [Emphasis added.] [3]

Comment:

The statement that the judge's "indiscretions in conversation" did not
affect his conduct of the trial indicates a hopeless confusion as to their real
significance. Obviously, Judge Thayer's remarks outside of court could have
had little or no effect on the course of the trial. Their vital importance lay
in the fact that they exposed the state of mind of Judge Thayer and his
intention to convict the defendants. In this respect they would have been
just as shocking to one's sense of justice if they had been secretly written
out, placed in a sealed envelope and then deposited in a bank vault.

[3] Vol. V, 5378l.

The Committee then calls the jurors to witness that the judge's "indiscretions" did not affect their opinions. Taken literally, this makes little sense, since they did not hear them. Probably the report really meant to state that the jury saw nothing in the conduct of the trial that reflected the sentiments expressed by the judge to "outsiders." Since the Committee excluded us from the secret session in which they interviewed the jurors, we do not know what questions were asked or what answers were given. We do know, however, as we shall see later in considering the report, that the Committee members themselves had an inadequate grasp of the record and insufficient knowledge of proper trial procedure to enable them to judge whether the trial was fair or not. If the jurors had been questioned by lawyers who had made a careful study of the trial, they might have seen many things they had not considered and perhaps modified their views as a consequence.

Obviously what shocked the Committee was not the hostile frame of mind implicit in Judge Thayer's talk, but only the fact that he let anyone know it. Nothing that the Committee said could have been more expressive of their unawareness of basic standards for the administration of justice. Nowhere in the entire report is there a hint that they knew of the words (or their spirit) penned by John Adams for the Massachusetts Constitution — that every man is entitled to be tried by a judge as impartial as the lot of humanity would admit. Once Judge Thayer had himself exposed to view his hatred of the defendants and his intention to secure their conviction, the Committee needed nothing further to find that Sacco and Vanzetti had not been accorded a just consideration of their cause. The Committee was not restricted by technical rules of law which the Supreme Judicial Court found a handicap. The governor would have been guided by their advice, whatever it was. However, when the Committee found a breach of the requirements of decorum when they should have found a breach of the essentials of justice, they not only doomed Sacco and Vanzetti, but also damaged the reputation of the Commonwealth for maintaining high judicial standards. To many it seemed unbearable that this should have been written by the president of Harvard and the ostensible head of the Lowell family.

Report:

But we do not believe that he used some of the expressions attributed to him, and we think that there is exaggeration in what the persons to whom he spoke remember.

Comment:

By "the expressions attributed to him," the report probably meant the reference to "anarchistic bastards" and "sons of bitches" as related by Professor James P. Richardson, and "bastards" as reported by Loring Coes to Robert Benchley as soon as Mr. Coes had emerged from the Worcester Golf Club.

No evidence was introduced at the hearings to justify the Committee in not believing that Judge Thayer had used the foregoing expressions. Nor had any member of the Committee or Mr. Ranney suggested that Professor Richardson was not telling the truth. Professor Richardson was holder of the chair of law on the faculty of Dartmouth College and a lawyer of long standing, and had been a member of the Massachusetts Constitutional Convention. We knew nothing of his talk with Judge Thayer until after he had written a letter to Governor Fuller dated April 19, 1927 (ten days after the defendants were sentenced), stating that he knew of his personal knowledge that Judge Thayer regarded the defendants in his court with abhorrence. Robert Benchley's report was wholly independent of Professor Richardson's and was also voluntary. No evidence was offered to counter it by Mr. Coes or anyone else. Mr. Benchley was a noted writer and the dramatic editor of *Life*. If the Committee did not believe the voluntary testimony under oath by men of the character of Richardson and Benchley, this could only be because it was at variance with what they wanted to find. As we shall see, this refusal to accept (or even to mention) evidence which did not suit their ends was typical of the entire report.

There was no evidence before the Committee that the witnesses to Judge Thayer's threats and diatribes had "exaggerated." Why should any of these witnesses "exaggerate" what the judge had said? Men like George U. Crocker, former treasurer of Boston, had even refused to give us a written statement. What was it that had been "exaggerated"? The Committee offered no explanation of this finding. Did Judge Thayer assure them in secrecy that reports of what he had said were "exaggerated"? If so, it would have been within the pattern of the report for the Committee members to accept it and to disbelieve, reject or ignore everything that conflicted with their conviction of the guilt of the defendants.

3. Genuineness of Fatal Bullet

Report:

Before the Committee, Mr. Thompson suggested that the fatal bullet shown at the trial as the one taken from Berardelli's body and which caused his death, was not genuine; that the police had substituted it for another, in order by a false exhibit to convict these men; but in this case, again, he offered no credible evidence for the suspicion. Such an accusation, devoid of proof, may be dismissed without further comment, save that the case of the defendants must be rather desperate on its merits when counsel feel it necessary to resort to a charge of this kind.[4]

Comment:

The general question of the integrity of the physical exhibits, including the fatal bullet No. III, has been discussed elsewhere. It need not be repeated here. Although the Committee did not know the whole story of the exhibit (discussed at length in an earlier chapter), it was aware of the fact that bullet No. III, which killed Berardelli, was the only one out of four lodged in his body that might have been fired through a Colt .32 such as Sacco possessed, and that the other three had come from a totally different type of weapon. Since the killer, alleged by the State to have been Sacco, was the bandit who pumped a number of bullets in quick succession at almost contact range into his victim and no witness claimed that this determined killer had fired two pistols, these facts prove that he could not have been Sacco and further raise the suspicions concerning the authenticity of bullet No. III. The Committee was also told of our late discovery that until the trial was underway, after the prosecution had in its possession the alleged mortal bullet for fourteen months, Mr. Katzmann had stipulated with Mr. Moore that he would make no claim that any particular bullet had been fired in any particular gun. There was also the sworn testimony of the expert Wilbur Turner that there was a tremendous difference in the marking of the base of bullet No. III from those on the other three bullets.[5] (Dr. Magrath, the medical examiner, had testified at the trial that he

4 Vol. V, 5378m.   5 Vol. V, 5225.

had marked the base of each of the four bullets seratim with the point of a needle as he extracted them.) I also reported my own observation of this difference to the Committee.[6] (The Committee did not know that the difference was noted by others, including Major Goddard, who had examined the bullets and shells in June 1927.) We fully expected that the Committee members themselves would examine the markings on the four bullets, especially as President Stratton had commented: "You should keep in mind that we can get the original bullets any time we want to. . . ." [7]

Was there "no credible evidence for the suspicion"? Against the background of peculiarities of the handling of other evidence by the prosecutor (called to the attention of the Committee), was a blind confidence in the genuineness of bullet No. III fully justified? (After Major Goddard had made his examination of the bullets and shells, both he and his companion William Crawford of the *New York World* readily agreed that there was nothing in the conduct of the trial which would lead one to place any great confidence in the exhibits.[8] Lieutenant John Collins (now captain), in charge of the ballistics laboratory of the Massachusetts State Police, is quoted by Francis Russell as stating that the markings looked different and that "the way they handled these exhibits from the beginning makes my hair stand on end." [9])

Instead of considering the possibility of a substitution, the Committee settled the matter with an adjective — our case must be "desperate." Indeed it was at least that. If there was any other word in the English language more expressive of hopelessness, I would say that the Committee's characterization of the entire defense case as "desperate" was a gross understatement.

4. Roy E. Gould (Post-Trial Witness Identification)

Report:

He was a by-stander through the lapel of whose coat a bullet was fired by the bandits, and who was questioned by the police. He was not called as a witness by the prosecution, but he was certainly close to the car, and has since made an affidavit to the effect that the men he saw were not the defendants.[10]

[6] Vol. V, 5317.   [7] Vol. V, 5228.
[8] Contemporaneous memoranda by Thompson and Ehrmann of conference on June 6, 1927.
[9] *Tragedy in Dedham*, 316–317.   [10] Vol. V, 5378o.

The report, following Judge Thayer's ruling, then found that Mr. Gould's evidence was "merely cumulative" (meaning that there were other defense witnesses who had sworn to the same thing) and was not "sufficient to demand a new trial." Standing by itself, this finding would not indicate a warped view of the evidence. However, the report then went on to give a special reason why it did not recommend action on the Gould evidence.

After stating that Gould had been in an unusually good position to observe the men in the car, the report stated that his evidence:

. . . is balanced by two other new witnesses on the other side. One is Mrs. Hewins, who stated to Mr. Thompson, as appears in one of his affidavits, that the bandit car stopped to ask the way at her house, and that Sacco was driving it. Sacco, if guilty, may have been doing so at the moment, or she may have mistaken whether he was behind the wheel or in the other place on the front seat.

Comment:

Mrs. Hewins was not a witness at all and certainly was not "new" so far as the prosecution was concerned. In the affidavit to which the report refers she is quoted as saying to Mr. Thompson:

. . . that before the trial she was interviewed by officials of the Government and so stated to them [that the driver was Sacco]; that she was summoned to court by the Government and *kept in court two days, and was then informed by the District Attorney or his assistant that her testimony was not needed, and that she might go home, which she did, without testifying in the case.* [Emphasis added.] [11]

The government never told defense counsel of the Hewins episode. Mr. Thompson discovered the incident on May 16, 1926, when he checked on Madeiros's story of the escape through Oak Street in Randolph.[12] Her home was at the fork, on the corner of Oak and Orchard streets. The incident was narrated by Madeiros in his deposition on June 28, 1926.[13] At the trial in 1921, when the halt had no apparent significance, Mr. and Mrs. Farmer had told of it. Mr. Katzmann had good reason not to use Mrs. Hewins's testimony. Having started with Levangie's testimony that Vanzetti was the chauffeur, and then being compelled to move Vanzetti around in the car to make a seat for the pale emaciated driver, he apparently decided that he did

11 Vol. V, 4540.   12 Vol. V, 4540.   13 Vol. V, 4643.

not wish to complicate his case with a witness who claimed that Sacco was the driver. Three different chauffeurs, including both defendants, would have been too many. As in several other instances, the Committee members regarded themselves as more astute than Mr. Katzmann. In their minds, a top-grade witness, such as Mr. Gould, was "balanced" by Mr. Thompson's hearsay report of a statement by a woman whose testimony was not wanted by the prosecution. However, the Committee had not yet completed "balancing" the missing testimony of Mr. Gould. There was another "new" witness on the other side.

Report:

The other witness is Mrs. Tattoni [*semble,* Tattilo] formerly Lottie Packard, who claims to have known Sacco when he was working in the factory of Rice and Hutchins where she also worked.

Comment:

Mrs. Tattilo no more than Mrs. Hewins was a "new" witness. As we have seen, she and her story were both well known in South Braintree. Mr. Katzmann and Mr. Williams were far too able as trial lawyers to put such a mad and uncontrollable witness on the stand. Apparently they did not even consider doing so. She would have ruined her testimony had she retracted the important part of her story, as she did before the Committee, and would have made a burlesque of the prosecution's case with some of her fanciful details, such as Vanzetti "hollering" to Sacco just before committing robbery and double murder, "Hurry up, there I have got to get through at half past three. I have some clams to dig." "If they going after clams, you wouldn't walk after clams." [14]

The Committee was again "smarter" than Mr. Katzmann. Mrs. Tattilo's testimony was "well worth consideration" "in this case." It also provided a good "balance" to cancel out the testimony of a sane witness who got a bullet through his overcoat from a bandit in the front seat, five to ten feet away.[15]

[14] Vol. V, 5122.   [15] Vol. IV, 3513.

5. Walter H. Ripley, Foreman of the Jury

Report:

Under the same motion was introduced an affidavit by William H. Daly, wherein he says that Ripley, when summoned as a talesman . . . in this case replied, "Damn them, they ought to hang them anyway." . . . He did not live to contradict the statement, and we believe that Daly must have misunderstood him, or that his recollection is at fault.[16]

Comment:

Daly was an old friend of Ripley, the foreman of the Dedham jury. There was nothing before the Committee to indicate that he had misunderstood Ripley or that he had remembered something he had not heard. This was only one of several instances where the Committee members nullified testimony favorable to Sacco and Vanzetti, sworn to by reputable people, merely by asserting that the witnesses must have "misunderstood" what they said they heard or imagined it out of a bad memory. May we not judge the character of the Committee report by this process alone?

6. The Proctor Testimony and Bullet No. III

Report:

The fifth supplementary motion for a new trial is known by the name of Captain Proctor, the police officer who testified as an expert on the question whether the fatal bullet found in Berardelli's body had been fired through Sacco's pistol. At the trial he was asked in regard to this matter as follows:
"Q. Have you an opinion as to whether bullet No. 3 was fired from the Colt automatic which is in evidence? A. I have.
Q. What is your opinion? A. My opinion is that it is consistent with being fired by that pistol."
In his affidavit of October 20, 1923, he says that while he was examining the bullet in preparation for the trial his attention was repeatedly called by the prosecuting attorneys to the question whether he could find any evidence that would justify the opinion that the bullet taken from the body of Berardelli — which came from a Colt automatic pistol — came from the particular pistol taken from Sacco, but at no time was able to find any evidence to convince him that it came from that pistol; that the District Attorney desired to ask him that question directly, but he repeatedly replied that if so, he would be obliged to answer in the negative. The two prosecuting attorneys in their affidavits denied

[16] Vol. V, 5378p.

that they had repeatedly asked him whether he had found evidence that the bullet was fired by Sacco's pistol; and Mr. Williams, who interrogated him, added that the form of the question was suggested by Proctor himself. It may be noted that Mr. Katzmann stated to the Committee, in answer to a question by counsel for the Commonwealth, that before Proctor made his affidavit he — Mr. Katzmann — had refused to approve Proctor's bill of $500 for expert testimony.[17]

Comment:

The report makes nothing of the fact that the two prosecutors conceded that Captain Proctor's account of the preparation of the question-and-answer testimony was correct except as to the word "repeatedly." Yet it was this prearrangement to avoid telling the jury plainly Captain Proctor's real opinion which precipitated so much condemnation of the trial in responsible quarters. Instead, the report concerns itself with insinuating that Captain Proctor gave his affidavit because Mr. Katzmann held up payment of his five-hundred-dollar bill for expert services. The Committee omitted Mr. Katzmann's further statement that Captain Proctor resented the fact that the case had been taken out of his hands and given to Chief Stewart.[18] (Captain Proctor's resentment would be quite understandable when he reflected on the type of witnesses and the kind of testimony produced by Chief Stewart to convict Sacco and Vanzetti.)

The Committee made no comment on Mr. Katzmann's ouster of Captain Proctor from his proper function. Presumably, the Committee knew that Captain Proctor had not been very helpful as a witness at the Plymouth trial of Vanzetti, where he chatted with Attorney Vahey about 12-gauge shotguns being used in "hunting birds and that sort of thing." [19]

The members knew that Proctor had refused to give an opinion at Dedham that Sacco's pistol had fired the mortal bullet and that he had been quoted as declaring in the Dedham courthouse that the wrong men were being prosecuted. They knew also that Katzmann was unable to deny that Captain Proctor had told him he believed the defendants to be innocent.

Was it not at least as important to inquire into Katzmann's purpose in removing the head of the State Police from the case as to speculate about whether Proctor's essentially truthful affidavit, favorable to the defendants, was made because his bill for services had not been paid? As a result of

[17] Vol. V, 5378q.   [18] Vol. V, 5085.   [19] Supp. Vol., 211.

Captain Proctor's untimely death shortly after he executed his affidavit, the question which the Committee did not probe — or even consider — will remain forever unanswered.

Why did the district attorney bar Captain Proctor from preparing for trial the case against the murderers of Parmenter and Berardelli?

Report:

Counsel for the defendants claim that the form of the question and answer was devised to mislead the jury; but it must be assumed that the jury understood the meaning of plain English words, that if Captain Proctor was of opinion that the bullet had been fired through Sacco's pistol he would have said so, instead of using language which meant that it might have been fired through that pistol. In his charge the Judge referred to the expert evidence on the question whether the bullet had been fired from Sacco's pistol, saying "To this effect the Commonwealth introduced the testimony of two experts, Messrs. Proctor and Van Amburgh." These two men did testify on the subject, the first saying that it might have gone through Sacco's pistol, the second that it did so; the experts for the defendants giving their opinion that it could not have gone through Sacco's pistol. It may be observed that the prosecuting attorney did not put the words into Captain Proctor's mouth, but asked him simply what his opinion was, and that Captain Proctor in answer used words that *seem not unadapted to express his meaning*. It does not seem to us that there is good ground to suppose that his answer was designed to mislead the jury. [Emphasis added.] [20]

Comment:

The assumption that a jury of laymen must have understood the technical meaning of the word "consistent" as the equivalent of "might have" is unrealistic and not justified by the evidence. Judge Thayer did not so understand it. The quoted phrase in his charge "to this effect" referred to the judge's words immediately preceding, that "it was his [Sacco's] pistol that fired the bullet that caused the death of Berardelli." [21] The Committee left out these words, thereby making it appear that the judge had not charged that Proctor's opinion was that the bullet had passed through Sacco's pistol. The McAnarneys understood Captain Proctor to mean that in his opinion, bullet No. III had been fired in Sacco's pistol. The Committee also ignored the fact that almost immediately after Captain Proctor used the word "consistent," the assistant district attorney led him into accepting the word as meaning *a positive opinion* that all bullets except No. III had been fired by the same weapon.

[20] Vol. V, 5378q–5378r.   [21] Vol. II, 2254.

Moreover, the Committee misstated the testimony of both Proctor and Van Amburgh.

Captain Proctor did *not* say that the bullet *might* have gone through Sacco's pistol. Had he done so, no one would have been deceived as to his meaning. He used the technical word "consistent," which not only conveyed a different meaning to the uninitiated, but served to fend off any inquiry by defense counsel which might have brought out that he had a *positive* opinion that bullet No. III had *not* passed through Sacco's pistol.

Nor did Van Amburgh give an opinion that the bullet had gone through Sacco's pistol. He went no further than to state that he was *"inclined to think"* that it had.

The Committee then turned to the 1923 affidavits and photographs relating to the No. III bullet and found that the evidence submitted by the government was "more convincing" than that offered by the defense. Even if the members were competent to make such judgment, this post-trial controversy had no bearing on the question as to whether the jury, in 1921, were misled by the trial testimony.

In another place also the Committee put forward its own reason for finding that the bullet No. III was fired in Sacco's pistol.

Report:

Then again, the fatal bullet found in Berardelli's body was of a type no longer manufactured and so obsolete that the defendant's expert witness, Burns, testified that, with the help of two assistants, he was unable to find such bullets for purposes of experiment; yet the same obsolete type of cartridges was found in Sacco's pockets on his arrest.[22]

Comment:

The record supports neither the assertion of "obsoleteness" nor the inference drawn from it. There never was any such evidence, and no such claim was ever made by the prosecution. Nor was the contention made at any other time when defense counsel could have answered it. The Committee's findings rest entirely upon a bit of misremembered testimony given at the trial in 1921 by defense expert Burns. On being asked by District Attorney Katzmann why he had not experimented on the same make of cartridge as had fired bullet III, Burns explained that he had been unable to pick up

[22] Vol. V, 5378w–5378x.

the same type of Winchester in stores between Dedham and Lawrence. Mr. Katzmann chided him for his lack of diligence. Even as late as 1923, defense expert Hamilton secured, fired and photographed at least sixteen of these allegedly unobtainable cartridges.[23] Sacco bought his mixed box of bullets in 1917 or 1918. The Winchester company discontinued manufacture of the type in August 1917, but since its new production was limited to war purposes, any Winchester cartridges bought at that time by private purchasers (including the bandits) would have come from the stock of the older type left on dealers' shelves.

This original argument based on "obsoleteness" must have come from the private interview with juryman Dever, who told me also that this was what convinced him of Sacco's guilt. The incident illustrates the unfairness of expecting jurors to recall accurately all of the testimony in a long trial without being allowed to take notes. Chiefly, however, it again is an example of the sloppiness of the Committee's investigation in not checking their findings with the record and of Mr. Lowell's persistent belief that he was more astute than Mr. Katzmann and was able to discover "proof" of defendants' guilt overlooked by that resourceful prosecutor. It also illustrates again the Committee's dangerous tendency to reach novel conclusions on evidence never tested in court or even revealed to defense counsel.

Report:

The counsel for the defendants produced Albert H. Hamilton and Elias Field, who informed the Committee that in an automobile ride Captain Proctor had told Hamilton that in his real opinion the fatal bullet had not been fired through Sacco's pistol. After the time of this conversation Captain Proctor made the affidavit already referred to, and in that, after quoting his testimony at the trial —
"Q. What is your opinion? A. My opinion is that it is consistent with being fired by that pistol."
he says "That is still my opinion." It seems to us improbable that Captain Proctor, who has since died, should have stated both at the trial and in his affidavit that his opinion was consistent with the firing of the bullet from Sacco's pistol, and in the meanwhile should have said in conversation that his opinion was exactly the opposite.[24]

---

[23] Vol. IV, 3631, 3689. In 1962 Mr. Braverman was still able to obtain from dealers various boxes of these "obsolete" cartridges. He sent me one as a souvenir. An excellent early discussion of this claim of obsoleteness occurs in Fraenkel, *The Sacco-Vanzetti Case* 374–377. For a later discussion, see Letter to the Editor from Herbert B. Ehrmann, 34 *Commentary* 72 (1962). See also Vol. II, 1435–1436.
[24] Vol. V, 5378u.

Comment:

It was hardly a sufficient reason for the Committee to reject sworn testimony before it on the ground that it was "improbable" that Captain Proctor would have stated what he was reported to have said. The whole Proctor episode as previously stated by him and admitted by the prosecutors was also "improbable" — as indeed is the entire Sacco-Vanzetti case.

Report:

One of the witnesses, Field, merely overheard Proctor's conversation with Hamilton about a subject with which he was not familiar; and the latter stated also to the Committee that Proctor told him that he believed before the trial the bullet was not fired through the Sacco pistol, which would be an admission not of a misleading statement but of deliberate perjury. This charge is inconsistent with Proctor's later affidavit, and we do not believe Hamilton's testimony on this point.[25]

Comment:

What does the Committee mean by saying that Elias Field, "merely heard" what Proctor had said? Mr. Field was a leading Boston lawyer of unquestioned integrity. How else would he have known what Captain Proctor said other than by hearing it? Is the Committee suggesting that he invented such an extraordinary story?

The report omits Mr. Field's further remark that Captain Proctor's statement "made considerable impression on me, and I went to one of my partners when I came back and told him." [26] I have in my possession a letter from Mr. Field's partner, H. Larue Brown, Esq., confirming the fact that Mr. Field reported the incident to him the same day that he heard it.

The report also omits a further statement by Captain Proctor which Mr. Field overheard. Mr. Hamilton and Proctor had been discussing various cases when the Sacco-Vanzetti evidence was mentioned, including the exhibits in that case. Mr. Field then related the following:

. . . Mr. Hamilton said to Capt. Proctor, "I think you ought to know" or "I suppose you know that I have been retained by the defense to study some of the exhibits in that case in connection with the pending motion for a new trial." And Capt. Proctor said in substance, "I don't care. I have been too old in the

25 Vol. V, 5378u–5378v.   26 Vol. V, 4976.

game, I have been too long in the game, and I'm getting to be too old to want to see a couple of fellows go to the chair for something I don't think they did." [27]

Since the above statement quoted by Mr. Field came from the veteran head of the Massachusetts State Police, who had directed the investigation of the South Braintree murders and robbery until Chief Stewart replaced him, one would have thought that it would have had a rather dramatic impact on the Committee. However, it apparently passed unnoticed.

Mr. Field's testimony as to Captain Proctor's real opinion that the mortal bullet had *not* been fired in Sacco's pistol was fully confirmed by Mr. Hamilton. Since Captain Proctor said it directly to Hamilton, the Committee could not dismiss Hamilton's testimony as something that the witness had "merely overheard." Instead, the Committee simply stated that they did not believe Hamilton because Captain Proctor's statement as quoted by him was "inconsistent with Proctor's later affidavit." Whether an opinion that a bullet *might* have passed through a particular pistol is inconsistent with a positive opinion that it did not may be debatable, but either way it is hardly a sound reason for rejecting Mr. Hamilton's testimony. It certainly is "consistent" with Mr. Katzmann's statement to the Committee that he could not deny that Captain Proctor had expressed an opinion to him that "these were not the men who committed that crime," [28] and with Judge McAnarney's testimony that Captain Proctor had exclaimed in the corridor of the Dedham courthouse that the wrong men were being prosecuted.[29]

7. The Cap Found in Pearl Street

Report:

The other significant new matter brought to the attention of the Committee by the counsel for the defense is the statement of Jeremiah F. Gallivan, former Chief of Police of Braintree, who said that in the cap found near the body of Berardelli, and claimed by the prosecuting counsel to be that of Sacco, the rent attributed by them to its hanging upon a nail in the factory, was in fact made by him in attempting to find a name under the lining before he delivered the cap to the officers investigating the case. This statement we believe to be true; but the rent in the lining of the cap is so trifling a matter in the evidence in the case that it seems to the Committee by no means a ground for a new trial.[30]

[27] Vol. V, 4975.   [28] Vol. V, 5084.   [29] Vol. V, 5055.   [30] Vol. V, 5378u–5378v.

Comment:

Chief Gallivan did not say that the cap was "found near the body of Berardelli." His testimony was to the contrary — that Mr. Fraher had stated to him that it had been found the night of April 16, more than a day after the murders and long after Berardelli's body had been removed.[31] (The Committee did not know that the *Boston Herald* for April 17 had reported that the cap had been found the previous evening in the street, exactly as Chief Gallivan told the Committee seven years later.)

Mr. Katzmann had used up a substantial portion of the record to make the jury believe that the tear in the lining identified this cap as Sacco's. He even produced a cap taken from Sacco's house which had a tear in the lining which Sacco testified he had never seen before. The tear in the lining of the Pearl Street cap may have seemed trifling to the Committee (*after Gallivan eliminated its supposed significance*), but it did not to Judge Thayer, who had made it one of his important reasons for denying a new trial.[32]

Possibly the members of the Committee thought the matter trifling because they believed the cap was Sacco's anyway. Here is what they said:

Report:

Then a cap is found on the ground *near the body of the man* he is accused of killing, which bears a resemblance in color and general appearance to those he was in the habit of wearing; and *when tried on in court it fitted, — that is, his head was the size of one of the men who did the shooting!* [Emphasis added.]

Comment:

The Committee again ignored Chief Gallivan's testimony that the cap was *not* found near Berardelli's body.

Another of the Committee's misstatements so fatal to the defendants is the flat finding that the cap fitted Sacco when tried on in court and that it was his head size.

There was nothing in the record to justify such a finding. To a cartoonist who sketched the scene when Sacco tried on the cap, it seemed to sit on his head like a "duck on the rock." The record indicated that Sacco's cap was size 7⅛, and the Pinkerton South Braintree reports indicated that the Pearl

---

[31] Vol. V, 5169.   [32] Vol. V, 4765.

Street cap was about size 6⅞. The Committee may be excused for not knowing the Pinkerton reports, but not for sending baseless false information to the governor that the cap was Sacco's size and fitted him.

8. The Madeiros-Morelli Evidence

Report:

The impression has gone abroad that Madeiros confessed committing the murder at South Braintree. Strangely enough, this is not really the case. He confesses to being present, but not to being guilty of the murder. That is, he says that he, as a youth of eighteen, was induced to go with the others without knowing where he was going, or what was to be done, save that there was to be a hold-up which would not involve killing; and that he took no part in what was done. In short, if he were tried, his own confession, if wholly believed, would not be sufficient for a verdict of murder in the first degree.[33]

Comment:

Factually, the foregoing summary is crucially deficient in that it bypasses Madeiros's statement that he was assigned the task of stopping pursuers, and for that purpose sat in the back seat with a .38 caliber revolver. Even as stated, however, the Committee's finding is legally inexplicable and astonishing. Both Mr. Lowell and Judge Grant were members of the Massachusetts bar. Not only was the above statement directly contrary to the law of the Commonwealth, but if they had perused the record of the trial, they would have read a clear explanation of it by Judge Thayer in his charge, in which he had said:

. . . the pistol fired by the hand of one conspirator was a pistol fired by the hand of each and every conspirator who was present aiding and assisting in the accomplishment of the alleged robbery.[34]

Mr. Williams in his opening had also dwelt on the equal guilt of all participants.[35] Only a few months before the Committee hearings, protests against electrocution of the three carbarn bandits had filled the newspapers for months. As a result, the Massachusetts law as to the equal guilt of confederates was well known to the Boston community, laymen and lawyers alike.

Before we proceed to a consideration of the Committee's handling of the

[33] Vol. V, 5378s.   [34] Vol. II, 2245.   [35] Vol. I, 78.

Madeiros-Morelli evidence, let us see how the report applied the law as to guilt of confederates in the case against Vanzetti. To do this, we must take up its finding on this issue out of order. However, it will give us rather a dramatic contrast between what they said when they wanted to discredit Madeiros and what they found when they wished to justify Vanzetti's conviction.

After reciting that Vanzetti belonged to the "same group" as Sacco, that he had a pistol "resembling" Berardelli's, that he had cartridges loaded with buckshot which "might" have been used in the "gun" sticking out of the back of the car (but were not), Vanzetti's falsehoods and armed condition at the time of his arrest and Officer Connolly's allegation that he "tried to draw his pistol" (omitted in Connolly's account of the arrest at the Plymouth trial),[36] the report turned to Vanzetti's alibi.

9. Vanzetti's Alibi

Report:

The alibi of Vanzetti is decidedly weak. One of the witnesses, Rosen, seems to the Committee to have been shown by the cross-examination to be lying at the trial; another, Mrs. Brini, had sworn to an alibi for him in the Bridgewater case, and two more of the witnesses did not seem certain of the date until they had talked it over. Under these circumstances, if he was with Sacco, or in the bandits' car, or indeed in South Braintree at all that day, he was undoubtedly guilty; for there is no reason why, if he were there for an innocent purpose, he should have sworn that he was in Plymouth all day. Now there are four persons who testified that they had seen him; — Dolbeare, who says he saw him in the morning in a car on the main street of South Braintree; Levangie, who said he saw him — erroneously at the wheel — as the car crossed the tracks after the shooting; and Austin T. Reed, who says that Vanzetti swore at him from the car at the Matfield railroad crossing. The fourth man was Faulkner, who testified that he was asked a question by Vanzetti in a smoking car on the way from Plymouth to South Braintree [Faulkner said *East* Braintree] on the forenoon of the day of the murder, and that he saw him alight at that station. Faulkner's testimony is impeached on two grounds: First, that he said the car was a combination smoker and baggage car, and that there was no such car on that train, but his description of the interior is exactly that of a full smoking car; and

---

[36] In summarizing the events supposed to show Vanzetti's "consciousness of guilt" of the South Braintree murders, the Committee members revealed their belief that Vanzetti was a desperate criminal by reason of his conviction at the Plymouth trial, saying: "On the other hand, all of these actions may be accounted for by consciousness of guilt of the attempted robbery and murder at Bridgewater of which he has been convicted." (Vol. V, 5378y.) The report did not discuss the evidence by which this conviction was obtained.

second, that no ticket that could be so used was sold that morning at any of the stations in or near Plymouth, and that no such cash fare was paid or mileage book punched, but that does not exhaust the possibilities. Otherwise no one claims to have seen him, or any man resembling him who was not Vanzetti. But it must be remembered that his face is much more unusual, and more easily remembered, than that of Sacco. He was evidently not in the foreground. On the whole, we are of opinion that Vanzetti also was guilty beyond reasonable doubt.[37]

Comment:

The foregoing statement is hardly an accurate summary of Vanzetti's alibi. No reason is given for finding that Rosen lied — his story was confirmed in a number of important respects; Mrs. Brini *never testified* to an alibi for Vanzetti in the Bridgewater case, but the Committee cannot be blamed for this misstatement, since defense counsel at Dedham made an erroneous stipulation to that effect; nor does it prove that two reputable people lied to protect a murderer because they freely admitted that they refreshed one another's reputation as to a particular date; the assumption that Vanzetti was conscious of guilt because he lied when he said he had been in Plymouth all day begs the question, since it is based on the Committee's disbelief in the alibi and does not disprove it; the reference to Reed fails to mention the fatal flaw in his purported identification, namely, that the man he saw spoke "clear and unmistakeable English." The statement that Faulkner's description of the train car "is exactly that of a full smoking car" was expressly refuted before the Committee by Daniel F. Ahearn, assistant trainmaster of the New York, New Haven and Hartford Railroad. Mr. Thompson had read to Mr. Ahearn Mr. Faulkner's description of the smoking car and asked him if it would fit any car on the train. To this Mr. Ahearn had said that there was nothing in the description that would compare with it except the small seat just ahead of the toilet.[38]

However, the inaccurate findings of fact in the above statement are not its most distinguishing features. Such errors seem to characterize almost the entire report. What is significant is the different views of the law as applied to Madeiros and to Vanzetti, and the strange new law as to proof beyond reasonable doubt that seems to have been uniquely phrased to fit Vanzetti.

For instance, if Madeiros said that he was one of the robber band, sitting on the back seat of the murder car, wielding a revolver for the purpose of

[37] Vol. V, 5378y–5378z.   [38] Vol. V, 5224.

shooting pursuers, this was insufficient to convict him. But if Vanzetti was in South Braintree *"at all that day, he was undoubtedly guilty."*

Faulkner's claim that he saw Vanzetti on a smoking car on the train coming up from Plymouth was refuted by evidence that there was no such car, that no ticket was bought or fare paid by a passenger from Plymouth or neighboring stations to South Braintree or neighboring stations on April 15, 1920, and by the testimony of all of the ticket agents in the Plymouth area that they had not seen Vanzetti on that day. Nevertheless, the report found that the identification was still valid, since such evidence did *"not exhaust the possibilities."* The defense had shown that Vanzetti could not have boarded the train from Plymouth or nearby stations to other stations in any of the known ways. What doctrine of burden of proof is it that requires a defendant to rebut unspecified "possibilities" or else risk having the discredited identification accepted as proof of guilt?

And finally, Madeiros could not be convicted even if he admitted to being an active accomplice in the murder car at the scene of the crime, but Vanzetti, although he was *"evidently not in the foreground"* was *"on the whole" "guilty beyond reasonable doubt."* These words may sound to lawyers like an opinion rendered to Alice by the Mad Hatter, but they constituted Vanzetti's death warrant.

10. *The Madeiros-Morelli Evidence Continued*

Report:

His ignorance of what happened is extraordinary, and much of it cannot be attributed to a desire to shield his associates, for it had no connection therewith. This is true of his inability to recollect the position of the buildings, and whether one or more men were killed. In his deposition he says that he was so scared that he could remember nothing immediately after the shooting. To the Committee he said that the shooting brought on an epileptic fit which showed itself by a failure of memory; but that hardly explains the fact that he could not tell the Committee whether before the shooting the car reached its position in front of the Slater & Morrill factory by going down Pearl Street or by a circuit through a roundabout road.[39]

Comment:

Since Madeiros stated that he sat on the back seat behind drawn curtains, there was no reason why he should have remembered physical land-

[39] Vol. V, 5378s.

marks in South Braintree. He had also stated that he had never been in South Braintree before or after the crime. We do not know what Madeiros said to the Committee members in their private conference with him, but on the record, in his confession and deposition, it would seem that his knowledge of "what happened" rather than his ignorance was "extraordinary."

Report:

Indeed, in his whole testimony there is only one fact that can be checked up as showing a personal knowledge of what really happened, and that was his statement that after the murder the car stopped to ask the way at the house of Mrs. Hewins at the corner of Oak and Orchard Streets in Randolph. As this house was not far from the place on a nearby road where Madeiros subsequently lived, he might very well have heard the fact mentioned.[40]

Comment:

The statement that the Hewins incident is the only fact that could be checked to prove Madeiros's personal knowledge is patently untrue. Omitting for the moment Madeiros's original contributions, which were not brought out at the trial, but which on investigation proved to be correct, Madeiros's description of the crime, as it would have appeared from his position as the occupant of the back seat, shut in by curtains, was almost perfect. Many details of his description are recounted in Chapter 25 in connection with Mr. Ranney's attempt to discredit the Madeiros story.

Even more important than Madeiros's accurate account of "what happened," however, was his contribution of facts which did not come out at the trial, but which, when "checked," turned out to be true.

The account of the Hewins episode came originally from Madeiros. If this, as the Committee stated, had been the *only* fact that could be checked, the Committee's explanation might be tenable, but in the mass of evidence of the truth of Madeiros's story, this hypothesis does not seem to make any sense.

The first mention of the use of two automobiles in the South Braintree affair, deliberately withheld from the jury at the trial, came from Madeiros. It was confirmed by the transcript of the "private" inquest. (Also by an analysis of the description of the fleeing automobile or automobiles by wit-

40 Vol. V, 5378s.

nesses beyond the Oak Street woods.) The report omits all mention of this fact.

Madeiros's story of the halt in the Oak Street woods to change cars led to the first notice of the fact that the escaping car lost considerable time between Randolph and Matfield. The Committee mentioned Mr. King's research study of this time factor,[41] but dismissed it as "based on somewhat uncertain data." However, it was the only accurate time data in the entire case — resting on railroad records and careful clocking of distances and different speeds. The Committee then accounts for the delay by the stop and turn around in Orchard Street at the Hewins house. However, this could not have taken more than a few minutes, even if the car had gone the full length of the short Orchard Street detour and returned.[42] The time lag must have been about twenty minutes. (Close examination of the testimony indicates that the Buick seen in South Braintree had no number plate in the back, whereas witnesses who saw a fleeing car after the Oak Street woods noted that it carried a rear license plate.) The Committee then delivered the coup de grace to the King study by saying: "It seems incredible that the bandits, as Mr. King supposes, should have spent something like twenty minutes in woods not far from the road and so short a distance from the scene of the murder."

What seemed "incredible" to the Committee was a tactic by professional criminals to throw off pursuit. The ruse would not have been worthwhile if the exchange had been made at a distance from South Braintree after the murder cȧr had advertised itself for many miles along the escape route. As a matter of fact, the State Police, according to the *Brockton Enterprise* for April 16, 1920, were working on the theory that the swap had been made in the Holbrook woods about three miles from the scene of the crime.[43]

The Committee continued in its attempt to discredit Madeiros:

Report:

How far do the other affidavits corroborate his statement? They state that Madeiros — who seems to have been rather prone to boast of his feats — had previously told Weeks that he had taken part with the Morelli gang in the South Braintree crime, and had talked with the Monterios also about it. The affidavits further state that he was acquainted with this gang, which consisted of

[41] Vol. V, 5378v.
[42] Mr. Fraenkel, for instance, did it in less than four minutes. *The Sacco-Vanzetti Case*, 532.   [43] *Ibid.*, 532.

a hardened set of criminals who had stolen shoes shipped from the Slater & Morrill and Rice & Hutchins factories, and were accustomed to spot the shipments when made at such factories; that on April 15, 1920, a number of that gang were out on bail for a different offense for which they were afterwards sentenced, and consequently could physically have been at South Braintree; that the photographs of Joe Morelli showed a distinct resemblance to Sacco and to whoever shot Berardelli, and that of Benkoski to the driver of the car — but identification by photograph is very uncertain; that Joe Morelli possessed a Colt automatic 32-caliber pistol.[44]

Comment:

The foregoing is an emasculated summary. The news that the New Bedford police, in 1920, had suspected the Morelli gang of the South Braintree murders is cut out of this report to the governor. In fact, the entire New Bedford episode is omitted, together with the incriminating implications of the appearance of a new-looking Buick in Mike Morelli's possession just before the South Braintree crime, its fleeting appearance in the late afternoon of April 15, 1920, the appearance a few days later of Joe Morelli's "Cole 8" bearing the number plate that had been on the Buick and the menacing attitude of the group in Fiore's restaurant indicating consciousness of guilt of something serious.

The summary mentions the gang's theft of shoes shipped from the South Braintree factories and their "custom" of spotting shipments, but shows no awareness of the fact that these thefts formed the link that tied the Morelli gang to the South Braintree crime. They explained how the robbers acquired the necessary knowledge concerning the location and the method of handling the payroll money by Slater and Morrill and Rice and Hutchins. We do not know whether the Committee understood this, but certainly the governor, who did not, got no help from their report.

Nor was there any mention of the (by then virtually conceded) fact that five bullets (not including No. III) had been fired through a foreign automatic of 7.65-millimeter caliber and that one of the gang had committed murder with just such a weapon in the same year as the South Braintree killings.

The Committee then proceeded to demonstrate that its members had missed entirely the impact of the Madeiros story.

44 Vol. V, 5378t.

Report:

They state that one of the gang was seen in Providence late on the afternoon of April 15th in a Buick car which, by the officer who so reported, was seen no more. In regard to the last item, the great improbability may be noted that bandits who intended to hide the car in which they made their escape should have first shown it in the streets of Providence after all but one of the members of the gang had already returned in another car.[45]

Comment:

The Committee's misstatement that one of the gang was seen in a Buick in Providence (instead of New Bedford) was not a slip. It sprang from a failure to understand the Madeiros-Morelli evidence. The whole idea of the escape plan was to keep the Buick, the murder car, out of Providence, which was the home base of the Morelli gang. The Buick was to be kept in New Bedford just before and immediately after the South Braintree affair — containing no robbers, no loot and bearing a Rhode Island number plate. The only mishap in an otherwise perfect plan came when the gang allowed the "Cole 8" to be seen in New Bedford carrying the number plate that had been on the Buick. Apparently they did not appreciate the alertness of the New Bedford police. Had Chief Stewart of Bridgewater not halted the investigation of the Massachusetts State Police by arresting a couple of anarchists in Brockton, it seems almost certain that those professional dectectives would have picked up the New Bedford trail and followed it to a complete and rational solution of the South Braintree crime.

The Committee members themselves, in closing their discussion, furnished the key to their chaotic handling of the Madeiros-Morelli evidence.

Report:

Even without considering the contradictory evidence, it does not seem to the Committee that these affidavits to corroborate a worthless confession are of such weight as to deserve serious attention.

Comment:

Since the confession was "worthless," it followed quite naturally that the corroborative material did not "deserve serious attention." This it certainly did not get — not even to the extent of being stated correctly.

[45] Vol. V, 5378t.

But what was meant by "contradictory evidence"? What evidence "contradicted" the affidavits corroborating the Madeiros story? Did the Committee have in mind the affidavits and statements of the Morellis? These did, indeed (to some extent), contradict the corroborating evidence; however, they also contradicted one another and were lies. It is to be regretted that the Committee did not consider the expostulations of innocence by the Morellis. If so, they might have distinguished between the consciousness of guilt as indicated by falsehoods told on their arrest by frightened alien radicals, the targets of a nationwide hunt, and the consciousness of guilt implicit in the prevarications of native-born professional criminals suspected, with good reason, of murder and payroll robbery.

11. Evidence Against Sacco

Report and Comment:

We have already commented on the Committee's handling of the cap found in Pearl Street, stated to be Sacco's head size, and of the mortal bullet alleged by them to be obsolete. The rest of the evidence against him, as cited in the Report, is practically the same as that claimed by Mr. Katzmann and summarized by Judge Thayer — the fact that he was armed, the lies told on arrest and the eyewitness identification. (This has also been fully discussed.)

12. Sacco's Alibi

Report:

In reaching this conclusion we are aware that it involves a disbelief in the evidence of his alibi in Boston, but in view of all the evidence, they do not believe he was there that day.

Comment:

Could the foregoing finding be attributed to anything but a deliberate avoidance of any discussion of Sacco's alibi? Contrast it with the report's treatment of Vanzetti's alibi. In that instance it sought to offset the evidence that Vanzetti was in Plymouth on April 15, 1920, by citing the testimony of Dolbeare, Levangie, Reed and Faulkner to indicate that he was in South Braintree. It sought to discredit by name at least two of the several

COTUIT. MASS.

Sept. 13. 1933.

Dear Sir;

The Committee, of which I was
a member, appointed by the Governor to investigate the Sacco-Vanzetti case had some
evidence not produced at the trial; but this
has all, I believe, been since published.
For example, two persons – not witnesses
at the trial – said said they had seen Sacco;
one in the car in which the murderers fled;
the other, who had previously worked with
in the same factory as Sacco and knew him
by sight, said she saw him in the morning

The Lowell letter

This letter was Lowell's handwritten reply to an inquiry regarding the reasons why
the Governor's Advisory Committee had concluded that Sacco and Vanzetti were
guilty. Not one of the reasons advanced by Lowell here was ever advanced in court.
Mr. Lowell implies that the prosecution was unaware of this evidence. Actually, the
evidence and its significance had been rejected by the prosecution.

waiting near the place where the murder was committed later in the day. Moreover, one piece of evidence — although known to the jury — was not mentioned in the arguments for the prosecution or the judge's charge, and is not stated in the printed report of the evidence because it appears only from the exhibits which are mentioned but not fully described in that report. The bullet that caused the death of one of the victims was of a type so obsolete that the expert for the defense was unable to find a specimen in the shops, but several of them were in Sacco's pistol and pockets at the time of his arrest some days after the murder. The jury became aware of this when they examined all these bullets, as we did long afterwards. The type was unmistakable.

I do not think that anyone really

impartial, as the members of our committee certainly were,
could go through all the evidence without being fully convinced
that Sacco and Vanzetti were guilty of the murder. Nor do
I doubt that if they had been Americans of old political
theories, that they would have been convicted without protest—

Yours very sincerely,

A. Lawrence Lowell—

witnesses who swore that he had been in Plymouth, and other alibi witnesses without naming them. Calling Vanzetti's alibi "decidedly weak," the report consumed about a printed page of the Holt Record in trying to disprove it.

On the other hand, Mr. Lowell with good reason had characterized the evidence that Sacco had been in Boston on April 15, 1920, as a "serious alibi." This was when he (erroneously) thought that he had "destroyed it." The Committee had attested to their belief that the alibi was "serious" by conducting its own investigation by reading newspapers (but not the one indicated by the testimony) and by unverified long-distance telephone conversations to prove that the "banchetto" to Commander Williams had been in May and not on April 15 as three alibi witnesses had claimed. The Committee had summoned to the State House two of these defense witnesses to prove that they had lied. When the bomb which the Committee members had expected to explode before Mr. Thompson and me blew up in their own faces, Mr. Lowell had apologized to the two witnesses and Judge Grant had assured us that the alibi was back where it had been before.

The alibi was not only not back where it had been, but was washed out entirely in the report. Under the circumstances, we had felt that the Committee was under an obligation to discuss the Sacco alibi and to advise the governor of the outcome of their investigation into it. When we found no discussion of the Sacco alibi evidence in the report, we reread it several times to be sure we had not overlooked it. Later we found that Mr. Lowell had given the reporter directions which caused him to omit from the record any mention of the vindication of Bosco and Guadagni, so that the transcript seemed to prove that they were liars and Mr. Lowell was right. For Mr. Thompson and me this was the crowning disillusionment. The others we might attribute to preconviction, or prejudice, or failure to understand the proper standards of judicial justice, or to gross carelessness. However, the omission of any mention of the evidence supporting the principal defense of the condemned Sacco was a symptom of a deficiency in character. It seemed to us as if the flower of New England had wilted before our eyes.

We should have been prepared for the Committee's failure to honor its obligations with respect to the Sacco alibi. The report's earlier treatment of Judge Thayer's expression of hatred of the defendants and his determina-

tion to convict them had shown the same indifference to matters of conscience. Perhaps because I was of counsel for Sacco and Vanzetti, the finding that this talk by the judge was merely "a breach of decorum" hit me
especially hard. I thought of the descent from John Adams to Lawrence
Lowell in less than a century and a half. The comfortable assumption of
progress which my generation shared was smashed by a phrase. Where were
we going — Quo Vadis? My mind went even farther back in history. In my
mood of disillusion I tried to imagine the prophet Micah declaiming,
"What does the Lord require of thee but to do decorum, love mercy and
walk humbly with thy God?" and of his fellow, the prophet Amos, admon-
ishing the "establishment" of his day to let "decorum roll down like the
waters." The distance from the Judean hills to Beacon Hill seemed no
longer measurable in millennia or in miles — but in morals. The thought
has stayed with me over the years. Many decades later, in referring to the
millions of human beings who had been subjected to manmade horror, the
mood of 1927 came again to the surface, causing me to exclaim: "We talk
of reaching the moon in a few years, when in over three thousand years we
haven't even reached the foot of Mt. Sinai!"

30.

The Governor's Decision

Then I and you and all of us fell down.
JULIUS CAESAR, *Act III, scene ii*

On May 4, 1927, we filed a formal application for clemency with Governor
Alvan T. Fuller. It was signed by Vanzetti alone. Sacco refused to sign,
although when it was read to him he stated to us that he agreed with it. He
now asserted that the authorities were determined to put him to death and
he would not join in a useless request to the governor to spare his life. It
was against his principles to make an appeal to government authority. Besides, he said, his death would put an end to his wife's suffering caused by
seven years of worry and anxiety. On one occasion, when I went to plead
with him to sign the petition, I took Mrs. Ehrmann along in the hope that

she might influence him. Sacco was adamant. It was when Mrs. Ehrmann asked him to sign, if not for himself, then for his wife and children, that he burst out, "Excuse me! I no love Rosina if I not true first to myself."

Vanzetti, on the other hand, took great interest in the composition of the petition. The subjects to be covered by it and their treatment were largely determined by him. Much of the material was almost literally in his own language, especially the parts referring to his own life, his own philosophy and the history of "libertarianism." We did some editing to make the petition read more smoothly. So did Vanzetti — to make it express his position more exactly. For instance, he struck out of a draft of the appeal the words "We are opposed . . . to communists and socialists" and substituted ". . . opposed to every theory of authoritarian communism and socialism; for they would rivet more or less firmly the chains of coercion on the human spirit, just as we are opposed to the present system, which is based upon coercion."

It may be doubted whether Governor Fuller understood what Vanzetti was trying to tell him. His education had not gone beyond the public schools and his thinking went along entirely different lines. Let us take a brief look at the man whose decision meant life or death for the condemned men.

Governor Fuller was a highly successful businessman. He had begun in the bicycle business but graduated early into the fast-growing automobile field. At the time of the Sacco-Vanzetti case, he owned an agency for Packard, then one of our foremost automobiles. He was rated a millionaire. More important to our story, he also had a second successful career — as a Republican politician. In 1915 he was elected to the Massachusetts legislature and later to Congress, where he was from 1917 to 1921. Returning to his home state, he was elected lieutenant governor of the Commonwealth, which post he held until 1925, when he took office as governor and served two terms through 1928.

Mr. Fuller was popular with the electorate because of his independence from "regular" politicians in his party. For the same reason, however, he was disliked by these same politicians. They were not happy when he announced his intention to seek the Republican nomination for governor. Nor was his candidacy welcomed by the "elite" set who felt that they had the prerogative of putting their stamp of approval on Republican candidates for governor. Mr. Fuller was not one of their number. However, his name was already well known and he was a "joiner" where it counted. He was an Odd Fellow, a Mason, an Elk and a Knight of Pythias.

At almost the last minute the anti-Fuller Republican leaders persuaded James J. Jackson, treasurer of the Commonwealth, to contest for the nomination. Mr. Jackson was strong where Mr. Fuller was weak, but, unfortunately, weak where he was strong. He was almost the ideal Republican candidate except for one thing — he was almost unknown to the electorate. Friends persuaded me to campaign for Mr. Jackson, which I did, with enthusiasm. We swung along the loop through the Massachusetts cities and towns from the Atlantic coast to the New York line and back again, sounding a calliope to draw crowds in every public square. Mr. Jackson lost by a fairly narrow margin, considering his late entry. Had I been able to peer into the future, the result of the campaign would have filled me with dismal forebodings.

I believe that Mr. Fuller's nomination and election was another one of those accidental happenings that, in retrospect, seemed to lead so inexorably to the deaths of Sacco and Vanzetti. Whatever view Mr. Jackson would have taken of the Sacco-Vanzetti evidence, I believe that he would have been more sensitive to the rising outcry against the unfair treatment of the defendants. For Governor Fuller, the only real question was whether he thought the men were guilty, not the way in which they were convicted. I believe that Mr. Jackson would have been more conscious of a "decent respect" for the opinion of mankind which would have impelled him to halt the execution. For Mr. Fuller, however, the worldwide protest was a challenge for him to demonstrate his courage and independence. The several bomb explosions while he was considering the case made sure of his decision.[1]

A glance at Governor Fuller's immediate past would have clearly foreshadowed the disposition of the Sacco-Vanzetti case in his hands if he thought the defendants were guilty. When Victor M. Berger, the Socialist Congressman from Milwaukee, was unseated as Congressman and refused a

---

[1] Had Mr. Jackson been elected, this would have probably changed my own future with respect to joining the defense of Sacco and Vanzetti in 1926. A similar coincidental chance happened the next year. Harold Williams, the assistant district attorney who had prepared the Dedham trial and tried it with Mr. Katzmann, became United States district attorney in 1925. He was kind enough to invite me to join his staff as an assistant. However, I could not accept because my senior partner, Edward S. Goulston, had recently died and I was needed by our firm.

seat after his reelection by an increased vote, Congressman Fuller defended the House action in these words: "Berger characterizes the action of the House as a 'crucifixion' and in a manner it is. It is the crucifixion of disloyalty, — the nailing of sedition to the cross of free Government, where the whole brood of Anarchists, Bolshevists, I.W.W.'s may see and read a solemn warning." [2]

In Mr. Fuller's mind, apparently, a "free" government should be solemnly warned that Congress will not accept freely elected representatives if their views on social or economic matters are obnoxious to the majority. This concept of "freedom" is not unknown today, but in the 1920's it was virulently active. Governor Fuller was one of its leading expounders. Sacco and Vanzetti belonged to the "brood of Anarchists" and, if guilty of murder, they could hardly expect clemency from him.

Another ominous hint of the fate of Sacco and Vanzetti could have been read in a report of a speech by Governor Fuller in *Success* magazine for December 1926 entitled "Why I Believe in Capital Punishment" in which he said: "One thing I have particularly emphasized; strict enforcement of capital punishment for those who have taken human life. Friends, relatives, even newspapers are enlisted in a campaign to win over the sympathy of the man supremely charged by the Commonwealth with the carrying out of its laws. Sometimes for two or three weeks these assaults on his sense of justice may continue." [3]

It is doubtful whether Governor Fuller had Sacco and Vanzetti in mind when he wrote the above words. The defendants had not yet been sentenced. He was probably referring to the passionate protests against the executions of the carbarn bandits, then pending. Governor Fuller had remained unmoved — at least outwardly — by pleas for leniency which had deluged him, even when the boys' mothers reportedly fell on their knees before him to beg for the lives of their boys. For him these appeals were probably the "assaults on his sense of justice."

This does not mean, however, that the governor would not have recommended commutation, or even pardon, had he been convinced that Sacco and Vanzetti were innocent. Had he believed this, I feel that he would have exercised the leniency vested in his office despite the swelling demand

[2] *Congressional Record,* 66th Congress, 1st Session, 382, 9148–9149. Quoted in Joughin and Morgan, *The Legacy of Sacco and Vanzetti,* 218.
[3] Joughin and Morgan, *The Legacy of Sacco and Vanzetti,* 251.

among the so-called "middle class" to "show the Reds" that they could not run the Commonwealth of Massachusetts. He had the courage needed to do this. However, he was also politically ambitious. For this reason there arose the theory that his decision was influenced by Calvin Coolidge's famous exit line as he left the national political stage, "I do not choose to run."

If we consider the course of the Sacco-Vanzetti proceedings until the question of clemency reached his desk, we can readily see how difficult it would have been for Governor Fuller to convince himself that Sacco and Vanzetti were not guilty. He might have some doubts about their guilt at times, but that is very different from belief in their innocence. He had before him the various opinions of Judge Thayer, heavily loaded against the defendants. He could get no help from the decisions of the Supreme Judicial Court, which, in turn, had been based on Judge Thayer's findings and rulings. When he received the unanimous report of the Advisory Committee, it became almost impossible for him to reject the opinion of the men he had appointed to advise him.

If it had been at all possible for the governor to free himself from the official documents of the case, all unfavorable to Sacco and Vanzetti, the method that he chose for his own investigation offered little chance of arriving at a different conclusion.

To begin with, Governor Fuller set himself the task of personally determining the guilt or innocence of the defendants. This was an issue clearly beyond his competence. He could not make the painstaking analysis of the lengthy record in the two cases, as we have done, or sift the true from the false in the multiple conflicts of testimony. Mr. Thompson begged him to abandon the effort and to concentrate on an aspect of the case which he could decide, namely, whether or not Sacco and Vanzetti had been accorded fair treatment by the Commonwealth. He explained to the governor at length that alleged truths arrived at by unfair methods cannot be trusted. However, it was apparent that the governor had the attitude of the uninformed layman, that a true judgment could be made regardless of how the evidence on which it rested was obtained or presented. He was therefore not interested in the unfairness of the proceedings. Were they guilty or not? And if they were guilty, why get excited about the fact that they were unfairly treated?

However, we had not yet learned the worst about the proposed investigation. The governor decided that counsel were to be excluded when he interviewed witnesses. We were not even to be told who the witnesses were or what they said to the governor. The Committee's blackout had been only partial, which was bad enough, but the governor's procedure left us in total darkness. Unfortunately, as we shall see, it also left the governor in murkiness where he could not see anything clearly.

Mr. Thompson again protested the proposed procedure and explained to the governor that no one could be sure of learning the truth from witnesses who were at liberty to say anything they chose without fear of being checked or even of being identified. Star-chamber sessions had been thoroughly discredited for more than two centuries. Nor was it possible for the governor to understand the real significance of what the witnesses told him in the absence of a lawyer who knew the record and could connect the testimony with other evidence in the case. Governor Fuller listened to Mr. Thompson's eloquence with uncomprehending admiration.[4]

The governor was one of those businessmen who believed that legal practice was the art of turning black into white (and vice versa), and it was easy

---

[4] Governor Fuller at times was attended by his personal counsel, Joseph Wiggin. However, Mr. Wiggin had no knowledge of the record so far as we know, nor did we know his attitude toward the defendants. He was friendly to Mr. Thompson, however, and tipped him off to the fact that the governor wanted to see some evidence that Vanzetti had actually received live eels at Plymouth, as his defense claimed. This led to the discovery of the American Express receipt book for December 1919. However, we learned from John F. Moors that Mr. Wiggin had repeated a rumor at a conference in the governor's office that Waldo I. Cook, distinguished editor of the *Springfield Republican* had been paid ten thousand dollars for writing editorials protesting injustice to Sacco and Vanzetti. Many such rumors drifted down from Beacon Hill, including one that Felix Frankfurter had been paid fifty thousand dollars by the Defense Committee for writing his *Atlantic Monthly* article.

Efforts to impugn the integrity of Frankfurter's article have continued until recent times. Unable to point out any errors in his report on the case, his detractors have resorted to charges that he was not a disinterested commentator. For instance, Mr. Montgomery, in his book *Sacco-Vanzetti: The Murder and the Myth*, claims that Frankfurter was a member of the Sacco-Vanzetti Defense Committee. To prove this he published what purported to be an authentic list of the Committee's members, ending with the names of Felix Frankfurter and John F. Moors. Neither was a member nor was there such a list. David Felix in his book *Protest: Sacco-Vanzetti and the Intellectuals* (Bloomington and London: Indiana University Press, 1965) repeats Mr. Montgomery's misstatement, but goes even further in an effort to discredit Frankfurter's great authority. He asserts that the article was based on defendant's brief and that it does not mention the record. To prove this, Mr. Felix points out that Frankfurter admitted that he took his facts from defendants' Bill of Exceptions, which, he says, is a "brief." This also is a misstatement, due, no doubt, to Mr. Felix's ignorance of Massachusetts practice. The Holt Record of the case, however, used by Mr. Felix, carefully explained that *a Bill of Exceptions is actually the record of the case* required to present the issues to the Supreme Judicial Court, and that it is agreed to as correct by counsel for both sides and approved by the trial judge. Mr. Felix could not have read the explanation.

to see that he thought that Mr. Thompson was one of the ablest practition-
ers. This was most unfortunate. Mr. Thompson's soundest arguments succeeded only in alerting the governor to the danger of being fooled by what
should have been a convincing presentation. When Mr. Thompson pointed
out the danger of listening to witnesses in secret sessions, the governor
smiled genially and observed: "Mr. Thompson, you are the most dangerous
person who comes into this room." He appreciated Mr. Thompson as a
successful lawyer — but did not really take in what he said.

When we learned by chance what witnesses were interviewed by the
governor, we wrote letters to him about them without any knowledge of
what they had said to him. One of those was Lottie Tattilo; another was
juror John Dever. This was a most unsatisfactory business.

The governor became much interested in the conviction of Vanzetti for
the Bridgewater attempt. In this he was getting close to the key which
might have opened the entire mystery of the Sacco-Vanzetti case. However,
he did not see it as such. He chiefly wanted to know why Vanzetti had not
testified at the Plymouth trial. He looked skeptical when I explained to him
the choice of risks which confronted Vanzetti in making a decision about
the stand. I told him that Vanzetti, as an alien ignorant of our legal practice, had to be guided by counsel. When Mr. Fuller still looked skeptical,
I said, "Governor, the defendants elected to testify at the Dedham trial and
Mr. Katzmann murdered them!" To this the governor commented, "I see
— they were damned if they did and damned if they didn't." This encouraged us to think that the governor understood the dilemma. If he did, he
soon forgot it.

On another occasion, the governor let slip a remark that one of the witnesses to the Bridgewater attempt (Cox), a friend of his, had (in his office)
positively stated that he identified Vanzetti as the "shotgun bandit."
When I told him that on the day of the holdup attempt he had described a
different-looking man and that when he first saw Vanzetti he was not so
sure about the identification, the governor remarked, "He had received a
threatening letter." When I reminded the governor that the alleged letter
had been received *after* the time I had reference to, he lapsed into silence.
The incident was typical of the kind of error that was bound to occur in the
absence of counsel who knew the record testimony.

When we received a copy of the Pinkerton Bridgewater reports, Mr.
Thompson and I spent a great deal of time writing a lengthy memoran-

dum to the governor analyzing their contents. Even today, the letter still constitutes a useful memorandum about the Bridgewater attempt.[5]

Shortly thereafter, when Mr. Moors was in conference with the governor about the case, the subject of Vanzetti's supposed guilt in the Bridgewater affair was raised. Mr. Moors asked the governor what he thought of the Pinkerton reports. To this the governor said, "What are the Pinkerton reports?" Mr. Moors then referred to the memorandum we had sent to him. The governor turned to Herman MacDonald, his first secretary.

"What do you know about the Pinkerton reports?" he asked.

To this Mr. MacDonald replied: "Oh, something about a cropped moustache."

This remained the alpha and omega of the governor's knowledge of the vital new evidence in the Pinkerton reports.

Word came to Mr. Thompson (as previously stated) that the governor had said to his personal lawyer, Mr. Wiggin, that he thought it strange that Vanzetti's defense at Plymouth was that on December 24, 1919 (the day of the highway robbery attempt), he was delivering eels to customers in the town and yet there had been no evidence that he had actually received any live eels, as the defense claimed. Mr. Thompson telephoned the word to me at Georgetown, Massachusetts, and I came in immediately. Aldino Felicani joined me in Boston because I could not speak Italian. On August 2, 1927, we visited every Italian fish store on Atlantic Avenue and then we went to the stalls at the fish pier in South Boston. No one seemed to remember Vanzetti. Discouraged, we returned to Atlantic Avenue and again combed the Italian fish vendors. This time, persistence was rewarded. A dealer at 112 Atlantic Avenue seemed to remember a customer named Vanzetti. He said that all of his old papers had been destroyed, but permitted us to look at a packing case on the second floor. We found nothing. It finally occurred to him that he had a box of old American Express Company receipts in the attic, under the gabled roof. We pulled out the box and began a feverish search until we found a receipt book for December 1919. Then the miracle happened! *Under the date of December 20, 1919 (a Saturday), there was a receipt for eels shipped to "B. Vanzetti, Plymouth, Massachusetts."* The eels would have been delivered in Plymouth on December 22 or 23, as testified to by witnesses at the Plymouth trial, including his landlady. This was exactly the evidence which the governor

[5] Supp. Vol., 339 *et seq.*

had wanted to prove Vanzetti's alibi. In order that the American Express receipt book would not go the MacDonald way, we sent it to the governor, in the care of Joseph Wiggin. That was the last we heard of the eel receipt. Like the fingerprints on the abandoned Buick, expressman Shelly Neal's story of the two cooperating cars in South Braintree, the Pinkerton Bridgewater reports, the notebook of Sergeant Jacobs in New Bedford and the record of the *banchetto* to Commander Williams in the North End on April 15, 1920, it was heard from no more.

A weird echo of the eel episode, however, did subsequently emanate from the governor's office. The fact that Vanzetti was actually selling eels in Plymouth on December 24, 1919, became fresh proof in the governor's mind that Vanzetti was guilty. Testifying in the case of *Commonwealth v. Canter*, John Moors quoted the governor as saying to him: "It is very easy to get in an automobile and ride from Bridgewater to Plymouth and be selling eels at 9:30 after being otherwise engaged [in highway robbery] at 7:30." [6]

Mr. Moors reported to us orally that the governor had then added: "It is only twenty miles from Plymouth to Bridgewater. A pretty clever ruse — start with eels in Plymouth, then [making a swooping gesture with outspread hands] dash to Bridgewater for the holdup, then [swooping gesture again] back to Plymouth to sell eels! Could there be a neater alibi?"

This sounded crazy to us, and yet it was no crazier than other hypotheses believed by other sensible men. For instance, that Sacco's request for a day off from his employer was actually so that he might have a little time to murder two men and rob them of a payroll on his promise to be early at work the next morning; or that Sacco and Vanzetti (supposedly successful payroll robbers) wanted Boda's jalopy for use in another payroll robbery the next day, forgetting, however, to bring along any 1920 number plates needed to put the car on the road.

We asked Mr. Fuller to send for General Richards of Providence so that the governor might learn from him about the various members of the Morelli gang. General Richards was the United States marshal who had gathered the evidence implicating the Morellis in the freight car robberies and had prosecuted them. He had also assisted me in my own investigation. As soon as he started to talk about the Morellis, according to General Rich-

[6] Supreme Judicial Court for the Commonwealth, No. 747 of 1929, Bill of Exceptions, 37.

ards, the governor stopped him, saying that he didn't care about that, but wanted to know what General Richards knew about these South Braintree murders. When General Richards said that he knew nothing of the shooting of Berardelli and Parmenter, the governor dismissed him. Had we been present, we could have explained the connection between his testimony and the Slater and Morrill payroll robbery. Without someone to relate one piece of evidence with another, Richards's story would have been meaningless anyway. Coming out of the governor's office, Richards reported to us that our clients were as good as dead.

During the governor's investigation, we watched and listened eagerly for clues which might point to his ultimate decision. Some of them were encouraging. For instance, we were sent word to be hopeful by Robert Lincoln O'Brien, editor of the *Boston Herald* and a friend of the governor. Mr. O'Brien's reasons for optimism were later spelled out in a letter to Albert J. Gordon, who had been a reporter on the *Herald* for years. O'Brien had talked with the governor at the Boston University commencement, where Mr. O'Brien and Mr. Fuller had both received honorary degrees. Reportedly the governor had said that Mr. O'Brien would be surprised at the way much of the prosecution's testimony had collapsed and that he was going to settle the case in such a way that he could live with his own conscience. He also told Mr. O'Brien that a son of one of the leading witnesses for the prosecution had been to him to tell him that his mother — the witness — was utterly irresponsible and mentally incapable of telling the truth.[7]

There was another wisp of straw that we thought might indicate the wind direction. In one of our conferences with the governor, he suddenly remarked, "Isn't Vanzetti an attractive man!" This seemed to indicate a frame of mind incompatible with putting Vanzetti to death.

We learned that the governor had called a meeting of the executive council for August 3, 1927. In order to reprieve the men or commute their sentences, the governor needed the "advice" of the council, meaning an affirmative vote of approval. If he intended to let Sacco and Vanzetti die, no meeting of the council was required. Therefore, we were again encouraged. August 3 was the date named by the governor for releasing his decision. To our consternation, however, on August 2 the ominous news leaked

[7] Louis Stark, *A Case That Rocked the World* (New York, Simon & Schuster, 1938), 351.

out that the governor had canceled the call for the council meeting on the next day.

In the evening of August 3, 1927, the governor released his own decision together with the report of the Committee. I was awaiting the news at Mr. Thompson's home. The decision was read to us over the telephone from the State House. It must be true that hope springs eternal, because we still had the capacity to be stunned by what we heard. Mr. Thompson, the veteran trial lawyer, took the decision with more apparent calm that I could muster. He was, however, boiling within.

We have already considered the morass of errors and wrong assumptions in the report of the Governor's Advisory Committee. The governor's decision ignored the entire case for the defendants.

The issuance of the report and the decision abruptly stilled the burgeoning doubts among the leaders of opinion in New England. Letters and telegrams of appreciation and congratulation poured upon the governor and Mr. Lowell. The report of the Committee was especially acclaimed, so great was the confidence in Lawrence Lowell. What more was there to say after a man of his character and standing had thoroughly investigated the facts and found the defendants guilty?

Whatever solace the Lowell report may have brought to the New England men who had doubted the justice of the Sacco-Vanzetti case, it did not assuage the conscience of the little group of women who had followed the proceedings. They had enough personal knowledge of what went on in the courtroom to perceive for themselves the misstatements and fallacies of the report. Their distrust of the trial and their faith in the innocence of Sacco and Vanzetti continued unabated. On the evening of August 22, 1927, when all hope was manifestly forlorn, some of them gathered in a home on Beacon Hill to wait out the last hours before midnight. When word was flashed that the end had come, they received the news in grim silence and then dispersed to go their separate ways.

The governor's decision marked the end of our fight as lawyers to save the lives of our clients. We continued, however, as informed believers in the innocence of the accused, to aid in the attempts to stave off the electrocutions. Mr. Thompson visited the condemned men on the evening of August 22, 1927. Returning to his office from the death house, he immediately wrote an account of his interview which has become a memorable document in the history of the case. Both of us then waited on the governor at the State House, where we made our joint plea for a stay of the execution scheduled for midnight. It was at the close of this meeting that Governor Fuller showed some understanding of the historical implication of the Sacco-Vanzetti case. As we left his office, I had remarked: "If these men are allowed to die, Massachusetts will never recover from the disgrace of permitting them to be executed under sentence imposed by a judge who cursed them for their beliefs while considering their case."

To this, the governor replied: "That is a complication."

In tracing the development of the prosecution's case from its origin in the weird story of an underworld contact, told to three detectives in a Brighton rooming house, we necessarily had to consider it in piecemeal fashion. In doing this we have considered, among other things, the forcing of identification testimony, untrustworthy enough to begin with; the omission of vital testimony and evidence; grave questions touching the integrity and even the authenticity of physical exhibits; the blatant rousing of prejudice; the use of unrestricted suggestion to get witnesses to change their testimony; the misstating of evidence and erroneous stipulations; and the failure to use any modern detection methods to protect the defendants from mistakes by witnesses. Nevertheless, it would be an erroneous approach to consider each such item separately. The Massachusetts Supreme Judicial Court followed such a procedure as to the matters raised in the Bill of Exceptions and attempted to justify each item separately. This was unrealistic. Even if it could have been done convincingly as to each point, this approach would have overlooked the crushing weight of the whole ensemble of alleged prejudicial matters.

The piecemeal examination of evidence against Sacco and Vanzetti has another distorting effect on a true perspective. It tends to throw into the background certain general considerations even more persuasive than particular parts of the trial evidence. In fact, if such general considerations had been in the foreground throughout the case, they might have determined how much credence would have been given to specific pieces of evidence offered by the prosecution. In the welter of discussion concerning particular bits of evidence, the jury and tribunals concerned all but lost sight of certain general considerations which should have raised powerful presumptions in favor of the defendants.

The following list of such matters is incomplete but may indicate some of the things which may have led Captain Proctor and the agents of the Department of Justice to the conviction that Mr. Katzmann was prosecuting the wrong men. This may involve some repetition, but some restatement may not be inappropriate as our story draws to a close.

Sacco and Vanzetti were not arrested because of any evidence or suspicion against them. They were caught in a trap set by a Bridgewater policeman to catch anarchists who kept a car in a shack near Bridgewater (the four points in Mrs. Vetilia's "vision"). They were unknown to the police.

Prior to their arrest, neither Sacco nor Vanzetti had ever been accused of committing any kind of crime. (Proof of this in court was made difficult by the Bridgewater conviction and the prejudicial stipulation agreed to by defense counsel at Dedham. Nevertheless, it was the truth and could have been noted in the Committee's report and the governor's decision.)

It was only *after* the arrest that the prosecution proceeded to compile evidence to detain, indict and try the two men. Some of the most crucial evidence did not even become part of the prosecution's case until after the Dedham trial had begun, fourteen months after the crime.

All of the resources of the Commonwealth did not produce evidence to identify the four alleged accomplices of Vanzetti at Bridgewater or at least four additional bandits in South Braintree. This resulted in the almost unheard of situation where, in the trial for crimes committed by multiple criminals, Vanzetti became the solitary defendant at Plymouth and he, with Sacco, the lone accused at Dedham.

In the matter of "consciousness of guilt" Mr. Katzmann (and Judge Thayer) ridiculed the defendants' claim that they wanted to take out Boda's old Overland in order to make arrangements to collect, secrete or destroy radical literature previously distributed. This explanation was consistent with the undisputed evidence offered at the trial about Vanzetti's trip to New York, Salsedo's violent death and the warning to the Boston anarchists to get rid of the literature. The prosecution was unable to produce evidence that the accused had some other purpose, or even to propound a plausible theory. This lack in the prosecution's case should have destroyed the episode as evidence of "consciousness of guilt" of the South Braintree crime. (The gap was filled by courthouse gossip to the effect that the old car, without even a self-starter, was wanted by Sacco and Vanzetti for use in another payroll robbery the next day. However, the rumor never showed one of its heads at the trial where defense counsel could have cut it off.)

A similar situation obtained with reference to the stolen payroll. The prosecution failed to connect the money in any way whatever with the defendants. While not essential, there is usually present in prosecutions for theft something that links the defendants to their acquisition of the stolen property. Frequently it consists in a change in their living habits. Nothing of the kind was shown with respect to Sacco and Vanzetti. Sacco had a savings account accumulated from his weekly earnings and Vanzetti had virtually neither need nor use for money. Here again the gap was filled by rumor. The defendants probably stole the money for the anarchist "cause." Again the rumored motive for the theft never reached a forum where it could be refuted.

Evidence of consciousness of innocence by the defendants received no notice. Yet it was more powerful than the alleged evidence of consciousness of guilt, which required certain unsupported assumptions as a base. The evidence of consciousness of innocence needed no preliminary findings.

For instance, Sacco could hardly have indicated his consciousness of innocence more impressively than by demanding that tests be made by experts to determine whether his pistol had fired the mortal bullet. The meaning of such tests had been carefully explained to him before he made the requests for a test.

When Vanzetti was arrested, he carried in his pocket a .38 caliber Harrington and Richardson revolver. The prosecution claimed that the weapon had been taken off Berardelli's body as he lay dying. Is it likely that a murderer would carry around for three weeks such damning evidence of guilt — especially if, like Vanzetti, he thought the police might arrest him at any moment as an anarchist and find the weapon in his pocket?

Is it a likely story to suppose that Sacco requested and received a day off from his job as edge trimmer in order to join a band of at least five confederates in a double murder and payroll robbery and then resumed his edge-trimming faithfully at his bench early the next morning?

Does it make sense to believe that Vanzetti, after receiving the eels from the American Express Company, cleaned and dressed them for delivery on December 24, but interrupted his deliveries on that morning so that he could speed twenty miles away to join a group of criminals in Bridgewater to commit a payroll holdup in that town and then speed back to complete the delivery of the eels previously ordered by his customers?

Vanzetti, when arrested, was drafting, with Sacco, an announcement of a public meeting in the city of Brockton at which Vanzetti was to address "fellow workers" on their wrongs. Is this the conduct of criminals who less than a month before had slain two men in the street in South Braintree in full view of scores of beholders?

Almost at the final hour, we learned from Mr. Moors that the governor had called for another test of Vanzetti's innocence of the Bridgewater crime. Would Vanzetti release his lawyers at the Plymouth trial, Messrs. Vahey and Graham, of professional secrecy so that the governor could talk with them? This was the immediate cause of Mr. Thompson's visit to the state prison toward the close of the day on August 22, 1927. Here is how he chronicled this portion of his interview with Vanzetti in his celebrated memorandum "Vanzetti's Last Statement" [8]:

I had heard that the Governor had said that if Vanzetti would release his counsel in the Bridgewater case from their obligation not to disclose what he had said to them the public would be satisfied that he was guilty of that crime, and also of the South Braintree crime. I therefore began the interview by asking one of the two prison guards who sat at the other end of the room, about fifteen feet from where we were, to come to the front of the cell and listen to the questions I was about to ask Vanzetti and to his replies. I then asked Vanzetti if he had at any time said anything to Mr. Vahey or Mr. Graham which would warrant the inference that he was guilty of either crime. With great emphasis and obvious sincerity he answered "no." He then said, what he had often said to me before, that Messrs. Vahey and Graham were not his personal choice, but became his lawyers at the urgent request of friends, who raised the money to pay them. He then told me certain things about their relations to him and about their conduct of the Bridgewater case, and what he had in fact told them. This on the next day I recorded, but will not here repeat.

I asked Vanzetti whether he would authorize me to waive on his behalf his privilege so far as Vahey and Graham were concerned. He readily assented to this, but imposed the condition that they should make whatever statement they saw fit to make in the presence of myself or some other friend, giving his reasons for this condition, which I also recorded.

In his argument on the night of August 22, after returning from the state prison, Mr. Thompson reported to Governor Fuller what Vanzetti had said.

[8] *Atlantic Monthly*, February 1928.

However, the occasion never arose where Mr. Graham or Mr Vahey were examined by the governor in Mr. Thompson's presence. Mr. Thompson also said that if the governor thought that the testimony of these men would make any difference, he should respite the defendants long enough to get Graham and Vahey to his office and let Mr. Thompson hear what they had to say — that they would not tell him that they knew that Vanzetti was guilty.

After Mr. Thompson's report to the governor, nothing further (to our knowledge) occurred with respect to his talk about releasing Graham and Vahey. The defendants were executed about an hour later. We do not know what the governor expected to learn by quizzing Graham and Vahey. It is possible that he wanted their version of why Vanzetti did not testify, since this question had become a positive obsession with him.

No explanation was offered for the uncontradicted testimony of over a score of witnesses to the alibis of the accused and other matters offered in their defense. These witnesses were reputable people (which a number of key prosecution witnesses were not) and many were unacquainted with the defendants. No reason was shown why many of these people should perjure themselves to protect murderers and robbers, other than Mr. Katzmann's charge at Plymouth that they were willing to tell a lie concocted by those "Italians up there."

And finally, there is the first and last question that should have been asked: Were Sacco and Vanzetti the kind of people who could and would have committed the double murder and payroll robbery at South Braintree? We have the opinion of experts in the field of crime who knew well the details of the South Braintree affair. Captain Proctor, head of the Massachusetts State Police, believed that Norfolk County was prosecuting the wrong men — and was fired from his proper function of preparing the case for trial. Agents in the Boston office of the Department of Justice viewed the South Braintree crime as the work of professionals. Even Tony Mancini, big job member of the Morelli gang, a hard-boiled professional and himself a prime suspect, immediately stated to me that Sacco and Vanzetti were not the type who would be involved in the South Braintree crime. However, the reader hardly needs "expert" opinion to assist him in answering this question. He now has sufficient knowledge of the nature of the crime and of the accused to judge for himself.

There is a last haunting question that emerges out of the Sacco-Vanzetti proceedings. It has no direct bearing on the case itself, yet it transcends in importance all other questions. It does not concern Sacco and Vanzetti. It arises from the fact that if the case troubles our conscience, we have no specific individual or group of persons on whom to unload our sense of guilt. Those whose unintentional collaboration brought about the tragedy represented a fair cross-section of the community. The poor and the rich, the ignorant and the educated, the humble and the elite were all involved. It may be possible to place responsibility on the personality defects of particular individuals, but not of the entire cross-section. Nor does it help to surmise (correctly, as I believe) that there were many others in the Commonwealth who would have behaved differently. They did not participate and therefore are irrelevant to our inquiry. We can, however, explain what happened as the unperceived effect of anti-Red hysteria and prejudice. When we do this, however, we arrive at a final question, with ominous overtones. If the twin passions of fear and hatred can pull the Commonwealth of Massachusetts away from its historic standards of behavior, they can do this anywhere, in any country, at any time. Nor is their power limited to the cracking of long-accepted standards of justice. They can be equally as destructive of ideals of honesty, of humanity, of peace. Therefore, the most troubling question that the Sacco-Vanzetti case asks of us is not what kind of men the accused were. This question may be important to a judgment about the case. It may help to clear the names of the dead men, as Vanzetti requested. Its implications, however, are limited to the case itself. For us, the Sacco-Vanzetti case poses an infinitely greater question. It probes to the very heart of human behavior. Have we the stamina to hold fast to our professed standards of conduct under the stress of transient manias and emotional excesses? For us, therefore, the question is not what kind of men the defendants were, but what kind of people are we?

The future of civilization may hinge on the answer to this question and, possibly, even the continued existence of the human race.

BIBLIOGRAPHY

In writing this book, I have relied mainly on the following sources:

1. Five volumes of the transcript of the record of the trial (at Dedham) of Sacco and Vanzetti and subsequent proceedings, as published by Henry Holt and Company, in 1929.

2. The Supplementary Volume, also published by Henry Holt and Company in 1929, containing:

   a) the stenographic minutes of the preliminary hearing against Vanzetti for the Bridgewater attempted holdup;

   b) the stenographic minutes (record not complete) of the trial of Vanzetti at Plymouth for the Bridgewater crime;

   c) the reports of the Pinkerton Detective Agency on the Bridgewater attempt;

   d) minutes of the inquest into the cause of death of Parmenter and Berardelli.

3. Reports of the Pinkerton Detective Agency on the murders and robbery at South Braintree (not published).

4. My own recollection and memoranda.

Because of the extent of this reliance on sources, I avoided, so far as possible, paraphrases and conclusions of other writers. In this connection I should like to point out that the portions of the trial records and reports cited throughout the book have been left unedited, except where obvious typographical and spelling errors would have caused confusion. There were, however, a number of instances where references to other books, articles and documents seemed pertinent and I have included these in the partial bibliography which follows.

For students of the case who desire a full list of references, I recommend the bibliography of G. Louis Joughin in *The Legacy of Sacco and Vanzetti*. Material published since the date of that work is now being assembled by Professor Joughin and will appear as a supplement.

Books and Periodical Articles

Bagdikian, Ben H., "New Light on Sacco-Vanzetti," *The New Republic*, June 13, 1963.

Beffel, John Nicholas, and Albert Wehde, *Fingerprints Can Be Forged*, Chicago, Ill., 1924.

Braverman, Shelley, "Forensic Ballistic Errors," *Gun Digest*, 1966.

———. "Investigation, Criminal," *Encyclopaedia Britannica*, 1966.

———, "Were Sacco and Vanzetti Framed?" *Guns Magazine*, May 1963.

Cook, Fred J., "The Missing Fingerprints," *The Nation*, December 28, 1962.

Dilnot, George, *The Story of Scotland Yard*, Boston, 1927.

Eastman, Max, "Is This the Truth about Sacco and Vanzetti?," *The National Review*, October 21, 1961, p. 261.

Ehrmann, Herbert B., "The Magnetic Point," *Harvard Law Review*, No. 3, January 1966.

———, *The Untried Case*, New York, 1933, 1960.

———, Letter re "obsolete" bullet, *Commentary*, Vol. 34, No. 1, July 1962, p. 72.

Felix, David, *Protest: Sacco-Vanzetti and the Intellectuals*, Bloomington, Ind., 1965.

Fraenkel, Osmund K., *The Sacco-Vanzetti Case*, New York, 1931.

Frankfurter, Felix, *The Case of Sacco and Vanzetti*, Boston, 1927.

Gunther, Jack D., and Charles O. Gunther, *Identification of Firearms*, New York, 1935.

Hatcher, Julian S., Frank J. Jerry, and Jack Weller, *Firearms Investigation: Identification and Evidence*, Harrisburg, Pa., 1957.

Hays, Arthur Garfield, *City Lawyer*, New York, 1942.

The Letters of Sacco and Vanzetti, ed. by Marion Denman Frankfurter and Gardner Jackson, New York, 1928.

Lyons, Eugene, *The Life and Death of Sacco and Vanzetti*, New York, 1927.

Massachusetts Law Quarterly, June 1965, Paragraph 16, p. 124.

Montgomery, Robert H., *Sacco-Vanzetti: The Murder and the Myth*, New York, 1960.

Morgan, Edmund M., and Louis Joughlin, *The Legacy of Sacco and Vanzetti*, New York, 1948; Chicago, 1964.

Musmanno, Michael A., *After Twelve Years*, New York, 1939.

———, "Was Sacco Guilty?" *The New Republic*, March 2, 1963.

O'Connor, Tom, "The Origin of the Sacco-Vanzetti Case," *Vanderbilt Law Review*. Vol. 14, No. 3, June 1961.

Outlook and Independent, October 31, 1928; November 7, 1928.

Russell, Francis, "Sacco Guilty, Vanzetti, Innocent?" *American Heritage*, June 1962.

———, *Tragedy in Dedham*, New York, 1962.

The Sacco-Vanzetti Case: *Transcript of the Record of the Trial of Nicola Sacco and Bartolomeo Vanzetti in the Courts of Massachusetts and Subsequent Proceedings, with a Supplemental Volume on the Bridgewater Case* (Holt Record), New York, 1929.

Stark, Louis, "A Case That Rocked the World," in *We Saw It Happen*, New York, 1938.

Thompson, Sir Basil, *The Story of Scotland Yard*, New York, 1936.

Vanzetti, Bartolomeo, *Background of the Plymouth Trial*, Sacco-Vanzetti Defense Committee, Boston, Mass., n.d.

————, "Last Statement" (to William G. Thompson), *Atlantic Monthly*, February 1928.

Warner, Arthur, "A Sacco Expert Revealed," *The Nation*, December 7, 1927, p. 20F1.

Newspapers

Boston Evening Globe, January 27, February 2, 3, 4, May 31, 1921.

Boston Globe, January 28, February 4, June 1, 1921.

Boston Herald, April 17, 19, 1920.

Boston Herald, January 28, 29, February 1, 2, 3, 4, 1921.

La Notizia, April 16, 1920.

Nickerson, Arthur S., letter to *Boston Herald*, February 4, 1966.

Legal Citations

American Bar Association, Canon of Ethics, 1908, Paragraph 5.

Attorney General v. Pelletier, 240 Mass. 364 (1922).

Attorney General v. Tufts, 239 Mass. 458 (1921).

Colyer v. Skeffington, 256 Fed. 17.

Commonwealth v. Center, Supreme Judicial Court for the Commonwealth, No. 747 of 1929.

Commonwealth v. Ryan, 134 Mass. 223.

Commonwealth v. Sacco, 255 Mass. 420.

Commonwealth v. Sacco, 259 Mass. 128 (1927).

People v. Hoffman, Indictment 33–1927, (Richmond County, New York Supreme Court, May 6, 1929).

General Laws, Massachusetts, Chapter 38, Section 8; Chapter 265, Section 18; Chapter 278, 533E; Chapter 453.

General Laws, Massachusetts, Section 29, Acts 1962.

General Laws, Massachusetts, Chapter 82, Acts 1964.

House of Representatives Resolves (Massachusetts), Nos. 1344, 1348, June 1928.

In the Matter of Arthur K. Reading, Supreme Judicial Court Docket #26194, Law 1929.

State v. Civitan (Hudson County, New Jersey, 1932).

State v. Israel (Criminal Court) Fairfield County, Connecticut.

Stopelli v. United States (9th Circuit, California, S Division, August 2, 1950, 183F. 2nd 391).

Unpublished Manuscript Material

Brown, H. Larue, letter to Herbert B. Ehrmann re Captain Proctor's Statement.

Felicani, Aldino, report on the De Falco incident, dictated per Dean Albertson of Columbia University, July 8, 1954. Copy in author's possession.

James, Edward Holton, "The Story of Mario Buda," report dated February 14–16, 1928, Harvard Law School Library.

Magrath, George Burgess, letter dated March 29, 1932, to Mrs. Katherine Codman. (In copy owned by the author the signature is diciphered as "Leroy" instead of "George.")

Musmanno, Michael A., report of visit with Chief Stewart, September 15, 1962. Copy in author's possession.

Myerson, Dr. Abraham, interview with Sacco, April 7, 1927. Copy in author's possession.

Pinkerton reports on South Braintree crime, Harvard Law School Library.

Plymouth trial jurymen, statements to Attorneys Moore and Callahan, Harvard Law School Library.

Sinclair, Upton, letter to Musmanno, September 5, 1962. Copy in author's possession.

Thompson, William G., letter to Judge Robert Grant, January 7, 1935. Copy in author's possession.

Thompson, William G., and Herbert B. Ehrmann, memoranda dated June 6 and June 9, 1927, of interview with Calvin Goddard.

INDEX

INDEX

A

Adams, Mr., 26, 29, 178
Adams, John, 502, 529
Affc (Afa), Carlos M., 354, 366
Agatkides, Nicholas, 15, 150
Aguglia, Mimi, 358
Ahearn, Daniel F., 518
Aiken, John, 159, 460
Akeke, Saul M., 23
Albertson, Dean, 162
Alibi, Sacco's, 348–387; Boston trip for passport claimed as, 56, 71, 349–374, 390–391, 524–528; *banchetto* as factor, 348–349, 359–360, 365–366, 374–387; witnesses, 357–387, 478; judge does not consider, 478, 480–481; Tattilo testimony against, 487–499
Alibi, Vanzetti's

FOR BRIDGEWATER ATTEMPT, 115–142; eel-selling on Christmas Eve as, 116, 383, 534n, 536–537, 542; neighbors' testimony supports, 117–138, 142; mentioned, 84

FOR SOUTH BRAINTREE CRIME, 329–348, 478; difficult to establish, 329–331; Thayer does not consider, 478, 480–481; Advisory Committee re-

port on, 517–519, 524–525
Alibi, nature of an, 329–331
Allen, J. Weston, 465
Alterio, Alberto, 419, 421
American Express Co., 24–26, 491, 534n., 536–537, 542
American Rescue League, 406
Anarchist and Communist aspects: accusations of Red propaganda, ix–x; exploitation by left-wing groups, x, 159; 1920's anti-Red hysteria, x, 11, 61, 138, 159, 288–290, 312, 454, 533, 545; Stewart's suspicions of Red involvement at Bridgewater, 11–12, 15, 150; Stewart pursues anarchist theory, arrests Sacco and Vanzetti, 43, 45–46, 49, 523; anarchist arrests alarm Sacco and Vanzetti, 47–49, 57, 288–289; Sacco and Vanzetti plan to dispose of radical literature, 48–49, 300–304; defendants believe arrested as radicals, 54–55, 128, 288–290, 293, 317, 322–328, 455–456; failure to trace money to anarchists, 60–62; cooperation between district attorney and Justice Dept., 60–65, 321–323, 325, 327, 433–434, 444–448; not a factor at Plymouth, 93,

W